Dark Clouds

Some Developmental Challenges Facing Africa

John W. Forje

Langaa Research & Publishing CIG
Mankon, Bamenda

Publisher:
Langaa RPCIG
Langaa Research & Publishing Common Initiative Group
P.O. Box 902 Mankon
Bamenda
North West Region
Cameroon
Langaagrp@gmail.com
www.langaa-rpcig.net

Distributed in and outside N. America by African Books Collective
orders@africanbookscollective.com
www.africanbookscollective.com

ISBN-10: 9956-552-35-6

ISBN-13: 978-9956-552-35-1

Acknowledgements

This book could not have been written without the wonderful inputs from my students as well as colleagues I have met during various conferences where some of the ideas were presented. I equally appreciate the comments made by various colleagues, and others. My views on clouds over Africa were formed after the completion of Century of Change and after attending the conference on the 10th anniversary of NEPAD in South Africa. I have been influenced by many people and many ideas. Several accomplished scholars with wide experience of African politics have broaden my way of approach, as I have been influenced by leaders like Kwame Nkrumah, Nelson Mandela, Patrice Lumumba, Tom Mboya, Odinga Oginga, Archbishop Desmond Tutu, Nnamdi Azikiwe, Steve Bioko, Obafemi Awolowo, S. A. George, Ndeh Ntumazah, Motomby Woleta, Samir Amin, to name but a few. The iconic writings of Chinua Achebe, Frantz Fanon, Mazrui Ali, Basil Davidson, Moss Mashamaite, Nyerere, Anta Diop Cheikh, Soyinka, Samir Amin, Joseph Ki-Zerbo, Chinuweizu, Asante Molefi Kete, Archie Mafeje, Adedeji Adebayo, Thandika Mkandawire and many others have significantly played an impressive role in shaping my thoughts.

At this stage, I want to pay special tribute to the staff and personnel of the libraries of Alvjso-Stockholm, the State's Library Lund, and the University Library Lund, (Sweden); Executive members of the Lund Horn of Africa Forum (LUHAF), Sweden, Abdullah Jama, Coordinator of the Horn of Africa Conference, Lund-Sweden, including Ambassador Count Pietersen; and John Legala Ghebdinga (Lund), whose rich library was equally exploited.

I am indebted, first to colleagues at the Faculty of Social and Management Sciences, University of Buea, who constituted a rich knowledge that can be; to post-graduate students at the Departments of Political Science, Anthropology and Sociology, Journalism and Mass Communications, Faculty of Social Sciences, University of Buea, and post-graduate studies, Pan-African Institute of Development (PAID - Buea, Cameroon), Students at the Department of Political Science, University of Yaoundé 11-Soa, students at the University of Bambili (UBa) Department of Communication, Development and Gender Bamenda-Cameroon and to all who in one way or the other, have been involved in the book coming to life in its present structure.

I could not have accumulated the fresh information and insights on which the book's analysis of significant external events in which direction the continent is floating and what must be done to save from it drifting far into an unknown deep sea without the help of so many publishing houses, organisations and friends. I am convinced working together; we can save the sinking boat as well as contribute to a 'blue sky' over Africa.

Many others have been generous with their time and thoughts over the years, all adding in various ways to my knowledge and my understanding of why Africa has to change to become a veritable player in the world and above all caring for its citizens. They include, Dr Ephias Ruhode of the University of Witts, South Africa, who in spite of his numerous activities found time to write the foreword, Prof Samgena Galega, University of Douala, Prof. Godfred Njimanted, Prof. Henry Kah Jick, Prof. Akoko, Prof. Muluh, University of Bamenda (UBa), Prof Fonchingong (University of Buea), and Francis Chamberlain, Lund-Sweden. Certainly, many others whom my memory could have bypassed or failed to record in extending my profound gratitude and appreciation towards the final product, which you are now reading. Their views and ideas helped in shaping my own thinking to a larger extent, as I bear the total responsibility for what is written here.

My children and grandchildren were encouraging as always; Noah has his usual enthusiastic self and of the continent of his father, while William gave me some great ideas. Mark junior's arrival graced and added new dimensions to my being. Gert, my son, kept pushing on with all kinds of jokes. My daughters Ellinor and Pauline where at the background as the driving forces supplying the latest information they could gather, and their brother kept telling me; *'dad take some rest'*. My better-half coordinated every activity and process in spite of her own commitments. I would like to record my deep appreciation to my family for their continuous support.

John W. Forje

Lund, Sweden and Bali Nyonga-Cameroon

Table of Contents

Foreword

As a University educator in the digital business transformation domain, I find Professor John W. Forje's book intriguing in many ways. Firstly, it reminds me of a learning course called 'Digital Business in Africa', which we taught during my time as Associate Professor of Digital Business at the University of the Witwatersrand's Wits Business School. Central to this learning module was to develop concepts, frameworks, models, and tools covered to address real-world digital business opportunities and challenges in various African contexts. As reported by Tedre (2011), the reality of a rural based agro-village in Africa is that there is:

- No electricity
- No landline phones
- No computers
- Poor public transport
- Poor road network
- Poor postal service

… but there are mobile smartphones.

It is in this context that the 'Digital Business in Africa' course finds itself as an element of the central theme in 'Dark clouds on the Horizon'.

Secondly, 'Dark clouds on the Horizon' is a clarion call to Africa's citizens to take control of their destiny. In this book, Professor Forje rightly identifies fragmentation of Africa's polity on one hand, and its tremendous potential for social and economic regeneration, on the other. For far too long, Africa finds herself at the mercy of nations in the north. It is one thing for the international community to celebrate the so-called end to colonialism, it is quite another to turn a blind eye to the debilitating effects of neo-colonialism. Many scholars and commentators reject the notion of a caring global community as advocated by the United Nations, but insist on defining neo-colonialism as the "new colonialism". In 'Dark clouds on the Horizon', Professor Forje decries the unprecedented political and economic slavery that Africa is reeling under. The book therefore calls not only for attention, but for participation of Africa's politicians, academics, the student community, civil society groups, policymakers, and captains of industry and commence, in the social, economic and political emancipation of Africa.

Thirdly, the book recognizes that Africa's development agenda should be situated at the confluence of politology, social innovation, and human development programmes. Professor Forje observes that societal forces such as the growing complexity of problems in Africa, do call for collaborative responses. Desperately needed are efforts at intellectual resource pooling amongst multiple players across the public, private and voluntary sectors in order to generate new structures to improving programming in governance across Africa. By following cognitive principles of political leadership as well as systematic harnessing of Africa's human and natural resources, Africa's citizens can attain genuine independence. Mapping a transformative pathway to inclusive prosperity in the entire continent requires a methodical pulling together of all human and natural resources.

Lastly, 'Dark clouds on the Horizon' is a reminder, that in order to achieve a much needed monumental revolution which transforms the human experience and a massive shift in society's standards of living, African leaders should be willing partners in the process. Professor Forje sends out calls for a rejuvenation of political and administrative systems globally, while placing African governments into focus. Improving social outcomes should underpin discourses at every level of political leadership on the continent. Deficiencies in social, political, and economic systems which manifest themselves in policy uncertainty, a large external debt burden, and general disquiet by Africans, should be subjects of political debates.

I find this book a beneficial read for society's entire cross section. The target audience include scholars, politicians, technological innovators, social commentators, and practically everyone that aims to drive the change agenda in Africa.

Dr Ephias Ruhode
Lecturer & Researcher in Digital Business,
University of the West of Scotland

MAP OF AFRICA

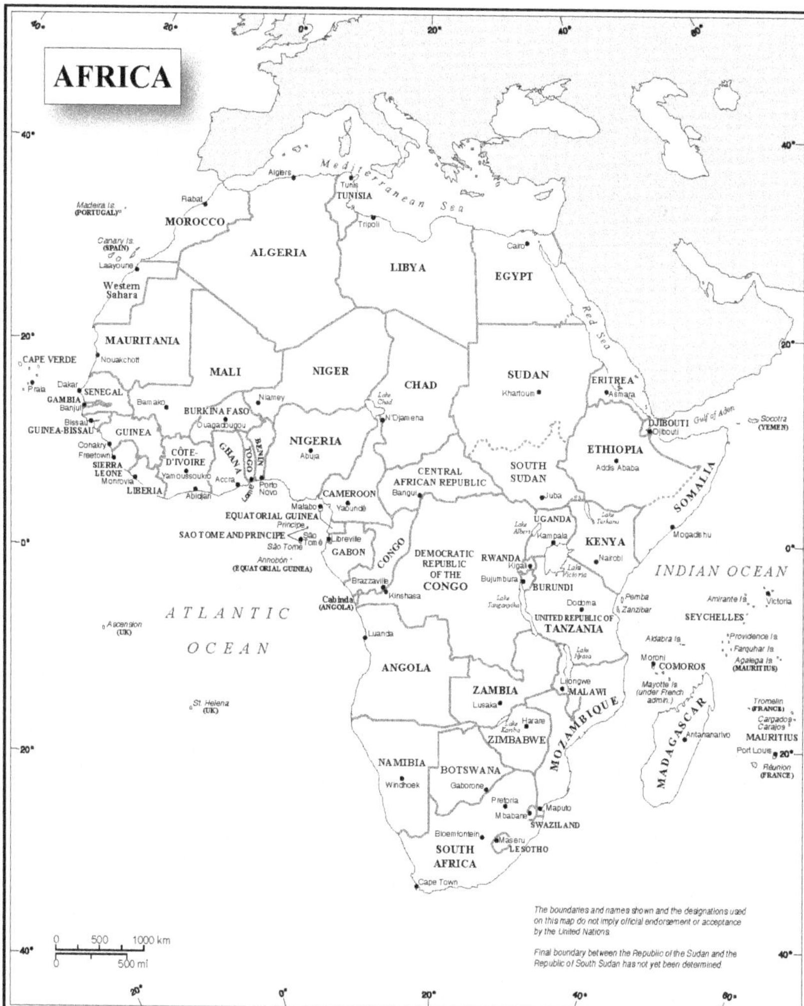

Map No. 4045 Rev. 7 UNITED NATIONS
November 2011

Department of Field Support
Cartographic Section

Source: Credit (Gegout Catherine (2021)

The Map of Africa is like a question mark; and Africa has many questions to answer; is it a continent; how independent is it; and shall the continent be ever independent and sovereign like the rest of the continents of the world?

"The seed you have is what you will sow the seed you sow is what you will reap. Go for good seeds. Be a learner and doer of good things." (I.U. Patrick)

Preface

Facing the Realities of Political independence A Noble Achievement…but. When will it be?!

"A turning point has now been reached in Africa's history. After years of patient effort to achieve he total political and economic emancipation of the continent by peaceful means, only limited results have been achieved, and it has become essential to adopt a more militant and positive strategy. Recent developments in Africa – for example, the outbreak of military coups and the continuance of Ian Smith's illegal government – have demonstrated the ruthless and insidious nature of Africa's enemies. The imperialists and neocolonialists are acting in strength and in unity; Africans must do the same. To know the enemy is to be equipped to defeat him. Economically, no saw in Aica, however less gifted by nature, need be afraid of its development and progress within the Union. For economic development on a continental scale implies harnessing and harmonizing Africa's vast physical and mineral resources for the benefit of the whole mass of the people of the continent. It is my view that, in the interest of African Unity, there should be no political or economic regrouping or blocs in Africa in alliance with any ex-colonial power or any foreign power for that matter; unless economic groupings in Africa are established only under the aegis and umbrella of an All-African Union Government, they will be detrimental to our Pan-African growth. Although political independence is a noble achievement in the struggle against colonialism, neo-colonialism, and imperialism, its effectiveness is superficial unless economic and cultural independence is also achieved. The road to the attainment of economic and cultural independence is beset with neo-colonialism which is becoming even more menacing to newly independent states than orthodox colonialism"

(Kwame Nkrumah (1967) in Foreword to Oginga Odinga (1967) Not yet Uhuru. An Autobiography, (pp. xiii -xv) **Heinemann, UK)**

Dark clouds on the Horizon are a collection of papers intended to provide the reader with some comprehensive and accessible summary of some burning issues constraining the sustainable transformation from a backward economy to a quality services delivery society. Ideally, the book is geared towards change in mindset focused on creating a humane society. The objective is to get a wide segment of society to understand the why, where, when and what of the underdevelopment/development saga; as it is imperative for the stakeholders to work as partners, friends and not as enemies and emblemizing resources that should be judiciously used in transforming the environment for the common good. There is monster-bird fly over Africa; the earlier the bird is bought down, the better for the people of the continent. Only then, and then will we in one voice shout and sing with one voice **"Our Beloved Africa is Free for Ever, free at last,"** recalling the birth of Ghana on 6th March 1957 on the Old Polo Ground in Accra. Or in the words of Martin Luther King Jr., ***"Let freedom reign."*** Yes, that will be the day the true and genuine Africa will see day light and be seated on the high table of the Security Council! By means of popular slogan such as *"Uhuru"* (freedom), *"Uhuru na umoja"* (freedom and unity), *'freedom,' 'liberty,' 'one man one vote,'* universal adult suffrage,' 'independence now' and 'Africa for Africans' the founding fathers of independent Africa succeeded in mobilising their people and politicising them to gain their liberty, freedom and sovereignty. Do not let their efforts be in vain.

More than sixty years gone, how independent, sovereign and free is the continent? The guns are thundering louder and louder across the continent; Africans are killing themselves more than ever before; many people are displaced and thousands perish seeking greener pastures in Europe. But the greener pastures are here with us. We voluntarily offer ourselves today as slaves to Europe sixty years after independence. We should ask ourselves, why? Where we are better-off before than today? The answer is blowing in the wind. May be Maya Angelou's book "All God's Children Need Travelling Shoes" gives a glimmer of hope; "...They believed she was descended from their 'stole mothers and fathers.' They wept, seeing their history in her face; they mourned 'for their lost people.' Angelou wept with 'a curious joy;' 'although separated from our languages, our families and customs, we had dared to continue to live...We had crossed the unknowable oceans in chains and had written its mystery into "Deep River, my home is over Jordan." Through the centuries of despair and dislocation, we had been creative, because we faced down death by daring to hope" (Susan Williams, 2021:24-25; Angelou Maya, 1986; 2008). The reality is that Africa is the bride or girl-friend every European nation wants for various reasons and interests. A Cameroon proverb goes thus; *"There is no virgin in a maternity ward,"* interpreted thus, 'when something happens there is always a cause for it, for example, everyone who is pregnant must have had sexual intercourse someday': even though technology is said to do wonders these days.

For these reasons, all kinds of seeds are sown in expectation of harvesting the best yields in the end. Here lies Africa's problems –

making the right decision on who should sow the seeds, why, when, where how and for what reasons.In particular, is the disease of the *'enemy in the house'* looking at the role citizen's play in destabilising their governments to please foreign governments? Or the role governing elites play in order to please the one who appointed him/her to remain in office. The numerous books on Africa, Susan Williams (2021), Fanon, Achebe, and many others highlight these weaknesses on the part of many Africans. For example, Susan Williams (2021:446-447) writes: *"Here was a chance, this fellow might get overthrown in the next couple of weeks and a really solid government comes in. The situation is very fluid, and the State Department also wanted 'to see if Gbedemah gets anywhere.... Gbedemah's conspiracy involved the America businessman Maurice Tempelsman and his agents in Accra...of the dealing between Grosse and Gbedemah. Gross was to play a key role in Gbedemah's plot."* Key role players in the struggle for the continent's independence suddenly became serious architects working for the destruction of what they fought so hard to bring to the people. We struggle for independence; we again struggle for destroying it; shame unto us for such acts of cruelty and destruction. Future generations will never forgive us for our self-articulate acts of today. Fanon (1963:50) writes: *"the leaders of reform have nothing else to say than: 'with what are going to fight the settlers? With your knives? Your shot-guns? It is true that weapons are important when violence comes into play since all finally depends on the distribution of these implements. But it so happens that the liberation of colonial countries throws new light on the subject."*

We equally saw the same scenario unfolding in the Congo during the short reign of Patrice Lumumba; in Cape Verde, and other parts of the continent; in Cameroon, the role played by S.T. Muna against Foncha and the people of Southern Cameroons; the struggle is ongoing with genocide as the highest price being paid by the people of Southern Cameroons, for example. We wonder, what has become of the people of this great continent. We are yet to overcome the *'slave malice,'* yet to wear the right-thinking cap; to forge ahead in the right direction, and avoid the famous *'Bafia Dance'* of one step forward and many backwards. It should be the reverse, 'one step backward and many sticking steps forward as the only way to overcome our predicaments. The *'dead hands'* of western destructive intelligence is hard-working on destroying the African continent. Professor Nzongola-Ntalaja George (a Congolese) feels keenly the deep scars left by Belgian occupation and then by the Cold War and neocolonialism.... the full disclosure of relevant documentation by the foreign powers that menaced the birth of his nation is an urgent necessity" (Susan Williams, 2021:505). Kwame

Nkrumah (1968) categorically outlines CIA activities in Africa, showing the death of Lumumba and other African nationalists as the covert operations of western machinations through their various cover agencies like the CIA. MI6, KGB, DGSE, among others. (See among others publications like Corera Gorden, 2012, Ronald Kessler, 2014, Blum William, 2003).

The loss of great sons and daughters of Africa who stood their grounds for the total liberalisation of the continent should not be forgotten. These men and women have contributed powerfully to the positive views of the continent. Philosopher, Molefi Kete Asante (2007) points out that "the ignorance of Africa is palpable, like a monster that invades our brains with disbelief, deception, and disinterest, yet is everywhere around us. We are victims of probably the most uninformed educated people in the world on the subject of Africa" and we allow ourselves to be used for our destruction! We all have a job to execute – the construction of a United States of Africa to sustain the unity, independence, freedom and sovereignty of African states. Ghana's independence gave impetus to oppressed peoples all over the world to fight for their freedom and liberty. There is a parallel between the liberation of Africa with American civil rights struggles. "A bottom, both segregation in America and colonialism in Africa are based on the same thing – white supremacy and contempt for life" (James Leslie, 2015). Speaking at the All African People's Conference (AAPC), Accra – Ghana, December, 1958, Patrice Lumumba, agreeing with the views outlined by James Leslie did not hide his feelings; "the conference reveals one thing to us -that despite the boundaries separating people in Africa from each other and despite ethnic differences, we have the same awareness, the same soul plunged day and night in anguish, the same anxious desire to make this African continent a free and happy continent that has rid itself of unrest and of fear and of any sort of colonialist domination" (Susan Williams, 2021:48). There exists a sort of detached complicity between capitalism and the violent forces which blaze up in colonial territory. What is more, the native is not alone against the oppressor, for indeed there is also the political and diplomatic support of progressive countries and peoples. But above all there is competition, that pitiless war which financial groups wage upon each other, notes Fanon (op cit.51). We should remember that knowledge is the garden: If it is not cultivated, it cannot be harvested. If we do not use the knowledge that you have, you cannot expect to gain anything from it.

Africans are challenged to focus on and accomplish the words **"Hands off Africa! Africa Must Be Free!"** boldly illuminating the platform of the rostrum of AAPC in Accra- Ghana 1958. We are waiting that coming day. This publication like many others ignites and incites us in that direction of the coming of the genuine independence, sovereignty and freedom of and for Africa, by Africans. We must acknowledge that efforts after more than half-a-century of Africa's independence, there is still audible disquiet in many African countries (the Congo crisis, the Biafra war; Sudan, trouble in the Sahelian countries; military take-overs in Mali, Burkina Faso, Cape Verde, Guinea Bissau, and the ongoing Anglophone crisis in Cameroon to list but a few) about what is generally regarded as structural imbalance within these so-called independent states and the perception that is inherent in this imbalance, is the tendency to the marginalization and exclusion of sections of the community from the centres of power, influence and material well-being of the people – the case of Anglophones in the Republic of Cameroon. How can we dispel this fear, create hope in the siege for desperation? As a continent we must build the courage, articulate and implement far-reaching endurable encompassing policies to grapple with the challenges of the time. In addition, we should know that is possible to consolidate the democratic gains so far made, especially that of rooting out corruption and inertia in the public service space in particular, and the entire country in general. Consolidating the gains made so far in the democratic process can only be achieved, if throughout our public and private institutions, we consistently and systematically nurture a culture of respect, morality, integrity and instil the code of work ethics and good behaviour. Finally, it should be noted that the process of good governance and democratisation, development and the rehabilitation of national pride will neither be effectively tackled nor confidently completed until we meet the outstanding challenges of restructuring and re-motivating our national institutions and services. It is no exaggeration to state that Africa holds the future for the world. But we must do more to hold that perception expected of Africa.

Freedom is not given freely on a platter of gold. When freedom is obtained, the leaders should listen to the voices of the oppressed. In this period of fundamental ferment, we can learn much by heeding the voices of those of those who are victimized by the existing arrangements of power and authority. We can learn about motivation, about struggle, and about the visions fighting to overcome oppression. We can also gain a critical perspective of the world system that traditional scholarly pieces do not provide – a perspective that forces us to constantly consider the human consequences of how the present system operates (Falk, et al. 1982:13). The poor performance of the system in post-colonial Africa could be seen as the 'Dark Clouds over Africa'. The dark clouds covering the region spells doom. We can state that colonial Africa gave birth to the Euro-centric agenda which has given birth to Ego-centric post-colonial Africa. Post-colonial Africa with Euro-centricism replaced by Ego-centricism or the combination of both plunges us into destructive effects of social, economic, cultural, and political trends are encompassing. There is no escape – even sanctuary on a space colony is a mirage. Post-colonial Africa seem not to grasp the extent to which Euro-centric plus Ego-centric manifestos subjects and pushes the people to the kind of existing geopolitical arrangements and condition of oppression the people find themselves. Their only possible rescue from going to the mortuary and back to the sanctuary is through a progressive Afro-centric accord. The old unjust order must be replaced with a just new national and world order.

The 'old' is gone, the 'new' has come and Africa has to be the new creation for human kind. If we do not have the sense of being futuristic, our past will control us. Dark Clouds over the horizon challenges us to have a certain vision in life, or else, we are as good as a sightless people heading on an unknown journey. For the past many hundred years, Africa has remained or made to be a sightless continent, and it has not changed even after independence, making her to set out on a journey without a compass, hence her destination remains uncertain. Africa have a vision. A progressive Afro-centric approach should be the vision. Believe in it, practice it, die for it. What you do not believe, will never form your behaviour. What you do not accept, will never become your asset. The progressive Afro-centric ideology provides the opportunity for the comprehensive restructuring of the continent. The wealth of the continent is like life, life is an opportunity, Africa mut benefit from it. Africa is a life, and it is beautiful, admire it and derive the best out of it. Now is the hour and time for Africa to solve her problems before it is too late.

Nevertheless, positive forms of transformation depend upon active and participatory politics. Any transformation of this sort will result from mass social movements. This prospect presupposes suitable awareness and committed leaders to educate the people and lead the struggle. A process that that needs to be more than intellectual. A process that must be felt in the heart as well as deeply planted in the mind and suggest entrenched positive and sustainable actions. What can and must be done? Those struggling against oppression are essentially hopeful; to them, social, political, and cultural change is possible. They believe in and act upon their own analysis, including its vision of an alternative future Post-colonial Africa is search for and must have an alternative future, and this has to begin with those who are representatives of ongoing movements of reform and revolution and evolution among the visibly oppressed, and then move to those who are trying to articulate an oppression that has not generally entered public consciousness (Falk, op cit.). A progressive Afro-centric agenda should activate public consciousness in fighting existing post-colonial African Ego-centric and Euro-centric policy and politics that inhibit the continent from getting its freedom and sovereignty.

The promise of a New African Order, in our understanding and the quest, arises from the centuries of enslavement, and colonial rule to the realization of a specific set of 'humane' values; peace, and economic well-being, social justice and ecological balance. The envisaged New Africa order values apply to means as well as ends. The New African Order as the means to overcome existing 'dark clouds over the continent' must be fashioned on the importance and active involvement of all; starting with the right choices we make as individuals; and as the most revealing new African order vision each of us makes in his/her life. Importantly, as well, those who give voice to the situation of oppression and seeking freedom and liberty are exemplary actors in the struggle for a progressive New African Order and a Just World Situation; to mention but a few, Nkrumah, Nyerere, Nasser, Nelson Mandela, Steve Biko, Sekoure Toure, Nnamdi Azikiwe, Awolowo: Remember Steve Biko's death, September 12, 1977, was a tragedy that forced many pros and cons opponents of apartheid from the path of violence. It is the Euro-centric against Afro-centric ways of existences. Euro-centric -. Ego-centric policies inclined and focused to quiet the Afro-centric policy, i.e., the persons whose acts and words dramatize the circumstances of oppression or many others. The force becomes a weaker, and hence the target. Steve Biko, Patrice Lumumba, Kwame Nkrumah and many other leaders who raised their voices against colonial, and Euro-centric policies towards Africa and its population was taking risks, often with any means of defence. It was a courageous undertaking for these leaders. Black lives matter. The Afro-centric agenda has a significant contributing part in the socio-eco-politico evolution of the region. Indeed, the programme, progressive Afro-centric is "defiance policy approach mechanism and agenda for the continent's sovereignty. The background of indiscriminate devastation these back to the face of hostility enter mission of western supremacy (Euro-centric policies) in dominating and controlling the Africa region.

The propagation of Ego-centric policies in post-colonial Africa makes us "guinea pigs," and we continue to remain dependent on what is dished out by the forces of Euro-centric agenda. The African landscape is dotted with conflicts, wars, genocide, abject poverty and misery. We need something concrete to protect ourselves against the invading forces of annexation and assimilation. (Nkrumah, 1970; Biko, 1978; Chineviz, 1978; Fanon, 1968, Memmi, 1965). We have set out on a long journey for a quest for true humanity; with the fervent hope of a progressive Afro-centric action plan should somewhere now and in no distant horizon see the glittering blue sky over Africa. Let the New Africa Order march forward with courage, determination and hope, drawing strength from our common past and plight and aspiration as the greatest gift possible for a brighter tomorrow with Africa as a sovereign continent in a just world system order.

The Algiers Declaration (4 July 1976) in line with the universal Declaration of the Rights of Peoples, attributes the central responsibility for the denial of human rights to "forms of imperialism" that have emerged in the post-colonial period "to express and exploit the peoples of Africa". The Algiers Declaration focus on reflection, and policy recommendation on five categories:

1. Basic human rights: food, housing, health education; the duty of governments to satisfy these rights taking into account the resource constraints and natural disasters (e.g., drought, flood);
2. Basic decencies: the rights of individuals and groups to be protected against genocide, for true, arbitrary arrest, detention and execution, o their threat; the duty of peoples and governments and their officials to establish an atmosphere where in these rights can be securely realized; Algiers Declaration
3. Participatory rights: the rights of individuals and groups to focus on policy recommend- participate in the process that control their lives including choice action of five categories of political leadership
4. …Security rights: the rights of individuals and group (including those unborn generations) to be reasonably secure about their prospects of minimal physical well-being and survival;
5. Human governance: the rights of individuals and groups to live in societies and a world that realises the rights depicted n 1-4, the

duty of individuals, groups, government and institutions to work toward to this end.

The non-adherence to these five or more categories of fundamental human rights creates scenarios for conflicts which can be dub as "alienation and affluence" most likely to be involved in systematic change. The disparity between rich and poor worlds, even if it gives to radical political movements, "probably does not imply any serious confrontation in the years ahead, for the underdeveloped countries even in concrete are unlikely to possess the serious toward serious military campaigns against one or more developed countries" (Kahn & Wiener 1967:363-365). Scientific and technological advances will change the structure of the dynamics of national and global order, increasing discrepancies between the rich and poor will be dominant reaction of the people of less developed world dependent of course on many economic, political and cultural factors. In short, the increasing discrepancies between the lives of those in poor continue and the rich nations (looking at the five pillars mentioned here) will be brought inescapably to the attention of even the most primitive and isolated communities by cheap and improved worldwide and isolated communication and transportation network. The dark Clouds on the Horizon is nothing but issues that pivot over, be little doubt that problems of development constitutions serious economic and moral concerns.

As the rich continue to get richer and the poor poorer, the world will be in an unstable condition. The situation will be even worse for Africa as the continent lacks the same opportunities to repeat the historic development of the rich nations even with the advantages of Gerschenkron "late comer advantage," even if aid were given, without skills and without capital there is little chances of it being used properly, since Africa countries have not yet attained the condition for economic 'take-off.' Dark Clouds over the continent is a culmination of 'despair,' requiring new injections and appropriate solutions for hope that goes far beyond our time. Differences exist and will continue to exist. These differences are fundamental to the debate and discuss on the Dark Clouds on the horizons and can be traced back to differences of opinion in three problem areas resources and technical change; the desirable political objectives and norms for society; and the economic, social and political processes whereby society evolves and changes. For Africa, the changes will be seeing a "Blue Sky" over the continent. Dark Clouds over the African horizon caries with a number of deadly sins, namely; reed, lust, gluttony, envy, wrath and slot which have o e swept away by a progressive Afro-centric manifesto, for the continent to see the blue-sky of justice, equality, peace, freedom and security. Attacking and curing these viruses – the pandemic that has brought the continent to its knees should be the research priorities of African universities, politicians and policy-makers. The time has come for the 'well-being' (Bache & Reardon, 2015; Fitzpatrick, 2018; Syrjala et. al, 2018) of Africans and for Africans to live well through the policy of a vigorously implemented progressive Afro-centric manifesto – which must be embedded with liberty and freedom, justice security and community as the obligations and mechanisms for counter-acting the euro-centric and post-colonial ego-centric ideology on Africa.

The vision for African reconstruction and renewal, the will of the people to undertake the task and human resource to go forward must come mainly from Africa and Africans. External business partners and friendly nations can be useful or virtually indispensable if they accept the context of cooperation and partnership. We should bear in mind that the darkest hour comes just before the dawn is not as trite a statement as it may sound. Analysis of problems in itself is a first step toward overcoming them, as is criticism both of decline and ways with coping with them. So too is a shift from almost fatalistic canvasses of uniform disorder to identifying areas of positive - even of fragile – continuity, of fighting back and at least tentatively successful initiatives (Green, 1995:293). The realities exist, can we herald a 'new dawn? Can the current odds of the tsunami of the 'dark clouds over the horizon be reversed so as we can see the 'blue sky' over Africa? Yes, it can. We have to be optimistic and not slip to carrying the sack of 'pessimistic' cross all the time. We have to develop a new development paradigm, where sustained development ensures that the full potentials of individuals are fully realized in an environment of self-confidence, dignity and fulfilment, and should centre on meeting the needs of the people guaranteeing their social and economic well-being" (Tomori, 1995:246).

Development and sustained quality livelihood – as heralds of the New African Dawn – "should be a process of self-reliant growth, achieved through the participation of the people acting in their own interests as they see them and under their own control; with its first objective being to end poverty, provide productivity and employment that satisfies the basic needs of all the people, any surplus being fairly shared" (The South Commission, 1990:13). We can equally draw solace from the views expressed by Sadig Rasheed (1995:254), "In spite of the gloomy record (Dark Clouds hanging over Africa) on the growth and development front; one must recognize that there is now creating willingness in the majority of Africa countries to undertake economic reforms. It is also evident that a great degree of financial ad budgetary discipline, more effective management of the economy, genuine encouragement of private initiatives and entrepreneurship and greater accountability and transparency vis-à-vis economic policies and issues are being practiced in an increasing number of countries." The dynamics and narratives of change must come from within and tailor guided by the people to best achieve quality livelihood. A well-articulated and implemented progressive Afro-centric agenda becomes the bridgehead to confront the Euro-centric/Afro-centric ego-centric policy hanging over the continent. It is the only way to dismantle the divide and rule action plans and to change the centre-periphery status-quo. The centre-periphery conception must be replaced with a 'win-win' accord. Our search therefore has to be directed towards a new strategy under the banner of a well-articulated and implemented progressive Afro-centric approach as the beginning of the end.

But the limits of the present approach to reversing the centre-periphery relationship is the growing state of eras building; the degree and attitude to which the periphery succumb to the centre; and as a result of the growing post-colonial ego-centric attitude of those at the helm of the supreme magistracy of African countries, who do not want to see another development trajectory materially possible that puts the last first and the first last. Power and bireledger are never relinquished easily, so 'unequal development' (Amin, 1976) will continue for a long time, and to break the chain of the 'lean years' (Barnet, 1980) even more difficult. Sami Amin (1960:1) points out that "If the 1960s were characterised by the great hope of seeing an irreversible process of development launched throughout what came to be called the Third World, and Arica particularly, the present age is one of disillusionment. Development has broken down, its theory is in crisis, its ideology the subject of doubt." Africa is in total disarray. It has to wake up and develop new parameters for her complex compound and complicated problems to receive a new life-coating for constructive change in order to have sustainable development.

Dark Clouds has only hinted at some of the implications. The focus of the book is on the influence and considerations which the Euro-centric agenda as derailed the transformation of the region into a quality services delivery continent, and why a progressive Afro-centric orientation is the way forward for a new African dawn. The New

African Dawn challenges the people to be better organized and better able to articulate their views and present their demands constructively to be able to achieve some tangent success. This the period of turning of the Euro-centric tide, embrace the Afro-centric agenda hole-heartedly, work and die for it, in order to bridge the existing development gap. It is time to make the best use of the 'late comer advantage, exploit the exploitation of the advances being made in science and technology; build the knowledge and skill capacities of the people, ensure that strong institutions and infrastructures are in place as driving mechanisms for the continent to move forward.

Critically looking at the status of human knowledge and skill capacity building in Africa discover that no other continent can boost of having a large citizenship number studying over the world like the continent of Africa. As such, Africa should be the citadel of knowledge. But because of the Euro-centric ideologically orientation, Africa has become the citadel of 'knowledge confusion." Post-colonial African development is struck with the worse 'knowledge confusion' one can imagine. What we witness so far, is that even with the knowledge and skill capacity acquired by Africans, only a limited role has been ploughed back to the society; 'brain drained' converged to 'brain gain' to latter be converted into 'destructive or delayed development' for the continent. There is an existence of 'tsunami of knowledge confusion' in Africa which delays the sustainable transformation of the continent. All these deliberate policies are designed to stifle industrialisation and modern economic growth and to perpetuate Africa's dependency on the metropolitan countries. Time and again, Dark Clouds over the Horizon stresses the issue that colonial policies were designed to provide markets in the colonies for manufactures of the metropolitan countries while promoting he countries as a source of raw produce. Industrialisation, the driving force of modern economic growth, could therefore find no fertile soil in Africa.

Current Euro-centric policies are out to ensure status-quo maintenance of the vision. What is required is an African counter-intelligence forward look policy approach. For now, Africa is threading on the wrong mindset, and is going to end up creating and sustaining the ideals of an underdeveloped continent, the wish of the developed countries. Therefore, a constructing a good mind-set is only created from good knowledge acquisition, skill and capacity building. It is therefore, imperative, for region to take the greatest possible advantage of the 'late-comer advantage' created by information and communication technology (ICTs) and ensure its good use of the wellbeing of the people. The Great New Brave African continent will be great and brave, but in the right use of strength, knowledge and resources. Dark Clouds is an appeal to the people to listen carefully and practice rightly the following views; 'If you do not go after what you want, you will never have it; if you do not ask, the answer is always no; if you do not step forward, you are always in the same place' (Nora Roberts). This is the vision and message of Dark Clouds and the urgent need for a progressive Afro-centric approach. Africa should develop on its own accord or it continuously be exploited and dehumanised by others. From the various publications cited, we see how Africa is continuously being humiliated and drag into the mud. The time has come to put an end to the talking and for concrete actions to begin. It requires dreaming the dream and seeing the visions. Essoka Peter (2014:4) makes an analogy between Joseph of the Old Testament and Martin Luther King Jr. "Joseph became the Prime Minister of Ancient Egypt, one which was unlike the Egypt of today. Martin Luther King Jr. dreamed of an America in which white and blacks and coloured people will move hand-in-hand someday and Americans shall live in peace as over-comes. His dream came true with a certain Obama as President. The process of total integration is ongoing except for some deliberate spoilers…The engagement of our leaders and people is seemingly illusionary. So how can an old man's dream come to pass of that wonderful country I saw in my dream? Fantasy! Perhaps we need more young men like Joseph and Martin Luther King Jr. not just to dream dreams but to see visions" and acting properly.

Africa must combine dream and vision and to ensure the realisation of both. African Union (AU) Agenda 2063 provides the dream and vision. We should see long before 2063 beautifully planned cities with impeccably clean streets across the continent; our cities glittering with unprecedented orderliness; four laned double-carrier highway with no check-points or some rude and unkempt gendarme, police and city-police workers bugging one to show one's papers or extorting monies from people with no good reason; corruption brought to the lowest possible minimum; quality services delivery in all institutions, (hospitals, schools, freedom of speech and the media industry; non-corruptible judiciary and school system) among others that enhance the quality livelihood of the people. We have the resources (human and natural). What we need do is to redouble efforts to building the human capacity and skills to give added value to our abundant natural resources as well as ensure we maintained a sustainable growth rate of more than 5% and rising. For now, our roads are scenic not highways. We continue exporting raw materials which the colonial powers disdained us to be. We should encourage within and between our countries; allow free movement of people and goods across the continent. Our building sites or 'grand-chantiers' are only visionary, our governance very tentative. The engagement of our leaders and people is seemingly illusionary. We behave as we are only passing through; the country is not ours! The AU and the 54 (or more) African states need to redouble their efforts to see that both the dream and vision come to pass on this wonderful continent of ours. How are we going about the vision of 2063? We should not only dream but work much harder than ever before. "This sounds fallacious perhaps stupendous o imagine the attainment of emergence especially when we maintain the pace at which we are moving, the attitudes of nonchalance, corruption and dubiousness which we hold dear" (Essoka, op cit.). It is sad to see underdevelopment and poverty in a continent of plenty. We seem to promote and even take pride in the poverty trajectories.

What future for Africa? Is the dream and vision we should begin to dream and wok towards its realisation? Colonial and post-colonial Africa relations seem to have come full circle, on the era of passive metropolitan-colonial relations, which prevailed at the end of the war, through the intervening period of decolonisation, rising expectations and active pressure for change, when the North was forced for a while into serious negotiations and into making what turned out to be some shallow concessions, and back again, after this false start, to a new era of Africa's abject dependence on the developed polity. Colonial governance subjected us to status of dependence. Post-colonial Africa has failed to redress the situation; rather, it has subjected us into a worse situation than before the independence of the continent. When will Africa be truly independent? All we see is a dehumanising and unyielding account of some of our citizens partaking in the making of a false African sovereignty and independence. We need to see the emergence of an independent Africa free from the yoke of colonialism and neo-colonialism. The continent needs a number of cross-cutting strategies critical for uplifting the performance of African countries which include; (i) building the human knowledge and skills including institutional infrastructure; (ii) improving the business environment; (iii) boosting science, technology and innovation in the sector by increasing investment in R&D; (iv) boosting power supply, and (v) improving on basic necessities for quality welfare, among others. Africa needs to improve on a number of political pillars in building a democratic society that respects individual liberties, freedom of speech, association and worship, and the rule of law. Such a policy strategy will enhance the dream and vision of AU 2063 Agenda.

The first African dream and vision was for Africa to be free from the yoke colonialism which was attained in the late fifties and sixties when most of the colonial flags were lowered and replaced by national flags. Since then, it was our place to build on that glorious achievements; and backed by the great sacrifices and determination shown by Africans it is only right for them to enjoy their hard-won freedom. The ball is in the court of Africans to respond positively in creating an enabling environment devoid of 'poverty, disease, and ignorance.' That vision is yet to be fully realized. AU vision Agenda 2063, national strategies such as 2025, 2030, 2035, 2040 etc., should make that dream a reality by ushering African states into the league o middle-income countries, where citizens enjoy widespread prosperity and in which the incidence of abject poverty becomes history. We should deploy our resources to build on independent Africa. This should be for us all individually and collectively commit ourselves to the realisation of the visions we have set before us. It is our duty working together in order to build a just, equitable and prosperous nation and continent. A project which can be achieved if we are focused towards our common future.

The problem with Africa is that we are not focused because it is not enough to be resolute in rhetoric without being resolute in actions. We have to walk the talk in our struggles against colonialism, neo-colonialism, poverty, injustice, inequality, exclusion and all other malice that makes us second class-citizens in the world. We have to be Pan-Africanist and the blood of Renaissance of the continent should flow in our veins. Pan-Africanism and Renaissances means Afro-centricism which implies the domestication of Euro-centric developmental activities. For example, Prof. Ali A. Mazrui (2005:13), notes: "…many of the ideas of the market economy, capitalism and free enterprise may be foreign to Africa. But domesticate them…. make them help Africa without harming us more. It is like domesticating a wild animal to make it more congenial to the home, and this time, the example can be used to domesticate foreign-styled universities. Our universities are originally very foreign in concept. So, to domesticate them is to make them more relevant to our society. A second major principle is to have a relationship with people of our own level of development, which I call horizontal cooperation, so that we do not just cooperate with the rich, but we find out from other developing countries what solution they have to some of their problems. We learn from India, China, or Latin

America, etc. This is a healthy horizontal cooperation or horizontal inter-penetration…partnership should include learning from other developing countries, not necessarily getting money from them, but learning skills from them, learning from their experiences. There are countries that started off at the same level as Africa, and they have spectacular progress – we should find out how."

Ghana gained independence in 1957 and it said the per capital income was the same as that of South Korea. Where is Ghana today compared with South Korea. Presently, South Korea is ranked the twelfth largest industrial power in the world, a position which giant African countries like Nigeria, South Africa, Egypt cannot meet. We cannot bypass a number of soul-searching questions, such; What went wrong and what is wrong with Africa even with its vast natural resource's endowment? How did South Korea and other East-Asian countries accomplish such great successes? Where and why did Africa fail? What should African nations do now? Can African nations catch-up with these countries? It is now the place of Africa to respond creatively, innovatively, constructively, productively, and masterly to the existing situation. It calls for a new mindset. Here human capital and knowledge building capacity is imperative. The views expressed by Makini Smith-Tchameni (2005:28-30) is important. "Despite the warning of the prophets of doom announcing their imminent demise. African nations are still flourishing and seem to have long days ahead. Paradoxically, the rise of globalization has run concurrently with awakening of nationalistic forces. On the African continent, the inability of neocolonial governments to create national consciousness within borders of micro-states, inherited from colonialism, has left enough room for the old and cherished concept of an African nations encompassing all continental Africans as well as the sons and daughters of Africa living in the Diaspora."

Africans being committed to 'African Renaissance' implies a strong desire to rebuild, revitalise, reconstruct and develop the continent and is people worldwide, education and skills building must be the strategic weapon for nation building. Defining education, Kwame Akoto states that 'education is the ritualized reaffirmation of the national identity, a national education system should be moulded and catalysed by the cultural and ideological assumptions, essential values, priorities and goals of that nation, both formal and informal, lies at the very core of the nation building efforts. It is through the educational system that national history is codified, interpreted and transmitted to the next generation. For Africa to be truly independent, requires a revolution, and for the revolution to succeed, a new mentality or mindset must be created simultaneously with a new material base in the country. Fidel Castro placed it plainly in these words, 'revolution and education are intertwined.' The goal of a colonial system of education is to reproduce the colonial elations of production. By maintaining this system, the independent African states are committing an act of cultural and historical annihilation and are seriously undermining the gains of independence (Smith-Tchameni, op cit.). This view is well-expounded by Mhango,2017, Talburt and Taore, 2017; Njogu and Adem, 2017; Laryea, 2017

A well-articulated and implemented 'progressive Afro-centric' Agenda will ensure the care and attitude towards human dignity by placing 'people first.' With no one being left behind. Africa should strive to restore and respect and safeguard the dignity of our people and to protect future generations so that they are free from suffering the fate we have been going through for many years. It becomes imperative to put an end to the kind of fragmentated society we have. A fragmented continent like Africa leaves the people at a cross-road of development or destruction. The choice now is ours; develop or perish! We need a solid shifting spanner to adjust to the realities of the situation; and knowing well that we are responsible for whatever choices made. Africa is challenged to have an optimistic view of its future. It is a continent that has undergone centuries of torture; and knowing no peace. Both in colonial and post-colonial era, peace has not been a frequent guest to our homes; rather, wars, conflicts, destruction and genocide are our permanent visitors. Karl Marx once noted that "war develops certain features earlier than peace. History has recorded on its pages wars that have lasted seven years, thirty years, and even a hundred years, The Congo crisis of the 1960s has yet to be resolved. The untold genocide in Southern Cameroons is entering its sixth year with no sign of ending. Indelible marks have been left in the annals of historical progress by two world wars of the 20th century, which took toll of 60 million human lives and destroyed immense material and cultural values.

The prospects of a Third World War started showing its ugly face on 24th February 2022 with the Russian-Ukraine debacle. Today the threat of a third world war beacon, which has been looming over the world for several decades, calls into question the future of humanity. The world has so far avoided this most terrible disaster. But the ominous flames of local wars (Cameroon, Guinea, Burkina Faso, Central Africa Republic, Mali, Sudan among others are flaring up in various corners of the world. Africa has become the epic Centre of conflict; The weapons of hum destruction are not manufactured in these conflict areas but imported from the developed polities, and used by developing countries in destroying themselves. On the strength of this fatal chain of conflicts in Africa, Western theoreticians and politicians assert that wars, conflicts are inevitable and eternal. We applaud that conflicts and wars are inevitable because these wars and conflicts keep the industrial wheel of western countries in constant rotation and profit making. The idea being floated around of send asylum seekers from Ukraine in the UK and Denmark to Rwanda is a new strategy of brawling war and conflict in this part of Africa in no distant future. We begin to wonder whether Africa learns from the annals of history. Africa should watch out.

In order to bring about a turn for the better, it is first of all essential to respect the sovereign right of every people to live and work under a socio-political system of its choice. Any attempts to challenge this right and impose a different form of state organization inevitably will lead to sharp conflicts as well as poison the entire national, regional and even the international atmosphere. It should be pointed out that conflicts and wars are waged due to a number of inter-related factors, search or acquisition of land and resources; Presently, there is no military industrial complex in Africa. There is of course, a powerful war industry machine in the developed countries supplying all kinds of weapons for human destruction in the continent. Finally, it should be noted that the danger of war stems from the imposition of the intrinsic Euro-centric ideology and the conflict arising from the clashes between Euro-centric and Afro-centric ideas. The clash of two different developmental ideas. The publication strongly advocates a progressive Afro-centric agenda that builds on number of our cultural heritage values like *'Harambee, Ubuntu, Batho Pele* among many others. The vision of Batho Pele is expressed in the belief set: *'We belong.* Batho Pele is all about and how to become involved in akin it forward. It is a collective responsibility of all to work for our common welfare and well-being which entails changing the way we think and work to a more service-centric attitude. The Batho Pele principles involves: consultation, services standards, access, courtesy, information, openness and transparency, redress and value for money. Therefore, in respect of consultation, for example, citizens should be consulted about the level and quality of the public services they received, whenever possible, should be given a choice about the services that are offered (DPSA-South Africa).

A well-articulated and implemented progressive Afro-centric agenda will ensure the care and attitude of human dignity by placing "People first' with no one being left behind. We should strive to restore the dignity of our people and to protect future generations from suffering the same fate we have been subject too during this many past decades. It is imperative to put an end to the kind of fragmented society we have. A fragmented society leaves us at the cross-roads of development and destruction; of hope and despair; of success and failure. We need to cultivate a new form of patriotism (Laryea, 2017), to fight for freedom (Talburt and Traore, 2017), to have a new critical perspectives on culture and globalization, (Njogu and Adem, 2017) and as Thandika Mkandawire (2015) puts it this way, "Africa must make serious attempts at recovery from a string of serious socio-political set-backs" and advocates for the role of universities as essential agents in the drive to sustained development. Knowledge acquisition and skill capacity remain the gate-way of sustainable development, quality services delivery and livelihood.

Colonial development has too often been jeopardized as a western construct, which, has come to be taken as obvious, casting indigenous development models in the shadows of pessimism. In post-colonial studies and popular discourses, little is known about decolonization of colonial development both in theory and in practice. There is little or no debate over what is meant by colonial development. This book argues that post -colonial understanding of development needs to be re-examined to radically deconstruct the dominant notion of development as a colonial construct. Development in colonial constructions misplaces what should be considered development rather propagates the interest of the colonial state in post -colonial contexts. There is a wide gap between the real development needs of the people and what is circulated as development, leading to crisis of development in post-colonial societies in Africa. The state of underdevelopment requires a dramatic retooling of state institutions, radical change in mindset and o state-society linkages. The degree of fiscal and political challenge to these development related activities weighs heavily on the types of decisions made about where to invest in human capacity and skills-building and strong institutions, however, and whether or not to build a social support base around development. African countries need a working model of development trajectories.

Based on the reality that Africa is greatly endowed with natural resources, these countries require (i) strong regime with powerful ruling coalition with a proactive civil society; (ii) reasonably administrative strong and powerful pro-regime; (iii) with weak regime with weak ties to society will produce poor development output; (iv) weak regime will undermine consolidation and produce disorganised or a weak social output. Most African countries suffers from the afore mentioned factors, leaving them extremely vulnerable to exploitation by external forces. Internal elements with the backings of external elements equally contribute to doing even more damage to the country. Africa has to reclaim its sovereignty, existence and independence. It is interesting to note that Africa is known to be harsh towards people with non-conforming genders and sexual identities. In pushing the *'mijadala'* – i.e., *'discourse'*, the continent should be more non-conforming with the Euro-centric agenda to reclaim its lost dignity, sovereign rights and independence. Being non-conforming means wearing the amour-dress of a progressive Afro-centric agenda. The continent is under pressure to occupy space that speak out and defend the African hegemony, defend it and promote the Renaissance and Pan-Africanism of the continent. There is no other way but threading the waters of our historical past and correcting where mistakes were made; mistakes which we ae paying heavily today. At the dawn of a new era or episode of the continent, we have to be move vigilant not to fall into the destructive trap of the past hundreds of years of imperialism, slavery, colonialism and the issue of neo-colonialism. Fighting the vices of slavery, imperialism, colonialism and neo-colonialism requires a new-mindset, commitment and determination, for, if there is a will there is way. We are challenged to develop a strong will to keep on the right track for our liberation, defending our dignity and sovereignty. It is a challenge we have to hold close to our hearts and to make the changes that breeds confidence, hope and courage in the people. Putting people first is the courage of discovering who we are and what we want to be. We need a new kind of leadership to provide and redefine our relationship with one another and with our society. For now, Africa remains the odd continent on planet earth. That cliché should be reversed, for Africa remains the most beautiful girl that is being courted by all. The beauty of the continent has also converged to being its source of destruction. Africa is and remains the continent to be to the world. The people should develop the unshakable will to continue exist, to live in peace and solidarity with the weakest, which is life insurance for the people. It is high time Africa has to come of age and head to where we want to be. Recognising that Africa is globalised makes urgent the achievement of African Unity, African Renaissance and furthering the course for Pan-Africanism. The old African dream remain, think and achieve it now or never.

The effect of this depiction of reality is that autochthonous development or indigenous knowledge system is emasculated and taken for granted, while the colonial development model circulates unquestioned and undermines the political and economic development of post-colonial societies. We are challenged to building a continent free from the yoke of colonialism; a continent with foresight and with the proper usage of the vast potentials of the continent for the common good of the people. As demonstrated again and again throughout the entire publication, the intention of the colonial government's was not to create a new and better Africa with a common ethos as this would reduce the centre-periphery dichotomy. The overall priority of colonial authorities was to cement the centre-periphery nexus, reduce the financial burden on British, French, Spanish, Germany etc., taxpayer, reduce bureaucratic duplication and enhance the financial purse of these colonial powers. Africa was the reverse bank for the colonial invaders. Even in post-colonial Africa is the reverse bank of the colonial powers or remains an inherent page in a colonial accounting ledger. We continue debunking on the state of the continent's poverty, ye the continent remains he accounting ledger of the developed countries, France in particular.

Something is wrong somewhere which has to be addressed. The tragedy of Africa is continue doing things as usual instead of being the new independent continent it should be. Seen within this context, Africa is yet to register its true "Uhuru" (Odinga Oginga, 1967). And as Kwame Nkrumah wrote in the foreword, "ordinary men and women throughout Africa, even those living in the most remote villages, are now talking the language of the African revolution. They speak of 'unity' and are prepared for the next, more realistic, phase of the struggle. In fact, a situation has arisen in which the people of Africa are ahead of their governments in that they have accepted the idea of unity while their leaders, in many cases, continue to hold back or to proceed too slowly. But pressure from below will inevitably force the pace onward and nothing can halt the process towards Union Government." Summing up Kwame Nkrumah's foreword and the book by Oginga Odinga (Not Yet Uhuru), our problem remains that of leadership and the people's commitment towards their freedom. It is for these and other reasons, that a progressive and well-implemented Afro-centric agenda and under focused servant leadership should "eradicate totally and completely foreign rule and domination from Africa and to fortify the continent against the turbulent world of power politics that we bent our concerted efforts towards unity" (Nkrumah, in Odinga Oginga, 1967:xv).

In 1963, Tom Mboya set the pace with "Freedom and After" which directly questioned what Africa was going to do with its 'freedom'! Here we are today many decades after still finding out what the continent has done with its freedom. Why is the continent more enslaved than before 'Uhuru'? What must be done to regain the continent's freedom? We find ourselves in a situation that strongly beacons for an 'African Mosaic' of civil society uniting to regain and 'rebuild' 'Uhuru' and ensure that 'Uhuru' is placed at the service and welfare of the people. So far, Africa has made a mess of 'Uhuru,' placing the people's aspiration in despair not hope for brighter tomorrow. 'Uhuru' was to bring us together and helping each other solve problems and build our common future. The hopes and aspirations of the people have been dashed with 'dark clouds' hanging over the continent. With the 'dark clouds' over the continent people re demanding a greater say in defining and controlling their destinies, seek greater accountability, participation and responsiveness from their governments, as well as challenging the growing power and value of the system in place for failing to defend their interests. Whatever the case, Africa will be free one-day as President Kenneth Kaunda in the African Writers Series No. 4 – 'Zambia Shall be Free' Heinemann, London, Ibadan, Nairobi. Currently, the imperialist and neocolonialist are acting in unionism which gives them unity and strength to forge ahead and implement with success the Euro-centric doctrine. To know the enemy is to be equipped to defeat him.

Defeating the enemy in this case requires good servant leadership and a progressive Afro-centric agenda as the key to the continent's economic, and political stability, peace and progress. The trouble with Africa is that though we know what we want, we fail to go after it the right way, scientifically and committedly. By not being scientific in our approach, we commit too many mistakes in the realization of what we want. The current Anglophone crisis is a typical example. No case for righting the wrongs of the problems done to a people by the UN is so glaring but failing because of failure to be objective and scientific in the approach of the people and leaders of Southern Cameroons in claiming their inalienable rights to self-determination, sovereignty and freedom. When confusion sets, and the leaders are divided, the oppressing party takes control. Complexity is often mistake for vagueness and sustainability is, like democracy, a complex idea. African countries must shift from the currently centralized authoritarian regime structure to a democratically elected representative government involving the creation of a system of checks and balances and respect for the rule of law. It does not mean that democracy is without flaw.

As noted by Winston Churchill in the British House of Commons in 1947, "Many forms of government have been tried, and will be tried in this world of sin and woe. No one pretends that democracy is perfect or all-wise. Indeed, it has been said that democracy is the worst form of government except for all those other forms that have been tried from time to time." Still, few would argue today that democracy has not been a blessing for humanity. No one can dismiss democracy – in all its form, with all their warts – for being vague. We just have to make best of the positive sides that it provides for our common good and well-being. The complexity of sustainability is daunting for many African countries. The changes it requires of us, in order to practice it, are every bit as revolutionary as democracy was more than two centuries ago (AtKisson,1997; 285-292 in John Burbidge, 1997). Since democracy is driven by, for and of the people, we have to embrace and make the best of it. Permit me pose the question which to many may sound cynical; why is the black race suffering the most when they pray more? Or are Africans suffering because they do pray honestly? Or are Africans suffering more because they use their energy blaming others for their predicament instead of critically and objectively x-raying at what is wrong with their way of livelihood and welfare? Why are other continents making significant progress and Africa is regressing in spite of its vast natural resources and a growth youth population – the market for the future?

Is there a kind of unholy alliance between African governments and the colonial masters? The religious faiths have their stronghold in Africa and rapidly expanding more than in any part of the world. The same goes with mobile or cellar phone. The expansion of the cellar and religion is phenomenon is fantastic. How are the people using the expansion of the cellar phones for the right purpose or as an instrument for criminality or devious activities? The expansion of the cellar phones does not correspond with the rate of economic growth which is falling far behind. The state of development and peace are grossly lacking, while wars, conflicts, human sufferings and destruction are on the rise throughout the continent. These are some of critical ad fundamental issues Africa should be addressing; why religion and the cellar phones and other modern technological gadgets are not accelerating the development process of the continent? It is pious to expect a post-colonial government to contemplate the long-term consequences of hanging on the colonial master's agenda of 'dependency' for the continent. We can only draw a poor balance sheet of the development process. With the overriding ideological principle behind Africa's independence, it has been difficult for the region to arrive at the unity and integration of the continent. It is not out-of-place to state that the struggle during the colonial era was characterised and inspired by the quest self-determination and regaining the dignity of the people that was drag into slavery; the post-colonial era is the failure to attain the unity and integration.

In short, African renaissance and Pan-Africanism seem to have taken a back seat in post-colonial Africa and especially after the demise of founding fathers like Nkrumah, Nasser, Nyerere, Nelson Mandela, Ghaddafi, Biko Steve and others. As demonstrated again and again in prior pages, the colonial government's priority was not to grant independence to Africa or to grant independence but to reconvert it through the Euro-centric agenda into something still under its supreme control. That is why post-colonial Africa has failed to create a continent of nations with a common ethos – unity and

integration. African Renaissance and Pan-Africanism is now relegated to the background. African nations are more or less paddling its canoe in different direction. Yes, there is the African Union to show; the African Common Free trade Area is there to show, but how effective is it. On the other hand, the entire continent is littered with conflicts of one kind or the other and the AU remains mute on these conflicts. Genocide is ongoing for example, the case of Southern Cameroons. We begin to wonder whether AU is out to protect the interests of the colonial lords? The continent's journey toward democracy remains questionable. After all, it is often true, as the French say, that 'the devil is in the details.' One of these devilish details is the growing gap between the African people in the rural areas in general and the governing political elites in the capitals of African people.

The problem of corruption is pervasive. The lavish lifestyle of the people's elected representatives across the continent speaks for itself. We are not talking about petty misfeasance. Corruption for example, is serious because it creates a sense in each African country at large and among the governing elites that we ae moving in the wrong direction with tremendous speed. Rephased differently, despite our limited progress towards democracy, markets, and the like, we are heading towards an entrenched centralised authoritarian, over-monopolistic criminal state. The hybrid nature of regime structure that has emerged in post-colonial Africa generates enormous stresses. The situation across the continent now inextricably bound up with a power struggle between the centre and the periphery. Then, there are the basic problems of state-building so clearly elaborated by Lucien Pye that have to be resolved: the issue of integration, penetration, distribution, participation, building consensus on power-sharing and so on. Seemingly, incompatible principles of political order (democracy, authoritarianism, populism, dictatorship etc.,) which coexist, and through powerful representatives in the governing elite vie for exclusive legitimacy. In all, democracy - 'government of, by and or the people' remains a dream for Africa. For now, 'democracy' is against the people. The conclusion in which all this points, at least in the short term, is that economic reform and democratic development will be making headway very, very slowly on the continent. There may be some countries where progress in the democratisation process will be fast and consolidated, while in other parts of the continent it will remain stock-on-the-runway without signs for a take-off.

Therefore, Africa still remains within the realm of a glaring need for 'transparency, accountability, responsibility and equity. For now, the viruses of underdevelopment, injustice, inequality and abject poverty is destroying Africa. Time to vaccinate the continent is now or never. Only Africans can put the continent on the right track of recovery and sustainable transformation. Therefore, every African must stand-up take his/her responsibility for the general well-being of the survival of the continent. It is a task we must be proud to commit ourselves diligently to achieve. The Global North is determined to uphold the current status-quo of superiority, dominance and control of the Global South at all costs. There are people in the Global South, Africa in particular aiding the Global North to sustain existing status-quo of the domination and exploitation of Africa. In (Isaiah 60:22) is written; *"The last one shall become a clan, and the smallest one a mighty nation: I am the Lord; in this time, I will hasten it."* When the time is right, the Lord will make things happen. The weaker will become the stronger and the stronger the weaker. We need to reawaken ourselves, getting of our entrench presence in the slumber land of captivity, enslavement and be free and dignified human-beings. It requires determination, commitment and a radical shift from the current mind-set to a progressive new mind-set in a new dawn. What future for Africa and the Global South Nations? Will the Global North Nations permit the Global South Nations have their liberty, freedom, sovereignty and dignity? Will the conquest and rule over the continent ever come to an end? Will Africa continue to be stuck on the run-way without 'take-off' to a new destination, the destination of sustainable quality services delivery and livelihood for all!

> *"Lord, Make me an instrument of peace, where there I hatred, let me sow love: where there is injury, pardon; where there is discord, union; where there is doubt; faith; where there is despair, hope; where there is darkness, light; and where there is sadness, joy. O Divine Master, grant that I may not so much seek to be consoled, as to console; to be understood, as to understand; to be loved, so as to love: for it is in giving that we receive, it is in pardoning that we are pardon, and it is in dying that we are born to eternal life. Amen"* (Attributed to St Francis of Assisi).

We are today faced with the situation of the bible and land; we have to decide what we want and how to get it the right way. The right way is being hard working, innovative, creative and entrepreneurial as the way out of the state of impoverishment in the midst of resource opulence. There has to be productive, transformative and reinventive understanding of our past, present and where we are heading. It beacons Africans to be constantly knocking at the door of knowledge, utilising improving on our indigenous knowledge system for the onward march to quality livelihood for all. Getting the land back, which we must, is equally a challenge of making proper use of it; just like making a proper use of the bible.

Adhering to the words of the bible is equally important in our transformation. It is only when people start misinterpreting the bible to suit their personal motives that the bible is given a wrong name. It is neither the bible nor the land that is at fault. The fault of our current pathetic status situation should be attributed to our 'love and quest' for money, not 'love' of the people and country; we have been overtaken by 'greed' and 'quest for power;' power wrongly used for destructive and not for the sustainable construction of the country. With such mentality, mind-set and attitude, the Global North will continue to rule Africa. With no overriding ideological positive principles embedded in leadership style postcolonial Africa, it is left to future generations to find and fashion a new way to rationalize the independence of the continent. The irony is that current leaders have established themselves as 'sit-tight' individuals who do not want to make-way for the young generations to take-over. Authoritarian power and wealth accumulation have become their preserved. Starting from the 1960s, post-independence African governments have failed to unravelling but perpetuated the Global North territorial consolidation by fracturing the continent. Since the passing to glory of Kwame Nkrumah, Ghaddafi,

Azikiwe, Nyerere, Nasser, Mandela, Steve Biko, etc.; and the replacement of Thabo Mbeki, Wade and others, the *"Great Dream of African Unity, Pan-Africanism and Renaissance Africa"* has suffered serious set-backs. Yet, it is too the continent's credit that it develops its own home-grown innovations and affirmative action plans for its independence that should help cut of the chain of domination by the Global North.

Perhaps it is pious to expect the Global North to contemplated the long-term consequences of its actions on the people of Africa. As demonstrated throughout the book, the colonial powers and the Grand Global North priority was and will never be to see the creation of a truly independent Grand and United African Continent. Without any doubts, the priority of the Grand Global North has always been to retain Africa as a raw material producing and supply region and a consumer of western products. This hidden or unhidden ideological orientation and policy action plans leaves a most indelible mark on the physic of Africans as second or even third-class citizens of the world. Dark Clouds on the Horizon continues preaching the gospel of a mindset for Africa in order to move forward; for the different countries to strategize and apparently build a unified Africa. A new balance sheet has to be drawn in colonial and post-colonial Africa that should usher peace, justice, security, hope, confidence, order and good government for the people. A balance sheet that places the people as the focus and centre or all development related activities. The people should give good government in place of tyranny and centralized authoritarian hegemonic administration, abolish human sufferings, ensuring that corruption is given the red card, peace and security assured throughout the country, that material prosperity entrenched with equity in benefit sharing of the wealth of the nation.

We should own these developments and ensure that generations yet to come have hope for a better tomorrow. We should not hand a 'false or a fool's paradise' to future generations. Africa is on the unfinished long journey to independence. The independence dream must be realized. Africa is in a crisis situation. Doubts are being expressed whether the goals of AU Agenda 2063 will be attained? A new post-independence revolution is imperative. The post-independence revolution and government should not be outside the boundaries of the ballot-box otherwise, it would subject the continent to the laws of unintended consequences. To a large extent, post-independence governments ravelled themselves with governance form that was against the people. Whenever any form of government becomes destructive of the democratic cradle of, by and for the people (failing to securing, practice and promote the inherent and inalienable rights of the people) when power from the consent of the governed, the future of that country is ruined forever. Africa seems not to learn from past errors making the future of the continent to be tainted with the colours of 'bleakness' and uncertainty. Yet, this is not the kind of future expected of Africa, for Africa, by Africans. Presently, desperate people ask if any solutions are in sight with Dark Clouds hanging over the continent?

How can the continent progress with more than 10 military French bases on the continent, and with more than 15 USA bases under the caption of AFRICON? These military bases are not for the protection of African people against external aggressors but for the protection of multinational interests of the hegemonic Global North in Africa. These military alliances and the establishment of military bases across the continent are to fan conflicts to under the obnoxious policies of divide rule. The divide and rule policies are to have hegemonic control over the natural resources of these countries. The concept of 'responsibility to protect,' which is enshrine in the African Union (AU) Constitutive Act of 2000 has suddenly been set aside for the Global North to have full control over African counties. Yet the Global North has not mobilised the powerful desire to reform Western-dominated institutions off global governance such as the World Bank, the International Monetary Fund (IMF) and the World Trade Organisation (WTO) and to create a more democratic and equitable world order for the common good of all. These Global Institutions are focused or geared towards protecting the interest of the global North, not the Global World. Can the African Union and the Global South monster a united front for the defence and protection of their interests?

A key challenge for Africa relates to how it can navigate tensions between its 'African Agenda' (promoting the unity of the region, security, and development on the continent and ensuring that Africa has a strong global role). For Africa to have a strong global role requires a thorough reexamination of its political, economic, social and cultural shocks occasioned by the coloniality of the global matrices of power. It has been mentioned several times and over, the key to the fulfilment of the interests of the hegemonic people of Africa is through a progressive Afro-centric agenda. A progressive Afro-centric agenda with a human face and with the people as the focus of activities. In all, here is no illusion that the Africa of the future we are about to embark on will not easy. A progressive Afro-centric Agenda will be only successful by our collective efforts with every African having a role to play. Dark Clouds on the Horizon signals an awaiting challenge; and we have no choice but the wish and determination to wade-off the 'dark clouds' so that we can all see the 'blue sky' in order to have improved and sustainable livelihood for every citizen. The Dark Clouds on the Horizon is a clarion call to build and strengthen our common determination, our common African heritage and our hopes for a more prosperous nation/continent offering a high quality of life to every citizen. From suffering the imperatives of imperialism, slavery, colonialism and post-colonialism, the people have exhibited their determination to fight for their freedom and sovereignty; their resilience to succumb to the new dictates of post-colonial governance rule by those in power remains the best hope for the future of the continent.

Therefore, the Dark Clouds on the horizon beacons us to remain resilient towards all intruding forces and to continue in the same spirit, the same determination demonstrated during the imperial, slavery and colonial era. Africa should stand united and to continue the struggle and resistance to wade off any form of recolonisation or brewing tsunami of recolonisation and enslavement. The vision of the progressive Afro-centric agenda is to consolidate the genuine sovereignty, independence and freedom of the African people. The progressive Afro-centric comes at the time in the history of the continent when we have a government of, by and for the people, when the opposition parties and the people agree on the need to move away *'from business as usual to business unusual'* for the overall interest of the people. The progressive Afro-centric Agenda should be the *'living ideological manifestoes'* that respond to internal and external changes and challenges but still remain focused on the goals of the sovereignty, independence and freedom of Africa. What we need most is the political leadership and support of the people to give added value to the new African vision. Giving added value requires a governance system of inclusion; a continent of justice, equality and caring or one another. Chad Norman (2022) points out that "the care of each other and the planet go hand in hand. This is the only way we will be able to pull ourselves from brink. We need a blueprint for right action: love, compassion, fortitude, and courage." We need a new dawn for the continent. Indeed, a new dawn for "Africa and the World" (Kornegay, 2020) working at the global geopolitical landscape from an African perspective, with a view to the opportunities and challenges facing the African continent.

Kornegay (2020) agues for the strengthening of continental integration and cohesion in pursuit of ideals that the African Union has enshrined in Agenda 2063. In this way, he calls on Africa to constructively engage – in a systemic and disciplined manner – with external powers to assert the continent's own interest which, in their faming, are also in the interests of humanity. A continent united in both purpose and action can be an active agent in shaping the evolving global order. The African continent has arrived at a defining moment; it is a question of now or never, a chance to take the bull by the horn, to step beyond not just the fear and failure of yester years but the divisive and polarised way politics and government have been practiced before and now. Africa in the post-colonial era of its history things have to be done differently to have a better and self-confident continent. An African continent of, by and for all Africans and friends of Africa. Africa has to be on the path of total and inclusive reconstruction, to ensure justice, equality, security and peace reigns for all; without which the continent will relapse into a non-repairable stage. The African continent is constantly x-rayed every day, scanned and rescanned for any progressive change being made, and how the continent can make it to the next level. Any progressive move depends on the new breed of leaders and the type of civil society response to the emerging leadership.

The work-load for the new leadership will be enormous and needs a well-spelled-out of does and do-nots for each country and the continent to regain its place in national and global politics. The pace of the transition could be slow, or old habits die-hard. The new leader will be bombarded with hundreds of decisions all of them evidently urgent that could improve the quality of the livelihood of the people. The new leader will be confronted with a rising expectations of the citizens who have been neglected for decades. Grief, resilience and hope live together. These are all parts of the 'dark clouds' on the horizon that have to be addressed for the people to have a view of 'blue sky.' Seeing the 'blue sky' is hope for a sustainable quality livelihood for all. Sustainable quality livelihood requires us working together, and working together leads to a blessed nation; a blessed nation is a nation of happy citizens with stability, balance, confidence, hope and determination to collectively wade-off any form of obstacles. Only when each African state is able to wade of obstacles can the continent become free, independent and sovereign. We have to become a people, a nation and a continent to be recognised. Africa is not recognised because the people are not united, they are losing their cultural value heritage to the Euro-centric agenda. We are victims of our own doing to state the least.

Therefore, a progressive and well-implemented Afro-centric agenda provides the way for the recognition of the people and continent. Any Afro-centric agenda must have as goal and orientation 'the people' as the priority focus of development and of our being on planet earth. Without such a focus, all is lost without any hope for better tomorrow. A successful Afrocentric agenda must build on justice, truth, equality, peace, security and hope; the current Euro-centric accord is construed within the ideological orientation entrenched with the viruses of fear, injustice, inequality, oppression, domination and destruction. Dark Clouds on the horizon beacons us to drift away from any policy strategy designed to foster such divisive and destructive goal-achieving ends. Democratic governance which is hailed the world over; its practice in Africa produces the wrong effects. Why is this so? There is always something new on the continent! The newness of something in Africa fails to be working in the overall good of and for the interest of the people and continent. On the contrarily, the newness is design for ushering failure.

Throughout the publication, we continue asking the question, when will Africa be independent? How can we construct a new Africa of, for and by the people? From the word go, the overriding ideological principle behind colonial rule was the creation of a fragmented region, and the granting of independence was to rationalize and legalise the fragmentation of the continent into smaller units and pitted each country against itself. The case of Southern Cameroons tells the story of pitting one region or section against the other. France has been excellent in splitting nations with the policy of assimilation and annexation and of subjecting its colonial territories to its hegemonic dominance. More injustice and oppression have been unwittingly done by colonial powers in their colonies just for the sake to securing their interests. A progressive Afro-centric agenda becomes more imperative than ever before for the restoration of the dignity and sovereignty of the people.

A progressive mindset calls or knocking on the doors for all to be actively involved in building and consolidating the dignity of the people and society. It is an indisputable fact of modern times that today the questions of development and progress cannot be resolved without the participation of all – the rich and poor, the urban and rural areas, the strong and weak. It has always been a wrong policy approach neglecting the contribution of the weak, poor and rural population. Development in Africa requires a holistic and integrated approach with no one being left behind. On the same note, the sustainability of planet earth rests on the involvement of all parts of planet earth - Africa, Asia, Latin America, and Europe. The newly independent territories have a favourable effect on the international situation. The state of Africa's under-development has roots in the policy of imperialism; the continuation of an identical policy approach in post-colonial Africa is shameful to state the least. The exclusion of the people are literally the causes of conflicts throughout the continent. At present, it is obvious that sustainable development, justice, peace and security can be safeguarded only by policies that are home-grown through inclusive dialogue and consensus of the people to forge ahead for the common good of society. The policy and politics of greed breeds exclusion and fans conflicts which when not carefully attended to can lead to disastrous effects and consequences to the country and people.

Development in colonial constructions misplaces what could be considered rather propagates the interest of the colonial state in post-colonial contexts. There is a wide gap between real development needs of the people and what is circulated as development, leading to crisis of development in post-colonial societies. The effect of this depiction of reality is that autochthonous development or indigenous knowledge system is emasculated and taken for granted, while the colonial development model circulated unquestioned and undermines the genuine political and socio-economic transformation and development of post-colonial African societies. The New African Order as the means of overcoming existing dark clouds over the continent must be fashioned on the importance and active involvement of all, and starting with the right choices they make as individuals, and as the most essential input ingredients into revealing and sustaining the 'New African Order vision each of us makes in his or her life. Importantly, oppression and seeking freedom and liberty remain exemplary actors. The forces that are promoting the policy of aggression, exploitation and destruction are quite strong. Africa has to build an equal countervailing force and resolutely oppose the Euro-centric agenda that has gained grounds in Africa. Guided by the common sense and the instinct for preserving African sovereignty and unity. Africa has to be extremely vigilant for misfortune is on the threshold knocking at the continent.

Alternatively, development is under-stood as equitable social wellbeing and progressive change. The term 'sustainability' has in recent times given additional impetus to development. As its foundational objective is exploitative, the colonial model is bereft of such core elements, leading to "development of underdevelopment." In the context of trade, Walter Rodney argues that colonial trade was nothing more than banditry. Thus, complex contradictions surround colonial development both as a social construct and colonial legacy structured to meet the needs and demands of the imperial power. As such, post-colonial notion of development underlies and defines the direction taken by post-colonial societies increasingly resulting in development backlash. This dominant challenge has resulted in crisis between the colonial and indigenous identity, emasculation of indigenous knowledge system, development crossroads, culture dislodgement, inequality and persistent poverty. If this is to change, post-colonial development critique must provide an alternative thinking of development which does not rely on extraneous trajectories rather more home-grown and self-reliant model is sought. It is ardent belief that the work of this book to call for a reconsideration of colonial development models. The continent has to move away from the entrenched Euro-centric to the progressive Afro-centric developmental agenda. Our indigenous knowledge system must play a leading role, combined with the changes in the advancements of the results of modern science and technology to provide quality services delivery to the people.

Political instability and state fragility have emerged as a tendency in countries with poor resource management records. In many cases, the sheer volume of revenues generated from the mineral resources has also taken the attention of decision makers away from institutional and human development, export diversification and value addition at the expense of local production, thereby deepening inequality and exacerbating poverty. In many African countries, natural resource booms have only to a limited extent set off a dynamic growth process. There is a general recognition that many African countries have relatively weak institutions, low human development status, poor public financial management, and inadequate oversight, and poor governance that leads to endemic corruption. For example, despite the huge energy resources, the continent faces enormous energy challenges that include low generation capacity and inefficiency, high costs, unstable and unreliable energy supplies, low access to modern energy, insufficient energy infrastructure, and lack of institutional and technical capacity to harness these vast resources to the benefit of the populations. Accelerating Africa's transition from traditional to modern sources of energy and ensuring access to clean and affordable energy is a development imperative.

Our national institutions since independence seem to have been rotting in a way and at the time of an accelerated pace in global scientific and technological advancement and efficiency. In an address, the former Secretary General of the Commonwealth noted on14 December 1999 "...be a source of much national discomfort that our national institutions have been rotting away at a time of accelerated pace in global technological reach and efficiency. Public services, national institutions of education, health, transport and communication, and many others, have over the years declined as their counterparts have improved in most of the other parts of the world". The East Asian countries, Singapore, Malaysia, and South Korea for example, were in many ways behind a number of African countries in respect of social and economic development indices. Today, these countries are years in advance of many African countries in many aspects of socio-economic transformation. The experiences of these countries exhibit how national development can gain from making public institutions and services target-chasing ad achievement-oriented.

Thus, the emergence of Africa to independence constitutes a testing of its strengths and weaknesses of within the international construct of nations, dominated by the colonial masters. The 'Dark Clouds' hanging over Africa equally provide crucial and incalculable test for the developed polities to show their genuineness of the granting of independence to their former colonies. By all means, the publication offers new and useful insights into Africa's division, European unity in pursuing their colonial agenda, the need for continental alignments of African countries in search for what they want and how to get it. They need a new sense of purpose and direction of some of the major forces and problems involved in their efforts of seeing that self-determination' works in their favour. Given the circumstances of Africa it is eminently comprehensible that there should be a determination on the part of many Africa statesmen to stand by the existing political structure of the continent even though any one can with ease poke his/her fingers through the loopholes with which it is riddled. Without doubts, the consolidation and utilisation of what presently exists seems a far sunder procedure than an effort to reconstruct the political map of the continent and run the immediate risk of creating even far greater and worse situation than the one which now. Africa has to be on the right mode of development not the wrong one of destruction. We should be making fast progress after independence not deteriorating. Otherwise, what was the sense for fight for our liberation only to be greatly enslaved stupidly!

We need and must x-ray ourselves critically, objectively and scientifically. Such a structure-functional analysis is essential to find out what has is going wrong with us. With such critical analysis, a new mindset, the people of Africa will triumph. We have necessarily approached the issues and problems of Dark Clouds on the African horizon from the perspective and view of the African people. But we do not see its interests as being in permanent conflict with those of the developed polities. Nor does the progressive Afro-centric self-reliance we counsel for Africa imply a turning away from the rest of the world. Neither do we believe autarky nor is domination a viable course for any or all of its countries. Our call for a progressive self-reliance is a call to make more effective use of Africa's own resources – human, physical, financial and organizational – as the basis of its development. We look to a new Africa and a world where there is no poverty and underdevelopment, where these vices are history; we also look to a world where Africa is an inherent part; a world and Africa in which there is no one part rich, developed and dominating and exploitative while the other is poor, underdeveloped and dominated.

How will Africa look like fifty or more years from now? With growing internal conflicts within African countries, coup d'état here and there (Burkina Faso, Mali, Guinea Bissau) which country is next on line; increasing internal conflict like the Anglophone crisis in Cameroon, Ethiopia and Tigre, the situation in the Central African Republic among others point in the direction of an unstable and chaotic continent that awaits the people. This publication should be seen and x-rayed as a contribution to Africa's endeavours in spurring it to respond to properly to current challenges; and to be prepared and well equipped in addressing coming. In no way do we pretend and advocate that it will be easy. Success is not assured; it is conditional on what African countries do individually and collectively. But united, focused and with good leadership something fruit and tangible can be achieved. As the saying goes, 'a single bracelet dos not jingle,' in short, smooth seas do not make skilful sailors. In a way, successful people are not people who had never failed or made mistakes, but they are people who failed or made mistakes and overcame their failures or mistakes and pressed on to achieve their goals. So, Africa should not give up at this point in time. The battle must be fought and won for Africa to be free, independent and sovereign; free at last. Being free, independent and sovereign takes out from what Patrick (2011: iii) proverbially way notes that *"if you don't have a certain vision in life, you are as good as a sightless person heading on a journey on his/her own."* Africa and her people envision that in

50 years' time, Africa and its leadership will have undergone a fundamental transformation such that Africa's natural resources that include the capacity of its people and cultural diversity will be sustainably managed and the integrity and diversity of Africa's ecosystems conserved. To achieve and sustain this vision, a discourse on transformed leadership to manage Africa's vast resources and deploy these on a sustainable trajectory to achieve the goals of Agenda 2063 and the SDGs 2030 becomes crucially important and therefore relevant for a focused dialogue.

The challenge for African countries is to mobilise and deploy their human potentials and capacity together with their resources more effectively and efficiently - nationally and collectively – to energise their transformational and developmental path, draw strength from joint undertakings, exploit global opportunities, as well as to make the international system responsive to their interests. We need good governance, current policies have to be changed, institutions reformed and strengthened, and new mechanisms created. It boils down to have a progressive new mindset as the tasks are formidable, but Africa has no other choice but to face these challenges – or face further marginalization, greater exploitation and untestable impoverishment. The current mindset turned towards the Euro-centric agenda is pushing the continent further into the abyss of underdevelopment and entrenched chaos, despair and hopelessness. The Dark Clouds hanging over the continent is getting darker and darker making it difficult having a glimpse of the blue sky. Without a good view of the 'blue-sky' sustainable development and quality livelihood can hardly come the way of the people.

I do believe and it is my fervent hope that the book in its humble way goes the mile assisting in attaining some of the objectives of a people-oriented development approach; its overall impact in building the United Sates of Africa and promoting the welfare of the people, within the limitations created by an enormous and unwisely amount of information and the constraints imposed by my own limited knowledge and understanding. However, looking back through the period of time, there is the realisation that many other well-meaning individuals and I may have helped shaped the situation by staying quiet for too long? If we had reacted differently to the early signs like Chinua Achebe and others did, on paranoia of things, may be, Africa could have been saved from its current abyss, a different continent shaping up. Some may ask, what happened to the gifted scholars, did the leaders listen to them? No, they did not because they were well entrenched in the doctrine of master-servant relationship and believe of being the replacement of the departed colonial masters. Quick concessions were made to hasten the transfer of power to the bourgeoise class; creating and absence of the cortical integration of the governors and governed, certain constellations of institutions established for particular groups in the framework of upholding an authoritarian ethnic governance structure to keep in place and silence the majority of the people.

Society had to be deculturalised from foreign values and our cultural heritage values and doctrines implanted to enable a smooth functioning of new gigantic machinery put in place for the day-to-day administration of the new state structure. This doctrine of political, economic, social and cultural hierarchy established is thus but one aspect of a systematized hierarchization implacably pursued. Our former colonial lords continue to increase their demands, accumulates concessions and guarantees and takes fewer and fewer pains to make the hold it has over these independent states; the result, of course, the masses have continued to stagnate deplorably in unbearable poverty, squalor and misery; but gradually being awaken to the unutterable treason of their leaders. A new Africa is in the making. The rise of a new Africa will equally force the leaders into an extraordinary lethargy. The Africa of tomorrow will face Europe like a colossal mass whose aim should be to resolve the problems to which Europe has not been able or do not want to find the correct answers too. They are in grind and held close to their hearts to uphold the status-quo of the "centre-periphery" notion where all the knees of African nations must bow to the almighty centre. Such expected structural changes may not come in our life-time; but it will one day. The struggle continues until victory will one day will be achieved.Of course, the wind of change could not stop the desire for the fight for sovereignty, freedom and independence forcing the people to react; and they reacted; unfortunately, civil society did not understand them. How many African leaders understood Kwame Nkrumah and others who candidly believed and strongly advocated for a United and Indivisible Union Government for Africa? It is only today that people are beginning to have a gist of what they stood and struggled for. If the ruling elites had been more or are more realistic and acknowledged the impossibility of shifting smoothly from a centralised dictatorial and foreign controlled state of their creation or imposed on them by the departed colonial masters to the democracy of their self-serving dreams, would they have been more respectful, less provocative, and be proactive? Or is African leadership today simply an example of how power corrupts? These questions are endless. But the answers point in one direction - only Africans have the answers to their problems. Answers that must be encompassing, progressive proactive Afro-centric approaches and cohesive strategic forward-looking and inclusive in the best endurable long-term interests of the people. This also requires an interface between The State, Civil society and the Private Sector including the International Community, for the continent cannot operate in a vacuum. In line with most authors, we do "denounce the hypocrisy of those who considered colonialism and its sequels, war, torture, as only a monstrous excrescence which had only to be circumscribed and reproved, whereas it was really a perfectly logical, perfectly coherent whole, in which all those who live within it were inevitably accomplices" (Francois Maspero, Paris, 1964, Foreword in Fanon, 1970:9). Susan Williams (2021) eloquently delivers a magnum opus looks at the role of Western powers in the colonisation and neocolonisation of the African continent.

New colonialism is about the subordination of African states in ways that allow foreign domination to continue without giving rise to challenges of recolonisation. The policy relationship between France and Africa is clearly outlined by Gegout (2021) in these words: France's relations with Francophone States in Africa in the 1990s-2000s, in the political, cultural and economic sectors, were deeply embedded in patronage. The Journal Agir lci-Survie (1995) transformed Houphouet-Boigny's concept of equal 'France-Afrique' relations into that of FranceAfrique to describe French policies towards Africa. French elite made economic and political gains from their privileged relations with some African leaders, and at the same time, African leaders manipulated those elite. They could ask their French fiends to support them politically, and to intervene militarily in their favour when conflict occurred. However, French foreign policy in Africa is moving away from some aspects of neo-colonialism: economic interests have been reduced and special relations are waning in importance owning to the investment of French judicial system in fighting illegal activities of French and African elites, the disappearance of personal relations and patronage, the desire of some African elite to study elsewhere than France, the use of English rather than French in some states.

On the whole, France continues to have a strong and total grip over its former colonies; which questions the status-quo of the independence of its former colonies. How genuinely and independent are former French colonial territories? Gegout (2021:137) states: "At the political level, relations between France and African states have been institutionalized since decolonisation, Franco-African Summits used to be held on an annual basis, and they still take place every two to three years. French elites will enjoy personal relations with their African counterparts. Some French officials were close advisors in African governments. For example, Colonel Mantion, a member of France's external intelligence agency, the Direction Generale da la Securite Exterieure (DGSE), had his own office within the CAR presidency. A French military adviser has been seconded to Alassane Ouattara's government in Ivory Coast since its inception (12/01/12). The Elysée has its own unit to deal with African Affairs, separate from the Ministry for Foreign Affairs. The French military presence in Africa can be explained by core realism military bases and close cooperation with African states in military affairs mean that France can use Africa as a strategic base. France has regularly maintained substantial numbers of permanent troops in Africa: 1300 in 1993: 9,000 in 1996; more than 6000 in 2013; and over 9,000 in 2017. In 2017, France still had three permanent military bases in Africa, namely in Djibouti (1,450 troops), Gabon (350) and Reunion (1600).

Susan Williams (2021:219) proceeds further in providing a compelling account of deocolonisation and the forces propelling the birth of neocoloniastion and those thwarting the chaotic situation (between Ghana and the USA) by providing ultimately liberating forward looking plans in these words: "Ghana and the USA, - The two had fundamental differences on the issue. The most fundamental differences were that of purpose. Ghana was seeking to protect the legitimate government of the Congo and was making considerable sacrifices in order to achieve that goal. The USA, by contrast, was seeking to undermine Lumumba and his government and to advance the perceived interests of the USA. In the process, the CIA took a key role." Africa suddenly declined into the state of no-recovery! Analytically, the Congo crisis became the linchpin for the launching of the neo-colonisation agenda designed to thwart and undermine Africa's independence and sovereignty – the starting point for "Dark Clouds over Africa."

It is not surprising that Kwame Nkrumah (1968) wrote these catching words on the C.I.A: "The activities of the C.I.A. no longer surprise us .... Further examples of C.I.A. activity...in Africa could be given. They would provide material for a book of their own." Africans must wakeup rom heir century long slumber; implying that the continent must now find itself, and speaks to itself through its own voices and actions. We must admit the reality that the continent or the 54 nations states are not a homogenous entity; we know too that enslaved people are still to be found on the continent, even with the so-called granted or a simulacrum of phony independence, with others who are still fighting to attain sovereignty and others struggling to obtain complete freedom but who live under the constant menace of imperialist aggression. Africa is a continent of diversity; with diversity as an asset not a liability as it is made to be known. These are the machinery for destruction. The assets of Africa's diversity are that the gives us the second largest land stretch in the world. The natural wealth of Africa is estimated to be greater than that of almost any other continent in the world. Therefore, this puts at an advantageous position. To draw the most from our existing and potential means for the achievement of abundance and a fine social order, we need to unify our action, efforts, resources, skills and intentions.

Most unfortunately, African states are moving in directions which exposes the continent to the dangers for imperialist and neocolonialism destruction. Therefore, to counteract the movements in the wrong direction and exploitation by the forces of neo-colonialism, there is need for a common political base for the integration of the policies-economic planning, defence, political (national, foreign and diplomatic relations), education, healthcare, agriculture etc. etc. which need not infringe on the essential sovereignty of each independent African State. In brief, a United Africa – political and economically should be construed n three objectives as depicted here.

- A common overall political, economic, science technology planning on a continental basis;
- Establishment of a unified security and defence strategy for self-defence. African countries should ask themselves which single country in Africa can today protect its sovereignty single handedly against an imperialist aggression, (not even South Africa)

An Untied Africa===➔

- The marriage of the two items above should be the structural foundation for a third approach – a unified foreign and diplomatic policies that gives a coordinated approach to joint efforts for the protection of the economic development of Africa for Africa to speak to the world with one voice for the continent to be taken seriously

One aspect of life that African people need to understand is that by working under a single common, political, economic, scientific and technological etc. command gives them greater bargaining strength; by working individually, weakens their position; we should not that the forces uniting us are far greater than the difficulties dividing us presently These views tie with that of former UN Secretary General, Kofi Annan's farewell address to the United Nations on 19th September 2006 in view of his retirement on 31st September 2006 in which he outlined three major problems facing the world, namely; (i) an unjust world economy; (ii) world disorder; and (iii) widespread content foe human-rights and the rule of law. Therefore, national governments and the international community need what Harry S. Truman's credo that "the responsibility of the great states s to serve and not to dominate the peoples of the world. We again revert to the reality and idea that "politics is call to serve" not be served. In the "Sayings of the Year," *(Observer, 30 December 1973)*, President George Pompidou of France had made the following statement: *"a statesman is a politician who places himself at the service of the nation and a politician is a statesman who places his nation and his service."* Of course, we can argue that politics exists both as an art and a theory, that s, as an academic discipline and as a profession, there is need to choose and underline that which interests our discourse. Francis Bacon further notes that "The knowledge of man is as the waters, some descending from above and some springing from beneath; the one informed by the light of nature, the other by divine revelation," When we put people first, we save humanity and that tells us what kind of leadership that befits a country and what type of politics that makes a nation great. Politics should be used for nation-building and not the destruction of the society. Paul Atogho Enyih notes that "it takes light to produce a shadow; it takes a fertile mind to conceive an idea and then an imaginative one to transform it into an act" (1999:17). We are all challenged either as a leader, politician, scholar, lay person or whatever status you find yourself in to use politics for the services of humankind.

The dividing line between Francophone and Anglophone Africa is that the French- speaking African leaders accepted in toto, the politics and polices of assimilation and annexation to be an inherent part of the extended French empire. Both Michael Crowder and Donald Cruise O'Brien state that, "French West African politicians in postwar years differed fundamentally from their English-speaking neighbours in that: "...the French speaking African leaders formally rejected independence in favour of greater participation in the political process of French Union or Community of which Africa would be a constituent part." It was not until Sekou Toure addressing the Fourth Congress of his Democratic Party of Guinea (PDG) in June 1958 that he voiced the word "independence" and this entered the political vocabulary or discourse in French-speaking West Africa. Generally, Africa started the journey to sovereignty and independence on two main temperament of African nationalism. One group, especially the English-speaking countries strongly advocating for self-determination and independence, the French-speaking states advocating for quasi independence under French hegemony. In a way an alliance emerged between Kwame Nkrumah (Ghana) and Sekou Toure (Guinea-Conakry), and both became brothers-in-arm for the unity and genuine independence of Africa. In 1958, the Ghana-Guinea union was formed; later to include Mali (Ghana, Guinea-Mali) which was then christened the Union of African states (UAS). We also see how Guinea paid the heavy price for saying categorically ***"NO"*** to the idea of a French Union which most of the French colonies gladly accepted. The consequences are clear for us to see today.

To make the political history or African nationalism short, the yearning for unity dates many decades way back in time past. From the first shirring's of the African awakening – African intellectuals, both at home and in the diaspora, had drawn one firm conclusion from their experiences. Africans had been through the harrow of slavery and colonial subjugation, not as Ashantis, or Igbos, or Zulus, or Fulani's, Fulbes. Kikuyus, but as Africans. Both slavery and colonial rule had also been greatly facilitated by African disunity, weakness and quest for money or hatred for love of country. The Charter of the Union of African states committed itself to a common foreign and defence policy, the defining of a common set of economic objectives, total opposition to French nuclear testing in the Sahara; support for other Africa countries waging anti-colonial struggles and the building up of African Unity." It is clear that even with all the differences in the mood and time, temperament and methods of approaches, at least, the anti-colonial struggle was already on course, the building on the foundation though not yet solid and firm, since it had many fronts, but the seeds for the struggle of African independence was already sown, waiting for it to germinate. The creation of the Organisation of African Unity (OAU) in 1963 by 32 independent African states was a positive sign towards African Union or a United States of Africa. The conversion of that group into the African Union (AU)that should take the mantle forward is a significant progress in the direction of a rating viable United States of Africa. The AU as of now is not the ideal organisation, but a process towards the total unity of the continent. In March 1959, Frantz Fanon lamented in an address to the Second Congress of Negro writers in Rome about colonial rule in making. Africa the absentees of universal history; he further noted: "If man is what he does, then we should say that the urgent thing today for the African intellectual is the construction of his nation. If this construction is genuine, that is, if it reflects the manifests will of the people, if it reveals the African peoples in their impatience, their national construction will necessarily be accompanied by the discovery and encouragement of universalising values.

The target readers of the book are all categories of society, from the lay-person, through the student community, policy-makers, political leaders, non-governmental organisation, the corporate world as well as seeking common grounds and understanding for a proper take-off. Each chapter can be independently read. In particular, I have eschewed the use of people-focused or citizen-oriented developmental approach as the common ground for good servant leadership to target the change, development, progress and sustainable agenda in transforming society. Here positive and responsible responses are required from civil society towards any form of comprehensive restructuring geared in the direction of improving the welfare of citizens. There is economic and social inequality the world over, much in Africa and between Africa and the rich industrial north. How can we change current thinking on increasing the divide between North and South countries? How can we change mentality in Africa in particular that it must take charge of its development path? The book like others attempts in a modest way of raising awareness in the direction of thinking about the disparities and the changes necessary in creating a more humane world. Hence the stands taken throughout the book are clear - developing an Afro-centric agenda for the people and within the confines of functioning within the 'global village' without losing our focused interests without losing our identity and quest for sovereignty, freedom and equality The basic fundamental human rights and freedoms must be respected – it is a universal and fundamental basic human-rights that does not discriminate whether black or white.

First, I have tried as much as possible to move away from the long-held view that the problems of Africa can be understood best with reference to colonial domination. The fact is that colonial rule did occur, destroying the cultural heritage and mental physic of the people, destroying their human personality and rendering them vulnerable to all kinds of exploitation. We can reconstruct that reality. It did happen. Nor has it subsided. How do we move away from existing construct to constructing a new sovereign Africa with an intact human dignity as well as deterrents ensuring the same mistakes do not occur in the new international environment of which Africa is a part? As noted by Ray

(1998:3) this view includes not only the notion that developing countries are somehow hindered by their exposure to the developed world, epitomised in the teachings of depreciate theorists, but also more mainstream concerns regarding the central role of international organisation and foreign assistance.

Accordingly, the school of thought holds that the problems of development in Africa must first and foremost be seen in a global context. After all, we live in "global village." Valid as this maybe, I weigh to stress equally fundamental issues that are internal to the structure of African countries. A sizeable section of this book is focused on the internal dynamics of change, development, progress and sustainability. It touches on the international aspects of development or relationship between Africa and the developed world. The reader who wishes to concentrate exclusively on any of these two stands will find comprehensive treatment as well. It remains an open-ended publication geared towards encompassing all views that contribute to the meaningful and total liberation of Africa. What is fundamental for the continent is to start cultivating new a form of leadership. There is no homogenous African state compared to some European countries like Denmark, Sweden, and Norway. African states are configuration of diverse ethnic entities. Therefore, leading, managing and leveraging the benefits of diversity in the continent is an imperative not just for individual organisational success, but for the survival of the continent. The continent is characterised by an abundance of diversity, both in its workforce and its natural resources, yet it remains one of the poorest continents (Ngambi, 2011). Unfortunately, its diversity which should be a blessing, an asset has only converged into a curse, a liability to the region. Something fundamental is missing and must be replaced or activated to set things in correct perspectives. A crucial missing aspect is the continent's current leadership, which constitutes the greatest challenges hindering Africa from realising her potential in the global space. There is a serious leadership gap cloud hanging over the continent. Africa needs more than ever before, ***Responsible, Accountable, Relevant and Ethical*** **(RARE)** leadership to pilot and defend its affairs, nationally and internationally. See section on leadership details.

Second stance concerns the conceptual or methodological approach. There is no common methodological approach. Each chapter builds on its own conceptual framework. However, a unified approach to the problems of development emphasis on adopting an Afro-centric view as against the currently practiced Euro-centric strategy adopted by many African countries and passionately is being pushed down the throats of Africa by the developed countries through its industrial military complex hegemony imposing its agenda of domination on the rest of the world, Africa in particular. At the same time, there is no countervailing policy strategy from Africa. Often, the continent reverts to the "blame theory" that does no good to the continent. Hence, the call for a new mindset as a significant game-changer to facing the plethora of difficulties that is confronting the continent. It is not that an Afro-centric or Euro-centric approaches are intrinsically bad or intrinsically good: the point is to understand the conditions under which they fall or function at an inefficient level to determine if appropriate policies grounded in an understanding of these conditions can fix such inefficiencies. These conditions, can be understood best by a serious appreciation of subjects that are at the forefront of development theory but need to permeate more thoroughly into policy formulation or textbooks; theories of incomplete transformation, of incentives, and of strategic behaviour (Ray, 1998:4). What the continent needs most are critical thinking, innovation, creativity, entrepreneurship, strategic planning, and comprehensive implantation process.

Based on these stances close to our hearts, "Dark Clouds on the Horizon," therefore, differs from other publications on development related issues in a number of aspects. Most of these differences stem from my personal perception and exposition and choice of subject matter. Apparently, I have not neglected the trajectory of historical development and the need for African countries carving their development approaches construed on the basis of drawing lessons from best practices of the old democracies, and of course, taking full advantage of the *"late-comer advantage"* propounded by Gerschenkron (1962). Africa does not need to develop the wheel but build and improve on the developed wheel for their wellbeing and the general good of humankind. The fact is that Africa cannot exist as an island implies it has to reach-out but on a different platform - no longer the master-servant dichotomy. It should be construed on the dichotomy of "master-to-master" or "servant-to-servant" dialogue as the line of approach or inquiry. Fair trade and not aid are what Africa is asking for. The current Master-Servant approach should be made history. Can it when there is new frontier line or recolonisation being hatched in Brussels. The old paradigm has shifted from Berlin to Brussels not to Addis Ababa, implying that the Berlin and Brussels doctrine is ongoing. The Addis Ababa line lost. It will not or never abate until a countervailing force is put in place. That is why a progressive Afro-centric agenda must henceforth be articulated and implemented to save the continent from further destruction. The 2012 Noble Peace Prize strengthens the exploitation agenda.

To what extent is Addis Ababa accelerating or confronting the emerging consensus on the exploitation of the continent? Can the 54 or more countries mount a common strong and united convergence strategy for the continent's redemption construct? Seen within these perspectives, African countries should perceive and understand the issues of underdevelopment/development in many ways but within the context of coming out of the underdevelopment cliché that hangs around their neck and how to cut of the chain requires a strong-saw. Attempts have been made in presenting analytical and comparative perspective on the various issues discussed. The issue of underdevelopment has to be faced squarely; the sad side of the story is that the continent is presented as poor in the midst of abundant resources. They are unable to give added value to these resources. And the resources have become a curse rather than a blessing to the people. Do not make our resources a curse. Frit weakens our effort towards improving the well-being of the vast majority of citizens. We strengthen our give resources as a great asset to the people, to the content and make proper use of it.

So, the continent is faced in many ways with the problems of how informal, imaginative institutions replace the formal constructs that are well established in the developed economies. A host of problems and challenges needing constructive and holistic solutions are imperative. The absence of proper understanding of the functioning of the global system gives rise to other features - the creation of widespread externalities. A common feature of the various problems yields a mental classification system - a way of seeing that different phenomenon stem from a unified source but requiring common solutions in meeting the basic needs of the people. The intensity in the escalation of the divide and inequality in the distribution of income and wealth-sharing plays a vital role in many transitional polities which can cause disruptions of wide magnitude. The ongoing conflicts in Cameroon, Ethiopia, Mali, Sudan and other parts of the continent testifies to the state of growing inequality between the "haves" and "have-nots," between the majority and minority; centre and periphery. In short, the challenges of the many faces of underdevelopment hang over these countries with little signs of constructive change. No single aspect of the socioeconomic transformation process must be left behind. It is an uphill task calling for mutual understanding and cooperation from all the stakeholders. Lucas (1988) points out that "the problem of economic development simply implies the problem of accounting for the observed pattern, across countries and across time, in levels and rates of growth of per capita income...but thinking about income patterns will necessarily involve us in thinking about many other aspects of societies too."

The book strongly emphasizes the destructive functional role of inequality and poor leadership impacting adversely on the quality wellbeing of the people. Africa suffers heavily from a deficit of images: we see the continent only through depressing news images headlines - people fleeing their homes to become refugees; abject poverty and poor services delivery, while the continent sees the West through Hollywood films. May be *'Nollywood'* will help create a better image of *"The other Africa,"* which no doubt will take some time. For now, the continent's 105 or more medical schools do not currently have the capacity to meet the urgent demand for doctors, nurses, midwives and other cadres of health workers. Meaning that Africa is a sick continent, requiring the best available surgical operations beds provided to African doctors. As a sick continent, the people are not healthy and productive. These complex set of factors - failing economies, high unemployment, low human capital development and poor human rights; armed conflicts, poor governance system constitute a fertile breeding ground for all sought of unproductive and destructive activities. The continent cannot become 'a service delivery entity' with such poor statistics and failed democracies. Why is the situation so chaotic and depressing? Why is the continent continuously degenerating into the abyss of underdevelopment, abject poverty and endemic corruption? Why, why, why. I wish we could understand the prevailing conflict situation; I wish we could understand the situation of the *'have-nots;'* I wish we could understand the situation of 'haves,' the powerful and rich. I wish we can understand our situation of 'unity in diversity,' diversity as an asset; not diversity as a liability. I wish we could understand the need for love for one another and country, justice, peace and equality have no price tack. I wish we could put behind us the prevailing orientation of *'love for money and cult'* against *'love for country and people.'*

It was Aristotle who noted in his book- *Politics* - "Why inferiors revolt in order that they may be equals. And equals that they may be superior;' concluding that such 'is the state of mind that creates revolutions;' and adding, "When some people are very wealthy and others have nothing, the result will be either extreme democracy or absolute oligarchy or nepotism will come from either of these excesses." These are some of the issues underpinning the Dark Clouds hanging over the continent. We move from one extreme to another. The Dark Continent has entered into an evitable best to bow with good grace. Only we Africans can bring grace to the continent. Either we do that or face the consequences of our common dilemma or inaction. We have no choice but obliged to build a solid fence, concrete pillars of which - The Afro-centric agenda rocks – justice, unity, peace and reconciliation; democracy government and political openness; social welfare and security; growth and development are necessary. We need a democratic state as "one in which all the people live in harmony and with equal opportunities;" a thing for which he is prepared to die for and a view justified by the fact that: "Man's capacity for justice makes democracy possible, but man's inclination to injustice makes democracy necessary" (Nelson Mandela, 1957).

The age-old definition of democracy remains, *"government of the people by the people for the people,"* which following our quest and practice of greed, we can add, "government against the people." The political conditionalities or vectors or constraints on development in Africa are simple to diagnose; Many African governments are working against the interests of their citizens. This is an inescapable concept or nexus in all serious discourses on the socio-eco-political discourses on the transformation predicament of the African continent. In a way, the concept has become by virtue of its implications, the bugbear of most African leaders and explains why they would like to hold-on-to-power for ever and ever. We cannot deny the fact that African states are inflicted with prolonged sight-tight-presidents, with the Central African Sub-region the worst affected. We need a new game-changer to reshape the socio-eco-political conditionalities of the continent. Some elements of the political conditionality within the domestic political systems include the following:

- Respect for fundamental human rights especially in accordance with the treaty provisions and other conventions to which African countries are signatories to – UN Charter, The African Union Charter and other international agreements:
- Greater political opening to encourage participation and the right of opposition with the system. This necessarily entails the establishment of multi-party politics as a step towards the re-emergence of democracy. Africa's return to multi-party politics has only contributed to a dominant one-party hegemonic state, Cameroon for example;

- Reform of the administrative and judiciary machinery of the state in order to eliminate waste, corruption and consequently enhancing efficiency, accountability, responsibility, transparency as well as improve on productivity. This implies also the undertaking of other 'institution building' measures to strengthen the state and also to extend its influence on areas where it is hitherto non-existent;
- Demilitarisation or cuts in military spending aimed at releasing resources for utilization in sociation in social and other more productive domestic needs. Military expenditure in African countries keeps rising compared to the declining expenditure on improving the social welfare standards of citizens. The more we focus on military solutions to socio-eco-political problems, the less we spend on the welfare of the people. See the high degree of expenditures on addressing conflicts in Africa – Boko Haram in Cameroon and Nigeria, the senseless war in Cameroon (Anglophone Regions), and the situation in Sudan, Mali, Central African Republic, Chad and name the rest.

The constitution of African countries parades these wonderful ideals or concepts but fail to practice, fit would mean a change in the current status-quo of total dominance to justice, equality and respect of the people. For example, The Preamble of the South African Constitution reads: "We, the people of South Africa Recognise the injustice of our past, Honour those who suffered for Justice and Freedom in our land, Respect those who worked to build and develop our country; and Believe that South Africa belongs to all who live in it, united in our diversity, we therefore, through our freely elected representatives, adopt this constitution as the Supreme Law of the Republic as to…." The constitution of Cameroon (1996), "We, the people of Cameroon, declare that the human person, without distinction as to race, religion, sex or belief, possesses inalienable and sacred rights; Affirm our attachment to the fundamental freedoms enshrined in the Universal Declaration of Human Rights, the Charter or United Nations and the Africa Charter on Human and peoples' Rights, and all duly ratified international conventions relating thereto, in particular, to the following principles". The Constitution of the Republic of Ghana (1992), states: "We the People of Ghana IN EXERCISE of our natural and inalienable right to establish framework of government which shall secure for ourselves and posterity the blessings of liberty, equality of opportunity and prosperity, IN A SPIRIT of friendship and peace with all peoples of the world; AND IN SOLEMN declaration and affirmation of our commitments to; Freedom, justice , Probity, and Accountability; the Principles that all powers of Government spring from the Sovereign Will of the People; The Principle of Universal Adult Suffrage; The Rule of Law; The protection and preservation of Fundamental Human Rights and Freedoms, Unity and Stability for our Nation......"

Looking at the proposed draft constitution of the Republic of Kenya Chapter One, Sovereignty of the People and supremacy of this Constitution, Article 1 (1) states: "All sovereign power belongs to the people of Kenya and shall be exercised only in accordance with this constitution. Article 1 (2) The people may exercise their sovereign power directly or through their democratically elected representatives. Article 1(3) Sovereign power under the Constitution is delegated to the following State organs, which shall perform their functions in accordance with this Constitution. (a) Parliament and the legislative assemblies in the country governments; (b) the national executive and the executive structures in the county governments; (c) the Judiciary and independent tribunals; and (d) the sovereign power of the people is exercised at (i) the national level; and (ii) the country level." The South African constitution reads thus:

> "STATUTES OF THE REPUBLIC OF SOUTH AFRICA-CONSTITUTIONAL LAW Constitution of the Republic of South Africa Act, ss. 1-3 No. 108 of 1996s -1- Preamble reads: We, the people of South Africa, Recognise the injustices of our past; Honour those who suffered for justice and freedom in our land; Honour those who suffered for justice and freedom Respect those who have worked to build and develop our country; and Believe that South Africa belongs to all who live in it, united in our diversity. We therefore, through our freely elected representatives, adopt this Constitution as the supreme law of the Republic so as to Heal the division of the past and establish of society based on democratic values, social justice and fundamental human rights; Lay the foundations for a democratic and open society in which government is based on the will of the people and every citizen is equally protected by law; Improve the quality of life of all citizens and free the potential of each person; and Build a united and democratic South Africa able to take its rightful place as a sovereign state in the family of nations. May God protect our People?
>
> *Nkosi Sikelei' i Afrika. Morena boloka setjhabasa heso. God seen Sui-Afrika. God bless South Africa. Mudzimu fhatutshedza Afurika Hosi katekisa Afrika*

Even the draft Constitution of the yet to be created The United Africa (UA) – The United States of Africa – proposed by African Civil Society, Yaoundé – Cameroon, 25th May 2005, the Preamble is embellished with these words: "We, the African People, **Moved and United** as one great people, from different peoples of the African continent, its Islands and its Diaspora. **Proclaim** that we are henceforth united by the dynamic nature of African Unity; **Acknowledge** that we are one people, constituted by centuries of historic march and marked by sufferings and multiple struggles; Celebrate with pride our unity in our rich diversity; **Proclaim** our unshakable will to transform the African Union (AU) into an authentic African Supranational State; **Acknowledging** that the OAU Charter, the Abuja Treaty instituting the African Economic Community and the Constitutive Act of the African Union constitute the minimum foundation of the political union to be realized;... In Article 8 (1) stipulates that, The United Africa must rely on itself for the development, well-being and happiness of its people; Article 8 (2). Every African, irrespective of where he/she lives, and his/her activities, has a duty to contribute to the development of the United Africa; Article 8 (3) Every African has the right to some of the natural resources of this continent, particularly the resources of the soil and sub-soil, for his/her personal well-being". (See African Civil Society Organisation, 25 May 2005).

Paradoxically, it was the cold war whose major thrust was to demonstrate the superiority of market and democratic values over doctrinaire socialism which had led many Western nations but particularly the United States, France and Belgium to close their eyes, as it were, to the political shortcomings in the countries closely attached to them - Kenya, Togo, Democratic Republic of Congo, Central African Republic, Cameroon, for example – where varying forms of authoritarianism and personal rule held sway. Two fundamental reasons seem to account for this emergence. In the first place we can make reference to what are the crisis of governance in Africa and, more specifically, the crisis of the African state. The second refers to the prevalent mood for change in the international system which in a way was triggered by the reformist inclination of degree of the former leader of the defunct Soviet Union, Mikhail Gorbachev - perestroika and glasnost concept setting the stage for the *'market and democratic revolutions'* that swept through the former Eastern bloc countries in the late 1980s. We cannot run away from the reality that there is indeed a crisis of mammoth proportions facing Africa because the evidence is overwhelming but the underlying causes of it have been subject to controversy aired often with an emotive and ideological outpouring. Scholarship which highlights the authoritarian and patrimonial character of rulership in African states is quite representative of mainstream academic opinion and in many ways is consonance with the Euro-centric analysis and path to development in Africa. The tendency of this type of political system and approach remains counter-productive to the socio-economic transformation of the region is sufficiently stressed and greatly underscores the structural basis of the book. Africa's democracy is fundamental to its good governance. It was President Franklin Delano Roosevelt who noted, "We know now that Government by organised money is just as dangerous as Government by organised mob." The organized mob is part of rigged elections that leads to state capture. State capture leads to Parenti's (1978:111) well-known statement: "When power is derived from the loyalty of others and wealth from the labour of others; where many citizens' failure is other people's success; and where noble intentions and ignoble effects exist in equal abundance, the power of a man is his present means to obtain some future well." We have to tackle and very seriously too, the flip sides of corruption as this are the great virus destroying the continent. The *'love for money'* overshadows the *'love for people and country'* Love-for-money is what is destroying the continent. Corruption is a tool for all – individuals, communities and organisations wishing to gain materially, or to improve their social or political standing in society where under normal legal and procedural circumstance they would otherwise not be able to. In all, corruption creates a *dog-eat-dog* environment making people prioritise survival all cost. These are of the inherent issues contributing to disgust, disunity and discontent within the society making the post-colonial state robust or fragile ready for collapse any moment. All the positive energies from within Africa must be integrated to ensuring that the continent achieves agency for navigating the contours of a difficult and challenging world construct. Africa is the only region with rawest deal in human history; all efforts must be made to ensure all of Africa becomes united with its fir, just ad new deal.

Catherine Gegout (2021:12) writes; "Before 2000, African affairs were hardly mentioned by officials at the Council of European Union (CEU). They are now assured regularly, and since 2000 five EU military operations have been conducted in African states. The European Union was present in the DRC in 2003 and 2006 and in Chad and CAR from 2008 to 2009. It has operated off Somali coast since 2008 and sent troops to the CAR from 2014 to 2015. Nevertheless, the mantra of the

EU officials is that "Africa's ills have to be deal with by Africans." Was the sudden EU interest a response to reaction to the creation of the African Union to ensure their significant presence to derail the smooth functioning of the African Union?

For instance, Richard Sandbrook (1985, 1986) strongly argued that as dysfunctional as personal rule – invariably patrimonialism – is to the development of capitalism. In Africa, its dismantling will raise problems for the personal ruler who relies on the resources generated by machine politics to hold the 'unintegrated peasant societies' which constitute the state together. But the problem is considered sufficiently grave to lead him to envisage survivalist remedies stretching from avoiding the state (self-reliance), through freeing the market to an evolution from above under a benevolent personal ruler as possible mechanisms for redressing the situation. The situation continues to persist pointing to the structural imbalances in the international division of labour dominated by global capitalism which places the continent at a particular vulnerable and disadvantageous position and begging for new dawn for genuine change in the continent. Perceived in this light, the crisis of the State in Africa is assumed by this hypothesis to merely reflect the crisis of global capitalism; the envisaged option is to disconnect the African states from the world. Samir Amin advocates the strategy of delinking to relinking.

Like some analysts argue, that the marginalisation of Africa from international exchanges represents a disconnection by default (Bach, 1991:245-51). The divergence in the appreciation of the underlying causes of Africa's state of underdevelopment, no matter which every angle the subject is viewed from, the inescapable analytical observation is that the calamity that has engulfed African states whose control seems to have been deliberately elevated to the point of becoming the essence of politics in Africa. By and large, most African states, since the dawn of independence failed to see the writing on the wall or the signal for the confiscation of their sovereign (state) right, and, through that, of the commanding heights or power of the economy by a strong man or a clique of powerful forces enough to impose their will on the rest of their societies. Callaghy, 1990:258) is categorical on this point, pointing out that; "A new political class began to emerge that used the state as its arena of action and source of power, status, rents, and other forms of wealth. The state was used to begin to build an economic base for itself… The result was neither an effective socialism or state capitalism nor a viable autonomous capitalism." Susan Williams (2021) eloquently and analytically delivers a magnus opus of the dirty tricks and role of western powers in the colonisation, decolonisation and neocolonisation of the African continent. Susan Williams (2021:219) meticulously book provides a compelling account of decolonisation and forces that sought to thwart the evolving chaotic situation in these words: "The most fundamental difference was that of purpose. Ghana was seeking to protect the legitimate government of the Congo and making considerable sacrifices in order to achieve that goal. The USA by contrast was seeking to undermine Lumumba and his government and to advance the perceived interests of the USA. In this process the CIA took a key role." The outcome is that Congo and Africa have gone the way the West wanted it to go. The legacy of the "Congo Scenario" is haunting and destroying the continent. Only Africans can change the gloomy situation. The fighting that gloomy situation rests on the strong emphasises of the Africa spirit of "Ubuntu" which stresses the virtues of humanness in humility, compassion, communalism and African patriotism that provide the veritable starting point for the development of the moral fibre to fight corruption which has eaten very deep into the social fabric of the continent.

Apparently, it must be admitted that there is no single cause for economic progress, but that a combination of factors - among them, as noted several times in the book; the improvement of the physical and human capital, the drastic reduction of inequality, and the creation of strong institutions enabling the background flow and respect of the rule of law, good governance and the right information reaching society being essential to constructive changes and performance consistently favouring and furthering the goals of development and sustainability in quality livelihood of the vast majority of the population. Lack of education and equal opportunities reinforces the cycle of poverty will only spiral out of control. However; catastrophe might be the last and most significant of our Nakbas. It can be avoided if we want. As political animals, the human being is far more engaged towards war, destruction rather than peace, justice, equity and development. From the capitalist perspective, we destroy to build in order to make greater profit. That can be termed as constructive destruction. Look at what is happening in Syria and other areas like Libya, Afghanistan, Iraqi, the Palestine occupied areas. There is western conspiracy and gross absence of unity among the Arab states.

Africa has since independence emerged as a conflict-prone zone. It is the battle ground for the acquisition of natural resources by the rich nations – East or West – making the people to be fighting, killing them and destroying their country as the powers that watch and jubilate. Our greatest mistake is to continue believing that the colonial enemy has lost its combativeness and its harmfulness by granting us independence. The belief, attitude and action have always been 'getting rid of the leaders' who want to liberate their fellow-country men and women. Nkrumah, Mugabe, Moumie, Biko, Lumumba, Ghaddafi and others must be silenced at all costs. Recall Lumumba's Congo's Independence Day speech: "…You aren't giving us anything. Why, can you take back these scars that you put on our bodies? Can you give us back the limbs that you cut off while you were here"? Africa has to learn and understand the "global game" being played by the colonial powers as they did in the Congo, in Rhodesia, South Africa, events which prompted Kwame Nkrumah while addressing the Fifteenth Session of The United Nations General Assembly,20th September 1960, criticising the UN on its failure to remove Belgian troops from the Congo and to end the secession of Katanga stated: "It is no more possible for a saint to be neutral on the issue of good and evil", he said slowly, but firmly, "than for the United Nations to be neutral on of legality and illegality," adding further; "imperialist intrigue, stark and naked, was desperately at work' to prevent reconciliation between Kassavubu and Lumumba. To do anything to damage the prestige and the authority of that government,' insisted Nkrumah, 'would be to undermine the whole basis of democracy in Africa'…with passion, he continued; "Now I, an African, stand before this august Assembly of the United Nations and speak with a voice of peace and freedom, proclaiming to the world the dawn of a new era" (Susan Williams, 2021:272-3). The UN created the ongoing political crisis in Cameroon 1961 today; it is silent to an extent and even enjoys the genocide and damages being inflicted on the people of Southern Cameroons. By being silent on the policy approaches of assimilation and assimilation carried out by France, the UB is failing to adhere to its founding principles: it is even undermining itself as a world body; failing to protect the weak against the powerful, the poor against the rich, and give voice to the voiceless. The situation confronts the UN with unescapable challenges, but more importantly with opportunities for serving the people. In short, the UN is protecting French interest as it did with Belgian interests in the Congo in the 1960s.

It is vital for all of us to work together and on all fronts against oppression, as fellow human-beings in partnership for the good of the environment. I believe it's necessary for both sides, rich and poor working together to keep people away from fighting each other. Push the poor and vulnerable toward servitude, poverty, and ignorance, while getting rich ourselves. Religion and ethnic diversity are used to keep people from real progress. For many decades, the powerful have declared war on the environment, human rights, rights to natural resources, rights to clean air, rights to sustainable environment and so on. Those who champion rights of the common people are by definition enemies of those elites and pay a heavy price for our resistance. On the global scale, human rights belong to those who have the military arsenal and can use it at will against the poor and weak. But life and struggle must go on. And life goes on too. Yet it is imperative that we work together to achieve true justice - and perpetuates for peace, change and development. Resuscitating the African economy is the wish of all, even the rich. But how to achieve it and ensure shared-prosperity is what divides the rich and poor. Ego-centricism and individualism paves the way for the violation of the fundamental rights of the people.

Various sections of the book have used as lecture materials. Revisions have been made and updated as well. The publication tries to adopt a coevolutionary national and world view as depicted in Figure 1. The Coevolutionary National and World View provide an interpretative/contextual understanding as well as an evolutionary perspective of opening up new ways of thinking about the structure and organisation of society. To begin with, as participants in society to understand the structure-functioning of the system, their limits, and how they can constrain interpretation and the accumulation of contextual knowledge in the past. Second, to devise structures and reward systems that enhances the use of the interpretive/contextual approach and to accumulate such knowledge. Third, Society would be better able to articulate with other bodies – local and national, public and private, scientific and non-scientific, indigenous and not – open to an interpretive/contextual approach to knowledge. Fourth, society would be better able to adapt to the ideas of universal principles of collecting information and making decisions are not getting in the way (Norgaard, 1991:18-19). African states are left at large. Fanon (1970:134) states; "The former colonial power increases its demands, accumulates concessions and guarantees and takes fewer and fewer pains to mask the hold it has over the national government. The people stagnate deplorably in unbearable poverty; slowly they awaken to the unutterable treason of their leaders." This is further discussed in the book by Catherine Gegout *(2021; why Europe Intervenes in Africa: Security, Prestige and the Legacy of Colonisation).* Europe intervenes in the affairs of the continent because we permit them to do. We are at fault with ourselves and development approaches. Africa should wake-up now before it is too late. Listen to the cries of Nkrumah, Fanon, Achebe, Sankara, Mandela and a host of other critical minds of Africa; draw valuable less from the historical past, understand the present and prepare for the future with open not closed eyes, ears and minds. Forward looking positive actions are required.

This awakening is all the more acute in that the bourgeoise is incapable of learning its lesson. And so, it is the appeal – come brothers and sisters so that we can jointly and constructive fight the good fight; we must find something new and different., bearing in mind that singly we can do nothing, but collectively we ca do everything so long as we do not imitate the wrong acts of Europe; so, long as we are not obsessed with the Eurocentric desire and the foolish idea of trying to catch with Europe. Can we catch-up with Europe? I wonder! Yet, it is very true we need a new model, and that we want good blueprints and best examples that suit us, not for the sake that they are best examples, but that these examples meet our wants and desires. We want our liberty, independence and freedom. We fought for it and it is our duty to preserve and protect it. At the same time, to bear in mind that 'the history of liberty is a history of limitations of government power.' Our governance system should not be construed on the ideological orientation of 'winner takes all.' It is this attitude that gives rise to the feelings of 'independence as failure or disappointment.' With the in-depth orientation of 'winner takes all,' it breeds corruption, making our society to become engraved in sin and addiction to corruption. To move forward we need an ethic governance environment that entails a system of 'horizontal and vertical accountability that entails a 'vicious circle,' in which each actor is both a watcher and is watched, is both a monitor and is monitored. Apparently, current Africa's democracy is afflicted with moral decadence and culture of "unethical materialism." Corruption is socially embedded in the 'logics' of 'unethical materialism' a system of mindless material acquisition of riches, whether illicit or not, and socially glorified by many in society. It is a system where altruistic social capital and socially useful citizens are subordinated to financial and material wealth. This has weakened social values, with broader public interests and social responsibility being subordinated to the enhancement of personal material gains" (Nsia-Pepra, Kofi, 2017:62).

For now, the ball is in the penalty-box space of African civil society to face the Herculean task in fighting to rid society of corruption. Facing the Dark Clouds over the African Horizon, requires a vital component of good governance and efficient management that values integrity, incorruptibility and accountability; shone, nepotism, cronyism, favouritism, and ensure the rule of law to demonstrate to the public the government's resolve to fight corruption and ensure equity in benefit-sharing. Good governance requires African people to make a paradigm shift from zero-sum game *'winner-take-all'* politics to the more inclusive *'win-win game* political system. Good governance rests on the temple of corruption control mechanism as the roof, with the following apartments (i) efficient administration; (ii) deterrent punishment; (iii) effective ACA; (iv) effective laws, with political *will* as the foundation. The foundation of good governance is inherent in matured democracies that foster political will to fight and curb corruption. What Africa needs is good governance values equity and inclusiveness that treats citizens equally and guarantees them equal opportunities. In Cameroon for example, apart from issues already mentioned, the country needs to remove the magnet-predatory of appointment, promotion, motion-of-support syndrome, to end corruption in politics through preventive and punitive measures.

Dear readers, these are some of the common current and future challenges of the Dark Clouds hanging over the African continent, which continue to be relevant not merely to yesterday and today but for tomorrow. What the Africa of today and tomorrow need most, is "the healing touch' to turn Africa from its past and present sufferings, into move it into a hopeful continent: Africa needs the *"healing touch"* desperately as ever before. It goes without stating liberation from colonial rule alone is not enough to build a nation. It remains an indispensable condition for nation building, even with that, it is not enough – Proper and genuine nation-building really begins after independence, and in Africa, it entails a multitude of many and varied things, the good, bad and ugly. To begin with, first, it entails accepting the ethnic factor throughout the continent. Therefore, it is only by dealing with the reality of ethnicity; we have to contend the forces of division from that quarters be kept in check. Therefore, Dark Clouds on the Horizon is book that should make you think and act positively and progressively for the good of the continent.

The African continent is engraved with many questions of (i) managing pluralism; (ii) making a virtue of African diversities. It means fostering social justice through equity, justice, truth and far play. Africa's diversities should be an asset not a liability, it should be seen in positive not negative terms as the world makes it. Therefore, any government which lays claim to legitimacy is expected to deliver a measure of social justice. In a key note address delivered to the Conference in African Diplomacy by the Secretary General of the Commonwealth on 24th March 1999, Chief Emeka Anyaoku stated: "In Africa, it is not only important that social societies be delivered; it is just as important, if not more so, that be seen to be delivered. It means fighting corruption so that society's rewards are seen to be based on merit. These are only some of the elements of nation-building even then, it is well to remember that nation-building is never laid to rest, never, fully, finally achieved – it is a perpetual chore." On the occasion of receiving the Nobel Price, Chief Albert Luthuli delivered the following speech at the University of Oslo on December 11, 1961 in these well-crafted words:

> "Though I speak of Africa as a Single entity, it is divided in many ways – by race, language, history and customs; by political, economic and ethnic frontiers. But the truth, despite these multiple divisions, Africa has a single common purpose and a single goal – the achievement of its own independence. An Africa, both lands which have won their political victories, but have still to overcome the legacy of economic backwardness, and lands like my own, whose political battle have still to be waged to conclusion all Africa has this single aim: our goal is a United Africa in which the standard of life and liberty are constantly expanding; in which the ancient legacy of illiteracy and diseases is swept aside, in which the dignity of man is recused from beneath the heels of colonialism which have trampled it. This goal, pursued by millions of our people with revolutionary zeal by means of books, representations, demonstrations, and in some places, armed force provoked by the advancing of white rule carries the only break promise of peace of Africa. What means have been used, the efforts have gone to end alien rule and race oppression."

Africa should draw valuable lessons from the views expressed by Kevin Williamson (2022). The USA "President is not the United States. He is not even the majority of the US Government – the Prime Ministers are not the United Kingdom; the Pope is not the church or the whole of Christendom. But there is still something in us that wants to vest the legitimacy and authority of key institutions in one man. Republicans already are talking publicly about the 2024 presidential contest (will it be Ron DeSantis? Will Trump be in the mix) and Democrats are engaged in mostly private speculation about whether Biden can or should run again." The West should equally learn from the views expressed by Barack Obama during his campaign for the presidency of the United States, "change will not come if we wait for some other person or if we wait for some other time. We are the ones we've been waiting for. We are the change that we seek." A new mindset and a comprehensive inclusive approach are most needed to reconstruct and rebuild the destroyed continent. For sixty years, we failed to acquire in-depth knowledge of the attitude of the centre-periphery dichotomy, and of life in Africa after the attainment of independence truly relay it to the people in Europe. We still have a long way to go in "seeking the political kingdom for other things to follow." Importantly, is to know that colonialism and the slave trade remain the greatest crimes and wrongs ever done to the people of Africa. We are obliged to do something tangible to address the situation and put an end to this horrendous act ever committed against the African people. Figure 1 - illustrates a coevolutionary world view in which innovations or changes occur in each of the components of the ecosystem: knowledge, organization, values, technology and renewable resources affects our development. First, we are participants in the development process and should know our roles; we should begin to devise structures and reward systems to such knowledge and participatory roles; third we should be better able to articulate and interact with other structures for an interpretive/contextual approach to knowledge; forth, we should be able to adapt to change for the collective good of society. Developing the right thinking is vital.

The various chapters are explicitly clear touching on some of essential aspects of (under)development issues poignant in all African countries. Collectively we can make the changes required. Individually, it will be a long and slow process benefiting only a select few. Here are some of the challenging clouds hanging over Africa. The way forward for the continent is to look back no more, but focus on developing, improving and sustaining the democratic process. This means changes, development, progress, service delivery and sustainability (CDPSDS) brought closer to the citizens. More partners must be brought on board to ensure wide courage and success. A collective dynamism, empowering the female gender, and giving greater space to the down-threatened population to be constructively engaged in the process of transforming society for their own good. Society has to be creative, innovative, productive and entrepreneurial. Just as the people show great passion about football, the same passionate spirit should be extended to 'democracy' and 'development' as the gateway to a service delivery society with sustained quality livelihood.

Fig. 1: The Co-Evolutionary World View

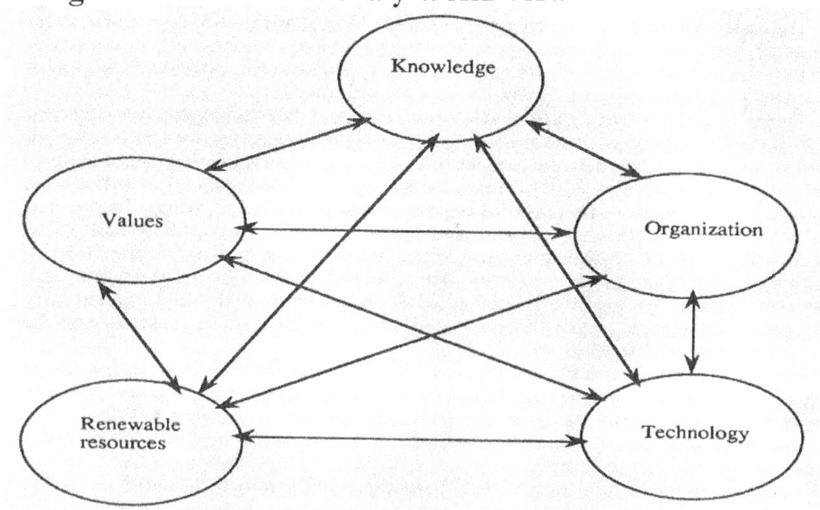

Source: Credit Kiriro Amos and Juma Calestous (1991:18) Gaining Ground – Institutional Innovations in Land-use Management in Kenya, ACTS Pres, Nairobi, Kenya, 1991)

We need pro-active policy agendas and implementation actions that put a smile on the human face to the growing globalised economy of our time. To properly appreciate the general discontent on the continent today, however, it is perhaps better to measures the precarious socioeconomic and political chaotic and hardship situation that has befallen the continent against the background of the tall hope (rising expectation) which the people were made to belief and the reality in the post-colonial Africa during the anti-colonial-struggles days - the dream of independence; a hope which has, from all indications, become shattered by the unfolding realties of the continent. Ade Ajayi (1982:5) was not indifferent to the situation, the mood and expectations of the people in the anti-colonial struggle days in what he called *"Expectations of Independence"* and quoted here in length: More than sixty years later, this expected rising expectation has converted into rising destructive frustration. Hopes, expectations, trust and confidence have all been dashed into an unknown abyss. We cannot run from the reality that the social problems – which indeed influence to become a source of increasing tension – seriously contribute to a worsening of the internal political crisis, which is also a crisis about performance and legitimation. The economic and social problems could also be blamed on the suppression, by the repressive, authoritarian state structures, the non-creative and innovative potential of the population, and on the lack of participatory forums and institutions at every organizational level of society and the state.

> *"Insofar as they appreciated what was involved in the independence movement, their basic expectations were to see an end to unpredictability and irrationality of the white man's world. Without the dubious advantages of Western education, they rejected the white man's culture, and for as long as possible, stuck to what they knew… Their notion of freedom was not an abstract ideal, but a catalogue of specific wants: freedom from unjust and incomprehensible laws and directives; return to their lands; and freedom to be left alone to live their lives and seek their own goals, especially in regard to land tenure and local government groupings that affected historical relationships. These wants developed and became specific with each new hope and each disastrous frustration. Soon, expectations came to include improved standards of living in housing and clothing, greater returns for their labour, better transportation for exporting and marketing their surpluses, education as a means to social mobility that would ensure a better life for their children and an adequate water supply, electricity, health care facilities and other such amenities of life"*

A wide range of groups, socialists, communists, liberalist and politically non-organised groups and individuals, laid the blame for the accumulation of social problems on the national leaderships and in their policies, which curtailed human rights and fundamental freedoms. The official reaction to this criticism often consists in implementing quasi-isolated liberalisation measures or announcing far-reaching democratisation policies that are never implemented. Such poor policy articulation and implementation process helps detect a basic rejection of the fundamental principles that ought to guide a modern (democratic) society, namely: observance of human rights; respect for individual and collective freedoms; the admission of broader sections of the population to share in the running of public affairs in equity in benefit-sharing of the state's wealth. Democracy must be at work and its output felt across the board. Democracy is a revolution of the individual, corresponds, in encapsulated form, to be the definition of democracy advanced by present-day advocates of a democratic, pluralist political system, at the heart of which stands the people, regarded as the holder of sovereignty. Topping the list of defining characteristics of democracy is the guarantee of human and civil rights, as is revealed by the call for state based on the rule of law, the prime concern of which would be to ensure equality of the citizen before the law. "Liberty, equality, fraternity" is a motto that is taken up time and again in this connection. Pluralism is regarded as another important element of a democracy. Democracy and good governance are the call of the African People.

For the average African, independence was expected to "usher a new era of basic rights and freedom long denied under foreign or settler rule" Nzogola-Ntalaja George (1987:76). Today, this amount to stating the obvious, asserting this has not happened, and may not happen for a long time to come. Hence, we have the "Dark Clouds over the Horizon" emerges from today's Africa (Abiola Lrele, 1992: 296). The evidence is evident everywhere in every street and alleyway throughout the continent, in the faces of the fleeing refugees, in the face of the wounded soldiers, in the stories of the orphan, in the 'barking' of the night marauders as they rampage almost freely even in the day times in Nairobi, Douala, Lagos, Johannesburg, Dakar, Cairo to list but a few. Here lies the frustration of the peasant who was asked a la Nkrumah, "to seek first the political kingdom with a promise of economic and social development to be added almost immediately." Neither a political kingdom nor economic development for the poor and excluded appears feasible today. But how did the continent get enmeshed in the present seemingly intractable mess? What, in their worlds, generated this problem that has bogged down contemporary Africa from making her a prominent member of the Third World always a toddler (Uroh, 1998:8)? Rising expectations have converged into destructive frustration, the results of the basis of the problems of poor governance and exclusion of the silent majority from equity in shared-prosperity.

Origin of the Dark Clouds

One should be clear from the onset that several factors both internal and external, converge to determine the present clouds which now is a serious crisis impacting negatively on the transformation of the continent. It would be wrong to state that Europe's conquest of Africa was not planed from its outset. There was a motive which still exists today; the motive of power, domination and acquiring resources. Of course, colonialism followed different waves, and each European country pursued their own interests. In all, we can state that they all had and still have a common interest. A combination of European curiosity about a legendary and mysterious overseas continent that provides the livewire for the industrial revolution changing the nature of the relationship to one of conqueror and conquered. For example, Max Siollum (2021:7) writes; "British colonisation of Nigeria was an afterthought. Britain was not the first European country to make contact with the land that would eventually become Nigeria. Portuguese explorers reached West Africa more than 65 years before the British did…However, it was events on the other side of the of the world, rather than Portuguese arrival in West Africa, which changed West Africa's destiny forever." Thus, Christopher Columbus arrival in the Americas while trying to find a sea route to India; and Europe's search for India inadvertently triggered the transatlantic slaved trade, set in motion a series of events that would lead to the decimation of the indigenous population of both continents and to the largest forced population transfer of history in history changing drastically the history of the African continent. Africa has since not recovered from that gruesome act by the European countries. We are confronted with at least two fundamental devils:

External Factors ==➔ Elements of Developmental Dislocations

(The slave trade with its dehumanization tendencies, leading to direct colonisation and all its contradictions which contributed to the delegitimisation of traditional and cultural values: the dislocation of the African economy; and after its neo-colonisation with the weakening of the Africa state construct.

Internal Factors ==➔ Poor and inconsistent activities of Africa's New (Ruling Class) Class) as well as the internal dynamics of the national politics within African States

(See Rodney, 1972; Fanon 1968; Nzongola-Ntalaja, 1987, Forje, 2020, Dumont, 1966, Sami Amin,1990; Claude Ake, 1989)

//

Implications for Development Conditionality's

//

* Rape of Africa before and after the colonial era
* Intensified dependency
* Imposed structural Adjustment Programme
* Decolonisation / recolonisation
* Globalization - highest stage of scientific imperialism;
* Increased political soldiering: (once the military assumes power that is, enters politics. Politics captures it and it immediately begins to reflect on an increasing scale the social contradictions of the society. The same features which discredited the civilian political formations and political regimes begin to assert themselves on the military).
* Militarisation of the continent – AFRICOM
* Centralised authoritarian hegemonic regime forms
* Total confusion in the structure – funding of the state
* Growing number of sit-tight presidents for life (STPFL)
* Corruption taking over and becomes the only way by which the citizen relates to state institutions;
* Growing instability, unpredictability and fluctuation in national and international economy, notably in interest and exchange rates, and growing uncertainty in capital markets;
* The continuous drain of the resources of Africa;
* Some quasi progress in the democratic process but rising tendencies in fake or contested election results

The world has become increasingly interdependent and, in a sense, integrated. But it has not evolved a system for dealing equitably with increasing integration. The South (Africa in particular) is still in a position of subordination and dependence, and this prevents the effective management of the new global challenges. A reform of the national and international system – particularly of international arrangements governing the flows of trade, money, finance and technology – is therefore an essential need of the world. It equally calls for a serious overhaul of the structure-functioning of national governance system so that we have a new world order in which one fourth of the people are affluent and three fourths are deprived hardly offers an enduring basis for peace and security. This is all the truer when the disparities between rich and poor are becoming wider. The imperative for moving towards a less unequally world is steadily becoming stronger.

Therefore, Africa needs a new vision – People-centred and self-reliant development in an interdependent world construct. The reality is that Africa is part of a world construct whose interdependence is constantly widening and deepening, and therefore, the vision should be of a co-operative world made more secure for its entire people. The goal should be a truly independent Africa and world environment organized on the basis of human equality and human variety in pursuit of jointly defined common purpose; where there is peace, security, equality, dignity for all persons and all peoples; where all can take advantage of scientific and technological advances; and where the resources of the continent (as well as the world's resources) are used in a sustainable manner to meet the needs of all rather than to satisfy the narrow interests of a few, so that poverty can be abolished with damage to the environment.

Our wish and vision for Africa is to achieve a people-centred development: a form of development that is self-reliant, equitable, where the rule of law and justice reigns supreme, governance is participatory, inclusive, open and sustainable. We envisaged a process of development based on a progressive Afro-centric approach that is executed and achieved through the active participation of the people, by the people, and for the people, in their own interests as they see them, relying primarily on their own resources, and carried out under their own control. Development must be conceived as a process which enables human-beings (Africans in particular) to realize their potential, build self-confidence and lead lives of dignity and fulfilment. Development does, of course, require sustained economic growth, for only in an expanding economy can abject poverty is eradicated. But development cannot be measured solely by the growth of the gross national product. What is produced, hoe and at what social and environmental cost, by whom and for whom – all this is just important as a higher GNP. Hence, the conditions of mass poverty, priority must be given to policies aimed at ending poverty, increasing productive employment, and ensuring that basic needs of all the people are met, with any surplus being fairly shared.

The gradual erosion of the compromises or social contract between the state and the people is due to articulate self-interests of the ruling class. Thus, the explanation of the failure of Africa as a whole should bring into play all the complexity of the interactions between specific internal conditions and the logic of the western capitalist expansion. As a result of ignoring current explanations, the views advanced by economists of the international economy and by nationalists of African countries remain superficial. The former lay emphasis of the system, like the corruption of the political class, the weakness of its economic foundations, the very low productivity of agriculture, still not up to the gel of animal draught, tribal fragmentation, and the need for African true capitalist business to gang up with the west for further exploitation of the working poor and excluded classes. All this hides their established agenda or the exploitation of the continent. There is unity among the developed countries about the exploitation of Africa. Divided and weakened as African nations are; the developed countries will continue to feed fat on the continent in many ways. African countries are not united in confronting the developed countries. Are we surprise why we are poor and remain underdeveloped? What we call independence is a sham and will continue be until we develop an Afro-centric new mind set, and implement its contents. We should move away from the entrenched notion of *'talking the talk'* into a serious stage of *'walking the talk.'*

The latter stress other phenomena, no less real, like the fact that the prices of raw materials on which depends the financing capacity on the take-off are deteriorating systematically. Governance has deteriorated into a defence of the elite privileges against encroachment by nonelites and continued efforts to subvert the rules to extract wealth from the economy for the benefit of the politically dominant class. The individual and his or her rights, protection, and duties as a citizen lie at the heart of this discussion and publication. Thus, the causes of human-rights abuses can, in this context, clearly be viewed as being rooted in the system: the notion of a structural wellspring for uncertainty of the law and the human-rights violation is confirmed when one analyses the situation in which abuses have occurred on an especially massive scale. There is no unity among Africa countries on how to tackle the dominating and exploitative policy of the developed polities towards Africa. We fail listening to the clarion call by Kwame Nkrumah and his fellow Afro-centric advocates raised on the need for the unity of Africa to be the goal for consolidating the independence, sovereignty and unity of the continent. Credibility, trust and honour are therefore at stake. African people seem to have lost trust, faith and confidence in their leaders. They feel neglected and disappointed. "Whatever goes into you mind affects your thinking; your thinking affects your performance, and your performance affects your future" opines Zig Zigglar. We should equally bear in mind that majority of the current population have a rose-tinted memory of colonialism. Above all, many Africans have a nostalgic reverence for British, French and Spanish rule. Many factors contribute to this. Thus, who saw bits of the colonial rule, compared to what is happening today do have a different image – an image of the disappointment of independence. Disappointment in the sense that independence has failed to deliver the basic necessities of quality livelihood. Compared to what existed before, some elderly citizens would even crave for the return of colonial governance. These narratives give the reader the impression that they are viewing the continent through the telescopic lens of colonial rifle, presenting it as a 'civilising mission' to the current corrupt governance system that plagues and reigns over the continent.

No one wants to return to colonial rule. The people want good governance, and leadership that caters for the common good of the people. All the people want is governance structure working for the well-being of the society and showing that colonialism and slavery was wrong. Without acting in that direction only strengthens the notion of colonial rule was to civilize the uncivilized and the protection of the people from themselves. Current poor governance substantial that. Why have African governments not subjected themselves to the Per Review Mechanism of the African Union? And we can ask ourselves, why are African governments and leadership acting the way they do towards their citizens? Current leaders and governance structure are out to defend foreign interests for articulate personal gains. These are acts that disappoint the people, craving for a return of British colonial rule. These are some of the expected reactions when leadership becomes greedy and thinks only in terms of articulate interest and defending the interests of those who provide their protection to better defend foreign interests.

Why do African countries shy-away from upholding and implementing Article 28 of the Universal Declaration of Human Rights of 10 December 1948, the conclusion of the 1981 African Charter of Human and People's Rights and all other agreements prioritizing human rights? There is need to revisit these Conventions, Agreements,

Resolutions and others to ensure that the concept of development be equated with that of a universal realization of all human rights. As long as other interests, of a kind not geared to people's – notably economic and political interests - determine the nature of development programmes, the latter will continue to be doomed to failure, as they have been up to now. We need to tackle the problem at their root – a course which necessarily requires radical changes in the existing international political and economic order. In view of the current and dramatic condition of our present global community, there is serious need to underline radical reformulation of development process for the common good of all humankind. We all need to live and eat together. If this chance is not exploited forthwith, the gloomy prophecies of the end of development and the end of human right could be true knocking at our doors any time soon.

Corruption has thus become an essential instrument and vehicle used to minimise mass efforts to prevent the implementation of perverse economic policies which benefit the ruling class, but, most unfortunately, plunged the masses further into state of abject poverty and misery. With the administrative institution grossly emerged with corruption, the ultimate result is inefficiency and incompetence among civil servants. The private sector equally becomes unproductive. Apparently, an important prerequisite for steady economic growth is an efficient civil service as the output function of quality services delivery to the society and the productive private sector. Therefore, the bureaucracy must be responsive to the needs of the entrepreneurial sector to foster, encourage and enhance innovation, job creation, employment and productivity in the economy. The past couple of years have brought to the limelight, deficiencies in African leadership which must be quickly addressed for the continent to take its rightful place within the community of nations. The country is bogged down with poor leadership and a condescending civil society to the whims and caprices of western powers. Africa will never progress with such bad scenarios. Our administrative sector needs proper medical attention. There is an urgent need for total restructuring and renovation of the public services sector which is the epic centre for the output functions of government. Government is judge by its output activities – that is, quality services delivery to the population.

The Disastrous Effects

What then are the main effects of corruption, and what is the appropriate prescription of this malady, this cancer which threatens to paralyse independent Africa? Available evidence suggests that among African countries which have been afflicted by corruption in various times are Cameroon, Nigeria, Ghana, Liberia, Sierra Leone, Morocco, Egypt, Somalia, Ethiopia, Sudan, Kenya, Tanzania, Uganda, Gabon, the Central African Republic, Malawi, Dahomey, Zambia, Zimbabwe, virtually, no African country is sparred from the viruses of corruption. It would be futile to continue with an infinitive list. The corruption virus is here to stay with us. And it is high time we get rid of it. This malaise has also crept into the educational field where, due to the devaluation of merit, motivation has generally declined among young people. Once the education system is corrupt, the entire system goes hey while in the corruption train. In contrast to earlier times when it was believed, recognised and evident that education was the key to the good life, there has been a general tendency everywhere in Africa to emphasise success without, however, relating it to merit, competence and diligence. In the wake of independence many undeserving people amassed wealth and got into positions of responsibility and influence by hook or crook, but mostly by crook. The trend persists to this day, and has even escalated to higher heights, with detrimental consequences. Yet, we continue blaming colonialism for our state of underdevelopment, more than fifty years after we gave them the red card. The red card of "seeking the political kingdom," to gain our 'sovereignty and freedom.' Fifty years after, we are returning that freedom and sovereignty. How have we lost our sense of direction? What are we doing to proof that colonialism was wrong in the first place, to begin with!

To put it crudely, but nonetheless realistically, it has become customary for job-seekers to have some connections or to present 'gifts' in order to get employment or promotion. It is hardly surprising, therefore, that we constantly have the wrong persons in posts of responsibilities in the country. Credibility, trust and honour are therefore at stake. These acts are incompatible with public morality as it involves the deliberate use of one's public position for wrong ends and reasons. In an address the Ghana Nation on the 26th Anniversary of the country's independence, Jerry Rawlings had this to say: "Somewhere along the line something went wrong (Ghanaians were happy, proud and hopeful (at the time of independence). Today, he/she (the Ghanaian) is treated with suspicion and contempt. What happened? Who did that to us? Who do we blame? None but ourselves…I am sure the earlier fighters for freedom did not seek to replace colonialism with political and economic irresponsibility, moral decay and spiritual blackout *(Daily Nation 7th March 1983)*. It should be noted that Jerry Rawlings staged a 'failed coup' in May1979. In December he stages another took power from Hilla Limann1981, introduce multiparty elections in 1992 and was elected president, as a committed socialist, and later introduced free-market reforms. He was re-elected in 1996 for a second term, but bowed in 2000 as the constitution prohibited a third term. A strong advocate of the Afro-centric ideological agenda, in him, people saw the 'solutions to the problems bedevilling the Continent.

His statement on 11th March 1983, tells us all: "Sixth March, 1957, was a day which held for Ghanaians a lot of promise. They were happy, proud and hopeful, not only because their country was the first Black Africa south of the Sahara to shake itself free of colonialism, but also because, by the historical fact of its new status, Ghana had assumed an African leadership. The people of this country were poised for action to make their country succeed. The foreign policy which the new Government pursued immediately after independence, especially in Africa advertised our country even more, and won us a fund of goodwill throughout the world. But somewhere along the line something went wrong; our politics and all went sour and our feeling of well-being disappeared. Twenty-six years after independence, where does Ghana stand? Again, not long ago, the Ghanaian could hold his/her high and push his/her chest out anywhere in dignity and pride. Today, he/she is treated with suspicion and contempt. What has happened? Who did that to us? Who do we blame? None but ourselves?" *(The Mirror, 12 March 1983).*

Kanu Genoveva (from South Africa) in a book published on "Kwame Nkrumah: The Man," (Delta Publications, Nigeria Limited) states: The real tragedy of Ghana today is that flattery and the tactic of telling the leader only what he is believed to want to hear have become a political way of life. If this is a fair judgement, then Ghana's coup-ridden political history during the last 16-25 years of independence clearly fall into a new perspective.... Twenty-five years after Ghana first shone out as the Great Black Hope, this is where the political maturity gathered in a quarter of a century has led them. Today the Black Star State is shrouded in the gloom and misery of self-inflicted wounds. It is not Ghana's proudest hour, nor is it Africa's happiest" *(Africa Now, March 1982).* Let us be candid and ask ourselves – what has independence brought to the ordinary citizen – quality of livelihood for a few, and horrendous status-quo of abject poverty and misery for the majority of the currently poor.

In an address to the Tanzania's ruling party (Chama Cha Mapinduzi), President Julius Nyerere on 25th January 1983, castigated the country's leadership for corruption and graft in these words: "Almost all leaders wanted lots of money and were being bribed clandestinely…. Such leaders are bribed because they are greedy. They are not running away from poverty by fighting it but by declaring war against the country's poor *(Daily Nation, 25th January 1983)*. Speaking to the Meeting of the Governing Council of the ruling Kenya African National Union (KANU) on 17th May 1983, President Daniel Arap Moi stated: "…I am determined to rectify the weaknesses which we have been witnessing in the government because of the conduct of these evil-minded people. In order to clean the system, I have therefore, decided that all elected leaders, including myself, will seek fresh mandate from the electorate …Because of greed and selfishness amongst some unpatriotic people who are entrusted with positions, it has proved very difficult to eliminate ***magendo*** (black marketeering) and corruption in the country – their activities have contributed to undermining our effort to reconstruct our economy *(Weekly Review, May 20, 1983)*. On the assumption of the highest office of the country (Cameroon) in 1982, President Paul Biya perplexed mesmerise and hypnotise the nation and the world with the slogan of, 'democratisation, moralisation and rigour' which was short lived. Since Cameroon held the world corruption golden medal of the 'most corrupt nation in the world' several times. The Nigeria corruption nexus of "419" was converted into the Cameroon (914) syndrome (see Forje, 2020). At the New Deal Congress in Bamenda 1985, which saw the death of the Cameroon Nation Union (CNU) and the birth of the Cameroon Peoples Democratic Movement (CPDM), the President had this to say: "democratization, understood as an illustration of political maturity, assumption of responsibility and progress is such that it should enable the citizen to find in the various party and public events, a school of tolerance where one learns to respect what is different, that is respect for others, their person their property, their rights and opinions *(See Cameroun Information, Vol. X11, No.3 1985,p48. Ministry of Information and Culture)*.

The rising expectation for every African country was high as independence approached. The morning after independence, rising expectation converged into destructive frustration. The hard realities of post-independent Africa started showing its ugly face. In a way, the colonial masters went, but left their ugly image and spirit behind; the new custodian of powers were now consumed of the left unholy spirit of the departed masters, and they started acting worse than the colonial lords. No doubt, the struggle will continue, because the blood of those who lost their lives will inject in the living, new strength of forging ahead with the unfinished battle for justice, equality, sovereignty, liberty and freedom. A government that repeatedly ignores the voice of civil society, with numbers as large as the electoral majority that voted them into office is doing nothing to nurture the growth of a young democracy. The shadow of democratic illegitimacy will haunt every leadership act and decision. On the other hand, abolishing a government, outside the boundaries of the ballot box, subjects a country to the laws of unintended consequences.

This leaves us with the unfinished march to Africa's independence. Africa has to an extent, made some progress but she is not there yet. The gains Africa made on 7 March 1956, and as noted by Jerry Rawlings, in (The Mirror, 12th March, 1983), the gains Africa made over the past sixty or more years are being pushed back and reversed, not by gun-toting racists advocates the Euro-centric ideologies, but by the diehards of those who propagate pushing at all cost neoliberalism... In this light, Africa has yet to achieve the Kwame Nkrumah's dream – *seek ye the political kingdom and other things would be added.* Kwame Nkrumah's death has still not brought the much awaited freedom; Lumumba's death has not saved the Congo its tragedies, Gadhafi's death has not brought pace to Libya, Mandela's transition did not resolved the xenophobic situation in South Africa, nor totally erased the hidden agenda of apartheid politics; all these and other iconic Africa leaders through their leadership move the continent at least one step forward; while the current leaders are dancing the Bafia waltz – one step forward and many more steps backwards. The struggle continues until the last colonial territory or idea is defeated. The weapon for its defeat is a progressive Afro-centric ideological orientation and implementation. African leaders should learn and draw exemplarily lessons from the iconic Archbishop Desmond Tutu, in the role for the death of the apartheid system and the eventual of South Africa's Truth and Reconciliation Commission (TRC).

The continent is bogged down with poor leadership and a condescending civil society to the whims and caprices of western powers. Africa will never progress with such bad scenarios. Our administrative sector needs proper medical attention. There is an urgent need for total restructuring and renovations of the administrative sector which is the epic centre for the output function of government. Government is judged by its output activities – service quality service delivery to the population. This is what differentiates governments in the developed and developing polities in Africa. We need, in order to make significant progress we need, what Aziz Pahad et al (2015) elaborates as a "call for alternative and progressive voices which are able to offer different interpretations and readings of the fast-unfolding events and processes, and are also questioning the prevailing assumptions and underlying logic of the Western 'liberal order'. These alternative and progressive voices are especially important for Africans, given the reality that Africa remains marginalized in terms of helping to fashion these relations, despite their direct impact on the lives and destiny of the one billion Africans. Furthering the debate, Kwandiwe M. Kondlo (2014) outlines perspectives of emerging and established African scholars in what one could describe as the debate on leadership and the articulation of the life of the mind in Africa's socio-economic, political and cultural life from the time of independence to date. While Nhemachena et al (2018) goes further to address issues of resistance and strategies from the early sixteenth century, when Europeans attempted to systematically exploit Africans, black people have emerged in a variety of organized and sustained resistance campaigns to assert their independence and identity.

On his part, Mentan Tatah (2017) addresses Africa in the Colonial Ages of Empire by looking at scholarly lives of academics researching on Africa are changing, constantly in flux and increasingly bound to the demands of Western colonial imperialism. According to Tatah Mentan, the effects of this existential situation of Africa compel serious academic scrutiny. For Mawere (2014). We have to look deep into the exploration of the practical problems resulting from Africa's encounter with Euro-colonialism, a reflect of the various nexus between indigenous knowledge, culture, and development, and indeed a call for the revival and reinstitution of indigenous knowledge, not as a challenge to western science, but a complementary form of knowledge necessary to steer and promote sustainable development in Africa and beyond. These studies and others point towards a common destiny – the call for a progressive Afro-centric agenda to restore Africa on the right rail for the development of the continent.

It tells us of one important thing; unity, cooperation and sharing whatever we have equitably for us all to live in harmony, security, peacefully and sustainably. We have to strive to be human in an increasingly dehumanized world construct. Given the current world construct, Africa remains a disaster-ravaged continent where the political leadership at east ought to *'declare a state of emergency.'* Current African leadership cannot. They want and have replaced the departed centre powers. Replacing the departed centre-powers makes Africa to be at odds with its own intentions. These leaders fail to adhere to the principles of truth, justice and peace, but trying to rewrite the history of the continent to suit their self-articulate interests and to please those who have placed them at the epic Centre of power and continue to protect their continuous stay at the helm of power. Our current leaders play the *'Centre-periphery'* dichotomy. We should remember that the privilege to speak the truth, loud and clear should be strongly exercised mainly to protect the weak, the poorest of the poor, survivors of an annihilation that is still being denied and whose explanation or justification is still being updated. To move forward in a grand way, we need a new mindset – denying, renouncing or refusing all responsibility for a crime whose magnitude has not yet been fathomed – gradually set in, uninterrupted from the Slave Trade to the current genocide (recognized and unrecognized) in different shapes ongoing across the continent and fuel inter alia, what can be seen as the second colonization of the continent by Africans in a grand style. These leaders should remember that 'one should not past your farm with a thief; you should not give a dog meat to keep.' Current leadership is deliberately paving the way for the destruction of the continent. In short, the wise servant leader is an honour and pride to the country, brings good things to the society, seeks peace, love and begets kindness and harmony. The current action of many African leader points in the direction of resolutely sliding with those whose audacity is costing the lives of many innocent citizens. We cannot cross-over from underdevelopment and exploitation to sustainable quality livelihood with such attitude or mindset. Existing mindset has been destructive to the kind of the country/continent we want. It is mind-set that entrenches our enslavement, colonisation and underdevelopment. The continent cannot liberate itself with such a dark cloud hanging over it.

We need a new progressive mindset; just as we need a new educational system with a progressive curriculum that builds and develops a new progressive, critical, innovation and entrepreneurial knowledge capacity building environment. Knowledge is power, knowledge is what builds society. The global society of the 21st century and far beyond is construed on a knowledge-based capacity driven by the forces of science and technology; as well as penetrates into developing our cultural heritage values which have been gradually eroded and destroyed by the forces of slavery and colonialism and neo-colonialism. The core cultural heritage values of our society have to be identified and maintained with 'pluralism and honour.' Instil ethics and moral. Inclusive participation, those limits seem to be tolerable and conducive to responsibility. Globality is generating a new culture which we should not allow o replace our indigenous cultural heritage values. Globality should aid us to deepen our knowledge in our indigenous cultural heritage values as a dynamic and evolving reality whose future shape can only be imagined. Therefore, it is imperative that we build our knowledge base capacity to meet the challenges of our time. We are forced to continuously repeat the issue of education and developing and implementing a 'curriculum' that response to the enhancement of the sustainable evolution of our society. Our higher education is in a mess, and what keeps it at bay must be given a new marching order to disappear from the Africa knowledge building capacity scene. Our universities cannot be found on the global university rating. According to the Times Higher Education (THE) has ranked the University of Cape Town (UCT) in its fifty-fifty position in the 2022 list of most international universities in the world, making it the only African university on the list. Congratulations to UCT. At the same time, we have to be candid and question seriously, what has been of the universities of Legon (Ghana); Makerere (Uganda)'Ibadan (Nigeria). African universities should feature on the top list for a number of reasons. First, Africa should be the citadel of knowledge and epic centre of research. Second, Africa is the only continent were the vast majority of is educated population has combed all corners of the global for knowledge acquisition; and yet her institutions cannot feature on the global ranking of universities. Africa universities cannot feature for a number of interrelated reasons, poor funding to the universities, corruption, interference of university system with politics; and confession of the university administration in building an authentic home-grown system for the progress of the country. We can only but encourage African universities to continue in striving towards academic excellence even under such had conditions; to continue to promote critical knowledge and scientific thinking, creativity, innovative and entrepreneurial thinking activities.

The Leadership Gap Status-Quo: The African Problem

"The history of independent Africa is characterized by persistent tendency by many national leaders and governments to disregard the necessity and relevance of public

morality in their actions and conduct. This is often done by resorting to tribalism and corruption. Apart from a few exceptions, many African leaders generally behave and act as though their countries and national resources were little more than their private or family property. In such circumstance's relatives, friends and ethnic colleagues generally get appointed to positions of responsibility and high income regardless of merit." (Gideon S. Were 1981:13)

"Countries that feature term-limits are less likely to experience conflict and more likely to enjoy stable government. The idea that "Big Men" must be allowed to stay in power to prevent chaos is simply false. Transfer of power is not a sliver bullet of course – they may just involve replacing a good and upstanding leader with a dubious one. But they have been shown to disrupt corruption networks, encourage leaders to respect the rule of law, and boost public for democracy" (The Eden, No. 1185, Monday 16 November 2020:12).

Sustainable take-off requires a proactive vibrant civil society, visionary servant leadership and productive and competitive private sector to trigger change, ensure progress, promote development as well as enhance sustainability culminating in proper service delivery and quality livelihood for the citizens. If Africa is to break with its grim status-quo, it has to do something different. It is commonly said that doing the same thing over and over again and expecting different results is a form of insanity. If African countries are to leverage their rich diversity in natural and human resources, they have to start doing things differently and innovatively. No country has ever achieved high levels of development through wrong imitation or through using resources that are not indigenous. But nations can learn from the best practices of other nations. Development starts from within the people and grows with the people; in the final analysis, the people harvest the results of their proper planting.

Leadership and political commitment are critical factors that would shape Africa's future and determine the success of Agenda 2063 and the SDGs. The leadership challenge for accelerated economic growth, transformation and sustainable development that Africa faces today is more complex, albeit no less demanding, than at the time of the struggle for independence from colonialism. There is a need for transformed and visionary leadership in all fields and at all levels: politics, business, industry, science, religion, education, and culture. The style of leadership that prevails, and the ways in which management and governance structures change and interact with national resources, will play an enormous role in shaping Africa's development trajectory. The dwindling and unpredictability of development assistance compels Africa to look inwards for domestic resources for the care of her people. The sustainable and efficient management of national resources is now an imperative for the achievement of at least 12 out of the 17 United Nations Sustainable Development Goals (SDGs). Restoring and maintaining the health of the natural resource base is not only needed to adequately feed current and projected populations, but to provide a better quality of life in the years to come.

Leadership competence requires the ability to think long-term and strategically too; to cast and communicate a national vision; and to manage the single biggest institutional apparatus in most countries – government. It is quality leadership that brings about nation building. Here Munroe (1998) states: "Quality leadership is key to a prosperous nation. And it is obvious that our nations are painfully in need of such leaders." Furthermore, quality, legitimate and just leaders are credible; and credibility constitutes a very important single most admired quality by the followers. Adei Stephen (2004:29) states: "Leaders do not only deliver on vision, strategies, mobilisation, and change management, but they are also credible and trustworthy… but in fact, it is credibility that enables them to engage their countries' attention for the long haul of transforming their national economies. "This is what we can style "legacy-building leadership." This kind of leadership is marked by three Cs, namely; Character, Competence and Care. Character denotes, trustworthiness, integrity, justice and principle-centeredness; Competence, the ability to deliver. Leadership as a function is to prosecute and to so competently provide the people with fundamental basic human needs thereby bring sustainable change on transformation in their daily lives. Care donates many things in many ways. It starts with valuing people as people, showing humility, love and patience. The raisons deter and object of development is to usher change in the lives of all citizens. The degree of care depends on one's motivation to be a leader in the first place. In Africa, often self-styled leaders cause so much mayhem and even loss of lives to attain power. We can also deduce this kind of leaders from what one can term a "servant leader" who are motivated by the desire to serve their politics. These are leaders who behave within the credo of *"politics is to serve."* As the African proverb goes, 'it takes a whole village to raise a child,' is implying that everyone in a community should be responsible for helping to raise a child. We are all responsible for developing the country. That is why servant leadership backed by a proactive positive responsive civil society will accelerate a comprehensive and sustainable transformation of the society. When a people do well, it gives a society character which goes with the country. In other words, what defines a society is the society's character which is inseparable from form the society and follows the society wherever and whatever it does. Therefore, we should not look where we fell, but where we slipped. In other words, we should not look at mistakes; we should look to what caused us to make mistakes otherwise we may repeat the mistakes many times over.

Government depends upon the assent of the governed to its legitimacy, and upon the co-operation of a significant portion of the elite in making the system work. In stating, as we have done, that traditional government formed a dome, high above the people, we must concede that this dome was, at any rate an echo-chamber. The voice of authority was heard, and was echoed by the chorus of the people. During the Western colonial period, this echoing chorus began to be pierced by dissentient notes; and after 1945 the discord was so harsh that colonial rule became impossible. The same scenario is taking place now. More than five decades after the attainment of independence, leadership and governor's failure to deliver the expected rising expectation of the people has resulted in dissenting voices, behaviour and attitude. The rise of dissenting voices could be seen as the 'Freedom Movements' calling for change, the need modifying in this respect. The ongoing situation in Southern Cameroons, Mali, Burkina Faso, Chad, CAR, etc. constitute part of the failure of the government of the day listening to the justified cry of the people in meeting their basic needs. Remember that even a tyranny governance system can only function with some degree of assent. One of the most pitiful revelations of the Nazi tyranny was the post-war discovery of the extent to which leaders of the Jewish communities in East Europe co-operated with their persecutors – for example, in providing lists of victims for the gas-chamber – in the illusion that, thereby, they might buy a respite for a Jewish remnant. The same scenario is taking place in Southern Cameroons.

The continent is still infested with the rise and stay of new *"Old Men"* in the helm of authority and power, castigating any form of the young ones onto the podium of power and governance. And so, when Presidents Yaya Jammeh of Gambia, Robert Mugabe of Zimbabwe and Omar al-Bashir of Sudan respectively were brought down in few years of each other, Africa appeared to be getting rid of the *old men* that had dominated the political scene for decades. The Central African Sub-region is host to the continent's long serving presidents. The iconic image of a young Sudanese woman demanding change from the roof of a car inspired hope of a new democratic dawn. The willingness of so many people to risk their safety demand a better future served as a striking illustration of a wide-spread desire for more responsive and inclusive governments. Africa's increasingly young societies appeared to be serving notice to their geriatric leaders that the era of *'presidents for life'* was over *(Eden, 2020:12, from the Africa Report).*

Africa is suffering from the disease of the *"Dictators Factory of Presidents for Life"* (TDFOPL). Today, the continent is host to the longest serving leaders of the world (Yoweri Moseveni, Uganda; Paul Kagame, Rwanda; Paul Biya, Cameroon; Obiang Nguema of Equatorial Guinea). It is interesting to note, in these countries, there seem to be a passive acceptance of TDFOPL nexus; or you may ask, why is there no greater opposition to the production and detainment of the *'old men in power"?* This is a million-dollar question requiring a million-dollar explanation. It is a puzzle in the political vocabulary of African politics. To begin with, and despite the clear quest and implications for democracy, criticism of these power grabs is often muted. On the one hand, surveys indicate that a greater majority of citizens want democracy and to live under a democratic functional governance system with multiparty elections and civil liberties adhered to; and fundamental basic human rights respected. On the other hand, one gets confused looking at the situation where for example, President Kagame of Rwanda commands considerable domestic support to remain in office while in Mali a coup d'état overthrows an elected president is greatly celebrated in the streets. This shows the two opposing faces of the continent. Africa is gradually returning the 1960s and 1970s, the age of *'coup d'état'* in Africa (look at what has within a short space time happened Mali, Burkina Faso, Equatorial Guinea. Africa should fifty years be celebrating the victory of independence and sustainable development in a grand style. We are not. Instead, we are even worse today than before. Why are these "coup d'état" taking place? Poor governance and bad management that gives rise to the disappointment of independence, and eventually rising frustration since the leaders have failed in meeting the desires and aspirations of the people.

In between, we have the spoils of the one-party syndrome and its falls cajoling citizens for them to harvest the best from the existing system. In Cameroon, it is the game of politics – scratch my back, I do the same for you - executed under the *"appointment, promotion, motion of support syndrome;"* and the 'centre periphery relationship. Contextualised within these scenarios, the most obvious answer is that many African governments are extremely authoritarian, preventing any form of criticism or opposition which bars many to speak-out openly against the regime. Or those who derive benefits will do everything possible to ensure the continuation of current status-quo – the patronage connection plays an important role as well. Pushing the discourse further, most of these leaders are experts in manipulating the threat of conflict to justify clamping down on critical voices; and often get away with slowly suffocating democracy. It can be argued that age should not be an issue; focus should be on the 'output' role of the delivery to the people. What looks like a good reason to sacrifice democracy today often turns out to have been a travesty tomorrow – even if you think that development is more important than human rights.

The problem is that the world's old men rarely continue to deliver when they enter their second decade in power. The reason for this is not so much age but the period in office. For example, President Trump's advanced years my help to explain some of his idiosyncrasies, but imagine how divided and dysfunctional the United States would be if he was allowed to govern for more than 40 years with no checks and balances. Leaders who cannot be held accountable are more likely to make policy mistakes, and less likely to correct them. When stagnating economies make it harder to sustain popular support and patronage networks, they also face fewer obstacles to using repression to remain to remain in power. The more coercion they use, the less willing they are to stand down and face possible prosecution for the abuses they committed in office. Transfers of power are not a silver bullet of course – they may just involve replacing a good and upstanding leader with a dubious one. But they have been shown to disrupt corruption networks, encourage leaders to respect the rule of law and boost public support for democracy (Eden, No. 1185, 2020).

The custodian of power in a country is the people. This candid fact runs through the constitutions of all African countries, but truly never respected. It remains the most violated aspect of the constitution. Therefore, civil society should be held responsible for the misuse of power by power-hungry leaders. Civil society should be held responsible for not showing the red card to leaders who usurp the state as personal property, transform the presidency into a royal dynasty – from father to wife or to son. We know the succession linage in a royal dynasty. The succession line in of a presidency is through elections and the people are the deciders. The transfer power in no way guarantees good leadership, but it dies help to prevent continuation of exploitative and incompetent government, government that claims or take it as given, the one in office, sees society as personal property that can be used anyhow without accountability. He/she is the State, and the State is him/her. Therefore, failure to halt the production line of dictators will mean that in twenty years' time, there will be more young people standing on cars across Africa trying to rid their countries of a new generation of authoritarian old men.

This publication advocates for a new African leadership approach that is responsible, accountable, relevant and ethical (RARE), if Africa is to galvanize its resources and create a better future for the continent - one where Africa operates as an equal competitive partner in the emerging global village (Ngambi, 2011:19, Forje, 2002). The continent pays heavily for suffering from gross deficiencies in leadership and a passive civil society. Poor leadership and uncoordinated civil society or events of mass peoples' actions impedes the democratic process. Democracy and constructive change demand comprehensive actions for a holistic system change which demands visionary leadership as well as proactive civil society working in the articulate interests of the collective good. It is call to positive action. This call is most important because any plan that is not put into action is of no real use at all. At least, it provides some useful ideas about critical issues on nation-building in Africa, by and Africa and humanity. What will people think of this book? We all have our different and varied opinions on how the continent should develop. Reactions will come from those who are enemies with their foreign supporters of the masses, of the continent's independence. There will be the false progressive persons who pretend to support the Afro-centric agenda: There the groups who strongly bank on the Eurocentric ideological orientation as providing the best way forward for changing Africa. The true progressive advocates of an Afro-centric will welcome this book and they will criticise it. The sum total of the criticism helps in shaping our perspectives for a better tomorrow. The criticisms will help the writer and others understand and are prepared to move forward in building the kind of society we want.

It is not wrong, to state the least; that the continent's diversity also contributes to its dysfunctionality seriously contributes to destructive conflicts and the collapse of the country. Hence, the major challenges facing the continent is not the absence of leaders, but the absence of appropriate and effective leadership and a vibrant, proactive civil society for its diversity and unity of people and resources. The point is lucidity outlined by (Mbeki 1998): *'I believe that what is at fault is not so much that we are at a loss as to what to do to realise the goal of development, but we have not evolved the social movement with its leadership, which will ensure that we do indeed make the necessary advances on this front"*. On the other hand, Africa's diversity and its potential strength in advancing its developmental strategies, in its stage of annexation and assimilation nexus are equally worrying. The inspiring speech of Kwame Nkrumah at the opening session of the First Meeting of the Educational Board of the Encyclopaedia Africana on September 24, 1964 at the University of Ghana comes to mind: "Africa had a noble past which astounded even the ancient Roman World with its great surprises. Yet, it was only much dilatory after a millennium and a-half of African history that we are now busily engaged in reconstructing for all the world to know, that racist exploitation and imperialist domination deliberately fostered a new and monstrous mythology of race which nourished the popular but unfinished image of Africa as the "Dark Continent," continent whose inhabitants were without civilisation, or any hope of future development – except by the Grace of foreign tutelage."

Leadership is the catalyst that keeps organisation and nations focused on their objectives and ensure that they deliver on promises to their clients and stakeholders, hence the argument advanced here and recommends an alternative leadership approach that should usher the benefits of this diversity and forge unity. The new form of leadership backed by a vibrant proactive civil society is (**Responsible, Accountable, Relevant and Ethical**) - RARE - Leadership and civil society. Responsible leadership cultivates an envisaged future in the hearts and minds of followers, and most importantly recognises when there is a need for change; Accountable leadership nut connected with the people one is responsible for. According to Maxwell (2010) asserts that connecting is the ability to identify with and relate to people in such a way that your ability to influence them is enhanced; Relevant leadership is one that is engaging and in touch with the environment It drives the organisation and national performance by analysing future trends (Beinhocker et al. 2009). And Ethical leadership maintains integrity, knowing core values and having the courage to live them in all parts of your life, in service of the common good. Ethical leaders need to demonstrate integrity to be authentic.

The leadership gap status-quo in Africa contributes to the rape, poverty, exploitation and marginalisation of the continent. The people remain poor in the midst of plenty. Their resources in no way improve the quality of livelihood of the population. The continent is caught in a developmental pause. According to the African Development Bank Group (2007) approximately 61 percent of the population leaves in rural areas, and in some countries less than 50 percent of the population have no access to safe water. Furthermore, poverty, poor health and other incidences of malaria and HIV/AIDS among others, high mortality and maternal rates; unemployment, and corruption characterise Africa. Not only is this worrying but jeopardises the transformation of the continent from a backward to a service society of the 21st century and beyond. Apparently, both internal and external factors contribute to this pathetic stagnation, with slavery, colonialism and poor leadership as well sharing in the blame (Ogbunwezeh 2006, Okafor, 2005). Looking at some of the external factors, we find that at independence, there were numerous and complex economic, social and political problems in practically all the newly independent states of Africa. Chief among these problems were unemployment, poverty, and inadequate educational and health facilities. In almost every case these problems were compounded in the years following the attainment of political independence. Another legacy of colonial rule was the prevalence of an economy that was characterized by irrational income inequalities, based on racialism, and in which the whites enjoyed a privileged dominant position. Internal, the external situation has not changed. We still have Black Skin, White Mask phenomenon. And so, "the ordinary citizens in most African countries live brief lives in squalor not appreciably improved over that of their forefathers….to begin with, the priorities of most developing societies are wrong or inconsistent with the broad perspective of bringing basic human needs to the greatest possible segment of society. The philosophical orientation of most political parties and trade unions in Africa lacks the mechanisms for mobilising human resources; rather they have become channels of exploitation, getting rich at the shortest possible time and by employing all means available. In short, there is a total lack of a 'sense of direction' (Forje, 1982). In other words, African leadership almost everywhere has failed to mobilise and utilize the vast human and other available resources for the greatest good of the greatest number of citizens.

Africa's wealth is legendary as Ogbunwezeh (2007) and others indicate: "40 percent of the world's potential hydro-electric power supply; the bulk of the world's diamond and chromium; 30 percent of the uranium; 50 percent of the world's gold; 90 percent of its cobalt; 50 percent of its phosphates; 40 percent of its platinum; 7.5 percent of its coal; 8 percent of its known petroleum reserves: 12 percent of its natural gas; 3 percent of its iron ore; 64 percent of the world's manganese; 13 percent of its copper; vast bauxite, nickel and land resources and millions of untilled farmlands". These outstanding statistics have not improved the wellbeing of the African population. It goes without saying that the success of failure of every nation is a reflection on leadership. Nweke (2010:12) is explicit in expressing his disappoint with Africa's leadership, and asks: "how can people so hungry for self-rule become so dispassionate about a future they had fought and lost so much to have? How can a people destroy the very thing they love so much with the same hands that they used in building it? Why should it be that Africa keeps going around in circles instead of moving forward?" This issue is echoed in Forje (2002; 41-60) - "The Disappointment of Independence" in which he outlines Africa's packed democracy and development which leaves the continent most vulnerable more than ever before. Today there is new form of recolonisation of the continent by the Chinese. Unfortunately, many an African president is motivated by the desire to cling to power at all costs - what is known as 'sit-tight-presidents?' The case of Cameroon, being a good example: characterised by failed policies and electoral manipulations and even ethnic xenophobic mindset attitude towards other citizens and regions. The ongoing Anglophone crisis (Cameroon) is just a tip-of-the iceberg of the vast problems the country is facing. These internal conflicts across the continent show how insecure the region is within the global construct are for its people. That is why it is imperative for Africa to adjust through a progressive Afro-centric mindset to greatly reduce the inherent Eurocentric agenda that keeps the continent as slaves even though slavery was banned many decades ago and independence granted to African countries in the 1950s. Africa has transverse for slavery, colonialism to independence and today it is back to re-colonisation and slavery. What is abundantly clears is that the developed countries are using the confused status-quo and plight of African countries to strengthen its dominance through the Eurocentric agenda and its influence over the development paths of African countries. Currently, African countries are being forced directly or indirectly to reshape their economic policies to make them compatible with Eurocentric design. This begs the question – will Africa ever be independent and sovereign? This question requires a million-dollar answer in which African countries must bear in mind that the successful and sustainable transformation of the regions on their shoulders – how they able to pulling their strength and opportunities to counter act existing weaknesses threats. With its vast strength and opportunities, backed with knowledge of the weakness and threats, Africa can successfully move to making the future more secure.

Neither national unity nor national consolidation can exist in such an environment. Therefore, the African continent need leaders able to reconcile diversity into unity, bolster development, tapping into the resources and needs and fears of the people, sensitive enough to recognise the needs and aspirations of the people and to respond accordingly, but does not micro-manage. This is the leadership that sets the vision and motivates everyone to rally behind that vision for the common good. Such leadership creates ownership among citizens, values morals, ethics and integrity and respects cultures as well as focuses attention on the developmental needs of the society and the nation it serves. The leader is servant to the people and not a master to be served by the population (Heide, 2007; Charan 2005; Dicicoo 2007; Beaty 2007, Ngambi 2010; Buckingham 2005). Such leadership focuses attention on the developmental needs of communities and nations it serves, and remains relevant in a value-adding way to all stakeholders and is of service to the community in which it serves. The diversity of economies within the continent precludes a uniform strategy, yet certain principles and objectives need to guide the development course of African countries. It is on this context that we strongly advocate the imperatives of a progressive Afro-centric approach, collective self-reliance as a more vigorous drive to strengthen co-operation among African countries is of supreme importance in the present circumstance to reinforce their capacity for growth. Africa's unity and solidarity are equally essential for improving its position within the world system of economic relationships. Thus, the publication is designed as a comprehensive approach to the multiplicity of problems confronting the region, its countries and its people have to overcome.

Each African country's development strategy must necessarily be specific to its stage of development, size, resources base, cultural heritage, and other national characteristics. But a strategy for self-reliant and people-centred development will need to be guided by certain common principles and objectives; the unity of the continent; the putting in place of a structure-functional democratic governance system; the fight against endemic corruption that has eaten extremely deep into the social fabric of the African society. The form, structure and contents of our educational system needs serious hauling to meet the changing pattern of the evolving global context and not forgetting taking along the essentials of the heritage of our cultural values – ethics, morals and other aspects that makes us Africans which we are. For now, educational or knowledge building system is sinking deeper and deeper into the bottom of the pit. The Times Higher Education (THE) has ranked the University of Cape Town (UCT – South Africa) fifth-fifth in its 2022 list of most international universities in the world, making it the only Africa University on the list. Congratulations UTC for flying the flag of excellence on the global arena.

Briefly, responsible leadership cultivates and envisaged future in the hearts and minds of the population, constructs a new mindset, foster unity and recognizes the need for change., they change the status quo, persuade and agitate for meaningful transformation (McKee 2002): Africa needs leaders you connect with people and accountable (A). Able to establish achievable goals and outcomes build a culture of high performance as well as provide feedback and consequences (Clark 2004). The continent needs Relevant (R) leaders who are in touch with the environment, continuously develops 'best practices' (Ansari 2002, Glatter and Kydd 2003) in pursuit of excellence. There is need for ethical leadership (E) as well as embedded with moral qualities to better overcome the destructive and unethical behaviour of citizens and close associates of those in administration.

To move forward, the continent must foster a new breed of leadership qualities to first decolonised existing colonial mindset, and breed a type of leadership that effects effectiveness, efficiency, accountability, transparency, trust, confidence as well as it injects positive influence in society. But effective leadership without proper understanding of management principle can, at best waste society's resources and at worst become toxic. Too many African leaders have become toxic elements. There is a call for the most effective leadership approach in a diverse political environment configuration like the African construct which makes the RARE leadership approach very welcome to foster sanity, unity and progress. Such leadership fosters what Ely and Thomas (2001) call integration and learning, also known as the learning and effectiveness paradigm. The issue is further expanded by Ngambi (2011) that leadership must foster a balance between engaging with current realities and developing leaders for tomorrow.

Africa needs a leadership style dedicated to educating, training, developing, retaining, rewarding talents, not mediocrity and serving the people. Such leadership does not support the incompetence that arises from misplaced loyalty, but is value driven and principled enough to reject any form of toxic behaviour, even from close allies (Cashman, 1997). In short, the continent more than ever before needs leaders who are adaptive fostering adaptation in order to thrive in tomorrow's world, embrace creativity and fosters discipline (Manev 2009). The

Centre for Ethical leadership (2007) describes ethical leadership as knowing your core values and having courage to live in all parts of your life, in service of the common good. To progress, all sectors of society, including the private sector, are in constant need of reform. The private sector is not free from fundamental thinking and action, characterised by aggressive and oversimplified language and a 'we are right, they are wrong' mentality. The public, private and civil society sectors need to do more of the same as well as inject even more energy and force. The ultimate goal or aim is to gain victor over the enemy - poverty, injustice, inequality, underdevelopment etc. instead of striving for harmony and the creation of a new equilibrium which will include the enemy; one can refer to dichotomy as masculine energy which divides one group against the other and which brings together. The State-Civil Society-Private Sector interface should be seen as a harmonious dialogue and approach that brings the ultimate benefit to the people. The complexity of development and sustainability is daunting. The changes are requiring of us, in order to practice it, and are every bit as revolutionary as democracy was more than was two hundred centuries ago. Just as the demand for democracy was more driven by (among-other things) rising levels of wealth and education among the common people, historical forces are at work that demand an embrace of sustainability.

Some good examples of the needed leadership qualities outlined can be seen with the roles of a few cases such as; Nelson Mandela exercised inclusive and visionary leaders; Kwame Nkrumah (Ghana) did the same as well as Nyerere (Tanzania), F W de Klerk demonstrated decisive leadership in his role in ending apartheid in South Africa; Thabo Mbeki articulated the idea of building a new progress and modernised Africa (Olivier 2003). The former Presidents of Namibia and Mozambique, Sam Nujoma and Joaquim Chissano respectively, not only built institutions of democratic law in their respective countries, but also ensured sustained economic growth. In addition, they joined leaders like Senghor (Senegal), Ahidjo (Cameroon) and Nyerere (Tanzania) and Mandela (South Africa) in relinquishing the posts of President freely or stepping down after their mandatory terms ended, and allowed their successors to be chosen in free and fair elections (Reedy 2002). In Cameroon, the outgoing President Ahmadou Ahidjo selected and appointed his successor Paul Biya in 1982. It is not surprising that the Mo Ibrahim Prize for African leadership with the criteria of providing exceptional leadership and leaving office when the country's constitutional term limit ends that has had the following as winners, Joaquim Chissano (Mozambique 2007), Festus Mogae (Botswana,

2008) Pedro Verona (Cape Verde, 2010) and with no former Head of State qualified for the 2012 award (because there was no winner qualified for the award in 2012) because none met the criteria needed to win this award, the selection committee announced that USA 1 million dollars special grant would be awarded to veteran anti-apartheid fighter, Archbishop Desmond Tutu (South Africa) for 'speaking truth to power'. African leaders are only speaking truth to the power of money and lies to their people with a manipulative and convincing style to remain in power for entirety.

Desmond Tutu continues to show himself to be the scourge of injustice, ready to rock the boat if necessary and speak out against those political leaders who he believes have lefty down their citizens and the wider world. The politics of succession is what is killing Africa. To avoid chaos, African leaders must follow constitutional procedures and respect and ensure that the rule of law prevails in society. In this respect, few countries have shown good examples, in the succession squabbles than others. Ghana for example demonstrated a high sense of succession responsibility after the death of President John Evans Atta Mills; so also, Ethiopia after the death of Prime Minister Meles Zenawi, compared with the situation in Malawi after the death of President Mutharika, or in Nigeria after the death of President Musa Yar'Adua in May 2010. Otherwise, it has been the struggle to remain in power for ever. It comes as no surprise Africa, especially; the turbulent Central African Sub-Region is the host to the world's many long serving presidents.

Political succession should not be a matter of *'do or die'* politics notes Noble Prize Laureate Wole Soyinka. Stability, predictability and continuity are important ingredients of good governance and are assured by a well-planned and managed succession strategy, including the respect for the rule of law. There are cases where the succession issues are turned into a dynasty from father to son like in Gabon after the death of Omar Bongo when he died in 2009, and the presidency was handed to the son Ali Bongo Omar (Foreign and Defence Minister); President Faure Gnassinge of Togo succeeding the father; and Joseph Kabila of the Democratic Republic of the Congo succeeded the father. Without the rule of law, there can be constitutional somersaults which bear all the hallmarks of what ridicules Africans before the world. Only outgoing USA President, Donald Trump seems to express such tendency of wanting to hold on to power even after defeat at the polls.

Most African countries' constitutions stipulate that in case of the death of a President, his or her deputy or the Head of the National Assembly will stand in until an election can be conducted to elect a new President. Some leaders, however, expect the designated 'her/his apparent' to display fawning personal loyalty. If he or she does not, political conflict can arise. In Nigeria, for example, Vice-President Atika Abubakar had a frosty relationship with then President Olusegum Obasanjo; the situation in Malawi with Joyce Banda, following her expulsion from the ruling party to pave the way for President's brother Peter Mutharika to succeed the brother. Goodluck Jonathan followed the footpath of iconic Kenneth Kaunda in accepting defeat before the elections results were announced. Many years after President Goodluck of Nigeria repeated the good act of Kenneth Kaunda. It replicates what Dr Endeley did to John Foncha way back in 1959. The shift of political power from the reigning Prime Minister, Dr. Endeley to the Opposition Leader John Foncha was smooth, friction free exhibiting the political maturity of the people of Southern Cameroons. That is how politics should be, functioning in the overall good of the people. Politics: is a call to serve not to be served as demonstrated by most of todays' leaders. Thomas Jefferson noted that: *"When a man assumes a public trust, he should consider himself as a public property"* (B. L. Rayner 1936, Life of Jefferson, p.356). Once he/she becomes public property, the defence of the public interests, or him/her mandatory. The best weapon is justice; that is, always doing the right thing. In the words of George Washington "the right is more precious than peace" (Speech to Congress, 2nd April 1917). The Chinese philosopher, Lao Tsu was realistic to seeing government efforts as improving the living conditions of the poor; and how to win the confidence of the people, by issuing the following advice to leaders:

> *": Go to the people; Live among the people; Learn from the people; Plan with the people; Start with what the people know; Build on what the people have; Teach by showing; Learn by doing; Not to conform but to transform; Not to relieve but to release"* (Tarh, 1988)

Following ongoing events in the country since 2016, the people as political pace-setter on the continent emerged in a double capacity as (i) the Jews in Egypt and (ii) the Palestinian in the hands of the Jews in the Middle East looking at the political situation in Cameroon today. The form and maturity of political leadership and the response of society towards such leadership is crucial in sustaining the state of peace, stability, growth and development. Our leaders should listen to the people and not to command them. Failing to listen to the cry of the people, they become obsessed with power. Obsessed by illegitimacy acquired through bad behaviour and corrupt means like fraudulent elections, most of the leaders make use of any means however, unscrupulous, that strengthens the power of the State to remain in office as long as possible. They often sought to prolong or defend the excesses of governance blaming the treachery of the governed. Blaming will never solve the problem. Africa is at the legitimate cross-roads of a harvest, a rich harvest that only requires building the socio-political-economic-techno highway of peaceful co-existing, of sharing, eating and living together. We no longer live together because we have foolishly or stupidly violated the values of our cultural value heritage – *ubuntu. batho pele, harambee* – and others. We have imprisoned ourselves with foreign cultures that we do not understand, and gotten divorced from our past which should be the building block for laying the foundation in preparing the future. A future which Nelson Mandela aptly narrates in the 'Long Walk to Freedom;' we have turned our backs and hearts to the power of *forgiveness, reconciliation and consensus.* We have no idol to emulate; no genuine servant leader to lead the people to the promised. The African today has been left at the gate of the palace of 'sustainable quality livelihood.' What counts in life as noted by Nelson Mandela "is not the mere fact we have lived. It is what difference we have made to the lives of others that will determine the significance of the life we lead." In short, we need leaders sending signals that something urgent must be done to hasten the economic and social emancipation of the African people. No African should be made to live like slaves in their own country, under any circumstances. The current state of abject poverty. The filthy inhuman dwellings which millions still live in throughout the continent must disappear. Here is a vast continent so rich in natural resources but with millions lavishing in extreme poverty. Simply put, liberation without repossession of land and its resources by the dispossessed remains a gigantic colonial fraud. The effects of the 1884-1885 Berlin Conference must be banished from the shores of the African continent. We live in an environment, like the South African situation where the 'victims of apartheid gave far more to 'reconciliation' than the perpetrators of colonialism and apartheid did.' The consequences of the wrong pollical response to the statesmanship to President Nelson Mandela by the representatives of the apartheid colonialist regime are that in South Africa today, there are 'two nations. One is the extremely rich and white settler minority. Another one is extremely poor, at 79.2 percent, the African majority

(Pheko, 2014:29). The same situation exists in other African countries, where the minority governing elites who replaced the departed colonial masters and a few rich and powerful persons control the wealth and power of the nations, compared to the more than 80 percent of population who are subjected to the whims and caprices of these 'nouveau rich and powerful'. Africa has to walk on to victory – sovereignty, human dignity and freedom.

Here is where we should give two cheers for embracing democratic governance because it admits variety and because it permits criticism. Our leaders should epitomize and promote a democratic governance culture on the continent. Why should society not give such cheers to a leader who propels ideals that enhance their quality of livelihood in all its facets? That is why it is necessary rejecting the Euro-centric ideological orientation which is no longer tenable to the African developmental approach. Every effort needs to be made with tenacity building of a strong, united, democratic and prosperous Africa. It is crucial for the new African leadership to ensure Africa's competitiveness, economic development and sustainability, technological advancement through improved human capital development, a proper utilisation of human and natural resources to create a decent and sustainable livelihood for all citizens, Society must be proactive as well as responding positively to RAREVS leadership style that the continent must deserve for its transformation. This is the time for constructive *'change'* in Africa. If African countries are leveraging their rich diversity in natural and human resources, they should start doing things differently and innovatively, creatively and entrepreneurially. Lee Keun (2016) encourages African countries to look at the Korean experience as one of the most remarkable stories of *"catch-up"* from very low to high levels of development. There are no other two ways out of the current predicament that has engulfed the continent. Bo Goransson et al (2016) look into the relationships between knowledge production and development in developing countries in Asia, Africa and Latin America. While Swann (2015) argues that innovation and wealth-creation are not monopoly of business but the contribution of ordinary people. The people must be galvanised in a different way. For its resources to create a better future for the continent, and for future generations, where the people will operate as equal competitive and cooperative partners in the global village ruled by a knowledge-based economy.

Finally, developing a RAREVS leadership governance style at all levels, individual, community, national regional and continental provides the best possible way forward to ensure sustainable development and quality wellbeing for Africa and Africans. The succession process in Ghana, Ethiopia and Malawi demonstrates three latest cases of smooth succession providing evidence that Africa is gradually graduating from the school of chaos into its transition right. Succession can be a frequent problem even in developed and stable democracies because it is all about political power. It is even more problematic if a leader dies in office. For instance, after the mess that surrounded the illness and death of President Yar' Adua of Nigeria. But why do African leaders hide their health status from their population? They fail to understand that once as an elected leader, your life becomes public property; but as public property, the public must equally respect and protect your life and privacy. It is within Africa's competence to banish hunger, poverty, ignorance, disease, insecurity and autocracy. Africa's inhabitants everywhere long for the day when these scourges will be banished forever from their midst. Do their leaders have the will, vision, courage and commitment to lead them across today's wasteland to the green pastures that lie on the other side? Will Africa be transformed into a land of integrity, rather than moral deprivation; of hope or rather than despair, of freedom rather than slavery, of wealth rather than endemic poverty?

African scholars often cite, justifiably; the numerous political and even sometimes military interventions of the Western powers, always hostile to the force of progressive social change on the continent, which always come to the rescue of reactionary and archaic forces. Not that these arrangements are structurally linked to the logic of internal conflicts and in that way, oppose the "external" to the "nation" whose contradictions are skipped (Uroh, 1998:29). The weakness of national scholar's dates back to the earlier colonial schooling which was designed for brainwashing and for the destruction of the cultural heritage and value systems of the people. The Rise of the new breed of African scholars is often viewed with scorn by the Grand West for making efforts to educate their people in exposing the weakness and destructive strategy of the West towards Africa. Hence the conspiracy hatred against and destruction of Kwame Nkrumah, Patrice Lumumba, Tom Mboya, Steve Biko, Sekoue Toure and a host of other nationalists. These leaders and scholars saw the light at the end of tunnel which the West did not want the majority of Africans to see and know how to hasten their enlightenment and strengthen the resolve to own their sovereignty and development construct. Thus, the independence of Africa started on a false note which continues today. The throes of the rapacious colonial agenda are not dead but waxing strong and planting seeds of conflicts, destruction and division within and among African peoples and states.

Caught between the growing power and prestige of a bureaucratic and technologically sophisticated elite and downward mobility pressure, mobility displacement rather than incorporation occurs in sectors close to marginalising groups. The more a bourgeoisie is subject to such pulls, the more it will change from a class in itself into a class for itself, a circumstance favouring authoritarian political regime (Cardozo &Falsetto 1979, Lipton, 1976). The marginalisation of women from top political leadership position in Africa is a course for serious concern. Though efforts are directed towards meeting the 30 percent quota, many countries are still dragging their feet. The politics of chauvinism still prevails hampering the process of balanced and sustainable development. Steady Chioma (2012) in a recent publication highlights key factors that have promoted female leadership in these 'male-dominated, authoritarian and war-prone' countries. She goes further to link motherhood with peace as a 'catalyst for female leadership' and notes that women's activism for peace focused on 'social and economic development with equity and justice. Using the concept of *'mothering the nation'* Steady argues that female leadership can 'humanise the state as well as provide a powerful alternative to the male-dominated status quo under which the continent is suffering from. Only two African countries can boost of having women as head of State – Liberia and Malawi, with Guinea's Rabioatou Serah Diallo as Deputy Prime Minister appointed in 2010. The female gender in Africa is making greater strides and the process must be encouraged to ensure a 50-50 parity in the developmental process of the continent. It should be strongly emphasized that parity does not entail competition, but partnership and complementary process of working together for the good of everyone. The male gender is part of the female gender and vice versa.

The criticisms of independent Africa, of its poor governance and state of corrupt middle classes, (which is has gradually engulfed the entire society) of the lack of economic direction, of the tenacity of rural community structures, forget that these features of contemporary Africa were forged long before 1880 and 1960. Equally, it is wrong to hang on colonial rule as the cause of what is happening today. Yes, some of the wrong seeds were planted long ago. What have African countries done to get rid of those bad seeds and plant good and health ones? That is the question we should be addressing and what this publication attempts to address in its own way; just as it joins other authors and numerus publications in creating greater awareness for a new attitude, behaviour and change (ABC) for reconstituting the Africa society. The African continent needs serious surgical operations if it has to leapfrog into the status and club of a developed polity.

Pursuing the discourse further, no wonder that neo-colonialism has perpetuated these features. The political teams which were in-charge of independent Africa were not necessarily artificially constituted of junior civil servants even among those which accepted the neo-colonial option. Their weaknesses were those of peripheral capitalism as it has been forged here. Suffice it to state that the responsibility of the metropolis was great. For when, despite the shortcomings of colonial society, the liberation movement had produced elites potentially capable of going farther, all effort was made to destroy these opportunities for Africa to get out of the rut. The Arab Spring is a continuation of the rut. The ganging up between Africa ruling classes and the global strategies of imperialism and of course, neo-colonialism is therefore, definitively, the ultimate cause of the failure for Africa to progress. One finds, in the workings of such unholy marriage, all the dimensions of the concern of the strategy of imperialism/neo-colonialism in the post-war 1945-1960 and post-colonial period, 1960-todate, in particular its geo-strategic dimensions. The post September 2001 events created new dimensions. Africa is going to pay the price with the eventual installation of AFRICOM on the Gulf of Guinea.

Rapidly going through and beginning from the Congo crisis of the 1960s, the Sharpeville massacre of innocent school children, the wars of independence on the continent (Angola, Mozambique, Zimbabwe, the collapse of the apartheid regime in South Africa, through the split of Sudan, the numerous military coup d'états throughout the continent to the Arab Spring and its fall outs, Western support to military and oppressive regimes in Africa all paint a gloomy picture of the plight of the people which the global system has failed to address And may never addressed issue that will keep haunting the continent. The issues haunting Africa is of great economic and political interests to the developed countries in various ways. We can justly ask why they must create stability and a peaceful environment in areas that feed them. It simply means cutting your nose to spite your face.

A new leaf has been turned and a new climax attained. The Organisation of African Unity (OAU) fulfilled its mission of decolonisation and handed over to the Africa Union (AU) charged with the obligation for creating an African Common Market (ACM) (Forje

1969) and an African Union Government (AUG). The debate on this new form of economic and political integration, is to my mind, be opened to constructive debate and engagement on new forms of integration and state-building that best suit's the continent. Special consideration deserves to be mentioned at this stage - the unity of the continent; the ending of poverty and corruption, good governance and the involvement of the people in governing, an end to conflicts, perception of ethnic diversity as asset not liability to nation integration, and the rest for the rule of law among others. Power sand politics in Africa should be geared towards creating an equal society - power to the people with equal opportunities for all: this ought to be the: guiding principle for the lost continent, to come to life. A new Africa has to be born with the views of Brazilian Archbishop, Helder P Camera's words in mind: *"I am not a technician, not in economy or sociology or politics.... Now I am always urging the youth of my country, the young university students and professors, to join interdisciplinary teams and to look for a model that will not be a servile of either capitalism or the present socialist model* (New York Times, October 1970:6).

Africa needs a rethinking of its development approach. A new articulated and strategically implemented way of doing things. This publication should be seen within this context. That is, a book conceived and written not so much to produce a new model as to provide a basis for broad-gauge and interdisciplinary discussion of the most pressing social, economic, and political problems facing African states today and tomorrow; in fundamental respects there are no significant differences and distinctions among other countries of the Third World - Asia and Latin America. This book is intended and designed to serve that purpose - an interdisciplinary approach to solving the continents plethora of problems. African societies must be futurists: they must endeavour to know in advance what they will be like, and technicians are inclined to be even more irritated by the resistance of human beings than by that of things. Africa has to be proactive and visionary in crafting their development path and destiny. There are no two ways; it is either or; develops or perishes? Africa is not going to perish but develop. It is our responsibility to see that is achieved. What are we waiting for? What is on offer? Why must we bother? What kind of legacy do we want to live behind? Taking the last question for example; we must bother because it is our obligations and responsibility to leave a better continent to future generations. We have to put 'people and the future first;' we have to unlock issues prohibiting our development process and path. We should not be the continent that is losing its mind, heart and head to the extent if even shrinking in economic and political impotence that other continents are less conscious of its existence. Africa should not continue perishing or exploited because of colonialism – in the brief, which is gone past since 6th March 1957. Since 1957, unfortunately we continue to hang on the "blame thesis" because of their "selfish behaviour." This only highlight the Westphalia state system is all about national government put their citizenry first and get punished if they don't. That is what our leaders are supposed to being doing.

Unfortunately, a new stage of power relationship and global capitalist polarisation has now begun, in which the logic of capital expansion strategically wants the African world structurally and provisionally 'marginalised and extremely exploited.' The structural adjustment programme was the start to the global marginalisation and exploitation of the continent. Thus, the debate on these new forms of polarisation should, is not open to a global debate of what the world system should look like. But one produced by the erosion of the former system, that of the post-war period, 1945-1960 without taking into consideration the events of the period 1960-1990, and especially post-1990 following the collapse of the Soviet Union and its satellite states. Factors influencing the new elements of the post-independence era 1960-to date, in my opinion include; the erosion of the self-reliant nation state and the resultant disappearance of the concomitance between the space of the reproduction of accumulation and that of its political and social management which was hitherto exactly defined by the borders of this self-reliant nation state;

- The erosion of the contract: centres - industrial regions / peripheries - non-industrialised regions and the emergence of new dimensions of polarisation:
- The late-comer advantage; the new nations transformation into a powerful economic block- the Asian Tigers, Brazil, India, South Africa and Nigeria posing serious challenges to the economic power base of the West; The Nolly-Wood film industry in Nigeria is posing serious threats to long-established Hollywood film industry in the United States of America. Africa is endowed with resources that can bring a serious and genuine game-changing nexus on the world scene. It is a question of how these resources are managed.
- The forces of globalisation accelerated by the power of information and communications technologies (ICTs) forcing

the world into a global village, with no nation any longer having a monopoly over information, and the construct of a world system based on 'knowledge' and less on raw materials though the latter continues playing a vital role in the transformation of a country.

Africa's position in the world pyramid is defined by the level of the competitive capacity of its product on the world market. Such competitiveness is the complex product of an amalgam of conditions operating in the overall field of reality - economic, political and social - and in this unequal combat the centres employ what could be called 'five monopolies' articulating the efficiency of their actions. These include the following:

- Monopolies from which contemporary centres benefit in the area of technology: monopolies which demand gigantic expenditures, which only the state - the big and rich states - can contemplate supporting. Without this support - which liberal ideology always ignores - and singularly support for military expenditure (industrial military complex), most of these monopolies could not be maintained;
- monopolies exercised in the financial institutions operating on the world financial market has given those monopolies an unprecedented efficiency:
- monopolies operating in the access to the natural resources of the planet; the dangers which the senseless tapping of these resources make the planet run now, and which capitalism - which is based on a social rationality in the short-term without more - cannot overcome, strengthen the scope of the monopoly of the already developed countries, which endeavour to simply prevent their wastage from reaching others:
- monopolies operating in the fields of communication and the media which do not unionise from the bottom of the world culture that they transmit, but still open up new means of political manipulation, the expansion of the new modern media market is already one of the major components of the erosion of the concept and practice of the democracy of the West:
- monopolies operating in the field of weapon of mass destruction; limited by the post-war bi-polarity, this monopoly is again the absolute weapon, whose use is reserved only for American diplomacy as in 1945 (Uroh, ibid).

These interrelated factors produce a new hierarchy in income distribution on the world scale, more unequal than ever, keep in an inferior position the industries of the peripheries and reduce them to an inferior position the industries of the peripheries and reduce them to the state of sub- contracting activities. The newly industrialised countries are no ay 'catching up' with the dominant centres where as those countries where as those countries in Africa are simply 'late' on this catch up even though the 'late more advantage (Gerschenkron 1962) plays in their favour. The former constitutes the heart of tomorrow's periphery whereas the latter can simply provisionally be kept on the fringes of the system.

Sadly, enough, Africa seem not to learn from history. Every development is like starting anew. Why do the policy-makers dread history; digging into the past to understand the present and mirroring the present to construct the future? It is here that the policy makers go wrong. It is from this neglect that Samir Amin (1990:1) was prompted to write: *"If the 1960s were characterised by the greatest hope of being an irreversible process of development launched throughout what can to be called The Third World and Africa in particular, the present age is one of disillusionment. Development has broken down; its theory is in crisis, its ideology the subject of doubt."* Pursuing the discussion on this line, Africa's state of backwardness remains a serious issue best described as crisis of "doubtful underdevelopment" or one of" mental decolonisation." It is therefore economic as well as political, equally socio-political as well as ethical and moral, which constitute a product of Africa's chequered history with the present manifestation largely shaped by the contemporary African environment with global context.

Africa's development has a chance if only structural changes take place within our mental decolonisation construct. Unless Africa changes its approach, unless all the various aspects of the Africa predicament are properly delineated and simultaneously tackled in a coherent and comprehensive way that we see their interface, the question of Africa's development would only remain an agenda on paper for some distant future. Africa has a chance as long as structural changes take place. Therefore, "the social, institutional, cultural and political milieu in which it is taking place (Hammelstrand 1994:16) must be understood in order to improve the standard of living of the people. The development of Africa is, therefore, how to make human-beings live a better life. Rephrased in another way, development must be human-focused quantitatively and qualitatively, increase or decrease as the case may be, inequality among the people - more or less marginalisation coming from or more democratic or authoritarian political regimes stretching their tentacles and so forth (Osia, 1987:37). In short, it is either the people develop themselves or they do not; *"in their own interest and by their own resources"* (Ake 1989:52). The crucial factors are autonomy, independence, self-reliant, pride, sense of direction, political will, and the ability/capacity to choose for one, either as an individual or as a society remains crucial as imperative. These constitute the only way by which the individual is the end, and not the means to an end.

Politically, and extremely unfortunately, Africa has transformed itself into an unthinking bunch, which, like a mirror has to be decided for by those in authority. Some African countries are not governed from the capital of the country but from abroad. The leaders on their part should be visionary, servant shepherd both responsible and responsive to led. Anything short from this construct is a degenerate political order d is anti-development. Without such an ideological orientation and priority setting, Africa will forever remain "a continent so disorganised as not to be able to feed from its own resources-will thus have to live by the world's charity as well as buying foreign food with her annual surplus that it should be spending for its own development" (Davidson 1974:73). Stated differently, Africa is poor in the midst of plenty. It has failed to give added value to its vast natural resource's potentials. The developed polities are exploiting the continent from the perspectives of this gross negligence on the part of Africa's poor leadership nexus.

Development cannot be attained by 'proxy.' Africa must develop its mental intellect to give added value to its vast natural resource's potentials. Building or developing the human capital to develop themselves; and this simply imply inter alias, which by themselves actively participate directly in the process that enhances and harnesses their development in the spheres already identified. It is a question of develop or perish by their own accord. Moosa Imad (2018) takes the argument of perishing further by exploring the contemporary doctrine plaguing the academic sphere, the principle of publishing or perishing; either Africa develops or perishing in the vast rapidly changing globalised knowledge based and regulated economy of our age. Bearing, the foregoing in mind, and contextualising the term development within the current dispensation in Africa, would among other things entail as the publication perceives it a progressive elimination of poverty, corruption, unemployment, injustice, absence of the rule of law, social inequality, authoritarian political structure, marginalisation, monopolisation of opinion by the state, exclusion, misuse of power and all other negative tendencies that have since independence, regrettably plagued though becoming the defining characteristics of the African continent.

No wonder, this pathetical situation prompted Ake (ibid) to state that the region is plagued by the chronic debt problems, the state of declining productivity and negative growth rates and worse still, the threat of starvation to over 150 million people on the continent. The North-South Roundtable notes; "Africa's economic and social performance during the 1980's was predominantly negative. This was manifest within Africa by severely depressed economic growth rate, stagnant agricultural production, deteriorating social sciences and a decline in living standards. Externally, it was marked by a rising debt burden, inadequate resources flow and a sharp fall in commodity prices for Africa's key exports" (North-South Roundtable 1991:3). Adding more caveat views to the saga, the (World Bank, 1989:1) had earlier noted that Africans are "almost as poor today as they were 30 years ago". Africa alone parades 32 of the 37 worlds 47 least developed nations: On the average, 1000 children are killed daily in the continent by some curable diseases such as dysentery, diarrhoea, cholera and what have you. The various manifestations this publication exposes on the crisis of development in Africa are what have contributed the rising degree of destitution and despair that have become the entrenched lots of the many on a continent blessed with plenty.

Rising destructive frustration is in the increase on the continent. Independence was expected to usher in a new era of the respect basic human rights and freedom denied under foreign or settler rule. The situation has not improved fifty or more years after independence. Without doubt, 50 years after independence neither a political kingdom nor economic development for the poor appears on the horizon and even feasible. But how did Africa get enmeshed in the present seemingly intractable mess? The first pointer is towards colonialism. Is it only colonialism that has pushed the continent to its current predicament? We should not only be look outward for the reasons why poverty and underdevelopment pandemic hangs on thc continent. We should look and concentrate to internal factors limiting the progress of the continent. This publication outlines some of the pertinent issues that have bogged down contemporary Africa making this prominent member of the Third World always a toddler. These are some of the questions the book examines. The reasons for this are almost obvious, unless we properly appreciate the basis of a problem; the book proffered solutions may be distant from the required remedies. We cannot deny that the "Rape of Africa" (Forje 1979) continues in a rather disguised but equally dislocating and plundering form. Kwame Nkrumah's development policies brought him into collision course with the USA and Britain whose intelligence services eventually plotted the over throw of the visionary African leader (The African Courier 2011:39). We can also talk of ***"The Peril of Africa."***

Finally, the book notes that colonisation opened the page of reorganisation or perhaps disorganisation of the economy of the colonised people to suit the economic interests of the colonial masters. To begin with, the dislocation took several forms: introduction of cash crops - banana, cocoa, coffee, tea, groundnuts etc. into the already vibrant western economy in Africa. Countries were made to become the hub specializing in specific crop production and equally restricted from trading among them. First this leads to disorientation in African agriculture. People shifted to the production of cash crops and consequently serious neglect of food crops production. The economy of the continent is intrinsically tied up to the whims and caprices of western capitalism with all its inherent contradictions. Capitalism is on the rise propelled by the forces of science and technology. Kingston William (2017) looks at integrating economic history, economic thought, patent-hoarding, venture capital and the changing global economy seeking to ask if modern capitalism might be an internally inconsistent system. Like Schumpeter Kingston is concerned that creative innovation might be stagnating into international ossification. Africa urgently needs creativity, innovation, and entrepreneurship sustainable productivity to be a veritable player in the globalisation nexus.

The last of the horrendous crime against humanity - apartheid - crumbled in the 1990s, but 'racial apartheid' was replaced by 'economic apartheid' known as the 'free market'; free market governs the continent. Africa has been delivered into the 'hands of the international capital.' The continent is enveloped in the hot air of international capitalism. The reality is that Africa has to stay alive; to do so require vigilance and responding properly to the wants and needs of the people; the people must be the chief actors in an honest, responsive and productive fashion bearing in mind they alone can make or mar their development path and benefit from what they have planted. The challenge is for the continent to clear the dark clouds. Africa has only one choice to do just that in an honest, truthful and justified manner that benefit all in society.

Africa's voices from all corners of the continent are calling for change. Are the leaders listening to the cry of the people? The response to this call is tackled within the context of developmental problems from a holistically perspective and within the contextual strategic shift to confronting the root causes of the regions state of backwardness. Without doubt, this demands a deep reappraisal of the socio-economic relations that have given raise to the continent's state of underdevelopment and exploitation. In addition, the people as an imperative factor are obliged to rediscover that the continent is part of the global hole or cosmos and cannot be bigger than the whole. Africa is not going to solve the global problem of climate change for example, alone but in unionism with the rest of the industrialised world. Western world mode of production driven by fossil fuels and other extractive activities, cannot be sustained without due consideration to others. Unfortunately, corporate interests are driving our fine planet towards a cataclysm. The interests of the marginalised must be seriously taken into consideration. The corona-virus is an opener and should be the game-changer for a better world environment and sustainable development for the common good of all. Diseases of this kind expose the vulnerability of the continent in many aspects, as it strengthens the quick call to the adoption of comprehensive, progressive Afro-centric developmental approaches. Gaster and Sorbom (2017) pushing the narrative far beyond a simple money-in-politics story line illustrating how corporation experts increasingly influence in the public sphere and often gain the upper hand vis-a-vis nation states.

With so much disenchantment with government and transnational corporations, the people of Africa must forge alliances among themselves and with their communities. Solidarity reinforced or reconstructed anew for people's sovereignty reclaimed in all spheres of endeavour. Why are African governments unwilling or unable to regulate the extractive industries? Rather these industries are the ones calling the shots, hiding behind instruments of state repression and enjoying impunity. Communities are criminalised when they protest against despoliation. The powerful live on the exploit of the silent poor majority. The answer lies in the people. Wake up, stand and fight constructively and orderly for your rights, be prepared to confront the wielders of power and the military arsenals. Not all will make it to the promised-land. There is a new wind of change blowing across the continent, from Banjul to the Horn, from Cairo to the Cape, the challenge is for people to unite and share-ideas as well as cultivate the habit of shared-prosperity. Getting involved in the political process is imperative to choose leaders through the democratic process not by the barrel of the gun to ensure that the dynamics of power so carved out is peaceful in the best interests of the people.

What this simply entails are that Africa cannot afford the luxury of national or sectional and self-sufficiency, any more than it can afford to formulate investment of development policies which leave better economic opportunities unutilised in one region in order to further much less available potentialities in another. The continent must sink or swim together. There is no other way-out but to consolidate resources for a common good. Consolidating resources entails having a vision and mission grounded on the ideological orientation democratic principles and virtues, non-ethnic and united, and which contributes to a nation and continent that is just and equitable, at peace with it and a world in which we share common values in spite of our diversities. Therefore, from Cairo to Cape, from Banjul to the Horn, Africa should be fully committed and dedicated to a common African interests and values under the African Renaissance Banner (ARB) which must adhere strictly to the following;

Patriotism➔Loyalty➔Dedication➔Sharing=➔(Ubuntu)Truth=➔.equity➔Integrity➔Justice➔ Peace➔>Integrated and A United Africa in its True Facets. Either the continent stands up as one or crumbles to oblivion individually. United it stands or fall we are doomed when divided. How do we ensure that we are united, remain united, stand-up as one person and speak with one voice!

With such a vision, mentality and ideological orientation, there is all reason to believe in Africa's bright future, destiny and sovereignty as an equal member of the international community. Without wish, the continent will continue to be regarded by the developed polity as an appendage to be recolonised and exploited with a difference. In a well-documented book, Williams and Le Billon (2017) show "how politics and power interact to limit the social benefits of natural resources endowments. They go further to stress the context-dependent nature of rent seeking and corruption by moving beyond the simplistic "resources curse" to highlight the key role of self-seeking local elites and of aid programmes that fail to cope with local political realities." Apparently, African political leaders show no "interest in the complex history and multi-faceted nature of value and valuation". In addition, "they fail to develop a pluralistic, transdisciplinary concept of "sustainability value" as the synthesis of different forms of usefulness, including exchange use, labour and function values" (Gale, 2018).

What is required of African leaders and the people is to build the transdisciplinary bridges so critical to solving their current problems and creating a sustainable and desirable future. In short, we have to explain how domestic interests and economic imperatives combine to securitizing resource politics in the continent. The continent has to embark on a comprehensive policy for sustainable growth, through strategic innovation and increased productivity of process goods. Kodama Mitsuru's (2018) examines how dynamic capabilities from both theoretical and empirical perspectives and practical applications can be a positive game-changer for the continent. We need to move from individualism and ego-centric to embracing an Afro-centric focused ideological orientation for the collective and well-being of all citizens. No one should be left behind. We should all join in the fight against poverty, underdevelopment, corruption and bad governance. President Paul Biya (Cameroon) on November 11, 1982, barely one day on taking over the reins of power from Ahidjo sent a powerful message to his Council of Ministers: ".to fight fraud and unlawful and unbridled quest for wealth, embezzlement, corruption…to ensure that our management is rendered sounder and more efficient." Bearing in mind that "poverty" is the common cause of corruption measures should be taken to drastically curb this pandemic that has eaten so deep into the social fabric of the society.

To put it crudely, but nonetheless realistically, it has become customary for job seekers to have some connections or to present 'gifts' in order to get employment or promotion. It is hardly surprising; therefore, that frustration and indolence have replaces enthusiasm and diligence in the public and parastatal service of independent African states. And looking at the United Nations 1999 Report on Human Development that categorically pointed out one of every two Cameroonian is poor; and considering that a poor and lazy person is often likely to adopt wayward behaviour as means of survival, it goes without that 50% of Cameroonians are embedded with the propensity to be corrupt. Enyih Atogho Paul (1999:110) makes the revealing statement: "Money can buy admission into professional schools! Money can buy grades in exams. Money can buy certificates. Money can buy positions and keep one in service. Money can provide the means for survival. And the gamut of bribery and corruption is complete. But when we realise that money cannot buy competence, we can imagine how much harm is being done to our whole society whose development and progress can only result from competence and selfless dedication to service" that contributes gravely to underdevelopment and exploitation.

All told, existing political, social and economic conditionalities can only serve as a facilitator for the transition to democracy and quality livelihood for the people of Africa. If these conditionalities are met, it certainly will constitute a more conducive environment than hitherto for redress the deteriorating conditions in this region. The Dark Clouds hanging over Africa will converge to a Blue Sky. Failure by the leaders and citizens in addressing the deteriorating situation only leads to greater destruction. We need a united front and joint cooperative acts to push out authoritarian leaders and ensure that we all submit to democratic action for our common well-being. Joint and cooperative actions confirm that political and economic conditionality remains a positive weapon for constructive change and a progressive forward march. The sad side of the story is the contradiction inherent in the fact that African governments act simultaneously as plaintiffs and defendants. They go further to act as torturers and murderers as well as indulging in windy rhetoric about human rights. A strong network has to be established throughout the continent inter alia for the defence of the weak and voiceless; a new political dimension should emerge across the board; one of joint transitional action that marshals slumbering forces, cluster them into groups, and transform them into units capable of engaging into setting the records right. For now, dictators, both old and new, are the only ones to be anything but overjoyed that the Euro-centric order has not withered. Advocates and supporter of the Afro-centric ideological orientation have a hell of work to do. This the time to sharpen tools, develop new strategies and launch a frontier attacks on the old and existing order. Let the act begin! Beyond this, it is important for every individual to reflect upon the determination of the forces propelling the Euro-centric agenda and to fashion out new strategies for a frontier offensive.

The Approach

During the past decades there has been a veritable explosion in the number of developmental institutions with critical voices for a complete turn about the kind of development activities ongoing which have not improved the lives of millions of people on the continent. We are less than three years to the Millennium Development Goals

(MDGs). The book is development-oriented. The approach is simple, straightforward - getting all the stakeholders actively involved in the process of 'people-focused' development approach.

The book is structure to meet the needs and expectations of readers with varying back grounds leaving much room for critical discourse. The reader is exposed to learn about the 'why,' when,' 'what' and 'why' as well as the 'how' of transformation. Who the actors are as well as the beneficiaries? Why development is bypassing the continent and what must be done to arrest the situation before it is too late? Each chapter can be read independently of the other with, of course, the guiding focus of creating awareness, and change in mindset, adopting a people-oriented and Afro-centric approach to development.

Apparently, it is time to accelerate preparations for both national and global agenda beyond 2015 that can build on the progress of the MDGs and meet the challenges facing Planet Earth. It is a publication that keeps the momentum beyond 2015 and is focused on moving towards a new national development agenda. How do we bring to fruition the targeted Sustainable Development Goals (2030) as well as ensure the full-realisation of African Union (AU) Agenda 2063? There is need to dialogue, to disagree to agree in order to create the necessary platform, holistic, comprehensive framework agenda to better move toward a new generations of development goals, define the core concepts and main elements of a new development paradigm; as well as ensure coherence in bringing the different process together for the common good of the people.

For these reasons, it is imperative to establish a framework for development cooperation within and among nations and between states, civil society, the private sector and international community. It is only through active participation of the relevant key stakeholders, the UN, AU, Regional Economic Communities systems and among political decision-makers that in unionism could further discussion and take concrete actions plans on what is needed in order to move toward a new generation of development goals that usher's quality livelihood to the people.

Structure of the book

Chapter One: Curiously, the chapter takes up the issue of a triple heritage of public policy, human capital development and Innovation as the sine qua non- to transforming the African state from a backward economy into a service delivery society. The role of government is imperative but does not exclude other stakeholders contributing to the process of building the continent's human skills to give added value to its abundant natural resource's potentials.

Chapter Two: Address issues of political economy and the kinds of foreign policies adopted by African governments to solidify or surrender their sovereignty. The issue of the "dependency theory" takes centre stage calling for an Afro-centric approach to the development of the continent. It is an issue of "de-linking to re-lining" with example from China.

Chapter Three: Science, Technology Innovation and Development: The chapter looks at the perils of (under) development, the significance and role of science, technology, innovation to the development process. The good, bad and ugly of current developmental approaches. It looks at the issues of state restructuring, the Euro-centric and Afro-centric perspectives of development.

Chapter Four: The Interface between the University, research institutes could see as replay of chapter One in a different way. The need for the continent to build scientific and technological prowess to facilitate and accelerate the development process. Of course, the continent does not need to develop the wheel, but to draw invaluable lessons from other countries that have been able within a generation to acquire scientific and technological capabilities enable them to be veritable competitors within the global knowledge-based system of our time.

Chapter Five: Looks at the dichotomy of religion which is tearing the world apart. How can share-values be beneficial to all be established bodies and society? Though the focus is on Cameroon, using the system approaches it branches its tentacles covering issues of justice, peace and security fundamental to all societies.

Chapter Six: The focus is on Mozambique in search for a New Economic vision. It makes efforts in the process and challenges in constructing a capable developmental state. The chapter could be seen as a continuation of earlier chapters from different perspectives. Why peace is necessary and why there is need for evolving on a common ground to quick start a new era for the continent? The challenging question is whether continent is learning from its mistakes?

Chapter Seven. The Challenge of Democracy –Africa is at the ross-roads of meeting the aegis of quality well-being or remains an enslaved continent. Services delivery is failing, insecurity is on the rise, and peace is a distant issue to the people. It is time to rethink and reshape our approach to development. This is the only way Africa can come out of its current dependency and slavery situation.

Chapter Eight: Emerging Perspectives on Democracy, Governance and Development probes into the growing consensus that modernizing the state and consolidating broader and functional institutional framework is essential in accelerating the pace for social progress. Building on the triple-helix of democracy, governance and development should be people focused in order to provide quality livelihood to all the citizens.

Chapter Nine – Pays attention on the emerging perspectives on democracy, governance and development in Africa. It gauges the rationale of the triple helix nexus.

Chapter Ten – looks at human capital development challenging us on the issues of truth we fail to accept. Are we empowering or disempowering our people?

Chapter Eleven –The Triumphant Agony and the Tragedy of Globalisation and Africa's Socioeconomic Transformation: Challenges, Changes and Prospects for the Future. How far have we come with our independence?

Chapter Twelve – looks at the dynamics of unleashing the people's power as a sign of the promise for a new democratic revolution and evolution. Peoples power should usher the new wind of change or a better Africa. Peoples power should be judiously used or the common good of society.

Chapter Leadership Ethos – Leadership is a crucial issues and Africa currently is suffering from leadership deficit. The continent is urgent need of 'servant' and not 'master' leadership in piloting the transformation process of the continent.

Chapter Fourteen delves into human capital, knowledge and skills building capacity of a society. It is the input to reversing the continent's current trend of exploitation and underdevelopment. Wrong education remains Africa's greatest tragedy.

Chapter Fifteen is on articulating a New Public sector reform towards enhancing quality services delivery. The African public service is in bad shape and needs to rehabilitate to become a veritable out-put window of the government for quality services delivery.

Chapter Sixteen could be seen as the conclusion or summary - Looking Back and Facing Forwards Challenges; Mapping A New Domestic and Foreign Order for Africa present the final phase of the paper suggesting the way forward. Where is the continent heading to? Are the right choices being made? Which are the prioritising and implanting **strategies?** How solidified are the instruments in place to wage the new battle of exploitation under aggressive development in

Brussels? Is the new honeymoon with China one way out or furthering the demises of the continent? How prepared or well-schooled are the foot soldiers on this tedious long journey of recovering the lost sovereignty, dignity and humanity of the people? Those who are waiting to see things work out, without working it out, may end up living a wasteful life. Be among those who make things work. Every African must become a good learner, a good worker and a strong believer in a new, prosperous and strong continent of tomorrow.

The Open Sore of a Continent.

It has been an incredibly rewarding experience as well as challenging task to bring together these diverse papers. Needless to say, there are many more dimensions and angles that could be x-rayed and included. Nonetheless, it is hoped that this collection of articles does convey several strong and important messages that moves the continent in the right direction. Africa is facing its biggest challenges yet; challenges that are critically fundamental about governance, rule of law, justice, equity and different view about what 'development' should really be about. Above all, there can be no way out of our predicament without daring to question the status quo - and making the impossible possible. The right choices must be made and then wait for - What Next for Africa? Africa will not perish even with gross-drain of its resources by the colonial state. Whatever form of treaties signed by post-colonial states with the colonial states should be scrupulously reviewed. If Africa is poor, it should not be feeding the colonial state. It is the wealth of African states that keeps the industrial wheel in constant rotation. For that reason, colonial states will continue fanning conflicts in post-colonial territories. Post-colonial states continue to remain the "chop-farm" of the colonial states. The case of France-Africa relationship tells it all.

Francophone-Africa should through the progressive start rethinking the renegotiation of the relationship to be 'win-win' outcome for both parties. The current cooperation ties to create an economy of alienation and disempowerment. The progressive Afro-centric agenda should be a new nationalism must seek "to de-Europeanise education and to disconnect Africans from the oath of tragedy, the tragedy of self-destruction, that Western education gradually leads them to, by first putting in place a system of education that reinstates the sanctity of the Inferior Other, and thus empowers the species being in its mission on earth within its culture specific context, especially that Western scientism in its aimless claim to be value free, even in the study of imperialism, a purposefully directed phenomenon by human beings against the others, is fast becoming a tool of self-delusion for Africans who blindly accept it" (Aseh, 2006:174). It is through the Western imposed system of education that our intellectuals have been deceived to mistake their ignorance for knowledge, unable to think ((Nkrumah, 1964:40).

Source: Credit - The Frontier Telegraph, No.0101, April 25 – March 10, 2014, pp1 and 7; Auth. No. E27/100/755/BRP, Cameroon Republic.

The picture depicts the attitude of France towards Guinea in 1958 to its current holding of former colonies as hostage to improving and sustaining the economy of France. As a side note; are African ruling elites forcing the suffering masses to pay for their plight and other predicaments which may not be of their making? One has to digest this in context of Jacques Chirac's speaking truth to African leaders, on 02/10/2005 in Senegal instructing African leaders to take up their destiny into their own hands. Using numerous examples Jacques Chirac pointed out without mincing words how the white man has killed, enslaved and continues to inflict sufferings and other damages on the black people, yet Africans fail learning lessons from such mounting of atrocities directed to the African people. Freedom is never obtained a platter of gold.. To what extent will Africans remain fools for ever under the servitude for the white man or seek freedom by completely casting of the "White Man's Burden" and becoming real and free people among other free people in other parts of the world. Chirac's speech remains a wake-up call for African leaders to rethink and restrategise their policies towards the Euro-centric agenda, the need for coherence and to develop the energy necessary towards sustainable solutions to their predicaments. A progressive Afro-centric agenda offers the best possible means and stop being the 'begging continent' in the world. As we continue feeding France reacts by destroying us in away.

That predicament constitute to what Wole Soyinka (1996) describes as the *"Open Sore of Africa"*. Post-colonial African authoritarian leadership has resulted not in nation building but in what could be termed 'nationless states.' African leaders failed to see 'independence; as a declaration of national unity' that needed all Africans 'displaying a nationalist political consciousness. Our African leaders operate in such a way that has robbed the continent of its moment of sovereignty and nationhood. The lost opportunity of Africa's independence by the blunder of African leaders, dashed hope for a democratic and independent Africa which will take many years for the region to recover. It is now left to the people to 'desanctify and dislodge authoritarian leadership and bad governance on the continent; to declare through the progressive Afro-centric agenda 'national unity,' *'political consciousness'* for the people to constitute a sovereign nation. What exist throughout the continent is total monopolisation of power by a select few. At the same time, 'corruption' is present not only at the top; it is a sickness that pervade every level of the African society; and with such prevailing realities, the 'Dark Clouds' over the continent will not drift away for the continent to see the 'blue sky over Africa. Therefore, within the context of the progressive Afro-centric agenda of a new national liberation struggle and change in mind-set, the struggle must begin with the cogent efforts at liberating our minds by effectively using education for mastery and control of our social and physical world rather than use it only as a means to a good life through employment in the public service or in the hitman's country through which, the white man in his superiorist claim to humanitarianism, controls our minds telling us what to say or do (Aseh,op cit.)

Dark Clouds on the horizon should give way for a 'Blue Sky' over Africa. Today we face the confrontation of two competing realities: *"Europe-centric" or "Afro-centric;"* 'the defeated or enslaved Africa' and the Afro-centric or the 'triumphant coming Africa.' A complex relationship exist, both in theory and in practice, the relationship between democracy and liberty, underdevelopment and development is a complex on that has spawned a certain degree of confusion among political leaders and scholars. On the one hand, liberty is sometimes treated a consequence of democracy; democratic governments, though varying among themselves in level of respect for human rights, are assumed to do a better job of protecting those rights hand do her authoritarian counterparts. On the hand, liberty is frequently treated as a precondition of democracy, to the point that most scholars include civil and political liberties is a third element (beyond participation and contestation) of the definition of democracy itself (Bova, 1997:113; Sorensen,1993:87-88; Aiddoo,1993).

Notwithstanding the crucial changes that have occurred and will occur in the political system and the state, democracy in Africa must still cope with serious problems regarding the institutionalisation and modernisation of its political parties. Political parties have become less ideological and class-based or ethnic-based. In a way, there is new competing or introducing force – the military – that have seen injected series of 'coup d'état' across the continent, the lasts being events in Burkina Faso, Mali and Guinea Bissau. Which country is next on the fire-line. Ideological principles and progressive programmes continue to matter, to, but they now count for less than factors like the pragmatic defence of social interest, the record performance in government, and the quality of the leaders that a party has to offer. These are some of the lingering issues that prolongs the state of 'Dark Clouds over the African continent; and which must be thoroughly address to send away the tsunami of the Dark Clouds.

Final appeal is that any form of lasting and sustainable change in Africa's fortunes is predicated upon and can only be achieved on the focus and ability of the people to address constructively and comprehensively with the root causes of the manifested political, economic and social malaise that has gripped the region for many decades. The continent cannot continue with the existing situation. Political repression, socio-economic injustices will only delay the amelioration of existing crises and exacerbate their negative effects. We can only but agree with the views expressed by Sadig Rasheed (1994), "positive change will be painstaking, and will take time to achieve. Perseverance in staying the course after introducing the elements and planting the seeds of durable change is an imperative. The key to the solution of Africa's perennial socio-economic and humanitarian plight is primarily and decidedly in the hands of the African governments and people. It would not pay to dodge that responsibility, or to attempt to shift it to others." The ball for change and progressively moving ahead lies now in the court of Africa, and African leaders and its citizens. It is time to take the opportunity and move forward in the right direction, stamina and focus.

Currently, something is wrong somewhere. Chris Uroh1998 posse the question: "Is there anything inherently wrong with Africa that the continent has remained immobilized in a milieu characterized with rapid transformation in other parts of the globe? Is Africa caught in a web of conflicting ideologies of development from which it cannot extricate itself? Is Africa a victim of ineluctable constraints and conspiracies? Is Africa doom? Or should we hope for better days ahead? How soon?" These are serious soul-searching questions needing urgent answers and immediate positive actions to drive the region forward. Some of these questions are taken up in the publication. The book shows how the interplay of economic, political and cultural factors, in and around Africa, has conditioned the African crisis; it equally proffers solutions. Drawing from the views expressed by Greta Thunberg (2020), "no one is too small to make a difference; everything needs to change. And it has to start today." Africa is on fire and calls for togetherness to drive the continent forward. Africa is split into two halves-what we may call the 'integrated periphery' and the 'marginalized periphery.' The integrated periphery is the periphery which is bound completely into the global capitalist system of the exporters of industrialised manufactured good; and this the case with major countries of Latin America and major countries of Asia, including China and India as well as most countries of South-East Asia, the so-called tigers or - what do you call them - Korea, Taiwan and soon.

The marginalized periphery is that part of the periphery, and Africa belongs to it, which has not even begun the movement to significant industrialization. Samir Amin sees this as a combination of four weaknesses of the internal societies and then nationalization movements and the working of the global system on the other hand. The weaknesses were the type of weakness of bourgeoisie or bourgeoisie, the populist general outlook of the national liberation movement, its shortcomings vis-à-vis the proletariat industrial nucleus, proletariat vis-a-vis the peasantry, etc. Africa now wears the coats of exporter of raw materials and dependency on aid for its developmental growth. These two bad scenarios can hardly contribute to the sustainable development of the region. We do not need to go far to discover the fragility of the continent, and why it cannot become a member of the club of developed nations until drastic turn-around in mindset takes place on the continent. Africa has and must change to regain itself and restore dignity and pride to the people; without which we are doomed forever. Currently, we are confronted and saddled with a host of far-reaching impeding factors; "including inept leadership, most of whom are lackeys of Western powers; with many reasons accounting for the state of affairs; an inferiority complex, economic dependence, the need for technical assistance, and chronic indebtedness" (Vakunta, 2006:33). Some of these factors are imbedded with far-reaching ramifications for the sustainable transformation of the African continent which include among others, the following:

- The sustainable transformation of Africa is being constantly hampered by the policy attitude of the colonial powers; the structural adjustment programmes imposed on African countries; the policy of the Bretton Woods Financial Conglomerates, the World Bank, International monetary Fund, etc. etc.;
- Stifling of domestic industries with unnecessary restrictions on the exportation of products from Africa to European markets, and high tariffs for the importation of finished products from the developed economies of Europe;
- Foreign interferences in the internal affairs of African nation-states;
- The existence or practice of poor governance in many African countries; including the weakness of the continental body – the African Union (AU) and its regional economic communities;
- African countries are debt ridden with debt servicing consuming a greater junk of the national budgets in Africa;
- The continent's dependency on the export of raw materials with little efforts in the processing of its vast natural resources.

A new way forward remains imperative if the continent is to overcome its barrage of impediments. Therefore, the current socioeconomic morass African countries are suffering require serious surgical operations including (i) African countries taking the future destiny into their hands; (ii) placing the people first as the priority in all policy articulation and implantation processes; (ii); (iii) ensuring the practice of democratic governance; (iv) building strong institutions and not individuals who are totally detached from the society; (v) a continuous policy of investing and building the human knowledge and skills capacity of the people; (vi) fighting poverty, corruption and inertia within the country. The productive capacity of the people needs to be strengthened especially in this age of knowledge-based global economy.

It is time we begin mapping a New African Order by learning from past historical experiences, to better understand present difficulties and to plan for the future. Many good examples abound which we can draw useful lessons from (see Zhang, 2018, Yusuf, 2017). The Asian Poverty Miracle by (Silber and Wan, 2016) provides some useful cases studies. Africa has the resources, the growing manpower which constitutes a rapidly growing market, but lacks the focus and vision to benefit from its God given natural resources. Rebuilding the African continent requires vision, focus, determination, leadership and responsive citizenship. The challenge now is how to rebuild Africa after centuries of destruction?

Africa's Complexities: Two Divergent Schools

"A sense of the past is essential to anyone who is trying to understand the here-and-now of development and underdevelopment. What is happening now is part of a continuing underdevelopment inherited from the past. But the past also provides influences. The past also reminds us of the importance of continuity but with a big difference. A new mindset drawn from past experience is the only to construct a better tomorrow. It is imperative that each member of society be obligated and responsible in constructing the sustainable future we all aspire now"
(John W. Forje, Lund-Sweden, 20 November 2012)

"The Freedom we know today would not have been possible had it not been for the contribution of Black, White, Indian and Coloured men and women, democrats, socialist, communist African's. Our freedom was made possible by many people around the world and African countries that walked to the cause of freedom in South Africa as they became convinced that apartheid was a crime against humanity."
President Cyril Ramaphosa, Speaking at the Official Memorial Funeral of Former Vice President F. W. de Klerk, 12th December 2021)

Morkaner – Nationalist, Comrades and Adversaries; The prophetic words of Solomon Kalushi Mahlangu as he was led to the gallows – when he said:" My blood will nourish the tree that will bear the fruits of freedom – will forever remain as an epitaph to the crime of apartheid."

Two Schools of Thought on African Nationalism

Two divergent schools of thoughts (i) Enthusiastic school; and (ii) The Markedly Subdued Mode emerged in African nationalism, these two discernible modes embedded variations in between

I. **The Enthusiastic School**: This school of thought with leaders like Kwame Nkrumah, Nnamdi Azikiwe, Julius Nyerere and others, saw the anti-colonial cause in a wholly perspectives. Colonial rule, whatever its incidental advantages was an anomaly; for a number of reasons; -
   a. It subordinated the interests of Africans to the interests of others;
   b. It impeded the meaningful development of African societies in such conditions;

c. Only independence could provide the basis for the regeneration of the continent;
d. Saw themselves as leaders of a people emerging into a new dawn, leading to the reality that existed;
e. The African personality, about which must have heard in the early years of independence, was a proclamation to the world that Africa has emerged to claim its place in the community of nations.

11 The Markedly Subdued Mood; African nationalism for this school of thought was characterized by markedly subdued approach; it was the dominant mode in the French-speaking colonial territories of Africa under the leadership of key personalities like Houphouet-Boigny, Leopold Senghor, Maurice Yamwogo to list but a few. The underlying principles of this school were 'caution.' In their hearts of hearts, they perceived the following line of approach; (i) working for self-determination but not independence; (ii) they held close to their heart - assimilation and annexation by France their mother. Their future was intrinsically hooked with 'Mother France,' which France used to draw the French accord of inherently link and domination by the colonial power.

The daunting complexities of the African continent are not abating. Not only is there a return to the Berlin conference of 1884, but it has also today converged in Brussels undermining the socioeconomic transformation of the continent. In addition, there is new development agenda - the invasion or new colonisation of Africa by China in the twenty-first century tells a different story. The Cold War between East and West has shifted to the African continent between the West and China and Africa paying the prize. When two elephants fight, it is the grass that suffers so goes the adage. Africa will experience that under a new technological age political dynamic in national and international construct of the 21st century.

On the other hand, Africa has lost its vision of sovereignty and unity due to poor governance and bad leadership. The continent is infested with 'sit-tight' presidents who have converted the peoples' properties into personal estates. Articulate self-interest overcomes collective interest and the common good. The predicaments of the continent are too vast to list. From the state of abject poverty, through the exploitation of the natural resources, to genocide in Rwanda, conflicts in Somalia, Sudan, and the Arab Spring, rising unemployment, piracy and insecurity the region becomes a fertile soil for exploitation from within and without. Apparently, how many are aware of the dramatic structural-functional changes ongoing in global politics about the re-colonisation of the continent? In 1994, the horrendous acts of 'apartheid' suffered a downward spiral signalling the end of slavery - the worse crime ever committed against humanity - the black people. It was believed with the end of apartheid and the emergence of. 'Black rule' in South Africa, the continent, from Cairo to the Cape and from Banjul to the Horn would after all thread on the sustainable path of regaining her lost sovereignty and independence. Africa is being recolonised in the age of enlightenment - there are more educated Africans today than in the fifties. Africans who have studied and lived in European countries should be in the forefront with people-focused ideas to better teleguide the transformation of the continent. This is not happening.

Unfortunately, the continent is embedded in perpetual underdevelopment, exploitation and poverty in the midst of plenty. The on-stoppable forces of globalisation make Africa more vulnerable in an already worse situation. All hopes for a better tomorrow seem dashed away. It is not surprising that rising expectation at the dawn of independence has been replaced by rising destruction, frustration and hopelessness Uncertainty and fear clouds the future of present and future generations. The only positive good news emerging out of the continent is the 'Rise of Women Power.' For too long women were stock-pilled on the minus side of the transformation continuum. Today, the continental organisation - Africa Union (AU) is under the stewardship of a woman fifty years after the creation of its forerunner, The Organisation of African Unity (OAU). The continent can boost of two female Heads of State - Liberia and Malawi - Sirleaf Ellen Johnson and Joyce Hilda Banda respectively, The International Criminal Court (ICC) is under the leadership of Fatou Bensouda; three Noble Peace Prize laureates. This is not had enough in the gender parity agenda (GPA), but present significant strides on the way of ensuring women as veritable partners not competitors in the state construct agenda. The hurdles and the triumphs of the continent should be forecast within the vision of optimism and hope for a better future.

Africa is on trial in the court of poverty, corruption and bad governance. It requires the expertise of all to produce the competence and actions necessary for saving the continent from more years of imprison in the under-development jail house. As the continent celebrates the 10 years of the AU and fifty years of the OAU, the people are challenged to construct a new mindset, behaviour and attitude as well as positive political will and concrete actions for change, development, progress and sustainability (CDPS). This is the age of change for Africa, and why new leadership bacons. Why should Africans develop Africa? Why the destiny lies in African hands? Why must we take a critical look at the failures of capitalism or mode of western development imposed on the region? Why have the ruling elites embraced this approach of development? In a critical analysis, Thandika Mkandawire (2015) (the First to hold the Chair in African Development at the London School of Economics) in a speech delivered at the thirty-second Aggrey-Fraser-Guggisberg Memorial Lecture had this critical analysis for the continent; " by tracing Africa's attempts at growth and development since independence era, her attempts at recovery from a string of serious socio-political set-backs, and advocates for the role of universities as essential agents in the drive to sustained development. Is it now time for the continent to choose its own political and economic philosophy that reflects African consciousness, inspiration incorporating the political integration and unification of Africa employing a common and collective solution guided by their cultural heritage for the good of the people? Why is the continent not using its Diaspora human power to forge ahead its development construct? What is actually wrong with Africa? These and other daunting questions raise the issue of good governance. Good governance following Anagwonye (2009) "cannot be attained without government structured to cater for the welfare and the happiness of the people, and the rule of law. Will it be a mirage where the law serves only in the interests of the rich, the privileged, the powerful and the advantaged at the expense or detriment of the poor, the deprived, the ignored, the cheated and the oppressed whether socially, politically or economically"?

There is the assumption that with a new breed of African leadership things may take a different curve for the better. There is some truth in this. We saw that coming when Ahmadou Ahidjo of Cameroon handed power to Paul Biya in 1982, which quickly inspired the people with the ideological orientation that was construed on the concepts of moralisation, democratisation and rigour, which unfortunately never was. We saw the changes Thomas Sankara ushered in Burkina Faso during his brief reign; just like Mohammed Mutala in Nigeria; and Jerry Rawlings in Ghana. Other success stories of leader abound. In contrast, we look at the regimes of Joseph Mobutu; Joseph Kasavubu; Moise Tshombe (Congo); Bokassa of Central African Republic). Leah Junck (2014) notes that in spite of South Africa's progressive constitution, citizen's intolerance of non-citizens, refugees and economic migrants has escalated in recent years. What is more, xenophobic attacks are covered in the public discourse as mere episodes of crisis and often rather rhetoric of national machismo than leading to an acknowledgment of the stories and experiences of people seeking refuge and being exposed to hostility on every day basis." Xenophobic attitude does not only exist in South Africa. It is common across the continent and world. These activities or developments put "Africa at a Crossroads" according to (Mutanga et al. 2018). Looking at Africa since the inception of the OAU and AU in which the authors from different perspectives look at the fundamental challenges for Africa given all that we know about pertinent issues, what should be done to ensure effective development in Africa?

The changing imperatives of international development – the reform of international finance institutions and the growth-development nexus (Gumede, 2018) need serious scrutiny. Tatah Mentan (2018) looks at the contradictions that exist between wealth of natural resources and the poverty of most of its peoples. These gruesome realities place Africa at a crossroad of development or decay. It is not only a change of leadership that is needed. There is an urgent need for change in 'mindset, attitude, behaviour and work ethics among others throughout the entire confines of society. The people must start reflecting why and how Europe is undermining African development? Why Europe Underdeveloped Africa? How Africa Developed Europe? Will Europe underdeveloped Africa again? Why Can Africa develop itself? In 1884, the Berlin Conference cemented and legalised the colonialisation of the continent. Europe has moved from the colonialisation of the 1884 strategy to another strategic agenda, criminalization of the colonialisation of the continent this time from Brussels, not through the slave trade but through neo-colonialism and enforced globalisation without a human face.

From our founding fathers to present day leadership, the issue of leadership has always taken centre stage. While putting blame on them for not piloting the state of affairs in the right direction and for the common good, blame can equally be levied on the people for failing in their obligations and responsibilities as the power and custodian of the society. Power lies with the people (Forje, 2009). With a population estimated at 60% of the African population aged under 30 years, the region remains not only the youngest continent in the world, but with a demographics calling for a new dispensation in African leadership and a continent having the longest serving Heads of States in the world, for example, Cameroon Paul Biya 38 years (1982-to-date): Mugabe 1980-

until his death): and a host of others. Before the Arab Spring 2011, leaders like Ben Ali, Mubarak and Gathaffi had been in power for many decades. What then should be the changing face of African leaders? Has Africa any future with the current development strategies being implementing? Are there other alternatives? Above all, does Africa want to develop, how when and by what means?

Colonialism has ended to put it mildly, so also apartheid. But there is still more work to be done. Freeing our mindset from mental colonialism is vital. An Afro-centric approach providing the way forward is imperative. The existing world order of might is right that the forces of imperialism impose on Africa is a cynical one. In it, Africa's role is essentially dual, take a look at the following: (i) to supply the raw materials needed to keep the wheels of the factories, markets and investment outlets for Europe, America, Japan and now China in permanent rotation;(ii) to act as buffer zones or shock absorbers to cushion and stabilise the crises of the global system are typically passed on to Africa. This dualistic strategic approach is undertaken mainly through lower prices for exported raw materials, higher prices for imported process goods, wilful manipulation of the values of the continent's currencies, exploitation of workers, higher interest charges on African debts and other inhuman acts and policies. In short, it is through the French policy *of 'assimilation at its greatest European stage and force.'* From the era of the Trans-Atlantic Slave Trade through neo-colonialism to the present stage of globalisation, the system has worked and is operating now to transfer huge sums of resources from the underdeveloped world to the advanced industrialised countries effectively ensuring that the affluence of the wellbeing of their citizens are kept artificially high. Seen within these perspectives, and in order to maintain this exploitative world order, imperialism does not hesitate to employ its enormous arsenal of economic and technology muscle and awesome military power to subdue any threat to the system

Why did the British and Western establishments find Kwame Nkrumah's comprehensive approach on Pan-Africanism so exasperating and infuriating one may ask? Take the case of Democratic Republic of Congo. It was the same desire to protect the global imperialist order that was behind the CIA sponsored Katanga secession that led to the brutal murder of Patrice Lumumba who was out to protect the independence and unity of his country. It was also the commitment to protect the imperialist order which was behind the CIA-sponsored overthrow of the democratically elected president of Chile, Salvador Allende, in 1971. The list is long. In Africa, the forces and politics of apartheid played the same role - the strategy of excluding all blacks from the process and benefits of development. The "hot pursuit" strategy was adopted to destroy all freedom fighters within and outside South Africa. Shaping the future of Africa requires a concerted Afro-centric approach and a development strategy that is people-oriented and people-governed with the people constructively participating equally in prosperity-sharing. From Banjul to the Horn, and from Cairo to the Cape policy strategies must be citizens-focused and Afro-centric principled. How do we exploit positively the knowledge of the Diaspora (the sixth region of Africa) in advancing the developmental process of the continent? How do we forge participation and partnership among the various stakeholders - state, private sector, civil society and the international community?

For now, we live in a global village with two worlds - the resources poor and a rich North; and the poor South with its vast resources. Adams A Nassau (1972: ix) writes: ".... the great bulk of mankind, however, was up to then largely untouched by the process and remained economically underdeveloped. This new era which dawned with the end of the war was characterized by a heightened and widespread recognition of two great truths: the possibility of promoting, on a continuous and long-term basis, and as a conscious purpose of policy, the economic betterment of mankind; and the inadmissibility of colonial rule of one people over anther, a nefarious institution that had taken root and spread through the previous centuries. A process of decolonisation was therefore soon to unfold that would see, in less than a decade, the freeing from colonial rule of hundreds of millions of people, representing over a half of mankind and occupying the great land masses of Asia and Africa...."

We live in Africa but two worlds, the abject and neglected rural area and population; and the rich and well cared urban areas and the affluent class. These disparities and polarisation call for quick and urgent sustainable solutions. The wake-up call can no longer wait. It is a tale of two worlds; two Africa; two Cameroon: two South Africa and so on. That has to change and is changing hopefully, during the past fifty years of Africa's independence; Africa has grown in many ways that are positive and progressive during that period in a way. But it could have been done better by taking advantage of the *"late-comer advantage."* The forces of 'capitalism' has submerged the 'late-comer advantage, or to state the least, the leadership of the continent have been overwhelmed with the 'greed' factor and not taking the 'late-comer advantaged factor even to increase their self-articulate interests. Following Dowden

Richard "Leaders do not emerge from nowhere. Could it really be coincidence that all of Africa's forty-odd leaders who came to power at independence were bad rulers who took bad decisions? Many were decent men who believed that they were doing what was the best. The new presidents inherited total power from colonial rulers, but the states they ruled were made up of old African societies, once self-governing and still held together by their own networks of power and influence. Trying to use the tools of a Western-style state to control these rooted societies was like trying to herd cats with a dog-training manual." This is not to hold a brief for failed leadership on the continent, but to situate the realities, a rose serious discourse and to further question why the new generation of leaders have not been able to right the wrongs of the past or made an attempt to create a new system that could replace the European rule imposed on Africa?

Polarisation on the two sides is so wide that a miracle is needed to pull the divided sides to common reasoning and understanding that it is in their best interest to work together for the common good of humanity. The new generation North and South, and particularly in the South with escalating and abject poverty must be prepared to craft meaningful policy strategies with a human face to put a stop to the pathetic situation. The future remains bleak if this not done now. Africa today requires not just sustained growth but economic transformation. Development has to be a collective action-oriented problem and solution requiring an African Power and Politics Programme Agenda (APPPA) - finding ways of being able to act collectively in their own best interests. It is about collective problem-solving in fragmented societies hampered by low levels of trust and high rates of social disparities

Woman Power Debate and its Significance

The Arab Spring begat what Bill Clinton once proposed for Africa to concentrate on "democracy and economic reforms," the term "new generation of African leaders," should be back on the drawing board as the continent celebrates the fifty anniversaries of the creation of the Organisation of African Unity (OAU) the forerunner of African Union (AU) which has just celebrated its 10 anniversaries in May 2012. We need leadership with a human touch. That human touch seems to come from women. Male leadership is important but so far has failed or unwilling to sacrifice for the greater good of humankind having been overtaken by articulate self-interest, greed and chauvinistic attitude. What is important is for both genders (male and female) working as a unit (partners in development) and not as competitors for the sustainable socio-economic transformation process of society.

Leadership change is necessary as we have seen women leaders at the helm of two African states, Ellen Johnson Sirleaf (Liberia) and Joyce Hilda Banda (Malawi) sworn on 7th April 2012. There is need for more. The 30% goal is not enough. For now, it is at least a good start; unfortunately, not many African countries have jumped on the bandwagon; but with their signs pointing in that direction. It is question of time and how the people can quickly consume and implement the right flow of information. But how exposed are the people to right information flow? The continent will be celebrating its 50 anniversary will women taking key decision-making position on the African political scene, Presidents Ellen Johnson Sirleaf (Liberal), Joyce Banda (Malawi), The AU Commission (Nkosazana Dlamini-Zuma) South Africa; Fatou Bensoudu (Gambia) Heading the International Criminal Court, (ICC); Asha-Rose Migiro (Tanzania, Deputy Secretary-General, UN, appointed in 2007) late Wangari Maathai (Kenya Noble Peace Laureate), Frannie Leautier Tanzania, CEO African Capacity Building Foundation; Ngozi Okono-Iweala, (Nigeria, World Bank and Nigeria's Finance Minister); Oby Ezekwesili (President, African Section, World Bank and co-founder Transparency International); Ferial Haffajee (Editor, City Press, South Africa), Bisi Adeleye-Fayemi (Co-founder of the African Women's Development Fund, AWDF), Helen Zille (South Africa - Leader of the Democratic Alliance, the country's main opposition party, Souhayr Belhassen (Tunisia - President, International Federation of Human Rights (FDIH), Ayaan Hirsi Ali (Somalia, Former MP in the Netherland); Mariam Aloma Mukhta (Chief Justice of Nigeria); in Sweden Nyamko Sabuni (DRC) elected to the Swedish Parliament in 2002 and appointed Minister in 2007; in France, Rama Yade (Senegal) Secretary of State in the Sarkozy Nicolas French Government: Ellinah Wamukoya (Swaziland) Africa's First Anglican female Bishop; Today, (2021), The Executive Secretary of the Economic Commission for Africa (ECA) is under the leadership of a women. In terms of gender parity or cresting opportunities for the female gender as partners in development, Rwanda remains a shining example. And African countries are urged to copy the good practices of Rwanda; and other countries making efforts in narrowing the disparity between the two sexes.

Many first ladies have been contributing their quota in advancing the course of social development, women's rights, empowerment, social justice and the sustainable transformation of society. Pokam (2011:26) notes that the new generation of First Ladies and a new function - a new profession perhaps - are in the process of emerging in most African countries. Most of these first ladies have taken over their husband's social policies and deal, for example, with poverty, women's rights and AIDS. These First Ladies are perceived as "Nation's Mother" in tandem with their husbands. These ladies play the role of an ordinary woman without being one, but in so doing they become closer to the people and so gain a better understanding of their needs. The question arises whether female gender empowerment affects African leadership. Male chauvinism for decades has drifted in the wrong direction, influenced by greed, wrong interpretation of culture (and) but guided by western influence the wrong way. The challenge for women was and is how to use their God-given feminine power in piloting their way through life but always seen as the "weaker sex" but with the phenomenon and reality of "bottom power" which men as the stronger sex fall victim off. Given this constellation, who is the stronger sex -man or woman? There is no stronger or weaker sex: they are all partners in development, contributing their share from their position of advantage. The sums total of these contributions are what makes the nation great and developed.

Mbewe Tom (2012) is right when he writes; "Extrapolated to cover the 'big' men (who govern for have governed) Africa in the post-independence era, who are said to have largely run the continent into the ground, how has the feminine power worked on them and their performance in office? How have suffered from the DSK syndrome - i.e., falling to pieces at the feet of women power? If yes, how has it affected their psychological wellbeing and, by extension, the way they govern? If no, how have they not been real men? For every real man tastes the power of woman power at some punt in his natural life. It is part of the growing up process," In addition, James Baldwin goes further to analysis *"bottom power"* as "money is turned out, was exactly like sex, you thought of nothing else if you didn't have it and thought of other things if you did. What do men do if they don't have It.?" inquired Baldwin, they do think of nothing else. The Nigerian writer Chinweizu (1990) writes: "Female power exists; in hangs over every man like a ubiquitous shadow. Indeed, the life cycle of man, from cradle to grave, may be divided into three phases, each of which is defined by the form of female power which dominates him: mother power; bride power, and wife power. We must remember the saying; the hand that rocks the cradle is the hand that rules the world." Chinweizu goes further to add that "marriage is the central institution of female power

- not political parties, parliaments, armies, business enterprises, bureaucracies, etc. The nest of family home, where a woman is both mother and wife, is the seat of female power - not the barracks, factories, offices or other such places where large numbers of persons gather together. In making marriage its central institution, female power has chosen the organisational form most suited to its nature and its needs." Society is not stagnant. It is dynamic. The notion that "it is not for a man to live alone" is pregnant with meaning - partnership, participation and equitable prosperity-sharing for the good of humanity. To exploit the universe, men and women require the assistance of each other without which there would be no procreation and replenishment of planet earth.

The Bible is equivocally clear on the partnership synthesis in transforming society. "It is not good for a man to live alone. I will make him a help mate…. Therefore, shall a man leave his father and mother, band shall leave unto his wife, and they shall be one flesh" (Gen.2:18, 24). Again (Gen.1:28) notes that after creating man and woman, God charged them to "be fruitful and multiply, and replenish the earth, and subdue it…" This implies that political gridlock must be avoided for the society to move forward holistically and in a sustainable pattern. The nine months a woman carries a baby in her womb for gives a special advantage of caring; hence the strong call and urgent need for caring leadership which women can provide. The male chauvinist attitude arises from the fact that God created a woman from the ribs of a man and therefore, should be subdued or controlled by the man. Or seen as the woman being a slave of the man; the 'weak sex' trajectory phenomenon. The trouble with Africa is the non-acceptance that 'men and women' are equal partners not competitors in the development process. A new mindset and a proactive agenda towards equality, participation and partnership are imperative to move the continent forward and in the right direction for the greater good of humankind. Africa is not only confronted with gender inequality, but a host of other inequalities that constraints its transition from a backward to a service society. The state of inequality contributes to the great divide within the society. Greater attention must be paid in the direction of eradicating poverty, corruption, poor infrastructures and other related development activities making the state of livelihood good for all. Much has yet to be done to improve the conditions of women in playing greater significant roles in the socioeconomic transformation of the continent. In this respect, attention should be paid to the activities of the United Nations Commission on the Status of Women (SCW57)

Elimination and Presentation of All Forms of Violence against Women and Girls in respect of:

- Raising awareness of existing commitments and standards for ending violence against women;
- Create a platform for sharing ideas and strategies that work and bring results;
- Identify key areas and issues where consensus needs strengthening, and
- Foster dialogue and build alliance to accelerate implementation and follow-up to outcomes of CSW57.

Violence against women takes many forms - physical, sexual, psychological and economic. These forms of violence are interrelated and affect women from before birth to old age. Some types of violence, such as trafficking across national boundaries. Violence against women is not confined to a specific culture, region or country, or to particular groups of women within a society. The roots of violence against women lie in persistent domination against women. Up to 70 per cent of women experience violence in their lifetime. Women aged 15-44 are more at risk from rape and domestic violence than from cancer, car accidents, war and malaria, according to World Bank data. Violence against women in police custody is common and includes sexual demands for sexual acts in exchange for privileges or basic necessities. The empowerment of women is a sine qua non to uplifting the continent out of its abyss. The rape and sexual violation of girls and women is pervasive in conflict ridden areas, for example, in Darfur region of Sudan, during the 1994 genocide in Rwanda where it is estimated that 250.000 to 500.000 women were raped; sexual violence was a characteristic of the 14 year long civil war in Liberia. In the Democratic Republic of Congo (DRC) approximately 1,100 rapes are being reported each month, with an average of 36 women and girls raped every day. It is believed that over 200,000 women have suffered from sexual violence in that country since armed conflict began.

Sexual violence in conflict is a serious present-day atrocity affecting millions of people, primarily girls and women. It is frequently a conscious strategy employed on a large scale by armed groups to humiliate opponents, terrify individuals and destroy societies. Women and girls may also be subjected to sexual exploitation by those mandated to protect them. Women as old as grandmothers and as young as toddlers have routinely suffered violent sexual abuse at the hands of military and rebel officers. Rape has long been used as a tactic of war, with violence against women during or after armed conflicts reported in every international or non-international war zone. Female genital Mutilation or Genital Cutting (FGM7C), i.e., several types of traditional cutting operations performed on girls and women are still practiced in many African countries. It is estimated that more than 130 million girls and women alive today have undergone FGM/C mainly in Africa and some Middle Eastern Countries. The practice of early marriage - a form of sexual violence is common and worldwide, especially in Africa. Young women are often forced into the marriage and into sexual relations, causing health risks, including exposure to HIV/AIDS and limiting their attendance in school. One effect of sexual abuse is traumatic gynaecologic fistula, an injury resulting from severe tearing of the vaginal tissues, rendering the woman incontinent and socially undesirable. Protecting the health of women is protecting the health of the nation. The woman is the life of the nation. Let us not be emotional and sensational but face and accept the realities. Just by thinking of the woman who carried you in her stomach for nine months should usher a new of thinking and respect for the female gender. That alone is sufficient to place the female gender high on top of our development priorities. The woman should be given special attention in their own way in contributing to the sustainable transformation of the society.

The FGM is a practice with a millennia-long custom that communities believe is an essential part of raising a girl properly. About 140 million girls and women worldwide are currently living with the consequences of FGM/C according to the World Health Organisation. Some 92 million girls 10 years old and above who have undergone the practice are in Africa. The practice has several immediate and long-term health consequences, with many women sufferings for years after being circumcised because of scarring and frequent infections. Most of these women have undergone severe kind of cutting, called infibulations, in which the clitoris is removed and the labia are stitched together to form a cover over the vagina. Only a small hole is left for urine, menstrual blood, childbirth and intercourse (Sambira 2013:20). Though advance reconstructive surgeries for patients who have gone through FGM7/C exist, the cost for most women in Africa is beyond their reach. Apparently, there is increased commitment and concerted action from governments to end the practice of FGM/C. A UN resolution aimed at intensifying global efforts to end FGM/C was approved for the first time on 26 November, with hopes that African countries will sign it and take ownership of the ban. Although there is renewed hope for a global ban on the practice, so far there has been little focus on solutions for many girls and women who have already undergone cutting. The possibility of reconstructive surgery is therefore a godsend to young women whose parts of their womanhood had been taken away, depriving them of feeling a complete human being. But must we descend to such a low-level behaviour towards women? Many women face multiple forms of discrimination and increased risk of violence. The cost and consequences against women are extremely high. They include the direct cost of services to treat and support abused women and their children and to bring perpetrators to justice. The indirect costs include lost employment and productivity and the cost in human pains and sufferings.

Much as we advocate cultural heritage being part of human development and identity FGM is not one of those cultural values that should be maintained in the 21st century and beyond. This is a crime against humanity requiring a holistic global effort to address. The move by Amnesty International Human Rights Action Centre, London hosting a conference with the theme, "Ending Female Genital Mutilation in Europe: Exploring Policies, Approaches and Lessons" (February 2013) should be a global move to defeat FGH. Britain's new anti-FGM programme is expected to reduce FGM by 30% in at least 10 priority countries in the next five years. The European Union added initiative of 13 million British pounds in fighting against FGM in European countries should be extended to cover countries where these acts are prevalent. In December 2012, the African Group against FGM led a resolution passed by the United Nations General Assembly banning the practice. The African Union should urge its members to do the same and stamp once and for all this serious crime against women. Countries such as Kenya are doing their bit to wipe out FGM with laws criminalizing the possession of the tools used in the act. Working with local; communities and education the people about the ills of FGM is essential in changing attitude, behaviour and creating a new mindset towards the practice. Cracking down FGM should be a priority in the process of human equality and the respect of human rights for all and by all. Gender equality and empowerment of the female gender is what we are expected to undertake to ensure a stable and balanced world nexus. Finally, we wait the great day when powerful nations like the USA, Russia, France, Italy and Japan will join the bandwagon for a female Head of State.

Building the Requisite skills

Human capacity development has to be greatly steeped up without which, added value cannot be given to our abundant resources. With Africa discovering more natural resources such as silver and platinum, there is a sense of urgency to leverage the continent's own ability to manage these resources. It requires a stock of well-trained human skills not only in these areas but equally in other aspects of development. Thus, the continent faces serious issues of capacity building and challenges, how they make the choices and implement policies will determine the degree and the path of success and the way forward for a sustainable society. It is time we start freeing ourselves from domination from mental colonisation and from the inferiority complexes. These are attributes or legacies constraining the sustainable transformation of the continent. We should wash ourselves clean of such bad legacies or memories. There is urgent need for bringing skills back home. Again, this requires improve our environment to attract Diaspora skills to help in training local human resources as the only way to catapult the continent from underdevelopment in the midst of plenty to a developed service delivery society. The Africa of tomorrow needs answers that are endurable. Therefore, the people must start rebuilding themselves today in tandem with all the stakeholders - state, private sector, and civil society, the international community working in partnership to seek solutions or create answers that are endurable for the Africa of tomorrow.

The cost of training abroad is a serious issue to be tackled by African countries. The solution is simple. Improve the learning environment in each country and the continent in general. This may help solve some of the issues of training and exporting the continent's human capital abroad. The views expressed by the Chonoko Ibrahim (2012) should be properly looked into: "The Students Association of Nigeria in Diaspora (SAND) calls on the Nigerian government to address the dangerous trend in higher education in the country in which huge sums of money are taken to other countries as tuition and school fees. Currently, more than 40,000 Nigerian students studying in various institutions of higher learning in the United Kingdom alone pay an average of 10.000 pounds (about N2.5 million) as tuition fees annually, thus contributing significantly to UK's revenue of 2. Billion pounds (N500 billion) it makes from foreign students ". It is time for African governments to 'take responsibility and evolve measures to salvage the situation so that the huge sums of money paid abroad could be channelled into higher institutions in Africa. It is imperative that

African governments start doing something in a different direction about education on the continent to avoid students traveling abroad or pay exorbitant fees to acquire quality education.

The SAND's idea goes with the vision propagated by the Vice Chancellor (Max Price) of the University of Cape Town - South Africa. An 'Afropolitan' University, according to Max Price; "The 'Afro' is obviously a reference to the university focus in the continent. The "Politan" signifies that it is not a retrospective look, a sort of naïve subsidy economy, safari economy views of the continent, but rather a cosmopolitan and metropolitan view of a continent that is developing fast and involved with the future. The cosmopolitan approach highlights that Cape Town has strong representation from the rest of Africa and the rest of the world that meets in the classrooms. Many of the high proportion of international students and staff are from other countries in Africa. That is also part of the Afropolitan Vision" (MacGregor 2012). Apparently of its 25000 student's population there is strong focus on research 68% of the students are undergraduates and 32% graduates. In 2011, the university produced nearly 6,600 graduates. It has a staff of 3000, and 1000 academics. The fees rang around R38-40.000 (USA4.000) compared to what is paid in the United Kingdom. The Cape Town example could be duplicated across the continent. Come to think of Africa's classical universities like Ibadan (Nigeria) Legon (Ghana), Makerere (Uganda) and many others that were centres of learning and excellence at independence and the immediate post-independence years which today have become shadows of themselves. Why are we moving from good to bad and eventually to ugly with our institutions at a time of the decolonisation process? By so doing, we galvanise ourselves to decolonisation in the 21st century.

There was the fighting spirit during the colonial era. A fighting spirit we stupidly lost after independence but develop another destructive fighting spirit, that of destroying our selves, instead of fighting and destroying poverty, injustice, inequality and xenophobic attitude. Durrani, (2018) writes about "British colonialism - people's resistance, the others being Mau Mau and radical trade union movement". Cloete et al (2014) takes us in the direction of knowledge of knowledge production and contradictory unction in African Higher Education. "The dominant global discourse in higher education now focuses on 'World-Class Universities – inevitably located predominantly in North America, Europe and increasingly, East Asia. The rest of the world, including Africa, is left to play "catch-up." These places the state of Higher Education and African Universities with serious problems to 'engagement' with which universities must grapple with. African universities and system of education has much to offer the high-participation and generously resourced system of the 'developed world." Olukoshi and Zeleza (1988) have written extensively on African Universities in the twenty-first Century. See also Zeleza (1997, Nyamnjoh, 2016) and other publications

South Africa has stepped up funding to bolster its post-secondary education to meet the needs of the country's economy and business with billions of Rand on Further Education Training (FET) colleges. State funding FET colleges has progressively increased from R3.1billion (USA35 million dollars in 2009 and it is epect3d to reach R5.2 billion by 2014 Bursary support has also increased from R312million in 2009 to R1.7 billion in 2012. By 2014 a total of R1.9billion in bursary will be provided to poor students. It is expected that 4million students will be enrolled at 50 FET colleges with 260 campuses across the country by 2030 as a goal of overhauling the countries to ensure the effective and sustainable continuation and functioning of the system and procedures for education in the country. The National Skills Fund Sector Education and Training Authorities (SETAS) has provided financial support of R2.5 billion (USA 28 million dollars) toward curriculum developments infrastructure refurbishment and construction on campuses. In addition, there is increased enrolments up from 427,435 in 2011 t0 657.690 in 2012. Occupational enrolments have increased by 84% due to funding from the National Skills Fund and the SETHS. Pouring money not colleges is not enough, but it is a start. We do need to enhance the profile of FET colleges among South Africans. We need to build capacity among the lecturing staff and provide further support as the need to build more FET colleges arises. If we had the resources to establish a FET college in each city or town, that would be a plus. For every engineer we need at least four skilled workers and our FET colleges do not have the capacity to the meet this demand (Makoni 2012). This generation has been part of the problem-creation of the plight of the continent as well as it must be an inherent part of problem-solving solution for the wellbeing of present and future generations. So serious is the disparity gap between nations and within nations that approaches to endurable solutions must go beyond borders. Take for example, the income disparity gap between Tanzania, Central African Republic and Switzerland. It goes without saying that low per capita incomes are an important feature of economic underdevelopment - perhaps the most important feature -

and there is little doubt that the distribution of income across the world's nation is extraordinary skewed.

This not the time for finger pointing; but one of seeking common grounds for common solutions in the great interest of humanity. Our environment must be preserved. Rural exodus curbed by creating the necessary infrastructure and other social amenities in the rural areas. The health of the people must be greatly improved. A healthy person reflects a health society. Africa is not a healthy region because the people are not healthy. The answer to this is articulating and implementing people-focused development activities; there is need or a comprehensive articulate and implementing policy approach hat accelerates he game-changing attitude of the people. We need to go "Beyond Appearance" (Harold-Barry, 2018) where he invites us to react upon our relationship with society; and repeatedly requesting whether we should put ourselves or others, and what happens when we ignore the plight of those around us; further inviting us to react on the nature of power, our interaction with it and our attitude towards it, do we gullibly agree to do what we are told without thinking or do we react on the consequences of apathy and inaction?

We need to give new directions for change in the dimension of Africa's dependencies (Mhango, 2017). Fighting the continent's dependency syndrome, means "Fighting for Freedom" as noted by Talbart et al (2017) which calls for "Patriotism and Nation-Building" (Philip Laryea, 2017) and "Fighting for Freedom". When we fight for freedom, we should as have noted by Mimiko (2017) in "Live with Happiness"; for the word needs love, happiness and well-being for everyone. For now, state policies are not people-focused. Most policies are tailored to meeting the exigencies of the Head of State and his cronies. This explains why the continent is stuck on the runway unable to take-off to the destination of a quality service delivery society.

Developing and using local languages should also receive greater attention by policy-makers as part of the transformation process. The views of the South Africa Minister of Higher Education and Training (Blade Nzimande) should be given adequate attention. Over the years, we have witnessed the gradual death of our languages, apart from English and Afrikaans, in the absence of their development as languages of teaching and learning, commerce and academia more generally. Many countries have struggled to develop and maintain indigenous language, particularly in higher education. The development of African languages is tied to social justice, which are an indispensable element of nation-building and the promotion of social cohesion in our country. The development of all official languages is a necessity for human rights and dignity, access and success at post-school institutions, preservation of our heritage, communication and culture (Makoni 2012). Therefore, it is crucial to view language not as a barrier but as an instrument of empowerment. According to the Russell Botman, (Vice Chancellor of Stellenbosch University, South Africa) "We need an 'Ubuntu of languages - an acknowledgement that a language is a language through other languages" and contributes to the transformation of the continent. How to live a multilingual world - that is the linguistic challenge of the 21s century?"

Rethinking education calls for more business focus. Africa governments must start rethinking its human capital development. All statistics suggest that the share of the working population with a degree or above is going to increase over the years. Therefore, government not only need to ensure the production of more graduate but also that the production of more graduates but also that the graduates so produced have the requisite skills and competence which are in demand in the global knowledge-based economy and society of the period. It is not just a question of completing courses for a degree; it is actually gaining the range of required skills that may not be the main focus of the degree but which are actually placing on in the best possible place to further one's career in the future. Therefore, African universities must do a better job of equipping young Africans to succeed in the 21st century and beyond with good education and skills. This is imperative more than ever before as skills drive our economies and they transform people's lives. But more education does not automatically translate into better skills and better lives. Importantly, education prepares for yesterday's economy or may be today's economy. But students are here for the future economy. They must be empowered with the right skills and training to face the future. After 14 years of civil war, Liberia is on the move to build its higher education system, following a powerful government delegation to the World Bank to discus and lay the groundwork for the structural change as depicted in the country's First Education Strategic Plan. Essentially the plan highlights the relevance and value of higher education to national development, by laying the groundwork for how it will endeavour to achieve the many envisaged objectives outlined in the plan (University World News 2012).

Dark Clouds on the Horizon does not provide even a tenth of the answers to the barrage of issues confronting the continent. In a way, it attempts to scratch the tip of the iceberg as it opens the Pandora box for objective discourses on the how, what, where when and why of the development trajectory or dichotomy of the continent's underdevelopment. No doubt, different answers to different kind of objectives are needed; but in reality, developing countries are all unique and very different, and generalisations of any kind could be misleading or, at best dangerous. However, they can forge their development under the concept of "unity in diversity" or "diversity in unity" for the greater good of humankind. All African countries were colonised or being colonised in one form or the other. This gives a common sliver-lining running through their struggles of sovereignty. The differences exist, but Dark Clouds on the Horizon settles on what is common may be the best way to confronting these problems, while not losing sight of idiosyncrasies, of which there are many, to state the least.

Finally, my comments or analysis are based with some minimal background in economic theory and political analysis but with a healthy dose of curiosity and sympathy for changing the face of the continent. And interest as part of the problem and solution. A deeper understanding of the book gives the impression of a very provocative and challenges of adopting an Afro-centric approach within the confines of conciliatory, cooperative and equity prosperity-sharing attitude towards the plight of the continent and in tandem with the greater good of humankind. We leave in a global village. Rephrased jinn another way, Clouds in the Horizon offers as honest as possible (like other publications in the field of social science and development politics do) few unambiguous answers. It guns for indigenous growth - hence the emphasis on Afro-centricism - the pace of development and growth determined from within Afro-centric may not offer the full answer, requiring a combination of indigenous and endogenous or Afro-Euro centric approach for the greater good of the people, not an Afro-Euro-centric approach that benefits only the rich in Africa and Europe.

Inequality like corruption has a built-in tendency to beget inefficiency, because it does not permit people at the lower strata of the wealth or income brackets to fully exploit their capabilities The great divide (which continues to widen) between North and South, and within the urban and hinterlands in African countries constitute a major stumbling block to the sustain transformation of the region. Low levels of wealth hinder or entirely bar productive educational choices limiting opportunities for creativity and innovations. Thus, inequalities in human feedback and reinforce the initial differences in equality. Inequality prevents the building of adequate healthy citizens which is certainly bad in it, but in addition contributes to inefficiencies in work productivity. These and other related factors and caveats explain why Africa is poor in the midst of plenty. However, if African countries are serious about their unity and developmental agendas, if Africa is serious about being a key player on the global arena, then it is time to take its continental organisation (AU) seriously and pay for it is infrastructure and functional capability. This is the only way of seeking African solutions to African problems - the Afro-centric approach. There is currently deep frustration among citizenry of the continent who watches with dismay their leader talks the talk and do not walk the talk, words upon words without concrete actions that significantly bring constructive changes to the continent so that these changes substantially trickle down changing the lives of the ordinary citizens. One begins to question or wonder how African citizens are expected to know and be inspired by the AU whose results are not visible; a tall order of serious challenges a wait's the AU new leadership.

What is important is to articulate a new dynamic form of development strategies benefiting all sides. Convergence of both sides for the common good is necessary. Globalisation, the catch word for development in the 21st century has taken-off thanks to the rate of technological progress which should be made to benefit Africa currently suffering from great deficiency in science and technology. We have to understand that technological progress is wrapped within two phases - technological progress for development or technological progress for human exploitation and destruction. The people have to make the choice. First, technological progress does not occur in a vacuum. The necessary enabling environment must be created to acerbate the process of technical change. In many cases technical progress depends on a number of interrelated activities; (i)gains in knowledge that are created by deliberate diversion of resources from current productive activity, in the hope that greater profitable production can emerge in the future; (ii) transfer of technical knowledge that occurs from the innovating firm(s) to the rest of the world. Africa for now seems not to benefit from both approaches, explaining the vulnerability of the region and why globalisation in its present construct constitutes the highest stage of scientific imperialism, used to destroying and derailing the region from making greater strides to quality livelihood. So far, we are using technological advancement for destructive purposes. Look at the amount monies being spent on weapons o human destruction in all he conflicts pone regions of Africa; Cameroon, Chad, Central African Republic, Mali, Sudan, Burkina Faso, Ethiopia etc., etc.

Education is not just a pathway to opportunity; it is a passport to inclusion and nurturing sustainable quality livelihood. Nurturing Africa's human development potential must be the top priority of all government policy strategies. For now, Africa remains a continent divided against it. Therefore, we all must be passionate where the continent is headed to and should go with a new-mindset, conviction and determination to restructure and do better. Here is where an Afro-centric approach cannot be dismissed. But an Afro-centric strategic approach does not entail being anti-west, even in spite of the horrendous acts of slavery, apartheid and other inhumane treatments inhibited on the African people. There are lots of difficulties and challenges. But Africa must be bold to stand out is grounds and overcome these challenges like the republic of South Korea and other East Asian "Tiger" economies teach us that a meaningful and sustainable growth surge can only be maintained by emphasising the development of our youth with skills and education. Education is not merely a problem for ministries to solve. In today's global economy context, failing to provide proper education will undermine economic growth and reinforce social inequalities as well as fan conflicts and instability in society.

Africa has some of the world's fastest growing economies, as highlighted in the 2012 Africa Progress Report, and this pace looks set to continue for the coming years. There exists a "twin crisis" in Africa's education. The numbers of children out of school may have dropped significantly between 2000 and 2009 but Africa is still likely to have 17 million children out of school in 2025, a decade after the world's 2015 target date for universal primary education. Meanwhile, many African children are receiving an education of abysmal quality. Far from equipping themselves for the global economy, millions of Africans emerged from primary school lacking basic literary and numeric skills. They face the prospects of marginalization, poverty and insecure unemployment. They easily fall into crimes and squalor. It is the place of the state to target those left behind. Importantly, a child's education should not depend on whether they are male or female, or whether their parents are rich or poor, or urban or rural. Public spending should target disadvantaged schools and regions. Financial transfer aimed at keeping children in schools - and young girls out of child labour or early marriage - all have a role to play. In addition, there is urgency for attention paid to the education of children in crisis in conflict countries (Burkina Faso, Cameroon, Somali, Sudan, Mali, Libya, Liberia, Central African Republic, Madagascar etc.) where conflicts that last a decade or more can set back education by a generation. The role of the international community is paramount in extending all necessary financial, logistic and infrastructure assistance to keep the "Education for All Promise" made in 2000 that by 2015 all children are able to complete their primary education.

As for those who the school system is failing them, a new approach 'second chance' is needed to ensure young people obtain the skills they need. For example, in Malawi, where only half of children manage to complete primary schools, as many as 10,000 students have taken part in such a scheme. By 2030, there will be three and have times as many young people in sub-Saharan Africa as there been in 1980. For today's girls' and boys' action must be taken now to equip them with the necessary skills for future challenges. With the ongoing political crisis in the two Anglophone regions of Cameroon where it is estimated that over 700,000 children are being deprived from having education, which is their basic fundamental human-rights. The situation is so pathetic that less than 30% of schools are operating in the rural areas; over 500 villages burned down; almost 27,500 people killed with hundreds of thousands of internally displaced citizens and refugees living in bushes and in neighbouring countries (See Eden Newspaper 03 December 2021, The Horizon, 09 December 2021 among others. Africa, this generation in particular, cannot afford to fail another generation. Sharawy Helini (2014) talks us through the continent's political and social thought. And Ndlovu-Gatshenoi 920130 interrogates with the African post-colonial condition focusing on the thematic of liberation predicament and long-standing crisis of dependence (epistemological, cultural, economic and political) created by colonialism and coloniality).

Investing in skills and education makes good business sense as a dollar invested pays back ten times over a person's lifetime, bringing prosperity to a family and society as a whole. Therefore, to achieve the goal of quality education and skills development, the government must take the lead to be supported by others - locally and internationally. The development strategies of African countries must target marginalised groups. Seen within these premises, policies must be closely linked with other policies, including a National Strategy for Accelerated Poverty and Corruption Reduction; emphasising varied types of training needs and recognising the importance of linking microfinance and skills development for those in rural communities. The challenges are clear; calling for proactive actions calling for proactive actions now to be given alternative pathways for the young to learn foundation skills. All young people, as earlier noted, need quality training in relevant skills at all stages of the education ladder; and school curricular should provide a balance between vocational and technical skills including Information Training (IT) and transferable skills such as confidence and communication which are indispensable for the work place skills strategies must target the disadvantaged - particularly young women and the urban poor.

Many African countries are turning to China and East Asian economies to learn how to help their youthful population lacking in most basic of skills can come out of their predicaments. For example, China recognised in the 1990s the importance of a solid education conferring dignity and the potential for self-realisation. The advantage with these countries is their cultural homogeneity which the fifty-four countries on the African continent. There is no single African country with a common cultural homogeneity. The cultural diversity in this respect acts as stumbling block to development. African countries north of the Sahara have an advantage with the 'Arabic' language compared to countries south of the Sahara. Swahili provides a new pathway as it spoken in a number of countries within Eastern, Central and Southern African region. Can that language be a continental flavour? By not only upgrading skills for industrialisation, but also focusing on productivity for small holder farmers and non-farm self-employment, the number of those living below the poverty line. Fell dramatically. The reward of this investment was strong and sustained economic growth. The investment also benefits young people through better earnings. These are some of the practices that Africa can draw valuable lesson - the effect of the "late-comer advantage." A holistic people-oriented policy approach is necessary to achieve the goal of China's development approach. Too many Africans are still barely scraping a living and need skills to find prosperity and quality livelihood. We should use the informal sector to create more jobs, improve on the livelihood of the vast majority of the citizens. Citizens themselves must be creative, innovative and entrepreneurial. We can ask whether Swahili can be extended to cover Southern and Central African regions; can the West African region come up with a common language that should help facilitate and unite the people? This is a challenge for the African Union's Academy of African Languages (ACALAN), the African Union's institution that deals with the continent's language policy and language policy implementation to continue looking into the problem.

Of course, the continent has achieved much in the past decade. It could have achieved more and do better than what exist. The continent needs only to grasp the potential skills training in the youths. It is a leap forward, but some distance from reaching the finishing line. According to the former British Prime Minister Gordon Brown, and now United Nations Global Education Envoy: "now is not the time for defeatism and despair;" but a call on the international community to "redouble our efforts." In the same vein, Pauline Rose, Director of the Education for All Global Monitoring Report, says the drive for universal primary education had enjoyed an initial "honeymoon period" with strong political backing and financial support. If that rate of progress had been maintained, the target would have been achieved. But at the current rate of change, it would take at least until 2030. The question to ask is simple. Why has it proved so difficult to providing primary schools? If the world can put a spacecraft on Mars, surely it can build and staff enough classrooms. This pledge on primary schools has now been a target since 1990. This sense of a fading national and international concern particularly since the financial crises constitutes a major problem to be addressed by all implicit partners. People seem to have lost interest and turned to other things. The corrosive impact of armed conflicts and political instability in Africa and other parts of the third world have also been a barrier. Come to think of the shooting in Pakistan of the 14-year-old educationist crusader Malala Yousefza, shows how cultural barriers and male chauvinism against the female gender attains a high peak. Such heights of inhumanity with cultural undertones must be discouraged and addressed through enlightenment, women empowerment does not entail underscoring men's right and competing with them, but a complementing as partners in development and well-being. Men and women are partners in development, not as competitors in development. Together, they build a home, a family, a society, a nation, and a continent we all want. That is the significance of living and eating together as one people, one country, and one continent.

While many Asian countries are making progress, there has been much less advance in Sub-Saharan Africa. Some African countries have made strides. However, the single biggest number of children out of school is now Nigeria (Africa's most populated country) notes the report, which states that there are 3.6 million more children missing in school than in 2000. Ethiopia can be given as example of what can be achieved, with "dramatic" reductions in out-of-school children. Tanzania trebled the proportion of national income spent on education and saw its primary school enrolment rate double. Tanzania is not the only country that appears as a success and yet languishes in a crisis of education;" a crisis cantered on quality, or lack thereof. Education is not about bums on seats, but about interactive and active learning. We need according to Roo Corbishley (Tanzania) to stop seeing the school as the panacea of education and start thinking of innovative ways in which young people can access the cognitive and non-cognitive skills and knowledge they need. South Africa is still grappling with poverty and massive inequalities. A huge educational deficit means blacks will continue to struggle in the economic arena, because of a lack of skills. This point is aptly analysed by Terblanche (2002); "the ANC's core leaders effectively sold its sovereign freedom to implement an independent and appropriate socio-economic policy for a menu of postage when it entered into several compromises with the corporate sector and its global partners. The unfortunate transitive must be retracted or renegotiated. Not much is done to revamp adult education. This group should not be left behind either; a large population within this group belongs to the female gender. Though over the past years, one has witnessed movements for freedom, human rights and democratic governance, the absence of and educated population cannot help in confronting the growing backlash of conservative groups, which seed and, in some cases, achieved significant political power in derailing the empowerment of the female gender as veritable partners in the development process. The challenges African women are facing call for support across the political divide and other democratic and social justice movements to intensify their support for the fight against illiteracy, support equality and to prevent a roll back on already hard-won achievements.

Education for all is a call that should not bypass any one since education plays a vital role in the progress and success of any human being and the nation. Therefore, engaging and empowering all the stake holders as agents of change in their families, communities, nation and the world at large is call and obligation we cannot run away from. Accordingly, "education is not only conditioned by time and space but should be consciously related to the needs of the particular society of which it is a function. The educational system itself must be fully unified and deliberately integrated as closely as possible with the life of society" (Huxley, 1944). The AU maintains that an African Research Council (ARC) could fill important gaps in the terrain of research in Africa and help the continent in its quest for better interface research and policy. If properly structured and managed, it could become a standard bearer for the best in African science - organising the production of research within defined fields, facilitating dialogue with policy communities, acting as a voice for African science in and outside the continent, and contributing to strengthening the institutional basis of science at the national, sub-regional and regional levels.

At the dawn of the new millennium the USA and European Union accounted for about 37% and 25% respectively of all global expenditure on Research and development (R&D), resulting in their together producing 76% of global scientific publications. By making similar investments, China had grown its contribution to global scientific publications to 10% over five years, second only to the USA in terms of its output of research, and rapidly increasing its share of patents, innovation and markets. In contrast, Africa's R&D investments are a mere 0.8% of global investments. The continent produced only 1.4% of the world's scientific publications. Little wonder, the continent has only 0.1% of global patents are currently owned by Africans. Only South Africa meets the 1% allocation of Gross Domestic Product (GDP) to research. The number of the countries is far away from the 1% envisaged target (Mashining, 2012). Looking at the comparative public spending on education as percentage of Gross Domestic Product (GDP) between 1980 and 1996 for some selected African countries we find the following:

Table: Comparative Public Spending on Education as Percentage of GDP

Country	1980	1985	1990	1995	1996
Botswana	6.1	6.2	6.9	8.4	10.4
Egypt	5.7	6.3	4.0	4.8	----
Ghana	3.1	2.6	3.3	----	----
Kenya	6.8	6.4	7.1	6.8	6.6
Nigeria	6.4	1.2	1.0	0.9	----
South Africa	----	6.0	6.5	6.8	7.9

Source: Jegede et al (2001:18)

African universities have lost their revered freedom even the right to have qualified lecturers, pursue the basic cannons of truth and take an independent and objective action without recourse to Government. They have been encumbered by unnecessary political entrapment and this has profoundly affected their morality and epistemological tactics.

They have departed from genuine scientific scholarship to leaking the boots of politicians for appointments within the civil service. This is very true of Cameroon where Professors and Lecturers were cajoled by the Ministry of Higher Education to sign a declaration supporting the candidature of the incumbent President Paul Biya during the 2004 and 2011 Presidential elections (Forje, forthcoming). The minister is a top scribe of the inner decision-making body of the ruling Cameroon Peoples Democratic Movement (CPDM). How can the academic community stoop so low to the dictates of a politician? Apparently, and most unfortunately, weak nations (Africa in particular) lack the capital base, international reach and financial clout to challenge some of the policies flagged by the World Bank, IMF, WTO and other bodies on some of their policies capable of hindering the continent's developme3nt. The aftermath is massive flight of professionals in areas they optimise their talent, thereby creating inequality and most importantly a development stasis in the developing countries. In this sense, globalisation for example, could be seen as a westernization of the world. In short, it is the highest stage of scientific imperialism as long as African countries have weak science and technology background. It strongly enhances the centre-periphery dichotomy. The periphery must condone to the dictates of the centre and the centre is subjected to the assimilating and annexing the periphery by all means possible.

A quick glance of student population and areas of study in seven universities in Sweden shows the following distribution (Table SA Mar Studenterna i Svereige).

Education is an agent of change which empowers its recipient to be creative and innovative as well as become a change agent. Therefore, 'humankind is the only point of departure and the only point of return' (Dennies Diderot). In the same vein, Rousseau (2000:6) emplacing the essentiality of education to human development points out; "we are born weak, we need strength, helpless, we need aid, foolish, we need reason. All that we lack at birth, all that we need when we come to man's estate, is the gift of education. This education comes to us from nature; from man or from the education of man, what we gain by our experience of our surroundings is the education of things."

Table So Mar Studenterna in Sveriege 2012

Universities	Student Population	Social Sciences	Humanities	Tech nical	Natural Sciences
Stockholm	48.936	63	25	74	17
Gothenburg	33.535	47	21	64	15
Lund	28.028	41	15	15	--
Uppsala	23.380	39	19	17	--
Linkoping	17,930	35	---	20	14
Umea	16.657	47	14	--	11
Malmo	12.394	56	12	12	--

Source: Svenska Dagbladet 28 September 2012, "So mar Studetentern i Svereige Hogskoleverkets Prognosis for 2012 of antal Student. Hoghskoleverket Ärs Report 2012"

What separates African Universities from their counterparts in the developed economies can be seen as one example, their strength or weakness of their libraries. According to Peretmode (2008), "Harvard University library consists of 80 individual libraries and has 15 million volumes. It prides itself as the largest academic library in the world. The University of California, Berkeley's library has 10 million volumes and maintains over 70,000 serial titles, while Stanford University library holds more than eight million volumes with 19 libraries. The University of Toronto library in Canada holds 10.5million items in its collection. On the other hand, no Africa, the university of Cape Town (South Africa) main library and nine branch libraries contains 1.5milion volumes and over 27.000 volume titles of which 6.094 are current. 30 electronic journal and 175 electronic research data bases. The University of Ibadan (Nigeria) has one million volumes of book, 60.000 journals and subscribers to 20 databases in its library."

This disparity in the state of higher education in Africa and the developed world shows how the continent's educational system has lost its operational utility and is trapped in the vortex of perennial politics and centralised authoritarian ethnic hegemonic preterianism. Instead of the universities being centres of excellence, critical debate, research and innovation, and the bastion of getting the people out of the squalor of poverty and ignorance or as people-processing institutions it has dived into the bottom-pit of entrenched ethnic party-politics and witch-hunting and pushed underdevelopment to illustrate its role in society. Could it be argued that it was from these perspectives that World Bank saw no need for university education in Africa? Or was it an entrench strategic conspiracy approach to keep the continent for ever as a raw material producing continent for western factories. The end result is that scholarship orientation and critical ideological toleration suffocated, just as dictatorship and centralised ethnic hegemonic rule became the vogue in educational administration and overtaken by corruption in the promotion of lecturer. Because of party politics in tension in the academic world, Cameroon has no plan in revitalising education in the 21st century. It is business as usual and as long as the status quo is maintained, the rest can go to hell. There has been no proper attempt to harmonise the British and French system of higher education. Even though France has moved to adopting the Anglo-Saxon system of education, Cameroon because of the French hegemony of assimilation hangs tight on the Napoleonic education system. Is the country really entering the 21st century and with which attitude?

China has progressed because of its stern adherence bedrock of education reform. It has increased research spending by 20% since 1999, and now spends about USA100.billion dollars in that domain. In 2006, 1.5 million science and engineering students graduated from Chinese universities. I believed that China would overtake the United States of America as the largest world economy in 2016. Again, the Royal Society of London in its 2011 report ranked China second only to the United States of America in the share of published research and may take the first position in 2013 (Akani 2012:97). Countries like Brazil, China and Japan have moved tremendously in overhauling their education system to ensure broad-based macroeconomic growth and to keep the country afloat at the cutting edge in the global economy (Obama 2008). There is need to put a human-face to the global economy. This should give the continent with visionary leadership and a pro-active Afro-centric strategic approach the necessary take-off to sustainable economy development, progress and quality livelihood to all its citizens. This is what the continent needs to overcome existing clouds over its development. In 2011 books published in the United States of America were as follows: Title published 347.00. Annual sales

USA dollars 27 billion. Export volume 240 million books*; Export earning USA 1.5. Billion dollars. Export volume does not include e-books. (Note (*) export volume includes new titles, old books still under copyright and out-of-print books published commercially. This total does not count self-published books and reprints published individually or demand, Progressive Economy, Week 1, and November 21, 2012. See also www.bowker.com/assets/downloads/products/isbn. Ouput.2001-2011.PDF)

The Noble Prize in literature is another barometer to measure where the continent stands in terms of academic standards. How do we fill the gap? Of course, it is only through creating an enabling education environment for the society. With Africa experiencing positive economic development, and there is increasing understanding of the important contribution's universities have to make if the continent's societies are to achieve the next stages of development, African universities can play a key role in facilitating the continent's economic development; but presently, they are still too weak in many respects. Therefore, governments and stakeholders have until recently viewed higher education and research as a "luxury" and a reserved preserved to the ruling and well-to-do classes, and meant for 'public officers' to maintain the elite/ruling class ld development status quo approach, which does not need serious public investment in higher education and training. Such thinking and behaviour contribute to weakening universities to the extent that major African universities once centres of excellence are at the verge of 'close to collapse.'

E-Learning as the solution

Can e-learning provide the answer to the state of the soaring situation of human capital development on the continent? E-learning has the potential for solving Africa's skill gaps; At the African Virtual University (AVU) was accessed in some 193 countries worldwide. The 21st century is providing increased opportunities for universities to turn to e-learning as an alternative to traditional classroom-based learning. Africa therefore, can leap-frog barriers to student enrolment by exploiting what e-learning offers. The 2000 Dakar Framework for Action (DFA) recognises the use of ICTs as a key strategy for achieving "Education for All" goals. In 2003, the New Partnership for Africa's Development (NEPAD) prioritised effects towards bridging the digital divided between Africa and the developed by fact tracking support to ICT initiatives in enhancing access to education. Technology is an enabler, not the solution in and of itself. Yet Africa and other emerging economies must address seriously the university space and environment to be competitive force in the global village economy of our time. E-Learning is effective with efficient, constant electric power supply not the kind of erratic power supply that exists in many African countries today. Second, how many people have access to computers and other gadgets? How efficient and effective is our electric power supply grid? How can we successfully make the e-learning an inherent component of our education system with an inefficient and chaotic power supply system as a tool for building the human capacity building process of the country?

Of course, challenges exist: (i) limited access to internet connectivity; (ii) high cost: (iii) intermittent power disruptions: (iv) lack of national and institution policies: (v) scare experienced human resources; and (vi) the perception that distance education may not offer the same quality as face-to-face education. However, given the pressure on Sub-Saharan countries meeting the demands for access to higher education and training human capital, with the progress made in laying fibre optics and using alternative sources of power, the challenges can be addressed in order to unlock the potential of ICT in education. The emergence of mobile technology is an asset Africans can count on. The AVU 2009-2014 Business Plan envisages creating an enabling environment that will unlock the potential of e-learning especially in Sub-Saharan Africa. So far, the AVU, between 2005-2011 implemented the continent-wide Multinational Project covering 12 universities in 10 countries, and the university is currently implementing multinational Project 11 (2012-16) covering 27 universities in 21 African countries, with the main objective of enhancing the capacity of universities to offer ICT integrated programmes in mathematics and science and to increase access to higher education and training.

Over the past decade, Africa has experienced unparalleled economic growth, putting the continent on a pedestal to become the growth frontier. Development experts predict that economies in Africa will continue to grow at an average of 6% even while the rest of the world is facing an economic slump. Apparently, the financial services, retails, telecommunication and construction sectors in Africa will attract more private benefit from Africa's economic boom. It goes without saying that, while there is much optimism surrounding Africa's growth potential, pessimism exist concerning qualified skills: the continent appear is lagging behind in training the necessary human resources to march its rosy economic growth prospects. If the continent is going to be a veritable competitive partner in the global economy, at least 12% to 15% of the work force should have attained tertiary education. For now, universities are currently overwhelmed by increasing student numbers. The rapid population growth of the continent accounting for this backed families unable to meet the cost of education for their children.

The introduction of parallel evening programmes has not solved the problem, as universities are struggling to deal with the growing student numbers. In addition, universities are unable to increase physical infrastructures and teaching staff to meet the soaring demands. It is here that distance education comes to the rescue of the demand for skill human power in Africa's economic take-off. Education and stability constitute the most single important factor in boosting an emerging economy. As the continent grows, the old political elites and establishment are being threatened by a youthful, growing middle class having extensive aspirations and demands more of its leaders. These challenges should be managed democratically and without a fall into security. The call is for African governments to march its commitments at the national and continental levels to invest in the people and uplift the quality wellbeing of citizens remains a serious output factor for governments on the continent. These are some of the necessary tools for the outputs of a structure-functional governance system badly needed on the continent.

Education must be tailored to the needs of society. Governments in partnership with other stakeholders must create the requisite enabling environment provide the required infrastructures. The economy is a sub-system of human society and so it is possible that socially or politically determined priorities may override strictly economic ones. This may lead to governments subsiding entrepreneurs or protecting them from competition by tariffs, quotas and preferential purchasing policies, even when it could be argued that the same results could have been achieved at a lower cost by allowing market forces to complete the task. The most common and preferred solutions should focus on the quality wellbeing of the people. An issue often missed in the development strategy of African countries. Stretching the issue further, the proof of the benefits of stability to an economy is in the figures. The countries where stability is strongest are those which have grown fastest. Ghana was the fastest growing economy in the world last year (2011) with 14% GDP increase; by one measure, South Africa GDP increase); by one measure, South Africa GDP now outranks that of Belgium and Sweden; Ethiopia expanded more quickly than China in the five years to 2009. Overall, Africa's collective GDP, at USA 1, 6 billon dollars in 2008, is roughly equal to that of Brazil or Russia (Ichikowitz 2012:34-35).

China's extraordinary economic development in the past couple of decades - which could be describe as China's Technological Rise: Myths and Lessons (Padmashree et al, 2012) has been the subject of intense policy and scholarship discussions. However, it is only recently that attention has turned to the growth of the country's technological and scientific capabilities in a wide range of sectors such as space exploration, super-computing and renewable energies. China is no longer just of the "factory" of the word but is rapidly becoming a major technological and innovation player. These are some of the best practices that the continent can draw invaluable lessons from and tailor their development accordingly but within their own socio-cultural and environmental confines. Africa can draw useful examples from the Korean case - Action Plan on Higher Education - where the country has invested heavily in quality education and the development of its human resources, particularly in the tertiary level. Judging from Korea has accomplished within a short space of time, a Korea-African Education Cooperation could play the hard-trick of implementing sustentative initiative to generate growth in the education sector. Cooperation of this kind could be inspirational on many levels; but it is a model untested outside of that environment, and some of the detail requires discretion. Of course, the continent has to be cautious. Korea has a homogenous culture. Africa has not. It is difficult to ascertain how South Korean education policies based on a unified cultural perspective will be applicable to the African environment, which is remarkably diverse at all levels - emotionally, economically, politically and demographically.

Sad enough, there is very little inter-university exchange programmes. Something has to be done in that direction. University inter-change programmes should be encouraging, so also Inter-university sports competition to foster mutual relationship and unity. This reminds me of the *"Outward Bound School"* at Man O'War Bay, Victoria, Southern Cameroons before the independence of a number of West African countries. The "Outward Bound School" brought students and civil servants from across West African English-speaking countries for a short period of training and learning the art of co-habituating) with a curriculum that included some form of para-military training, social and community work etc.) But importantly, for people of the region to learn to one know one another, how in living and eating together. On arrival at Man O' War Bay the students are sorted into teams or sections of approximately ten each, with a leader and assistant appointed for each group. From then on till they leave the Centre these young men, of different religious, tribes, social, and geographical background, must learn to work together. Each section receives marks throughout the day and the section with the highest marks has its pennant raised on the flagstaff at the beginning of each day's activities. The School was geared in fostering mutual understanding of unity in diversity; learning how to live together; and working for the common good of the community and humankind.

What is important is for Africa to draw inspiration from the Korean experience, not to copy it in every detail but to build an education system that are appropriate to Africa's needs and realities. For now, the Korean government is providing support to African countries in the area of ICT, including masters' scholarships to African students who benefit from two-year programmes in Korea, education research awards via the Association for the Development of Education in Africa (ADEA), and training programmes in ICT. With the objective of cultivating next generation leaders in the field of information and communication technology ICT, Korea is well placed to impart some of its experiences to the continent. Seen within these perspectives it would be necessary for Korea to increase the scope of the Next African Leader Programme (NALP) through a scholarship initiative. NALP provides courses in ICT and economic development policy - areas in which Korea is globally competitive.

Citizen journalists are becoming a potent force for building open and democratic societies. Presently, a simple smart phone offers the public a journalist's toolbox just a few years ago cost thousands of dollars and filled a car trunk. In environments where poor infrastructure, minimal access to technology, and small-scale economies impeded the development of mainstream independent media, and in countries where repressive governments limit the ability of professional journalists to operate freely, citizen journalists are helping to fill the gaps. This shows the power, influence and importance of emerging technologies on the body politics of societies - Africa in particular - where there is great need for informing and educating the public. These citizen journalists can provide a corrective, alternative view that expose corruption, maladministration and bad governance, fosters accountability, and documents abuse of power. Just as they can serve to challenge mainstream forces, however, they can also be tools for government's propaganda, as in many developing countries, where loyalists have flooded social media sites and blogs with pro-regime sentiment. Citizen journalism also poses a problem for advocates of quality, accuracy and objectivity, as they typically lack formal training or knowledge of the essential roles of independent media plays in ensuring accountable and transparent government. The world has changed. Today's Africa and sit-tight president are forced to change with it or be thrown out -The Arab Spring and its aftermath, for example. Demonstrating resilience and a keen ability to adapt, leading authoritarian regime are developing subtler and sophisticated methods to retain power. To surprises dissent, mass brutality has been replaced by selective safety inspections and tax independent civil societies and opposition groups, witch-hunting of the opposition and critical scholarship opinions or positions goes unabated.

New economic resources at the disposal of authoritarian regimes in Africa have enabled them to bolster their authoritarian attitude of governance. Meanwhile, the democratic world has been slow to acknowledge and respond to the emergence of these of these views, nimbler regimes. A kind of coalition of the willing emerges because of the convergence of articulate self-interest to exploit the silent majority. Liberation technologies are now an instrument for change. This is a valuable tool at the forefront of this bourgeoning field of study. It looks at the popular dichotomy of 'liberation' versus control' with regard to the Internet and the sophisticated dimensions of such control. Yet, it is imperative for us all to work together and on all fronts against oppression, whether of fellow human beings or of the environment link. I believe it is necessary for all stake holders to unit forces and keep people away from fighting each other; fighting which pushes them towards servitude, poverty, and ignorance, while getting rich ourselves. Religion and ethnic diversities are used to keep people from real change, development and progress. For many decades we have declared war on environmental rights, human rights, rights to natural resources, rights to clean air, rights of sustainable environment and so on. Those who champion the rights of common people are by definition enemies of those elites and humankind pays a heavy price for resistance. On the global scale, human rights belong to those who have the military arsenal and can use it at will against the weak and poor. Human rights belong to the developed countries and not the developing countries. But life and struggle go on. And life goes on too. Yet it is imperative that we work together to achieve true justice - a prerequisite for peace, change, development, progress and sustainability. Without justice, there is no peace; and without peace, there is no development; and without development, there is equitable quality livelihood and services for all.

Resuscitating the African economy is the wish of all, even the rich. But how to achieve it and ensure shared-prosperity are what dividends the rich and poor, strong and weak. In defining what poverty is in a given context and also frames poverty and underdevelopment as a universal challenge as all countries will have their stock. The state of poverty must be tackled nationally and globally to ensure social sustainability and inclusive green growth; and by exploring different facets of national resources management at the macro level and seeking to challenge the prevailing concept, fostered by the expanding discussion on the green economy growth, that creating greater prosperity in terms of jobs, narrowing resources equity gaps and efficiently using natural resources are innately complementary. We need to address, and explore the impact of resources for rural development - energy and land - how structurally defined policies supposed targeting access have in fact often created or produced other forms of inequalities and entrenched the economic exclusion of indigenous peoples as well as significant socio-economic and socio-cultural costs. Though there is significant difference in the economies of African countries, sub-regions, common challenges exist in terms of:

- The power asymmetries created by heavy reliance on one or few key sectors comprising large and well-organised and powerful international private sector alliances:
- The effective economic governance by resources flows determined largely by external and globalises market dynamics;
- The varied cost of maintaining an attractive investment environment;
- The multiple social environmental costs generated by such resources - intensive growth; and;
- Challenges of having a functional Common Market; as well as political governance system;
- Repairing or breaking away from such pathways as short and long-term policy options (See UNDP, 2012).

The Diaspora - An Emerging New South in the North/

There is an emerging New South in the North. Tapping into the expertise of the Diaspora in constructing a new Africa is a must. Just as more Black Americans are moving from North to South, creating what could be called a "New South" in the United States of America, that zeal should be mobilised in creating and strengthening Renaissance Black Continent (RBC) or a United States of Africa. Today, many blacks have become governors, congressmen and women and are numbered among the wealthiest citizens. There is Afro-American President Obama) occupying the White House. In Britain, we have Lord Boating of Akyem (Ghana) and Wembley (UK) the first black British Cabinet minister; in Poland,(John Abraham Godson) the first ever African member of the Polish Parliament; a number of Africans are members of the British Parliament (Adam Afriyie, Ghana; Kwasi Kwarteng (Ghana); Chuka Umunna (Nigeria); Helen Grant, First Black Female MP appointed Under-Secretary of State for Justice and for Women and Equalities; Chinyelu 'Chi' Onwuraf, Nigeria, Junior Shadow Minister for Business, Innovation and Skills after winning the 2010 elections); Canada has Maka Kotto (Cameroonian) the first Africa appointed Minister of Culture and Communication in September 2012; and in Sweden, there is the first black women (Democratic Republic of Congo) as a member of the Swedish cabinet; Chuka Umuma (Nigeria) Member of the British Parliament. The list is long portraying the changing circumstances of the time but emphasising the communality of humankind and not the colour of the skin. This and other developments show how Africa is developing Europe; and that knowledge of developing the centre should rechannelled to moving the periphery out its currently captive situation to that be being a free person.

The diaspora as the six regions of the African continent have enormous potentials to offer the continent in various ways in advancing the continent's struggle towards maturity. Originally, we saw and treated the 'diaspora' as *'brain drain;'* but that *'brain drain*; can and should be turn into *'brain gain.'* We can see the "Diaspora" as Africa's prodigal sons and daughters. Let us be candid and honest to ourselves; most left the continent in search for greener pastures abroad; some left because our governance system failed in providing the requisite, enabling and conducive environment for the realization of their dreams and desires. Others left for curiosity sake, as explorers. In all they left as hunters and are now returning home with their bounties. For the past many decades, the struggle for national liberation ideologies and the eventual granting of 'independence' has failed to meet the rising expectations of the people. In short, Africa's independence as a result of failure to meet rising expectations has been rubbished, and national-determination itself declared as passé! Africans, since 6th March 1957 has been told that it has only one choice: either get integrated fully into the globalised world or remain marginalised. The spectre of marginalization haunts Africa; Africa leaders are left with limited options; *"either you embrace and ride on the 'globalisation bandwagon or be doomed in the sealed room of 'no return."* Even with the AU vision of 2063 Agenda, African countries are falling in line one after the other to this *'sweet-bitter'* Euro-centric agenda, which in away is disowning their own nationalist agenda.

Our brothers and sisters abroad are endowed with knowledge and other capacities that should be exploited to the advantage of the people; their know-how should be used both in the public and private sectors for the ultimate advancement of the country and continent. It requires and urgent putting in place the necessary mechanism that would grease and smoothen their resettlement and reintegration in to system to make them useful to all. But when the very basic are not available, it scares them from returning home. It thus remains an issue of 'brain drain and not 'brain gain' that should help uplift the continent from its current slumber-land to a booming continent. Here lies Africa's missing link in the capacity building metaphor.

The Missing Link

Capacity building in Africa remains the most pertinent developmental challenges facing the continent. It remains the challenge of the time and in the distant future. Africa must develop its own capacities; the COVID-19 pandemic is a pointer that the world tomorrow is going to become difficult for Africa to compete in. Now is the second, minute, hour and day for Africa to prepare itself for the pending challenges. Technologies and markets re being revolutionalised; we are destroying or neglecting our indigenous knowledge systems instead of improving on it at an era when Africa is going to become more integrated into the global market -- no less, and not prepared or well-armed. To that challenge, Africa needs the right of technically skilled and excellent people, institutions and infrastructure. Let us be realistic and face the truth: development cannot come from outside –external support helps –but development progress is organic and must be home grown. Development can come our way when we grow it. This is not being done. Therefore, the right capacities and enabling environment must exist for that to happen. Development should be or is like democracy: development of the people, by and for the people.

Most importantly, Africa should be more and more in control of its economic destiny, less vulnerable to external shocks, many of which it has seen during the past couple of decades; and must exert more efforts to be more competitive, creative, innovative and productive in the global market areas. There is a missing link, from slavery – imperialism – colonialism – independence – neo-colonialism and now the struggle for Renaissance Africa to regain the lost Africa; these various stages and changes in emphasis in development strategies – from state-led growth through basic human needs to structural adjustment tells a story of change and development. Politically from the OAU to the AU signify different approaches to the transformation of the continent with varying approaches to the transformation of the region with varying levels of failures and successes.

Failure or success fundamentally all lacked one essential ingredient: the failure to incorporate, as a central feature, the building of indigenous Africa skills, knowledge and institutions. Capacity building has continued to be the missing link; dependency on foreign aid and human capital takes pride of place in the vocabulary of the leaders, policy planners of independent African countries, signalling the reality that Africa is yet to be free and independent and for an unforeseeable future will remain colonized and exploited by external forces. Externally, colonized and internally living under a centralised hegemonic authoritarian governance system shows how vulnerable the weak, the poor and excluded are; and how the continent is treated differently and suffers as a result. Africa is suffering from *"crisis management"* and there is no positive *"crisis response"* from the colonial or administering powers.

Let us ponder and ask ourselves why is the continent experiencing the presence of 100,000 experts or technical advisors in Africa many years after independence; at a time when many Africans with skill competences are in the diaspora under the notion of "brain drain" re in Europe and the America's? The trend should be in the opposite direction. Dependency on 'technical assistance' is in the wrong direction and with wrong intention and destroying the continent. Therefore, there is need for serious changes in attitudes; both by Europe and America; and by African countries. A reciprocal change for an attitude entails assistance becoming an opportunity for an African picking up a skill, for African institutional infrastructure to be built, for Africans to execute the job and for Africa to grow out the quagamia of abject poverty and underdevelopment. Changes in attitudes entail the donor countries giving up the control tactics and strategies in the choice, design, execution and assessment of development projects. Development projects should be "an African priority," not a European priority; the implementing mechanisms – an African priority, not externally-devised. Africa's capacity building remains an acid test for Europe, America and the rest of the developed polities.

There have to be fundamental changes in attitude on both sides of the ale. Is the developed world ready to see Africa shaping its own features? Are the developed countries ready to get out of their current perception as enslaved people ready to be civilised? Are both sides ready to make long-tern genuine commitments to the continent's development? We should bear in mind that capacities will be built over decades, not over-night; and it cannot be done on the cheap. Africa needs a social foundation for its capacity build endeavour until the mind-set of African countries are in the right direction, their development will never go right. Africa should change its mind-set for good or improve on its good mind-set. This is the time for Africa to discipline itself, without which the region will end up being disciplined by the condition which it finds itself. So, Africa is self-disciplined to better restore, reconstruct the African continent. In short, capacity building is a serious test of and for African government this requires serious change in attitude in many cases, especially in the proper utilization of indigenous capacities created ad tapping into indigenous knowledge or continues to face the consequences of dependency on foreign aid in different forms.

For the past sixty years or more since the wind of change started blowing across, have these governments listen to themselves, see what is happening and are prepared to learn and inject new visions that should be the new game-changer for a new Africa. African leaders are challenged to answer two fundamental questions on capacity building: (i) where should Africa in the new mode of being sensitive to the continent's priorities and needs begin? The current policy analysis, the right kind of management structures in place remains essential to supporting progress in every other sector. Whatever the case, an integrated analysis/management function remains the sine qua non. It is extremely important for African countries getting the policy/management interface right for other activities to follow more easily and smoothly; (ii) how should this evolve and what must be done to ensure the sustainability of the process of human capacity build?

We need to have vision; for there exist no mystery about human capacity building initiative? The goal or the vision can be 5, 10, 15, 20, 30, 40- or 50-years' policy strategic plan and implantation process. All these policy measures require management skills to ensure their realisations. Management skills require knowledge development. Our institutions of higher learning have an important role to play and must be given all the resources that are needed for the smooth functioning of the establishment. The 11th Conference of the Association of African Universities, 28th February 2005 meeting on the University of Cape Town, South Africa, on the theme; *"Cross-border Provision and the Future of Higher Education in Africa"*, the appeal made by President Thabo Mbeki of South Africa, calling on higher education practitioners to consider themselves as architects of the New African World; and for collaboration among all stakeholders in an effort to make knowledge relevant to the needs of the continent remains important as we strive towards a solid capacity building and resources development in Africa (see Thandika Mkandawire 2005).

One will not stop the repeating the clarion call for capacity building and human sources development as e central challenge of the highest priority now facing Africa, the people and world community, as we seek in our different ways to grapple with the multifaceted developmental crisis now hovering over the African continent. The socio-politico-eco power dynamics have to be adequately addressed (Mkandawire, 2005; Assie-Lumumba, 2006). Forward on the continent has to move; and should be guided by the words of Kim Kyons; "Yesterday is a cancelled cheque, tomorrow is a promissory note; today is the only cash you have. So, spend it wisely" (Patrick 2011:64). Africa should be doing the right at the right time to overcome the burdens of colonialism and neo-colonialism. Spending the cheque properly and appropriately calls for a comprehensive structured movement from fragmentation to unity; from conflict to peace, from inequality to equality and from injustice to justice. Building an inclusive holistic society should be the goal. This requires 'outreach' cross the divide, to ensure sustainability and stability as many societies both in the developing and developed countries are undergoing rapid substantial change. This process of change hangs on the consciences of the leaders in Africa and the western world. There has to be a growing awareness to spur them into positive action in defence of beliefs than emphasis freedom, equality, community, dialogue, and tolerance. We are all challenged to work in the direction of creating an atmosphere of understanding and solidarity among the people on either side of the divide that transcends division based on race, nationality, class, religion and political orientation, East, West, North or South.

United Kingdom Prime Minister Tony Blair's Commission for Africa (2005) castigated the intensive placed on African state for practicing 'bad governance', lack of responsibility and accountability, thereby, ignoring the role of imperialism and neocolonialism in the exploitation of the continent's resources and supporting of nondemocratic states when it suited their interests. In addition, Africans are told they have no capacity to think and articulate correct policies that should uplift their countries. Hear him; "Africa's history over the last fifty years has been blighted by two areas of weakness. These have been *capacity* – the ability to design and deliver policies; and *accountability* – how well a state answers to its people." Characterising this statement, Mkandawire and Soludo (1999: vii) painfully pointed out (i) major irony of African development history is that the theories and models employed have largely come from outside the continent. No other region of the world has been so dominated by external ideas and models."

Pushing the dialectics of the discuses further, Africa continues witnessing a proliferation of political, economic and policy initiatives being forced down the throats of the people of the continent since the granting of independence to former colonies. The globalization bandwagon has instead intensified the divide between the developing and developed polities; and subject Africa into a new deeper form of colonization through policy initiatives like Enhanced Structural adjustment Facilities (ESAF); Highly Indebted Poor Country (HIPC); G8 Plan of Action for Africa (G8PAA); the Poverty Reduction Strategy Papers (PRSPs); The Comprehensive Development Framework (CDF); the Millennium Development Goals (MDGs); and the Sustainable Development Goals (SDGs) all with the hidden agenda of keeping Africa where it belong as a "Chop Farm" the developed countries. To keep the military industrial complex in constant rotation, the slogan and ideological orientation had to be developed, *"war on terror"* led by the USA created the avenue for African leaders to destroy the lowly but rising strides of a new democratic governance on the continent; empowered 'sit-tight dictatorial regimes to enforce the governance by bayonet" in order to remain in power for entirety. African countries instead of increasing their budget on human capacity and infrastructure development, rather and substantially increased its defence budget for silence any form of protest requesting for greater improvement on the democratic governance structure. In a way, the end of the Cold War" produced conditionality's for the "destruction of democratic governance and management system that could improve the status of the quality livelihood of the population. One would have expected the new conditionality's to strengthen, deepen and enhanced the embracement of multi-party democracy; the adopting of the strict practice of the principles of accountability, transparency and the rule of law, which constitute the core of "good governance" (Olukoshi 1998)

While African countries were struggling to meet the suggested 'new conditionality's, socio-economic-politico conditions of the people only worsened and even encounter productive reduction. Was the Blair Commission a new strategic device to hide the failures of the West; to buy time, hoping to hit the balance to favour to continue and strengthen their grip on Africa? Was the Blair Commission to destroy the Africa Union /NEPAD like the structural Adjustment Programme was put in place to counteract the Lagos Plan of Action (LAP) the most articulate ambitious development policy paper ever articulated on the continent at the time? Adebayo Olukoshi (2006:45-50) is right to have joined hands with other critics of the "Blair Report or Commission for Africa, 2005" with seven-point arguments; which I call the *'seven deadly sins committed against Africa'*: -

- *Why was it deemed imperative creating the commission in the first place when African governments had adopted NEPAD and were seeking to unit themselves behind it;*
- *Was it a deliberate decision so conspicuously to exclude the African Union, which politically is by far the most credible organ of the collective will of the Africa people and which, on all the issues covered by the Commission, has had a clear point of view developed?*
- *It is really possible to change the fortunes of Africa from externally-driven initiatives such as those represented by the Commission;*
- *Of what use is the pleas for an increase in aid flows to Africa if no commensurate effort is made fundamentally to reform ad system itself?*
- *Would not a lot be gained by increasing not just African access to Western markets, but equally importantly, also improving the terms of trade for African agricultural exports;*
- *In all matters pertaining to the development of Africa within an environment of peace, security, and stability, had not the time come to stop chasing shadows (such as those associated with the omnibus notion of 'conflict, 'resources' flows) and refocus attention on fundamental issues that speak to the structural roots of the problems addressed by the Commission, issues such as the hole sale re-invention of the state beyond the watch-dog role that is too frequently attributed to it, the thorny issue of citizenship, and the urgent need for a workable macro-economic and macro-social policy environment that will promote domestic accumulation?*

- *The recognition by the Commission of the central place of higher education in the development prospects of all countries represented a welcome re-statement of a position that was obvious to all except the World Bank which strove in the 1980s and 1990s bot to undermine African higher education. (The position of the World Bank was that Africa did not need higher education but to invest in primary and vocational education – so that they could continue their exploitation spree of sending experts to Africa).*

It is interesting to note that a commission is always established by Western powers when Africa initiates comprehensive and progressive policy strategies that should alter their status from a developing into a developed polity. It would be interesting to see what the West has in its selves as counter measures against for the growth of the Africa Free Trade Area, the biggest economic trade area in the world. Second, how African leaders will react- positively or negatively to measures that restrain their economic advancement and improved quality livelihood? That would constitute an interest topic of and for research. It is time Africa leaders should put on their 'thinking cap' and reflect on some of the fundamental initiatives taken like the Lagos Plan of Action (LAP); The African Alternative Framework to Structural adjustment Programme for Social-Economic Recovery and Transformation (AF-SAP) and the African Charter for Popular participation in development. These policy documents were articulated in the light of Africa's perceived necessities for the improvement of the continent, but often thwarted by the West in order to attain its hidden agenda. African scholars, Adebayo Adedeji, (1983, 1990, Mkandawire & Soludo 1999) and others have been critiques of West policies towards the continent.

African leaders fail to not that their crisis problems cannot be fully grasped unless it is situated and addressed in its proper historical context. It is time for the people of the continent to focus on the changing perceptions of public management in Africa. Effective management requires purpose and direction. These are the issue to be addressed and needing the urgent attention of the people of Africa issues that touch the conscience of the developed world not to remain aloof to the plight of Africa, which Europe has contributed to set motion, but remaining silent in finding workable solutions. The Lagos Plan of Action (LPA) adopted by a Special Meeting of African Heads of States, continue to preoccupy the ECA in 1980s; and even through it stress self-reliance, it was still moulded largely in what government should do. The controversy between the ECA/OAU, on the one hand, and the World Bank on the other, limited the ability of the ECA and African governments to fully embrace the orientation that had spontaneously taken place in African Society (Hyden, 1995:80-1). The two bodies fail to realize the fact that the objective of development around which consensus should coalesce is responsible well-being by and for all. When it comes to policies and practice, less agreement can be expected. What ought to be done, and how it should be done, is sensitive to conditions. Any tentative outline of consensus here is more open to challenge, and more likely to shift and vary. The goal of and for development should be responsible and sustainable well-being for all. Sustainable responsible well-being entails an overarching and intertwined range of activities, requiring massive shift in priorities and thinking taking place – from things and infrastructure to people and capabilities These include – well-being, livelihood, capability, equity and sustainability.

To begin with, (i) the objective of development is the well-being for all. And well-being simply entails good quality of life. Well-being, and its opposite ill-being (which the continent is cloth with), differ from wealth and poverty Well-being and ill-being are words with equivalents in many languages; (ii) livelihood security is basic to well-being; and livelihood can be defined as adequate stocks and flows of food and cash to meet basic needs and to support well-being; (iii) capabilities are means to livelihood and well-being; and refers to what people are capable of doing and being –the means to livelihood and fulfilment; and their enlargement through learning, practice, training, and education are means to better living and well-being; (iv) equity is fundamental and this regard, the poor, weak, vulnerable and exploited should be given pride of priority by putting the last (i.e. weak and vulnerable) first and the first last (i.e., rich and well-to-do); this requires a good, conditions and change must be sustainable – economically, socially, political, institutionally, and environmentally (Chamber, 1997:10-11). Thus, a holistic approach is required to ensure all policies and actions, with sustainable well-being and sustainable livelihoods as objectives for present and future generations.

Africans are on the move towards the mountain of hope and development. The Diaspora remains an important part of the African continent. They have to be treated with care and encouragement, not to forget their biblical cord back home. Christina Atekmangoh (2018) like others probing into the role and usefulness of the Diaspora, in a book on transitional migration (familiarly called 'bush falling') and remittance flows to Cameroon. With the current dire economic state, Cameroonians increasingly aspire to travel abroad to make a living. There is the notion of the moral economy, transnational remittances….

remittances are understood to be a composite of financial, material, and cultural flows – maintaining and transforming social and kinship ties." The Diaspora have an obligation to 'Mother Africa,' just as 'Mother Africa' has responsibilities to the Diaspora by creating an enabling environment for their home coming to Mother Africa. Give them a voice; encourage them to return home; tape into their knowledge skills. Show that they not forgotten; it is not an issue of the prodigal son. It is a question of how the Diaspora can drive change and driving change as noted by Gibbon (2014) takes us the basic law of physics – how the application of a relatively smaller lever can shift weight, create movement and initiate change far in excess of its size. How we can use the Diaspora to achieve remarkable change.

The era of the Ku Klux Klan is over; the Apartheid era is over: Slavery era is gone. The era of segregation, social injustice and discrimination should be placed on hold, tried and judged by a rising era of social justice, good governance and focused-humanity - thereby bringing back the denied rising expectations and the promises of quality livelihood during the pre-independence era. That is why the potentials of the Diasporas must be adequately exploited to beef the human capital skills of the continent to meeting its challenges; and in taking advantage of the current economic 6% or more growth rate; and solidify its economic and technical skills foundation in the rapidly expanding global knowledge economic development of the 21st century and beyond. Can the emerging Black South in the United States be transferred to new Diasporas in an emerging Renaissance Africa of the 21st century?

Yes, it can and is done to restore the lost hope and give vitality to the people to prepare for a brighter and better future. But the drive and incentive for building this incredible new African world - or town - around us is not just indulgent or artistic. It will not come on a platter of gold. It will come through hard work, prorating setting and the determined will to succeed. There is also an element of self-interest and self-preservation driving transition, the 'stick' to the beautiful vision's 'carrot.' Africa's economic tycoons at home and abroad (Ibrahim Mo Foundation, the rising Black Economic Empowerment (BEE) middle class in South Africa - the Cyril Amphora, Mzi Khumalo, Tokyo Sexwale etc. the Nigerian millionaires etc. etc. should be mobilised to see the usefulness of developing Africa for Africa's competitiveness in the global economy of our time. Facts and figures about Black Europe show that 70% of Black Europeans live in just seven nations, England, France, The Netherlands, Germany, Italy, Spain and Portugal with the following breakdown, Table 1. Facts and Figures About Black Europe; and the impact of globalisation, where blacks are penetrating in the European countries; they gradually making imprints in other European countries as well as East Asian region. Is Africa on the road to colonise Europe? Will this change the entire dynamics of power relationship in the world? Answers to these plethora of questions can only be provided by futurologists.

Table 1 Facts and Figures about Black Europe

Country	Population	Blacks
England	60,975,000	1,785,000
France	62,106,000	2,500,000 - 5,000,000
The Netherlands	16,405,400	500,000
Germany	82,218,000	350-500,000
Italy	59,619,000	243.000
Spain	46,158,000	228,000
Portugal	10,618,000	148.000
Ireland (Dublin)		30,000*

Source: Stephen Small. The Empire Strikes Back. (See also African Courier (2011, no.80, vol.14. p26)

* Dublin (Ireland) some 30,000 Africans have settled in the country within the past decade, making it the fastest growing Black community in Europe

A further breakdown shows that Blacks in Germany, the foundation of today's black community dates back to the 1890s, when many Africans were brought from the continent to be trained for future service in the administration of the then German colonies - Togo, Cameroon and Southwest Africa (today's Namibia) and Tanzania. Although many of these predominantly male African immigrants returned home, many others remained, married German women and formed families. Other immigrants of African origin, mainly artists and students, from England and the United States, joined this group. After the World War 1, Africans served in the French forces that were stationed in Rhineland and many married local women and had children. In the 1960s, when most African countries became independent, Africans came to Germany mainly to study or receive training for the postcolonial development efforts of their countries. Another form of immigration emerged as Africa's political upheavals of the 1970s, and the economic downturns and wars of the 1980s and 1990s, forced many young people in flee their homelands to seek a better life elsewhere. Many came to Germany to seek political asylum either as a temporary safe haven or a chance to resettle.

Today, the community of people of African descent in Germany is made of Africans, Afro-Germans (offspring of German-African parentage and Africans who grew up or were born in Germany), African-Americans, Caribbean Blacks, and lately French and British citizens of African origin, who as European Union nationals have come to live and work in Germany. The immigrant population of Greece - largely Black Africa - increased from 2% to 7% in one decade. In Ireland, some 30,000 Africans have settled within the past decade. An area near Parnell Square in Dublin has been dubbed *"Little Africa"* (See Stephen Small and African Courier 2011). The main destination in 2005/2006 for some selected African countries included the following; see Table 2 Main Destination for African Women in Europe 2005/2006.

The growing number of Africans in Europe has not been hitch-free, facing numerous challenges like the Blacks in America. However, according to Muammar Mubarak (2011) "...There is very high tolerance for racism and discrimination here. Many of us have succeeded and there are growing numbers, but not without difficulties. A number of children of the African Diasporas are organising to return to Africa through investments. Is the future there, in Africa?" The decision by the AU to create Africa's six regions is a welcome move and the necessary enabling environment should be created to incorporate the willingness of Diasporas returning home. African countries are faced with the challenges of creating growth and jobs for their rapidly increasing youth populations, while simultaneously have to import skilled workers for specific industries such as oil, gas, mining, telecommunication and much more. The economies of many African countries are facing labour and skills shortages, even in the face of entrenched unemployment and underemployment. The growing mismatch between skills and labour market needs in the coming decades constitute a serious uphill task for these countries which must be addressed now to reap the benefits of demographic dividend and its expanding economic growth (Lee and Mason, 2006).

Table 2 Main Destination for African Women in Europe 2005/06

Population 15+		Total	Recent Emigrants	Women	High Education	15-21	Total
Country	Thousands						
	1000	%	%	%	%	%	%
Cameroon							
FRANCE	58.8	53.0	27.8	58.4	35.9	19.7	33.1
USA	25.1	22.6	41.0	49.7	58.2	16.6	11.1
Italy	4.3	3.8	47.9	45.5	26.1	-	2.1
Gambia							
Spain	19.5	44.7	19.9	33.0	-	15.0	5.8
USA	9.6	21.8	17.6	41.1	31.8	17.2	5.6
Sweden	2.8	6.4	25.0	40.9	12.8	18.0	2.6
France	1 6	3.6	16.2	43.9	8.5	7.6	1.0
Ghana							
USA	97.5	39.2	27.4	43.5	41.9	14.0	62.3
UK	75.1	30.1	29.6	48.3	46.6	12.1	53.3
Italy	27.4	11.0	22.3	45.2	-	16.7	16.4
Canada	18.6	7.5	17.4	49.4	48.3	20.1	15.8
Belgium	6.0	2.4	-	-	-	-	2.5
France	5.3	2.1	17.0	52.3	15.1	17.7	4.2
Netherlands	4.6	1.8	56.1	-	-	-	-
Austria	3.2	1.3	-	-	-	-	-
Australia	2.5	1.0	28.2	45.9	44.1	19.3	1.7
Switzerland	2.3	0.9	-	-	-	-	1.5

Kenya							
UK	118.8	51.5	6.0	50.3	41.2	5.4	125.5
USA	69.3	30.0	33.0	49.4	51.1	18 .4	37.5
Canada	21.4	9.3	13.5	67.7	61.6	11.3	19.1
Australia	8.1	3.5	31.0	48.8	59.9	15.4	6.1
Malawi							
UK	17.8	78.8	-	53.3	51.7	11.7	
USA	2.8	12.1	14.3	42.5	50.7	17.5	1.7
Austria	0.6	2.7	31.7	51.1	64.4	14.4	0.3
Canada	0.5	2.2	19.5	51.5	75.2	14.9	0.4

Source: OCED I-Library (2012 Connecting with Emigrants. A Global Profile of Diaspora - Africa, 05-1 2012.

In 2010 people's ages 15 to 34 accounted for 43% of all international migrants in the less developed economies, compared to 29.1% in the developed countries. In mid-2011, the top 10 countries with the youngest population were in Africa. The young growing African population is also increasingly mobile - searching for job opportunities across national borders. As such Africans are the most mobile in the world - their mobility has to do with conventional reasons such as labour, or trade, marriage, education, pilgrimage and status, among others. Poles of economic growth such as Botswana, Cote d'Ivoire, Gabon, Ghana Libya and South Africa continue to attract large number of migrant workers. Emigration to OECD countries (and new destinations like China, Argentina and the Gulf countries) has also increased steadily during the last decades. Much of this migration is irregular and unregulated (Olsen 2012). With Sub-Saharan African economies built on the informal sector and the increasingly educated and increasingly mobile youth mainly unemployed or underemployed, the conclusion points in the direction of 'stand-alone policies based on country-led development growth for capturing the demographic dividend have slim if any chances of success.

Therefore, a holistic and comprehensive human development approach, backed by regional skills pooling based on mobility and flexibility should be developed in order to ensure a match between supply and demand in the changing labour dynamics and to ensure sustainability in the economic growth of the continent. Educating the human capital and creating jobs are the greatest challenges facing the continent. The potential of diasporas as source of economic and social development in origin countries and whether diasporas could help foster development depends on their characteristics such as size, composition, skills and degree of concentration but also on the degree of integration into the destination countries and the economic, political and social environment in origin countries. Governments of origin and destinations can indeed facilitate the improvement of diasporas by supporting networks, by facilitating communication with the country of origin, by creating an enabling environment, or work directly - by easing skill mobility and use. In this regard, the capacity to characterise profile of Diasporas is instrumental.

Intra-regional mobility in the African labour market dynamic is crucial for understanding the role of labour market integration; it is rarely understudied; yet crucial for the economic take-off and growth of the continent; At the same time, there is an increasing youth unemployment on the continent leader to increased outflow of young Africans in search of jobs in the developed economies. A human capital development approach and human resources pooling services as an investment, increasing productivity and competitiveness is imperative if the continent has to maintain and improve on its current economic growth. The cankerworm of corruption must be eradicated. Eradicating corruption and bad governance are the required steps to eliminating poverty and improving the wellbeing of citizens. Critically and categorically, African leadership almost everywhere has failed to mobilise and utilize its vast human and other available resources for the greatest good of the greatest number. Without any hesitation, the continent's backwardness and poverty is perpetuated by the bankruptcy of its leadership. A kind of leadership that has created and continues to perpetuate a shameful situation in which the continent presently excels as a refugee and forgotten entity. Every country in the world is rich and poor; it is what you make of your richness and poverty that determines the status and quality livelihood of the people.

Briefly stated, the poverty and backwardness of Africa are the direct result of wrong priorities and policies nexus of the leaders and governing elites. Africa nations are not, therefore, poor because there are naturally poor, nor because their citizens are lazy. Unfortunately, we have been brainwashed to believing in our state of poverty. We have graciously accepted the label status of poverty, primitive, backwardness accorded us. And as if our cup of sorrow was ordained to flow, the continent has also acquired the dubious honour of being a morally decadent continent, thanks to the very nature of its leaders since independence. Corruption as the epic climate of our activities has aggravated the issue of nepotism, personal aggrandizement, brotherisation, tribalism, favouritism, inequality, injustice, discrimination, and thousands of other prescriptions of the same social evils and ills that constitute 'Dark Clouds over Africa' and what are making up the African Problem. And the African problem is nothing short of issues related to depravity, or addressing it differently, the devaluation of public morality whose main pillars forever are honesty, integrity, justice, trustworthiness and diligence. Dark Clouds over Africa has much to do with *'corruption, dictatorship and economic mismanagement.'* These ills challenge every African to turn over-a-new leaf, by embracing justice, ethical and moral values, equality, honesty, integrity, diligence, competence. The most serious setback is the 419-corruption virus that has eaten extremely deep into the body politics and fabric of the society. We need a new mind-set of critically two well-known contrasting paradigms, which are the *'top-down'* blueprint and *'bottom-up'* learning process approaches to development. A progressive Afro-centric policy vision will push forward the *'bottom-up'* development process in contrast to the Euro-centric agenda that purports the *'top-down'* or *'centre-periphery'* approach. This can be illustrated by advancing the following:

Centre-periphery	**Afro-centric**
Things-Oriented	*People-focused*
Top-down	*Bottom-up*
Blueprint	*Learning process*
Measurement	*Judgment*
Standardization	*Diversity*
Underdevelopment	**Development**

This table shows that development theory and practice are in constant flux; the speed with which the key concepts come and go and fashions flourish and fade confuses alarms and breeds cynicism. In the 1990s other concepts like: accountability, civil society, entitlement, governance, human rights, livelihood, ownership, participation, people-centred development, stakeholder, sustainability, transparency, well-being play key roles in fostering quality livelihood for all. The coming new coming Africa presents challenges as noted by Havel 1992: "it is not that we should simply seek new and better ways for managing society, the economy and the world. The point is that we should fundamentally change how we behave." The views expressed here are challenges directed to uppers, to the powerful, to the structures of power. It is to upend the normal, to stand convention on its head, to put people before things, and lowers before uppers. Imbalance is needed to establish balance. The personal, professional and institutional changes implied entail reversals of much that prevails as normal.

We leave in a world of unequal exchange and exploitation of the weak nations by the stronger ones through the gospel of capitalism. Capitalism was from the beginning an affair of the world-economy and not of nation-states. Whatever, the case, the tendency of the capitalist mode of production to become worldwide is manifested not only through the constitution of a group of national economies forming a complex and hierarchical structure, including an imperialist pole and a dominated one, and not only through the antagonistic relations that develop between the different 'national economies' and different states, but also through the constant 'transcending' of 'national limits' by big capital. That capital constitutes the 'wealth the nation' eloquently discussed by Adam Smith. The world economy is characterised by large disparities in wealth both among and within nations. The misery of underdevelopment that exists in Africa, Asia and Latin America contrast with the affluence of North America and Europe, where waste is abundant and where many people suffer from the problems associated with overdevelopment. In Africa, the new governing elites now make it their duty to transfer that waste in Europe into their respective countries though the acts of corruption. In short, the governing elites in Africa are acting worse than their departed colonial masters.

Today, many people live in conditions of abject poverty, their lives dominated by hunger, disease, illiteracy and absence of hope. Cameroon (with the five-year crisis and politics of genocide in Southern Cameroons) presents a very good example of people leaving in fear, insecurity and with no hope for a better tomorrow. South African abolished apartheid but a new global apartheid has emerged.

Advocating for a progressive Afro-centric developmental approach should be the way for negotiating the future for the millions of the power who have been betrayed by their leaders. A well-articulated and implemented progressive Afro-centric manifesto sends strong messages to the Euro-centric entrenched agenda that it is the beginning to the end. The down trotted need to wake-up. This calls for acts of defiance or civil disobedience not through the deployment of arms, but peaceful resistance. More than half-a-century of the independence of African countries should have been devoted to development and of putting the last first. Rather, it has and continues using large amounts of monies in buying weapons of human destruction. Many years of independence has been years of destruction, spending billions cast away instead of uplifting the quality of the livelihood of the people. What the progressive Afro-centric manifestoes should begin by the diversities and narratives that underscore three cardinal points; (i) system-maintaining approaches; (ii) system-reforming approaches; and (iii) system-transforming approaches. What is emphasized here, however, is the issue of a new mid-set that attitudes toward change with respect to the depth and extent of national, and continental are the essence of a new world endeavour. Africa is obliged to keep its house clean, take its responsibilities and stop the current globe-trotting with a begging cap in hand. Our African proverb tells us that borrowed water cannot fill the bath. Our living is determined not so much by what live brings to you as by the attitude you bring to life; not so much by what happens to you as by the way your mind looks at what happens.

Corruption Nexus - A Cancer to Development

> *"Inequality is not just killing those with less political voice. It is also killing the planet. This makes the strategy of privileging profits over people not just unjust but monumentally stupide. Economics will not 'grow,' and markets will not deliver 'prosperity' to any one, no matter how powerful, on a dead planet." (Jeyat Ghosh, 17 January 2022)*

Corruption like bad governance remains the continent's greatest enemy spreading its tap roots deeper and deeper into the marrow of society. One can but agree with the German based organisation (GTZ) that it's hard for most of us to imagine living in a country where corruption and violence are present on a daily basis and public life becomes paralysed by crisis. It such contexts, the human right to education is often violated. But these may also be the contexts where education is needed the most. Education is known to have a large potential for resolving conflicts, consolidating peace, and preventing future crises. On the other hand, in countries affected by crisis's, education can have served negative impacts and may increase conflict, e.g., if it is for ethnic political propaganda or increases social inequalities.

Corruption remains the greatest cancer in the developmental construct of the continent. It is clear that a thief acts alone, but a corrupt person always needs a partner. And they are increasing number of partners in this flourishing trade. Come to think of the Internet scammers, or the custom officers, taxation officers and others who extort monies from individuals and the state to enrich them. The state official who instead using the budget for the activities assigned for diverts the amount into his private account. It takes two to tango. Corruption kills and murders Africans every day. And we need to deal with it as a form of murder. When funds for hospital or water project are diverted to the private purse of some corrupt individual how many people die from preventable diseases? The biggest untapped resource is not in the ground. It is the people, but this future is stolen because of the injustice of this world. Why we take serious issues with African based corruption. We must overstate that it is very easy, and sometimes a trick to hide massive bleeding of African resources. When we challenge corruption, we must understand the hideous forms in which it takes. In the words of Martin Luther King Jr., "ultimately a genuine leader is not a searcher for consensus, but moulders of consensus." Leaders that are more concern with wealth acquisition as opposed to development receive support from the capitalist and industrial military complex in bleeding their citizens to death.

Following Transparency International (TI) (2009) corruption creates hatred among people. In African countries corruption has become cancerous which is destroying the economy and life of the peoples and by this creating hatred shires and distrust in government institutions. Only five out of 180 countries in Transparency International survey 2009 could be classified as clean as many as 19 countries are highly corrupted an another 100 are almost corrupted at every sector (TI 2009). Against this background, people are becoming conscious and creating hatred spheres which are helping the rulers of those countries to be aware of the scenario and making anti-corruption policies to combat corruptions which are a positive sign (Forje 2004). The ruling elites in Africa should not take advantage of the fact corruption is world-wide and that "recent scandals involved British MP's expenses, charges of nepotism, worries over lobbying companies, and the access of interest groups to MPs; prominent cases of corruption such as match fixing in snooker, spot fixing in cricket, cheating in rugby, and irregular payments associated with the transfer of football players have made the UK public see sports as the second most corrupt sector in the country" (Boating 2012:34-35) is a prelude for them to plunder their citizens to death

Which is the way forward? The one determination the continent mutt have is to make the system and its institutions function appropriately: and also, to make Africans protect their rights. Only education, discipline and good leaders with responsible citizenry can salvage the African predicament. Therefore, proactive leadership is needed to drive Africa's reputation and competitiveness. Eradicating the state of corruption entails educating the people and looking forward. The continent has to focus on developing, improving and sustaining the democratic process. It is imperative in this process not to repeat the mistakes of the past. Importantly, to get African leaders restrain from addiction to power - the sit-tight presidents - who want to remain in power forever. With good governments the continent can move mountains. In short, the Africa of tomorrow needs answers that last and in the overall good of the people. "Financial crisis has brought into stark relief the price of complacency about corruption in Europe and the failure to prevent, detect, and sanction against legal and illegal forms of corruption"

Because corruption is a worldwide phenomenon, it does not imply Africans should carry the corruption flag of the world. For many in Europe, corruption is assumed to exist only in other countries, particularly in places such as Africa. Recent surveys have shown that corruption is also a "major problem" in Europe, and there is a strong correlation between corruption and the ongoing financial crisis in the Euro-Zone. Even in countries with a high raking status on the TI corruption index like Sweden, corruption within the education system among students had been on the increase over the decade. Following the Swedish Daily Newspaper (Dagens Nyheter, 8th December 2012:1,8and 9) cheating and other examinations fraud among university students has increased and those doing distance studies ..." i takt med att tiotusentals nu plugger på distans eller gör hemtentor; via nätet ökar möjlighteerna att fuska drastiskt genomgåang visar att metodorna - som oftast går ut på att anlita 'spoksrivare' - blir fler och mere refineries. DN har talat med en man som via nätet erbjuder sig att skriva uppsatser for 150 kroner per sida, minst godkänt utlovas (Jällhage & Kärrman

2012:8-9). Students who have been found plagiering or undertaking some orthodox activities at the country's institutions of higher learning include the following:

Year	Number
2001	68
2002	75
2003	112
2004	215
2005	261
2006	294
2007	269
2008	302
2009	303
2010	406
2011	517

Source: Dagens Nyheter, Stockholm - Sweden, pp8-9

The number of students undertaking their studies by distance education has increased in the last decade, from 26 000 to about 90 000 in the year academic year 2010/11. According to the University Commission statistic, at least every five students are undertaking his/her education through distance education. About one third of the 143 000 students, are combining distance education and camp studier." This should not be a thing to propagate within the educations system for Africa to copy. We can also in a way correlate corruption in Africa with poverty and exclusion. There are many lessons for Africa to draw the views expressed by Boateng (op cit.26-32). For Africa where corruption has become endemic in most countries, there is a high price to pay for failing to combat corruption - as shown in Greece, Italy, Spain and Portugal. No matter how strong a nation's economic and political foundation, corruption, or the failure to fight it, can bring dire consequences. Africa's state of underdevelopment has much to do with corruption; it impacts on the structure-functioning of good governance and the rule of law. Throughout the continent we can depict at least four (4) fundamental inhibitors of governance and rule of law, namely;

- Corruption in society, (government) and the immunity of its Chief Executive;
- The undemocratic nature and structure of the institutions, especially those conducting elections
- Structural deficits in the system of the dispensation of justice;
- The corrupt nature of the education, legal and security establishment.

The corrupt nature of our education institutions especially, higher education breeds many uncomfortable situations in the country and hen these institutions are corrupt, the society can never develop or make significant progress in the direction of sustainable quality livelihood for all. The constitution of African states has beautiful clauses for the fight against corruption, but they never executed through the acts or existence of a corrupt judicial system. These institutions are not independent; here is he gross absence of justice and the rule of law. Because a government exist does not entail there is the presence of good government and the fact that there is the existence of a rule of law, and does not mean that the laws are good. Good governance cannot be achieved with a government structure to cater for the welfare and happiness of few people; and the rule of law will be a mirage where the state serves only the interests of the rich, the privileged, the powerful and advantaged at the expense or detriment of the poor, the deprived, the ignored, the cheated and the oppressed, socially, politically or economically (Anaywonye, 2019:247).

Disturbingly, across the continent, "public procurement is a corruption hotspot. Public procurement has long been considered the government activity most vulnerable to waste, fraud and corruption due to its complexity, the size of the financial flows it generates, and the close interaction it entails between the public and the private sectors" according to Transparency International. The continent needs many whistleblowers in exposing corruption, wrongdoing, and mismanagement in both public and private sectors. But these whistleblowers need protection. Transparency International, emphasis again; "protecting those who have the courage to speak up and according to their conscience and contribute to a vibrant democratic culture. It is an instrument whose usefulness is being increasingly recognised across the globe."

Good Governance and Leadership

Development is an ongoing process and we must continue to ask the right questions and search for the right solutions as well as make the right choices and right action procedures to overcome contemporary predicaments to better more forward. Therefore, dialogue and mutual understanding between the implicit partners - Africa and Europe - is imperative for both sides and humanity. Serious political will and actions are required to ensure the proper convergence path for the good of all. It is necessary, therefore, to integrate in an intuitive and not very abstract way, theoretical and empirical literature and practices that should guide emerging economies to overcome their current underdevelopment challenges. The development paradigm ball is in the court of emerging economies (Africa in particular). Even though the developed economies need from these emerging economies the raw materials much require for their growth and sustainability as well as ensure endurable quality livelihood for their citizens.

Good governance is at the heart of the effective and dynamic development in any society or organisation and is crucial in ensuring transparency and ultimately greater stability and sustainability. It is also the cornerstone of effective policy-making, particularly at a time when scarce resources call for greater efficiency, creativity and accountability with a government's policy mechanism. Yedder Omar (2011:66) notes that most leaders who brought the continent to independence were not the people to establish Africa as democracies. They were good with independence but should not have stayed much longer. When they stay much longer as has happened in the majority of cases, things go wrong in a very big way Of course true as this may be, have the younger leaders fared any better?

Leadership plays an equally important role in governance. Just as in the case of inequality, poverty is both of intrinsic and function significance. Clearly good leadership is major deficiency in the developmental paradigm of the continent. It is clear that good leadership is essential in piloting the continent out of its current predicament. Most people would say that the removal of poverty is a fundamental goal in economic development. Hence, the characteristics of the poor and the appropriate measures of poverty are important considerations in policies that must be sharply targeted towards the poor. Therefore, the issue of leadership in giving a sense of direction and having the vision of what society needs the most is paramount in the transformation of the continent. Leadership is not only intrinsic; it has enormous implications for the way in which the entire society functions. Some of these functional implications are discussed throughout the book and linked with governance and leadership. Keep away greed, there is justice, peace and development. We share and live peacefully as one unit even with diversity, we sow. Just as the discussion of poverty is tied up with inequality so also is injustice with greed. At the heart of all discourses on leadership, governance, poverty etc. is the notion of 'interests' and 'access' to goods or services, a critical threshold in the transformation of society, or, more generally, access to goods and services below which individuals are declared to be poor. The continent is in a catch-twenty-two situation beaconing for change. And that change is to build effective systems in their capacity to govern, which in turn, hopefully, should help to reduce poverty and corruption through improved governance. Therefore, Africa's destiny lies in Africa's hands. For now, Africa remains a scar on the conscience of the world, which should not be an excuse for African leaders to continue bleeding their people to death: and no responsible leader can turn their back on Africa. There is an urgent need in rebranding Africa, with new leadership. Embracing the idea that there exist vast opportunities open to the continent but that the people must do all they can to promote the ideological strategic approach of Africa-centric narrative. The continent needs strong governments and strong oppositions. That it is vital and imperative as well as desirable for the countries to create a situation of bipolarity, with a strong and unified opposition that can play its role of providing checks and balances, and curbing the high degree of inefficiency and poor governance.

The truth is that the Libyan situation greatly exposed the vulnerability of Africa in so far as resolving its problems and resisting Western or external interventions and exploitation of the continent's resources are concerned. Seen within these perspectives, Africa will never scale up to the challenges of the 21st century and to the great needs of its people. Therefore, good governance, development and progress, and use of new technologies provide an opportunity for Africa to brave existing predicaments as well as prepare for unseen challenges. However, we must note that new technologies are only a tool. Innovation will not come from there. Human capital development and good leaders provides the gateway to transforming the society. In respect of education, at least six values *(humility, integrity, passion, excellence, diversity and compassion)* must be implanted in the mental psychic of the people. A good example cold e seen with the dignity of Joseph Murambe (Rothmyer, 2019) who in 1966 after serving as Kenya's

Foreign Minister and Vice President resigned from the government on grounds and conclusion that "the country had made a wrong turn away from a concern for the poor and ideals he believed in, telling friends he could no longer "be part of corruption in this country." Durrani (2018) echoes the mistake of turn as the brings to the front "pillars of resistance to British colonization – peoples resistance, the others being Mau, Mau and radical trade union movement, party together and showing several aspects of peoples' resistance to colonialism and imperialism – before and after independence, and this includes resistance by nationalists, students and workers facing enumerable difficulties to achieve their goal."

Political leadership and the quest for independence created a state of high rising expectations which could not be fulfilled in the post-colonial period. Here leadership seems to be the hidden factor among others perpetuating failure. It is evident that poor leadership lowers subsequent processes of transformation. In addition, the people inflict poverty on themselves. Here we also see the correlation between leadership and poverty: or poverty connection between inequality and growth. And poverty with self-inflicting factors. There is evidence that inequality lowers growth and fans hostility and underdevelopment. High inequality creates a political demand for distribution and sustainable transformation of society. Just as the rich get richer, the elite get more westernised and the poor, who constitute 90% of the population get poorer and more desperate seeing serious decline in their living standards and jobs prospects disappear. The trouble with Africa, which is quite disturbing, is the continent being monopolised by a few thousand ruling elites and their external partners; while the majority of the people are suffering and living a state of constant uncertainty. The continent needs agents of change - education, good leadership and responsible citizenship.

Africa's cultural heritage anchors a sustainable future. Culture is dynamic and not static but adapting to the changing times and space without losing its fundamental values. Undergoing transition from a resource-based society to a knowledge-based energy society calls for determination, vision, courage, taking the right decisions and movements now. With education and enlightenment come power, change, development, progress, sustainability and quality livelihood. With ignorance, society is buried in the annals of exploitation and perpetual underdevelopment. This is not what the continent needs. The continent must work hard to attain these new values of developmental and management thoughts for it to progress. The tension between self-articulate interests and human-centred models of development and management must be addressed now and in favour of people-focused development activities incorporating new lines of thinking, research and disciplines - strategy, leadership, good governance, knowledge management to list but a few - in the body politics of the continent. Africans must thus be shepherded from the unsavoury aspects of colonialism and centralised hegemonic ethnic governance system. They should also tread on the path of a pro-active conscious and sustained development. The eyes of the people should be open to the true nature of imperialism and centralised ethnic hegemony governance system. The concerns of Africa in the 21st century is more than colonial freedom. The need for reconstituting our mindset is primordial in the series of changes the continent and people should undergo.

The political, social and economic problems shaping the continent's situation - the prospects of sovereignty and control over natural resources - has emblazed themselves on the dependency situation as a whole; for colonised peoples thought the world are confronting the dangerous politics of European imperialism which is now being expanded to include Chinese dominance. China's penetration into Africa is little more than a façade designed to hide its intension and to spite Europe. But both are the same birds, same colours though with a difference, with more nefarious intentions to exploit and keep the continent as the supplier of resources and consumers of foreign products. Africa is the loser if it does not stand up. It is time to "Lift up the Torch of United Africa" (Fanon) and a call to the people of Africa to reject an international community dominated by the colonial powers of the West. The truth is that Africa's situation is indicative of a general pattern of exploitation and coercion of the weak by the strong and is extended throughout the continent by the ruling elites, or agents of the developed countries to ensure control over the continent's resources, especially oil, copper, uranium among other precious materials. The hypocrisy of the developed countries is evident. It is hidden under the global relationship that promises bringing Africa into the 'modern word' through the process of the 3Cs - *Commerce, Christianisation and Civilisation.* Even in the wake of this purported progress after the so-called granting of independence to the colonies, Europe's colonial powers maintain its superiority through 'the systematic use of violence, exploitation and racism. Come to think of events in Libya of recent and in the Democratic Republic of Congo in the past and present. Or the case of Ivory Coast, the conspiracy between the UN, and France against the Ivorian struggles for sovereignty. The silence of the UN in the struggle or he self-determination of the people of Southern Cameroons, a problem created by the UN and the failure of UK Government, backed by the success of France in pushing forward its politics and policies of assimilation and annexation; and the acceptance of the centre-periphery dominance y he people under the tutelage of French dominance.

In the face of such oppression, Africans bear the responsibility to respond to this aggression by vigilantly acting to obtain their freedom. This can only be done through empowering themselves with the weapons of education, determination and visionary leadership including all other available means. The African people have no future in a community that sees their struggles for quality livelihood as everything from 'naïve' to 'illegitimate.' The continent requires proactive positive action. What is required now is taking concrete steps to mitigate the severity of the situation the continent is facing. Failure to begin with addressing urgent social, economic and political concerns and clean-up the country will only exacerbate and unnecessarily prolong the African sufferings. Demonstrable political will is required from national governments and continental organisations - the African Union, NEPAD - to implement proactive Afro-centric policy strategies. There are endless opportunities for the continent to kick-start its development upsurge to uplift the people from the squalors of underdevelopment. Resilience is needed to achieve freedom, development and progress. No matter how high the price for freedom and development and how long it might take to achieve, it is possible to achieve to it as long as the will is there. All the continent need is to set out in a new direction and where the people leave the tragedy of underdevelopment and exploitation behind and work together for a better future regardless of ethnic origin and diversity, political differences and religious orientation, warming up the past is of no use to anyone, but looking forward for the common good is what matters.

African governments must more than ever before be bold and committed to the sustainable transformation efforts. This requires embarking on an ambitious science and technology development programme aimed at contributing to the well-being and improved quality of live for the African citizens. In this regard, the African Union Conference of Ministers in charge of Science and Technology (AMCOST) must push forward-looking policies that secure the continent's competitive advantage and leverage on the continent's capabilities by focusing on research and development to respond to the challenges and needs. Seen within this perspective, NEPAD should do likewise as an innovative way to exploit and utilise Africa's existing scientific excellence, promote greater participation and involvement of the continent's scientists, researchers and institutions in implemented Africa's Science and Technology Consolidated Plan of Action (CAP). It is vital that governance be differentiated from management that reputation risk, innovation and competitiveness are balanced correctly and that oversight of effective academic governance be improved including the setting of standards. Under a modern and effective governance model, the education system must justify its value before the country. It is this accountability role that gives the university/education system their added value. But such changes represent a huge challenge for policy-makers in Africa.

Challenges and Responses

There is to my mind a further justification for a proper diagnosis for the continent's development challenges and why the continent must take actions now to address existing predicaments. Again, the point must be made; development does not fall from policy-makers heaven. The people must work hard for it; make the right choices and ensure implementation. The challenges to developmental environment should provoke a comprehensive and quick response from the political establishment, policy-makers, civil society, the research community and the various stakeholders. The challenges and responses come nearly always from the environment and from using technologies, but more often from shifting political and social forces. Development is a social activity. Policies must be directed in that direction - the wellbeing of citizens. How society is managed is a direct reflection of the social forces which are brought to bear on the rulers. The political climate is changing rapidly at both the national and global levels. The trend in recent decades towards more participatory and people-oriented and democratic governance reflects very strong the 'end of the past' and the prevailing world-view that democracy provides the best and highest form of governance and best way for attaining sustainable quality livelihood for the citizens. Therefore, adopting an Afro-centric approach provides the best possible option for the continent. The continent should look back to the developmental path of China, South Korea, and the rest of the Asian countries and draw invaluable lessons. These lessons should be fashioned according to the vision and purpose of development in partnership with all the forces in the society.

The contribution or lack of resources and the tempting offers from abroad to researchers is part of the explanation for universities' problems in Africa. The fact that many university staff take on extracurricular teaching assignments at other - usually private institutions to supplement their incomes, also contribute to the weakening of the academic core in universities in Africa. Positive developments point in the direction of centralising of an AU proposed research Council based on the model of the European Research Council. This is a noble idea if only corruption is rooted out of the system with good governance as the key role criteria for awarding research grants. For now, the great concern is about the 'brain drain phenomenon' from Africa, which has for decades been losing academics and professionals - up to 20.000 annually following a World Bank Report. Hence strengthening African universities could be one way of stemming the loss of academics that leave in search of better working conditions and wages. Many African countries have an economic growth rate of more than 5%, implying many more jobs requiring academic training than before. In addition, the discovery of rich petroleum and other mineral resources position African countries on the verge of major income revenues. How should they use these incomes? They are two possible options.

They can choose to go the way that oil-rich Angola and Nigeria have done and focus solely on the extraction of oil and gas. But these countries are characterised by great inequality and lack of development outside the oil economy. Or they can choose a different path, broader development strategy in which research and higher education played a major role. In short follow the Norwegian example. Countries like Ghana and Mozambique for example, their situation offers an opportunity to aim at a comprehensive development plan which is not only rooted in the oil sector, but looking at development from a holistic perspective. In 2016, commercial-scale oil production will begin in Uganda. But with only a quarter of all of its children in secondary school, how can more of the people, especially girls, benefit from its new wealth? How have the people of Cameroon benefit from its oil-wealth when for example, the education system is in shambles - poor infrastructure, over-crowded class rooms, poor university infrastructure, inadequate teaching staff to name but a few of the ills plaguing the education and other sectors. Countries with the new-found oil riches should draw examples from best practices from various parts of the world to evade being victims of poorly utilised revenues coming from the resource's potentials of the country.

Importantly, it is for African countries themselves, their leaders, politicians, policy-makers, and other stakeholders including university authorities and researchers to make those development choices. Africa must avoid as much as possible, move away from replicating the typical scenarios where the developed economies dictate to countries and universities in Africa how to develop. This should not be the goal and path of development cooperation in the 21st century (see Rönning 2012). Corruption as pointed out is cancerous to the development path of the continent. Poverty should be eradicated. Exclusion should be arrested. Ethnic diversity is both a curse and a blessing. It should be made a blessing to accelerate the transformation process of the continent. The role of governments should not be underestimated, nor should government bypass the people in the governance system. However, a government is organised, a democracy, autocracy, monarchy, republic or hybrid of any of these, it will find that there are interests it must satisfy if it is to achieve its objectives, as well as its wishes to satisfy for reasons of friendship, political affiliation, philosophical direction, return of favours received or some other reason.

Accountable government has eluded the politics of African government. The logomachies of these governments are weak making the people to leave in perpetual poverty, fear, underdevelopment and uncertainty. In countries with elected or failure to reconcile the 'must' with and 'want' will lead, eventually, to electoral defeat. If changing the government through an electoral defeat of change through an election the government through an election is impossible, other means will be used and history suggests that they will eventually succeed (Legge & Hindle 2004:220) The potential for economic growth in Africa is undoubtedly immense but issues that need to be guarded against and appropriately addressed as political instability and necessary on the one hand and poverty corruption on the other. The politico-entrepreneurial nexus as a way for restructuring the way forward is what the continent should bang on. The politico-entrepreneurial nexus may after-all be good for Africa's countless resources, spatial material and human make it a great destination and land of 21st century opportunity. Africa holds the future, and the future of the world is Africa. Africa is the emerging lion. This should be good news for Africans. How to make good use of the emerging Lion, elephant or crocodile is the question only to be answered by the people and their leaders?

However, we should bear in mind that the current economic changes in selected African countries do not necessarily reflect every citizen is better off. But that is even true everywhere even in the powerful economies, USA, Japan, Europe etc. The important thing is to see the day when all human beings have equally opportunities for prosperity and quality livelihood free of fear and uncertainties. Sadly, under the current monetary economic system, there is no way this planet's resources can sustain yet another consumer society at the levels and methods western countries now employ. "Policies should reflect on issues that helps improve the livelihood of citizens, through knowing and learning existing social structures, including gender relations, the problem of social elites and advantages of utilising already existing systems of labour training" (Utas 2012). The emerging economies of East Asia and the Chinese example provide a golden opportunity for African countries rethinking the fundamental issues about their socio-economic development. This is the time for African to change; for the 'dead hands' of destruction are hitting hard on the doors of the continent, preventing the take-off of democracy governance. "The destruction of Africa's hard-won democracy remains pitiless, despite powerful popular resistance. By rising up, arms in hand, against an externally backed regime of corrupt and self-serving leaders, the people sought to uphold the egalitarian and developmentalist ideals of independence together with the political legacy" of progressive African nationalist leaders (Nzogola-Ntalaja, Georges, 2007)

Africa as an emerging market implies interesting news for the people. Why? As we have seen across much of Asia, economic growth has accomplished what decades of wellbeing development efforts failed to do, lifting hundreds of thousands out of poverty. If this happens to Africa which is likely to occur, the world would be transformed. "The case of Africa as the world's new economic tiger is made in the Fastest Billion - The Story Behind Africa's Economic Revolution," a data-packed collection of essays to be published at the end of the month and brought together under the aegis of Renaissance capital and investment firm with Russian roots and global ambitions." Presently the United States faces a fiscal cliff and political gridlock. Europe is tenuously poised between years of painfully slow growth and outright collapse, and even China would slowly be facing a decline. Africa is on a tear. "It is the only region in the world where growth is accelerating. Keeping aside South Africa, the rest of the region is actually growing very rapidly. In this case, Africa is following the path to economic development that has been trod in recent decades by countries like Brazil, China and India - only in Africa the transformation is happening even faster," (Freeland 2012).

To begin with, let us look at where Asia was in the early 1970s, where it is today. Placing development in Africa within the context of African countries, the region will go on for the next 30 years keeping aside imposed destructive activities of the west in respect of promoting conflicts in the continent. Keeping that aside. Africa has and will be making progress or remaking itself. For example, Kenya has halved infant mortality in five years which took India 25 years to achieve. Africa's place in the world will be utterly changed. By 2020 it is believed Nigeria will be the most populous country in the world and the African economy will be bigger than that of the United States and Europe combined. Who says the "African Lions" are not on the move to structural changes leading sustainable development? The progress and potential of African economies are there; and it is left for the people to make the best use of the current improving situation and ensuring that the momentum for continuous development is not lost.

Conclusions:

The Coming New African Hour

Judging from the views presented, and based on development within the new European construct - from Berlin to Brussels, and given the new rising tides of Africa, will Europe continue undermining African development or will it be a veritable partner to ensure that Africa's progress adds to its own development? The future of the continent takes centre stage in the development agenda of Europe like in the 1884. The balkanization of Africa by 13 European countries has moved to 27 countries - The European Union (EU) in Brussels. The current ambitions under the Economic Partnership Agreements (EPAs) are providing a new colonial strategic approach to the recolonisation of the continent.

"If the EPA is meant to develop Africa, it needs to be owned by Africans Currently, even in countries that have signed or initiated the document, there is little or no public discussion by the private sector, parliaments and civil societies. One hopes that if that if EPAs are to be domesticated, it will not be the kind of charade of rent crowd consultations that were designed to rubber stamp the poverty Reduction Strategy Papers (PRSPs). We now know better and must therefore o better" (Soludo, 20112:17). Kwame Nkrumah understood it and challenged the global capitalist system. "The real nature of American and British imperialism but, more importantly, he was prepared to confront it in Africa. And the British and Americans were also prepared to use all means at their disposal to block or even eliminate Kwame Nkrumah. For them, the stability of the global capitalist system was at stake, and they would fight tooth, nail and claw to protect it. And in doing this, they swore, as they have continued to do, that they would never allow any model of a successful alternative to neo-colonial dependency to take root or British" (Adam Nasser Gamal 2011).

Africa should avoid getting itself into a state of economic apartheid. Apartheid was ended in 1994. Unfortunately, a new economic apartheid is in the making. Pilger (2012) is categorical on this as he notes; "This economic apartheid is now replicated across the world as poor countries comply with the demands of western "interests" as opposed to their own. The arrival of China as a contender for the resources of Africa, though without the economic and military threat of the US, has provided further excuse for US military expansion and the possibility of world war, as demonstrated by Barrack Obama's recent arms and military budget of USA 737 billion dollars. The first African-American president of the land of slavery presides over a perpetual war economy, mass unemployment and abandoned civil liberties; a system that has no objection to black or brown people as long as they serve the right class. Those who do not comply are likely to be incarcerated," To a large extent "Clouds on the Horizon" puts pressure on all of us for real change. It is our duty to get involved irrespective of outstanding in society, lobby at all levels, public officials, parliamentarians, politicians, religious leaders and governments to get start thinking in terms of a people-oriented development agenda. No contribution in the direction of creating awareness and influencing people towards a *PEOPLE-ORIENTED DEVELOPMENTAL APPROACH FOR THE CONTINENT IS SMALL*. Little drops of water form a mighty ocean we are told. The essential thing is to start from somewhere. It is a journey of hundreds of thousands of kilometres. Essentially, the first step must be taken here and now without which we can never arrive at the destination. A house is not built in a day. The planning and the foundation must begin properly to get the structure elected.

Together we can make a difference; we can change the situation by finding constructive and comprehensive solutions for the common good and help build a safer, more secure future. Our differences and diversities should not be a barrier, but an asset in creating a continent for many people with different priorities but shared-values. Whether in addressing local, national, continental or global challenges, we have to be focused passionately on the humankind, about many different issues and how to seek endurable solutions to them. It is the idea of humanity that binds us together and our core values, such as national, international cooperation, share-values, share sustainability and prosperity, the rule of law, democratic accountability, and good citizenship creating an environment of ethnic and religious tolerance, fundamental fairness provides the best way forward for a sustainable planet. It is hoped that Dark Clouds on the Horizons like other publications provides some of the tools for positive action on issues affecting our presence and existence on planet earth. Development as a collective-action problem and addressing the real *CHALLENGES OF AFRICAN GOVERNANCE AND DEVELOPMENT* should take pride of place in our thoughts and actions. Collective action and working together is vital. Working together and the process of collective action problems is an approach concerning the particular conditions that lead to the under-provision of public goods of collective benefits, including many of the preconditions for successive development. Such goods are non-excludable; those who do not contribute to their production cannot be excluded from their benefits. There is, therefore, a free-rider problem that weakens the motivation to contribute. It is, however, pertinent as well as crucial for all to contribute and be part of change process. Now is the time for change – AU Agenda 2063 should begin here and now with the full participation of Africans a home and abroad.

Small-scale communities often have institutions that prevent the distribution of open-`access resources. Modern states do provide goods to some extent, even in the poorest countries. However, in Africa collective action problems remain widespread and re at the heart of the challenge of development. They exist at all levels, affecting the choice of presidents, bureaucrats and business communities as well as those of civic actors and peasant households. They are often subject to ameliorative action - but not if they are approached in a 'best practice' mode or using a principal-agent conceptual framework that assumes away the principle of challenge (Ostrom (2005)

Viewing people-oriented development as a multi-layered collective action problem offers a clearer way forward. Still, it poses further challenges to the way development is seen and the modalities delivered. The book tackles some of these issues of development in its own way and in line with the wishes and aspirations of the people. The principal-framework takes reform into safe and relatively generic territory - the wellbeing of the people, and what they should do. Addressing collective action problems is more challenging because such problems are specific to each situation and generic remedies will not work (Olson, 1962). What is needed is a detailed knowledge not only of the actors and settings involved, but also of its extent to which solutions may need to be practical hybrid institutions that borrow from local cultural repertoires. Ministers, parliaments and voting publics at both ends of the development assistance relationship need to be convinced that development progress is about overcoming institutional blockages, usually underpinned by collective action problems (Booth 2012). Undoubtedly, getting engaged in these kinds of ways are difficult for actors that are not thoroughly embedded in the relevant situations.

African leadership currently trapped in the ideological vortex of ethnicity and ethno-nationalism, and allured by corruption, Estacada-generating overseas tours and a consumption driven economy should start rethinking their development strategy. "The times cry out for the leaders to guide the people safely in a world where, without vision, more people and (institutions) will perish in more different ways than have ever perished before" (Akani, 2012). African leaders must painstakingly overhaul the educational edifice and governance structure in line with the needs and demands of their people 's development and global changes. The current governance structure fails to give the people the opportunity to impact on the socioeconomic transformation of the society. It inhibits opportunities for active participatory involvement and ownership. Participation and ownership require the reconfiguration of the existing structures of theory and a proactive Afro-centric approach to facilitate efficient utilisation of resources and ensure sustainable standards of local delivery of the global vision. The organic edification approach - an approach that builds on the people's ways of doing things own their development; and exhibit consciousness that has been a veritable instrument in socio-economic strides paving the way for quality livelihood.

By and large, in spite of the difficulties being encountered by the continent, the Dark Clouds hovering over this part of the globe, also has a new positive cloud over the continent, so Africa can see the 'Blue Sky' or a better tomorrow. Sindjoun (2010) writes; "What is at stake is not to be pessimistic or optimistic about Africa. The epistemological challenges are to understand what is going on. By focusing on converging African realities, on issues of the state, civil society, gender and development strategies, the authors of the book show under which conditions the African hour is coming. At that level, the commitment for political science meets the commitment for Africa," The Coming Hour which is showing the blue sky, is a period for serious and meaningful 'post-independence and post-conflict reconstruction and development era that requires a progressive Afro-centric implemented agenda. The coming new Africa should create a healthy and equitable society for us all. The African hour should be one of *"Free at Last," "Free and United"* to serve the oppressed people of Africa with the help of God so that everyone enjoys eternity! It is a matter of deep regret that in the face of the new onslaught against Africa's independence and sovereignty, there are few Africans available to take on the intellectual proponents of the neo-imperial scholars imbued with a critical mindset and commitment to the agenda of a progressive Afro-centric ideological orientation and implementation action plan. The new coming African hour should be one on which we reflect on the people's journey on emancipation in search of African self-understanding and transformation. On the other hand, the new coming hour should also lead us to celebrating the contribution of African people in their struggle for identity, self-knowledge, self-control and self-emancipation. The struggle in the field of knowledge as the real weapon or sovereignty and independence will continue until Arica and humanity are fully emancipated from the remnants of Eurocentrcism and westerns intellectual dominance which people like Kwame Nkrumah, Steve Biko, Nelson Mandela, Nyerere, Frantz Fanon, Claude Ake, Archie Mafeje, Mazrui Ali, and many others fought so much; and of which, many are still fighting for to ensure the genuine emancipation of the African people and the continent from the hands of the developed polities.

Where Do We Go from Here?

Where do we go from here - that is the question? Africa stands at a cross-road. The emerging powers footprint is evident in a renewal of academic discourse and scholarship on African politics. This extends even beyond the reaction of theory and epistemology and donor foundation as well as civil society groups on and beyond the continent is preoccupied with how to respond to the rise of emerging actors. Are we heading to the sanctuary or the mortuary? That is the question hanging on the Dark Clouds over the continent

- How are African countries reacting to the rise and penetration of new colonial powers to the continent?
- How should the behaviour of these new colonising powers be interpreted?

- Whether the rise of the emerging powers constitutes an opportunity for or a threat to the future of Africa's development?
- To what extent is the antipathy and xenophobia attitude towards emerging powers and potentially vis-à-vis other actors is a reflection of competition among the petty bourgeoisie and the society?
- How sustainable is the role of these emerging powers in Africa?

It must be recognised that Africa's traditional relationships with the developed north are being challenged by the competing interests from the South, most notably, China, India, Brazil, the Gulf States and economies in South East Asia including South Korea and Malaysia. How this shift should be interpreted has become the subject of intense speculation as it has also given rise to a belief that the continent is in the middle of a "Second Scramble." The debate of a 'second scramble' is only part of the discourse. It is anchored by ideological dispositions that define the way the scholarship is presented. Can one identify the new actors as the "new imperial powers" to perpetuate and solidify Africa's underdevelopment status?

On the other hand, we can question who is benefiting from the new marriage with the new colonising powers and how? How the interests of Africa's ruling classes are being strengthened by their relationships with these new Southern actors? To what extent are the interests of the new actors being enhanced? And what are the consequences for the rest of use especially the currently marginalised population of African society? How does the ruling class define their "national interests," that of their citizens and that of the new powers or actors? To what extent is or how sustainable is the role of these emerging powers in Africa? Are these new bodies working in the interest of Africa or their own interests? In going forward, we are construed to return to the degree of how the new relations with these new actors should be conceptualised? Is Africa developing any countervailing strategies towards mitigating the hidden destructive agenda of these new imperial powers? How prepared is Africa in receiving their new august guest - which could either be any enemy or a friend? It is important for Africa to build a set of development strategies on how to receive their newfound friends or enemies. Here the universities play a vital role of critical objective debate, educating and informing society of the pros and cons of the visitors. Society needs to be sensitised and integrated in a broad-based approach - interrogate in order to understand and disaggregate the short-term, medium-term and long-term consequences of their engagement with Africa. We need to know how the new entrants into the continent's socio-economic-politico landscape would help to create a just, stable and equitable Africa society. What master plan and where does Africa fit (see Southall & Melber eds. 2008).

For now it can be stated that the new entrants to Africa adopt a conservative approach with liberal undertone and character, seeing their role as building an environment of peace in Africa through economic development; they have come to align their involvement in peacekeeping activities with their overall development cooperation strategy fine-tuned in which poverty eradication, socioeconomic governance and boosting infrastructure that improves market access are identified as key contributions to a stable and profitable region (Kuo 2012). One can but agree with the statement, "as Africans we must think with our hearts, but also with our heads in order to bring back the confidence and the candle spirit we had in the 1960s. If we can get that right, as one billion people with a common destiny, we will be bigger than China" (Leauther Frannie 2012:24). This takes us back to the key issue of human capital development, here the issues are clear as noted by Juma Calestus (2012:29); "Africa's educational systems have so far paid little attention to training in engineering fields and related business knowledge. His short fall is likely to be filled by finding new ways to tapping into the Africa's Diasporas."

Seen within this context, African engineering students and scientists must learn how to produce weapons for development and not weapons for human destruction. An issue taken up further by Archbishop Desmond Tutu (2012:26): "how can we continue to spend billions on instruments of death and destruction when a small part of that could ensure children everywhere have clean water? Young people are our hopes," for the future, we are today destroying their lives to satisfy our ego. In Cameroon, for example, government is acting in a way of radicalising the youths towards destructive frustration. What is the government doing to solve the Anglophone crisis? The Government by believing in a military rather than a socio-political approach, it sends the wrong message to the people and youths; propelling them to adopting a more destructive and hateful attitude towards government; destroys their sense of belonging, kills patriotism. Government fails in doing the right things of building and putting trust, hope and patriotism on the doorsteps of the people. Briefly stated, current policies are not geared towards building trust, confidence, justice and a sustainable polity; rather, we are working consciously towards the destruction of the polity.

In Cameroon, for example, government is acting in a way of radicalizing the youths towards frustration and destruction. The measures adopted in solving the Anglophone crisis is inappropriate and only pushes people towards the acts of disintegration. By believing in a military solution, this sends the wrong signal or message to the youths. Patriotism and nationalism are killed and the youths adopt a more destructive and hateful attitude towards government; it destroys their sense of belonging. Government fails in doing the right things of putting people first, building trust, confidence and hope in the people. Patriotism is not placed on the doorsteps of the people. In short, current policies are not geared towards building a sustainable society, rather, policies are designed consciously or not towards the destruction of the society.

In the same vein Ace writer, Chinua Achebe (2012:31) notes; "The great challenge for Nigeria (Africa*, *my inclusion*) is how to convince 150 Nigerians (*one billion Africans**) to put aside competing interests" and work for the common good of society. Disunity is Africa's greatest deficit. While Europe is work towards the divided continent following World War 1 and 11, the East-West conflict that resulted, Africa still believes in the ethnic-statehood concept fashioned and propagated by the colonial masters and washed down the throats of Africans. We remain a continent without our own identity apart from the international passport colour of being black. Change in mentality and mindset is required to move forward the continent in the right direction. There is need to establish a new socio-political environment. This is the time to do so. The opportunity to establish a new political culture is being threatened by vested interests, partisan politics and ideological polarisation. There is an urgent need for redefining Africa as the emerging of a New African Continent (NAC). A new leadership is necessary. "We are working to promote economic growth whilst optimising environmental integrity. We have decided that we can no longer rely on our oil and forest resources if we are to offer the Gabonese people (Africans, ***my inclusion***) a prosperous sustainable future" (Onidima Bongo Ali 2012:10). Can we imagine the word without Africa? But can African capitalism without a human face propel the continent onto a veritable global economic player? Truly, Africa has the opportunity to play its rightful role in the global arena. How to play that role is the question? But as the President of Malawi, Joyce Banda points out, "it is my view that there is an urgent need in the country

(Africa, my inclusion) to change the way we do things" (Banda 2012:14). Or as Noble Peace Laureate points out, "I believe in the power of African women. We should not wait for the UN resolution to do anything for us" (Gbowee Leymah, 2012:16) laments. As we lament, remember that one thing above all about annexation and assimilation constitute what we can call, divide, destroy and govern which in another way is to "separate development" or living and not eating together, an act which is unforgiveable.

As earlier noted, corruption and poor governance stand in the way of the continent becoming a serious global player (see Highlights - ECA7SRO-CA) which is a tip of the corrupt iceberg on the continent). The war against corruption, bad governance and financial crimes will begin to produce results when the leaders begin to demonstrate the fear of God and place the interests of the people first and theirs last. The wealth you accommodate illegal means you might not live to enjoy (Adeboye Enoch, 2012:26). The goals for the fatality of hope must be sown today. Justice sow's development and good governance ensures and consolidate progress and sustainability for quality livelihood of the people. Though the continent is the world's next great growth engine - hundreds of thousands are at risk of being left behind. Today while Africa's economies are modernising, its rulers too often are still not. They are tied to the aprons of centralised hegemonic authoritarian rule. This explains why the continent has so many long serving presidents in the world. In many countries, corruption and impunity + and the inequality that results - are still routine. "With very few notable exceptions, our leaders are not part of accountable and responsible governments. It is still, if they perform abdominally, so what" notes (Desmond Tutu op cit.).

Above all, the continent's leaders are, by one important measure, less accountable than they were in the past. But young Africans are the ones to shape the future, judging from the Arab Spring, when sclerotic, corrupt regimes that oversee strong overall growth failed to share the gains or greater freedom with a connected and well-educated youth. All these ingredients exist in potentially even more explosive proportions in Africa South of the Sahara. The average Africa is 19, while the average Middle Easterner is in his/her 20s. Foreign aid has cubed up development on the continent; at the same time, hundreds of thousands of Africans are better educated than ever before and many more will soon join the rank and file expecting more rewarding jobs.

By 2016 there will be over one billion cell-phones in use on the continent, giving nearly every African has access to the most powerful and essential tool of the 21st century rebellion. It is a recipe for simultaneously entrepreneurialism and revolution. The youths are taking the change challenge into their hands through the use of ICTs gadgets, following a survey at the Kwame Nkrumah University of Science and Technology (KNUST) Kumasi-Ghana. According to Braw (2012:10), 74% of Africans today have mobile phones compared to 4% some 10 years back. This figure is likely to rise to 85% by 2015 following a survey undertaken by Royce Rands. Nigeria has 93 million mobile phone uses and the number will increase in lips and bonds in the next couple of years. Karrer-Rueedi & True (2012:13) looks at the empowering micro-entrepreneur and small business through mobile phones. Millions of local and entrepreneurs in developing countries are able to expand their multi-scale businesses by overcoming institutional hurdles and infrastructural constraints. Even though there are still many challenges that have to be addressed, existing experiences with mobile phone technologies clearly shows that it is able to add more value to local knowledge and this led to social and economic development.

The use of ICTs gadgets is making strong entry and impact in administrative service delivery, E-governance through internet opens avenues for most governments to deliver services, creating opportunities for government to put in place e-government initiatives and information and communication technologies for the people to further enhance public sector efficiencies and streamline governance system to support sustainable development. Among the e-government leaders, innovative technology solutions have gained special recognition as the means to revitalise lagging economic and social sectors Governments must increasingly begin to rethink in terms of e-government - and e-government - placing greater emphasis on institutional linkage between and among the tiered government structures in a bid to create synergy for inclusive sustainable development. An important aspect of this approach is to widen the scope of e-governance for a transformative role of the government towards cohesive. Coordinated, and integrated processes and institutions through which such sustainable development takes place.

Africa has taken a giant step in the use of mobile phones, far more than more than Europe did. Nearly every street vendor has a mobile phone and makes money out of it. The use of laptops is moving in that direction especially among students. Students now contact various enterprises offering their services to solve problems if any faced by these enterprises. There is truth to the optimism about Africa. But if you do not share the benefits, there is a price to be paid. And it is paid in blood. At the same time, there is a new 'Great Game' being played out in Africa. Yet much of the West ignores this geo-strategic giant. Business increasingly dominates foreign interest in Africa. Investment first outpaced aid in 2006 and doubles it. These new technologies, far from replacing radio in developing regions, are presenting new opportunities for broadcasters and listeners, and are offering a renewed promise to fulfil the vision of radio as a truly two-way medium (Girard 2007: Myers 2011). In the context of Sub-Saharan Africa, the boom in mobile telephony, with Africa being the fastest-growing mobile market in the world (GSMA 2011), has facilitated the rise of radio call-in programmes and the ease with which listeners can now connect directly with broadcasters to give feedback, ask questions and have a say. Satellite techniques enable the transfer of information over fast distances in an instant, and in some cases allow news and information to reach people in a political environment characterised by extreme censorship.

For decades, radio broadcasters have acted as development knowledge brokers, often producing programmes paid for by the international agencies that target key development themes such as health, migration, environmental sustainability and poverty reduction. The convergence of radio and new ICTs opens up opportunities and pathways for broadcastings to act as knowledge intermediaries, transforming knowledge in increasingly horizontal ways and providing access to information exchange. While there is enormous potential for radio broadcasters to harness new technologies to facilitate improved knowledge sharing and brokerage, very little is known about the best ways to achieve this. As a result, there is often a disconnect between technology drivers and the potential beneficiaries in developing countries, and further assessment of the technologists themselves and the social, political and cultural context in which they are embedded is required (Chapman and Slaymaker 2002).

What we see is a convergence between the radio and other ICTs in merging at an ever-increasing rate, all over Africa. Mobile phones, especially, are playing a critical role in the daily experience of Africans today and can even play life-saving roles, as Wallace Choma from the University of Cape Town found when he looked at the xenophobic and elections-related violence in South Africa and Zimbabwe. Another good example comes from Uganda. It was found that by adding automatic SMS (Short Message Service) texting to radio campaigns abut HIC/AIDS prevention, people were more likely to come forward for voluntary counselling and testing than they did as a result of the radio campaign alone. In Ghana, it was fund that there was potential for better-targeted agricultural advice for the rural radio audiences with the addition of Freedom Fine. However, the convergence process is happening slowly and is still subject to the well-documented digital divide. In Burkina Faso and >Benin, only 8 per cent of radio stations streams their audio content on the internet. Comparatively, South Africa is vastly better-equipped in this respect, but even here, it was found that old disparities governed by geography, income and gender still prevail. The urban and commercial radio stations - normally the riches ones - are tending to embrace the internet and other convergent technologies much more than the poorer rural and community-type stations - which therefore reinforces the disparities of access for rural populations and minority language-users.

A common pattern across the continent is that governments are failing to convert growth into jobs. It is believed that 275 million out of a total of African work force of 382 million are either unemployed or in informal day-hire work. By 2020 a youth surge propelled by the world's highest birth-rates, which will raise Africa's population from 1 billion in 2009 to 2 billion in 2050 will add a further 122 million Africans of working age. That will be a boon if they had to work. In the same period, it is calculated that Africa will create just 54 million to 72 million more jobs. If current trends continue, it is going to take Africa until 2066 before employment levels reach those of East Asia. It is a risk. People need opportunities. While the continent is experiencing economic growth, there is also a warning about the incendiary effects of growing inequality. Already there is a serious prevalence of inequality between the rich and poor and between North and South. This divide is a time-bomb. The divide that has opened up the rift between the rich and poor in China helps fuel hundreds of anti-government protests a day. This year the Indian State has faced a tide of anticorruption demonstration. The lessons from these stars of globalisation are the massive social improvements are inevitably massively socially disruptive when corruption blocks growth's gain from being fairly shared, discontent can become explosive. (See Perry Alex 2012: 31-37) Africa is overripe with corruption. It must stop if development is to come the way of the people.

So, the continent with its history of detached elites, the path of prosperity will likely be bumpier. And the looming prospects of 300million jobless young, and the imperative for any African government looking to mitigate the turbulence is clear. The next phase of the continent's development is job creation. What will it take to fill that void? The same thing must be done with the continent's traditional extractive industries which are capital intensive, and more in sectors like tourism and retail areas which employ more labour. The challenges are numerous and have to be tackle simultaneously to make any significant impact of the transformation process. Failure not to act, means missing the wind of progressive change. In the wake of our great mistakes, we find ourselves in serious retrogression, bitterness between our citizens, divisions grows to an alarming height, the economy is pushed into serious decline tango, confidence ebbs away; unemployment issues, insecurity becomes the order of the day, life is unstable; government becomes increasingly insecure and dictatorial and intolerant of any more that points in the direction of constitutional and legal procedures, increasingly violent and suppressive attitude of the security forces – police, military etc.; education is reduced to an instrument of both subtle and aggressive indoctrination.

This is our Africa in the age of globalization; and when Africa should be an epic centre of a great recovery of greatness. Africa is today at the fringes of world society; it is decaying. Sad enough, we continue to praise centralized authoritarian regime structures which is part of the cause and failure of post-independent Africa. And whereby, government is using the "Ku-Klux-Klan" approach to subdue the population. For every step taken in trying to force through a wrong government system on the people, very falsely, so called achievement we try to fashion, is cancelled out by numerous wrong barriers or policies adopted in order to remain in power for ever. In Cameroon, for example, and in light of the Anglophone crisis which government dismissed lightly as two cubes of sugar soon to dissolve in a bucket of water, is now haunting those who wrongly believed that the deployment of military arsenal is the solution to socio-politico-economic problems. The war is five years old today with more than 30,000 lost lives. Over 700,000 children unable to attend school; almost a million as internally displaced persons and refugees in neighbouring countries (Nigeria for example). Five years gone, and there is no end in sight for the Anglophone crisis or war for self-determination and independence. Our governments have failed to stand-up to the times of times, but swimming in the sea of flux, moving from one political, economic, legal miscalculations and illegality to another.

Sub-Saharan Africa with its 54 states and 3000 languages is inevitably a place of diversity and opportunity. It is a continent of entrepreneurs that must be awakened. Where does Africa get its spirit of enterprise when and if you are constantly scratching for a living, you are an entrepreneur. This is what the Africans have failed to exploit. The cultural heritage and indigenous knowledge of the people must be seriously exploited to kick-start a number of development related activities for the transformation of the region. Again, we are back to square one - the development of the human potentials of the people for their development. Rethinking the nexus of institutional structures and social innovations for the sustainable development of the continent is what should occupy the minds and visions of leaders, policy-makers and academics. Human capital development should be the new medication for Africa's state construct. With good human capital development, the emerging continent should be bursting in its new freedom and sovereignty; that should throw into the dust-bin centuries of serf-dominance. We should through AU Agenda 2063, national development plans this century, Africa's age of the dawn of her fulfilment of the hopes, expectations and desires of the people –free at last, Africa is free from scourges of poverty, misery, oppression, injustice, exclusion and marginalisation.

The world's emerging economic powerhouse, with their own experience of the shades and tones of transition find it easier to digest Africa's simultaneous potential and pitfalls. China has taken the lead. Two-way trades with Africa - often in infrastructure for resources swaps that have given the continent an infrastructure basis make over that runs from roads, ports and railways to airports, hospitals and dams - hit USA166 billion dollars in 2011. Also, in pursuit of the continent's oil and gas, coal, timbers, minerals and farmland are India, Brazil, Malaysia, Turkey and the Gulf States. Here is the new great game being played on the continent - leading to the second scramble of Africa (Perry 2012 31-37). This is Africa's moment to reconstitute, reconstruct, restructure, regain and re-own its development path, and sovereignty. Now is the time that Africans must sent out the clarion call to the world that the continent is no longer for sale? The region must begin on a new platform, the energy to harness and enhance the peoples' capacity to create new jobs, build new education institutions, centres of excellence for healthcare of the people, build alliances within and across borders to repair damages and meet threats of different structures and magnitude. It is a long road ahead, but together the continent will get to the Promised Land - sustainable quality livelihood for the citizens and by the citizens. The continent's false start should remain part of history but also as signpost for constructing the future. The long-term search and goal of the continent should be peace, security and development and that this destiny is shared by all citizens as new dawn of African leadership beacons with all brightness and the true strength of the continent remains its people and wealth and the enduring search for democracy, liberty, justice opportunity and equality.

The continent's post-independence leaders continue holing on State-led import substitution industrialisation as the key to rapid economic growth (UNECA, 2010). Industries so created remain uncompetitive and unsustainable and efforts to spur industrial development largely vanished with the economic crisis of the 1980s and 1990s. This can be attributed to the minimal emphasis placed on science, technology and innovation (STI) in the industries on the continent during the time. The period between 1980 and 2000 is characterised by the implementation of very unpopular policies to liberalise Africa's economies. In particular, was the imposed privatisation and liberalisation policies promoted by the World Bank and IMF under the Structural Adjustment Programme (SAP) which contributed to the collapse of much uncompetitive state-owned enterprise reduction of foreign firms and loss of jobs and revenues in many countries? Although there are some strong and valid arguments that it could have been implemented with a 'human face,' one cannot deny that it is the investment that followed these draconian policies that are now bearing fruits. For example, African exports continued to grow despite a large contraction in 2009 due to the global crisis, as they rebounded by 25% in dollar terms in 2010 outstripping world export growth of 21% (UNECA 2012).

The continent is faced with the impediment to growth. Africa is inching toward integration, towards regional and continental integration. Africa is faced with inadequate infrastructure which limits its economic progress. With such constraints, it cannot successfully compete within the existing global based knowledge economy even though it is a region to man of the essential raw materials being exploited by the developed economies. Focus of attention should be on infrastructure which should be broadened beyond financing crisis to include efforts to improve efficiency and productivity. It is a draconian task which African countries face requiring severe strains needing concrete actions to reignite sustainable growth. African countries must move aggressively to diversify their economies away from dependency on commodity exports. It should be noted that Africa's surge of progress cannot persist with a strong education and health systems. Therefore, with concerted action and courageous leadership backed with a progressive Afro-centric there is a bright possibility for many African countries to continue to make substantial development progress in the coming decades. Now is the time to reset policies to address current challenges and ensure the resumption of the continent's strong rising path for the region to reap its substantial economic potential and provide quality livelihood to the largest possible number of citizens. Responsible well-being for the uppers can be sought through altruism and generosities, putting the last first, and through disempowerment, putting the first last. Too many uppers, disempowerment seems loss; but often all can gain. Disempowerment can liberate uppers from professional prisons and personal stress. Many ways are needed for the powerful to gain from less power. For new behaviour, there is no time to wait. There is a vanguard to join and new high ground to explore.

The book present serious challenges to the 'haves,' to the powerful, to the structures of power. The have-nots are not left out. It is a holistic struggle for the common good. Imbalance is needed to establish balance. In the words of Vaclav Havek, (1992) and who points out "it is not that we should simply seek new and better ways for managing society, the economy and the world." The Progressive Afro-centric manifesto should be a vision for African reconstruction and renewal, the will to structurally and comprehensively walk the talk, as going forward will only come primarily from Africa and African institutions insulated from day to day demands of short-term coping. The outstanding and most relevant question is neither how do we salvage our predicament nor who is to blame? Rather it is crucially important to ask what more? What different? What next? We are all guilty in different ways; just as we should be committed to finding common grounds and solutions to send away the dark clouds over Africa. We have to gun for a new African agenda, of coping, capacitation, co-ordination, co-operation, participation, and equity-sharing for our common good.

Recommendations

- Ensure the practice and prevalence of good governance: the rule of law, social justice and equitable shared-prosperity;
- Human capital development and proper utilisation of such skills, as well as making use of indigenous knowledge;
- Stimulate job creation and employment as increasing youth un-employment is creating a requirement for services and rights related to quality wellbeing of the people
- Serious attention should be paid to the state of existing mismatch between skills and labour market demands, as well

as making use of the potential of the workforce of the continent.

- The empowerment and mobility of women needs to be encouraged as this has immense potential impact on the growth and developmental path of the continent
- Restructuring the education curriculum to meet the needs of the continent's evolving socio-economic challenging goals and competitive role in global development; training people who go out to create jobs and not as job seekers;
- Empower civil society and the media for better objective responsible reporting and citizenship
- Educating Africans to be able to rise to the challenges posed for its development by the accelerated processes of globalisation that the world is caught in;
- The international system responding responsively and positively to the developmental challenges of the continent;
- African voices are calling for change and leaders must respond accordingly to desires and wants of the people in a holistic and constructive pattern.

References

Abiola Irele (192) "The Crisis of Legitimacy in Africa", Dissent (Summer) 1992

Adams A. Nassau (1973). Worlds Apart. The North-South Divide and the International System. Zed Books, United Kingdom.

Adebayo Adedeji (1976) Africa: The Third World and the Search for a New Economic Order. Third World Lectures, Turkeyen, November Georgetown, Guyana,

Adebayo Adedeji (1983) The Evolution of the Monrovia Strategy and the Lagos Plan of Action: A Regional Approach to Economic Decolonisation, Addis Ababa, Ethiopia.

Adebayo Adedeji (1990). The African Alternative: Putting the People First, ECA – Arusha,

Ade Ajayi J. F. (1982) "Expectations of Independence" Daedalus, Vol. 111. No. 2.

Adeboye Enoch (2012) New African, No.523, December 2012, London, p.26

Adei Stephen (2004) The Promise of Leadership: The Chances of Ghana Having the Leadership to Move the Country from Third to First World. Combert Impressions, Accra, Ghana.

African Courier (2011) "European Blacks - Facts and Figures about Black Europe, No. 80. Vol.14, June/July 2011. (www.theafricancourier.de)

African Development Bank Group (2007). Selected Statistics on African Countries. (www.afdb.org/en/…/Selected-Statistics-On-African-countries/ (accessed 20 September 2010)

Adam Nasser Gamal (2012) "Independent Africa - 50 Years On. Why Kwame Nkrumah Was Overthrown" The African Courier, April/May 2011, p16

Aidoo Akwasi (1993) "Africa: Democracy without Human Rights," Human Rights Quarterly 15, November 1993): 908-9

Akani Christian (2012) "The Effects of Globalisation on Nigerian Education", Global Advanced Research Journal of Social Sciences, Vol. 1 (5), pp092-100, October 2012

Ake, Claude (1989) The Political economy of Crisis and Underdevelopment in Africa. Selected Works of Claude Ake (ed.) JAD Publications, Lagos - Nigeria

Amin Samir (1990) Maldevelopment: Anatomy of Global Failure. United Nations University Press, & Zed Books Ltd. New Jersey, Tokyo, London.

Amin Samir (1976) Unequal Development. Monthly Review Press, USA

Anagwonye C. Ben (ed.) (2009) Greatest Speeches of African Black Leaders. Mindex Publishing Company Limited

Ansari, A. (2002). Best Practices in Open and Distance Learning Systems in India: An Assessment. India Journal of Open Learning 11(2); 247-261

Arkhurst, Frederick S, (ed.) (1974) U.S. Policy toward Africa. Praeger Publishers, New York, USA

Asante Molefi Kete. (2007). The History of Africa: The Quest for Eternal Harmony. Routledge, London

Aseh Nfamewih (2006) Political Philosophies and Nation-building in Cameroon. Unique Printers, Bamenda, Cameroon.

AtKisson Alan (1997) "Why Civil Society Will Save the World" in John Burbidge (ed.) (1997) Beyond Prince and Merchant. Citizen Participation and the Rise of Civil Society. Pact Publications, New York. Pp285-292

Atekmangoh Christina (2018) "Les Mbengis" – Migration, Gender and Family. Transnational Cameroonian Migrants' Remittances. Langaa RPCIG, Cameroon.

Assie-Lumumba T. N'Dri (2006) Higher Education in Africa: Crisis Reform and Transformation. CODERSIA Publication, Dakar - Senegal

Bach, Daniel (1991) "Avant-propos', Etudes Internationales (Numero special Afrique La deconnextion par default. XX11.2. 245-251

Bache Ian & Louise Reardon (2018) The Politics and Policy of Wellbeing. Understanding the Rise and Significance of a New Agenda. Edward Elgar Publishing, Cheltenham, Glos. UK

Barnet Richard (1980) The Lean Years. Simon & Shuster, New York, USA

Biko Steve (1978) I Write What I like. Harper & Row, USA

Biney, Ama. (2011). The Political and Social Thought of Kwame Nkrumah. Palgrave Macmillan.

Beinocker, E., I. Davis and l. Mendonca (2009). "The 10 Trends You Have to Watch", Harvard Business Review 87(7):55-60

Boateng Osel (2012) "Corruption - A Greater Problem in the UK", New African, 46th Year, No.520, August/September 2012, London, pp43-35

Boateng Osel (2012) "How Corrupt is Europe?" New African, 46th Year. No. 520, August/September 2012, London, pp26-32.

Booth David (2012) "Development as a Collective Action Problem: Addressing the Real Challenges of African Governance" Policy Brief 09, Africa Power and Politics, ODI, October 2012, London

Bova Russell (1997). "Democracy and Liberty: The Cultural Connection," Journal of Democracy, January 1997, Vol. 8, No.1, pp-112-126;

Blum William (2003). Killing Hope: US Military and CIA Intervention since World War 11. Zed Books London,

Braw Elisabeth 2012) "Här Är Afrikas Framtid: Appbyggande Ungdom," Metro, 28 October, 2012, Sweden p.3 (www.metro.se)

Callaghy, M. Thomas (1990). "Lost Between State and Market. The Politics of Economic Adjustment in Ghana, Zambia, and Nigeria," in Nelson M. Joan (ed.) Economic Crisis and Policy Choice: The Politics of Adjustment in the Third World. Princeton University Press, New Jersey, pp257-319

Cardoso Henrique Fernando & Faletto (1979) Dependence and Development in Latin America. University of California Press, Berkeley,

Casshman, K. (1997), "Authentic Leadership", Innovative Leader 6(11) November 7.

Centre for Ethical Leadership (2007). Ethical Leadership.

(http://www.ethicalleadership.org/philosophies/ethical-leadership, 7 September 2010)

Chambers Robert (1997) Whose Reality Counts? Putting the First Last. Intermediate Technology Publications, Southampton Row, London, UK

Chapman, R & Slaymaker, T. (2002) ICTs and Urgent Development Reviews of the Literature Current Interventions and Opportunities for Action. London, Overseas development Institute

Chinweizu (1978) The West and the Rest of Us. NOK Publishers.

Chonoko Ibrahim (2012) "Nigeria Students want to Stop Money drain in Higher Education", University World News, African edition, No.00249, 25 November 2012.

Chinweizu (1990) The Anatomy of Female Power

Clark, N. (2010). Emotional Intelligence and Learning in Teams," Journal of Workplace Learning 23(3)125-145

Clapham C. (2006) "Fitting China in" Brenthurst Discussion Papers 8, Johannesburg, Brenthurst Foundation.

Cloete Nico, Peter Maassen and Tracy Barley (eds.) (2014) Knowledge Production and Contradictory Functions in African Higher Education. Africa Minds Publishers, South Africa.

Corera, Gordon (2012). The Art of Betrayal: The secret History of MI6. Weidenfeld and Nicolson, United Kingdom

Davidson Basil (1974) Can Africa Survive, Little Brown & Co., Canada.

Department of Public Service Administration (DPSA) Republic of South Africa, Pretoria.

Dowden Richard () Africa: Altered States, Ordinary Miracles

Durranu Shiraz (2018) Peoples Resistance to Colonialism and Imperialism in Kenya. Vita Books, Kenya

Ely, R.J. and D.A. Thomas (2001). Cultural Diversity at Work. The Effects of Diversity Perspectives on work Group Processws and Outcomes" Administrative Science Quarterly 462:229-273

Enyih Atogho Paul (1999) Politics: A Call to Serve – Essay, EDI'ACTION, November, 1999, Yaoundé –Cameroon

Essoka Peter (2014) "The Irony of Vision 2035", The Guardian Post, No.0601, Friday, May 09, 2014, Yaoundé-Cameroon, p4

Falk Richard, Samuel S. Kim & Saul H. Mendlovitz (eds.) (1992). Toward A Just World Order – Vol.1. Westview Press, Boulder, Colorado, USA

Fanon Franz (1968) The Wretched of the Earth, Grove Press, New York

Fawehinmi Gani (2007) Creating A Sane Society: Impact of Good Governance and the Rule of Law in Anaywonye C. Ben 2009- Great Speeches of African Black Leaders.

[Epicurus as a Build to Contemporary Social Reform. Edward Elgar Publishing, Cheltenham, Glos. U.K.

Forje W: John (2009) Here the People Rule. Political Transition and Challenges for Democratic Consolidation in Africa. Nova Science Publishers Inc, New York, USA

Forje W. John (2002). "The Disappointment of Independence," Future Research Quarterly, Fall 2002, Vol. 18, Number 3, World Future Society, Bethesda, Maryland, USA.

Forje W. John (1979). The Rape of Africa at Vienna - Lund Sweden

Forje W. John (2004) Cameroon Without Corruption. The Search for A New Vision. Niba Publishers, Bamenda, Cameroon (New enlarge edition in press).

Forje W. John (1969) An African Common Market, in New Africa – Africa Trade and Development, Vol. 11, No.3/4. 58 Paddington Street, London ppii-vi

Forje W. John (1982) "The Underdevelopment of the Underdeveloped Regions of the World: Exposing the Politics of Poverty and the Politics of Affluence", Trans African Journal of History, vol. 11,

Forje W. John (Forthcoming) Mainstreaming Gender….

Freeland Chrystia (3012) "Africa: The Next Economic Tiger," 19 October 2012. For further details, see

(http://blog. Reuters.com/chrystia-freeland/2012/10/19Africa-the next-economic-tiger/).

Gale P. Fred (2018) The Political economy of Sustainability. Edward Elgar Publishing Limited, Cheltenham, Gloucestershire, UK

Garsten Christina & Sorbom Adrienne (eds.) (2017) Power, Policy and Profit: Cooperate Engagement in Politics and Governance. Edward Elgar Publishing Limited, Cheltenham, U.K.

Gbowee Leymah (2012) New African, No.523, December, 2012, London. p16

Gegout Catherine (2021). Why Europe Intervenes in Africa: Security, Prestige and he Legacy of Colonialism. Hurst & Company Publishes, UK

Ghosh Jeyat (2022). "Inequality Kills" 17 January, 2022

Gibbon Trish (ed.) (2014). Driving Change: The Story of the South Africa Norway Tertiary Education Development Program, African Minds Publishers, South Africa.

Girard, B. (2007) Empowering Radio, Good Practices in development and Operation of Community Radio: Issues Important to its Effectiveness, Program on Civic Engagement, empowerment and respect for Diversity. Washington DC. World Bank Institute (WBIST)

Glaller, R. & L. Kydd (2003). "Best Practice" in Educational Leadership and Management Can We identify it and Learn from It?" Educational Management Administration & Leadership 31:231-243

Green Herbold Reginald (1995) "Not Farewell but Fare Forward Voyagers: Africa into the 21st Century", in Bade Onimode & Richard Synge (eds.) (1995) Issues in African Development: Essays in Honour of Adebayo Adedeji at 65. Heinemann Books, Nigeria, OLC & African Centre for Development and Strategic Studies (ACDESS) Ijebu-Ode, Nigeria, pp264-303

GSMI (2011) African Mobile Observatory 2011, London: GSM Association

GTZ (2012) "Education and Fragility." Bonn - Germany, 2011.2012

Goransson Bo, Claes Brundenius and Carlos Agulrre-Bastos (eds.) (2016) Innovation Systems for Development. Making Research and Innovation in Developing Countries Matter. Edward Elgar Publishing Limited. Cheltenham, Gloucestershire, UK.

Hammerlstrand Ulf (1994) "Perspectives, Controversies & Dilemma in the Study of African Development", in African Perspectives on Development, James Curry Ltd. London

Harold-Barry David (2018) Beyond Appearance: Reflections on Principles and Practice. Weaver Press, Zimbabwe.

Highlights - ECA/SRO-CA (2012) No.123. La lutte contre la Corruption dans le secteur des pme en RDC, highlights No.123- 30 November 2012

--------- (2012) Les Institutions nationales de lutte contre la corruption dans les pays d'Afrique centrale (B) Highlights No. 122, 30 November 2012

--------- (2012) Les institutions national de lutte contre la corruption en Argue central (A) Highlights, no.121, 15 November 2012

---------- (2012) Instruments region et initiatives au niveau sous regional pours la lute contre la corruption, o. 120, 13 Novembre 2012 (see AAKARA@uneca.org)

Huxley, Julian (1944) One Living in a Revolution. Chatto & Windus, London

Holden Paul & Martin Plaut, Who Rules South Africa's, Jonathan Ball Publishers SA, and Biteback Publishing, UK.

Ichikowitz Ivor (2012) "Modernising Police Makes Economic Sense", New African 46th Year, November 2012, No.522, London, pp 34-35

James, Leslie (2012) George Padmore and Decolonisation from Below: Pan-Africanism, the Cold War and the End of Empire, Palgrave Macmillan Limited, London.

Jegede S. et al (2001) Nigeria's Tertiary Institutions and Human Rights Committee for the Defense of Human Rights (DHR) Lagos, Nigeria

Juma Calestus (2012) New Africa, No.523, December 2012, London, pp29

Junch Leah (2018) Like A Bridge Over Trouble Water. Langaa RPCIG, Cameroon

Jållhage Lenita & Kärrman Jens (2012) "Studentfusket Ökar Kraftigt", Dagens Nyheter, 8 December 2012, Stockholm, Sweden, pp1, 8&9).

Kahn H & A. J. Wiener (1967) The Year 2000. Macmillan Publishers, London

Karreer-Rueedi Emam A. & Trub Dariu (2011) "Empowering Micro-Entrepreneurs and small Businesses Through Mobile Phone in Emerging Markets and Developing Countries" ATDF Journal Vol.8, Issue 3/2 "012 pp 13-18

Kingston William (2017) How Capitalism destroyed itself. Technology displaced by Financial Innovation. Edward Elgar Publishing Limited, Cheltenham Gloucestershire, UK

Kessler, Ronald (2014) Inside the CIA. Pocket Books, New York

Kodama Mitsuru (2018) Sustainable Growth through Strategic Innovation. Driving Congruence in Capabilities. Edward Elgar Publishing Limited, Cheltenham, Gloucestershire, UK

Kornegay A. Francis (ed.) (2020) Africa and the World: Navigating Shifting Geopolitics. Mapungabwe Institute (MISTRA) Publishers, South Africa

Kuo, S. (2012) "Not Looking to Lead", Beijing View of the Crisis between the Two Sudan's", in Wheeler Tom (end) (2012) China and The Two Solutions. SAFERWORLD Briefing, August 2012. (See also http: //www.safeworld.org. uk/downloads/pubdocs/China-South/20 Sudan%20briefing%20 English. PDF)

Langaa Vitorino Patricio (2014) Higher Education in Portuguese Speaking African Countries. African Minds Publishers, South Africa.

Lanyea Philip (2017) Patriotism and Nation Building. Sub-Saharan Publishes, Ghana

Lee Keun (2016) Economic Catch-Up and Technological Leapfrogging. The Path to development and Macroeconomic Stability in Korea. Edward Elgar Publishing Limited, Cheltenham, Gloucestershire, UK

Lee Roland & Mason Andrew (2006) "What is the Demographic Dividend?" Finance and Development, Vol.42, No.3, September 2006, IMF Washington, USA

Legge John & Hindle Kevin (2004) Entrepreneurship. Context, Vision and Planning. Palgrave Macmillan, London

Leauther Frannie (2012) CE= - African Capacity Building Foundation. See New Africa, No.523, December 2012, London, pp24

Lipton Michael (1976). Why Poor Stay Poor. Harvard University Press, Cambridge,

Lucas R.E (1988) "On the Mechanics of Economic Development," Journal of Monetary Economics, 22, 3-42

MacGregor Karen (2012) "Top-Ranked University Goes 'Afropolitan'", World University News, Issue No. 249, 25 November 2012.

Makoni Munyaradzi (2012) "South Africa Minister Urges Debates on African Language Use in Higher Education," University World News, Issue No. 100, 25 November 2012.

Makoni Munyaradzi (2012) "South Africa: Financial Support Further Education and Training Colleges Soars", University World News, Issue 00250, 2 December 2012

Mandela Nelson (1957) A Speech at Oxford on June 14, 1957 and reported in The Times of London 0f 15 June 1957

Mashininga Kudzu (2012) "African Union Task Force Proposes Continental Research Council," University World News, African edition, Issue No.249, 25 November 2012.

Mawere Munyaradzi (2014) Culture, Indigenous Knowledge and Development in Africa. Reviving Interconnections for Sustainable Development. Langaa RPCIG, Cameroon.

Maya Angelou (1986, 2008) All God's Children Need Travelling Shoes, London; Virago Press

Maxwell, J. (2010.). "Servant Leadership Lesson: John C. Maxwell at Chick-Fill-A. Leadercast

Mazrui A. Ali (2005) "A True African of the World" Interview, The African Union (AU) Magazine – The Watchdog of Africa, June 2005-August 2005, Pretoria – South Africa, pp12-19

Mbakwe Tom, (2011) "Women Power. How does it affect African Leadership?" New African, 46th year, No.508, July 2011, London, pp10-20 (www.Africa.com)

Mbeki, T. (1998). "Statement of Deputy-President Thabo Mbeki to the African Renaissance Conference, Johannesburg, 28 September.

Mboya Tom (1963) Freedom and After. London (See Danish Title translated by Preben Hansen – "Afrika frit og hvad sa? Birger Jorgensens bogtrykkeri, Kongens Lyngby -Copenhagen-Denmark

Memmi. (1965) The Colonizer and the Colonized. Orion Publishers, New York, USA

Mentan, Tatah (2017). Africa in the Colonial Ages of Empire. Slavery, Capitalism, Racism, Colonialism, Decolonization, Independence as Recolonisation, and Beyond, Langaa RPCIG, Cameroon.

Mentan, Tatah (2018). The Open Veins of Africa. The Dynamics of Extractive Accumulation by Dispossession in 21st Century Africa. Langaa RPCIG, Cameroon.

Meyers Todd (2017) The Ways We Stretch Toward One Another. Langaa RPCIG, Cameroon

Mhango Nkuzi Nkwazi (2017) Africa's Dependency Syndrome, Langaa RPCIG, Cameroon

Mimiko Abbas Olubansile (2017) To Live with Happiness, Safari Books, Nigeria

Mkandawire Thandika (ed.) (2005) African Intellectuals: Rethinking Policies, Language, Gender and Development. CODESRIA Publication, Dakar – Senegal.

Mkandawire Thandika (2015) Africa: Beyond Recovery. Sub-Saharan Publishers, Ghana

Moore, Barrington, Jr. (1972) Reflections on the Causes of Human Misery. Beacon Press, Boston, USA

Moosa a. Imad (2018) Publish or Perish. Perceived Benefits versus Unintended Consequences. Edward Elgar Publishing Limited, Cheltenham, Glouceshershire.UK

Myers, M. (2011) Voices from Villages: Community Radio in the developing World. Washington DC; Centre for International Media assistance.

Mubarak Muammar Johnson (2011) "France - Are We Really French?" African Courier, June/July 2011, No.80, Vol.14, Germany, pp28-30. (See www.theafricancourier.de)

Munroe Myles (1998). Becoming a Leader: Everyone Can Do it. Bakersfield Pneuma Publishing

Mutanga Savious Shingiriral, Thokozania Simelane and Munyaradzi Mujuru (eds.) (2018). Africa at Crossroads: Future Prospects for Africa after 50 Years of the Organisation of African Unity/African Union. Africa Institute of South Africa, Pretoria, South Africa.

Naidu S. (2011) "The Emerging Powers Dimensions of South Africa's Second Term on the UNSC, in South Africa in the United Nations Security Council 2011-2012. Promoting the Africa Agenda in the Sea of Multiple Identities and Alliances. http://www.safi.org/funded__projects/deliberating-south-african-role-united-nations-security-council-unsc

Ndlovu-Gatshenoi J. Sabelo (2013) Coloniality of Power in Post-Colonial Africa. Myths of Decolonisation. CODESRIA, Dakar-Senegal.

Ngambi Hellicy (2011)." RARE Leadership: An Alternative Leadership Approach for Africa" International Journal of African Renaissance Studies. Vol. 6, Number 1. June 2011, Routledge Taylor & Francis Publishers and UNISA, Pretoria, South Africa, pp6-23

Nhemachera Artwell, Tapiwa Victor Warikandwa and Samuel K. Amoo (eds.) (2018) Social and Legal Theory in the Age of Decoloniality. (Re-)Envisioning Pan-African Jurisprudence in the 21st Century, Langaa RPCIG, Cameroon

Njogu Kimani, Adem Seifudein (eds.) (2017) Critical Perspectives on Culture and Globalization, Twaweza Communications, Kenya

Nkrumah Kwame (1967). Challenge of the Congo: A Case Study of Foreign Pressures in an Independent State

Nkrumah Kwame (1968). Dark Days in Ghana, Panaf Books, London.

Nkrumah Kwame, (1970) Conscientism: Philosophy and Ideology for Decolonisation and Development. Monthly Review Press, New York.

Kwandiwe Merriman Kondlo (ed.) (2014) Perspectives on Thought Leadership for Africa's Renewal. Africa Institute of South Africa, Pretoria – South Africa.

Norman Chad (2022) A Mater of Inclusion. Mwanaka Media and Publishing, Zimbabwe.

Norgaard B. Richard (1991) "Science, Environment and Institutional Change", in Amos Kiriro & Calestous Juma (eds.) (1991). Gaining Ground: Institutional Innovation in Land-use Management in Kenya. ACTS Press, Nairobi=Kenya, pp7-20

North-South Roundtable (1991). The Challenge of Africa in the 1990s. Report of the North-South Roundtable Consultations, New York.

Nsia-Pepra Kofi (2017) "Flawed Democracy: The Bane of Ghana's Success in Curbing Corruption", in Africa and Francophonie, 2nd Quarter 2017, Vol. 8, No.2, pp62-78

Nweke, O. (2010)." The Failure of African Leadership." (http://talkafricagh.wordpress.com)

Nyamnjoh B. Francis (2016) #RhodesMustFall. Nibbling at Resilient – Colonialism in South Africa. Langaa RPCIG

Nwokedi Emeka (1993) "Political Conditionalities: Vectors or Constraints on Development in Sub-Saharan Africa? In Rainer Tetziaff (ed.) (1993) Human Rights and Development. German and International Comments and Documents, EINE Welt, Germany. Pp 161-186

Nzogola-Ntalaja Georges (1987) Revolution and Counter-revolution in Africa: Essays in Contemporary Politics. Institute for Africa Alternative, With Zed Books, London and New Jersey

Nzogola-Ntalaja Georges (2007) The Congo from Leopold to Kabila: A People's History. Zed Books, London

Obama B. (2008) Change We Can Believe In. Conogate, Edinburgh

Odinga Oginga (1967) Not Yet Uhuru – An Autobiography, Heinemann Educational Books Ltd, London, Ibadan, Nairobi, New Delhi

Ogbunwezeh, F. (2006). African Poverty as a Failure of Leadership. (www.glopbalpolitician.com accessed 20 September 2010)

Okafor, E. (2005)." The failure of African Leadership, Cause of Africa's Problems. (http://Africa unchained.blogspot.com)

Onidima Bongo Ali (2012) New African, No.523, December 2012, London, pp10

OECD (2012) Connecting with Emigrants. A Global Profile of Diasporas

Olsen West Sofie Anne (2012) Demographic Window of Opportunity in Africa - And the Role of Migration. Policy Brief, October 2012 Danish Institutive of International Relations (DIIS), Copenhagen - Denmark.

Olukoshi Adebayo (1998) The Elusive Prince of Denmark: Structural Adjustment and the Criss of Governance in Africa. Nordiska Africa Institute, Uppsala – Sweden.

Olukoshi Adebayo (2006) "African Perspectives on the Commission for Africa Report" CODERSIA Bulletin, Nos. 3 & 4, Dark, Senegal, pp45-50.

Osia Kunirum (1987) "Black Africa and the Dilemma of Development", Journal of African studies, Vol. 14. No.7 (summer) 1987

Olson Mancur (1962). The Logic of Collective Action, Harvard University Press, Harvard USA

Olukoshi O. Adebayo and Zeleza Tiyambe (1988) African Universities in the Twenty-First Century. Vol.1 and 2. Codesria, Dakar, Senegal

Ostrom Elinor (2005) Understanding Institutional Diversity. Princeton University Press, USA

Pahad Aziz, Garth le Pere and Miranda Strydom (ed.) (2018). Promoting Progressive African Thought Leadership. Africa Institute of South Africa, Pretoria, South Africa

Padmashree G. et al (2012) "China's Technological Rise: Myths and Lessons of Global Debates on Innovation, Technology Transfer and Intellectual Property," International Centre for Trade and Sustainable Development, June, 2012. (info@ICTSD.ch).

Patrick, I. U. (2011), 186 Quotes for Success. Success Impact Publishing, Benin City, Edo State, Nigeria.

Perry Alex (2012) "Africa Rising" Time Magazine 3rd December 2012, Pp31-37

Petermode, V. F. (2008) "What is Higher Education,"! 0th in the series of Inaugural Lectures of the Delta University, Abraka, Nigeria (see also Akani, op cit. 2012 (http://garj.org/garjss//index.htm.

Pheko Motsoko (2014) "Farewell Madiba! Ut Challenges Remain," New Africa, No.535, January 2014, London, pp28-29

Pilger John (2012) "Apartheid Didn't Die in South Africa. It Inspired a Global Order Upheld by Force," New Statesman, September 21-27 2012, London, p.57

Pokam de Prince Hilaire (2011) "Woman Power Versus Political Power", New African, 45th Year, No.508, July 2011, London, pp26

P0pov Vladimir and Peter Jutkiewicz (eds.) (2017) Mapping a New World Order. The Rest Beyond the West. Edward Elgar Publishing Limited, Cheltenham, Gloss, UK.

Ranelagh, John. (1986). The Agency: The Rise and Decline of the CIA: From Wild Bill Donovan to William Casey. Cambridge Publishing, New York, USA

Rasheed Sadig (1995) "Reversing the Odds in Africa: Towards a New Ethic in Development Co-operation with Africa", in Bade Onimode and Richard Synge (eds.) (1995) Issues in African Development: Essays in Honour of Adebayo Adedji at 65. Heinemann Educational Books Nigeria PLC, & ACDESS, Ijebu-Ode, Nigeria, pp249-263

Rasheed Sadig (1994). Development's Last Frontier, What Prospects – Four Essays on African Development, ICIPE Press, Nairobi - Kenya

Ray Debraj (1998) Development Economics. Princeton University Press, Princeton, New Jersey, USA

Reed, G. (2004), "Toxic Leadership", Military Review (July-August) 67-71)

Reddy, J. (2009). A Conceptual Framework for African Leadership Development.

Rodney Walter (1972) How Europe Underdeveloped Africa, Tanzania Publishing House Limited, Dar es Salaam, Tanzania.

Rothmeyer Joseph (2018) Joseph Murambi. A Legacy of Integrity, Zand Graphics, Kenya

Rousseau, J. J. (2006) Emile, Everyman. Edinburgh

Running Asle (2012) "Stronger Universities Needed to Support Development," University World News - Africa edition, Issue 00249, 26 November 2012. (See also http://forskning. No: www.forsknin.no)

Sambira Jocelyn (2013). "Reconstructive Surgery Brings Hope to Survivors of Genital Cutting. New Advances Can Give Women More Normal Lives," in African Renewal, January 2013, Vol.26. No. 3, United Nations, New York, USA, pp20-21

Sandbrook, Richard (1985) The Politics of Africa's Economic Stagnation, Cambridge University Press, Cambridge

Sandbrook, Richard (1986). "The State and Economic Stagnation in Tropical Africa," World Development: 143, 319-32

Sharawy Helini (2014) Political and Social Thought in Africa, CODESRIA, Dakar-Senegal

Silber Jacques and Wan Guanghua (eds.) (2016) The Asian 'Poverty Miracle'. Impressive Accomplishments or Incomplete Achievements? Edward Elgar Publishing Limited, Cheltenham, Gloss UK

Sindjoun Luc (ed.) (2010) the Coming African Hour: Dialectics of Opportunities and Constraints. African Institute of South Africa, Pretoria.

Small Stephen (). The Empire Strikes Back

Smith Edwin N. (1927). The Golden Stool: Some Aspects of the Conflicts of Culture in Modern Africa, London Edinburgh House Press

Smith-Tchameni Makini (2005) "The Role of Education in Nation Building" African Union (AU) Magazine. The Watchdog of Africa, June 2005-August 2005, Pretoria, South Africa, pp28-30

Soludo Chukwuma (2012) "From Berlin to Brussels: Will Europe Underdeveloped Africa Again?" New African 46th Year, No.516, April 2012, London, pp10-17

Southall, R. & Melber H. (eds.) (2008) A New Scramble for Africa? Imperialism and Development. University of KwaZulu Natal Press, South Africa.

Sorensen George (1993). Democracy and Democratisation, Boulder, Westview

Stedy Chioma Filomina (2012) Women and Leadership in West Africa. Mothering the Nation and Humanising the State. Palgrave, Macmillan Publishers, New York, NY, USA

Swann G.M. Peter (2015) Common Innovation. How WE Create the Wealth of Nations. Edward Elgar Publishing Limited, Cheltenham, Gloucestershire, UK

Syrjala and Haana Mari Leipmaa-Leskinen (2018) Seen Deadly Sins in Consumption. Edward Elgar Publishing, Cheltenham, Gloss UK

Talburt Tony and Traore Moussa (eds.) (2017) Black Resistance and Identity. Sub-Saharan Publishers, Ghana

Tarh, B. N. (1988) "Focus on Rural Development", Cameroon Tribune, January 26, 1988.

Thandika Mkandawire & Charles Soludo (1999) Our Continent, Our Future. CODESRIA, Dakar, Senegal.

The African Courier (2011) "Independent Africa: Fifty Years On. Why Kwame Nkrumah Was Overthrown." The Courier, April/May 2011.

The Eden Newspaper (2021) "CND Toronto Declaration Outlines Way Forward for Southern Cameroons Synergy", Eden No.1234, Tuesday 07 December 2021, Limbe-Cameroon

The Horizon (2021) "Toronto Leadership Retreat; Southern Cameroons Leaders Opt for Multilateral Mediation to Achieve Peace: No. 0653, Thursday, 09 December 2021, Yaounde-Cameroon, pp1, 3, 6-7

The South Commission (1990) The Challenge of the South. Oxford University Press, United Kingdom.

Thunberg Greta (2020). No One is Too Small. Amazon Books,

Transparency International (2009) Corruption Perception Index. Bonn - Germany.

Traoe Moussa and Tony Talburt (2017) Fight for Freedom, Resistance and Identity. Sub-Saharan Publishers, Ghana.

Terreblache Sample (2002). A History of Inequality in South Africa

Tomori Siyanbola (1995) "Evolving a New Development Paradigm for Africa" in Bade Onimode and Richard Synge (eds.) (1995) Issues in African Development: Essays in Honour of Adebayo Adedeji at 65. Heinemann Educational Books, Nigeria PLC & ACDES, Ijebu-Ode, Nigeria, pp239-248

Tutu Desmond (2012) New African no.523, December 2012, London, pp26

United Nations (2001) International Migration and Globalising World. The Role of the Youth Population. Technical Paper 2001/1. Department of Economics and Social Affairs, Population Division, New York, USA

UNECA (2010) A Technology Resurgence. Africa in the Global Flows of Technology. UNECA series on Technology transfer for Africa's development. New York, Geneva, united Nations.

UNECA (2012) Unleashing Africa's Potential as A Pole of Global Growth, Addis Ababa, Ethiopia, United Nations.

UNDP (2012) International Policy Centre for Inclusive Growth (IPC-IG)

Uroh Chris (1998) Africa & The Challenge of Development: Stewart Graphics, Ibadan, Nigeria.

Utas Mats (2012) Urban Youth and Post-Conflict Africa. On Policy Priorities. Policy Notes 2012/4. The Nordic African Institute, Uppsala, Sweden

University World News, (2012) Issue No. 249, 25 November 2012

Vakunta Peter (2006) "The Trouble with Africa", CODESRIA Bulletin, Nos. 3 and 4, Dakar, Senegal. Pp32-34.

Villafaria, Frank (2009). Cold War in the Congo: The Confrontation of Cuban Military Forces, 1960-1967. Transaction Publishers, New Brunswick, New Jersey, USA

Vusi Gumede (2018) Inclusive Development in Africa. Transformation of Global Relations. Africa Institute of South Africa, Pretoria – South Africa.

Were S. Gideon (1981) History, Public Morality and Nation-Building: A Survey of Africa since Independence. University of Nairobi – Kenya.

Williams Aled and Le Billon (eds.) (2017) Corruption, Natural resources and Development. Edward Elgar publishing Limited, Cheltenham, Gloucestershire, UK

Williams Susan (2021) White Malice: The CIA and the Neo colonisation of Africa. Hurst Publishers, London

Williamson D. Kevin (2022) "There are No Easy Cures for What Nils Our Body Politics" National Review Politics and Policy, January 30, 2022, 06.30 am.

Wole Soyinka (1996). The Open Sore of a Continent: A Personal Narrative of the Nigerian crisis. Oxford University Press United Kingdom.

World Education Blog (2012) Education for All Global Monitoring Report 2012 - Education Must Not Fail another Generation, 5th November 2012

Yedder Ben Omar (2011) "Life After Office", New African, 45 Year, No. 509, August/September 2001, London pp.64-66

Yusuf Shahdid (ed.) (2017) China and the Global Economy. Edward Elgar Publishing Limited, Cheltenham, Gloss, UK.

Zeleza Tiyambe (1997). Manufacturing African Studies and Crisis. CODESRIA, Dakar - Senegal

Zhang Fan (2018) The Institutional Evolution of China's Political and Economic System. Government vs. Market. Edward Elgar Publishing Limited, Cheltenham, Gloss UK

Chapter 1

Innovation That Matters: Towards Pro-Poor Innovation – Putting Public Policy and Values into Science and Technology for the Benefit of All in Emerging Polities.

Introduction

"The efforts of the African governments and people in addressing their plight can be facilitated of hindered, and these efforts can succeed of falter, to the extent by which the international community is willing to help rather than hinder Africa in initiatives to deal with the root causes of its problems and create the enabling external conditions that are so vital to contributing to positive change and to accelerating such change." (Sadig Rasheed, 1995).

Government Insights – Where Are We?

Despite the common misperception local, national, regional governments are important breeding grounds for progressive science and technology solutions and innovative sciences. The truth is people nod governments have always built and maintained some form of science and technology systems the world over. People and governments have become pioneering thought leaders in areas such as system consolidation, the expansion of services oriented architecture (SOAs). The challenges and opportunities provided by the competitive knowledge-based global economy makes it imperative for every stakeholder to intensify cooperation and innovative activities enhancing the development and proper utilisation of science and technology in promoting growth, creating employment opportunities leading to sustainable quality wellbeing of citizens. Reality is that technological development is founded on meeting the wants of the rich. Scant attention is focused to the vital needs of people in the developed countries.

There is need for emerging economies to take advantage of advances provided by science and technology to enhance and harness their transformation process or what Gerschenkron [1962] calls the "late-comer advantage". Africa, for example does not need to invent the wheel but take advantage of what exist and learn from best practices and failures of nations that have passed through the tunnel of underdevelopment and are today classified as developed economies. In contrast to Rostow's Stage of Economic Growth [1960] to improve on the quality wellbeing of their population, as advances in science and technology creates new short-cuts for improving the livelihood of the people. Proper policy articulation remains vital but here lies the problem. What form of policies is put in place to create the necessary enabling environment for the development and utilisation of science and technology for development not for destruction? Whether we like it or not, the world is rapidly changing. Technological advancements increase productivity, income, quality of living and life expectancy. For now, and the truth is that technological development is focused on meeting the wants of the rich countries and the ruling elites of developing nations. Scant attention is paid to the vital needs of people in transitional polities. And yet within these societies lies hidden talents that could be developed to add to the growing pool of technological know-how.

The International Council of Science (ICS) argued some decades back those developing nations lack an infrastructure base for exploiting technology to their advantage. As such increased investments in universities and research institutes are necessary. Most African countries are not only poor in terms of measures of human wellbeing but also in terms of indicators of technology, spending a small proportion of their Gross Domestic Products (GDP) on research and development (R&D), often less than 1%, compared to high income countries that spend around 2.5%. The number of scientists in some African countries is less than 50 per 100,000 people, compared to over 3000 per 100000 in the developed economies. As a result, even indigenous knowledge cannot be properly used for the transformation and benefit of society. Apparently, Africa is research desert yet to be exploited. It can be argued that to enable sustainable development people need to work with the market system and not against it. This implies the understanding market mechanisms, understanding innovation processes, and then working with key stakeholders to enable business models that will deliver on human need rather than on consumer want. We have yet to scratch the tip of indigenous knowledge and impart its findings in the development process of African states which in turn will equally benefit the market sector and humanity in general.

Forward-looking measures on research into, improving and utilising indigenous knowledge can buffer food systems from stress – or at least reduce the frequency and intensity of the most damaging strains. Indigenous knowledge, creativity and innovative capacity of the poor are often relegated to the background as having no scientific values or nor market impacts. We fail to understand that creativity and innovative strength of the poor has been their only weapon of survival all these years. Valuable lessons can be drawn from this survival attitude. The most effective social protection policies raise returns to core productive assets – in Sub-Saharan Africa, labour and land – and the people out of poverty, inducing their need for social support and building their capacity to withstand recurring shocks. Developing indigenous knowledge and linking social protection to incentives and other measures that improves creativity and innovation and enhance the rural poor who are often farmers access to technology, stabilise rural markets, and commodity prices, and build up rural infrastructure makes the bottom billion and markets more resilient. The poor remain vulnerable to external shocks due partly to natural causes and partly to poor policy articulation that fails to take into consideration the situation of the poor in society. Crises happen, and poor communities must be ready to manage risks and cope with shocks. Social protection-such as insurance, employment protection, food and cash-for-work programmes, food assistance, subsidies, and social transfer-can determine whether crisis-struck households survive or succumb. The basic rights to life itself are being violated in African countries to an intolerable degree. Building a food secure continent for example, requires fundamental change – change that will be most effective if accompanied by a shift of resources, capacities and decisions to the rural poor and women. When the female gender and other vulnerable segment of society gain a voice in the decisions affecting their lives and livelihoods, their capacity to innovate, produce, trade and use resources is materially enhanced. Knowledge and organisation remain the key and weapons to open the public space and accelerate the transformation process of African countries.

We cannot deny the fact that the arrival of Information and Communication Technologies (ICTs) during the past decades was accredited to widening the gap between the rich and poor. It has also improved the situation in transitional polities who are exposed to greater connectivity with the rest of the world more than ever before. So far innovations seem to fail and be applied in developing countries where there is a real need. Recalling the words of E. F. Schumacher, "new technologies are developed only when people of power and wealth back the development" [1973, 1974] process. Arguments can be advanced for and against Schumacher's concept of 'small is beautiful.' This has its attractions; otherwise, the concept would not have survived so vigorously for so many years. There is a lot of truth in this statement. Innovation activities for the local people are not given the attention they deserve because the ruling elites do not consider the rural poor as human beings. In short, current development policies are not human-oriented, if they are, things would radically change in the direction of improving the livelihood of the people. Science and society together have the responsibility to ensure that the restraint of science in the discovery of new knowledge in certain fields could hamper development that leads to proper living stands for the rural poor.

The rural poor who can afford modern gadgets of communication can improve on their livelihood as information technology puts an up-to-the-minute knowledge about market prices and conditions at farmer's fingers, increasing their leverage, while cooperatives and producer's associations can provide platforms for collective bargaining. New knowledge, inputs and farming techniques can liberate the poor from cycles of low productivity and poverty. As earlier noted, technology is a double-edged implement; improper-utilisation can lead to serious consequences leaving the poor in a more vulnerable state than before. Good governance leads to many advantages for both the rich and poor. Good governance leads to inclusion and participation. Participation and voice grow stronger when political, economic and social power is widely dispersed. Bringing the excluded into the development process is essential as it leads to alleviating the plight of the poor and ensuring security for all.

In an OECD Report in the 1980s, *"Technical Change and Economic Policy"*, it concluded that a framework of slow rate economic growth, combined with large-scale unemployment, under-development and inflation, the process of technical change is disruptive, or what Schumpeter described as "creative destruction". Technological advances during the past decades have injected structural changes making it possible for transitional polities to make positive strides in the direction of improving the livelihood of their citizens. Unfortunately, these advances are not being proper utilised or deployed in meeting the needs of the rapidly increasing bottom billions. Creative destruction should be converted into 'creative development' for the benefit of the bottom billion. A new national and international economic and political order becomes imperative. Without that we shall not be able to come to grips with the increasingly strong challenges and plight of the developing countries within the global economic and political construct of the 21st century and beyond. The justification of world politics, world markets, world crisis, and world problems, to cover the series of problems on a world scale – energy, food, population growth, unemployment, diseases, health, shelter, resources depletion – overlap and interlink. Thus, the world system approach is best suited to handle the problematique. Handling that problematique begins with constructive inputs by national governments. What kind of policy strategies are put in place for the transformation of society? Policies that risk aggravating the plight of the poor and insecurities for example, the current scramble for land in sub-Saharan Africa should be avoided. Western large-scale investment and technology are used to displace the vast majority of the rural poor all in the name of development that satisfies the articulate self-interests of the few rich and powerful.

National strategic policies should be backed by a comprehensive and positive responsive approach from the developed economies in seeking common solutions to global problems. It should not be left to market forces. Collaboration and coordination of planning and other related activities [Fues & Wolff, 2010] will help in redirecting investment capital and research activities and in the satisfaction of basic needs with priority for the socially and economically weakest groups currently suffering the absence of appropriate infrastructure. When policies are pro-poor oriented the innovative capacities of the rural people, or people who do not matter will be discovered which eventually become inputs in the market process; through the efforts of a productive private sector. Such discoveries lead to a triple heritage which forms a vicious circle:

education (university) =➔research institution) =➔ private sector interface) =➔Civil society needs met)➔ equality of life improved)➔ increased productivity) =➔growth assured, and the cycle continues

Individual hidden talents have to be discovered; there is lack of infrastructure-base for developing and exploiting technologies (especially indigenous knowledge) and increasing investments in universities and research institutions to convert research results into consumer products. The private sector becomes the channel for the conversion process. The private equally should invest in higher education and research institutes; big enterprise should equally beef up their own research departments. All these presuppose collaboration between the state, private sector and civil society working as one body in building the scientific, technological and productive capacity of the society.

What is the role of innovation and technology in social, economic and political development? Historically, social, economic and political development (especially the creation and distribution of wealth) has been associated with the four factors of production: land, labour, capital and entrepreneurship. Land, resources and labour are in abundance on the continent, but capital and entrepreneurship are lacking. Therefore, land, labour, resources and the ingenuity of the people must be harnessed backed by investments in education, technical training and technology. Schumpeter's [1942] hypothesis on the role of evolutionary technical change in economic growth is still influential if controversial. African countries need to penetrate into this hypothesis to constructively structure and ascertain the developmental path of the continent. Low innovation leads to low income, low growth and poor competitiveness of transitional polities in the global market; poor economic growth leads to unemployment and lower living standards. It is a vicious circle which can only be adequately addressed through a comprehensive people-oriented policy approach. To ensure growth and quality well-being, it is imperative to enable sustainable development; people need to work with the market system and not against it. There is an urgent need for the education system and policy approach to discover hidden talents in the rural and urban areas among the people and to bring "indigenous knowledge" [Gordon & Krech, 2012] into the fulcrum of modern science and technology.

In short, transitional polities must articulate and aggregate policies geared towards understanding market mechanisms, understanding innovative processes and then working it with key stakeholders to enable businesses models that deliver on human needs rather than on consumer want. Here we see the importance of the interface between the universities – research – private sector – civil society intercourse. Such intercourse is essentially important for emerging economies, to tap into its indigenous knowledge and link with what is available in the market. With existing technology this is a major challenge since business models [including supply chain, logistics are already established and which] transitional polities grossly lack, to accelerate their developmental goals. Developing indigenous technologies as a way towards pro-poor innovation opens a window of opportunity for a vast majority of the people to connect with the modern world, increase employment opportunities and economic growth and ensure sustainable development. Developing countries have to address numerous fundamental issues all at the same time, and often far beyond their capacity; climate change, environmental depletion and protection, sustainable development, democracy and others – all influence by the role and impact of science and technology. For poor and vulnerable rural communities, innovation through local experimentation and adaptation in agriculture and other practices provides important means for survival, which can later be translated into large state productive units.

The African Human Development Report 2012 makes clear that sustainable increases in agricultural productivity protect food entitlements – the ability of people to access food. Furthering human development requires nutrition policies that unleash the potential of todays and future generations. Also, communities must be resilient enough to absorb shocks and have the power to make decisions about their lives. Sub-Saharan Africa has ample agricultural land, plenty of water and a generally favourable climate for growing food. And in the past 10 years, many African countries posted world-beating economic growth rates and became among the fastest movers on the Human Development Index. With these endowments and important economic and social achievements, why is the region still food insecure (Figure 1) and grossly underdeveloped? Source: [UNDP 2012] Africa Human Development Report 2012, UNDP, New York USA.

Has the continent neglected its indigenous knowledge in alleviating the plight of the people, especially the bottom-billion or what? Is Africa consigned to a lifetime of underdevelopment and food insecurity for example? The knowledge, technology and resources for closing the food security deficit are available today, and break through will continue to emerge from research and development. It is not just a question of distributing seeds and fertilisers. The problems that add up to the mountain of problems on the continent are pervasive, from poor policy articulation, neglect of the deployment of indigenous knowledge, human capacity building, commerce, transportation etc. An effective response to challenge this broad-range of questions cannot be narrowed down to a single intervention, discipline or institutional mandate. It takes a holistic and coordinated response across sectors, within and between nations.

Africa's greatest problem is deficit leadership. Servant visionary leadership is needed to give new directions and orientations for the continent to recover itself and to know what it wants [Okombo et al, 2011]. For too long, Africa has remained a dehumanising region, hunger and the spectra of famine which has virtually disappeared elsewhere in the world continues haunting many parts of the continent, poor governance, ethnic division fanning the improper utilisation of resources, the cankerworm of corruption epidemic like an HIV/AIDS tsunami is here to stay all because of an African leadership vacuum and the triumphal of western strategies of hegemonic domination. This challenge presented by this book joining many others to 'uppers, to the powerful, to the structures of power for a serious change in mind-set. It is to upend the moral, to stand convention on its head, to put people before things, and lowers before uppers.' Like Vaclav Havel (1992) points out, "it is not that we should simply seek new and better ways for managing society, the economy and the world. The point is that we should fundamentally change how we behave." The coming new high ground of Africa presents serious challenges in status-quo; nested in other changes which confronts the dominance of the uppers: rapid spread top-down as a fashion brings bad practice: dominant and superior behaviour, rushing, upper-to-upper bias, taking without giving, and arousing expectations which re not met, (Chambers, 1997:210).

A progressive Afro-centric agenda will generate synergies of three pillars – methods, behaviour and attitudes, sharing and partnership - that reinforces each other. Empowerment of the masses should be the goal. Empowerment is identifying the weak and enabling them to gain skills, confidence, and knowledge and have hope for a brighter tomorrow. It will also have the effects of challenging the status-quo of the uppers. As such and in this light, responsible well-being for the uppers can be sought through altruism and generosity, putting the last first, and through disempowerment, putting the first last. A progressive Afro-centric agenda should begin by balancing the game changer environment, as disempowerment for the uppers will mean loss; but often all can gain. More ways are needed for the powerful to gain from the less powerful. For new behaviour for both, there is no need to wait. There is a vanguard to join and new high ground to explore (Chambers, op cit.). We need to bring bad practices, behaviour and poor attitude to an end, and how to ensure and assure improved quality and sustainability for quality livelihood for all. Here lies the golden opportunity for the continent to reconstruct itself and join the club of quality services delivery nations of the world. This is what is expected of African leaders and the population to gun for. It also requires addressing number of interwoven questions. We have the golden window of opportunity to collectively change things for the good.

Some Soul-Searching Questions

The challenge faced by emerging polities is multi-related, calling for holistic, concerted and comprehensive and far-reaching priority policy strategies

- How can policy be developed linking indigenous know-how to development?
- How can African countries enable new science-led technologies to deliver products which fulfil human needs rather than consumer wants?
- Does Africa want to develop: how, by what means, by whom and when?
- Can indigenous technological know-how deliver social and economic progress?
- How can science led new technology be made available to poor people?
- How can local innovation accelerate the economic take-off of transitional polities or how can local innovation be fostered and valued alongside the wider development of high technology, which is commonly associated with globalisation?
- To what extent can the provision of information and accompanying model for work facilitate the adoption of new technologies in transitional polities?
- What are the impediments to new technology in developing countries?
- How do we move from local or pilot projects to large scale production?
- Defining of innovation approaches and yielding positive results
- What breakthroughs do we need for creating a new, innovation economy?
- What are the key challenges in integrated indigenous knowledge into mainstream?
- Are women not innovators and why are they neglected?
- Where and who are female researchers and innovators?
- Ways of turning innovation and technologies into business opportunities
- How do we institutionalise innovation and how do we build innovation systems?

Comprehensive and sustainable answers are needed if the continent is to break the long cycle of underdevelopment and exploitation by forces from within and without. Women have been sidelined. Yet we cannot deny the reality that women across generations have participated in the reinvention of our economic future in the areas of technology, research and technology are the means to a more sustainable future. The key catalyst to innovation is the human spirit, and we tend to suppress the spirit and ingenuity of women. Therefore, policies should explore the imaginative and creative ways of how women can be active participants in the innovative economy. How can the system encourage more innovative women whose works impact our lives at micro or macroeconomic levels?

Policy Articulation and Implementation

By focusing on the poor and quality wellbeing, systemic policy architecture and action-research on developing indigenous knowledge can begin to see the light of day as contribution towards innovation related activities providing meaningful insights into change across the system. How policy can put public value into science and technology and improve the livelihood of the poor. Second, policy architecture on pro-poor focus can equally pave the way for social entrepreneurship which is crucial to development. This involves designing new technologies or technological approaches to such specific requirements of poor people; these creates basis of small businesses or used to help people meet their basic needs. Is the underdevelopment of the new nation-states to be attributed to the misuse of political power or the misuse of science and technology? Or have in different ways contributed to the current state of affairs? What is being done to remedy the situation? [Forje1984:141]. Third, policy articulation begins with what we want, what are our development priorities; what resources we have, and how we intend to use these resources; leadership role and vision and responses of civil society towards their own wellbeing. Is society challenging existing institutional structure with a purpose of putting in place a better functional alternative?

A better functional alternative that can stimulate more young people to launch their own businesses is crucial. Consequently, creating jobs and contributing to the growth of the economy and quality wellbeing of citizens should constitute an inherent part of the strategy. Policies should challenge women to think big, audacious, imaginative and creative in ways to further impact our economic transformation; there is need for women to be active participants in the innovative economy of our time. Opportunities for policy change may arise with new actors, but this may also raise questions around participation of marginalised voices. According to Keeley and Scooners [2003] "policy processes are viewed as complex, non-linear and 'uneasy' driven by actors with diverse sets of interests who subscribe to particular narratives in framings of problems and their situations". Kingdom [1995] shows how a crises situation can provide a policy window bringing about rapid change when there is a convergence of interests or values, agendas and actors". Source: UNDP [2012] Africa Human Development Report 2012, UNDP, New York.

Taking the agricultural sector for examples, policies need to focus on income, market structures, institutional rules and governance that enable the poor to buy and trade food in fair markets. It also means reinforcing essential human capacities in health and education. Focusing policies on these areas entails unleashing a dynamic vicious cycle of food security and human development [Fig 2] and paying particular attention to the creativity and innovative knowledge of the people. Sub-Saharan Africa still trails the world in human development, but the quickening pace of change and the new economic vitality in the region offer grounds for renewed if guarded optimism [UNDP 2012]. Policies must be vigorously implemented. Poor implementation breeds fertile grounds for corruption related activities. It is for these reasons that the African Charter on the Values and Principles for Public Service and Administration, Article 12 (1, 2, 3, 4) Preventing and Combating Corruption is categorical and determined to bring sanity in the public sector of African countries [AUC)), 2011]. Corruption is a cankerworm in the development process of the continent. A true development process can only start when governments start listening to the people and not to the polluters, the power of the people can no longer is undermined. Innovations that advance women's economic resilience support women in overcoming entrepreneur barriers and produce a more equitable flow of financial and non-financial opportunities and benefits.

A crisis situation exists; Africa is poor in the midst of abundant resources; globalisation is challenging the very existence of third world countries. The gap between the rich and poor is widening. These and many other related questions beacon for urgent answers; answers which are broadly overlapping with the overall research questions of the pro-poor innovation for quality wellbeing.

a. What are the state and other development partners or stakeholder's motivations for improving the quality wellbeing of citizens?

b. What are the experiences of these countries over the past 50 years?

c. What efforts have they made on people's lives, values, relationships and behaviours?

d. What do they see as new emerging challenges and the space for change?

e. What is the perception/reaction towards the policy strategies of the government, development partners and o the private sector etc.?

There is what is known as 'local knowledge' which must be tapped into. African countries face similar challenges in developing their economies but the differences are as deep as the similarities, and these matters in business. Therefore, policy articulation should be focused on what advantage exists for the people. Seen from these perspectives, innovation policy strategy must target any person showing the potential for any new activities or creativity, which can create jobs, earn income for the people, increase growth and improve the quality wellbeing of citizens in general.

Unleashing economic change from all fronts requires looking into indigenous knowledge, building human capacity through education and training design to cater for business, entrepreneurship, enterprise creation and consequently sustainable enterprises as well as incorporating modern science and technology. The pro-poor innovation strategy could be seen as new form empowering the poor by converting their creativity and innovation into mass produced products. It is a way of reviving neglected hidden but emerging economic activities with an eventual vast potential. Focus on pro-poor innovation could be seen as a New Growth Path [NGP] designed to achieve a 'step change' in growth and transformation of economic conditions of African countries from a solid foundation. It should be pointed out that with the state of soaring unemployment rate especially among the youths and women, policies are necessary to ensure that this vast increasing population is absorbed into various forms of income generating activities. The public service sector cannot employ all these beaming youths with high school and university qualifications who roam the streets unemployed. Many African countries have witnessed, via unfortunate riots throughout the Arab world, how impatient the youth has become to politicians promises that yield nothing.

Government policies across the continent are failing to create jobs and proper utilise their trained human capital.

Innovation policies should be a path to new ideas, increase productive future and sustainable development. We need innovative policy strategies targeting the real challenges and promoting Africa's long-term economic and social development – its "recovery" development. The "recovery" of the development of Africa must span all areas of activities. Take for example the 'hand-dyed' fabrics of Malian women capturing markets and creating beauty and profit [Ighobor & Haidara, 2012]. Or a farmer who develops a 'bee-have' using local material after learning about a 'bee have' suitable for more commercial bees. Or the case of a young man who develops the process of charging "mobile phones" in the village using bicycle wheels for generating electric power. Or the case of a boy able to light a village with simple devices of constructing dam from a river as source of generator. Or the case of "Kick-Start" – a non-profit organisation in Kenya that develops, adapts and markets low-cost technologies in Africa that are bought by local entrepreneurs (often farming families) and used to establish small businesses. There is a mobile device in hand-pumps in Kenya to record breakdowns a mile step in ensuring that these water hand pumps are quickly repaired to give water and life to the vulnerable rural population. Such innovative ideas should be exploited and disseminated across the continent.

They create new jobs and income for poor people; examples of products include a brick press, oil press, treadle pump and hip pump among many other items. The fundamental basic needs of the rural poor are met through the first stages of Schumacher's "small is beautiful," though the argument of the irresponsibility using the cheap term 'the techno fix" is unacceptable for those who held on to large scale production and profit-making. The economic down-turn of the 1980 as a result of World Bank/International Monetary Fund imposed structural adjustments saw the collapse of many small and medium enterprises (SME) and these enterprises have since faced little investment and abysmal profit margins. A pro-poor innovation policy strategy can breathe life to the awakening of SMEs and with a New Growth Path change the lives of many people. African countries require making hard choices and shared determination to achieve a 'step change' in growth and transformation of economic conditions of the bottom-billion citizens. The hard choices and shared determination to achieve quality wellbeing for citizens could propel many ambitious youths into the world of entrepreneurship.

Many of such local examples abound throughout the developing world which can be improved and turned into commercial usage for income generating activities. These innovative activities use local knowledge and available local resources and things that are easy to use, repair and maintain. These few examples show how adapting simple technologies can provide alternative means of income generation in rural areas which later spread to become commercially available through the aid of further university research and private sector engagement. These are examples of Participatory Innovation Development Approach (PIDA) which can be transformed from supporting and realising the potential for local people innovation and further on to large-wider scale development activities. Public engagement with emerging creative activities of the local people can boost income generating activities. Such dialogue provides full understanding and solutions to the plight and complex nature and problems being confronted by the rural and urban poor and to both economic and behavioural changes in society. African countries have a large stake in backing new national innovation architecture for all economic activities, agriculture, food security, local industries among others based on better market access that can bring incomes to families.

Equally, it helps researchers to appreciate, take into account the need of the poor and seeks proper solutions that give added value to the creative initiatives of people. Mechanised agricultural though important may not be priority needs of the people in feeding themselves. Their local or indigenous knowledge comes to play, appreciated and of value to them. Mechanised agriculture comes with other problems if not properly addressed, storage, processing and cost, unemployment in the agricultural sector, among others. For the poor and vulnerable communities, innovating through local experimentation and adaptation in farming, handicrafts and other related activities and practices is an important means of survival. How can local innovation be fostered and valued alongside the wider development of high technology, which is commonly associated with globalisation? Because of its low state of technological development Africa lacks the capacity to compete within the new global knowledge-based economy construct. Innovation policies must focus in addressing these shortcomings. Partnership with the various stakeholders provides the best avenue of ensuring sustainable development and improved quality livelihood. Therefore, in summary, a new policy option for the continent is called for as depicted in Table 1: Strategic Policy Options and Envisaged Usage.

Table 1; Strategic Policy Options and Envisaged Usage

Policy Options	Usage
Stimulating individual Action	Creating and providing incentives, innovations to the vulnerable groups to develop their skills and talents; Getting all involved Making use of indigenous knowledge
Expanding Public Service	Human capital development Quality services delivery Funding research and innovative related activities
Expanding the Private Sector	Converting research results into consumer goods; Increasing productivity Making proper use of indigenous know-how; Sustainable use of resources
Engaging Civil Society	**As link between state and the private sector** Defending the rights of the people through proactive and not passive actions Mobilising approach reinforcing creativity and innovation among the people
Generating Public Action on Human Focused Policies [National and Global]	Behavioural Change – New Mindset Gender equality and strong legal rights for women and other vulnerable groups National and International Policy engagement Departure from western-centric, profit maximisation attitude to a new Global order, and responding positively to the needs of transitional polities. **Creating a new Global Political and Economic Order for the benefit of all**

Source: Forje [2012] Based on Analysis in the Paper

State-Civil Society-Private Sector Nexus

Why do African policy-makers shy away from funding indigenous initiatives developed and owned by the people for their common good? A true revolution for constructive development on the continent can only start when policy-makers (governments) start listening to the people and not to external partners, even though they are needed in the development process. The power of creativity and innovative ideas of the people can no longer be undermined but given added value and properly exploited if Africa is to steer and own its development. The people's indigenous knowledge must constitute an indispensable aspect of the socio-economic transformation and sustainable development process in enhancing the quality wellbeing of the citizens. Table 1 presents a summary of the fundamental issues in questions and approaches to resolving some of the outstanding conflicting problems that leads to the serious divide between the rich and poor, developed and developing economies rural and urban areas.

African governments must focus on pro-poor innovative processes that places food on the table, create more jobs (by linking grass-roots innovation to the productive mainstream) and other related activities. Small is beautiful and can become big. It is from these small or local innovative ideas that can be replicated and expanded into large scale industrial output. A new form of social entrepreneurship eventually develops through a harmonious linkage of state-society-private sector intercourse. Unfortunately, policies are not people-focused but oriented towards profit-making at meeting the wants of the rich in society at any cost. Technological innovation and entrepreneurship are crucial to development. Sustainable development is vital to the quality wellbeing of the citizens. A new entrepreneurial approach to development emerges with a proper fusion of these three sectors (state, society, private sector). This involves converting local creativity and innovation into designing new technologies and adapting existing ones to suit the specific requirements of poor people, which are bought by poor people to form the basis of small businesses or used to help people, meet their basic human needs.

Strategies for poverty reduction need to recognise the role that innovation plays in achieving social change in the country – that is able to lift more people out of poverty. The interface between the state, civil society and private sector and other emerging players should be supported with all possible means, political, economic and technological, to help build African science and technology innovation capacity. How all this is effectuated – the policies, the support mechanisms, and the incentives – will be complicated, given that indigenous knowledge has been relegated to the background in the development process in African countries. However, with the escalating state of poverty, attitude and behaviour are gradually changing towards greater interface between state-civil society-private sectors as providing a sustainable way forward for the development of the continent. It should be pointed out that as the continent's innovation capacity grows, a central question is whether techno-nationalism will grow, or whether impulses towards global collaboration and exchange of new ideas will prove stronger. Given that globalisation is rapidly changing the world construct, it can only be assumed that these emerging 'science powers' will be reshaping global science and innovation. Therefore, African countries need to strengthen the political case and practical mechanisms for closer integration and beneficial collaboration between the triple heritages, *state-society-private sector,* as constituting the foundation on which the continent should build its development capacity.

Africa's centres of human capital development must work with the people to shape science and technology contribution to improving the wellbeing of the people especially, the currently bottom billion-poor down-trodden. The rich and poor nations must work together, just as indigenous knowledge must collaborate with modern science and technology in shaping human ingenuity in ways that are not just about trade, markets and economic competitiveness, but also about using global knowledge to address shared environmental and social challenges. With concerted and well-structured interface between the various stakeholders working together, more ideas, in more places around the country and continent must be good news for innovation and creativity of the people can and should be brought to fruition for the common good of humanity. The impulse to developing the indigenous capacity of emerging societies and to collaborate with advance western science and technology must win out over the drive to compete if vital benefits are to be achieved for good of everyone. Africa's priorities for sustainable development should begin with developing indigenous knowledge and marrying it with modern technological development. Policy needs to be backed up by good communication, so that local people understand and act on new opportunities.

Developing indigenous knowledge requires building up the human capital of the poor. In this present transition period, social responsibility is expressing a unity between science, technology and society bringing the maximum benefit to the poor. We have to recognise that "African institutions are weak and a continental leadership vacuum pervades. The continent is currently failing to assert itself as a key player, spearheaded by strategic leadership, speaking with one voice on matters of vital continental interests. This lacuna is being exploited by Western powers, notably the so-called P.3 and the US, France and Britain, as a theatre for reinstating a colonial global order. Even in the wake of an unprecedented economic decline on the part of the powers, they use military might and political verbosity to realise what the Americans have long regarded as their "manifest destiny" [Landsberg 2012]. There has to be an African destiny. Only Africans can shape that destiny. The *'top-down'* and the *'bottom-up'* progression for a cordial meeting point should spread so that equitable sharing of national resources can take place for the overall good of the people and progress of the country.

Persistent Challenges and Emerging Threats

Misguided policies, weak institutions and poor governance are the deeper causes of the continent's plight today. Working towards a sustainable and secured future requires comprehensive people-oriented policies, and enabling environment placing it on the path of improving wellbeing of citizens. For decades, the policies of African governments and their development partners relegated indigenous knowledge and pro-poor policy approaches but opting capitalist consumer focused development profit-making strategies that benefited the ruling elites and the multinationals. Wrong priorities cloud Africa's path to sustainable development.

Many advocates of pro-poor innovation fear a globalised world that is exploited by large corporate enterprises and powerful countries, now including China, Brazil and India. Perceived threats include loss of local knowledge and powerlessness of low-income economies and their enterprises in the face of cheap goods produced elsewhere. Pro-poor innovations such as drought – or disease-resistant crops or effective and cheap drugs are often not prioritised. One response has been to turn the perceived threat into challenge – to harness the power of big business through public-private partnerships (PPP) [Wilson, 2007]. For the people to reclaim their lost power hijacked by the ruling elites [Forje, 2009] they also need to be organised and rally under the common banner that binds them together. The adoption of a new \Kenyan constitution in 2010 expanded human and democratic rights in various areas of life. Unfortunately, many Kenyans (most Africans in general) are still not fully aware of those rights. It is the place of the increasing number of FM Radios to educate society on the rights. "Information and communication technologies have generated many benefits, but their distribution around the globe has not been even" [Beebe et al (eds.) [2003].

Poor people have the weakest voice in defining understanding of public need, from which pro-poor policies are formed. Public policy to support growth an innovation thus largely ignores employment generation and the scope for technological paths that support 'pro-poor' growth. This shows the importance not just of the public sector holding the private sector to account, but of the private sector to account, but of the public sector itself being accountable to poor people. The globalised world can offer opportunities for pro-poor innovation – fair trade and ethical goods, markets, for example, offer opportunities for pro-poor innovation without having to compete directly with corporate giants of the new Asian powers. Local knowledge is crucial for survival, but for poor people to be agents of their own development, it is not enough. Innovation concerns the production and application of knowledge. The production of knowledge is achieved by exposing what we know to what we do not know [Wilson, 2007]. Therefore, policy formulation must strive in the direction of making the people know what they do not know. In this sense two kinds of knowledge network are potentially important inputs to pro-poor innovation, namely;

- Networks (local, national or international) where people in the same sector, such as farming, can share and compare their knowledge:
- Networks where people in different knowledge domains share and compare their understandings of problems or challenges, they have in common

Wilson (op cit.) notes that motivation is an essential potential of pro-poor innovation to be realised. Volunteered motivation is not enough: institutionalised incentives are also needed. The areas play a key role in this respect, namely; (a) the public sector, where incentives for pro-poor innovation is linked ultimately to some form of democratic governance accountability. This is important if public-private-partnership (PPPs) are put forward. Governments are unlikely to make serious demands on the private sector if they are not committed themselves: (b) innovation is an essential element of the capitalist economy, where market competitiveness and profit-seeking are the incentives. Corporate business will engage in pro-poor practices if they are seen, for example, to enhance brand image locally or amongst well informed consumers globally: and (c) employees motivated by the 'professional challenge of contributing to a better world can be found in the private and public sectors. Apparently, solutions to most problems are often within not out there. Unfortunately, Africa seems prone to seeking outside solutions. The country ends up spending huge amounts of money and time on things we could have disposed of with ease had we looked in the right place. Besides, we create new problems. It is good, though, to listen to external views, however, it is equally good, if not imperative and better, to begin by listening to those around us. They are the people in charge. What is their understanding of the situation? It always helps to analyse and understand things from their perspective before seeking external intervention. Thus, the pro-poor innovation policy strategy is within the society, and yet the views of the neglected are not sought as the first step in addressing their plight.

Given our unequal, globalise world construct posing major challenges for pro-poor innovation for which the mechanism of PPPs is not necessary the answer. Rephrased differently, the poor are a menace to the rich. For decades, policies of national governments and international governments continue to neglect the development of the rural poor but concentrated in developing urban areas with damaging legacies which included in effective post-colonial development plans geared towards exhausting the natural resources of the country. The imposed World Bank/IMF structural adjustment programmes helped in destroying the indigenous knowledge of the people as large human development deficits were created especially among the vulnerable poor. In addition, skewed allocation of natural revenues and foreign aid that overlooked agriculture and the health statues of the rural poor destroyed the sovereign rights dignity and wellbeing of the people. For now, development policies evade accountability. Answering to the people equals accountability. By this we "mean a system which ensures that governments are answerable to their people for the way they run the country. Too often in the past Africa governments have responded not to the interests of all their people but to those of elites, parties, tribes or other particular group Sometimes they have even put the demands of the international donor community before the concerns of their citizens" [Commission for Africa, 2005].

Accountability is the necessary counterpart to voice. When accountable authorities answer to engaged communities, social justice is served, the rural poor people start filling the missing gaps and there is assured form of development that benefits the poor. Governments must be answerable to all their people including the poorest and most vulnerable. Clearly there are not felt to do this at present. The issue of policy formulation or transformation on the continent is littered with broken promises and squandered opportunities. Pro-poor innovation policy strategies should be seen through the periscope of multiple perspectives necessitating the state of development from a wide range of geographical, social, political, institutional and economic starting points [Burns 2011:14]. Empowerment, social justice and gender should be given adequate attention in policy formulation. For example, building a food secure continent requires transformative change – change that will be most effective if accompanied by a shift of resources, capacities and decisions to smallholder farmers, poor communities and women. There are strong links in developing the potentials of indigenous knowledge, mutually reinforcing links between expanding women capabilities – through better education more direct control over resources and a more decisive voice in decision-making – and enhancing food security, improving the informal sector which are the main sources of the livelihood income of the poor as vital input sectors in the national economy. For development to proceed equitably all sectors of the society must be involved in the choice and use of science and technology, all must be aware of its limitations and all must enjoy its benefits. The nexus is that Africa must grapple with at least four major trends which deeply affect its current state of underdevelopment that if not resolved will largely determine and enhance its poor future. The four fundamental issues being:

- Human resources development and institutional infrastructure /capacity building;
- improving the agricultural sector through scientific, technological and industrial development;
- improving or developing indigenous knowledge and encouraging innovative and creativity that leads to entrepreneurial development:
- Establishment of democratic governance

These four factors are interrelated. In different ways they contribute to the place of human capital formation within the framework of the evolution of super-technology and mega trends for the 21st century. The general picture of the continent is a gloomy one. As with any general picture, it does not tell the entire story. The need to embark on a radical restructuring policy strategy, though this may be extremely difficult and painful, is imperative. Africa has no other choice but to undertake comprehensive radical strategic people-focused policies for the common good. It entails protecting the peoples' interests and ensuring sustainable quality livelihood for all. Achieving sustainable quality livelihood requires empowering all individuals to share, learn and express their concerns and ideas in a cooperative and inclusive manner. Constructive engagement of the various stakeholders is imperative. It will thereby facilitate a movement towards empowering all individuals and institutions to contribute towards their own livelihoods, communities and environment. The challenge is to address fundamental societal imbalances currently defined by a small centre of society wielding disproportionate access to political and economic resources compared with the vast silent majority of individuals. Unfortunately, the privileged power elites consequently perpetuate socio-political orders that reinforce their prosperity to the exclusion of and detriment to those on the peripheries. What emerges is crippling paradoxes and inefficiencies that undercut societies throughout the African continent, which include among others the following:

- Rapid economic growth coupled with rampant income inequities leading to a state of abject or endemic poverty;
- National, continental and global surplus of agricultural resources in the wake of increasing incidences of famine; it is sad that many people on the continent go to bed hungry every day;
- Revolutionary technological development that fall to reach those individuals with the greatest need;
- flawed democratic political mechanisms that restrict pluralistic participation and contributing to poor governance that ends up in what is fashionably known as 'failed' or 'collapse' states.

The challenge for the continent is developing a broad-based social platform for mass engagement and constructive interaction between the various stakeholders in society as well as partnering with forces or institutions that respond positive to the needs and aspirations of the people, with the hopes of informing policy recommendations that encourages renewed commitments towards share-humanity and a more peaceful continent and the world at large.

Conclusion and Recommendations

Creating a Better Climate

Policy formulation that bypasses pro-poor innovation strategic approach remains harmful to the economic take-off of African countries. Therefore, policies are needed involving poor people in growth related activities. Where incomes are unequal most of the benefits from growth go to the wealthy. Growth will not reduce poverty unless poor people are able to participate in it. For now, policies are articulated with inbuilt failure or squandered capacities and missed opportunities. The African continent is littered with opportunities. If Africa is to take advantage and establish its own sovereignty and create its development dynamic path, it must start by exploiting existing opportunities in the country. African governments should take the opportunity to build on what they have, improve on it so that in their development endeavours whether it be political, economic or otherwise they are able to stand on their own feet and avoid the consequences attendant with imposed policy strategies that often come in the form of bailouts and other imposed conditionality.

With the IMF and World Bank anticipating average growth rates of more than 5% across sub-Saharan Africa in the years ahead, Africa's strategic importance to the world economy is rising fast. It is little wonder that the region is being courted by traditional and emerging trading partners more assiduously than ever before. Here is an opportunity for African countries to roll out constructive strategic policy approaches that benefits the poor and which puts people at the centre of development. What this set out to achieve is simply give voice to the voiceless, tapping into their creativity and innovative prowess for their wellbeing as well as contributing to economic growth and improved quality of wellbeing for the rich and poor. Perhaps a national democratic revolution is imperative in restoring the people's dignity and right to existence within the system of global governance to better end her marginalisation as well as to the claimed benefits of the process of globalisation. It has been recognised in the paper, that little attention is paid to the bottom-billion, and the neglect of indigenous knowledge is to an extent extending the poverty status of the bottom billion. The following issues have been highlighted: (a) searching for and improving the talents of people in the education systems at all levels, and in particular in the universities and research institutions; (b)ensuring effective links between academic institutions, research centres, civil society and the private sector or public enterprises: (c) creating appropriate mechanisms for policy formulation, ensure the development of indigenous knowledge, science and technology policy so that there is the optimal allocation and utilisation of resources to meet national aspirations and goals; (d)ensuring the fruitful application of indigenous knowledge and science and technology in rural development to harmony with tradition technology: (e) fostering scientific temper, incentives not only in modern science and technology bit also to indigenous knowledge: and last but not the least, the need to interrelate the humanities, social science, science, and technology is greater than ever.

A holistic approach is imperative. In this way, we shall be able to emerge from the lightless suburb in which the status of the poor receives greater attention, and not left standing among the ruins with only sorrow and abject poverty to bit on. We should be able to see with new eyes of hope and emerging society. The end of the exploitation and neglect of the poor in Africa is much overdue. Now is time for genuine change and new mindset for constructive change. Only the

African people can affect such a change. For now, Africa is like an orphan. It beacons for a common agenda and visionary leadership. Pro-poor innovation for Africa – is its good luck or bad luck, despite our despair at the leadership vacuum across Africa, and how the continent can empower it within the existing global construct. Africa needs policy constructs that can reverse the marginalisation of the region. A good place is to start by building on and giving value to indigenous knowledge. Africa has to reclaim its cultural heritage with indigenous knowledge as the innovative arm for sustainable development.

Africa's educational system and its institutions of higher learning should take the lead; but the sad side of it is that poor leadership contributes to poor institutional capacity building. For example, between 1970 and 1995, the University of Makerere–Uganda, once a top leading university in Africa plunged into abyss during the reign of Idi Amin. During the SAP era, many universities on the continent suffered the same fate, backed by the notion that the World Bank propagated the idea that Africa did not need universities. The measures of repression inhibit an atmosphere for conducive learning environment for the continent to have qualified human skill capacity and quality to move forward with its development agenda. Development should not be limited to the satisfaction of basic needs. There are other needs, other goals, and other values. Development includes freedom of expression and impression, the right to give and receive ideas and stimulus. There is a deep social need to participate in shaping the basis of one's own existence, and to make some contribution to the fashioning of the continent's future. Restructuring of the political, economic and management system is answer to the challenge of the time. To wade off the 'dark clouds' requires us arming ourselves with the requisites tools necessary for fighting the battle and seeing the 'blue sky.' Considered pivotal to the sustainable transformation and quality livelihood of the people, education and skills building should be given the long overdue attention it deserves. Important consideration should be focused addressing the education of the female gender and the youths. Too often, neglect of this group of citizens continue to delay the transition process from backwardness to progressive development. Knowledge acquisition should be taken to the hinterlands, giving the kids the opportunity to go to school within their community. With knowledge and skills, the youths can be gainfully employed.

Recommendations

- Recognise and support the creativity and innovative activities of the people;
- Support the people to gain confidence and a voice
- Private sector organisation should be encouraged to fund pro-poor research by offering them incentives as tax concessions;
- Better links between the public, civil society and private sectors be encouraged, including research partnerships between universities, research institutes and the private sector
- The media industry remains an excellent means for disseminating livelihoods-related innovation
- Reconstitute the leadership vacuum and ensure that the sheep is herded with a voice and shepherd leadership
- Encourage social entrepreneurs to develop simple business plans, and marketing strategies to guide their business.
- Policy needs to be backed up by good communication, so that local people understand and act on new opportunities;
- Alter the structure of the African economies in such a manner to create greater diversification, internalize the forces and impulses of growth and enhance the capacity for individual and collective self-reliance;
- Empower the broad masses economically and, invest in human capital;
- Invest in institution and infrastructure building.

References

African Union Commission (AUC) [2011] African Charter on the Values and Principles of Public Service and Administration, Addis Ababa, Ethiopia.

Beebe Maria, Banji Oyeyinka et al. (eds.) Africa Dot Edu. Its Opportunities and Higher Education in Africa. Tat McGraw Hill Publishing Company limited, New Delhi, India

Burns Danny [2011] "A Methodological Strategy for reimagining Development: Enabling Complex Systemic Patterns to Surface through Multiple Voices", in IDS Bulletin – Time to Reimagining Development? Vol. 42, No.5, September 2011

Chambers Robert (1997) Whose Reality Counts? Putting the First Last. Intermediate Technology Publications, United Kingdom.

Commission for Africa [2005] Our Common Interest. The Commission for Africa. An Argument, Penguin Books, London.

Forje W. John [2009]. Here the People Rule. Political Transition and Challenges for Democratic Consolidation in Africa. NOVA Science Publishers Inc, New York, USA

Forje W. John [1989] Science and Technology in Africa. Longman World Series on Science and Technology, .10, Longman Publishers, Essex, United Kingdom

Forje W. John [1984] "Politics, Society and Science Policy in Sub-Saharan Africa: in Maurice Goldsmith, Alexander King, Pierre Laconte (eds.,) [1984] Science and Technology for Development: The Non-Governmental Approach, Proceedings of the CISTOD World Congress, Tunis, April 1983, Tycooly International Publishing Limited, Dublin, pp141-150

Fues Thomas & Peter Wolff (eds.) [2010] G20 and Global Development: How Can the New Summit Architecture Promote Pro-Poor Growth and Sustainability? German Development Institute, Bonn, Germany.

Gerschenkron A [1962] Economic Backwardness in Historical Perspective. The Belknap Press of Harvard University Press. Cambridge, USA

Gordon M. David & Krech Shepard (eds.) [2012] Indigenous Knowledge and The Environment in Africa and North America, Ohio University Press, USA

Ighobor Kingsley ^ Haidara Aissata [2012] "Malian Women Create Beauty – And Profit", African Renewal, April 2012, Vol.25, No.1

Keeley, J. and Scooners, I [2003] Understanding Environmental Policy Processes: Cases from Africa. Earthscan Publishers, London

Kingdom, J. W. [1995] Agendas, Alternatives and Public Policies. Longman, New York 2nd edition

Landsberg Chris [2012] "Africa, The African Union and The Fading Western-centric Global (dis) Order", Thabo Mbeki Foundation, News Letter, Vol.2, May 2012, South Africa

Okombo Okoth et al [2011] Challenging the Rulers. A Leadership Model for Good Governance, East African Educational Publications. Nairobi- Kenya.

Rostow W.W. [1960] The Stages of Economic Growth

Schumacher, E.F. [1973], Small is Beautiful. Abacus, London

Schumacher, E.F. [1974] "Economics should begin with the People Not Goods" Futurist, December 274.

Schumpeter, J. A. [1942] Capitalism, Socialism and Development. Harper & Row, New York

Wilson Gordon [2007] "Threats, Opportunities and Incentives for Pro-Poor Innovation". Id21 Insights 68, September 2007

United Nations Development Programme (UNDP) [2012] African Human Development Report 2012. Towards a Food Secure Future, Regional Bureau for Africa, 1 UN Plaza, New York,

Chapter 2

Decolonisation and Recolonisation through the Political Economy of African Foreign Policy: Challenges, Prospects and the Way Forward

Abstract

The perpetuation of the dependence, underdevelopment and poor governance is causing visionary African leaders to rethink their development strategies and scholars to redesign and reshape their analytical perspectives. This is the ideal way forward. But unfortunately, recent events especially with the aftermath of the World Bank/IMF imposed structural adjustments, the global financial melt-down and the progress made by African countries in the recent past decade, cast doubts as to whether the continent wants to be free or remain a colonised entity forever. The paper departs from the perspectives that colonial rule or slavery is not dead, that poor policy articulation leads to the recolonisation of the continent at the peak of scientific advancement ever known to humanity. It questions why Africa is poor in the midst of plenty, and why development is evading the country. The paper seeks to explain and identify alternative strategies as Africa moves towards a very difficult future with the unstoppable globalisation bandwagon. It goes further to opine that 'globalisation,' the highest stage of scientific imperialism, and the race to meet quality livelihood is behind the new recolonisation policy of the develop economies, which subjects Africa to a new kind of dependency. The conclusion is clear; Africa has to own its development path, claim total sovereignty over its independence, develop its human capital and make judicious use of its rich natural resource's potential and human capital to better ensure the quality wellbeing of its citizens. Proactive strategic policy measures are advanced as the way forward for Africa regaining its hard-won freedom from colonial rule.

Keywords: slavery, governance, policy, leadership, civil society, international community, science and technology, human capital development.

Many salient factors and apparently contradictory features have marked Africa's political economy since independence, continuity and change, without a difference. First, despite the cry for continent to own its development trajectory, things continue to be as usual and even getting worse. There has been change, within new economic entrants exploiting the vast resources of the people almost at a given way price. The second salient feature of Africa's political economy is its increasing focus and wishes to construct regional economic integration as spring board for an African Economic Community or Common Market, despite continued and expanded incorporation into the global economy. Increasing continental influence through Regional Economic Communities (RECs) and global respectability may be the product but at what cost? All the same, continental influence and global respect in the face of a deepening incorporations into and dependence on the global capitalist economy represents an anomaly. For while natural resources have led to great influence, deepening incorporation and dependency have increased under-development, conjointly producing what one scholar aptly calls; *'affluence and underdevelopment'* [Fadahunsi, 1979]. The ruling elites are craving for affluence but engraved in underdevelopment and baptised with the vices of corruption.

That the African economy should be accorded "greatness" in international politics is a contradiction in terms unless of course we are dealing with an illusion of greatness. Why this anomaly? Africa's natural resources potential should and must be accorded the symbol of "greatness" and not its economy if one has to go by the analysis of 'Africa's Bill Gates' computer Wizard Phil Emeagwali [Emekalam 2010:43], and that 10 million Africans in the Diaspora have an income roughly equivalent to Africa's gross domestic product [Emeagwali 2010]. There is a great need to empower the youths [Lema 2009] and that means developing the private sector. The paper attempts to answer the question of anomality' and to relate it to the conceptual orientation premises of *continuity and change* in the continent's political economy policy. It takes off from the premise that structural conditions arising from the incorporation of the continent into the global capitalist economic system give rise to dependent social formations providing the historical dynamic in the evolution of the African continent and political formation had, over time, called into existence regional, transnational and national-nationalistic bourgeoisies each with its conflicting occupational interests groups, bureaucratic, commercial/ industrial, and technical/worker elements The argument goes thus; continuity in the substance and change in the style of foreign relations and political economy is the product of interactions both between the global economy and the continent and between the latter and domestic social formations. Since the global economy presents the same conditions and restraints to successive governing groups, who eschew fundamental change in the political economy but rather share the same basic approach, objectives and strategy of development, the responses have been the same: continuity in the search for 'multiple entry visa; into the global economy rather than 'exist visas' [Mazrui 1981, Fadahunsi 1979].

Exit visa could be seen in terms of 'de-linking' as opined by Samir Amin, for Africa to gain its genuine sovereignty and dependence. Because of the dependency phenomenon, new entry visas are issued to economic viable countries that never had colonies in Africa, Chine for example. The Chinese move to penetrate into Africa sends worrying signals to the West. In short, the Chinese resurgence in Africa is not only transferring the continent's political, economic and social landscapes, but is sending nervous shivers into Western governments, hitherto the dominant forces in Africa. Nevertheless, the ball is now in Africa's court – to fully embrace the new-kid-on-the-block, ort hang on to friendship and policies by maintaining the status quo. This time, Africa needs to play its cards right [New African 2008:12-18]. Has Africa accepted the dragon - China's fait-accompli or will an emerging African lion roar back. Is Africa receiving China on a new dependency attitude with a difference or as role model filling the missing gaps left by the departed colonial powers?

Situating the Recolonisation Trajectory

> *"Legitimacy is gone, citizens are alienated, naked power and bribes erode the law. In turn, the strongly centralised state has lost much of its effective grip, because its legal directives are ignored, except under duress or when they seem to be opportune." (Jane Vansina 1982)*
>
> *(Vansina Jane (1982) |Mvasi's Trials", Daedalus, Vol.111, No.2, 49-70)*

The encroaching and unstoppable forces of 'globalisation' inject a new dimension in the political economy of African states. New elements are introduced and new entrants into the exploitation spree of African resources have established a strong grip on the continent in terms of meeting social needs of the population which national governments had failed to do so. The new entrants now capitalise on the weakness of Africa's dependency theory and in the belief of filling the missing gaps or vacuum created by the colonial powers' failure in fulfilling the social contract with their colonies. However, economic melt-down and the current financial crisis faced by some member states of the European Union, the old colonial masters, have led to increase in protectionist and restrictive trade policies, shrinking foreign investment and contraction in foreign aid, all of which threatens growth and poverty reduction hitherto achieved. Thus, the developed economies are seeking exist visas in terms of reduce foreign aid, but seeking multiple entry visa for the scramble for natural resources. Other contradictions in the political economy of African states are the sudden loss of its cultural heritage and value system and its total acceptance of foreign cultural value belief systems. Its natural resources have become a curse rather than a blessing. Otaviano Canuto & Mathueus Cavaliani [2012] note that "an abundance of natural resources is intuitively expected to be a blessing, Nonetheless, it has been argued for some decade that 'large endowments of natural resource – oil, gas, and minerals in particular – may actually become more of a large, often leading to slow economic growth and redistributive struggles".

While the crisis persists especially in the euro-area, there are signs of recovery and growth in other regions of the world. The need to reverse these negative trends and re-launch the continent on the path of sustainable recovery informed the focus of the African Regional Conference on the Global Financial Crisis on the strategies and lessons that can be learnt from those countries with and outside Africa that have rebounded strongly and have moved to the front burner of recovery from the global economic meltdown [AAPAM 2012]. Inconsistency in the nation states' policy articulation and implementations creates room for controversy in its political economy of African foreign policy. On many occasions they are unable to speak with one common voice and vision. Articulate national self-interests take place of pride. Absence of a common voice and vision is equally exploited by the new entrants into Africa, rendering the continent a failure in the club of nations. Those African states have emerged as failed or collapse entities come as no surprise.

As for now, Africa is ill-equip to face the force of globalisation, the highest stage of scientific imperialism. But Africa cannot escape the scourges and opportunities offered by either the vices or virtues of globalisation. Presently, the continent is not prepared for constructive transformation and in creating the structural basis for enhancing and sustaining the quality wellbeing of its population. There is losing of sense of direction as well as having wrong priorities in our developmental approach. A new mind-set is required. And we must be ready to admit our faults and weaknesses and tell the truth at whatever cost to oneself may be a source of tremendous power to change.

The Development Dilemmas

The issue of recolonisation of Africa comes two fundamental states amongst others. Sekou Toure, the Founding President of the Republic of Guinea noted years back "to win and proclaim a nation's independence but keep its old structures is to plough a field but not sow it with grain for harvest"[1962:147]; and that of President Samora Machel, of Mozambique; "to decolonise a state means essentially to dismantle the political, administrative, cultural, financial, economic, educational, juridical and other systems which, as an integral part of the colonial state, were solely designed to impose foreign domination and the will of the exploiters on the masses" [Joseph 1976]. Fifty years after, most African states exhibit with no regret the standard of decolonisation or recolonisation proffered by Presidents Samora Machel and Sekou Toure epitomising a state that has yet to be independent or decolonised. But why this attitude. The developed economies have conspicuously strategically positioned themselves ensuring the failure of these states. In addition, these states have conspicuously articulated and aggregated policies that directly or indirectly play into the hands of the developed countries.

Africa's dependency on natural resources is not a health sign, especially when the continent can neither determine the prices of these natural resources nor that of imported finished/process products. Nkuepo [2012] notes: "natural resources dominate Africa's economy, leaving other sectors neglected and underdeveloped. Political economic factors also contribute to Africa's poor performance vis-à-vis the free flow of goods and services. These obstacles need to be significantly reduced by 2017 if Africa leaders are serious about establishing a Continental Free Trade Area (CFTA) but can this be done".

Contradictory Perceptions

Two or more contradictory views persist on the recolonisation of the political economy of the continent's foreign policy; namely; one is that of turning their backs towards their former colonial masters and embracing the new colonisers who are out to continue the unsustainable exploitation of the resources of the continent. The other is rejecting the ideology of class struggle as a means of resolving the outstanding contradictions in the emerging post-colony. Here also one could add the behaviour of the new ruling class which is not different from the oppressive attitude of the departed colonial masters. The problems of the continent are clear. First the bourgeoisie class is not sufficient large to take control of capitalist development. The means of ownership of the mass of production in industry commerce and transport is concentrated largely in foreign hands. If domestic resources are properly mobilised and utilised, i.e., savings are accumulated; they can be used to obtain the capital held by the foreigners. Second, foreign capital has been increasingly difficult to come by partly because of the economic meltdown and increased competition. Third, the political control and management of these state capitalist enterprises. Fourth, the large population of the bottom billion and their exclusion from the development process inhibits their potential resources and skills (indigenous knowledge) being used to at least accelerate the process of change. The ruling elites believe the rural areas and uneducated class have nothing to offer.

There has to be a profound paradigm shift and serious diversification of the economy a shift from dependence on export raw materials to some form of local processing of these raw materials. For example, "seven Africa countries – all highly dependent on mineral exports and with low economic and institutional development – are at particular risk of falling victims to the resources curse, Burkina Faso, Democratic Republic of Congo, Ghana, Mali, Mauritania, Tanzania and Zimbabwe" [Haglund 2012]. A resource improperly used becomes a curse for the people. The countries of the continent continue to carry all their eggs in one basket which is dangerous for its political economic transformation and growth explaining why quality livelihood of the people is not improving but regressing. Apparently, Africa is faced with serious political, economic, cultural and social (PECS) obstacles.

- Political obstacles	Poor governance	P
- Economic obstacles	Poor infrastructure	E
- Cultural/social obstacles Diversity		CS

The economic obstacles - also known – as infrastructure obstacles constitute a serious threat to intra-African trade are a consequence of Africa's poor development, exploitation and marginalisation. A new political economy approach is imperative if the continent is to get out of its predicaments. Seen within this context, it is imperative that African governments have to work with the private sector to develop archaic infrastructures and put aside the belief that only government can provide public services like roads, rail and communication systems, social institutions like healthcare, drinking water, housing and others. The state has somehow siphoned the benefits from the resource's potential of the country to those who control the corridors of power. Articulate self-interests are what are guiding the political economy of African states. Thus, and abundance of natural resources is intuitively expected to be a blessing. Nonetheless, it has been argued for some decades that large endowments of natural resources – oil, gas, and minerals in particular – may actually become more of accurse, often leading to slow economic growth and redistributive struggles.

In many cases, these capitalist enterprises and finances become the property of the Head of State. This is to record that state capitalism is one form of political patronage. Other forms of patronage occur via appointments to various state corporations, government, and membership of the Political Bureau, among others. For example, writing of the situation in Ivory Coast which is typical across the continent, states: "the growth of state capitalism, through the many societies' d'état and departments of government, provided opportunities for economic activity to complement what had previously been only political and administrative roles…." [Cohen, 1974:62]

Confronting the Challenges

To begin with, the permissiveness of the state towards foreign capital, economic growth, profit, the embourgeoisement of the ruling and the urban classes together with longevity of the regime and interrelated and mutually reinforcing and contributing to woes of the state. The attitude of Wall Street [seen here as the ruling class] towards the Main Street [the bottom billion] breeds destructive frustration, social impasse and other factors contributing negatively towards state construction. No doubt, there are now growing indications of the degree to which economic growth has been purchased at considerable socio-economic and political cost. In short, the continent is confronted with the crisis of peripheral capitalism, inequalities, greed, recession, abject poverty, endemic corruption, and all forms of insecurity and social conflicts threatening the legitimacy and existence of the state.

First, economic growth has and continues to be highly uneven. The inequities of incomes and opportunities may me more glaring between North and South, between rural and urban areas, but there also major differences between rural zones as well as occupational and educational groups. Development related activities are often ethnic-oriented following the whims and caprices of those controlling the realm of power. Second, political conflict has developed following the return to political party pluralism giving serious rise to social conflict, ethnic differentiation and hatred. Third, insecurity is on the increase, corruption in some cases even legalised, and poverty abounds everywhere with the silent majority getting, and the loud minority richer for every passing day. Fourth, it gives room for maverick politicians to exploit the situation for self-interests, and would sacrifice everything possible for the continuation of bad governance that perpetuates the chaotic situation. The chaotic situation was aptly analysed way back by Joseph [1976:13];" with the political and social hegemony exercised by the local ruling class, and depoliticisation and repression of the\masses and of radical organisation, only an as yet unforeseen conjuncture could lead to the sweeping away of this dismal legacy." Some of the states face serious problems of political succession giving rise to exacerbated tensions. Ghana should be praised for the smooth transition of power following the death of President Atta Mills as compared to what happened with the death of the Presidents of Togo (Eyadema), Nigeria (Sani Abacha and Yar' Adua) and (Bingu Wa Mutharika) of Malawi. Such smooth democratic transition gives greater credence to the governance system, enhances government's legitimacy, credibility and gives greater value to both foreign political economy and national development strategies and as an instrument of attraction to foreign investors and the mobilisation of domestic resources and investors. Ghana's democracy has come of age and should be consolidated. This is a best practice for other countries to draw useful lessons from Ghana's maturity in the democracy and good governance construction.

It is clear these crises are embedded with revolutionary transformation is imminent. The 2011 Arab Spring being a typical example. Failure in addressing the issues of economic crisis breeds political instability. Failure to attain to the issue of social inequality, greed, exclusion breeds chaos, conflicts and instability leading to state collapse. The continent's political economy and governance should address inequality, discrimination, exclusion and division within the society. Africa should strive towards a political economy and governance policy that becomes the engine of growth and development. Therefore, the current economic crisis presents golden opportunity for new mindset and constructive change.

Six Steps to resist the resources curse

- understand and manage broader macroeconomic impacts;
- use mineral receipts to invest in productive assets;
- understand your local economic and social impacts;

- manage expectations through effective communication and consultations;
- understand your local economic and social impacts
- strengthen accountability mechanisms.

Time for Fundamental Economic Changes

If there has ever been a time for restructuring, renewal and change is now as the continent is caught between the devil and the hard rock. The current economic crisis is a catalyst for structural changes to create a more resilient Africa. Choices and the right ones have to make today not as to compromise the wellbeing of future generations. Recolonisation through the political economy of Africa foreign policy is exacerbated by a number of interrelated input factors absent on the continent which both the old colonial masters and new colonisers exploit to their advantaged as depicted here:

Impeding Factors Accelerating Underdevelopment and Exploitation
Economic diversification: Vast majority of African countries {economies} lack globality competitive industries and services Conflict: Political tension, conflict and violence weakens the capacity of African states to engage in intra-regional trade, and even work together Infrastructure: Infrastructure deficiencies hamper trade and communication within and between countries Financial Constraints: Most countries are financially weak with vary non-convertible Currencies. The use of multiple currencies impedes the progress of the continent Language Barriers: Like the multiplicity of currency, too many languages pose serious problems forcing the continent to depend on foreign languages Dependency: Dependency on export of raw materials and aid subjects these countries to wrong treatment by the developed economies and donor countries // // // // **Impedes intra-African trade and political unity** **But** **Accelerates external trade with the consequences of exploitation, dependency and domination**

Forje [2012]

In 2008 the financial bubble that had, in fact, been growing since the early nineties dramatically burst. Most of us are fairly conversant with the issues leading to the crisis and their specialised terminology. We now realise the weaknesses of financial deregulation. We understand about reckless attitude of Wall Street against Main Street and should lament human greed that has gripped the ruling class, and the disproportionate amount of financial influence wielded by the few. We can even relate to the unparalleled spending spree embarked upon by the governing class who never think about the day of reckoning to come. Yet we continue to marvel with the escalating degree of the corruption pandemic and its impact on growing abject poverty in society. African financial institutions find themselves unable to support intra-regional trade, mainly because of a weak capital base limited knowledge and inexperience in managing countervailing risks, and limited correspondent banking relationships. The continent is plagued with multiple and non-convertible currencies inefficient payment mechanisms insurance requirements and customs guarantees. While currency conversion makes trade more expensive, the non-convertibility of some currencies makes many things tremendously time-consuming scarring away potential investors. The continent must change its current mindset by

- gunning for democratic governance and quality services delivery to all citizens;
- restoring public rights over corporate privileges;
- taking equity, social justice and inclusion seriously;
- ensuring social justice and the rule of law;
- bringing the female gender and other marginalise groups to the plus side of the development continuum;
- changes in mindset;
- changes in fiscal and regulatory policies;
- intensifying regional / inter-African economic and political integration

The political focus on economic globalisation and deregulation growth has led to marginalisation as it excludes actors in society, mainly poor people, especially women and indigenous peoples whose priorities are not determined exclusively by the price system. It is true the voices of the bottom billion are never heard and respected. The fight against corruption and poverty has not achieved its purported goal, rather poverty and corruption intensify than ever before and the methods for the fight against this pandemic canker worm destroying the social fabric of society have been revealed to be defunct. In some countries the creation of anti-corruption commissions are just dogs that bark but cannot bite. Most of such institutions are completely controlled by the executive. And so, the plethora of predicaments plaguing the country continues unabated. In some countries these commissions have been able to bring sanity into the functioning and accountability of the government.

A new fresh air of good governance is now possible though there is still a long way to go. The first steps in the right directions have been taken. Another Africa is possible if we so want. The very reality in the lives of the citizens of all 34 AU member states and their respective leaders is that of a hopeless people incapable of solving their development problems on their own. The lives of the citizens are just as good as they were under the colonial masters, with the leaders still under coercion from colonial influence on how the citizens and their economies are managed. The fact is 'yes,' there is a change in the guards of who run the colonies, but they still sustain the domineering interest of the colonial masters with the collaboration of US power under the guise of the 'international community" [Yekin Kofi 2012]. There is an urgent need to work diligently with the various stakeholders to craft a new way forward and rescue the people from sinking deeper into poverty and global marginalisation. Africa needs proactive strategic policy measures and visionary leadership to lead the people out of their current state bondage. The mindset that has grown from the impunity that has accompanied the Africans has kept them on a curse of self-annihilation. As a result, other mantas have grown aimed at forgetting history, forgetting humanity and anything connected to keeping them in the commons of history, humanity - alive and well. The tragedy unfolding in front of our eyes is not just about the excesses of one financial environmental disaster. It is about the continued and deliberate silencing/sidelining of Africans by a tiny dictatorial fraction that, for centuries and generations has always gotten away literally with the murder of its citizens.

Conclusion

Where Do We Go from Here?

The particular political economy of African states which is marked by an unbridled state and foreign private capitalism in close collaboration with external associates has allowed unscrupulous exploitation of the continent's natural resources. The entry of new exploiters revamps the recolonisation of the continent. African countries have failed to develop a strategic policy of *'win-win'* with these new colonisers, but instead gun for a 'loose-win' approach and attitude. The penetrating impact of globalisation with a weak technological base, poor human capital development and dependence on a single resources or export of raw materials exacerbates the plight of African countries [see Rodney 2012, Tandon 2012].

As the current economic meltdown and recession reverberated through the devaluations of the currencies of the developed economies, they have brought the contradictions of dependent growth and concomitant conflicts to the open. Faced with a deteriorating revenue base and open skirmishes, African states have intensified their overtures to the People's Republic of China while still hanging on to former colonial masters in the West, as well as they have engaged in occasional defensive radicalism and are now beginning to gradually open up to a stronger Regional Economic Communities (RECs) and continental organisations like the African Union (AU). New Partnership for Africa's Development (NEPAD) as a new and emerging trump card, and as a way of reviving the flagging economy and exerting political influence in the emerging global knowledge-based economy of the century.

Are African countries becoming reformist or playing the hide and seek game that benefits the ruling class. Creative and strategic thinking are need more than ever before to get things right and moving on the continent. The continent is faced with the tension between independence and dependence. "The uprising across the continent is the result of common experiences of decades of declining living standards, mass unemployment, land dispossessions and impoverishment of the majority while a few engorged themselves with riches" [Firoze & Ekine, 2012; see also Amin Samir 2012]. However, this requires constructing and consolidating a democratic governance system; building up its human capital; intensifying state-civil society-private sector interface; involving female gender as serious contributors to the transformation of the continent; devolving indigenous knowledge and building up the technological skills of the people; mobilisation of domestic capital and proper use of natural and human resources; the need for visionary servant leadership. No doubt, one can but strongly shares the views of Nilsson [200923] that a crisis is a terrible thing to waste. A crisis is a catalyst for strong structural changes. An economic crisis has important cleansing effects in helping to facilitate painful restructuring. It is probably the case that if the financial crisis had not happened last year, we would have had to invent it, otherwise the magnitude of reconstruction would be overwhelming. Ultimately, out of the economic crisis, the new wave of globalisation, new ideas will flourish, but the time for restructuring and renewal is now. Africa has to take great advantage of the economic melt-down to reconstruct itself.

The financial crisis is no longer just financial. Africa is going from a financial crisis to an economic crisis and with a political melt-down looming in the horizon. Dramatically decreased growth will bring

African countries to the verge of bankruptcy and instability. Rising destructive frustration is on the horizon. The Arab Spring is a good pointer to countries south of the Sahara to draw valuable lessons and begin to adjust accordingly. Continued poor policy articulation and aggregation, back by the current attitude of 'greed' exhibited by the ruling class, the economy will be in a shamble for a long time yet. Of course, we cannot rule out the issue of 'hope,' though the destruction Africa faces is deep, destruction or economic meltdown in its turn generates new, albeit frightening forces that can produce tremendous creativity. Colonialism held the people of Africa down for many years, the people bounced back; the apartheid system held the black majority in captivity for many decades, but the resilient and fighting forces bounced back. Today, Africa is the future of the world and how we use that golden opportunity to construct ourselves matters a great deal. We have to construct a different continent. Now is the time to do so. The message the paper conveys is simple; Africa is in the midst of transition to a new African Order but what kind of New African Order? Africa must unite: but behind whom? Globalisation means interconnectedness and that cooperation is the only way to sustainability and survival. If there is one thing the economic meltdown and the dismal development strategies so far adopted and should teach Africa, is that no one country would be able to go it alone at the expense of the rest.

In short, Africa must unite to regain its legitimacy, sovereignty, credibility, and to make the best use of its natural resources for the common good. Let the virtues of globalisation be exploited to the advantage of the present people without compromising the wellbeing of future generations of Africa. We need a New Political Economy Renewal: From Means to Ends. This is the only way to design a new what may be called 'Practical Imperative" for the good of society. The political economy foreign policy must operate to treat the people, whether yourself or any other person, in every case as an end, never as a means only. The need for a happy and s sustainable continent in which people would treat each other in this way – as ends in themselves, not just as means to something else – or call it Africa as a 'kingdom of ends.' The challenge for Africa is that of tackling all problems simultaneously; abject poverty, endemic corruption, famine, energy, employment, health care, education, road, rail and communication infrastructure, housing and conflicts. With regards to conflicts, there is no chance of endurable peace without development, shared-prosperity and social justice. The exits gap and social divide should be adequately addressed. The take home message is simple. Driving home, the practice of democratic governance, and stimulating economic growth to improving the quality wellbeing of the people. The state has a crucial role to play, and must exert responsibility in many different areas in order for development to take place. The state has to play a controlling role in development while permitting private ownership and entrepreneurships at the same time.

African governments should strive toward the ideal proposed here. The conviction is that the performance and services of governments to the African people will rise dramatically if it does. That is the renewal we all look forward to. The conviction is that of government performance with effective and efficient service delivery to the African people. The people of Africa are expecting nothing short but sustainable development, justice and equity,

Recommendations: Time for Renewal

- putting in place a democratic governance system is imperative, though not the panacea, but a constructive and comprehensive means towards a sustainable end;
- Stimulate state-civil society-private sector nexus, not to make government business like, but to make it more government-like;
- The bureaucracy as the output mirror of the state is concern with public goods [service delivery] acting within the framework of public law, political will and democratic consent. not serve "clients," but serve "citizens" who have common purposes and rights, and among these are the right to be treated equitably- [equity, fairness, openness, due process and accountability are among the foundations of public administration: together with other principles, they make public management an activity fundamentally different in nature from its counterpart in the private sector];
- The state, civil society and private sector should operate within the confines of" people," "accountability" and "service" (PAS);
- There is needed to create a Council of Administrative Development and Renewal (CDR); to push ahead the sustainable transformation of the continent;
- Intensify Regional Economic Communities (RECs) for economic integration of Africa; as well as reduce dependency

on the export of raw materials; diversification and processing of these raw materials should be the goal;

- There is need for a common currency; and need for a more progressive African political body that speaks and defends the continent
- Utilise the potentials of the Diaspora; as well as reduce the continent's dependence on foreign aid; intensify the mobilisation of domestic resources;
- A new political economy should be a joint responsibility and obligations of all the stakeholders- state, civil society and the private's sector, not excluding the international community

References

AAPAM (2012) "Call for Papers – Global Financial Crisis Africa in a Post-Crisis Global Economy – Lessons and Strategies for Africa's Transformation" Rwanda, October 2012, Nairobi-Kenya.

Amin Samir [2012] The People's Spring. The Future of Arab revolution, Pambazuka Publishers, London

Cohen A. Michael [1974] Urban Policy and Political Conflict in Africa. A Study of the Ivory Coast. Chicago, USA.

Emeagwali Phil [2010] "How Do We Reverse the Brain Drain"? Keynote Speech delivered on October 24, 2003, at the Pan-African Conference on Brian Drain, Eisah, Illinois, USA and reproduced in Renaissance World, 1st April-31st May 2010,

Emekalam Kelechi [2010] "Meet Phil Emeagwali, 'Africa's Bill Gates' and 'Father of Internet". Renaissance World, 1st April – 31st May, 2010.

Fadahunsi Akin [1979] "A Review of the Political Economy of the Industrialisation Strategy of the Nigerian State 1960-1960", Political Science Departmental Seminar, Ahmadu Bello University, Zaria, Nigeria, April, 1979].

Firoze Manj & Ekine Sokari (eds.) [2012] Africa Awakening – The Emerging Revolutions, Pambazuka Books, London

Haglund Dan [2012] How Can African Economies Turn the Resource Curse into A Blessing?" Bridge Africa, Vol.1. Issue 3, July 2012, pp7-9

Joseph Richard [1976]. "The Gaullist Legacy: Patterns of French Neo-colonialism, Review of African Political Economy, Vol. 6. May-August 1976, p.12

Lema Forje Catherine [2009] "Empowering Youth Through Entrepreneurship", Cyprus Journal of Management, Vol.14, No.1, Autumn 2009, pp26-45,

Mazrui Ali [1981] "Exit Visa from the World System: Dilemmas of Cultural and Economic Disengagement", Third World Quarterly, Vol. 3, No. 1, January 1981, pp62-75

New African [2008] "China – Africa: Why the West is Worried", New African, No.471, March 2008, London, pp12-18

Nkuepo Joel Henri [2012] Reducing Non-Tariff Barriers to Trade in Africa", Bridge Africa, Vol. 1, Issue 3, July 2012

Nilsson Sten [2009] "The Time for Restructuring and Renewal Is Now". Potions, Summer 2009, pp22-23

Otaviano Canuto & Mathueus Cavaliani [2012] "Natural Wealth Is It Invariably a Curse?" Bridge Africa, Vol. 1. Issue 3. July 2012, pp4-6

Rodney Walter [2012] How Europe Underdeveloped Africa, Pambazuka Publishers, London (this classic remains an essential introduction to the dynamics of Africa's relations with the West].

Shaw Timothy M. & Aluko Olajide (eds.) [1984]. The Political Economy of African Foreign Policy. Comparative Analysis, Gover Publishers Aldershot, England

Tandon Yash [2012] Ending Aid Dependence. Pambazuka Publishers London

Tandon Yash [2012] Development and Globalisation. Daring to Think Differently. Pambazuka Publishers, London

Toure Sekou [1962] Africa's Failure and The World, Foreign Affairs, Vol. 41. No.1, October 1962, p.147

Wadada Dani Nabudere [2012] The Crash of International Finance – Capital and its Implications for the Third World, Pambazuka Publishers, London

World Bank [2011] The Changing Wealth of Nations: Measuring Sustainable Development in the New Millennium, Washington, DC, USA

Yekin Abdul Ali Kofi [2012] "Africa Must Unite but Behind Whom?" (Pambazuka.org) July 2012, London

Chapter 3

Rethinking Science, Technology, Innovation and Development: *Facing the Good, Bad and Ugly:* Challenges and Prospects Impacting on Africa's Development – Looking Back to see forward

Abstract

No society develops without innovation, entrepreneurship, science and technology. Africa is no exception. It is not just having the science and technology base; its utilisation as a tool for African solutions to African problems is vital in improving the quality livelihood of citizens. The paper looks at the good, bad and ugly of science and technology placing the African citizen at the centre of development and decision-making at the national and international levels to better consolidate its sovereignty and development. Briefly stated, science and technology are considered the most effective means to enhance growth as well as change the dynamics of socio-economic development of nations. Therefore, scientific and technological developments have profound and long-term impact on income distribution, economic growth, employment, commerce, industrial structure and other aspects of society. It goes further to present the case of building the scientific and technological capability of the continent from the perspective of an intermarriage between:(i) indigenous knowledge; (ii) tapping into the inherent knowledge and skills of 'reversing migration' or reverse brain drain into 'brain gain' and (iii) learning from the global pool of scientific and technological skills. The comprehensive combination of these interrelated factors provides the structural basis of African solutions to African problems as the primary agenda. The challenging question is how to use science and technology for the development of the continent not for its destruction? How can Africa improve on its indigenous knowledge and blend these with modern scientific and technological global knowledge to accelerate, enhance and restructure the socioeconomic transformation of a so-called backward economy into a service delivery society. It argues that the burden and endeavour to place the African citizen at the centre of development and decision-making is far from a successful venture due to its weak scientific, technological, industrial, non-competitive and entrepreneurial status within a global knowledge-based economy of our century. It concludes that building the scientific and technological anvil of the continent provides the best leverage for seeking African solutions to African problems and consolidating its sovereignty, integrity and unity without which Africa is condemned into the annals of a failed, collapsed and fragile continent, in spite of existing vast resources potentials exploited a marginalized by the those who command both the vices and virtues of science and technology power. Without a solid scientific and technological base added value cannot be given to the wealth of resources potential the continent has in improving the living standards of the people. A framework for understanding and acting upon solutions advance is presented, taking into account a variety of institutional, intellectual and international perspectives.

Keywords: science and technology, indigenous knowledge, human capital development, policy articulation, visionary leadership, unity, good governance and rule of law.

Introduction

> "Just as energy is the basis of life itself and ideas the source of innovation, so is innovation the vital spark of all human change, improvement and progress.
>
> (Ted Lewitt)

The Reflexive Turn: The Perils of (Under) Development

In the past couple of decades, the great divide between the weak and strong nations, the rich and poor within and between African countries, and between Africa and the developed countries has attained serious dimensions that one begins to question why? This paper is notably interested in the implications of what could be term 'sensitive' fields of development that fails to deliver quality livelihood to the poor, deprived and neglected. At the same time human intellect has made tremendous strides in the domain of science and technology. It has been possible to send humans into outer space, but unable to feed the growing new mouths on planet earth. The trajectory between scientific achievements and quality living standards of the silent majority is put into question. How come that Africa with vast natural resources and given global advancements in science and technology, Africa is still classified as underdeveloped leading to failed, collapse and fragile states littering the continent?

The continent of Africa holds a central position on the world stage. One of the most significant events in the life of the international community in the most recent decades has been the emergence of the African countries in the 1960s which were formerly colonies. By these acts they took their place on the world's raster of independent nations. In 1950, there were four independent states in Africa: Ethiopia, Liberia, Egypt and the Union of South Africa. Today, there are 54 states, with the eventualities of more in the making. Whatever the changes the continent is gripped with many challenges in an upheaval unprecedented in modern history! What is evidently clear is that there are two distinct Africa's. One is the Africa of the headlines; the Africa torn by coups, mutinies, war and turmoil. This is the Africa that, to some, seemed to confirm the worst forecasts of the pessimists. But there is another Africa that remains largely peaceful and intent on its drive for modernization, political evolution, social and economic development. That is the Africa that will endure. The challenges are how to ensure that good Africa survives and the test of time! Presently, political revolution is one of the tremors shaking the region. African society itself has been undergoing a transformation which, while less spectacular, is no less profound. To lead this great transformation, requires new leaders with vision and the ideals of the placing the people first in all developmental changes. We cannot deny the fact that some progresses have been achieved towards realizing the dream of sovereignty. Much could have been achieved if only the leaders were focused and detest hanging on the Euro-centric developmental approach. Together, we should collectively work towards that goal by creating an enabling environment for all citizens to be active contributors in the process of transformation for the common good.

Taking a critical look, the paper questions why fifty years after the attainment of independence, Africa has not been able to craft policies construed on the ideological principles of African solutions for African problems? While we can confidently assert that formally the age of colonialism and apartheid is history; yet the deep-seated scars it has left and structural frames erected have not been done away with completely. More than fifty years since the historical events at the polo ground in Accra - Ghana, the endeavour to place the African citizen at the centre of development and decision-making is far from a successful venture. The argument is that the continued underdevelopment of the continent and its marginalization in the global arena is attributed to its state of its fragility in the domain of science, technology, entrepreneurial ship, industrialization, management and good governance. A weak scientific and technological base inhibits any form of added value to its vast range of resources potential. The complex relationship between the economy, society and the environment and scientific knowledge requires a multi-disciplinary approach as it also calls for skilled communication to be address technological issues as well as the socio-political framework within which problem solving necessarily takes place. Apparently, globalisation of science and technology strongly associated with political economy of the late 20th and early 21st century, has been dominated by "bottom-up" processes, driven largely by purely scientific dynamics of commercial considerations, and notes Allam Ahmed and Josephine A. Stein (2004). There is an urgent need to bridge the development gap between the developed and developing countries, alleviating poverty to provide a more equitable and sustainable future for all becomes imperative requiring the incorporation of indigenous knowledge and scientific knowledge.

The second caveat is the weakness of African states and its institutions hindering the growth and use of S&T in the development process. Osia (2004) points out that since independence African countries are caught in the modernising waves of development ideologies. They have not been able to absorb or understand the implications of these modernisation theories that have evolved from the cold war rivalries of the super powers. In addition, they lacked strong institutions to dissect and put in place the necessary policies measures to effect development the way they want and according to their needs. Institutional weakness – the administration, judiciary and educational establishments due to political influence and manipulations remain weak and shadow of them unable to articulate and inject strong guide lines for any meaningful take-off. It is obvious that African states, though independent, are incapable of making independent decisions as to what model best suit their situations. Without an iota of doubt, African countries are operating from a weak political, scientific, technological and economic platform. The intellectual, technological, economic and political prowess of the developed polities constitutes a serious ideological scramble for Africa and the domination of the region for a very long unforeseeable period. A new mindset is necessary to redeem the continent from its current predicaments.

In the field of 'research politics' the reflexive turn has also been distinguished by the renewal of the Afro-centric agenda like the forces exerted during the era for self-determination struggle. This renewal is to place in correct perspectives the different types of relations between the different actors or stakeholders. The anthropology of development as seen through the periscope of 'Africa's solutions for African

Problems' which underpins OAU/AU at 50 and beyond has for the past fifty years been polarised between a radical critic of the developmentalist enterprise (or approach under the canopy of Afro-centric) and coached within the context of Euro-centric (devices formulated by the liberalist to accelerate the globalisation bandwagon) show the uphill tasks faced by African countries in making the right choices. It is imperative to bridge the development gap between the developed and developing polities, as well as alleviating poverty in transitional countries to provide a more equitable and sustainable future for all. These activities require novel integrated approaches, especially serious change in the mindset of the people in developing countries to fully incorporate existing indigenous knowledge and new scientific knowledge. Therefore, international cooperating in science and technology from the village blacksmith, traditional healer to the most sophisticated western science and technology must be considered as the key tool for enhancing sustainable development and improving on the livelihood of the people.

Why the Euro-centric approach still holds sway is due to the legacies of colonial rule and the forces of globalisation; the acculturation of Africans into beholding everything West as right and good for the continent. The assimilation of Africans into the cultural setting of the West leads to policy articulation that works against the sustainable transformation of the continent. These policy architecture benefits the West and not the continent. Africa is not an island; it has existed, will continue to exist and interact with other continents of the world. It is from these perspectives that a triangular structural approach is adopted to build, improve, enhance, harness and utilise science and technology in the transformation of the continent from what could be termed a backward entity into a service delivery society.

Therefore, developing the continent's scientific knowledge by building on its indigenous know-how and backed by the 'late-comer' advantage creates the avenue of systematic scientific knowledge as an increasing important factor for the development of the continent through its transitional phase and its years of consolidation and maturity. Africa is not creating its own science and technology but to tap properly from existing knowledge of which she has been contributor centuries past. The first university in the world was located in Africa. It was organised around three great Masajids or Mosques. The University of Timbuktu (Mali) was the world's first university established in the 12-century located in the city of Timbuktu in Mali – West Africa.

Unfortunately, the *"Golden Age of Africa's Scientific and Technological Knowledge'* contribution did not last long due to the invading forces of imperialism, capitalism and colonialism. Neo-colonialism is equally threatening the reawakening of a new scientific and technological age expected to be provided by the Diaspora and intensity in building a solid human capacity background. The continent is left at large scrambling to pick up the broken pieces not through strong men but through strong and functional institutions and visionary leadership. Colonial policies and reinforced by post-colonial policies created the African university as an ivory tower (designed to replace the departing colonial masters) living in splendid isolation from the realities of the rest of society, wrecked as is often the case, by political strife and social dislocation, contributing very little to the sustainable transformation of the society. Political party interests and ethnicity infiltrated the university; and combined with schisms within the university, created stubborn structures that thrived on the persecution of those who failed to stay within the prescribed political and ideological boundaries.

The African university lost its intellectual, scientific, investigative research credence, became a haven of petty-bourgeois ambitions, aspirations and fantasies, engendering a culture of careerism and fierce competition, fertile breeding grounds for the transmission of political repression and intellectual persecution. Political and intellectual witch-hunt rears their ugly heads. Scientific discourses, research, innovation was down played to the delight of the West. The victors, those supporting the Euro-centric and ethno-centric or ruling political party forces were rewarded with the transient privileges of promotion and corporate appointments until they, too, slipped and felled in the continent's treacherous political quicksand. A new but challenging dawn awaits African scholars to show-case their lost prowess in the field of scientific inquiry and scholarship.

As a result of imperialism, capitalism, colonialism and neo-colonialism, political party and ethnicity infiltrated the academic environment rendering it hopeless in providing leadership and sense of direction and orientation for attaining a strong and capable scientific and technological transformation process. The intellectual space of African scholarship was and is narrowed and weakened. It is still today. Hovering above are the rumbling clouds of state authoritarianism and exclusion. The Cold War conflict backed by the economic recession that gripped many countries further compounded the problems of intellectual production research, innovation and productivity as the academics and their universities began facing unprecedented hardship.

Political party politics and ethnic tendencies facilitated the production of power by the political class by fostering the divisive power of communal consciousness and foreclosing the disruptive power of class and other social solidarities. The power of the sword became mightier than the power of the pen. So African intellectual virtues crumbled and relied on Euro-centric dictates of transforming the continent. The impact of this on education and scholarship in general is not hard to imagine. Africa is stuck on the runway unable to take-off towards being a capable developmental state on the long journey to a service delivery polity. African scholarship lost ifs sense of direction and purpose of being the true beacon of guiding the development of society. Call this the **'Sad Era'** of Africa's transformation.

The hot-pursuit of critical scholars contributed to the **'brain drain'** phenomenon or what could be seen as 'The Perils of Academic Tourism" (Zeleza, 1997) which can now be converted into the **'brain gain'** phenomenon or the motion of the '*rebuilding of Africa*' to kick start or revamp the scientific and technological transformation and reconstruction of the continent. The return of the African Diaspora and infusion into the society is a constructive process and the right search for African solutions to African problems. The irony is that, while the expatriate western scholar is seen and accepted and even respected for their contributions; the returning African scholar is treated with disrespect, and little fanfare that accompanies the arrival of the western expatriate scholar in African countries. In other words, there is the advocacy for African solutions to African problems, but not put into practice. Apparently, the AU has accepted the Diaspora vas its sixth region. Inherently, the Diaspora ultimately constitutes a significant part of African solution to African problems. Rhetoric's should be converted into practical actions for conflict to benefit from the technological, financial and knowledge-prowess of and from the Diaspora. The gross neglect of scientific and technological research and innovative aspects of the African university over the years is a contributing factor to the destruction and inhibiting the developmental process of the continent. Africa should be in search for science and technology for the sake of humanity, for take the people out of the scorn of endemic poverty and corruption constraining the sustainable transformation of the continent.

An Afro-centric and the late-comer advantage provide windows of opportunities to galvanise and fill the lost scientific and technological terrains of the continent. The creation of the continent's sixth region (Diaspora) gives credence for the search of African solutions to African problems. African countries must realize that there is no substitute for good quality education. Otherwise, progress will be installed or continue to wane. Countries like China, Thailand, Indonesia, Singapore and others continue to invest heavily in technical education, reaping the result by biding fare-voyage to the economically impoverished states clothed in poverty. Is there any reason why Africa cannot do same, given that it is a more resource-rich continent than those countries that have moved up the ladder of economic growth?

There is a widely shared and lasting concern for at least three aspects of technological progress. First, how Africa assures its participation in continuous technological innovation and adaptation in order to stay economically competitive in the world of the 21st century and beyond? This entails a number of interrelated activities; (i) building the requisite human capital: (ii) a search for sources of innovation and technological amativeness as well as its vigorous implementation process: Second, how can Africa integrate new technologies into its social body and avoid the effects of de-humanisation and degradation of work that since the industrial revolution have been the frightening aspects of technological innovation? In other words, how scientific and technological knowledge is used to improve on the wellbeing of the people? Third, how can the continent be a major player in the globalisation bandwagon of the 21st century? What role can improve indigenous knowledge contribute towards Africa owning its development? Can the cell-phones of today be seen as Africa's crude forerunner contribution from the "African Talking Drum" to modern communication system?

What is the contribution of the continent in world transformation after it's lost *'golden age of scientific and knowledge'* capabilities? Natural resources are not the problem of the continent; but giving added value to its natural potentials is the outstanding question that must be addressed and quickly too. In short, seeking African solutions to African problems by developing its knowledge industry and aided by the global pool of scientific and technological advancement provides the best way forward. Here lies the challenge. What policy measures can best be articulated and aggregated to ensure that the continent is part of the evolving scientific and technological community of nations? Can you imagine learning computer science without access to computers; or learning chemistry without the necessary test tubes and other appliances? The exact nature of education prepares a country's future workers in a fast-changing global job-market is desirable. A new, progressive and enabling education environment is urgently needed in Africa.

Human capital building must take advantage of the present information superhighway. Similarly, the dichotomy between the liberal arts – learning art, music, science math – and vocational specific job skills must be revamped for an approach that leans towards modified arts with an emphasis on coordination and leadership skills. The rise of the Asian Tigers in the 20th century has shown that success or failure in the global economy does not depend on natural resources alone. In essence the basic ingredient for developing competitive supremacy lies in knowledge embodied in managerial, leadership, and technological competence (Hax, 1989). African countries must bear in mind that there is no substitute for education. Constant learning and skills upgrading remain advantageous for individuals and societies. Therefore, society must be equipped with the knowledge to transform their ideas and skills into enterprising ventures. The Asian Tigers are reaping the results of serious investments in human capital development especially in the fields of scientific and technologically development. That is why Africa should its human capital base to better exploit and making the best use of the late-comer advantage.

The solutions provided here focus on technology, the impact of culture and its effect on the adoption of technologies. In addition, technologies do not come cheap. There is nothing like free lunch. Making proper use of and overcoming resistance to technologies calls for good training. And that technology is not here to replace human beings but facilitate an ease the drudgery of work. The relevance of technology in the African setting can be questionable as well. Technology has to be relevant to needs of the people. We cannot deny the fact that most imported technologies are not necessarily relevant to the pressing needs of the society. If a technology does not fit the task it is intended for the society, obviously problems will emerge. To a large extent, the continent has not done well to refining technologies to ensure their suitability to the continent's need and the rapidly changing environmental setting.

Though these questions of scientific and technological progress have been with us for generations, this paper is just adding another brick to a great building of cumulative understanding. Africa has no choice but to address seriously its deficiencies in the domain of scientific, technological and entrepreneurial standing. Far from closing some of the theoretical or empirical questions of our general understanding, the paper has its own theoretical perspective and tries to come to terms with specific dimensions of organizational transformation and technological innovation using the Afro-centric platform as points of reference. The Afro-centric departure platform is focused on the direction of African solutions to African problems from a collaborative and adaptive perspective. Diversity rather than uniformity characterizes this paper. Importantly, the reader carries the important message that organizational transformation and technological innovation are highly multifaceted and complex requiring collaborative efforts across different disciplines.

Drawing from and building on other scholars, competition and allocation of economic resources were believed automatically to create the equilibrium growth path – which made economic thinking so attractively simple and deterministic. Also, the forces producing the theoretical outcome were believed to create the reality leading to its destiny of economic and technologically rationality (Borum & Kristensen 1989). The issues concerning capitalism, socialism, and democracy (Schumpeter (1943) generates heated discourses about what determines growth, what determines the pace of technological development, when and at what point societies take-off into the era of modernity and of rapid industrialization? Poor policy articulation leaves Africa wanting in the domain of science, technology, innovation and entrepreneurship. It impedes its transformation into a service delivery society.

Africa is caught within the trappings of capitalism, socialism and democracy in transforming the continent into a veritable player within the global context. David Landes 'The Unbound Prometheus' (1969) presents a very clear and deterministic view on economic and technological rationalisation and yet his conclusion (p544) presents doubtful rather than affirmative picture: "If there are some general conclusions to be drawn from this, it is the complexity of economic development. This is a process that, particularly when it takes the form of industrialization, affects all aspects of social life and is affected in turn by them." Africa is within the ambit of the theorems of change and needs all available know-how to accelerate the change paradigm. That is why the 'development of the wheel' and the 'late-comer advantage' interface provides a consolidating drawing board and pool of knowledge to draw from in its search for development.

Drawing from the *'late-come advantage'* advanced by Gerschenkron (1962); what Africa requires is organisational transformation, good management, visionary leadership and technological innovation. According to Schumpeter, such processes were dependent on the gifted individual, the entrepreneur, who in a flash of genius transformed our way of organizing, or made a technological innovation. Apparently, innovation is the ability to see change as an opportunity – not a threat, and innovation distinguishes between a leader and a follower. While the West went ahead to innovate, Africa remained as a follower – hence, the Euro-centric dominant developmental approach. The challenge is to reverse the trend, hence the Afro-centric paradigm backed by embracing the 'reality theory' and discarding the *'blame theory.'* The reality theory is building on the Afro-centric to ensure the unravelling of the unequal level of economic and political development vis-à-vis the developed world that strongly propagate ad benefit from globalisation even though globalisation remains indispensable for the sustainable growth of all nations. We must not gloss over the fact that the tragic history of colonialism, slavery and the remains of its administrative apparatus have resulted in governments being unable to follow a path of, or generate conditions for, sustainable development as noted by Osia (1987). Thus, the trajectory of institutional and structural weaknesses of African states, and the wrong developmental approach adopted, the expected growth and development (rising expectation) have failed to materialize, resulting in destructive frustration. Since independence, African states continue experiencing endemic coup d'état, gross exploitation and underdevelopment. Strewn on the broad canvass of African states' political history was the debris of unfulfilled expectation, socio-political discontinuity and instability (Osia 1998). Inherited economic theories remain inadequate to the internal viability of economic development and transformation of African countries.

How do we transform a potentially rich backward society into a veritable service delivery society? How do we create a pool of gifted individuals, the innovators, the researchers, the entrepreneurs, who in a flash of genius can best transform our way of organizing, managing or make constructive changes within the society? Africa is challenged and faced with the incremental process of learning *'by doing'* and *'by using.'* What must Africa do now and what must it use to accomplish its objectives – African solutions to African problems? The message of this paper, however, is simple but straightforward; one of differentiation and of variety, as it constructs a typology based on the movement towards an Afro-centric construct that groups different types of technological learning behaviour connected with indigenous and informal knowledge creating the way for the continent to evolve within the ambit of global scientific and technological changes for the good of its people in particular, and humanity in general. It is imperative that African countries must strive to strengthen their institutional and infrastructural capacity, improve on governance system making it to be more inclusive and participatory ensuring that equity and justice prevails. These should be the major focus areas of the developmental process of the continent; a process that S&T plays important roles. Sixty years after independence, our underdevelopment is man-made. This challenges the continent to articulate and develop its own pace for its own goal and vision not Ibadan to continue dancing and propagating Euro-centric notion of development which only advances and makes supreme the economic interests of multinational corporations of the industrial west. The developmental interest of the developed polities is its own interest, not that of African countries. The bottom line is that "the process of globalisation is uneven, contradictory and certainly not linear," notes Goddard et al (2003).

No country develops without a scientific, technological and entrepreneurial foundation. Western domination of Africa through science and technology acquires a new holistic dimension – a factor abundantly in evidence with globalization. You have to be scientifically and technological equipped to draw maximum benefits within the globalised knowledge-based economy. Modern technology and intensified industrialisation are regarded by many as the best and surest solution to the problems of persistent backwardness. Sophisticated technologies alone cannot offer the right incentives (Forje 2011:101). Hountondji (2002:278) contends that "the one essential shortcoming of scientific activity in the colonies was the lack of an intermediate state. We missed the central operation of theory-building and nation-building."

Africa only had the first and third stage of the process: (a)the data collection, the feverish gathering of all supposed useful information; and (b)a partial, occasional and limited application of the research outcome to some local issues. The medium stage took place in the so-called 'mother country,' the colonial metropolis." Africa was only a receiver not producer of knowledge and scholarship. By the late 1990s and even in mid-2000 a number of francophone countries were still using syllabuses designed in the late 1950s and early 1960s. Not only were such syllabuses obsolete and irrelevant given the strides of intellectual advancement the world over; but only created greater difficulties for the transformation of the continent. These countries have become entrenched in what is known in Cameroon as *"the Bafia*

Dance" – the rhythm and movement of taking one step forward and two or more steps backward.

Developing the medium stage (building centres of excellence, research institutes, universities, building the requisite human capital etc. would have laid the basis for a scientific and technological take-off for Africa. Two things went hand in gloves – the theoretical vacuum and the industrial vacuum used to characterise economic and development activities were missing and are still missing. Africa lacked these vital inputs in its developmental phase. It still lacks fifty years after Ghana's independence and the creation of the continental organization, Organisation of African Unity/African Union (OAU/AU) creating a deep hole in the scientific and technological advancement of the continent. Though policies were articulated but these countries failed to marshal the much-needed political will and finances for the realisation of technological targets. And provide the thrust to promote technological innovation in well-defined key sectors and advancing new technologies in energy, information technology, agriculture, and biotechnology among others that have generic influence in the economy i.e., these integrated product areas that have multi-sectoral repercussions because of a strong existing web of interconnectedness, the so call filieres.

The entire strategy was based on the control of knowledge production both at the centre and at the periphery of the system, which constituted the colonial pact. The globalization wind only strengthens old ties. The technological trajectories of countries depend on a multitude of factors. Key among them is knowledge, and specifically its production, absorption and exploitation (PAE). The colonial strategy was designed to prohibit the smooth execution of the trinity of (PAE) within the colonies. Even the 'late-comer advantage' advanced by Gerschenkron (1962), African countries is not able to mobilise and utilise science and technology for their developmental process due to the factors earlier numerated. The Lagos Plan of Action (LPA); the recommendations of the First and Second Conferences of African Ministers of Science and Technology (CASTAFRICA 1 and 11, Dakar 1974 and Arusha 1987) respectively together with other recommendations on the issue at national, regional and continental levels provide the framework for advancing the scientific and technological prowess of the continent. These recommendations seem to have fallen on deaf ears, since these documents continue accumulating dust on the shelves. The 21st century provides a new contestation and role of technology and knowledge in the socioeconomic transformation of any country or continent. The other continents (Asia, Latin America, for example) are significantly transforming themselves from the so-called third world into a first world society.

They are gradually consolidating themselves into a powerful block. Bear in mind that some of these countries were behind African countries in the late 1950s and early 1960s. The story and situation are dramatically different today. What went wrong? There has been the 'Rape of the African Paradise' by current custodian of power. This makes it impossible for providing solutions to the continent's problems. There is the synergy issue – development at its most successful is an integrated process that depends heavily on the synergies that merge from collaborative efforts. For example, within the present fragmented MDG scenario, some positive interaction will inevitably arise from the independent pursuit of different Millennium Development Goals (MDG) and targets, but even this interaction will need local interventions in poverty reduction, health, education and gender equality coming together for the same groups of people.

This convergence is made less likely by the reality that goals are compartmentalised into responsibilities of different line ministries nationally, sub-nationally and locally, which means that the potential for simultaneous actions in the same location, working with the same communities and households, is unlikely. Convergence between indigenous knowledge and modern scientific and technological knowledge is a necessary condition for Africa's optimal achievement and participation between the state, civil society and private sector for the provision of quality services delivery to the people. The role of science and technology impacting on the people requires strong political will and commitment by the people and leadership and the interventions designed purely based on the needs and resources of the society.

Knowledge needs to be understood to become useful. Its absorption, the process of learning, takes place in more or less formalized ways. Indigenous knowledge is often passed on through the spoken word, and the relationship between teacher and apprentice may be highly idiosyncratic, by contrast, knowledge transmission and generation I organized societies is structured around a system with layers of education, training and investment in research (Lorentzen 2006:183; Forje 2011:101). Apparently, Indigenous Knowledge System (IKS) should be married with modern science and technology to give greater advantage and scope for exploration. The problem facing

African scholars in this regard is to come up with African epistemology. Ali Mazrui's 'triple heritage'; Achebe's (1966) A Man of the People; Armah's (1968; 1970; 1972) bitter trilogy, The Beautiful Ones Are Not Yet Born, Fragments, and Why Are We So Blest; Wa Thing's (1982, 1986, 1993) and others contributes to the development of the continent by deafening critique of the moral bankruptcy of Africa's post-colonial ruling elite into a furious commitment towards their overthrowal in Petals of Blood and Devil on the Cross. All these barrages of post-colonial novels in Africa are master piece publications of delegitimating: rejecting the Western imperium of Euro-centric approach, but also rejecting a fake nationalist project of the post-colonial national bourgeoisie. That is why these paper stresses on a progressive Afro-centric people-focused developmental approach as the authentic way forward for the continent to harness and utilise science, technology, innovation and entrepreneurship for the sustainable transformation of the region.

It is therefore, imperative that IKS and their underlying world view should be unearthed, developed and harnessed for the cultural, social and economic transformation of the continent. The experiences in other developing countries such as South Korea and Singapore demonstrate that knowledge is the foundation of sustainable development. This explains why resources poor countries like Denmark, Belgium, Holland and others are developed while Nigeria, Cameroon, Democratic Republic of Congo, Sudan and others are not. Africa needs to develop the critical mass to give added value to its resource's potentials. And to find long-lasting solutions because other countries are developed and it is standing still or even declining in the wake of great advances made in the domain of science and technology. What are the forces impeding the developmental take-off of the continent? Why should Africa remain the least developed continent?

Facing the Reality: Not the Blame Theory

The reality is that Africa remains an underdeveloped polity in search of good leaders, policies and a determined will to escape from the annals of colonial history as a backward entity. Facing the 'reality theory' prepares the continent to abandon the world of underdevelopment and exploitation. To attribute the continent's failure to transcend the frontiers of underdevelopment to others is missing the point as well as dodging from scientific inquiry as a tool for constructive development. On the other hand, Africa was the cradle of civilisation and centre of learning long before the creation of centres of learning in Western Europe, for example;

Universities	Country	Year of Creation
The University of Timbuktu	Mali	(Before 859)
University of al-Karaounine	Morocco	859*
University of a-Azhar	Egypt	970 - 972*
University of Bologna	Italy	1088*
University of Oxford	Britain	1096*

Source: * Vick & Khalil (2013). Faith and the Campus, Time Magazine, Vol. 181, No.22.

What went wrong that the continent is at the tail end of human capital development? The blame theory comes as a result of the forces of imperialism and colonialism impacting negatively on the socioeconomic transformation of the continent. Nations rise and fall. So, has been the faith of Africa. Therefore, Africa should not hang on the *"blame theory"* but exploit and adopt the *"reality theory"* as providing the best possible way forward. Unfortunately, post-independence educational policy builds on the 'blame theory; or fans the 'Euro-centric' approach to the transformation of the continent. African countries continue buying this destructive developmental approach. The buying of the Euro-centric approach can be attributed to a number of interrelated factors; (a) greed or articulate self-interests; (b) share ignorance; (c) inferiority complexities the slave trade mentality and (d) leadership deficit. Hence, a new mindset is imperative to accelerate the process of change and the realisation of African solutions to African problems. African problems are not decreasing for that matter. They are mounting for every passing day with no solutions in sight. A sense of urgency and policy implementation must ensure building on the orientation of power to the people, good governance, the rule of law, human capital and infrastructure development, social justice and visionary leadership.

The *'blame theory'* is clear; the colonial powers did not want to see educated Africans and did everything possible to maintain the educational hegemony so as to dominate the colonies. That is history today and should be thrown into the trash bag or else the continent cannot make constructive progress. Therefore, the 'reality theory' is that colonialism created the 'pushes and pulls' of academic labour migration and the destruction of indigenous knowledge. Two outstanding universities created before the independence of African state, Legion (Ghana) and Ibadan (Nigeria) in the late forties provided the breeding ground for West Africans in search of higher education. At independence, the universities most of which were created by the newly independent states as factors to churn out personnel for the Africanisation of state apparatuses and as emblems of cultural modernity, enjoyed cosy relations with the new nationalist rulers, many of whom were themselves intellectuals, or at least aspiring ones.

Mbeki (1998) is categorical on the issue, noting that: 'to perpetuate their imperial domination over the peoples of Africa, colonizers sought to enslave the African mind and destroy the African soul. They sought to oblige us to accept that as Africans we had contributed nothing to human civilization except as beasts of burden in much the same way as those who seek to convince them that they have a place in the human society, but only as beasts of burden and bearers of children. In the end, they wanted us to despise ourselves, convinced that if we were not sub-human we were, at least, not equal to the colonial master and mistress and were incapable of original though and the African creativity which has endowed the world with an extraordinary treasure of masterpieces in architecture and the fine arts. A people capable of such creativity could never have been less human than other human beings, and being as human as any other such people can and must be its liberator from the condition which seeks to describe our continent and its people as the poverty-stricken and disease-ridden primitives in a world riding the crest of a wave of progress and human upliftment."

Zeleza (1997:12) is explicit on this as he opines: "The conflicts in the wider society are condensed and reproduced in the university. Societal polarisations, combined with schisms within the university, create stubborn structures that venerate and thrive on the persecution of those who do not stay with prescribed intellectual and ideological boundaries. The university, as a haven of petty-bourgeois ambitions, aspirations and fantasies, engenders a culture of careerism and fierce competition, fertile breeding grounds for the transmission of political repression and intellectual persecution. Periods of civil conflicts and social strife often reinforce the university community's fratricidal struggles for the limited spoils of academia. Political and intellectual witch-hunts rear their ugly heads. The victors, those who support the successful forces, are rewarded with the transient privileges of promotion and corporate appointments, until they, too, slip and fall in Africa's treacherous political quick sands." Apparently, we have to acknowledge the range of constraints that militated against the development of post-colonial states. In this respect, it can be noted that; "post-colonial Africa inherited weak states and dysfunctional economies that were further aggravated by poor leadership, corruption, and bad governance in many countries. These two factors, together with the divisions caused by the Cold War, hampered the spread of accountable governments across the continent (Krugman 1999, Landes 1969, Mbeki 1998; Shiva 2001).

The politicisation and ethnicization of the African university and labour market helps to generate and reinforce the Euro-centric approach that sustains academic labour migration which can be used as a reversal of the *'brain drain'* into the *'brain gain'* input into building the scientific, technological, and entrepreneurial skills of the continent. It is here that indigenous initiatives must be forced to canalise Africa's renewal ambitions into a more focused and condensed framework for science and technology to play a pivotal role in the transformation process. If Africans hold on to the 'blame theory,' it is because; colonialism help ruined their cultural heritage, knowledge systems and other values that distanced them from the trappings of quality livelihood. In this regard, Africans should be forgiven for being sceptical about learning about leadership from societies that until 50 years ago had occupied, exploited and deeply damaged most of Africa as colonial powers.

When confronted with the leadership failures, many Africans angrily point out examples of corrupt and destructive leadership outside the continent. At the same time, Africans seem to be very slow or reluctant to seek leadership models in their own past, especially during the period just before and during the early phases of colonialism. The absence of visionary servant leadership is like the absence of science and technology, innovative and entrepreneurial skills to advance the continent from a backward economy to a service delivery society. This by hanging on the 'blame theory' does more harm than good to the sustainable development of the continent. Of course, the 'blame theory' cannot be disregarded totally; rather valuable lessons can be drawn from this to strengthen the 'reality theory' resolve as the path to construct the foundations of Africa's engine of growth to a develop polity. Learning from the ***'blame theory' plus exploiting positively the 'reality theory' plus good leadership leads to constructive take-off to building a capable development state and eventually, a service delivery society hence, an African solution for African problems.'***

The *'reality theory'* is simple; Africans wanted independence, they got it. It is left for the people to articulate a new way forward, by departing from the Euro-centric approach handed on the dawn of independence.

The responsibility of developing Africa rests squarely in their shoulders. This they can do by adopting an Afro-centric, people-centred strategic development approach. The past is past and Africa must look neither to the East or West, nor South or North but look forward to the unfolding future under the canopy of globalisation propelled by the increasing advances in science and technology. Why must Africa look forward, not backwards?

A number of interrelated factors have to be pierced together, namely: (i) colonialism certainly was not interested in empowering the people or teaching them what they needed to know in order to make informed choices: (ii) what has Africa done right to prove that colonial rule was and is wrong, devastating and inhumane? (iii) if they have to be part of the global community and ensure a sustainable quality livelihood for present and future generations, there is only one way forward; making the right choices and getting the right answers on issues that matter on the onus of shaping the continent for the next fifty or more years; and by using the necessary implements to shape the future.

The reality is that science, technology, innovation, entrepreneurial skills and developing the requisite human capital provides the concrete outcomes to accelerate the economic and developmental take-off for Africa. Development can only start, when you liberate your mind from dependency, servitude and inferiority complexes, you can make progress towards the hall of quality livelihood. The sad side of the story is that Africa has abandoned its indigenous knowledge, cultural concepts, like *'harambee, ubuntu, and batho pele'* and even failed to incorporate modern science and technology and to broaden its view and approaches of how technological knowledge is created in the economic process. Africa is therefore challenged in the following aspects among others to ensure, promote and realize the ideals of African solutions to African problems:

- science and technology policy for Africa;
- technological innovation, entrepreneurial and organization change;
- social experiments with modern science and technology;
- reviving indigenous knowledge and skills; and giving added to it;
- human capital development

All these interact in its recourse to the social context in terms of educational system, labour market relations, national, regional and continental development as explanatory factors of development of specific types of competences and inter-organisation relations needed for arriving at the ideal of African solutions to African problems. If we are to seek African solutions to African problems, we compelled to develop a progressive Afro-centric approach, attitude, mindset and behaviour towards work, ethics and responsibilities. The ideological orientation of African solutions to African problems has any meaning when we can do things ourselves and should be waged on the platform of 'war' against underdevelopment and exploitation providing the only basis where soldiers cooperate and unite with another in spite of their diversities and levels of well-being to attain a purpose, overcome the enemy and claim victory.

Apparently, the believe is that approaching the question of explaining science, technology, indigenous knowledge, innovation, entrepreneurial and organizational transformation by local circumstances and specificity is a needed change in the orientation of social change, which too often has treated cases and local development as illustrations of universal theories. What we need is the time-consuming in-depth study of variety and specificity, which then eventually can constitute the basis for future studies and analysis into new grand theories. Our researcher / scholars need to penetrate deeper in our indigenous knowledge seeking ways and means of marrying it with modern scientific knowledge.

How can Africa use science and technology to reach the goals of African solutions to African problems? In short, how can Africa evade the quanqamire of underdevelopment through the application of science and technology? Rephrased in another way; what type of knowledge-generation across the continent that most directly bear on the innovative content of Africa's barrage of underdevelopment debacles that helps marginalizes its place within the community of nations. The conflict between East and West did not make things easier for Africa either. African countries were forced into a coupling the process of economic reforms with donor demands for political democratization. But the resulting misappropriation, misallocation, embezzlement, and wasteful marginalization of the foreign resources inflows provoked an Aid-debt spiral that potentially threatened to destabilise the West's financial and banking system. The glacial pace of reforms was partly due to the opportunities for resistance by African governments that were created by the Cold War environment. There were palpable fears among African leaders that the reform policies would precipitate serious social and political problems for their respective regimes. These fears were reinforced because most of those at the helm of national affairs had only a very limited understanding of the nuts and bolts of the reform package in their technical dimensions. The educational and health sector were serious affected by cuts, yet these are two vital areas necessary for the sustainable transformation of the continent.

- Science-based knowledge ========➔
- Disembodied knowledge } Building the necessary technological
- Embodied knowledge } basis and capacities for ASAP
- Learning-based knowledge =======➔

Change has become inevitably and technology presents a great opportunity for the African continent, but everything we need we either dig it or grow it, so beware to look after it. African governments are faced with numerous challenges; how to choose to pursue reforms that promise uncertain and short-term costs? How do political leaders evaluate their chances of getting away with them? These and other related questions lie at the core of the state restructuring dilemma, particularly when confronted with making the right choices between Euro-centric Afro-centric approaches to development.

State Restructuring

In a sense, state restructuring refers to steps taken by government to improve services delivery through good government, accountability, transparency, the rule of law and new management methods and administrative approaches. It may even become imperative for the state to take drastic measures as layoffs departmental merger or closures, disinvestment from less service delivery units and of course, the introduction of new management and administrative methods. Restructuring African universities is an imperative assignment if science and technology should have any impact in the transformation of the continent.

The Educational curriculum of the continent needs to undergo drastic transformation to reflect the essential and urgent needs of the society. It should not be education for education's sake, but education with a purpose of change, construction and development leading to sustainable improvement of the quality livelihood of the people (Ajayi et al. 1996, Ngara 1994). The brain drain has sapped Africa of its intellectual resources and increased the continent's dependence on western expatriates, who are far more expensive to recruit and maintain than their African counterpart. On the other hand, the brain gain empowers the continent with new resources and other knowledge input factors that accelerate the transformation of the region. The case for creating serious and sustainable Pan-African networks of intellectual exchange is overwhelming and this should be an input factor for African solutions to African problems.

According to the World Bank Report (see Blair and Jordan 1994), "some 23,000 qualified academic staff are emigrating from Africa each year in search of better working conditions ". Africa is training its human power for the continued development of the West. This should be a worrying figure for Africa in 2014 because of the realisation that Africa's best brains are constantly engaged in the socioeconomic development of other parts of the world. To crown it all, Africa is exporting both its human capital and natural resources. It is no surprise to state the least, where the continent finds itself at the development/underdevelopment ladder. To halt the flood of African experts to overseas countries, the leadership of the continent must create the right and enabling working environment. Here lies one of the lollipops for the 'brain gain phenomenon. Relying on Africans to solve Africa's problem is simply another way of practicing self-reliance and sustaining the independence of the continent. In the absence of African experts, the task of transforming Africa remains a difficult assignment, and probably would never be executed (Obijiofor 2001). Closely associated with the engagement of African intellectuals and experts must be an aggressive policy on the development of indigenous knowledge, science and technology culture and infrastructure in creating Africa's samples of "Asian Tigers". The need for African Lions or Leopards is an imperative input factor for its development take-off. Africa has no other choice but to critical re-examine its position of science and technology and the development of indigenous knowledge to aid the development process of the continent. The continent must be willing to invest heavily in human capital development, science and technology and in particular in the new communication technologies. The future of Africa lies ultimately in the continent's ability to properly utilize its wisdom (indigenous knowledge) experiences, history and traditional values in transforming its people and societies.

Given that we live in a globalised world with its increasing competitive trajectories essence of capitalist economies, states are compelled to constantly reassess their policy and liability structures and making such adjustments as deem appropriate to ensure continuations in the realm of power. When the various structures of the state make similar adjustments at the same time, they aggregate into a visible economic and political phenomenon at the local, provincial and national levels. Here is where Africa has been lacking, enhancing dependency on Euro-centric development approach to the detriment of the African people. While the ideological orientation of ASAP is indeed a major change in policy orientation, it is still awaiting its clear articulation. As such it remains a murky concept without a precise definition making its implementation inconsistent and at times downright impossible. It is not only a problematic approach to utilize conceptually but it also tends to lack the requisite political, financial and resource backing. There are occasions where the principles of ASAP have been used as as an excuse by the 'the West' for not engaging in the socio-economic transformation of the continent. These examples range from reluctance in addressing the inhumane apartheid governance system in South Africa or the illegal white minority regime of Ian Smith in the then Rhodesia (Zimbabwe) or the genocide situation in Rwanda, among others. It is a forgotten genocide in Cameroon and these questions whether Africa countries ever learn from history?

For African countries, the late 1970s and through the 1980s and 1990s, saw a wave of such adjustments – the famous or infamous structural adjustment programmes (SAP) sweeping across the continent. In the 1990s on wards state restructuring came to represent a deeper process of change. In a broad sense, state restructuring represents a deeper process of change; State restructuring is a fundamental transition in the internal administrative set up of state institutions and in relationship between these institutions and other social and economic actor to improve on quality services delivery. State restructuring is a highly political process (Gourevitch & Shinn 2005). At one stroke, it affects power relations within society, the social and political pact embedded in the post 1980s system, and ultimately the competitiveness of nations. Governments have the power to slow or accelerate the process and to shape its direction through myriad policy instruments.

Since the 1990s, a transformation in global socio-politico-economic environment has made state restructuring dilemma more salient. Financial deregulation across the African continent and technological change has led to a rise of global inequity. Conversely, political leaders are held responsible for poor quality services delivery and social dislocation. Measures taken by the state to facilitate the process of restructuring, the acquisition and development of technological capability to facilitate the attainment of quality livelihood of the citizens, both the removal of obstacles and the adoption of new inducements are the focus of this discourse – with the goal of arriving at African solutions to African problems and also learning from best examples or practices around the world that ushers great dividends to the people and continent.

With the second wind of change blowing across the continent after the 1990s, a transformation in the technological capability and capacity in Africa is on course to becoming a capable developmental state This requires investment in human capital development and infrastructure. Africa has the advantage of building on the Gescenkronian concept of 'late-comer' advantage; and therefore, does not need to invent the wheel but take advantage of its existence by learning from the successes and failures of today's developed polities. For African governments tapping into the Gerschenkronian late-comer advantage; digging deep into the annals of its indigenous knowledge will eventually bring promise of technological change, increase competitiveness and ensure greater and equitable social welfare boils down to African solutions to African problems. Educational curriculum must be tailored on the realities of the plethora of problems facing the continent and it light of its strength, weaknesses, opportunities and threats.

Presently, the continent's educational curriculum is Euro-centric. It has and must be Afro-centric or else the continent will perish in the wave of the globalisation arsenal. Our universities are equally challenged to plug into the late-comer advantage, build on existing indigenous knowledge and come up with cross-cutting research activities and results that benefit the continent and humanity. Africa is a research desert with plenty of things yet t discovered. Building our universities and research institutes to world class establishment should be the concerned of every ministry of higher education, health and agriculture in the continent. What did our universities learned from the outbreak of the "Ebola" disease and the ongoing pandemic - "COVID-19" which has brought the world down to its knees! Why have our universities not been able to come-up a cure for the "malaria" disease which has and is a serious killer on the continent? Our institutions of higher-learning should now be the locus for sustainable development. These institutions have the vast opportunities of the 'late-comer' advantage to come up with cross-cutting research activities and results that benefit the continent and humanity.

Africa is a research desert with plenty of things yet to be discovered; add this to its wealth of century old indigenous knowledge system, the continent has much to offer to herself and the world at large to ensure sustainable development for all. All these activities require vision, investments and the political will to carry through envisioned activities. Of course, these activities require significant financial and infrastructural investments. According to Adeli (2004) "the subject of sustainable infrastructure systems will receive increasing attention in the coming years because of (a) the need to rehabilitate the aging infrastructure of the nation, (b) the public demand for prudent and optimism utilisation of the public funds, and (c) the national consensus and concern for preservation of the environment. Sustainable development is now a global concern and enterprise. Sustainable development has many important facets including cultural, societal, environmental and political. But scientists and engineers can contribute significantly for sustainability."

Economic recovery requires building a strong scientific, technological and innovative background. Indigenous knowledge is an asset not a liability as some makes it. The development of such inherent knowledge backed with modern scientific and technological knowledge is an added vantage to quick start the continent on its upward climb to quality services development. No development can be expected to be deep and dynamically sustainable without the entrenchment of technological preconditions. Rostow (1959) heightened the significance of technological change in stimulating growth-oriented dynamics in an economy. Gerschenkron (1962) emphasises this with the "late-comer advantage" to advance and accelerate their take-off. Of course, Schumpeter (1943) sees technology as the quintessential factor and fundamental driving force of all economic systems. Gee (1981) asserts that industrial revolution in the United States dating back to the Industrial Revolution and have witness major role that American technology played in the economic resurgence of West Germany and Japan since World War Two.

The developing countries in particular realise that, in order to reap the full benefits of an increasingly technological world, they must align their governmental infrastructure for effective utilisation of technology imported mainly from the industrial countries. On his part, Timamy (2007: vii-viii) sounds a note of warning here, calling for a new approach to the sustainable transformation of the continent, as he notes: "Has Africa ever paused to reflect why she stormed out of the meeting in Seattle? Was it not becoming apparent to African leaders that the West's legendary inaction on the subsidies front was a manifestation of the latter's desire to have her cake and eat it too? Was it not becoming obvious to Africa that the West was using all manner of gimmickry to preserve the global status quo inimical to her? Had it not occurred to African leaders that their economies were, to a large measure, the only ones embracing the neo-liberal conditionality's with virtually no reciprocal movement being observed on the other side.

The technological imperatives in Africa's quest for economic renewal are issues that should haunt all policy-makers and stakeholders genuinely keen to see Africa's constructive and participatory role play in the global setting. For now, Africa has shot itself in both feet running the risk of immobilising its entire body almost completely, and conceptualising technological change in very narrow terms. The heterodox view of science-technology-research relationship has to be recognised and create new windows of opportunities to push the science and technology package in the development process of the continent. Africa has been reaping a whirlwind for centuries under successive regimes of organised spoliation. The seeds of this degenerative decay have been sown at different times during her evolution. What Africa needs most is a National Code of Science, Technology and Research (CSTR). The NEPAD initiative on Science and Technology should be given greater credence, more than the ill-fated Lagos Plan of Action (LPA that never took off but remains Africa's well best and well-crafted policy plan for the continent's technological take-off).

Apparently, the marriage of Science, Technology, Research, Innovation and Entrepreneurship (STRIE) is an imperative for Africa to claim ownership over its development agenda. Africa's present condition of (deepening poverty in the midst of plenty) and precarious destiny awaiting it need to be blamed ultimately on the leaders, even though powerful exogenous forces share the guilt of responsibility of Africa's malaise real and potential. Without developing the science, technology, research, innovation and entrepreneurial base of the continent, African leaders would be condemning several generations of Africans to a life of the "walking dead" grinding poverty and other incalculable risks. Scholars are implored to show commitment to the problems of the continent, to study its institutions and values, in short, to provide solutions to the national/continental problems of economic development and political integration.

A major drawback on the continent is the gross absence of text books that adequately reflect the state in Africa which constitute a threat to the cultivation of consciousness among students. Existing history textbooks in particular tend to portray the history of the pre-colonial era as static. The treatment of the period since independence also leaves a lot to be desired. The factors behind the failure of scholarly research in African history to raise the levels of historical consciousness among the general public are quite complex but not forthcoming. They are determined by general economic and political developments in each country and the specific processes and practices involved in the production of social knowledge. This has equally had a spill-over in other subject areas.

In this paper, the introduction of a novel conception of technological flows and marriage with indigenous knowledge seem as the 'golden bargaining process and development' (GBPD). De facto, the Gerschenkronian concept offers politician a deal whereby the society taps into the abundant and takes advantage of cheap indigenous knowledge and marries this with modern technology to accelerate the development process of the continent and to `guarantee quality livelihood for all citizens. The paper focuses on the Gerschenkronian 'late-comer' advantage to move away from the Euro-centric to the Afro-centric as a progressive force change, a range of policy options available to all African states. Africa can take full menu of the recipes offered by the 'late-comer' advantage; pick out parts of the menu and add new ones; throw out those ideas that work contrary to the good of the people and continent.

The 'Golden Bargaining Process Development (GBPD) constitute a conditional displacement where African countries cannot ignore the new global forces, a range of policy options are available for their export. They cannot also dismiss their indigenous knowledge construct as cultural input factor in development. There is need to marry the two. Hence, the paper underscores the variety of choices in the force of this new challenge and the differentiation of pathways within hitherto stable clusters. In this regard the paper concentrates on a number of puzzles looking at the differences among African countries and he developed societies with relatively similar at one stage in their political economic structures by concentrating on the following assumptions.

- What explains the variation in national responses to the GBOD, even among relatively similar economies?
- Why should Africa implement deep changes in its post-Cold War era – structure, Euro-centric to Afro-centric structure and thinking without constructively changing its course?
- Why can Africa amplify the external signals and sweep aside both the longstanding discourse and structure?
- Which are the existing opportunities, potential needs and indigenous knowledge to exploit and expand upon for the advancement of the continent?

- What other alternatives exist for the country to transform from a backward to a modern society?
- How can Africa use its strength, weakness, opportunity and threats (SWOT) paradigm to develop, enhance, and harness its resources for the betterment of its people?
- The continent is not out for territorial conquest, but the defeat of backwardness and all that it entails; where do science, technology and indigenous knowledge fit into addressing these challenges impeding the progress of the region?

The Euro-Centric Predicament

Imperialism, colonialism and capitalism is not meant to liberate the African people but condemned them to the hell of poverty, enslavement and underdevelopment. Euro-centricism is designed to cement the assimilation paradigm. The theories of development on the continent have been effectively set by the West and meant to benefit the West, with African scholars reduced to followers, or at best, critics of each new intellectual fad emerging from the Africanist centres of the West. Western imported paradigm pervades all social science in development paradigm; Africa has no option but to follow. This has killed indigenous knowledge and skills (Braby & Tobin (2005). The Euro-centric ideological orientation excludes any form of recovery plan for the continent. Why have the developed economies not articulated a "Marshall Plan" of recovery for Africa like the USA recovery and reconstruction did to Europe? There is the Tony Blair "Our Common Interests: The Commission for Africa (2005) with no serious financial injection into the African on the basis of the Marshall Plan. It is clear such financial injection that uplifts the continent has also implications for development in the developed polities and its hegemony over Africa. With all the fine words and intensions, nothing concrete is being done to uplifting the current poor economic status of the economy of African countries.

Chapter seven of the Blair's report (p.75), states; Africa is the poorest region in the world. Over the last thirty years its people have, on average, seen virtually no increase in their economies. The message is clear: without economic growth, Africa cannot make substantial reductions in poverty." On pages 93-94, the Blair Report. Resurrects the Hippocratic Oath taken by doctors through the ages. "First do no harm, is one popular summary of the Hippocratic Oath taken by doctors through the ages. The maxim should also be applied to the responsibility that the rich world has towards Africa. The trading relationship between the developed and developing words has long been one dominated by a complex web of rules, taxes, tariffs and quotas which massively bias the entire business of international trade in favour of the rich." Here lies the secret nexus of the centre-periphery dichotomy; the periphery must bow to the dictates of the centre. But to hide the hidden agenda behind the Euro-centric philosophy, the report on (page 94) states: "...As well as helping Africa's capacity to trade competitively...G8 and EU countries must compete more fairly." With globalisation as the imperatives of 'Scientific Imperialism,' how can African countries compete on equally footing with the developed countries – when fair and balanced trade does not exit; when the agricultural sectors of G8 and EU member countries 'are heavily subsidised and protected in the economies of the industrialised world. Rich countries spend around US$350 billion a year on agricultural protection and subsidies – which is 16 times their aid to Africa. The European Union is responsible for 35 percent of this, the United States for 27 percent and Japan for 23 percent" (p94).

Africa countries are deceived with 'aid' given them but behind the 'aid' agenda lays other motives which falls in line with the Euro-centric doctrine. The only way to counter-act the Euro-centric agenda is through a progressive Afro-centric functional agenda. The Afro-centric agenda should focus on 'cleaning away the road blocks to begin with; first by developing a new and critical 'mind-set' that is embellished with the nexus of 'putting people-first' especially those currently at the bottom of ladder, so that they can with hope, confidence and trust begin climb up the ladder in pure security and confidence. Up-rooting the road blocks is off-rutting order into the existing chaotic system of governance – that is, Africa "has many internal barriers to trade, which damages its ability to grow its way out of poverty. Second, Africa is living within the contour of bad governance; excessive bureaucracy, cumbersome customs procedures, and corruption by public servants using bribes and other means of extorting monies from people to supplement their salaries (even if these salaries are not meagre). These are some of the many African road blocks that inhibit integration within and between nations to ensure sustainable development. Improving infrastructure is essential to the sustainable transformation of the continent. It is extremely difficult moving goods or travelling within and between African countries. It is much easier to travel abroad than from one part of the continent to another or even within a country. This hinders trade within and between countries. A lack of trade between African countries is a serious problem as only 12 percent of all African goods go to other African countries; improving that requires improving communication, infrastructure, reduce internal trade barriers and so forth.

Mazrui (1973:183) notes that the balkanization of the continent by European colonial administrations sowed the seeds of internal unrest and destroyed the intellectual capability of the people decades after the attainment of independence: "it was in Africa that Europe practiced the art of partition at its most elaborate. Where Europe attempted to unify those who were different, it sowed the seeds of future separation. Where Europe divided, it sometimes left behind latent passions for reunification – and political killings at the grassroots level have resulted from such division. In short, balkanization is a breeding-ground for political violence, including the phenomenon of assassination. And balkanization is what Africa is burdened with for the time being." Ashby et al (1980:159) in expanding this skewed relationship notes: "the limited industrial expansion and relative agricultural stagnation in poor countries is seen to have evolved historically from international relations of colonialism and unequal power, and hence exchange, between producers of raw materials and industrial capital goods. These relations have sustained a distribution of wealth and power within poor nations."

The Gerschenkron paradigm offers a policy of technology windows, which fit within a progressive forward looking Afro-centric approach that indicates propitious conditions for political action. This paper advances Strategic Political Autonomy (SPA or Afro-centric (SPAC)) within the framework of people-focused development strategy as the key concept that best measures the degree of political onslaught available to entrepreneurs and action with key groups. The Afro-centric vision should be seen within the context of (strategic political autonomy (SPA) defined as the political space available to empower African leaders and governments to embark on the path of political entrepreneurship in relation to providing quality service delivery to the people. The Afro-centric empowers Africans to dig deep into their indigenous knowledge to expand their scope of development. The late-comer advantage is drawing from modern science and technology and marrying indigenous knowledge which draws closer to the people's way of life. This empowers the people to be active players in the sustainable transformation of the continent.

Apparently, the argument is advanced that the Euro-centric orientation is construed on the principles that Africa is part of the global construct implying that African problems reflects a current global political, economic, and social interconnections and interactions with science and technology providing the answers. African problems are not solely Africa and as such require global solutions. True to an extent; African economics are invariably integrated to the global economy and Africa can do little on its own by way of autonomously deciding on the terms of the management of its economies - but in reality, this is not the case. The West determines everything and dominates. Africa's bargaining power is severely limited in setting the price of commodities that it offers on the world market. The prices are determined by the vagaries of the global economy on the world market; it turns out that price fluctuation is decidedly a global issue that the notion of ASAP is less likely to address. Since the sovereignty of the continent is undermined, there is an urgent need to search for other alternatives. ASAP provides such alternative. The disunity of African states contributes also to its marginalisation in global politics. African countries failed to listen and pay attention to Kwame Nkrumah's speech delver at 10.30, on Friday 23rd September to the General Assembly of the United Nations 1961 on the Congo crisis in these words: "...he called for an end to colonial rule, for support for the legitimate government of Lumumba and for the UN to use only African nations and troops to create an African solution to the problems of Africa."

"African Solutions for African Problems," nonetheless provides hope and should be hailed as a watershed moment for the African political landscape in which there is an 'arrival of Africans' resulting in 'a paradigm shifts from the beggar mentality' to one that is proactive and self-assured. It is a discourse and strategic approach that should mobilize and help Africans to claim ownership of challenges on the continent which are not necessarily experienced elsewhere in the world or in the same manner for that matter. It is a mantra that should instil a new mindset and drive toward finding more homegrown or localized answers to the state of underdevelopment and all that it entails – poverty, drought, and disease while simultaneously investing in capacity building. It is a claim of agency and policy independence that should intriguingly help to firmly place Africa and the African agenda within an increasingly global complex political landscape. Will ASAP pave the way for African unity as well as underscore a multi-faceted struggle against neo-neo-colonialism as well as motivate the people to emerge as its own leader in the 21st century by finding African solutions to the plethora of problems and challenges facing the continent? But corruption stands out tall as the one single fundamental factor retarding the progress of a nation and its socio-economic development. The reason for corruption is simply among other issues that African governments are:

- embedded with tendencies of fascism;
- the rule of law is smoke-screen and hypocrisy of the worst order;
- the government pays lip-services to democracy and its basic tenets;
- elected representatives failing to play their roles as people's voice in parliament; they trail to be servant leaders, making politics an instrument for becoming rich overnight instead of serving the people elected them;
- as a result, the country is being governed by proxy.

Finally, by all these acts and backed by the non-challant attitude of civil society, the people (as the true custodian of power) the people continue to suffer in silence. In the case of Cameroon, one can reasonably question when an Anglophone will be President of Cameroon. Since the 1961 Cameroon has hard two presidents, all francophone (i) Ahmadou Ahidjo 1961-1982; and Paul Biya (1982 to-date). The exclusion of an Anglophone to head the top-job of the country is not due to incompetence but to France's mechanisation and hegemonic control and tight grip over the politics direction of the country under its tutelage. The exclusion is part of the ongoing war and genocide in the country. That exclusion of an Anglophone at the helm of the country's governance structure has psychological effect on the war. These are worried some and put into serious stress the unity of the country. The unity of Cameroon and many other African countries must be taken as a religion in the sense that not only should we believe in unity – living together but eating separately – true and genuine unity means living and eating together – doing things to promote unity not things that enhance the promotion of disunity.

However, apart from foreign-induced (Euro-centric) obstacles, to the continent's development, one must also identify internal problems such as the continent's history of incompetent leaders. Therefore, the need to cast away the 'blame theory,' and moving forward in the spirit of the 'reality theory' as the best developmental approach. The reality is that incompetent leaders in Africa have shown themselves to be visionless, vicious, dictatorial and unaccountable. Hence, one must hold them responsible for dragging Africa backwards while the rest of the world is moving forward. Lack of accountability and responsibility leads to gross corruption and acts of economic misdemeanour. To experience, scientific and technological development constructive and encompassing social change, Africa needs a new crop of dedicated and selfless leaders who possess the vision and drive to steer the continent's socioeconomic development. Without this there can be no progress. It takes such leadership to transform a country as South East Asian countries have demonstrated. There is no reason why Africa cannot repeat that development approach even better.

The example of Lee Kuan Yew comes in mind for creating the structure and base for modern Singapore. So also, the situations of Malaysia with Mahathir Mohammed and Suharto Sukarno in Indonesia. Africa suffers from a dearth of such leaders. The Asian experience should be a strong and veritable lesson for Africa. These countries have proved that the dominant and only path through which modernisation or development could be achieved is – human capital development, industrialisation, urbanization and capital-intensive technology – the central pillars of Western socioeconomic values, as highlighted by (Servaes, 1986; Walsh, 1993; Levy Jr., 1992' Little and Reed, 1989) among many others. Adherence to these values is now the cornerstone and the major factor influencing the development of certain countries like China, Brazil, South Korea, Mexico and others.

The Afro-centric Progressive Action Agenda

"Five centuries of European expansion into Africa has made Africa a ravaged satellite of Europe. As a consequence, African culture has lost its autonomous centres, lost its independent bearings and become eccentric" (Chinweizu 1987). The Afro-centric approach provides the sources of freedom and constraints determining the actions of African political entrepreneurs with science and technology as the underlying instrument to wage the battle against underdevelopment, exploitation and poor living conditions. There has been a failure in the political economy of producing historical knowledge for schools and the transformation of the society. African scholars were an enthusiastic, energetic lot anxious with the inspired rhetoric of their pens (Mazrui 1979). They too believed in the new nations, if only as a prelude to the Pan-African vision of continental unity. This intellectual ferment and faith were underpinned by buoyant economic growth.

Unfortunately, advocates of ethnicity facilitated the production of power by the political class by fostering the divisive power of communal consciousness and foreclosing the disruptive power of class and other social solidarities, while at the same time the consumption of these class threatened the integrative imperatives of nation-building. The development of the country became highly ethicized and politicized, a subject treated with great suspicion and even hostility. African political leaders lost patience with scholars asking awkward questions about neo-colonialism (Zeleza op cit.; Forje 2011).

An Afro-centric approach rekindles the Lagos Plan of Action (LPA) and the AU Commission's Plan of Action 2004-2007 promoting human resources development, capacity building and science and technology as tools for development. AU agenda 2063 should and must be properly implemented to guide Africa to the good logical end of a capable development quality services delivery society. We have no choice but to pursue AU Agenda 2063 to the end. The visions of the LPA and the AU's Science and Technology Consolidated Plan of Action (2005) should pave the way forward for:

- enabling Africa to harness and apply science and technology, related innovations and entrepreneurship to achieve sustainable development;
- ensuring that Africa contributes to the global pool of scientific knowledge and technology innovations must be adequately implemented to accelerate the socioeconomic transformation of the continent;
- the development of Africa will not start in earnest until the struggle over development agenda is determined by Africans and this requires a comprehensive and concerted drive towards a progress Afro-centric agenda.

Building a technological base from the anvil of an Afro-centric perspective creates the bases and holy marriage with the technology of 'modern' society which can be likened to a landscape with huge altitudinal variations between the mountains and plains. Most of us journey through this landscape every day. How do these variations affect the continent? Do the heights make Africa giddy and the plains depress the continent? Do our ears buzz and stomachs turn at each rapid change? Science, technology, innovation and entrepreneurship can be seen with this periscope. They have certain inherent positive and negative sides all depending on its usage.

Technology as a curse or blessing can be seen from the perspectives of the 'trinity of technology' – (the technology of mobility, the technology of violence, and the technology of destruction/ development). Technology for developmental peace missions, improving quality livelihood in a polarised, fragmented and underdeveloped continent goes under what we have been discussing – The technology of knowledge and its appropriate usage leads to the technology of development' which accelerate the progressive nature of the continent. The technology of mobility and violence leads to the destruction of the nation and can be likened with the Euro-centric agenda for Africa. The technology of mobility and violence practiced by the apartheid regime in South Africa inhibited the fundamental human rights of the people. However, there also emerged a positive side of that dreadful governance system which makes South Africa the most developed African state. African state importing the arsenal of the technology of destruction is not different from the apartheid regime structure for the represent the Euro-centric agenda. (Forje 2011:107).

Rapid technological advancement and wrong application raise alarming questions about humankind's biological stability. The question is how can the technology of mobility and violence be converted into the technology of development and construction? The technology of violence (Euro-centric agenda) is destroying the sustainable socioeconomic transformation of the continent. With ongoing political conflicts and instability across the continent, for example in countries like Chad, Mali, Somalia, Southern Sudan, Central African Republic and others, the inflow of the technology of destruction escalates, while the technology for development diminishes. With the technology of knowledge and development, integration of countries and development accelerates and encourages people to travel and sleep with theirs close. How does Africa construct good roads that facilitate travel within and between African countries? How does Africa harness the airspace to accelerate faster connectivity among peoples and nations? How can Africa use technology to break down barriers, promote mutual understand and peaceful coexistence among people and nations? How can the continent deploy technology to build trust, confidence and reliance on the governance system?

The importance of knowledge, technology, innovation and entrepreneurship in Africa's transformation remain crucial. Articles 72-80 of the African Union Charter see science and technology as a vital weapon in accelerating the socioeconomic transformation of the continent. The important factor is the conversion of the technology of mobility, violence and destruction into the technology of development, reconstruction leading to a better and sustainable quality livelihood of the people. The European countries are fast advancing with the establishment of European Spoliation Source Scandinavia (ESS) at the University of Lund – Sweden, which will attract 5000 researchers yearly.

Technology is an instrument for nurturing the continent's talent and resources. Therefore, Centres of science and technology excellence must be constructed now. It should be pointed out that a continent with well-developed scientific and technological environment is the key to sustainable development and quality livelihood.

Admittedly, science and technology are not the panacea for development but no country has ever transformed itself without the use of science and technology as a catalyst for changing the structure of the state. Africa is no exception. The following issues are a vital for the transformation and sustainability of the continent cannot be tackled without the development of science and technology. As a late-comer, the continent has the advantage of learning from the failures and successes of other nations that have walked and continue to walk down the path of economic transformation in its bid of seeking African solutions to African problems with the blessing of knowledge, inventions, production and other related activities from other continents.

- Peace, security and development;
- National, regional and continental infrastructure
- Pan-Africa centres of research and universities – higher education, human capital development (drawing lessons ESS – Scandinavia and cases in success stories from different parts of the world.
- Fighting epidemics and pandemics (health status of the people – HIV/AIDS, malaria, tuberculosis etc.)
- Climate change, desertification and coastal erosion;
- National, regional, and continental infrastructure;
- Free movement of people, goods and services

Africa cannot neglect, dismiss or reduce the role and impact of science and technology in the transformation and sustainability of the continent as a vital player in global development. We must equally intensify the development and use of our indigenous knowledge system; marry it with modern science and technology and see how rich the continent becomes. It facilitates the assemble of activities, structures and resources that together gives credence, power, strength, intelligence to place the continent within the range to achieve progress and being ahead of other nations. Take the simple example of the indigenous innovation, creativity and usage of the **'African Talking Drum'** for transmitting messages from one hamlet, or village to another. Africa failed to give added value to this medium of communication. The poor status of the continent's research institutions failed to use the concept of 'policy windows' to further propitious conditions for sustainable development. As a result of poor human capital development and low institutional infrastructure, the process of 'learning-based knowledge could not be deplored to generate and store experiences. Our traditional doctors (the herbalists) have been forgotten. They should be brought into the scene to help improve of the health of people; encouraged to work hand on gloves with modern science and technology (medical doctors, researchers etc.) to discover the inherent medicinal values of our vast natural plants and crops.

On the other hand, African ingenuity was overcome by western research, inquisitiveness; creativity, entrepreneurship and productivity in converting the 'talking drum' into a valuable instrument of world-wide connectivity medium of communication (wwwcmc) – the cellar or mobile phone of today which is an indispensable part of modern pattern of livelihood. Many of such examples abounds where Africa has missed being a veritable cutting-edge technology society. The knowledge of talking drum was not transformed into productive innovation as the basis of advancing small and medium and eventually large-sized enterprises. How can the continent use such latent indigenous knowledge activities to contribute to the understanding of the accumulation of knowledge and learning as preconditions for technological development? There is a connection with the four different picture of knowledge-generation that directly bears on the science, technology and innovative activities of a society. It should be emphasized that indigenous generated knowledge is of great importance. However, intensive development and user contacts are also important, both prior to the development process itself; we must not forget our roots as the foundation for our existence and wellbeing.

Whatever the case, whether the Euro-centric or Afro-centric approach, the good, bad and ugly exist all depending on how and for what purpose you use science and technology. Therefore, uncoordinated and ill-focused Afro-centric Agenda can be more disastrous. When it is disastrous, no solutions can be provided for African problems. With Euro-centric paradigm, Africa has for too long been swimming with disastrous solutions to African problems, with the continent's continued underdevelopment coming as no surprise. The non-take-off of the Lagos Plan of Action (LPA) constituted a blow to the scientific and technological transformation of the continent. Some of the critical issues needing urgent and serious structural adjusting in Africa include; -

Weak strategies for science innovation; Outcome of inadequate and inappropriate higher education curriculum and research strategy systems; this could be explained by poor educational infrastructure; poor enabling environment; poor financing, inappropriate education curriculum not tailored to the realities, needs and challenges of the continent – with the eventual consequences of the 'brain drain' phenomenon though this could be converted into a 'brain gain' input development factor;

Critical Issues In Africa needing ==➔} Urgent Attention	Poor policy formulation and little attention paid to science, technology, innovation and entrepreneurship related activities; lack of national reliable data on scientific and technical potential (human resources; institutions, programmes etc., promoting indigenous knowledge); Prevalence of micro-nationalism, resulting in rivalries, instead of cooperation and integration based on comparative advantage; Communication barriers (infrastructure, telecommunication, erratic energy supply, poor internet connectivity; poor library facilities, high cost of educational implements, etc, Poor harmonization of initiatives which inhibits the promotion of science and technology throughout the continent Poor state of university-research institute-civil society and private sector interface Creating an enabling environment for the advancement of science, technology, entrepreneurship, innovation, proper working climate for researchers, lecturers etc. as well as encouraging the female gender to be interest in science and technology related disciplines - physics, mathematics, chemistry, etc.)

Developing the scientific and technological capacity and capability of the continent should be given top priority by all – individuals, municipal councils, civil society organizations, private sector, national governments, Regional Economic Communities (RECs), NEPAD and the AU. The adoption and implementation of a forward looking and cutting-edge strategy for science, technology, innovation and entrepreneurship would be justified in various sectors like agriculture and exploitation of natural resources which currently constitute the mainstay of the economy of the majority of African countries. Importantly, lessons should be drawn from Bill Gates (1995:257). "Citizens of the information society will enjoy new opportunities for productivity, learning and entertainment. Countries that move boldly and in concert with each other will enjoy economic rewards. Whole new markets will emerge, and myriad new opportunities for employment will be created."

The Good, Bad and Ugly

The good of science and technology lies in its usage to narrow the growing gap between the poor and rich; to improve the wellbeing of all citizens and to ensure a safe and peaceful world environment. So far, the good of technology has been advancing the wellbeing of the West and exploiting the South. There have been fall outs of western science and technology for the transformation of Africa no doubt, just as it has been used for the destruction of the continent. Therefore, science and technology could also be the devil on the cross symbolizing the bad and ugly. The widespread of military arsenal in destroying the continent shows the bad and ugly sides of technology. On the other hand, the speed at which Research, Science and Technology (RST) for example, in connection with the virus of the COVID-19 Pandemic, show the good of science; one only wish that the efforts of RST did or is doing for the search of a cure for COVID-19, be extended to searching for the cure of the long-standing disease like malaria which has been serious headache or menace to the people of developing countries.

Africa needs to go back to the drawing board, apply the full aspects of the Lagos Plan of Action, Recommendations from CASTAFRICA 1 & 2, the AU Commission's Plan of Action 2004-2007 promoting human resources development, capacity building and science and technology as positive and vital tools for development and other vital recommendations from various national and international for a should be fully implemented. The vision of the S&T Consolidated Plan of Action (2005) on

- enabling Africa to harness and apply science, technology and related innovations to achieve sustainable development;
- ensuring that Africa contributes to the global pool of scientific knowledge and technology innovation must be adequately implemented to accelerate the socio-economic transformation of the region and enhance its quest for a union government;
- Encourage the use of indigenous scientific knowledge system as well incorporate this into modern S&T for it to play a more growing role within the continent and the world at large. Bear in mind that indigenous scientific knowledge is closer to the people, and they have hope and trust in it, just as it is more affordable to the people.

Science and technology as a curse or blessing can be seen from the perspectives of the 'trinity of technology' (the technology of mobility, the technology of violence, and the technology of destruction/development).The technology for developmental peace missions, improving quality livelihood in a polarized, fragmented and underdeveloped continent goes under the good of science and technology for enhancing wellbeing in all its facet – the 'technology of knowledge' and its appropriate usage leads to the 'technology of development' which accelerates the progressive nature of the continent The technology of mobility and violence leads to the destruction of the continent. The technology of mobility and violence practiced by the apartheid regime in South Africa inhibited the fundamental human rights and liberties of the people. The 'tactics' of hot-pursuit was (chasing the freedom fighters within and beyond national environs) was facilitated by the technology of mobility and violence – the use of weapons of destruction.

Africa is at war with underdevelopment. But the arsenal of the technological weapon is directed not to fighting underdevelopment and poverty but towards the destruction of the sources of livelihood for the citizens. The spread of military weapons has given rise to the privatization of security and military functions leading to the demise of the Modern Nation-states in Africa (Small 2006). African states have not undergone the standard process of internal territorial expansion and acquisition, nor have they undergone the process of forging mutual constraints between rule and the ruler as did their European counterparts. Instead, African states were constructed by colonialism, a process whereby the African continent was arbitrarily carved up into zones of foreign power influence and jurisdiction, separating and uniting diverse and incompatible social groupings under the rubric of 'state' (Clapham, 2002)

The bad and ugly of science and technology is that it has made the continent's resources become a curse not a blessing. The Niger Delta Region presents a glaring example – The curse of oil. How the Oil Conglomerates have used science and technology to amass wealth but leaving the people in the Niger Delta Region in the lurch and death, and providing wealth and abundance to a select few. (Obayiuwana 2012:10-15). Nigeria's Ogoniland needs billions of dollars and more than 30 years of serious work to restore the devastated ecosystem and rehabilitate its impoverished inhabitants. Technology is available but will not be used to clean up the mess created by western quest for profit within an African setting. Imagine if such high oil spill occurred in the West. But environmental and public health impacts of oil contamination have been ongoing in the area for over 50 years, bringing close to USA$500bn in revenue to the Nigerian exchequer and ten times more profit to the oil companies with no guaranteed quality of life to the ordinary citizens of that region. The Chinese re doing the same in Africa today though they please us, so to say, with certain infrastructure which we pay heavily with our resources.

Africa's expenditure on military arsenal for destructive purposes far outstripped expenditure on science, technology, research, and innovation, the weapons necessary for the development of the continent. Rostow, clearly placed a special premium on the technological factor in the take-off of economies gripped by inertia like that of Africa. Glee (1981) goes further to point out how foreign countries remember the miracles of technologically based industrial innovation in the United States and the major role of American technology in the resurgence of West Germany and Japan since World War Two. While there is nothing wrong for Africa to get to the moon, the first priority is to get into the villages, eradicate poverty and diseases, and improve on the health of the people by properly using science, technology and indigenous knowledge in alleviating the plight of the suffering masses

The developing countries in particular realise that, in order to reap the full benefits of an increasingly technological world, they must align their governmental infrastructure for effective utilization of technology imported mainly from the industrialised countries. Such development trends emphasis the good of technological development and its usage. Clearly, Africa's prospects for realizing sustainable economic renewal depend on how her leaders *'take the developmental bull by the indigenous knowledge, scientific and technological horns.'* Taking the developmental bull by the horn means taking science and technology and improving indigenous knowledge the right way to the people in the hamlets and all corners of society.

It is not out of place to insinuate that (the bad and ugly) of science and technology can be seen in the escalation of small and medium weapons that are manufactured in the West and used to fan conflicts across the continent. These weapons threaten the peace, security and development process of the continent. Some leaders use them to prolong their illegal stay in power. Various challenges face civil society actors in Central Africa for example. Many leaders in the sub-region have autocratic tendencies. As a result, the state infiltrates the group and often seeks to influence the operations of civil society, co-opting some actors to act on behalf of its interest or frustrating the efforts of organization that criticise the weaknesses of governance structures and human rights. In Cameroon, critics have accused the government of using strategies such as 'divide and rule' to penetrate civil society. In the Democratic Republic of the Congo (DRC), the political context has influenced the structure and character of civil society. In Nigeria, the destruction of the environment by oil companies gives rise to arms insurgence as the only means of survival by the people of Delta Niger Region. The situation in the Great Lakes Region is not different. The Horn of the continent is notorious for its piracy and use of weapons for destruction and destabilizing purposes. The Central African Sub-Region constitutes one of the most dangerous places on the continent. Many of these groups have borrowed the structure of political parties and governments. In terms of governance, some civil society organizations have leaders who make unilateral decisions on rules and procedures for their operations (Dahre2012; Paterson & Saunders 2011, Ekiyor & Mashumba 2006). With such prevailing situations, why should Africa not be classified as a failed continent? A failed continent – Africa is because we have conditioned ourselves to be slaves and failures perpetuity. This is the new hour for Africa to reimagine, recreate restore, rebuild, renovate itself and move forward ad one unit to make the best of its resources (human and natural) for our common good.

Conclusion

Tomorrow is the Product of Today's Actions

> *"A dramatic power shift is coming, and all nations face one inescapable rule – survival of the fastest."* (Alvin Toffler)

A Call to Action

The future of Africa is intertwined with how well prepared it is today particularly in the domain of science and technology in order to take advantage of the 'globalisation bandwagon' propelled by advance in Information and Communication Technologies (ICTs). A global village has come to stay creating an avalanche of 'hyper-competitive knowledge-based global economy. Competitive knowledge and comparative advantage evolve from 'knowledge-intensive,' value added technology that creates new products, processes and services. Given the evolving scenarios, it is essential and imperative that the continent find ways and means of acquiring knowledge. It does involve even employing unconventional means of acquiring the knowledge, which comprises acquisition of technological secrets from those that have it by any means. Stealing technological secrets is nothing new. It is a booming enterprise providing a way to equalize the gaps between the haves and have-nots (Toffler 1993). A number of developed polities have perfected the trade to an art form. There is nothing wrong for continent to join in the lucrative trade and hunt for the best in order to accelerate the fastest way for technological transfer. Africa needs technologies that mesh well with local cultural practices as such technologies have a greater probability of being accepted and properly used by the citizens. The future of the continent ultimately lies in Africa's ability to utilize its wisdom, experience and cultural values to transform its people and societies. As noted by Ellinor Forje (2018:15) valuable lessons can be learnt for China: "Chins, because of the tremendous strides it has made in the last30 years, combined with it having the largest population in the world, has lifted more out of poverty than any other country, as highlighted by The Economist in 2013".

The challenge now is building 'strategic alliances' to better overcome what could be seen as the continent greatest deficiency or what former Executive Secretary of the UN Commission for Africa, Amoako termed Africa representing the world's most serious challenge. The technological know-how for mass production is wanting. As a result, the 'haves' are constantly in the midst of far-reaching technological frontiers while the have-nots continue to wallow in self-pity and outdated methods. Therefore, in breaking out of the doldrums of the old economic policies that have not worked and will not work, requires certain issues be addressed: an emphasis on excellence at all levels; a focus on cost effectiveness and value creation; and effective partnering. All these must be incorporated and harnessed if Africa is to participate in the latest global technological frontier (Olanirum, 2011; Forje1988). Africa with stigma of *"ghetto of the world"* should be converted into the *"paradise of the world."* Indeed, Africa is the paradise of the world that the people fail to make it to be.

While science and technology and research hold a long-anticipated hope for Africa for the most vulnerable in society, it has to be combining with a number of other interrelated factors to produce the much-anticipated results – visionary leadership, a functional democratic governance system and environment, effective and efficiency energy supply, good road infrastructure and other transportation means, sustainable food production and self-sufficiency; human capital development among many others. It is tall task but necessary to proper the continent into the new global order of development and wellbeing. The earlier the leaders and the people hatch a progressive open mindset to confront the barrage of task, the better. It requires commitment and the resolve to start somewhere. It should be the pride of all Africans to make the continent the most admirable place on planet earth in the 21st century and beyond. Yes, Africa can make it. That is when we can see, talk and harvest the fruits of Africa solutions to African problems. "The application of indigenous knowledge system would accelerate the stages in Rostow's modernisation theory from take-off to maturity. However, it is critical to note that establishing knowledge production through effective ICT policies is the first essential step towards take-off "(Forje & April, 2015:92).

Science, technology entrepreneurship and indigenous knowledge will not be parachuted down from heaven or from outside. Whatever the generosity of the developed polities, transformation of the continent rests sole with Africans. It is the responsibility of African leadership visualise a realistic vision for the future of Africa. The current pessimistic scenario that dominates Africa's present and future exacerbate the current crisis by depriving Africans of their self-confidence. African solutions to African problems give an ideological optimistic orientation and not for the continent fall prey into false illusion like the 'rising expectation' of independence that converge into rising destructive frustration the morning after the new national flag was hoisted.

African solutions to African problems entail a new constructive scenario for the continent to construct the virtual state model, in which the state reflects the will of the people; and in which the people are totally involved, committed and concentrate their resources and strength in crafting a true, participatory democracy, equitable development and shared prosperity. In short, Africans are challenged to construct a society that is not **'deformed, distorted, disarticulated, destroyed and dissatisfied** (the 5 D's). The present construct of continent is one that has culminated in the effective marginalization, destruction and exploitation of Africa in the global-capitalist system and its domination by profit and hegemony-seeking transnational corporations. The goal or *raison d'etre* of the state should be people-focused (Afro-centric) and not serving external interests (Euro-centric). National and Regional cooperation should be enhanced and states should show willingness of surrendering some degree of sovereignty in social and economic spheres to a continental body. Without this in mind, the African Union (AU) has no meaning to the continent. Education and culture must not be politicized and a strong work ethics must evolve with due respect to the rule of law and practice of a good governance system. Africa must strive to be a 'winning continent' striving to become a sustainable global player in the global village of our time. The promotion of technical entrepreneurship and technological innovation is most needed now as a strategic approach for restructuring the economy, ensuring economic diversification, job creation, redistribution of wealth, increasing production and improving international competitiveness.

A good player does not lack a 'team'. Africa should employ the strength, weakness, opportunity and threats (SWOT) approach to build convergences and alliances to foster its position and as winners not losers in the globalised economic and technological knowledge-based economy of the 21st century and beyond. Let us pay attention to the views expressed at the 2017 African Unity Renaissance Conference in Pretoria, South Africa by Mammo Muchie (2017): We equally need to draw valuable lessons from the views expressed by Gunnar Myrdal (1957): "Underdeveloped countries should not accept economic theory uncritically for much of this theory is a rationalisation of the dominant interest of the industrialised countries." Our institutions of higher learning should step-up their research and critical thinking on how to advance the socio-political-economic transformation of the continent and stop relying on what is dished out from the developed countries to Africa. Technological advancement changes the dynamics of the development process, making the contribution of technological progress in modern economic growth and rising per capita income widely acclaimed and recognised. Africa should avoid what Harberger, 1998) sees as "mushroom-process" characterised by a spurt of economic activity in a particular sector or industry. The East Asian countries provide outstanding examples for African countries to emulate. They have within a short period successfully transformed their economies from low-income to middle-income level and its production structure entails substantial technological sophistication. We are blessed with abundant natural resources (the envy of the developed countries) but remain extremely underdeveloped. We need to ponder deep and investigate how changes in the structure of our economy should generate additional growth to improve on the wellbeing of the people.

We are thus challenged to – '*provide glaring examples as the new growth pole of the world 'It is time to un-think to rethink, un-learn to re-learn, un-design to re-design, un-engineer to re-engineer and un-science to re-science and un-political economies with human and nature wellbeing as the priority of priorities to bring about an African integrated sustainable development not to make Africa forever fail or fall. Let us unite to make free Africa forever, colonized Africa never.*' It is time to rekindle the lost glory of the continent, to place it on the right developmental track, to ensure innovation, creativity, entrepreneurship that opens up entirely new possibilities for long-term changes in economic growth and economic structure. We need to get our political governance system ad dynamics right. In this regard, it is highly recommended that African countries ensure political stability and good governance as a fundamental precondition for socio-economic development.; second, African states should rebuild and maintain infrastructure and seek to acquire technical and managerial skills for better performance of public institutions; third governments should demonstrate transparency, accountability, build confidence and trust to show the proclivity to political, economic and social strife that dives investors away, opines (Gambari, 2000).

On the field of Africa's transformation and the sustainability of the continent, it should be fare-well to the past and fare-forward voyagers to Africa's future far beyond the 21st century. African countries must create an enabling environment to better continue improving their chances for growth, development and sustainable wellbeing. Good governance, transparency, accountability and participation of all in the processes are important to attract investors and remain the only veritable way of transforming Africa. The Africa we envisaged should agree with H. G. Wells that the future depends upon the outcome of "the race between education and catastrophe." The sustainable transformation of the continent rest on the hands of the people through a progressive Afro-centric developmental approach that includes all the citizens and these citizens enjoying equal benefits of the progress of the nation. Therefore, our leaders must work feverishly in the hope and desire that their children, children will enjoy a better life than they will ever know. Most unfortunately, our current mind-set is not turn toned in that the direct. Rather, we continue perpetuating the *'Euro-centre-periphery dichotomy.'* The reasons why Africa not develop; and the reason why the developed countries would prefer regional economic groupings as this would offer them greater advantage of exploitation and domination.

The enormous and increasing differences in the economic, political and technological power between Africa and developed world are a reflection of the international division of labour, which has condemned Africa to specialise in low-valued added, low-technology production and exports of raw resources. We strongly also believe that, in the process, a fairer more rational and more lasting world economic system can be built. Just as African countries cannot develop without a more favourable international environment, lasting stability in global relations calls for progress in the continent and greater global equity. In short, this call for a New World Political, Economic and Technological

Order (NWPETO). The reform must be construed on *'win-win'* approach for developed polities and African countries. That 'win-win' constitutes central setting up arrangements to provide for the transfer of adequate resources from the North to Africa. The reform or call for a NWPETO should include contingency mechanisms to ensure the orderly continuation of development efforts in the face of unexpected shocks. The NWPETO also requires fair international regimes for science and technology (S&T) and for the management of the environment and the global commons. International institutions should be made more democratic, more effective and more supportive of development efforts in Africa.

Africa needs to articulate a holistic policy towards a strategy of liberation, bearing in mind that he modern economic and social system has been confronted since its origins with contradictions it has never managed to surpass. There are ae nations that relate with Africa on the basis of (i) profit, and (2) with the human feelings with the concern for the genuine transformation of the region. The latter group is small, but mostly welcome and needed. Of course, the transformation of the African continent begins by struggles at its base. For without the beginning of changes in ideological, political and social systems on the level of their national bases, any discussion about African Unity, globalisation, polarisation and regionalisation remains a dead letter. African countries need to overcome a number of contradictions which sets he inevitable exigencies of labour, subordination, imposed by the rule of profit against the people's aspirations to be masters of their human destiny. It is only through their struggles that Africans can force their enemies to adapt to the specific logic of their interests – which finds itself in conflict with that of the ideals of capitalism in two aspects: (a) with respect to the distribution of the fruits of economic growth: it imposes increases in the remuneration of labour, both individual and collective, on a parallel with increases in productivity; (b) regarding the principles of democracy; it promotes their implementation in social domains for which they were not intended originally. Africa is failing on the democratic and social reform domains. For the New Brave Africa to emerge, it must respond positively towards democratic and social reforms. Africans must work and aspire to improved material conditions and the respect of human rights, they want, simply, to be the masters of their society, in order words, to liberate themselves from the fundamental economic alienations to which they are submitted.

References

Achebe, C. (1966). A Man of the People. Heinemann, London

Adeli Hojjat (2014) "Editorial Viewpoint: Science and Technology for Sustainable Development". World Review of Science, Technology and Sustainable Development, Vol.1, No.1. 2004, pp108-109

Ahmed A. and Stein J.A. (2004) "Science, Technology and Sustainable Development: A World Review", World Review of Science, Technology and Sustainable Development, Vol. 1. No. 1. Pp5-24

Ajayi, J. F. A., Goma, K. H. and Johnson, G.A. (1996) The African Experience with Higher Education. The Association of African Universities, Accra – Ghana.

Armah, A. K. (1968). The Beautiful Ones Are Not Yet Born. Heinemann, London

Armah, A. K. (1970). Fragments, Heinemann, London.

Armah, A. K. (1972). Why Are We So Blest? Heinemann, London.

Ashby Jacqueline, Klees, Steven; Pachico, Douglas; & Wells, Stuart (1980). "Alternative Strategies in Economic Analysis of Information/Education Projects," in McAnany, Emile G. (Ed.). Communications in the Rural Third World: The Role of Information in Development. Praeger Publishers, New York

Blair, Robert & Jordan Josephine (1994). "Staff Loss and Retention at Selected Africa Universities: A Synthesis Report," AAFTHR Technical Note No.18, Human Resources and Poverty division, Technical Department, African Region, World Bank, Washington D.C.

Borum Finn & Kristensen Peer Hull (eds.) (1989). Technological Innovation and Organisational Change. Institute of Organisation and Industrial Sociology, Copenhagen, Denmark

Braby, N. & B. Tobin (2005). "Protecting and Strengthening Traditional Knowledge Innovation Systems," Work 17. 2(2005)

Chinweizu (1987). The West and The Rest of Us. PeroPress, Lagos - Nigeria

Clapham, C. (2002Z). "The challenge to the State in a Globalised World," Development and Change, Vol.33. No.5, 2002, pp782-786

Dahre Ulf Johansson (ed.) (2012). Predicaments in the Horn of Africa. Media Tryck, Lund University, Lund -Sweden

Ekiyor Thelma & Mashumba Noria (2006). The Peacebuilding Role of Civil Society in Central Africa. Policy Seminar Report. The Centre for Conflict Resolution, Cape Town, South Africa

Forje, Ellinor (2018) "Unblocking Africa's Underdevelopment Through the One Belt One Road Initiative", in Thokozani Simelane & Lavhelesani Managa (eds.) (2018) Belt and Road Initiative: Alternative Development Path for Africa. Africa Institute of South Africa, Pretoria, South Africa, pp7-23

Forje, W. John (1979). The Rape of Africa at Vienna. African Participation in the 1979 United Nations Conference on Science and Technology for Development. ARGD Publication, Lund- Sweden

Forje, W. John (1987). Science and Technology in Africa. Vol. 10. Longman World Series in Science and Technology, Longman Publishers, Essex, UK.

Forje W. John (2011). "Science and Technology for Enhancing Sustainable Development: The Instrument for Accelerating the Construction of a Union Government for Africa n Problems and Prospects," in Forje (ed.) (2011) Century of Change. Symposium on African Unity. Nova Science Publishers Inc. New York, pp89-126

Forje W. John (1988). Science and Technology in Africa. Vol. 10, Longman World Series on Science and Technology, Longman Publishers, Essex. UK

Forje W. John (1979). The Rape of Africa at Vienna. African Participation in the 1979 United Nations Conference on Science and Technology for Development. ARTGAD Publications, Lund-Sweden

Forje W. John and Yazani April (2015) "Rethinking Africa's Development Through Science and Technology: A Partnership Opportunity for South Africa and China" in Funeka Yazani April and Garth Shelton (eds.) (2015) Perspectives on South Africa-China Relations, Africa Institute of South Africa. Pretoria, South Africa, pp83-104

Gambari, I. (2000) Globalisation and marginalization: Africa and the International Community. A Keynote Address at the 2000 Commencement at the University of Bridgeport, Connecticut, p.35

Gates Bill (1995). The Road Ahead. Penguin Group, New York

Gee, S. (1981) Technology Transfer, Innovation and International Competitiveness. John Wiley & Sons Inc., New York

Gerschenkron, A. (1962). Economic Backwardness in Historical Perspectives.

Goddard, C.R., Cronin, P. and Dash, K. C (eds.) (2003) International Political Economy: State-market Relations in a Changing Global Order. Lynne Rienner Publishers, Boulder and London.

Gourevitch, Peter and James Shinn (2005). Political Power and Corporate Control. The New Global Politics of Corporate Governance, Princeton University Press, Princeton NJ.

Harberger, A. C. (1998) "A Vision of the Growth Process", American Economic Review, Vol. 88. Pp1-32

Hax, A. (1989). "Building the firm of the Future," Sloan Management Review, 30, pp75-82.

Hountondji Paulin (2012). "Introduction: Decentring Africa" in P. Hountondji (ed.) Endogenous Knowledge Research Trails, CODESRIA Book Series, Dakar, Senegal.

Krugman, P. (1999). The Return of Depression Economics, Penguin, London

Lagos Plan of Action (LPA). Lags Plan of Action for the Economic Development of Africa 1980-2000, Addis Ababa, Ethiopia.

Landes, D. (1969). The Unbound Prometheus, Cambridge University Press, New York, USA

Levy Jr., Marion J. (1992). "Confucianism and Modernisation," Society, Vol. 29. No. 4, May/June

Little, Reg and Reed, Warren (1989). The Confucian Renaissance. The Federation Press, Sydney.

Lorentzen Jo (2006) "The Knowledge of Numbers: S&T, R&D and Innovation Indicators in South Africa" in Vishnu Padayachee (2006). The Development Decade? Human Science Research Council, Cape Town, South Africa.

Mazrui, A. A. (1978). Political Values and the Educated Class in Africa, Heinemann, London

Mazrui, Ali A. (1973). "Thoughts on Assassination in Africa," in Prosser, Michael H. (ed.) Intercommunication Among Nations and Peoples. Harper & Row Publishers, Inc. New York

Mbeki, T. (1998). Africa: The Time Has Come. Tefelberg Publishers Ltd. Cape Town, South Africa

Muchie Mammo (2017) 'Still on The Journey to Regenerate Africans: The 7th AU Conference, May 22-24 2017, Pretoria, South Africa

Ngara, E. (1994). The African University and Its Mission. The Institute of Southern African Studies, Lesotho

Obayiuwana Osasu (2012). "The Rape of Paradise: The Only legacy that Oil has brought to the Niger Delta is Death," New African, No.513, January 2012, London, pp10-15

Obijofor M. Levi (2001). "The Future of Africa Lies in Home Grown Solutions," in Olugbenga Adesida & Arunma Oteh (eds.) African

Voices – African Visions. The Nordic African Institute, Uppsala – Sweden, pp131-146

Olaniran A. Bolande (2001). "Africa in the 21st Century: A Case for Innovative Use of Technology: in Olugbenga Adesida & Arunma Oteh (eds.) 2001. African Voices – African Visions., Nordic African Institute, Uppsala, Sweden, pp147-160

Osia, K (1987) "lack Africa and the Dilemma of Development", Journal of African Studies, Vol.14, No. 2, p.38

Osia, K (1998) "Leadership, followership and accountability" in Nwaneri, A. (ed.) Nigeria: Visions for the Future, Macmillan Nigeria Publishers Ltd., Ibadan, p236

Osia, K. (2004) "Globalisation and the politics of unequal development". World Review of Science, Technology and Sustainable Development, Vol. 1. No.1 pp.25-36

Paterson Mark & Saunders Chris (2011). South Africa, Africa and the United Nations Security Council. Centre for Conflict Resolution, Cape Town, South Africa.

Rostow, W. (1959) The Stages of Economic Growth, History Review, August

Schumpeter, Joseph (1943) Capitalism, Socialism and Democracy. Unwin Publishers.

Servaes, Jan (1986). "Development Theory and Communication Policy: Power to the People." European Journal of Communication, Vol.1. No.2, June

Shiva, V. (2001). Protect or Plunder, Zed Books, London.

Small Michelle (2006). Privatisation of Security and Military Functions and the Demise of the Modern Nation –State in Africa. Occasional Paper Series, Vol. 1, No.2, ACCORD, South Africa.

Timamy, M.H. Khali (2007). The Political Economy of Technological Underdevelopment in Africa. CBAAC, Lagos – Nigeria and DPMF, Addis Ababa, Ethiopia.

Vick Karl and Ashraf Khalil (2013). Faith and The Campus. Islamists, Secularists, Democrats and Generals All want al-Azhar University. The Outcome of their tussle could determine the future of Egypt." Time Magazine, Vol.181, No.22, 2013, pp22-25

Wa Thiong'o N. (1977). Petals of Blood. Heinemann, London

Wa Thiong'o, N. (1982). Devil on the Cross, Heinemann, London

Wa Thiong'o, N. (1986). Decolonising the Mind. The Politics of Language in African Literature, Heinemann, Nairobi – Kenya

Wa Thiong'o, N. (1993). Moving the Centre: The struggle for Cultural Freedoms. James Currey, London.

Walsh, James (1993). "Asia's Different Drum," Time Magazine, 14 June 1993

Zeleza Tiyambe Paul (1997). Manufacturing African Studies and Crises. CODESRIA Book Series, Dakar - Senegal.

Chapter 4

The Interface between the University, Research Institutes and the Private Sector as Appropriate Technological Link for Africa's Developmental Take-off: Changing Attitudes, Changing Behaviours and Pushing Forward Development

Abstract

With the growing knowledge-economy of the globalise world, higher education (human capital development) is no longer seen as a luxury that transitional polities cannot afford. Without a constructive holistic linkage between education, research and enterprise, Africa will be stuck on the run-way, unable to take off to the destination of quality wellbeing of its citizens. Such a move requires a comprehensive policy strategic basis and the determined political will to bid fare-voyage to underdevelopment and exploitation, by making science and technology and indigenous knowledge the anvil for change and progress. The paper argues that the "late-comer advantage" [Gerschenkron 1962] provides the solid foundation on which Africa can draw valuable lessons from the failure and successes of today's developed economies in fashioning the continent's development path. It is a question of tapping the available resources of the people and making good use of such resources. The vision of Africa is not racing to the outer space but to the rural areas and hinterlands that have been neglected to better improve the quality livelihood of the people. The strategy is construed on the interface between educations, research institutes and enterprise depend on the potential for accelerated growth by using appropriate the vast natural resources of the continent. In short, education gives added value to natural resources potential. There is an urgent need for articulate appropriate policy formulation and implementation strategies in building the science and technology base and using it for development, not destruction the paper argues. The role of indigenous knowledge and technological prowess must marry modern technology to give a breakthrough for the people to own their development and in meeting basic human needs. Proactive strategy policy measures are advanced

Keywords: Appropriate technology, policy articulation, human capital development, indigenous knowledge, cross-cutting issues, gender equity, quality livelihood,

Introduction

Unleashing a New Developmental Plan

"What has become embarrassingly clear, after three decades' ad more after the attainment of independence by the majority of African countries is that the generality of our people has been excluded from any significant contribution to the determination of national directions."

(Professor Adebayo Adedeji, formerly Executive Secretary of the United Nations Economic Commission for Africa, in a Lecture in Kaduna, Nigeria as reported in West Africa, 11-17 November 1991)

Africa in 2012 celebrated the 10th anniversary of the African Union (AU); in 2013, the continent will be celebrating the forerunner of the AU, the creation of the Organization of African Unity (OAU). The two events rekindle an epoch-making period in the life of a continent highlighting the need for the region to move in the direction of constructing a capable developmental state. It is clearer that the continent has walked a fault-finding journey towards realising a society that truly reflects her geographical structure both socially and economically given vast natural resources potentials. It is sad to notice that the continent is poor in the midst of plenty: their natural resource is a curse rather than a blessing to the people. Yet a new world of production is emerging based on linkages among state-university-society and industry or the triple helix, as the basis for constructing a new development path. How entrenched or equipped is Africa in this new development agenda designed to ensure sustainable livelihood for the population. Newly industrialising, de-industrialising, and re-industrialising nations share a mutual interest in fostering knowledge-based economic and social development by creating inter-institutional ties and boundary-spanning mechanisms with goals of ensuring sustainable quality wellbeing for the citizens.

In this respect, Africa remains the least developed continent in the world. The focuses of the paper are too critically and objectively probe into why the continent is underdeveloped; what must be done to reconstruct its current image of backwardness rift with conflicts, diseases and exploitation. We have to continue asking questions that trigger more dialogues in our search to alleviate socio-economic ills that overshadow and undermine the freedom, sovereignty of the continent. The basis of argument is the absence of focused leadership; poor human capital development and lack of political will are some of the contributing factors to the continent's marginalisation and exploitation within the prevailing global construct dominated by the forces of capitalism as executed by the developed polities. African countries need to ponder deeply into the Adam Smith (The Wealth of Nations, 1776) which is the bible of capitalism and underpins Africa in the garage as a raw material producing and exporting continent; to fashion out a new approach to addressing their predicaments as well as to probe into Olowu and Wunsch (1990) The Failure of Centralised State being practiced in many African countries.

While the continent does not have to develop the wheel, it has failed to exploit to its advantage the views advanced by Gerschenkron [1962]. The "late-comer advantage" must be dissected from the forces of globalisation. The public-civil society-private sector interface is weak or non-existing unable to forge an entrepreneurial spirit for transformation. Apparently, globalisation is the highest stage of scientific imperialism forcing African countries to open their doors without consolidating their indigenous knowledge as bases for their take-off. To this date, indigenous knowledge, which has generally been passed from generation to generations by word of mouth, is in danger of being lost unless it is formally documented and preserved. The future of indigenous knowledge, which reflects many generations of experience and problem solving by countless indigenous people across the continent, is uncertain. The loss of indigenous knowledge would impoverish society because, just as the continent/world needs genetic diversity of species, it needs diversity of knowledge systems. Thus, indigenous knowledge forms a solid basis for state-civil society-private sector interface in developing a sustainable basis indigenous knowledge is a protective shield for countries without the scientific and technological capacities of the developed world. For Western development, protectionism was the rule. For the transformation of Africa, globalisation is advocated which simply implies opening up Africa for all at all costs and closing the gates of the West to African products. The Blair Report – 2005 and Adam Smith – Wealth of Nation, 1776) tells it all. Actions to rectify these trade imbalances must be taken especially in areas like (i) tariffs, (ii) scrapping subsidies, (iii) for African countries to diversify and avoid dependency on export of raw materials. The Wealth of Nations like all other similar publications echoing the same views implants a western "culture of imperialism" in Africa; and Africans have graciously embarrassed the imported culture as against destroy their own. We have to understand the wider framework of culture and its penetrating impact as this becomes of special importance when cultures as different as those of African and

European peoples. The colonies existed for the colonial trade; and it was in the very nature of the colonial trade that not only was wealth drawn from African produce to be spent in Europe and not in Africa, but also that most even of the consumer goods in Africa cities had to be imported from Europe. Exports were of primary products with little or no local processing, refining or manufacture (Brown, 1995:26).

It is argued that Africa's future development must in fact be constructed on the roots wherever they were still alive (Achebe et al.1991); In 1989 the UN Economic Commission for Africa pointed out that not markets, nor states, nor parastatal institutions, but human beings in their own households and community associations must be the 'fulcrum of development' (Brown, 1995:7; UNCS 1989:2-3) the point at which all the levers of change should be brought to bear. It can be argued that 10 years of the African Union (AU) and 50 years of the Organisation of African Unity (OAU) is a short span in the life of a continent. Admittedly, the continent is a vast mass, and we must acknowledge and embrace the reality that it consists of diverse nations with many and diverse nations harbouring varied past geo-political historical construct, but with a shared common identity of colonial rule and the need to create a new identity after the shackles of colonial domination was cut (so to say) by the granting of independence to former colonial territories. But how independent these countries are being a different ball-game? However, Africa is in dire need and requires concerted policies and visionary leadership to redress existing socioeconomic imbalances of the past and present but also time, perseverance, cooperation and focused ideological orientation.

Using the SWOT approach, Africa has the means to develop provided new mindset architecture is put in place. Focusing on a people-oriented approach, the stigma of underdevelopment and backwardness can be erased within a generation. The Asian countries did it; China has done it. These countries are able to feed their citizens possessing far less the natural resources potential of Africa; why not the African Lions owning their development construct and providing quality wellbeing to their citizens. African countries continue to face difficulties with regards to poverty alleviation, job creation, quality human capital development, proper health care system, good shelter among many other deficiencies that impact adversely on the quality livelihood of the people. The problem faced by the continent is numerous. Solutions are many as well. The obstacle is how to fashion out the right solutions to these barrages of problems that persistently manifest themselves on daily bases.

The absences of political will, visionary leadership at the national and continental levels constitute a serious barrier in mounting a common and united front in the struggle to establish the continent within the global construct and context in changing the fortune other region. Here is a region blessed with vast opportunities but lavishing in abject poverty, misery and a pack of shame hanging over its head. As pointed out by Heraclitus (c.500 BC) "Nothing is permanent but Change." In the last century, change accelerates and the future becomes harder to foresee. As instant communications spread, and power and wealth concentrate, so ideas spread faster. A balance-sheet of development and human well-being shows achievements and deficits. Power and poverty are polarised at the extremes, with a global over-class and global underclass. An evolving consensus converges on well-being, livelihood, capabilities, equity, and sustainability as interlinked ends and means. Huge opportunities exist to make a difference for the better. The challenge is personal, professional and institutional, to frame a practical paradigm for knowing and acting, and changing how we know and act, in a flux of uncertainty and change. New power, knowledge and social and economic polarization coexist on an unprecedented and scandalous scale. Seen within this context, a progressive Afro-centric agenda is mapping a new African Order that should be the game-changer for the continent and for situating its appropriate place within a "New world Order" as eloquently discussed by Popov and Dutkiewicz (2017). The sovereignty and human rights of the African people must be protected by all means possible.

The conceptual premises build on the interface between institutions and development (Fig1)and interposing the discourse between the stages of development [Rostow,1960] and the *"late-comer advantage"* [Gerschenkron 1962], and interfaced with the place of indigenous knowledge as cultural heritage and anvil possessed by the people to also stimulate their developmental onslaught.

Fig.1 the Interface between Institutions and Development in Africa

University <=======→Research<=======→ Private Sector
//
Civil Society
Policy Articulation & Implementation
Research, Science and Technology
Indigenous Knowledge system
//
Conversion Process
//
Developmental State
//
Quality Wellbeing of Citizens

It is argued that by linking indigenous knowledge to the development process, creates the avenue for challenging archaic cultural values that impedes particularly female gender contributions and involvement in the development process. Appropriate technology, the research knowledge of the people should be harnessed and put at the services of the people for their common good. The hidden creativity, innovative and productive capacity of the people must be developed and harnessed for the sustainable development that addresses the needs of the people and communities. Pharmacologically-rich plants known to the herbalist - indigenous knowledge - can rival conventional medicines. For its commercial purpose requires the input of the private sector. Increased participation of women in science and technology is therefore advocated not only as a matter of equity but as a critical means of building diverse capacities to tackle the multidimensional challenges of development. The scientific system in Africa is so deficient in female input and this has serious implications for the kind of science and technology that must be applied to Africa's transformation at this critical time in the continent's development. The challenging problems of the region touch upon survival and dignity of humankind. The problems pivot around food production, nutrition, health, education, and the environment, all of which can be addressed through the application of science and technology that takes into account the multi-dimensional situation of the continent.

This is a crucial and critical strategy of utilising the continent's human resources in the most efficacious way. Africa is politically free but mired in deep misery of economic deprivation, poverty, ignorance and disease. The most pervasive problem of Africa today is deep-seated multi-dimensional poverty – poverty of the material kind, poverty of a positive vision for the future, [Makhubu, 1997; Odhiambo, 1994, Forje 2009; Bangura, 2011]. When policies are pro-poor oriented the innovative capacities of the rural people, or people who do not matter will be discovered which eventually become inputs in the market process; through the efforts of a productive private sector. Such discoveries lead to a triple heritage which forms a vicious circle:

> *education (university) = research institution) = private sector interface) =civil society needs met) è quality of life improves) e increased productivity) =e-growth assured, and the cycle continues*

A dynamic private sector can also exert a positive influence over both democracy and development and well-functioning democratic institutions can help the private sector take advantage of economic opportunities. Well-functioning legislative environments and public access to information provide a healthy environment for business. The private sector can be a player in the functioning of democratic institutions by engaging in policy discussions to enhance the creation and development of democratic practices that are supportive of business. Productivity and growth in the private sector contribute significantly to the sustainable transformation of society. Cooperation in research, science and technology offer potentially powerful means to inform policy designers for national and international agreements as well as it provides the sort of joint creativity and capacity-pooling needed to advance and apply knowledge to national, continental and global problems. The speed at which researchers, scientists, and the entrepreneurial world collaborated to looking for a vaccine to the COVID-19 pandemic which brought the world to its knees tells us what humankind can achieve when they develop the will to work together.

Individual hidden talents have to be discovered; there is lack of infrastructure-base for developing and exploiting technologies (especially indigenous knowledge) and increasing investment in universities and research institutions to convert research results into consumer products. Thus, the behaviour of the private sector can also reinforce democratic governance by respecting the rule of law, enforcing property rights, ensuring transparent procurement, and by working through business associations and public-private dialogue to guard against the erosion of these institutions by misguided political actions. State-civil society-private sector is a vital development approach. Development like democracy cannot be imported but grown internally taking into consideration advances in human knowledge, and respect for universal fundamental rights, the use and protection of the global commons (environment) without compromising the rights of future generations. The appropriate technology here is developing the talents of the people, taking into consideration the availability of modern science and technology as a catalyst for multiplying knowledge and improving the livelihood of the people. The paper contributes to an understanding of the efforts of African countries to improve slowly from what is now by no means a desperate state, through evolutionary processes, perhaps the problems and approaches to their solutions will be seen as not very different from those of energy, poverty, pipe born water and healthcare, which are approached with a similar slowness and hesitation in the developed economies. And from that perception may emerge the mutual respect necessary for cooperative solution of the present problems of the continent. It should be noted that there is no 'one size fits all' approach to achieving these outcomes, but bit is vital to ensure that interface between the various stakeholder's interface inventions is embedded with;

- informed by the various actors, disciplines and other societal related activities;
- are tailored to the specific needs of the society;
- involving the people or actors equally in decision-making;
- creating a conducive environment for co-operative activities.

Though there is a growing recognition of the importance of university-civil society-private sector cooperation, lack of adequate institutional infrastructure, appropriate scientific equipment and finance have often prevented African countries from benefiting from this type of interface. Thus university-civil society-private sector nexus is illustrated in Fig 2. depicts the need and necessity of the various stakeholders to cooperate so that educational institutions can adapt their training programme to the needs of industry, developing research programmes that promote innovative processes and technology transfer from institutions to industry and for industry to produce goods meeting the needs of citizens. Cooperation between the various key actors (see Fig 2- Cooperative Partners in University/Private Sector Interface) becomes imperative in achieving quality wellbeing of the people.

Fig 2. Comparative Partners in University Industry Partnership

Public sector institution **Private sector institutions**

University and Research Research Laboratories

Science, technology and culture

// //

Research Park Zones

||

PRODUCTS

||

CONSUMERS

Improved Quality Wellbeing

Certain constraints however, exist as the university and the private sector have different objectives and invariably the university should provide the initiatives. Whereas university research aims at extending the limits of knowledge and seeking logical explanations, the private sector concerns with applications that lead to commercial production. For the private sector, the value of know-how is the business that can be made out of the application of knowledge. The private sector's expectation is to own knowledge by protecting it through patents. Financial result is top most important for the private sector. For the university, the wish is to publish his/her discoveries in renowned journals. Society and the private need education. This requires cooperation between the different actors. Africa remains the most scientifically and technologically underdeveloped region of the world. Yet it is the richest in terms of indigenous that remains untapped. According to Prof. Daniel N. Latum (1985:401-408), "From the very beginning, it is necessary to emphasise that all aspects of a people's culture must be interrelated, since they are synchronized elements of the means and results of the struggle to live – and live well – in a given ecologic milieu (physical, social, spiritual, intellectual, cosmic)". Dr. Bienvenu Logmo (1985:409-424) writing on the importance of African Traditional Medicine, states that is an "undisputed and undeniable heritage of our culture, is no longer in doubt. Unfortunately, this medicine is more and more like a lost soul drifting between primary and sophisticated health care; or even being seen simply as a 'clematises' and pious whish". We need to foster the harmonious linkage between indigenous knowledge and modern scientific and technological know-how to improve the welfare of all citizens. To develop and improve of it is to marry indigenous knowledge and modern scientific development. It is therefore seen that successful cooperation would require effective communication and mutual understanding between the stakeholders.

The role of the media is to educate all. The revolution in information and communications technology which is progressing at an incredible and indescribable speed continues to by-pass many Africa countries due to lack of foresight and moribund institutional structures. The state of ignorance in Africa can be greatly reduced by developing human capital and using modern information gadgets. Africa needs to wake up to the realisation that we have squandered a lot of opportunities for growth, development and equitable-sharing of the results of development which has failed to trigger down to the bottom billion. We need to be more people-focused. This requires a harmonious interface between the state-civil society and the private sector to constitute a formidable force and ensure that the combined talents of the people (men and women, including indigenous knowledge) is put into good use and is not frivolously wasted. There is a tendency amongst Africans to endlessly repeat pointless tropes rather than respond to the myriad market failures on the continent (bad roads, bad education, poor health system etc.) with innovative business solutions. This is where public service-civil society-private sector nexus comes in as a motivating instrument to performance management and service delivery. Contradictions between university/research institutions and the private sector pivots on the following perception as shown on Table 1 – Contradictions between Objectives.

Table 1: Contradictions between the Objectives of Private Sector and University

University	**Industry**	**Impact on Civil Society**
New discoveries	new applications	
New knowledge	Added value	
New financial means for additional research	financial benefit === ==== ====== ➔	**Wellbeing: Poor or Good**
Basic research	Applied research	//
		but approached from
Long term	short term ==============➔	different values perspectives for different objectives/goals
Know how, what and why	Product driven	
Publications	Secrecy	
Free public good	Protection, patents ============➔	
Academic Freedom	Commercial approach	

Source: Extracted with my additions from Ntim Benjamin [1997] "UNESCO's Role in Promoting Linkages between Universities and industries", in Science, Technology & Development, Vol. 15, Numbers 2&3 August/December 1997, p32

Services to society are rendered but from different value perspectives and intentions. The challenge is how to harmonise divergent objectives for a common purpose, i.e., the researcher continuous efforts in producing knowledge, and the private sector's goal of profit-making are married towards the common goal for the sustainable wellbeing of citizens. The role of the private sector in advancing the transformation of the continent cannot be dismissed lightly. Though the state has always been the major player, the private sector is a force to reckon with. Given the increasing needs of the population, the state no longer has the sole monopoly in services delivery. Outsourcing is required. Other partners must be taken on board. There is need for an African Civil Society Private Sector Renaissance to spur an African Miracle Development Process which should evolve into an Afro-centric developmental approach. The question to be asked is whether state-civil society-private sector partnership in Africa still has a common Agenda to advance its developmental onslaught in the best interest of the continent.

Developing the Entrepreneurial Spirit

The Gerschenkron concept should be the stimuli for developing an entrepreneurial spirit in African education construct. Science and entrepreneurship are the bases of economic transformation and growth. Drawing from the experiences of Alexis de Tocqueville [1851], "what astonishes me in the USA is not so much the marvellous grandeur of some undertakings as the innumerable multitude of small ones", should tell Africa how to promote activities and culture of creating these multitudinous initiatives where leaders like Franklin [1901] as a polymath inventor, statesman, scientists and business person gave the country a new vision and direction of development. Weber [2002] deployed the ideas of Franklin to develop his ideas about the relationship between Protestantism and the origins of capitalism. Weber's hangs on thought and action – underscoring the origins of the entrepreneurial traditions expressed in business and social improvement activities.

Our education system must be rigorously restructured. Technical education and entrepreneurial training should be given priority in the education curriculum of African countries. Lessons can be drawn from other countries, for example the "entrepreneurial education scheme in Brazil (the Pontifical Catholic University of Rio de Janeiro – PUC) and the University of Brasilia. Strategies should be articulated to address the complex social problems of anomie and alienation to resulting in dropout from education and disconnections from the world of work in many societies:

- spread of the cooperative education projects and entrepreneurial initiatives in a much broader way at the secondary level as well as pushing it into the university level;
- transforming higher education, following experiences from other countries – Brazil's entrepreneurial academic model, by making it into an activity for all students.
- improving on the country's indigenous knowledge and skills and linking this to modern technological knowledge

There is need to build on existing indigenous knowledge system resources, adapt modern technology to create new ones to establish riches of technological innovation and secure the African place within the competitive economy in an increasingly global knowledge-based economy. Building and improving on indigenous knowledge system requires interplay between African scientists and research with indigenous people in all spheres of activities; especially, in health, agriculture, environment, culture. What can modern science and technology learn from indigenous people and vice versa? We have lots of knowledge outside there which must be taped, stored for future development. When such collaboration does not exist, the tendency is likely the disappearance of indigenous knowledge with society becoming poorer due to its stupidity of not linking modern and traditional knowledge. Society is the poorer when indigenous knowledge disappears.

The SWOT Approach

Articulating and aggregating an African Miracle Development Process requires a critical analysis of the strength, weakness, and opportunities and threats (SWOT) Table 2, challenges the continent with the issues and hard choices it has to grapple with.

Table 2: Facing the Challenges of SWOT in the Transformation of Africa

Strength	Virgin area still to be researched and tapped;
	Provides development opportunities for other continents;
	Holds the future of the world;
	Valuing African people;
Weakness	Poor policy articulation and aggregation;
	Weak leadership, poor governance system; African leadership vacuum and western triumphal; over developing countries
	Inadequate human capital development;
	Colonial legacies constraining the development process;
	Unshared-prosperity: widening gap between the rich and poor;
	Undeveloped private sector – poor infrastructural development;
	Uncontrolled population explosion can back fire and retard the development;
	Absence of a committed and vibrant media industry to educate the people and put forward critical objectives as watch dog of failing government policies;
Opportunities:	The late-comer advantage – Africa does not need to develop the wheel;
	Vast untapped natural resources potentials;
	Fast growing youth population creating a strong labour force;
	Provides bases for the world's fastest growing economy;
	Diversity as 'asset' not 'liability' in state construct and the development process;
	Bright future for Africa provided it does its homework and in the peoples' interest;
Threats	Globalisation – a 'curse' but can be converted into a 'blessing';
	Weak scientific and technological background;
	Poor state construct;
	Poor human capital development and weak institutions;
	Bad governance – leading to the exclusion of the people in the development process;
	The West will continue using all means available to promote its agenda, policies and interests in then name and principles of globalisation;
	Recolonisation of Africa in the age of scientific and technological awakening;
	The politics of globalisation should be critically scrutinised;
	Self-articulate interests of the leader's/ruling elites;
	The forces of post-modern imperialism and the new colonising powers
	Hostile international environnement ;

Source : Forje, 2012

The Need for Cooperation

The inexhaustible potential of the research desert of Africa has much to offer and serve humankind's economic and social progress and help eliminate hunger, disease, economic backwardness, and other national and global problems. Africa and the rest of the world could then comer nearer to attaining the long-term objective of sustainable development by exploiting usefully our natural resources and putting this at the services of humanity. Our education and health system need to be upgraded to world class. We need in respect of such improvements, the following action plans;

- National, inter-African, and international cooperation so as to (i) enhance basic research and launching of inter-country, inter-continental and interplanetary research;
- Use of research results for the common good; we should draw valuable lessons from the COVID-19 pandemic;

- Development and utilisation of technology for human purposes – developing and
- improving human welfare.

With these and other research activities, humankind could come nearer to attaining the long-term objective of industrialisation and globalisation. In all, Africa could with the rest of the world be moving towards new research cooperation for sustainable development (NRCSD). With such a vision, we can rest assured that "humankind is tired of the confrontation being forced on it by the powerful; and of the oppressive fear for the future because of the oppressive present. For the African people, their hopes are linked to ideas which will lead to a continent and world without fear and war, to a continent without poverty and weapon, but a continent where the military weapon is 'development, justice, security and quality livelihood for all citizens.' Every Africa, I strongly believe, supports peace, development and justice, and rejects military structures for destruction. Africans reject warlike attitudes and welcome peaceablessness, mutual understanding, trust and the art of living and eating together. I strongly pray that leading circles in the West take these realities and facts into consideration; and act in concert for the common good of all humankind.

A critical look at conflicts in Africa shows that African countries are not at war with one another; but they at war within each country. For example, Cameroon is at war with itself not with another country. The same situation prevails in Ethiopia, Central African Republic, Mali, Chad, Congo, Tunisia etc. etc., On the other hand, why must African nations be at war with one another; or why must there be internal wars within each African nation? The war should be against poverty, corruption, poor services delivery, injustice, and inequality. The Afro-centric doctrine should create the new African dream of living and eating together. This is what Africa needs most is collaboration across the board. It is such interface between research, science, technology and entrepreneurship that quickly could come up with a vaccine for the COVID-19 pandemic. We need this kind of collaborative action plan or research activities to conquer long-time devastating effects of killer diseases like malaria. We need the following actions in light of:

- A heightened activity of the African people as well as their determination to achieve through joint and collaborative efforts or change for the better in every African nation and the continent for a change for a better Africa, and the world at large;

- A comprehensive set of measures which should block the escalation and penetration of Euro-centric agenda on Africa;
- Increased willingness by the people of Africa to take control, responsibility and accountability of the interests of the African people;
- The urgent need for the continent to speed up of political dialogue between the different faction in society; that despite their differences, they can and must work together for the common good of the country and continent. They must be poised between peace, justice, equality and development; avoid the forces of confrontation, but encourage peaceful co-existence to maintain a harmonious social balance in society.

African countries should commit themselves to the triumph of political reason and good will I national and international relations. Therefore, peaceful coexistence, the equal and reliable security of all sides, the reduction of the level of military confrontation and overall military and political tension in the world and the inadmissibility of hegemonies in any form – there should be the maim aims of the continent's objections to Euro-centric hegemonic agenda being pushed down the throat the throats of African countries. The only reasonable way out of the existing situation is for the immediate adoption of a comprehensive-progressive Afro-centric agenda to halt the Euro-centric offensive that is penetrating throughout the continent. We have to articulate the search for a reasonable out of the current dilemma that has gripped Africa. By and large, Africa has to make a choice how to limit and put a stop to the policy strategy of the military industrial complex and its grip over the continent. The research institutes and universities of Africa should ponder deep into the quick search for the COVID-19 vaccine and step –up greater collaboration and research in other areas that improves the well-being of the people. In addition, it is also a challenge for African governments to beef up funding's in research and for higher education training on the continent. Thirdly, for the private sector to be an inherent and vital component in the development process.

Either Africa shapes policy in the direction of promoting a progressive afro-centric approach or perishes under the weight of Euro-centricism towards the continent. With this in mind, Africa must attempt to sow the following seeds; -

- Only through an Afro-centric agenda can development come the way of the people;

- Only through a progressive Afro-centric agenda can we put an end to the invulnerability of the whole western agenda;
- Africa should through the Afro-centric agenda make the weapons of Euro-centric agenda 'ineffective and obsolete as well as developing the will to eliminate the hidden agenda or faces behind the mask;
- The implementation of an Afro-centric agenda should help accelerate unprecedented technological, scientific and developmental breakthrough that will take Africa to the heights of progress and prosperity and ensure sustainable development for a stronger and united Africa;
- A stronger and united Africa – is the basis for the brighter future of the continent;
- African countries should draw valuable lessons from the progress made by a number of East Asian countries, which were behind the continent some fifty or more years ago;
- The West has developed the attitude and policy of keeping Africa on the edge or fringes of underdevelopment, which the continent seems to accept and adjust itself to such conditioning. The collaborative search for vaccine for the COVID-19 pandemic is good pointer for cooperative relationship between research, science, technology, private sector and society;
- Can the COVID-19 pandemic be the game changer in forging cordial and collaborative actions in research, science, technology, indigenous knowledge system, the private sector – all efforts put at the services and benefits of humanity.

What is Africa to be in the next fifty years? I strongly believe that with the coexistence of our diversities, of opposing blocs, a great deal that is useful can be done and achieved for Africa and world development. We need to exploit to the maximum things that draw the two sides together for a win-win situation of the developed and developing countries, for science, research, technology, private sector, civil society interface. The problem is that the legacy of colonial past remains a stumbling block to development. There are certain stigmas on the continent, some cause by the new independent state, others by the laid down stigma arising for the many years of colonial rule. Africa due to its colonial past, each country has its experiences which differ in the way of life and way of thinking; the people have the inalienable rights to live in peace and in a continent that is constantly being exploited by the well-to-do countries.

Whether advocates of the Eurocentric or Afro-centric schools of thought have one thing in common; we were all colonized, neo-colonialism is with us; we are underdeveloped; we are suffering from the weight of poverty; we cohabit with poor health, communication facilities to mention but a few of the predicaments facing the region. These are some of the gifts given us by the west which we have to live with. We should on our part, given the realities we experience on daily basis to rethink, re-strategies our different position to genuinely and collectively do something productive towards improving and concretising our situation. We should from our different points make attempts to convince the developed countries that the current policy approach constitutes a serious threat to our well-being; that improving the situation is also creating room for a 'win-win' outcome that does not threaten but also consolidate whatever advantages or gains made so far. Different threats exist, just as different gains exist for the different parties concerned. Therefore, the rich and poor countries should genuinely work towards the common goal of: -

- Total elimination of poverty, misery, injustice and inequality;
- A radical reduction in defence budget allocation;
- A radical increasing on the budget on social spending that leads to greater improvement in the quality of services delivery and livelihood;
- Putting an end to conflict and doing things possible that promotes peace and stability;
- The pledge by states to jointly and harmoniously fight the ills and consequences of poverty, underdevelopment; and for states to be thirst not to go to war against their citizens because of differences in opinion;
- War does not solve socio-economic-politico problems, but justice, peace and the art of listening (inclusive dialogue) between and among conflicting parties provides the best solution for any form of conflicts;
- The ideological orientation of working towards a treaty or doctrine on the non-use of military arsenal against the people and the maintenance of the peaceful co-existence and relations among people.

We should bear in mind that peace cannot be built on the basis of superiority of strength but on the anvil of justice and equality. The system of subordination of one to another is built on superiority of strength. Peace is possible only on the basis of justice, respect, equality, strength along with the refusal to use military force and the elimination of military arsenals. The best way to put an end to the poverty and underdevelopment of Africa is to put an end to poverty and underdevelopment, simply to stop it.

Conclusion

The paper briefly reviews various input factors international, regional and national strategies and mechanisms for promoting university-civil society-private sector interface for the ultimate wellbeing of the people. African countries have a strong base and advantage to advance their scientific and technological take-off if only they know what their development priorities and needs are. The drawback is the absence of the political will in constructively engaging the people and creating an enabling environment to ensure a functional and financial relationship between the implicit actors. Science and technology are embedded with vast potential needs to be developed to the full in meeting national and global challenges of sustainable human development. Failure to develop the potentials of the people only prolongs the state of underdevelopment construct the continent is facing. There is need to openly recognise that Africa institutions are weak and a continental leadership vacuum pervades. The continent is failing to assert itself as a key player, speaking with one voice on matters of vital continental interests. This vacuum is being exploited by Western powers, financial conglomerates and business organisations. We have to strengthen Africa's cohesion, and therefore its capacity to act in unity, around a broad, progressive agenda.

Sustainable human development and quality wellbeing for the people calls for shared-prosperity, better development and sharing of scientific knowledge including indigenous knowledge), across society and between nations backed by a sustained commitment to a people-oriented development approach on the part of state, civil society, private sector and international community towards a common human course. The interface between state-civil society-private sectors provides the best possible means for the continent to galvanised its resources, (human and natural resources), for the sustainable development of the continent and as a meaningful partner in global construct. Local innovations and development may only require critical interventions and hand-holding efforts for their transition into wider development. Design intervention may also help to bring in the much-needed empathetic understanding and holistic vision to connect and integrate the various efforts towards a positive outcome. Since indigenous knowledge and local innovations are essential to development, they must be gathered, organised and disseminated, just like scientific knowledge that emerges from research and development. Of course, there are problems or challenges involved, such as the management and preservation of indigenous knowledge related to methodology, access, intellectual property rights and the media and formats in which to identify, codify and preserve it for further scrutiny and further innovations. Of course, solutions to these problems can be found. That is a challenge to research and researchers to fashion out. A consolidated interface between state-civil society-private sector partnerships should provide the need stimuli for indigenous knowledge to have a kick-start for the development of the continent.

Presently, the development construct of Africa is weak, uncoordinated, embedded with derogatory perception, undervaluing of Africa and Africans by non-Africans impedes the sustainable transformation of the continent. A new mind set is imperative for African to reclaim its place in the world of the 21st century and beyond. Developing and proper utilisation of its human capacity potential is the key to a successful road map to sustainable development approach. What is required is visionary leadership in piloting state-civil society-private sector connect for the developmental construct for the future of the African continent.

Recommendations

It is strongly recommended that strategic policy measures be put in place that will enhance state-civil society-private sector nexus in building the science and technology bases for the continent's take-off to sustainable development. In this regard, the following are recommended.

- Comprehensive and concerted policy formulation and resources allocation;
- Human resources development and capacity building;
- developing indigenous knowledge and its linkage to main stream science and technology development;
- Indigenous knowledge should not be discarded but improved upon and integrated into the development process;
- The private sector taking keen interest in developing indigenous knowledge, creativity and innovation; this can lead to new areas of product development for the sector;

- Intensify cooperation within and among African universities and research institutions;
- developing the requisite infrastructures, including sustainable performance – level financing;
- giving the neglected bottom billion a chance in sharing knowledge, skills, talents and other values enhancing the development construct of the continent;
- Existing vacuum in African leadership should be bridged;
- ensure the right of the masses of the African people to participate in the process of governance and development;

References

Achebe Chinua et al (eds.) (1991) Beyond Hunger in Africa: Africa 2057 – Conventional Wisdom and an African Visio. James Currey.

Alexis de Tocqueville, [1851], democracy in America. A. S. Barnes Co. New York, NY

Bangura Ibrahim [2011] "A Critical Assessment of Development Views of Gender in Africa," Africa Peace and Conflict Journal, University for Peace, Vol. 4, Number 2, December 2011, Addis Ababa, Ethiopia, pp54-65

Brown Barratt Michael (1995) Africa's Choices: After Thirty Years of the World Bank. Penguin Books. UK

Franklin, B. [1901; 1771] Autobiography of Benjamin Franklin, Macmillan Publishers, New York, NY

Fishwick, W. [1985]. Strengthening Cooperation between Engineering Schools and Industry, Paris, UNESCO

Forje W. John [2009] State Building and Democracy in Africa. A Comparative and Developmental Approach. Nova Science Publishers Inc, New York

Gerschenkron A [1962] Economic Backwardness in Historical Perspective. The Belknap Press of Harvard University Press. Cambridge, USA

Higgins, T. [1991]. "The Geopolitics of Research Finding in Europe, USA: Some Policy Aspects" International Journal of Technology Management, Vol.6

Lantum N. Daniel (1985) "Cameroonian Cultural Identity Expressed Through Science and Technology" in The Cultural Identity of Cameroon. Papers presented at the Colloquium of the Second National Cultural Week, 13-20 May 1985, Ministry of Information and Culture, Department of Cultural Affairs, Yaoundé-Cameroon, pp. 401-408

Logmo Bienvenu, (1985) "The Contribution of Traditional Medicine and its Pharmacopoeia", in The Cultural Identity of Cameroon. Papers presented at the Colloquium of the Second National Cultural Week, 13-20 May 1985, Ministry of Information and Culture, Department of Cultural Affairs, Yaoundé-Cameroon. Pp409-424

Makhubu P. Lydia [1997] "Women's Participation in Science and Technology for Development in Africa" Special Issue of Science, Technology and Development, Vol.14, Numbers 2&3, August/December 1997, pp95-103

Makhubu P. Lydia [1993] "The Potential Strength of African Women in Building Africa's Scientific and Technological Capacity", Paper presented to America Association for the Advancement of Science Symposium on Science in Africa. Washington, DC.

Ntim Benjamin [1997] "UNESCO's Role in Promoting Linkages Between Universities and Industries", in Science, Technology & Development, Vol. 15, Numbers 2&3 August/December 1997, p32

Odhiambo, R. Thomas [1994]," Redefining Africa's Priorities for the 1990s: An Agenda for a Science led Development Strategy for Africa", Strategic paper for the Second Presidential Forum, Maputo, Mozambique

Popov Vladimir & Piotr Dutkiewicz (2017) Mapping a New World Order. The Rest Beyond the West. Edward Elgar Publishing, UK

Rostow, W. W. [19600]. The Stages of Economic Development, London

Weber

Chapter 5

Re-imagining Faith-Based and Civil Society Organisations as Agents of Development in Transitional Polities in Africa. Challenges and Prospect for Shared-values in the Future. Lessons from Cameroon

Abstract

Situating the Paradigms

Africa is caught between the devil and the deep blue sea. It remains a continent trapped between development, under-development, decay and destruction; between peace, chaos, conflicts and war. So far development and peace has evaded the continent. It has embraced conflicts, poverty and other vices partly not of its own making and partly due to imposed pattern of development as a result of the articulate self-interest of forces beyond its control. By and large, Africa presents a contradiction of itself. First it is a continent characterised by hunger and starvation, yet a continent blessed with vast natural resources potential that cannot be matched by any other continent on planet earth. It remains the least developed continent. Human ingenuity and advancements in science and technology impacts little on improving the quality wellbeing of the people. The knowledge, technology and resources for closing the food security deficit are available today, and breakthroughs will continue to emerge from research and development. It is a continent that has become the jig-saw of super powers, making its natural resources a curse rather than a blessing to sustainable transformation of the region and the quality wellbeing of citizens. Looking at the continent's deficit in all facets, the paper probes into the issue of peace and development which has evaded the region, the continent's embracement of conflicts and why dialogue between theories and practices seem to have failed throughout the continent. It critically and objectively explores the ways in which specific approaches to peace and policy agendas play or interact for good or worse on the continent. The absence of war does not entail peace. The existence of democracy does not imply development. Other parameters are needed to ensure the linkage between democracy and development to usher maximum benefit to society. A number of African countries have escaped the scourges of conflicts. But these nations still know no peace. Peace therefore goes far beyond wars and conflicts. Other parameters come to play but often not seen as crucial input factors or ingredients to sustaining the peace. The search for peace begins by putting in place the paradigms and parameters that make life worth living – food security, health security, shelter, job security, security to life and property, security to freedom of speech and worship, among others. Why have these fundamental factors essential to human existence evaded the region? Why has the continent known no peace and remains underdeveloped? Why is the continent poor in the midst of plenty? Why has conflict overridden the continent? Why has the continent been a war and refugee ridden zone? Why there is no dialogue between theories and practice as far as Africa is concern? A new mindset among the various stakeholders is called for. Proactive and strategic policy measures are advanced.

Keywords: peace, conflict, governance, poverty, dialogue, development, equity, war, shared-prosperity, justice

Introduction

In Search for A New Paradigm

The article discusses the methodological principles which underpin the paradigms for the search for peace dialogue between theories and practices given that the continent is caught between the deep blues and devils the trappings of underdevelopment, development, decay, destruction; between peace, stability, chaos conflicts and war. It notes that Africa presents a contradiction of itself. First as a continent characterised by hunger and starvation, yet a continent blessed with vast natural resources potential that cannot be marched anywhere in the world yet engraved with poverty and poor livelihood for the vast majority of citizens.

It remains the least developed continent. And a region ravaged by conflicts with the largest people on the run in the world. The refugee camps in Kenya, Cameroon, Chad, Somalia, Sudan, and other parts of the continent present a true story of the continent not being at peace with itself. There is a greater need re-imagining the search for peace; the need for dialogue, consensus as well as the strength and limitations promoting and impeding the transformation of continent from being a 'cursed region to one of a blessed region's as it holds the future of the world given it vast natural resources potentials and opportunities for development. The new scramble for these resources and investment opportunities are catalyst for conflicts as well. Peace is not sustainable by economic empowerment alone; its pursuit must include community mediation, conflict resolution and peace education. Social justice must reign and shared-prosperity incarnated in the governance system. Due to poor governance, the continent is riddle with deep-rooted problems, corruption, poverty, hunger, diseases. For peace to reign there is need to unlocking the baggage's of factors that impede development and quality wellbeing of citizens.

Seen from this perspective of the continent's deficit and gains the paper probes into the issue of peace and development which have so far evaded the continent and why it has embraced conflicts and chaos; and why dialogue between theories and practices seem to have failed throughout the continent. It critically and objectively explores the ways in which specific approaches to peace and war policy agendas play or interact for good or worse on the continent. The absence of war does not entail peace. The existence of democracy does not imply development. A whole-government approach is essential but not sufficient. It needs to be accompanied by radical changes in participatory rights in decision-making and the commitment to guarantee and protect citizen participation. The rights of access to information, public participation and access to justice are essential to sustainable development and peaceful coexistence. Other parameters are needed to ensure the linkage between democracy and development to usher maximum benefit to society. Apparently, some African countries seem to have escaped the scourges of conflicts. But these nations still know no peace. Neither have they experienced development; Cameroon is a typical case in point. Peace therefore goes far beyond wars and conflicts. Implying that other parameters come to play but often not seen as vital puts to sustaining peace and development. Indeed, the search for peace begins by articulating and putting in place paradigms and parameters that make life worth living – food security, health security, shelter, job security, security to life and property, security to freedom of speech and worship among other things that sustainable improves the quality wellbeing of the population. Good governance is not created through elections and institutions building alone. Peace-building is as much careful economic development as it is social change. Substantive economic transformation involves addressing the issues important to a multiplicity of stakeholders. The failings of good governance to address the challenges often point to the inadequacies of effective decision-making of governments or inclusive bodies that fail to create effective action on a systemic scale that threatens peace but heralds a state of war. Marching theory and practice on peace means getting people adopting a positive attitude towards peace and not conflicts so that people can be at peace with another. Therefore, "democratic governance and full respect for human rights are pre-requisites for empowering people to make sustainable choices." [UN, 2012].

Political and economic exclusion breeds conflict and instability. Shared-prosperity evades most of the people. Social injustice blurs relationship between the rulers and ruled. The political economy of conflict and war is such that the state and non-state actors, for example, benefit from violent conflicts. Rebel groups exerting power in a nation state through the exploitation of extractive industries have a disincentive to work towards peace. In such situations, peace-building requires international cooperation to prevent the financing of violent and prolonged conflicts by stemming demand for the rebel-controlled resource on global markets. This explains to a large extent why a country like the Democratic Republic of Congo has known no peace since independence. The theory of peace and its practice are two different things on the continent. Building theory and practice nexus for the sustainable development of the continent should be seen from the perspectives of fostering equitable and sustainable development or reconstruction in Africa. For a country's politics and development to be fully functional, there has to be 'total and perfect peace' seen to rest on solid and sustainable foundation of justice and not peace that is viewed to be merely 'cosmetic.'

Cameroon illustrates a perfect example in this context. What exist in Cameroon is 'cosmetic peace' attributed to the high level of police repression of manifestations and expressions of grievances and the imprisonment of or threats on political opposition leaders or critics of the administration. The cosmetic peace which Cameroon is said to be experiencing compared to her neighbours in the region and interpreted in certain quarters as an 'island of peace' or 'haven of peace' can be questioned in many aspects. The recent transfer of power following the death of the President of Ghana, Prof. Atta Mills July 2012 shows the linkage between theory and practice. Ghana has exhibited its political maturity on the democracy scale compared to what happened in Malawi after the death of President Bingu WA Mutharika in April 2012.

System Approaches

The paper departs from the conceptual and analytical framework of system approach as important input factors addressing issues that are engaged with and are always enmeshed with other issues; that there are meta-level patterns and norms which affect these issues, that one assessment of them is often dependent on where we place the boundaries of what we view and that unintended consequences can emerge from the inter-relationships [Burns 2011:13]. Mutisi [2010] argues that well-being in a society is an imperative in contextualising the issue of theory and practice. Therefore, development-peace-building has become a common term in the lexicon and practice of development, post-conflict building and reconstruction. Underdevelopment and violent conflicts including natural disasters destroys national and local economies, ultimately reducing productive capacities and eroding livelihoods. The case of the tsunami in Japan, conflicts that erupted following post-elections in Kenya in 2008; wars in Liberia, Sierra Leone, and the greed of capitalism in Niger Delta Region in Nigeria among many other activities. The issue of theory and practice is blurred by what we may term 'greed' or 'articulate self-interests' and the 'collective good.' In spite of efforts to promote an ephemeral peace by ignoring some of the dimensions of sustainable development, one should not lose sight of equally relevant factors of articulate-self-interests in perpetuating conflicts [Berdal and Malone 2000]. Collier [1999] focuses on the need for development, specifically on the 'hardware', such as a rebuilding economics, infrastructural development, and promoting macroeconomic stability. Here is where theory and practice part ways in Africa. Even in countries that have not been subjected to conflicts like Rwanda, Burundi, Democratic Republic of Congo, Central African Republic, Liberia, Sierra Leone and a host of others, there are still gross absence of linking theory and practice to improve on the quality livelihood of the population. The conflict is between 'real peace' and 'cosmetic' peace.

Cosmetic peace breads a dysfunctional governance system lacking the separation of power with total autonomy in the discharge of day-to-day functions and responsibilities. For close to fifty years of independence in many African countries, the governance system has been under the charm of political deceit and dishonesty. In some countries this developed into full fledge wars and even genocide [Burundi and Rwanda]. For peace to penetrate into the annals of the governance system in Africa it must be fertilised with the sperm of justice, shared-prosperity, and humility and under the canopy of democratic governance. The sustainability of peace requires visionary leadership, people-focused public policy orientation, a vibrant civil society and a productive and competitive private sector. The international community plays a significant role as well. The plight of the Ogoni people and others in the Niger Delta Region is partly contributed by the international industrial military complex, (capitalism, the search for resources and domination). The establishment of African High Command by the United States of America is to defend its economic interests in particular and that of the West at the expense of the suffering bottom billions in the region, country and the continent.

Poorly articulated development policies or its execution may have unintended effects, especially if they interact with existing systems of exclusion, inequality, deprivation, and marginalisation. As such, the nexus between theory and practice on peace should be seen from the perspectives of delivering the goods or constraining the goods based on the factors of either 'greed, articulate self-interest' or 'collective interests for the common good.' The general interest has given way to individual interest thus threatening the basic fundamentals of peace and peaceful co-existence among nations and peoples. This presents the controversy between theory and practice. Is the nexus between theory and practice on peace in Africa able to address the fundamental issues of poverty and inequality which are the major driving forces for contemporary conflicts in Africa? Even ethnic conflicts have economic dimensions. Second, the absence of justice within the governance system perpetuates conflicts. Therefore, the nexus between peace theory and practice is equally linked to the kind of judiciary system of a society. Against this background, there seems to be a consensus that it is not enough to simply make peace, but that this peace must be just and address not just the causes of war, but also issues such as hunger and poverty [UNDP 2005; Smoljan Jelena 2003; Guy Jackson 2006] The governance performance, management and delivery systems plays a very crucial part in determining the outcome of the theory and practice of peace. When the government's performance and delivery system is unjust, unequal, discriminative, conflicts are bound to arise.

Defining the Relationship and identifying Problems

Undoubtedly, theory and practice of peace are important features of modern state construct and statehood. Representing the heart of any state, peace gives nations their legitimacy and the mandate to govern. Ideally, peace provides protection for the population, and the state and its institutions command and control them to that end. In democracies this control would ensure that the people would not undermine the state since the controlling institutions are products of the will of the people. Potentially, however, undemocratic regimes and autocrats could face threats from either outside or inside the country, either from the upper echelons of their own ruling elite or from society itself [Gandhi & Przeworski [2007]. The gap between theory and practice is seen in the governance system of most African countries. Theory is one thing, practice another. The gulf between the two weakens the governance system, leaving institutions weak or fragile and making them competitive against each other, instead of coexisting to protect the state.

A majority of African states has at some point tried to develop socialist systems whether they called it scientific socialism or African socialism. Others hold on to civilian authoritarian or purely military regime structure. Looking at the issue of theory and practice, in the 1980s, no fewer than 35 of 63 African states called themselves socialist at various times [Pitcher& Askew, 2006] called themselves socialist at various times it is clear that "these experiences have left a problematic legacy since socialist regimes tend to highlight regime security even more than other autocracies, often by putting the party and not the state in charge of national security affairs and the army. Communist countries simply would not tolerate anything like a military outside the political realm, since in previous decades they considered it the armed wing of capitalism and the defender of the bourgeoisie. In the eyes of communist leaders, therefore, it was totally legitimate to turn the military into an instrument of the Communist Party, a tool to modernise society and advance socialism. As the case of Ethiopia dramatically illustrates, this dynamic led to a militarization of society and a politicisation of the military intelligence, and other security services" [Dehez, 2010:59; Zwede,1998]. The inter-state conflict between the two Sudan's is a case in point creating serious animosity between the states and citizens threatening their peaceful co-existence. Many of today's intra-state conflicts, especially in Africa, occur where there is an abundance of resources and where the central state authority is weak and failing or manned by greedy leaders.

Search for Peace

Marrying theory and practice under a good governance system paves the way for peace. That is proper performance management leads to peace and development and improved quality wellbeing of citizens, which contributes to stability continuing the vicious circle. In other words, peace is obtained and maintained when greed gives way to collective good; when human fundamental basic needs are assured for all; when shared-prosperity and social justice exists in society; when the international community respond positively to the desired needs of the people and not through oppressive policies that enhances their greed and articulate self-interests. Theory and practice are compatible when good governance, justice and shared-prosperity exists.

Democratic governance, the practice of development the right way, is therefore a key component of peace and post-conflict reconstruction. Development assistance has been used not only to reduce economic inequalities between groups but also to diminish economic incentives to fight. It has also been used to fan conflicts. The international community is using development assistance as a conditionality to promote economic and political practices that both strengthen peace-building as well as promote conflicts. When development assistance reaches previously disadvantaged, newly empowered groups, it has the potential to fuel resentment among other groups. Peace is not sustainable by economic empowerment alone; its pursuit must also include community mediation, conflict and peace education [Nelson & Karbo, 2019: vi]. The idea of imposing democracy on countries contributes to the gap between theory and practice. While democracy has over the years emerged as providing the best governance system, it is also loaded with inherent complications or cultural value and environmental contexts that impedes is transfer from one country to another. Thus, the theory and practice of democracy may differ from country to country with the only common basic universal tenets being the respect of fundamental human rights. State fragility directly or indirectly is a contributing factor to the state of poor nexus between theory and practice. Furthermore, there is no common communality among academics on 'theory' and 'practice.' The concept 'peace' remains elusive, simply because peace is never fully achieved, it is not an end-product, but rather a constant process of negotiation among different actors, regarding the terms of their relationships in a myriad of different arenas or environments. The formation of a new government in Zimbabwe between the ruling and opposition parties is a good example. The search for peace as a process and the various forms of conceptualisation and empirically practiced can be addressed from the following approaches;

- peace as the outcome or dominant scholarly work and policy agendas;
- examining and investigating how peace is constructed as a concrete and common aspiration that shapes social interactions in daily life;
- peace in theory and practice; does it exist, and can it be achieved? What is the role of external forces influencing the process of peace or creating an atmosphere of war?

Peace outcome as a scholarly discourse and policy agenda ties with issues of human rights, basic needs, justice, equality, security, governance, quality of livelihood, etc. issues already discussed. Scholars are concerned with the scientific bases of the nitty-gritty of the construct, structure and functioning of the state in meeting its social contract with the people. What type of state construct is practiced by African countries? African countries practice from quasi form of democracy through socialism to authoritarian governance system, with myriad failures and successes. Examining how peace is constructed as a common aspiration for improving the quality wellbeing of the people is reaffirming the need for government's responsibility to its citizens in respect of:

Material needs
Spiritual needs
Cultural needs
Reaffirming the need for Government =======➔ Economic needs=====➔ Impacts on the wellbeing of people and relationship with other nations
Social needs
Environmental needs
Governance needs

State construct, structure and functioning and the role of government improving the quality well-being of citizens could be deduced from the constitutions of nation states, for example, the South Africa Constitutional Act 108 of 1996, clearly states the government performs the following functions;

- lay foundation for a democratic and open society in which government is based on the will of the people and every citizen is equally protected by law;
- improves the quality of life of all citizens and frees the potential of each person;
- builds a united and democratic South Africa, which is able to take its rightful place as sovereign state in the family of nations

System changes or the need to transform the way in which government functions if not properly carried out can trigger conflicts, chaos and instability. Numerous challenges and opportunities exist for the development of the state and improving its output activities. A new paradigm reforming the public service is needed for it to be more efficient and effective in services delivery characterised by management of outputs in achieving policy objectives and outcomes in the most cost-effective manner. The public service as the output machinery by which government is judged has to be performant – effective and efficient in-service delivery and in utilising limited resources in new ways to heighten the effectiveness of government in addressing the needs of communities. The renewed focus of government on all levels is not contained so much in what they do but how they operate

[Osborne & Gaebler, 1992: xxi]. The situation in Syria depicts the impact of external forces influencing the process of peace achievement/failure in theory and practice. The International Criminal Court (ICC) is another example seen from the perspectives of justice which eventually can contribute to state of peace or war '[Jabre and Moni, 2012:42]. Or the ongoing situation in Eastern part of the Democratic Republic of Congo presents another example. In these and other cases, articulate self-interest plays an important role influencing the outcome. The case of Malawi turning down to host the AU Summit for fear donor countries will withhold their aid because of the stance European countries have threaten to take against the President of Sudan, Omar EL-Bashir. On the one hand, Europe demands peace as a means for development. At the same time, it fans activities that points to war, creating serious dichotomy between theory and practice.

Thus, the word 'peace' conjures myriad images, which include a world free of violent conflicts stemming from ethnic, cultural, religious, or political differences. For others, the promotion of democracy, justice, and human rights are additional and equally important factors of peace. According to Elias and Turpin [1994:4] peace can generally be categorised as either 'negative' or 'positive'. Negative peace is defined as the absence of war or other direct violence. Negative peace on the other hand promotes the idea that war is inevitable, the idea that a weaker state will not attack relatively powerful states and collective security. Positive peace insists on the promotion of social justice. Positive peace is attained when social justice is present and promoted. In a world of positive peace, war is absent, and human rights protected, but weaker states cannot be sure that protection from powerful states will guarantee their security. As such, peace is not secured. If 'peace' is perceived as a snake with two heads (positive and negative), then theory and practice cannot mesh to ensure a single entity which adds to the controversy. Even judging from the parameters of peace as implying social justice and human rights, or equating social justice with the definition of human rights, as the protection of civil and political rights, and a world that operates on as argued by Elias and Turpin [2004] human rights are complementary and can lead to the establishment of positive peace. In essence, peace is not just avoiding war; peace is also about observing and promoting human dignity [Bangura 2004; 2002]. What exists in the absence of war or a state of positive peace, in developing countries, is structural violence seen as underdevelopment and institutionalised poverty, and the recognition of and environmental preservation as essential to peace. With the state of persisting poverty, environmental destruction and inequitable relations between the developed and developing countries, the human rights of the people are threatened and even violated. This is what is happening in the Niger Delta Region, DRC, and elsewhere on the continent which compromises the issue of theory and practice and peace for the people of the region.

Conclusion

The preceding discourse has been edging towards a common proposition that theory and practice is presently contradictory, controversial, challenging and posing serious problems plaguing or fostering democratic, economic, development, and good governance and peace on the beleaguered continent – Africa The argument so far alluded to is that regardless of the kind of knowledge used to analyse a problem the conclusion of the analysis is a problem, the conclusion of the account remain to a large extent, the same. Africans must seek the right solutions to their problems and must not depend on solutions from external source. He external bodies can provide some useful guidelines to how we address and conflicts and differences. The final solutions must come from within.

Contextualising the African situation, there is need to go beyond this discourse by insinuating distinctly African flavour and knowledge of the "baobab tree" approach as offering move constructive approach to realising theory and practice which in modern parlance is reconciliation. Therefore, theory and practice for justice and peace in Africa needs a holistic incorporation of the cultural heritage and indigenous knowledge of the people; and a conscious need to revitalise in the hearts and minds of Africans (Bangura, op cit. 15). In line with this argument, we have concentrated in building security, hope, confidence in the post-conflict reconstruction of the continent. Efforts to establish peace, justice and meaningful socio-economic development and participatory democracy have not been quite successful. There is lot of work to be done. Political parties and the party system that should underpins Africa's democracy must have the potential to build cohesive and prosperous continent. Countries with a dominant one-party system strain the system as well as its tested it and its institutions fortitude. There is need to re-orientate the governance system towards a form of open and inclusive governance system. Africa's current state of underdevelopment and state of growing abject poverty is an indication of the enormous challenges the region faces in this rapidly changing globalised based knowledge economy.

References

Burns Danny [2011] "A Methodological Strategy for Reimagining Developments: Enabling Complex Systemic Patterns to Surface through Multiple Voices" in IDS Bulletin, Time to Reimagine Development? Vol.42, No.5, September 2011, Institute of Development Studies, Wiley Blackwell.

Collier Paul [1999]" Doing Well Out of War", Paper prepared for the Conference on Economic Agenda in Civil Wars, London, 26-27 April 1999.

Collier Paul & Anke Hoeffler [2001] "Greed and Grievance in Civil War", World Bank Policy Research Working Paper No. 2355, May 2000

Dehez Dustin [2010] "Intelligence Services in Sub-Saharan Africa. Making Security Sector Reform Work," Africa and Francophonie, Vol. 1. No. 3, Fall 2010, pp57-63

Elias Robert & Turpin Robert [1994] Rethinking Peace. Lynne Rienner Publishers, Boulder, Colorado, USA

Gandhi Jennifer & Adam Przeworski [2007]." Authoritarian Institutions and the Survival of Autocrats," Comparative Political Studies No. 40, No. 11 (1 No ember 2997, pp1279] pp 1279-1301

Government of South Africa [1996] Constitution of South Africa, Government Printer, Pretoria, South Africa

Jabre Lee & Moni Jaye [2012] "Is Africa on Trial? The Role of the ICC Examined," New African, 46th Year, No.519, July 2012, pp42-46

Jackson Guy [2006] "Nobel Prize Links Poverty Reductions to Peace", Agence-France Press, 13 October 2006

Nelson Catherine & Karbo Tony [2010]" Editorial Note: African Peace and Conflict Journal, Vol.3. No.1, June 2010, University of Peace African Programme, Addis Ababa, Ethiopia, pp v-vii,

Mutisi Martha [2010] "Building and Sustaining Peace: The Development-Peace building Nexus in Post-Conflict reconstruction in Africa". African Peace and Conflict Journal, Vol. 4. No.1. June 2010, University of Peace, Addis Ababa, Ethiopia, pp25-34

Osborne, D. & Gaebler, T. [1992] Reinventing Government: How the Entrepreneurial Spirit is Transforming the Public Sector, Plume Books, USA

Pitcher M. Anne &Askew M. Kelly [2006] "African Socialisms and Post-socialisms," Africa 76, No.1. [2006]:1-14

Sachs Jeffrey [2007] "No Development, No Peace", Sunday Times Online, 24 July 2007;

Smoljan Jelena [2003] "The Relationship Between Peace-Building and Development", Conflict, Security and Development, 3-2(2003), 233-50

UNDP [2005] Human Development Report 2005: International Organisation at the Crossroad – Aid, Trade and Security in an Unequal World. United Nations, New York

UN Secretary General [2012]. UN Secretary General's High-Level Panel on Global Sustainability. Resilient People, Resilient Planet. A Future Worth Choosing, New York, p.15

Zwede Bahnu [1998] "The Military and Militarism in Africa: The Case of Ethiopia," in Hutchful Eboe & Abdoulaye Bathily (eds.) [1998]. The Military and Militarism in Africa, Codesria, Senegal, pp258-63

Chapter 6

Mozambique in Search of a New Political Economic Vision within the Context of the Current Global Crisis: Challenges and Prospects in Constructing a Capable Developmental State in the Future

Abstract

The quest for a new political economic policy for a transitional polity like Mozambique is quiet challenging but urgent. There is an imperative need for innovations within the public sector in light of the current global context. The global consensus on the urgency for reinventing government is not only manifested in the research efforts that are focusing on how to improve the performance of governance and public administration institutions. It is also seen in the innovators' readiness to come together to share information and knowledge about their innovations to minimise wastage of resources and time in re-inventing the wheel. It has dawn on most people concerned with the improvement of performance in the public sector that although innovations in government are circum- scribed in scope, they have the potential to trigger a bigger process of transformation of the State and produce general positive benefits for citizens through improved service delivery. Mozambique finds itself at the cross-road of development. With its chequered historical past, and given strides made since independence, current global economic crises attempt to constraints the country's movement towards a capable developmental state. The country's policies are constrained by the global economic crises, making ineffective attempts at reducing poverty, vulnerability and real inequality, in modifying productive structures, in reallocating income between social groups, and in reducing patterns of dependency and instability. The only way for Mozambique to become a capable developmental state is to engage on the path of good governance, harness its human and natural resources and own its development and independence. The paper takes a critical stand at the policy lessons and policy formation on the role of the state in reinventing itself in producing a developmental road map that exploits the human and natural resources of the country to the overall benefit of the common good of citizens. It adopts both the SWOT and SLEPT conceptual framework in setting the right plat- form for the emergence of new forms of economic, political organisations, new dynamics of demonstrations and expressions of social struggle outside of the formal institutional framework, related with waves of unemployment and social frustration, particularly among young people. With the mentioned conceptual framework of SWOT and SLEPT, it will have contextualized crisis caused by 'failing state' reflected in lack of good governance, fiscal discipline, failure of the social protection model and deregulation of finance capital. It will equally look at the crises from the perspectives of the social mode of accumulation capitalist reproduction which, naturally, is of a political nature and has political as well as economic implications affecting models and options of the state and of representation, affirmation and political struggle. Finally, the paper concludes that there is no shortcut to effective delivery of services except to have the best talents equipped with ethic, moral, transparent, accountable, integrity virtues and values within the public sector, and private sectors in particular, and the country in general. For the public sector to meet quality services delivery it has to be innovative, creative and productive. Ultimately, the ability of the government to provide services effectively and whither the economic crises are for the state to be proactive, inclusive and having a democratic a political public administration.

Conclusion and Recommendations

We need to recognize that the march towards a new political economy of inclusiveness will be resisted in many ways – particularly when it threatens authoritarians or those opposed to economic democracy. The economic and social transformation of the country depends to a large extent, on the people's mindset of owning their development and properly utilising both their human capital and natural resources for the collective wellbeing of the citizen

Based on the marriage between SWOT and SLEPT, a new conceptual frame is introduced as:

SWOT + SLEPT + NPMS + RIG + ROG ➔ Capable Developmental State ➔Meeting the Needs of the People as the Frame of Analysis and Sustainable Development.

Proactive strategic policy measures are advanced for Mozambique as a future capable state in respect of quality services delivery state.

Keywords: new economic policy, civil society, integration, human capital development, state-civil society-private sector interface, economic crisis, innovation, rule of law, charter on democracy, national. New economic order

Introduction

Confronting the Challenges - Building State Capacity

The critical question facing Mozambique after many decades of the struggle for independence is that of constructing a capable state embedded with the virtues of empowerment, good governance, democracy, vibrant civil society and productive private sector. The current global economic crisis adds to the plight of the people in rebuilding a holistic state and consolidating its independence as well as owing its development path. By necessity, post-independence reconstruction incorporates a wider approach beyond re-establishing peace and security as well as ensuring economic growth. It entails a structural-functional governance system. The place of the state has taken a new dimension. The crisis of failed states on the continent challenges existing conceptions of the state's place in the world and its potential contribution to human welfare. It should be acknowledged that economic potential and stability in Mozambique can only be realised if government interventions are underpinned by a stable and capable public service capable of delivering quality services in key socio-economic realms leading to sustainable quality well-being of citizens. Attaining quality livelihood entails hard work, constructive and comprehensive strategic policy and planning [Forje, 2009]. Current global economic crisis only adds to the plethora of challenges face by the country. How can Mozambique overcome these challenges? What must the country do to own its development path? This paper hopes to address the whole gamut of building state capacity as means of reinforcing its bid in overcoming the global crisis impeding Mozambique's transformation towards a sustainable state structure resting on building strong and capable institutions in the following areas;

- Building institutions and structures of the public service;
- developing human capital and proper utilization of such critical skills;
- mobilising domestic resources;
- mainstreaming gender equality in the development process;
- Challenges and pressures for employment and rapid urbanization;
- utilising indigenous knowledge in the development process;
- Good governance and the rule of law, and shared prosperity;
- Promotion of broad-based participation – state-civil society-private sector interfaces;
- fostering political and economic unity within and between African states [see Forje 2009; World Bank 1997, Hyden 1983].

It is generally acknowledged that African countries are abundantly endowed with natural, material and human resources to enhance and facilitate their envisaged rapid transformation and development. However, several challenges exist in the execution of national development strategies and plans in a country like Mozambique arising from the inability of the country to effectively and efficiently mobilise, fully utilise critical human resources for the enhancement of national capability and global competitiveness. How Mozambique defines and solves the strategic problems facing it determines its present and future development and security. Currently, leaders and the institutions they serve drift towards solving immediate problems from an ad hoc perspective with perhaps too little concern for long-term consequences. Transitional polities at their best when confronted with cleanly bounded issues and a known end state or perceive objective. Legitimate concerns about the most appropriate way to defeat the enemy- poverty, underdevelopment, inertia, corruption and exploitation - win battles for of poor-quality livelihood, and secure the foundations for political and economic victory must occupy and dominate the vision and thinking of African leadership, because success in these areas will eventually lead to a capable developed state.

Mozambique like other African states is faced with the great task of how best to prepare to meet societal expectations – the needs of the bottom billions, confront long-term strategic challenges, and to remain effective, efficient, transparent and accountable at the helm of governing the country, even those punctuated by conflict, requires a different mindset, new political will and a different approach. Mozambique finds itself within the complexity of a growing strategic hostile environment demanding new approaches and coherent options to forge ahead this forward march requires (a) new state activities to match its capability; greater focus is badly needed to improve effectiveness; choosing what to do and what not to do is critical; which involves choosing how to do things – how to deliver basic services, provide infrastructure, regulate the economy, or just whether to do them at all; and (b) looking for ways to improve the state's capability by reinvigorating public institutions. The choices here are many and must be tailored to the circumstances of Mozambique. The first priority of Mozambique is getting the fundamentals right.

It is not surprising, that the people of Mozambique are putting the state under scrutiny, asking what government's role ought to be and, critically, how that role should be played. Thus, the paper explores why and how some states have been more effective than others at playing a catalytic and sustainable role in economic development and in the eradication of poverty and other vices of underdevelopment. Getting priorities right entails building strong and functional institutions among others in streamlining the role and activities of government. The global financial crisis illustrates that there are fundamental problems with how the corporate world is conducted. Today, there is growing tendency that the level of public trust in the corporate world is decreasing. The conduct of Wall Street has not only shown that they are largely addicted to dirty games but also, they have invested huge sums of money in attempts to undermine the sustainable growth of developing countries as well as confuse public opinion on system change in areas where they make the most profit and ruled by dictatorial regimes. Most developing countries end up with growth without equity and essentially jobless growth. Main Street pays the price in the end. Mozambique is paying the price of Wall Street and also poor policy formulation and execution.

Mozambique's long years of struggle for independence led to the destruction of most of its infrastructure and available human capital. Rebuilding lost resources and healing the wounds of the past requires a sustainable political process of reconciliation and a new mindset for governance system which must be all inclusive, caring and sharing. The global system over the past decades has not made the reconstruction process easier either. In the past couple of decades, the global financial crisis, sub-Saharan Africa made some remarkable gains, Mozambique for example, in achieving economic growth and stability. Growth averaged more than six percent, inflation had fallen to single-digit levels before the fuel and food price shocks of 2008, while comfortable external reserves positions were maintained. However, like the rest of the world, Africa was not isolated from the impact of the global financial crisis, which inadvertently jolted these positive developments.

Major impacts include: precipitous decline in global commodity demand, increase in protectionist and restrictive trade policies, shrinking foreign investment and the contraction in foreign aid, all of which threatened growth and poverty reduction hitherto achieved. These were the result of vulnerability to external resource stocks suffered by all emerging economies, even though Africa came out slightly better than most other regions [AAPAM 2012]. The challenge for Mozambique is searching for a new development agenda that can greatly reduce if not eliminate is vulnerability to external forces. Forces which continue to hold the country and continent hostage in the now established global knowledge-based economy. Globalisation adds to the woes of the developing economies. The resources of the continent are open for exploitation, often at giveaway prices. Trade restrictions imposed by the developed economies helps in retarding the economic growth of the country. Yet these countries are forced to open up their markets for products from the developed economies at high prices Mozambique has neither done extremely well nor badly in the struggle to revamp its economic drive towards becoming an emerging economy. What is clear is that there are positive signs on the wall requiring a new vision under the agenda of good governance and the people owing their development construct for the common good.

Conceptual Framework

The conceptual frame builds on the strength, weakness, opportunity, and threats (SWOT) analysis supplemented by the science, labour, economic, political and technology (SLEPT) approach. The combination of these two approaches is contextualised and localised with the Gerschenkronian *"late comer advantaged"* [1962], in contrast to the Rostowian [1960] *"stages of development"* [1962] concept of developmental path for transitional nations. These together with other relevant materials set out the structural basis for Mozambique in addressing the economic melt-down and its consequences on the country's transformation and growth. This show how overarching theories of risk and its management need to be modified or supplemented to account for detailed variations or approaches for the state to maintain its hegemonic approach towards a modern state construct. Mozambique could be seen as a *'risk society'*: at the same time, we are said to live in a *'regulatory state'* [Majone 1994]. The idea of the *'regulatory state'* is that a new institutional and policy style has emerged, in which government's role as regulator advances while its role as a direct employer or property-owner may decline through privatisation and bureaucratic downsizing. The two ideas of *'risk society'* and *'regulatory state'* could, indeed be linked in so far as risk and safety is often held to be one of the major drives of contemporary regulatory growth. In turn, development of risk regulation is interpreted by many to reflect broader political and cultural change.' States are still the main holders of political authority in the world: And are likely to remain so. In the long-term, the vitality and viability of the State of Mozambique depends on its ability to perform the task of transforming the society from an agrarian into an industrial/service delivery society, by adapting itself to changing realities. This is the biggest test facing the country.

Indeed, the more democratic Mozambique becomes – the more genuinely representative of, and accountable to, the people – the greater also will be the country's political legitimacy. And therefore, it is entirely proper as well as inevitable; the State of Mozambique will remain the main political master player in reforming and pushing forward the economic transformation of the society. Other actors are needed to accelerate the process of sustainable transformation. Mobilisation of domestic resources and promoting the role of the private sector being a vital input factor in accelerating the process for reconstruction and development. The country has the choice to take risk and uphold the status of a regulatory state, in the reconstruction process or succumb to the dictates of the forces of the economic melt-down and remain underdeveloped forever. Will it have the capacity to bear the brunt of economic melt-down and the evolving crisis and consequences that entails?

Douglas [1990:7] sees risk as a political weapon used by a society poised between the cultures of individualism and egalitarianism, to blame those who wield power in the state and big corporations for what happens to the rest of us. From this perspective the increased salience of risk and regulation reflects a cultural shift away from 'hierarchist' world-views over matters of trust and blame [Douglas & Wildavsky 1982; Power, 1997:141]. Power argues from the perspectives of development an "audit society" responding to the risk and regulatory failure by "greater investment in formal generalisable systems of control rather than by developing non-standard capabilities for acting on informal sources of intelligence." The argument is that patterns observable in the financial world, where more elaborate and formal audit systems are adopted after every collapse to offer greater 'assurance' about system robustness, are developing in many other domains of social life [Hood et al, 2001]. In other words, Mozambique must take the bull by the horn as a 'regulatory state' in institutioning broad based democratic reforms as the best remedy for confronting the impact of the economic melt-down as well as crafting new strategies for its development path. Risk regulation regimes must be based on:

- Role of government; developing anticipative whole-society solutions through open, responsive, representative, participatory and inclusion governance system incorporating all the basic virtues and values of democratic governance [support. develop popular participation]
- Justice Model: rule of law with an independent judiciary, respect for human rights, justice for all and aggregate social welfare utilitarianism, protecting the worst-off, give them priority
- Involvement of other stake holders: incorporating other stakeholders, civil society, private sector and the international community. [Agenda 21 on local consultation over global environmental change for examples. In this case the development of a new world order – thinking globally and acting locally].

As earlier noted, a risk regulation regime-centred approach to looking at the economic melt-down and its impact on the sustainable eco-social transformation of the State of Mozambique is intended to be a middle way approach to national institutional analysis This together with the SWOT & SLEPT approaches are designed to capture the variety issues left out but pertinent to resolving existing problems. The country has many advantages to forge ahead with its reconstruction agenda just as there are many challenging impeding factors. Marrying the SWOT and SLEPT approaches highlight the opportunities and constraints facing the country. Hard choices with people-oriented focused strategies must be made by the government and people of Mozambique. The same goes for the rest of the continent.

The SWOT Approach

Articulating and aggregating an African Miracle Development Process requires critical analysis of the strength, weakness, opportunities and threats (SWOT) at the disposal of the state and its partners. Table 1, challenges the Mozambique/continent with the issues and hard choices it has to grapple with.

Table 1: Facing the Challenges of SWOT in the Transformation of Africa

Strength	Virgin area still to be researched and tapped; Provides development opportunities for other continents; Holds the future of the world; Valuing African people;
Weakness	Poor policy articulation and aggregation; Weak leadership, poor governance system; African leadership vacuum and western triumphal over developing countries; Inadequate human capital development; Colonial legacies constraining the development process; Unshared-prosperity: widening gap between the rich and poor; Undeveloped private sector – poor infrastructural development; Uncontrolled population explosion can back fire and retard the development; Absence of a committed and vibrant media industry to educate the people and put forward critical objectives as watch dog of failing government policies;
Opportunities:	The late-comer advantage – Africa does not need to develop the wheel; Vast untapped natural resources potentials; Fast growing youth population creating a strong labour force; Provides bases for the world's fastest growing economy; Diversity as 'asset' not 'liability' in state construct and the development process; Bright future for Africa provided it does its homework and in the peoples' interest;
Threats	Globalisation – a 'curse' but can be converted into a 'blessing'; Weak scientific and technological background; Poor state construct; Poor human capital development and weak institutions; Bad governance – leading to the exclusion of the people in the development process; The West will continue using all means available to promote its agenda, policies and interests in then name and principles of globalisation; Recolonisation of Africa in the age of scientific and technological awakening; The politics of globalisation should be critically scrutinised; Self-articulate interests of the leader's/ruling elites; Poor regional integration; The forces of post-modern imperialism and the new colonising powers Hostile international environment ;

Source : [Forje 2012]

A look at the SLEPT approach produces the following factors that marry into the transformation and growth of the country. It should equally be noted that the absence of a proper mix will contribute to chaos, conflict, dissent and instability disrupting the sustainable transformation of the country, see Table 2.

Table 2: Contextualising the SLEPT Approach

Social	as a result of the long struggle for independence, Mozambique inherited a divided polity with destroyed social institutions. A climate of hate ensured. The social fabric of society has to be reconstituted within the direction of an ideological orientation, of One Nation; One People, One Destiny, and One Mission for the Common Good. Social and cultural values must be made to play an important role in the transformation of the society. But old and archaic destructive cultural norms and values must be swept under the carpet or reform to meet the exigencies of the time. Social waves of frustration must be addressed through a policy of inclusion and shared-prosperity.
Legal	The legality of the nation must be established and respected as sovereign entity with fixed boundaries, enjoying all the full rights of a sovereign state within the international community of nations. The constitution of the country enshrines its legality. The country must operate within the confines of its constitutions and agreed international treaties, commitments and obligations it has so committed itself to. The rule of law and respect of the legal instruments of the state must be upheld to ensure justice for all.
Economic	Given the country's natural resources potentials, the economic basis is strong but requires skilled human capital to give added value to existing resources. There is an urgent need to serious diversify its economic structure. Building the necessary infrastructures: roads, rail and communication net works, healthcare, education, water, energy are ingredients for a strong economic take-off and sustainability. The marginalised female gender component must be entrenched a viable economic factor. State-civil society-private sector partnership must equally be intensified. An enabling environment created to stimulate local as well as foreign investors. Issues of escalating waves of unemployment must be adequately addressed
Political	Good governance should be seen a necessary but not sufficient panacea for transforming and sustaining the country. Other input factors remain imperative in this long process of nation-building and guaranteeing and sustaining quality livelihood of the citizens. Leadership, mindset of the people; constitute a positive responsive international community towards the country play in different nuances in ensuring the legality and development of the country. A policy of reconciliation is vital. Healing the wounds and inclusive governance restores trust, confidence and respect in the state. Strong institutions are vital. Checks and balances in the operation of the government imperative. The hegemony of centralised authoritarian ethnic/regional rule avoided and discarded at all cost.
Technology	Technology is a serious deficit in the process of the country's transformation. Without the necessary technological background, the country cannot become innovative, productive and competitive in the fast-growing global based knowledge of the economy of the 21st century and beyond. Globalisation is construed and successful on the imperatives of a strong scientific and technological background. Indigenous knowledge and other local skills should form part of the up build of the scientific and technological capability of the country. A new public management system is inevitable to face the challenges of transformation in a context of international crisis and internal reconstruction process.

Source: Forje [2012]

A critical analysis of both the SWOT and SLEPT approaches should give clear indications of addressing pertinent issues such: what now for Mozambique and which way forward for the country; what the relevance, tendencies and dynamics of foreign investment and its relationship with natural resources and domestic processes of capital accumulation; Is the country evolving on the basis and strategise of a 'win-win' situation and are the other options; what must the state do to better contain rising destructive frustration; how can the rise of social movements be properly used in building a new climate for state construct?

Contextualising the Situation

Confronting the current global economic crisis and ensuring the sustainability of the country's development path entails a multifaceted process. The components of the road map for constructive engagement should embrace the good governance, state-civil society-private sector partnership. Within a comprehensive framework of good governance, state-civil society-private sector interface, the proper bases for constructing;(i)efficient service delivery construed on the principles of subsidiary services that can be effectively provided at lower levels of government (distribute public power) to better achieve more effective and responsive government:(ii)construct a government structure in which diverse groups can live together in peace and harmony enhancing minority or marginalised individuals, groups or regions to identify their space in the system;(iii)build up an integrated partnership with the various stakeholders to ensure mechanisms increasing innovative, productive and competitive means within the global market.

To begin with, the country needs an army of trained human capital to build, improve and sustained its development efforts. Second, proper use of such human skill and natural resources must be put into proper usage. Third, the need for an inclusive democratic governance system is imperative in the process. Fourth, the issue of shared-prosperity remains crucial in establishing and sustaining trust, confidence and respect for government and the institutions it incarnates. Fifth, state-civil society-private sector interface provides the structural basis for promoting and sustaining development and growth as catalyst for ensuring the quality livelihood of the population. Sixth, the rise of social movements can be of positive and negative impact on the transformation of the society. The failing of the state reflects a lack of fiscal as well as social indiscipline, failure of the social protection model, infiltration of the cultural heritage and value system by external cultures – western culture for example.

Mozambique has the resources but lack the skilled manpower to give added advantage to its natural wealth potentials. Therefore, an education curriculum designed to reflect the priority needs of the country must be put in place and effectively implemented to ensure rigorous attainment of its objectives. Without the requisite human capital, a functional governance system, harmonious interrelationship between the state-civil-society-private sector triple helix, the country will not be able to claim ownership of its development. A vital component in the state-civil society-private sector dichotomy is that of fully engaging the female gender as a veritable part of the development process. Certain cultural taboos impede their contributively role in state construct. Therefore, improving on their human capital development will give added vantage to the role they currently play. Resolving the global international crisis requires total mobilisation of domestic stakeholders as veritable forces in kick-starting the process if economic growth. There is need to build a new social mode of accumulation as well as strengthen formal institutional framework related with the waves of addressing the scourges of unemployment and social transformation.

Emerging from the crisis requires fundamental challenges and comprehensive changes in the political, economic and social construct of the mindset of the people. New patterns of work attitude and behaviour leading to production, competitiveness and equity in wealth distribution must be injected the work habit and attitude of the various actors. Strong institutions are needed to ensure compliance to the rule of law and behaviour. The currently over-bloated public service sector must be made to be productive, effective and efficient in serves delivery and as instrument for attract foreign invests as well as encourage domestic investments. The challenges and changes require a functional democratic good governance process, visionary servant leadership and a vibrant civil society operating as control mechanisms for government output related activities. The politics of inclusion, transparency, accountability, responsibility and shared-prosperity are necessary instruments in piloting the activities of social movements and ensuring that these social movements contribute to educating society in the efficient usage of services provided by the state as well as their re4sponsibilities and obligations in state construct. The dependency attitude on foreign currency income on one type of export commodity should pave for diversification, encouraged, domestic consumption and forging greater trade links with African countries is on the development menu.

Globalisation may have destabilised African economies, but it has also brought along new economic opportunities mainly for highly educated to tap. In this hash economic climate, African women's access to higher education also represents a crucial policy initiative for fighting Africa's war of survival. Apart from the human resources that remained untapped, women's underrepresentation also calls into question the very purpose of tertiary education; the fundamental reasons for pursuing and transmitting knowledge for which the ivory tower dotted across Africa were established. The question must be asked, where are women located as students, scholars and teachers? This is a crucial question which the few women who make it through higher education and the even fewer number who end up as arbiters of knowledge continue to wrestle with. The struggle for academic freedom, which the majority of Africa male scholars give their solid support, must go hand in hand with women's struggle to find their place in academia (Okeke, 2006:79-92).

Conclusion

Charting the Way Forward

Mozambique is at the cross-roads of development or decay. It is left for the leaders and people to craft a society that truly befits the countries transform process. The choice is that of the people to make or mar the quality live hood of present and future generations. The way forward for Mozambique is to build on the positive sides of SWOT and SLEPT approaches and marry this with the New Public Management Service, Rigour in the Governance System to ensure effective and efficient service delivery, sustainable development and quality wellbeing for all citizens as depicted here.

SWOT + SLEPT + NPMS + RIG + ROG ➔ Capable Developmental State ➔Meeting the Needs of the People as the Frame of Analysis and Sustainable Development.

Lessons can be drawn from other success stories throughout the continent and in different parts of the world. For now, Mozambique can exploit the late-comer advantage advanced by Gerschenkron [1962]; institute an inclusive democratic governance system backed by proper utilisation of its human capital and natural resources potentials. The ultimate goal of solving the crisis is to ensure sustainable quality livelihood for the people. Seen within this context transformation should be people-oriented and focused. Mobilisation of domestic resources is imperative. Mozambique has to realise the issue of interconnectedness and construct its development strategies accordingly. The words of Samora Machel, former President of Mozambique, should be at the centre of the continent's development strategy: "*To decolonise a state means essentially to dismantle the political, administrative, cultural, financial, economic, educational, juridical and other systems which, as an integral part of the colonial state were solely designed to impose foreign domination and the will of the exploiters on the masses*" [Richard Joseph: 1976:12]. This statement with that of the former President of the Republic of Guinea, Sekou Toure [1962:147]: "*to win and proclaim a nation's independence but keep its old structure is to plough a field but not sow it with grain for harvest*" should ring the bell for Mozambique to fashion out a development strategy that puts in place appropriate measures to address issues of accumulation, transformation, development and other international crisis.

As the current global financial crisis and recession and inflation and the devaluation of foreign currencies have reverberated through the Mozambique economy, they have brought the contradictions and dependent growth and concomitant conflicts to the open. Faced with a deteriorating revenue base and open skirmishes, the state has should intensify its overtures to the developed economies on the one hand, and engaged in occasional and defensive radicalism, as it has also opened up for supranational regional integration, (NEPAD, SADC, AU etc.) as a way of reviving the flagging economy and political influence, which, could be seen as a way of domestic resources mobilisation for a new state construct. The Mozambique state is becoming reformist. With downturn in global financial crisis, and eventually in economic growth and with growing home demands for profound' changes in political and economic governance promise to make the future of the country and eventful one, with implications for more creative adaptations in the country's development construct which this paper has attempted to scrutinise.

Recommendations

- There is an urgent need for the country to deepen its democratic process, ensuring open and inclusive governance, shared-values and shared-prosperity;
- State-civil society-private sector interface must be intensified;
- Efforts must be made to ensuring that Mozambique owns and control the means of production and development;
- The need for developing a new education curriculum to intensify and develop the country's human skill and its proper utilisation in the process of nation-building.

- Regional integration should be fostered and encouraged as a corner stone for sustainable transformation and improving the quality welling of citizens;
- Articulating and implementing a comprehensive and progressive Afro-centric agenda for the sustainable transformation, integration and unity of the continent.

References

AAPAM [2012] Call for Papers Write Up – Global Financial Crisis: Africa in a Post-Crisis Global Economy, Rwanda October 2012

Douglas Mary [1990]. Risk and Blame. Routledge Publishers, London.

Douglas, Mary ^ Wildavsky, A. [1982] Risk and Culture. University of California Press, Berkeley

Forje W. John [2009] The Challenges of Administrative Political and Developmental Renewal in Africa: Emerging Issues. Nova Science Publishers Inc, New York, USA

Forje W. John [2009] The Challenges of Administrative and Developmental Renewal in Africa: Essays on Rethinking Government and Reorganisation. Nova Science Publishers Inc, New York, USA

Forje W. John [2009] State Building and Democracy in Africa: A Comparative and Developmental Renewal. Nova Science Publishers Inc. New York, USA.

Gerschenkron Alexander [1962] Economic Backwardness in Historical Perspectives. The Belknap Press, Harvard University Press, Cambridge, MA

Hood Christopher, Henry Rothsteen & Robert Baldwin el al. (eds.) [2001]. The Government of Risk: Understanding Risk Regulation Regimes. Oxford University Press, Oxford.

Hyden Goran [1983] No Short to Progress: African Development Management in Perspective. University of California Press, Berkeley, USA.

Joseph Richard [1976] The Gaullist Legacy: Patterns of French Neo-colonialism", Review of African Political economy, vol. 6, May-August 1976, p.12

Majone, G. [1994] The Rise of the Regulatory State in Europe", West European Politics, 17:77-101

Okeke E. Philomina (2006). Higher education for African Women. Prospects and Challengers: chapter 5, in All A. Abdu, Koble P.

Puplmpu and George J. Sefin der (eds.) (2006) African education and Globalisation. Critical Perspective, Lexington Books, USA
Power, Michael [1997]. The Audit Society, Oxford University Press, Oxford
Toure Sekou [1962] Africa's Future and the World, Foreign Affairs, Vol. 41. No. 1, October, p.147.
World Bank [1997] World Development Report 1997: The State in A Changing World, The World Bank and Oxford University Press.

Chapter 7

The Challenge of Democracy after the Rising Spell of Africa's Independence and Sovereignty

Introduction

Facilitating or Hampering Development!

The African continent is at the cross-road of developmental challenges, from a backward to developed polity. Meeting the aegis of Quality Wellbeing (QWB) of citizens and evolving broad understanding of the linkages between democracy and development. The implications for these linkages and multifarious effects impact differently on societies depending on the geo-politico-economic architecture of the society. For example, Cameroon may fare better or worse than Chad, Ghana, Gambia, Nigeria, Mali, Botswana, Lesotho, Sudan, and Kenya in one area. The common challenge faced by these nations is that of making services work for poor people, but too often they fail. So far, many African countries have failed in unleashing a new plan that makes services work for all.

Services are failing poor people in many ways. First, while governments devote about a third of their budgets to health and education, they spend very little of it on poor people – that is, on the services poor people need to improve their wellbeing – education and health. Public spending on health and education is typically enjoyed by the non-poor. Second, even when public spending can be reallocated toward poor people – say, by shifting to primary schools and clinics - the money does not always reach the frontline service providers. The corruption epidemic being major constraining factors. We are a tree that bears fruits. Each one of us nurture the tree that produces the fruits which can either be bitter or juicy. The fruit reverts to a seed, the seed of another generation that will ripen. And so, life continues. It is our place to ensure that we continue to nurture the fruit for our common good. The continent has a peculiar history - the history of slavery, imperialism and colonialism (SIC). Slavery, imperialism and colonialism remain the greatest crime ever committed against the people of the continent. We live with the legacies of SIC. No single African can be held responsible, but it is important to identify the real perpetrators of the crimes in order to expiate the insult and rebuild the continent. It is not the perpetrators SIC that will rebuild the continent, for that goes totally against their original intention, which was and is keeping the continent as the supplier of raw materials and consumers of western finished products.

The most outstanding and challenging question is how to reconcile the people to rethink and rebuild themselves? We need to know our past, to understand the present and to prepare building a better tomorrow. We need to enrich our discourse on SIC; just as we should ask ourselves, do Africans hate one another or are made to hate each other? What have we, after fifty or more years of self-independence, done or trying to do to probe into SICS and seeks setting the records in the right perspectives? As Africans, we need to double re-think our situation. We must admit that SIC has divided us, injected the hate attitude in us and this impedes our unity faculty and moving forward as a society, nation and continent. The architects of SIC hold together, we sufferers continue splitting ourselves even in the wake of what is ongoing. We need to get on new train, profess a profound, implacable love for one another, even though there may some particular signs to show with one another. For now, admittedly, relations among us are not what they should be. We have to make a distinction and draw a line between (a) blame and (b) reality; as well as make clear distinction and line of demarcation between the actions of the state, those of its servants and the society. The state as oppressor continues to commit crimes against the very essence of its people. This is the level of crime that is unbearable. With such policy attitude, Africa can never be free, sovereign and independent.

Society has handed powers to the state; the state fails to act to the interests of society; rather the state is in alliance with the promoters of SIC. To be blunt, the African state has transformed the people "as part of enterprise of massive destruction of human life and introduction of venality as resource of economic, political and social promotion. To lend legitimacy to its action, it chose to target a portion of its stigmatised" (N'Daide, 2006:37). The African state that replaced the departed masters, positions itself as the Centre from where it spreads the ideological orientation within the periphery by covering up its key role in the administration of absurdity and manipulation. The state perpetuates the 'hate' attitude as an instrument of divide and rule as it gives it leverage to thwart with the democratic process. In some cases, thwarting the democratic process as a solution to remaining in power has even taken a new dimension, the resort to military arsenal as the indirect way of governance and of remaining in power. This macabre is staged through second-rate subordinates such as governors, administering authorities the security forces lacking consciences. We may see this as 'the darkness of the human.' It is important for us to examine ourselves and to stop complaining if we want to make progress. It is in the memory of the African people we should appeal to their capacity to stand up as one strong and united unit to raise the tragedy and build a new society.

However, there seem to be a kind of silver-lining at the core of some of the challenges these former colonial dependencies encounter, such:

{a}Decreasing trust in vital state institutions of representative democracy – {executive, legislative, judiciary, political parties etc.}

==============➔ {b} Rise of populist politics, or hybrid regime obviously feeding on the delivery capacity of many democracies;

Challenges of Governance Democracy, Elections and Development

{c} Growing perception of domestic democratic processes becoming less relevant in the light of power external influences generated by the forces of globalization; hardly controllable financial flows, trade protectionism, mass migration and the rest.

// //

{d} Deepening North-South divide – polarization – exploited by forces opposed to democracy, the wellbeing of the people in the South, but greatly engraved in promoting the hegemonic idea that democracy is a Northern and Western construct or prerogative only to be managed by them

// //

=============➔ **Confronted by the Realities===➔Democracy and Development Landscapes changing rapidly in many ways**

The literature floodgates on democracy, governance, elections and development are enormous; thanks to the rapid technological achievements that information and communication technologies (ICTs) places at the disposal of humankind, though many in the South have yet to exploit and benefit from these developmental gadgets, and the very nature these concepts impact on livelihoods. It is futile to even begin penetrating into the annals of the vast abundance of literature in these domains but to constantly keep abreast and in mind the wealth of literature existing and yet to be published remains abundant and inclusive. These concepts will continue undergoing semantic evolution as the human horizon and intellect expands.

Within the scholarly research of the topics addressed here, we see important changes over time. The first change is that these topic areas have been define increasingly broader ways. They have not been static. Progress can be recorded over time. Practically, there is more draw-back despite the volume of published materials. More are yet to come. Implementation has not gotten pace with the research results produced due to articulate self-interests of the individuals / leaders. In short, the performance of government more or less is reduced in some countries that are enemies to change. This however should not be a discouragement from addressing the issues from the perspective of constructive and efficiency-related measures for the common good. In other words, the performance of governments can be looked upon from internal and external views dependent on whether the focus is on the internal governance structure or externally influenced. Good performance of governments includes attention to different administrative values: efficiency, but also effectiveness and fairness in improving the quality wellbeing of citizens. Therefore, government performance includes a number of dimensions (internal-efficiency, internal-effectiveness, and internal fairness).

Before, development was construed with the prefix as synonym of economic growth, today it is broadly understood as a process leading to the continuous improvement of the quality of life of the vast majority of the people, particularly the bottom billion poor and excluded. The concept has expanded to include dimensions of human rights, the reduction of disparities in the distribution of wealth and income, issues of participatory democracy and social democracy as system of governance and gaining more grounds as pillars of a governance system expected to deliver on social and economic and development. African countries should draw valuable lessons from this; build on our progressive cultural heritage and values system to construct our society. Africa has to decide what it wants and not to depend on the dictates of the developed polities which we have been doing for the past many donkey years; it has not improved but rather made our situation worse. The realities on the ground should hasten a new line of thinking, inject a progressive mindset and spirit of seeking amicable solutions to problems.

Contextualized within this construct, issues on the impact of democracy, development and vice-versa converged in the direction of at least three fundamental accepted universal principles.

- democracy and development are desirable, constituting values to pursued in their own rights
- development being more than economic growth;

UNIVERSAL CONVERSION===➔} democracy is more than institutions; and mechanics of democracy expected are to deliver in terms of quality of livelihood

PRINCIPLE'S

// // // //

Constructing a better Continent:

//

=======➔} **AFRICA AND ITS PLACE IN THE WORLD**

It is clear that the outstanding challenge facing Africa is how to enhance a self-nourishing relationship between the governors and governed within the prerogatives of authority, accountability, transparency, rule of law, responsibility, empowerment, inclusion and equity in shared-prosperity [Diamond, 2008; Forje 2009]. How to end dependence on aid, which Samir Amin's perception on aid is an "instrument of imperialism's strategy of domination rooted in the mind-set and development strategy of countries dependent on aid' [Tandon Yash, 2008].

Africa's destiny is shaped by how much Africans construct a sense of common identity based, not on the narrow lenses of state race or religion, but construed on the continent's belief in democracy, governance and unity as the most viable policy option to mediate, reconcile, and accommodate our individual and collective interests. In this case Africa is caught in making the proper choice between the different models of democracy – whether democracy means some kind of popular power (a form of politics in which citizens are engaged in self-government and self-regulation) or an aid to decision-making (a means of conferring authority on those periodically voted into office) [Held 1995]. Contextualising Africa in this light, three basic variants or models of democracy stand before it for selection:

- direct or participatory democracy, a system of decision-making about public affairs in which citizens are directly involved. This is the 'original' type of democracy that exist in ancient Athens, among other place; the earlier African traditional society;
- liberal or representative democracy, a system of rule embracing elected 'officers' who undertake to 'represent' the interests of views of citizens within delimited territories while upholding the 'rule of law;
- a variant of democracy based on a one-party model (although some may doubt whether this is a form of democracy at all) as practiced in the collapsed Soviet Union and East European countries, and fashionable system in many African countries in the immediate post-independence years until late into the 1980s

The challenges are numerous, impacting differently, but at the same time challenging each society to articulate, implement and evaluate policies that takes it from the minus to the plus-side of the development continuum. However, there is a common basis of departure in situating the problems plaguing the continent. The issue of development and instability of African politics can be explained in part as a function of the attitude of citizens, governance system, regime change, leadership style and succession. Of course, these are themselves a function of many other factors, some of which may be found in the traditional explanations of the failure of politics in Africa. Success depends on the interplay between many centres of power and participants internally and externally. Without cordiality between the various actors, it is difficult to see the continent getting out its current mess. This is briefly illustrated in Table 3. Communality of the Dimension of the Challenges and compounded by at least three problems in terms

Table 3: Communality of the Dimension of the Challenge

The Role of the Political **The Impact of Globalisation** **Society** **on Democracy**	**the Role of the international** **Community**
Parties, Parliament and others opportunity for building parti- pation Policies towards sustaining citizen's participation and involve able development – State to advance the institutions construct of democracy national and inter- national	Opening up the broader creating an actors in formulating space for the more democratic societies of the African political society to participate and shape its national development priorities and owning it

Compounded by a variety of forces =========➔}	• the crises of modernisation, especially because modernisation, especially because modernisation in the new states brings rising frustrations from the oceans of unfulfilled expectations {Pye 1966}: • the politics of scarcity [Weiner 1962}: • the failure to build self-sustaining political capabilities {Almond and Powell 1966}; • the dual or simultaneous process of modernisation and political decay {Huntington in Welch 1967, Englund & Nyamnjoh 2004; Moss 2007

Forje [2012]

Fundamentally important, it must be appreciated that democracy is by no means a domain where a divide can be drawn between "donors" and "receivers." No country donates "democracy and no country receive democracy" from abroad. It is an upsurge idea that the North should civilize the uncivilized South on democracy. This remains a colonial harmful paradigm to be unlearned. Democracy has to be 'home grown' but bearing the virtues of the universally accepted basic tenets of respect for fundamental human rights, rule of law; separation of powers, checks and balances, majority votes and minority rights, free media industry, among others.

The West or North is not free from rigged or flawed elections either. Let us take a look at the last presidential elections in the United State. Look at the events that followed concerning the handing of power to the newly elected president. What prevailed is the existence of strong institutions and strong individual. But this is no excuse for the South and Africa in particular to be an ardent contributor to flawed elections and other electoral malpractices, poor governance failing to deliver quality services to the citizens. Democracy building and consolidation is contingent on strong institutions. Democracy and elections are processes, not events with the key elements in building democratic culture in Africa is anchoring the ongoing practices in unambiguous and predictable processes and strong institutions supported by popular participation. Constructive engagement is called for. This leaves us with serious soul-searching questions concerning the evolution and consolidation of democracy in Africa. The attitude of the outgoing president showed what is common in Africa – a system of strong individuals lording electoral results over the people, in the absence of strong institutions that are not corrupted. Strong and democratic institutions prevailed when Richard Nixon was forced out of office. The military did not step-in to take power and the governance system. Can we in Africa draw valuable lessons from these two events in the United States? The incident in the Capitol Hill could have led to a chaotic situation in the USA. The America system was once again put to test.

Some Soul Search Question on Democracy

We cannot deny the fact that much progress has been made in the process of democratic consolidation on the continent fifty years after these states started obtaining their independence and sovereign rights from the colonial master to govern themselves.

- Is Africa ready for democracy or has democracy bypassed the continent?
- Is African democracy representative?

- Is African democracy encompassing and responsive?
- Is African democracy responsible?
- Is African democracy delivering?
- How socially and political empowered are the people?
- How do we retain legitimacy in fragile states?
- Does Africa risk civil war by promoting democracy?
- How do we bridge (in) security and (under)development?
- Do good intentions prevent conflicts?
- Why African countries cannot conduct clean, free, fair, transparent, competitive elections with results acceptable to winning or losing parties?
- Why is development evading the continent?
- What is actually wrong with the continent?
- Are there hopes for a better Africa?

From these barrages of questions, it is clear to conclude that democracy, elections, governance, leadership and development is in state of 'crisis' or in recession in different parts of the world and more pertinently in the African continent. It is on the rise in certain parts of the continent even with the Arab Spring 2011 which has given it greater impetus. For those countries trialling behind to be alert and embrace the basic tenets of democracy. Apparently, what is evident, however, the popular problem is not the lack of popular support for the ideas of democracy but the way in which vital institutions of democracy are functioning, for example

- Elections are 'stolen;'
- Political parties are often perceived as top-heavy, corrupt, male-dominated and ineffective – gripped by the politics of the 'belly'
- Parliaments are powerless and complacent, becoming a hand clapping institution failing in defending the interest of the people and failing to operate as checks and balances to the whims and caprices of other state institutions - executive, judiciary, and slaves to the military establishment thereby failing to exercise the oversight role;
- A politicised, ethicized public service administration failing to deliver quality services to the people; unable to connect governor to governed;
- Failed judiciary system that the highest bidder gets justice;

- A captive civil society that thrives on the 'politics of the belly' and even compromising its authority of custodian of power in society;
- A weak private sector, non-competitive, non-innovative and non-productive in the age of globalise knowledge-based competitive economy;
- An international community totally hostile to the aspirations and needs of the poor in South, and believing democracy must be transferred to the South wily Nelly.

A new dawn for Africa beacons with all intensity and vigour. Africa's renewal and renaissance calls for constructive and holistic policy strategies and comprehensive implementation zeal involving all the stakeholders and at all levels. Democracy and development need and require deeper insight. However, a tall list of crucial questions cannot be overlooked.

- Democracy and development for whom, by what, means and how;
- Who is shaping the agenda?
- Have the down-trodden a voice in the process;
- Can the electors rely on their elected representatives to set the priorities right and ensure authentic realisation;
- Who are the owners of democracy and development?
- To what extent is ownership of democracy and development democratised

Ownership to democracy and development needs to be democratised, open and transparent. National ownership has converted into individual property. State property becomes the sole property of the Head of State who dishes out development related projects as a personal gift to the people and a condescending civil society responding with 'motions of support' and thanks to the Head of State of a constructing a road, providing a university, pipe born water, build a classroom, a health centre for the people, typical of Cameroon. The taxes paid by citizens become the wealth of the Head of State. For all practical purpose, "ownership" has been reduced to ownership by the executive branch of government or those who walk the corridors of power. This is the case in both developed and developing polities. State institutions and political actors in Africa failed in a constructive discourse in shaping the development strategies and agendas.

Strategies and Agendas

In most African countries, Cameroon for example, political parties and parliament are the weak links of democracy. What constraints these two bodies are the issue of 'syndromes aptly analysed by Forje [Forthcoming, 2012; Haynes Jef, 1993]. The institutions of political parties and the legislature cannot be bypassed in constructing a capable developmental state. The continent needs institutions and political actors that are entrenched and not alienated from national issues. The ongoing political impasse in Cameroon show how alienated the elected representatives especially in the Anglophone speaking part of the country are. It highlights the simple reality; which these so-called elected representatives are totally disconnected from the sufferings of the peoples they are supposed to represent. These elected representatives fail to speak truth to the powers that be.

Building strong institutions with active political actors, and political processes, such as election, is critical in ensuring that if a politician loses today, it will be rational and cost effective for him/her to trust the political system to afford him/her another chance in the future. Institutions that get involved in elections, management bodies that lack capacity, public trust and legitimacy; political parties that have weak internal processes and lack internal democratic systems; acrimonious inter-party relations and weak civil society involvement in the electoral system. This tells us that democracy is much more than electing leaders periodically through competitive elections. It is about acceptance of a culture that institutionalises certain basic freedoms and liberties; freedom of association, assembly, expression of ideas, political organisations; and property rights. In short and simply stated, democracy is about affording the individual the possibility and hope for change, that is, change they can trust in, rely on and build on a strong and democratic foundation as the bases for transformation. Democratic governability is the bases for efficient institutions. Democratic governability refers to democratic systems where decisions necessary to resolve social problems, can be enacted, implanted and sustained because they are arrived at through institutionalised democratic procedures that fully consider the views and interests of relevant political and social actors. There is need to unlock the democracy and leadership deficit in Africa.

What Africa has to come to grips with, appreciate and set countervailing forces is that globalisation, colonialism, imperialism, apartheid and slavery have one thing in common: they extort the weak and vulnerable states and/or the disadvantaged segments of population. There is urgent need for African countries to develop national capacities – human development, research investment, infrastructural development as logical and pragmatic actions towards entering global competitiveness and overcoming existing state of underdevelopment. The state of underdevelopment subjects the people to foregoing their fundamental basic human rights. This gives room for the powers that be to constantly dribble them; making things to fall apart. Since we canonised strong individuals and not strong institutions, things continue falling apart, when the individual no long controls the realm of power.

How do African countries make development more sustainable? How do the people find common grounds in accelerating their transformation process – political, economic, social and technological? These countries are challenged to create new 'vaccines' for development and to ensure that the vaccines are equitably administered to all. Power to the people with equal opportunities for all to ensure the vaccines attain maximum results. Africa needs new vaccines, new rules and new players to wade off its underdevelopment and poor governance turbulences. What is required is a transition to a new national construct of reformed institutions and new governance mechanisms that can harness diverse energies and resources in a cohesive way for the common good of all. How can the continent develop? The book continues to insist in the quality livelihood of the population, by getting the progressive Afro-centric approach back on the track for the sustainable transformation of the continent. There are numerous opportunities, if only African leadership and people get their axes together the right way for the right purpose. All we need do is to search for the suitable metaphors for the sustainable transformation of the territory. We have to search and think for policies that work well and how and for whose interests? Again, the emphasis on the progressive Afro-centric approach that should lead to insights and discoveries, from a closed to an open and participatory society; of seeking unity in diversity enhanced by self-critical awareness; personal responsibility; and sharing.

Development - Democracy Nexus

Is development the sine quad none of democracy or vice versa? The two are inter-related and impact on each other, in a variety of ways what do we mean by the term "development."

Democracy ⇐============⇒Authoritarian Rule
Development Underdevelopment

// //

Sanctuary <============> Mortuary

Africa is confronted with two scenarios. Sanctuary and Mortuary which unfolds as such;

On the one hand and what is required

Democratic governance =====================➔}
People-oriented and focused development
Inclusion/participation SANCTUARY
Shared-prosperity
Justice - the rule of law
Power to the people with equal opportunities ========➔}

On the other hand, and what Exists

Bad Governance =========================➔}
Inappropriate development strategies
Exclusion
Articulate Self-interests MOTUTUARY
Non-respect for the rule of Law
Power and money in the pockets of a select few ======➔}

The nexus of democracy and development remain clear. Both are deeply intertwined in spite of the difficulty of identifying a direct, caused and quantifiable relationship between them. More importantly, they are increasingly understood today as including each other to a great extent and building upon each other. Both democracy and development are political processes requiring long-term, context-specific and integrated approaches, and they need to be owned, shaped and pursued by those who demand them and who will be their ultimate beneficiaries. Enhancing the capacity of democratic institutions to deliver on the reduction of poverty and inequality is the key to reclaiming of their credibility [IDEA 2008]

Following Bardham [2008] democracy can facilitate development. There are several key features of democracy directly favouring socio-economic developments namely

=➔Democracy's implicit system of checks and balances as an uncontested mechanism for avoiding catastrophic mistakes: Come to think of China's Greet Leap Forward and the Cultural Revolution.

=➔Democracy as an embedded effect on fairer distribution by exporting capitalist excesses to greater pressure

=➔Democracy functioning as a tool for conflict management and fostering sustainable development and welfare for all

We may ask when democracy sneezes do development catches the cold or vice-versa. Or when there is a smile on the face of democracy or development; what is the reach on either of those two concepts/construct and impact on society. The franchise came to Africans both male and female on the attainment of independence. So, Africa made quick stride in this domain, especially the female gender. They should be proud of it as they were the voting power behind the attainment of independence. Ad should perfect this stride of involving all in the process of governance and development. We can, of course, give credit to those African countries, for example, Rwanda Angola, Mozambique that top the list of female representation in parliament and cabinet. We all know the support of Ghanaian women to Kwame Nkrumah. The massive women vote in Southern Cameroons for the reunification of British and French Cameroon in 1961 for example. Unfortunately, responsive government seems to evade the continent. Africa must gun for a system of government that is responsive to the enthusiasm of franchise which the African people showed on the eve of independence. The destructive frustration of colonial rule was to be replaced by "rising expectation" after independence. Grossly this failed to materialise. We preached Afro-centricism before independence and canonised Euro-centricism after independence. How confused we are about what we want and how to get what we want.

Sadly, enough, rising expectation has been converted into destructive frustration. A system of government can never be really successful unless it has the active support of the people who are being governed, or at least of a substantial portion of them. "Here the People Rule [Forje 2009] outlines the issue within the context of; Attitude (A). Behaviour (B) and Change (C) ensuring also that civil society is proactive, responsible and fulfilling its obligations as custodian of the nation When democracy sneezes do underdevelopment catch the cold or vice-versa? Or when there is a smile on the face of democracy or development, what is the reaction on either authoritarian rule or underdevelopment and how do these concepts/constructs impact on society? With independence, greed, individualism, self-articulate interests took pride of place over the collective interests of the people, making society be more divided than before the advent of independence. Love for people and country was replaced with love for money, hatred for people and country. Africa failed in consolidating the principles of attitude, behaviour and change for the total and comprehensive reconstruction of the battered continent after the granting of independence to former dependencies. Here we are today with a more divided people and continent even though we pride ourselves foolishly with an African Union that propagates the doctrine of Euro-centricism not Afro-centricism. We begin to wonder, who controls the AU? Does AU work for and in the interest of Africa or the developed polities?

Progress has been made in Africa on the path to consolidate the democratic process. More could have been achieved had the leaders not been confused with the conversion of or minister presentation of politics with dynastic governance system. The essential problem of African democracy is we may conclude the essential problem of democracy everywhere in the world at the early stages of transformation from one system to another. In the African case, it is a transformation that is mixed with trying to marry African traditional governance system with western governance system. Comparatively, democracy has succeeded in North-Western Europe and in few countries outside Europe because it has become entwined in the traditions of the people.

Africa 'is on the march' and at the same time confused because throughout the continent traditional ideas are being given up and replaced with ideas imported from Western cultures. African countries should deepen African cultural values without any pollution. Freedom from colonial rule should mean deepening African cultural governance system. What we have seen from 'freedom from colonial rule' has turned out to be the introduction of 'anarchy' which nobody wants. It is anarchy that is destroying the continent. Africa wants change. Change must come to the continent. The people are the ones to create that change, protect their freedom from colonial rule, reverse the African governance system and ensure that the quality livelihood of the people is not compromised. What are most needed are political stability, unity, discipline, reconciliation, moral ethics, economic growth and progress. Successes in these areas will significantly contribute to improved and sustained quality livelihood for all citizens.

Democratic government is a difficult process because it relies so much on the good faith of ambitious politicians who are subject to a good many temptation. It is by spurning these temptations to the abuse of power by the leaders that society will emulate and evolve on a better note. Weakness in that domain gives rise to corruption. Corruption at all strata of society is what is destroying democratic consolidation on the continent. Internal cohesion must develop without which politicians will continue to exploit divisions and sectional differences to keep themselves in, or to attain power. One cannot blame an African electorate, any more than one can blame an Asian electorate, for possessing ideas and emotions which has been handed down from generation to generation. It would be surprising if ambitious politicians do not make use of existing divisions or sectionalism in society for personal gains.

What is more, as we have seen, political propaganda before independence fosters the impression that independence will immediately usher improved social and economic conditions, though any such improvement will be narrowly limited to classes which are already favoured. By understanding and resolving these difficulties that order can reign. Africans are human beings like others. They have the same defects as political leaders in other countries. But this is not an escape route not to do things that proper and good for the people. No doubt Africa leaders have the same devotions to the public good and the same ambition to improve the lot of their fellow citizens [Jennings 1963] Problems exist and will continue to arise, These problems of solutions. Vision is necessary to look for the right solutions to problems. Solutions can be helped by constitutional devices, but their successes depend essentially on the people (men and women) who give them effect.

Fifty or more years of independence has shown the strength and weaknesses of the continent's march in the democratic culture. The threats are there like the opportunities exist to overcome these threats and challenges impeding the constructive march to democratic consolidation. What seems lacking is a breed of people who are energetic, imaginative and devoted servants of their citizens. Visionary leadership constitutes an essential party of the democratic process, so also the role of civil society. A marriage between the two will drive mountains. These two key components seem to have missed the harmonious marriage from the eve of independence. The divorce is what is costing the continent heavy in its resolve to the many challenges it is facing. Political independence failed to bring economic independence and genuine liberation to the people.

Of course, we can critique the anti-colonial movement and struggles without throwing away the historical and political victories it brought to the continent. Without these struggles many of us may never have had the opportunity to go to school or even realise that what we were experiencing was neo-colonialism. On the other hand, the 'new generation' of African leaders have brought about many positive changes. May be their 'historic mission' has been to stabilise neo-colonialism [Biney & Olukoshi 2010]. We all need a new mind-set to straighten *'things that fall and continue falling apart.'* This is one of the greatest challenges facing the continent. New leadership, new civil society, new mind-set is required to restructure and move the continent positively and constructively forward. That is the change we have to gun for in the second phase of the independence of the continent. The challenge is that Africans who, now more than ever, must let reason and rationality triumph over sentiments and parodical attitudes. Perhaps now more than yesterday, Africans need to begin asking themselves what they have personally done to promote and hasten the advent of a more prosperous, a more harmonious and united continent.

A change that should adequately address the core development questions including leadership, citizen's role, slow-growth puzzle, issues in economic reform as well as the role of international aid. Regionalism and Africa's place rightful within the global economy and politics is imperative. Some of Africa's underlying inherent issues include: (i)Africa has had and continue to have an unlucky history and faces many structural factors that impede development, but with a change to harness the region's other advantages and work around these obstacles: (ii)transforming the African state to improve accountability and the management of resources is key to attracting larger aid flows and foreign investor as well as mobilising domestic investors; (iii) aid should be increased, but also made to become more effective, in addition to diversify the economy of African countries; reduce the export of raw materials, embark on processing these raw materials at home, stimulate inter-African trade among other trade inputs: [iv)a shared responsibility between the region and the world to ensure that the former is able to take advantage of global economic opportunities. Existing regional groupings have neither fostered regional trade arrangement nor succeeded in boosting trade within the continent.

The obvious of falling on the *'blame theory'* looms high. But we cannot dismiss the factors of a number of inter-related factors, i.e., bad legacies, big men and others. Post-colonial Africa started with the legacy of colonialism, the role of 'big men' and personal rule, conflict and civil war, and contemporary political change and democratisation all impacting on the transformation process of the continent. To a large extent, structural adjustment visibly improved macroeconomic management across Africa, notwithstanding the role played by conditionality. Importantly, Africa must make development more sustainable [Munasinghe 2007] and to ensure sustainability in the quality livelihood of the peoples. Factors impeding the eradication of the frontiers of poverty must be addressed. Therefore, hanging on the 'blame theory' is not the solution. A lesson for Africa is learning from Singapore. The case of Singapore is interesting. As a resource-starved nation transformed itself from a dirty-poor backwater into today's pleasant garden city-state of 'first world' facilities emerged (Yew).

Former USA Secretary of State Henry Kissinger in his foreword to Lee's book wrote some profound truths that Africa and the world should care to listen to: First, he concedes that the "long established nations of the West have fallen prey to the temptation of ignoring history and judging every new state by the criteria of their civilisations. It is often overlooked that the institutions of the West did not spring full-blown from the brow of contemporaries but evolved over centuries which shaped frontiers and defined legitimacy, constitutional provisions, and basic values." Second. Kissinger notes that "in mitigation, Africa's apparent slow march to development is not unique. It takes time, even centuries, for institutions to evolve; and all countries, including those of European stock, went through this history. History does matter. The institutions of the West developed gradually while those of newest states were put in place in elaborated form immediately." Third, Kissinger continues: "In the West, a civil society developed side by side with the institutions of the modern state. This made possible the growth of representative institutions, which confined the state's power to those matters which society could not deal with by its own arrangements. Political conflicts were moderated by overriding purposes."

Apparently, Kissinger is right to an extent. Africa more often not neglects history- everything seems to start a fresh. However, one thing stands crystal clear – the Gerschenkronian theory of the 'late-comer advantage' (the use of science and technology) that Africa can use to overcome some of its developmental dilemma. Kissinger's assessment of Singapore in comparison to Africa is so pertinent that it deserves extensive quotation here; "Most post-colonial states like those in Africa have no comparable history. Tasks which in the West were accomplished over centuries must be completed in a decade or two and under much more complex circumstances. Where the common natural experience is colonial rule, especially when the state comprises diverse ethnic groups, political opposition is often considered an assault on the political validity of the state rather than of a particular government. Singapore is a case in point. As the main British naval base in the Far East, it had neither prospect nor aspiration for nationhood and beyond." the collapse of European power in the aftermath of the Second World War redrew the political map of Southeast Asia. In the first wave of decolonisation, Singapore was made part of Malaya until it's largely Chinese population proved too daunting for state attempting to define its national identity by a Malay majority. Every great achievement is a dream before it becomes reality, and his vision was of a state that would not simply survive but prevail by excelling. The Singapore of today is testament of the acts of Lee Kuan Yew. Annual per capital income has grown from less than USA dollars 1,000 at the time of independence to nearly USA dollars 30.000 today. It is the high-tech leader of Southeast Asia, the commercial enter-spot, the scientific centre. Singapore plays a major role in the politics and economics of Southeast Asia.

There is no better lesson for Africa than looking at Singapore and other countries within the Asian Tiger's miracle of economic growth and societal transformation from a backward to a modern society. Rising expectation was at the door steps of the people just as the people accepted tight discipline, honesty, hard work as the price of prosperity. But what happens when the system is no longer in a position to deliver its side of the bargain? Of course, things begin to fall apart and the rise of 'failed or collapsed' state becomes eminent as witnessed in Africa. The struggle was for independence but without proper preparation on to make independence succeed. Independence was handed to African countries. Yet the second challenge of how to manage the brutish rule of colonialism into 'freedom' when the winning and drinking days were over, when the constraint on society begins showing its ugly face and the state incapable of meeting its side of the social contract with the people? This in nutshell is the challenge facing African leaders and will continue to hunt future leaders unless a drastic turn-around approach is prioritised and implemented to underpin endeavours for constructing a sustainable state structure.

Political leadership in Singapore took the bull by the horn with the determination of transforming the country into a 'service economy' with a matching resolution that in its chosen areas of specialisation, the country would be second to no other country in South-East Asia. In this regard an elite economy called for elite specialists and so the educational system was fundamentally restructured to produce an elite class of administrators, managers, and entrepreneurs with the necessary drive and dare to spearhead the country's progress. Hence a special premium was placed on knowledge and skills. Information and knowledge gathering were accordingly made the concern of everybody in a leadership position (Anafu 2011:66). It goes without saying that only education, discipline and good leaders including the citizens themselves can save Africa. Equally important, Africans must begin to appreciate their Africanness within and outside the continent. The sad side of the issue is failing to appreciate our Africanness party is responsible for some of the problems besetting and plaguing the continent. We continue to see ourselves first through the prescient of our nations – Algerians, Cameroonians, Ghanaians, Nigerians, Kenyans, South Africans etc. before reducing ourselves further into ethnic musculatures of Ashanti's, Ibos, Mande, Kikuyu, Yoruba, Zulus and so on. We have allowed xenophobic attitudes to take pride-of-place in the continent's development endeavours. Serious soul searching into our behaviour and attitude to re-dynamise the efforts toward the "Africa Must Unite" agenda is needed. At the national levels ethnic and institutional xenophobia is encountered in various government departments and even among the police and other uniform persons as well in society at large.

In Cameroon for example, it is the *"come no go"* phenomenon – the hatred implanted by the political establishment between the people of the North West and South West Regions or between the Anglophones and Francophone's. Xenophobic attitudes attained its highest stage in South Africa in 2008 and of recent the maltreatment and killing of a Mozambican citizen. Because of the unstable situation in Zimbabwe, Somalia and other countries, citizens from these and other parts of the continent have been victims of xenophobic attacks, prompting former President Thabo Mbeki (a staunch Pan-Africanist) describing the situation as a 'national disgrace' (Commey 2013:18). Growing xenophobic tendencies is Africa's lingering time-bomb doing more harm than good to African Unity. We cannot be craving for African Unity when we hate ourselves and dance to the dictates of the west by adhering to the Eurocentric agenda of divide and rule; to better continue their exploitation machinery which renders the people poor and submits to the total propaganda machinery of the West.

We need at this venture to develop some quality treats that puts into proper perspectives our vision for a better and united Africa. Some these treats include: (a)courage and honesty; courage and honesty does not mean the absence of fear, but rather the ability to make and take the right decision and action even though you feel afraid; too honest to yourself and to others and to stand your grounds without fear or favour; (b) accountability, transparency and responsibility all add to making the person you are; (c) generosity – we need to share with others – we always have something that we can share – move out the greed, self-articulate interest and individualistic attitude. These are some of the things destroy the continent, retarding the progress of the people, making them subservient to the dictates of the developed polities. That is why the African continent can dance to the music being played by France; why the developed countries call the shots in African affairs; why the Chinese are digging deep into the political annals and destruction of the continent in a very subtle way; with the bottom line, why Africa remains poor in the midst of plenty.

Being generous imply giving with the heart, without any hidden agenda of deceit or schemes to receive plenty in return. More often than not, those who have the least are the most generous toward others, because they know what it is like to have nothing. Rephrased in another way, Africans have the biggest heart, the hearts of forgiveness (hence we have to a large extent, forgiven the West for committing the most outrageous crimes against Africans – slavery, colonialism and today, neo-colonialism; (d)patience – is a great quality that many admire, but it is also one of the most difficult to put in practice. Generally, we Africans lack that art of patience – always in a hurry of doing things; wanting things to be on our times and way. We should bear in mind that we are not the only occupant of planet earth. It is extremely important to note that the country doesn't revolve around us, the wealth of the country does not belong to those who wield power; it belongs to the entire community. The absence of accountability, transparency, patience, generosity, breeds the art of corruption and destruction; (prudence and temperance -the ability to determine whether or not a particular action is good or appropriate, idea at the specific point in time. Having temperance is being abstinence from something, what it actually means is moderation. It means finding a middle-way and balancing the self in the face of a situation. Most of the conflicts in Africa could easily be solve if the powers that be and the various actors exhibit the arts of prudence and temperance. The ongoing senseless war in Cameroon is a typical example of the lack of patience, prudence, temperance in thinking that the use of bad language, show of military strength, display of majority provides the quick solution to the problem. Five years have gone by without the 'two cubs of sugar dissolving. The powers that be underestimated the resilience of the people on what they consider a just struggle against marginalisation, annexation, assimilation and majority against minority.

The entire continent is on fire. There is no peace in Mali, Sudan, Cameroon, Central African Republic, Ethiopia, Chad, and other parts of the continent. The issue now is how the continent can navigate out of the stalemate of poor governance? It is true that deep-seated social and economic failure underlie some of problems being faced by Africa countries, but it is also accurate to say that these problems themselves are in key respects political ones, for which political solutions must be found before there will be any chance of improving the socio economic structures that can improve livelihoods and keep people at home (Banseka, 2006:34-41) in peace, security and justice. While there is no perfect democratic country, but this should be no excuse for us not to gun towards respecting and adhering to the basic tenets of democratic governance. Our vast rich natural resources have become curse not blessing to the African people. As noted by Former ECA Executive Secretary Adebayo Adedeji (1999:41); "What African countries have lacked during most of history as independent states are leaders who are unifiers, chiefs in the true sense…pursue a policy of inclusion rather than exclusion and are seen by one and all to be of the highest integrity and beyond suspicion."

References

Abbas Hakima & Niyiragira Yves (eds.) [2009] Aid to Africa: Redeemer or Colonisers? Pambazuka Press, London

Adebayo, Adedeji (ed.) (1999) Comprehending and Monitoring African Conflicts. The Search for Sustainable Peace and Good Governance, Zed Books, London

Anafu Moses (2011). "Why the Enduring Admiration for Lee Kuan Yew," New African, November 2011, pp64-67

Banseka Cage (2006)" Painful Good-Bye to Home: Governance Failure as a Precipitant to Emigration from Africa" CODERSIA Bulletin, Nos. 1& 4 Dakar – Senegal,

Bardham K. Pranels [2008] "Democracy Facilitating or Hampering Development?" in IDEA [2008] Democracy and Development in a Globalised World. Stockholm-Sweden, pp17-19

Biney Ama & Adebayo Olukoshi (eds.) [2010] Speaking Truth to Power Selected Pan-African Postcards by Abdul Raheem Tajudeen, Pambazuka Press, London

Commey Pusch (2013) "Xenophobia. South Africa's Lingering Time bomb," New African, No.530, July 2013, London pp16-19

Diamond Larry [2008] the Spirit of Democracy: The Struggle to Building Free Societies throughout the World, Times Books

Diamond Larry, Juan Linz and Seymour Martin Lipset (eds.) [1988] Democracy in Developing Countries, Lynne Rienner and Adamantine Press

Englund Harri & Nyamnjoh B. Francis [2004] Rights and The Politics of Recognition in Africa Zed Books, London

Forje W. John [2020] Cameroon Without Corruption. The Search for A New Vision Lambert Academic Publishing, Germany

Forje W. John [2009] State Building and Democracy in Africa: A Comparative and Developmental Approach. Nova Science Publishers Inc. New York

Forje W. John [2009] Here the People Rule. Political Transition and Challenges for Democratic Consolidation in Africa Nova Science Publishers Inc. New York, USA

Haynes Jeff [1993] "The State, Governance, And Democracy in Sub-Saharan Africa", Journal of Modern African Studies, 31.3 (1993)535-39

Held David [1995] Democracy and the Global Order. Polity Press, Cambridge, UK

Huntington Samuel [1967] "Political Development and Political Decay," in Welch [1967] Political Modernisation, Wadsworth Publishing Co.

IDEA [2008] Democracy and Development in a Globalised World. Stockholm, Sweden

Jennings W. Ivor [1963]. Democracy in Africa. Cambridge University Press, Cambridge, UK

Munasinghe Mohan [2007] Making Development More Sustainable: Sustainomics Framework and Practical Applications. MIND Press, Colombo, Sri Lanka

N'Gaide Abderrahmane (2006) "Reconciliation, Justice or Pardon: Mauritanians Face Their History", CODERSRIA Bulletin, Nos. 3 & 4, Dakar-Senegal, pp37-41

Pye Lucian [1966]. Aspects of Political Development, Little Brown Series, Boston

Moss J. Todd [2007] African Development. Making sense of the Issues and Actors, Lynne Rienner Publishers, Inc. Boulder, Colorado

Tandon Yash [2008] Ending Aid Dependence. Pambazuka Press, London

Weiner, Myron [1962]. The Politics of Scarcity, University of Chicago Press.

Welch, R. Claude [1967]. Political Modernisation. Wadsworth Publishing Co.

Welch, R. Claude [1970] Soldier and State in Africa, Northwestern University Press

Wright Jason [2007] "Democracy and Growth. A Case Study in Failed Causal Interface," in Gerardo L Munch (ed.) Regimes in Latin America Theories and Methods. Oxford University Press, New York and Oxford

Yew Kuan Lee () From Third World to First – The Singapore Story: 1965-2000.

Chapter 8

Rethinking the Nexus of Institutional Structures and Social Innovations for Sustainable Development in Africa

The African continent with its vast potentials of natural and human resources is caught in the flux of underdevelopment, exploitation, marginalisation and poverty within the midst of plenty Poor governance contributes to the non-utilisation of the vast potentials of the continent for the good of the people and humanity. The paper argues that sustainable structural transformation leading to change, development, progress and sustainability (CDPS) hangs on the balance of forging a comprehensive interface between indigenous knowledge, entrepreneurship and public/ private sector participation and partnership. To begin with the continent needs strategic transformative reforms in its knowledge and institutional governance structures for change, developing and enhancing national and intra-African knowledge flows and networks within the rapidly expanding global economy based on knowledge. It tackles the issues of emerging national and global changes, global recession as well as shifts in national and global partnership. Finally, the nexus of institutional structures and social innovations for a sustainable developmental and progressive state construct in Africa is embedded within the parameters of developing the human knowledge and capacity of the people which must start at an early age. Strong institutional and infrastructural development must be part of the process. Conclusion; without developing our human potentials and adapting our social cultural heritage to the virtues of modern science and technology, Africa will remain stuck on the runway of underdevelopment. The continent must work towards a proper development take-off. A new mindset and forward-looking people-oriented approach and visionary leadership inspiring change is imperative for the continent's breakthrough to a quality service delivery society

Keywords: human capital development, public/private sector partnership, regional economic groupings, leadership, science and technology

Introduction- What sort of Africa?

"A basic feature of the contemporary world is the acceleration of S&T development because of its impact on the nation and international position of each country, and, of course, its part in shaping economic and political development. Hence, the struggle for scientific and technological progress, particularly in less-developed regions, is a

prerequisite for balance and stability, for establishing international relations on an equal footing, and for the sovereignty and political independence of each nation."
(John W. Forje, 1998:33, in N. Pillay and C.H. Prinsloo, 1998)

" Black Consciousness is an attitude of mind and a way of life, the most positive call to emanate from the black world for a longtime. In essence is the realisation by the black man of the need to rally together with his brothers around the cause of their oppression – the blackness of their skin – and to operate as a group to rid themselves of the shackles that bind them to perpetual servitude. It is based on self-determination which has ultimately led them to believe that by seeking to run away from themselves and emulate the white man, they are insulting the intelligence of whoever created them black. The philosophy of Black Consciousness therefore expresses group pride and the determination of the black to rise and attain the envisaged self. Freedom is the ability to define oneself with one's possibilities held by black not by the power of other people over one but only by one's relationship to God and the natural surroundings"
(Steve Biko 1978)

Undermining or Understanding Our (Under) development Saga!

Africa is at the cross-roads of decay or development. Despair or hope. Decay if she continues with its existing incoherent policy strategies construed on the principles of articulate self-interest: development if she embarks on a citizen-centred policy strategy of inclusion, participation, human capital development, shared-prosperity, rule of law and social justice. With such a comprehensive, inclusive and open mindset she will impact her citizens with new ideas, new states of mind, attitude and behaviour for change, development, progress and sustainability (CDPS). Such inclusive forward looking and encompassing development strategy will bring present and future generations all closer attaining great heights and reaching all the places we have never been, - sustainable quality livelihood. The challenges of the continent are multifarious, just as there are multifarious solutions available. Making the right choices and implementing appropriately policy decisions is what stands between sustainable development and decay, hope and despair. Hence the need for new paradigms and pathways, including visionary leadership style focused on citizen-centred developmental approach for economic growth that is inclusive of social and environmental sustainability. The recently published World Bank Report (2012) aptly concludes that 'inclusive green growth is necessary, efficient and affordable, the search for solutions needs to shift from search for more financial resources, to getting smart'.

Getting smart means building the human resources capacity of the people to pilot and own their development pathway: as well as seeking sustainable solutions to empower and advance the case of women, youths and children.

Leaders around the world have continuously echoed that 'technological innovations will be central to the creation of a new and more sustainable development.' Therefore, embarking on the right kind of science, technologies, innovations and entrepreneurship is at the heart of sustainable development (UNESCO 2012, UNEP 2011, UNDP 2012, and UNCTAD 2012). Underscoring the selection of the right science and technology is the role and place of human capital development in the process of quality services delivery and sustainable livelihood for all citizens (AUC 2011, Beebe Maria et al 2003). Well into the 21st century, women in Africa continue to face boundar8ies in terms of access to education, employment, healthcare, security and safety. These boundaries are particularly acute on the continent; where well over half of the population is female. Women of Africa who face these obstacles every day also hold the wealth of potential and power; take the right actions to find the resolutions necessary. Women's human capacity should be developed, empowered and encouraged to take-up science related disciplines. A discipline that bypasses the female gender as of now. Presently, Africa's deficiency in human capital development is alarming. The continent should gun for knowledge, influence, improvement and progress. Without substantial increase in human capital development, the continent can neither be a veritable player in the global scene, nor take advantage of the virtues of globalisation. Currently, the continent is suffering from the vices of globalisation because of its weak science and technology basis, poor human capital development, low innovation and entrepreneurial skills (Forje 1989, Beebe et al 2003, Gerschenkron 1962, LPA 1980).

Africa's state of underdevelopment has much to do with inappropriate policy formulation. The continent is quick in the implementation of inappropriate policies. This is largely due to the lack of political will to implement policies geared towards citizen-focused development agenda or negotiated agreements and international commitments: global mechanisms and institutions that favours balanced or binomial relationships between the global north and the global south with knowledge, technologies and innovations predominantly flowing from the former to the latter: and general inequities in the distribution of skills and capacities for innovation and wealth creation. Africa cannot afford to remain recluse of the emerging global realities and social economic, environmental and technological change: neither should the continent remain a global consumer of knowledge, technologies and innovations in the new global architecture that is emerging today. The general feeling is that the global governance architectures be it at the socio-political, economic or environmental realms leaves the continent disadvantaged in many ways. The First African Forum on Science, Technology and Innovation (STI) jointly hoisted by the Government of Kenya, United Nations Economic Commission for Africa (UNECA), The Association for the Development of Education in Africa (ADEA) and the United Nations Educational, Scientific and Cultural Organisation (UNESCO) emphatically called on African countries to strengthen among other things, design STI policies and programmes to implement strategies to support growth, employment, sustainable and human capital development. No doubts, institutional construction and infrastructure - roads, rails, and secured, efficient and sustainable energy supply among others are needed to spur development. Each country should start anticipating the creation of "Science Parks." This requires cooperation, partnership, and participation of the State (Ministries of Higher Education, Scientific Research, Commerce and Trade, Universities etc.), individuals, and the private sector.

Conceptual Departing Premises - Scraping the Path of Dependency

A study of this kind entails incorporation of many disciplines and theoretical conceptual issues. No single theoretical approach provides the way forward for Africa in addressing its plethora of problems. The focus is on the virtues of capitalism and socialism impacting on what path of construct the continent should build on. Colonial and post-colonial Africa has been brain-washed to adopting the capitalist approach is the path of transformation. The objective assigned to the paper is to draw on the best of these two contesting views on which a developmental capable state with the final objectives of moving away from a backward to a service delivery society. The overall focus is getting out of the dependency construct that has and continues to fashion the development path of the continent. Hence the conceptual departing premises focuses on the developing a conceptual approach from some existing literature and practices of two approaches, capitalist represented by Adam Smith (1776) and Rostow (1960) the socialist represented by Marx () and Rodney (1967) and to build on the

(Gerschenkron ,1962, and Amin….) as a middle way to transforming the continent. This provides a comparative analytical approach on the different manifestations, causes and effects of contemporary Africa path to development.

As a result, it combines different and multi-disciplinary approaches in retrospective and prospective terms. Finally, it gives the continent a multi-layer analysis for African countries, the reason and meaning or the adoption of an inclusive concept of institutions for the countries in terms of structural or informal social capital, patterns of behaviour, norms and perceptions with a focus not only on a macro- but also meso- and micro-levels model comprehensively tilted on the quality livelihood of the citizens While European capitalism collectively moved in between the frontiers of free market and welfare (Britain), or between the so-called Protestant type capitalism or social capitalism (Germany, Scandinavian, France) or small entrepreneurships and network capitalism (Italy) and transition capitalism (Eastern Europe). African capitalism concentrated on Wealth accumulation for the individual. The absence a middle-class at independence accelerated the State to proceed on capitalist path without a human face which implied privatising state properties in the interest of the Head of State and his new African stets should have at least evolve on the path of the Scandinavian model or cronies. The trying a combination of free market and welfare (capitalism with a difference or human face).

It is hoped that with a paradigm shift through visionary leadership focused on the people, a new form of African capitalism with a human face or structured refined socialism with competitiveness and the challenging and hybrid forms of transition able to create a strong economic and social convergence among all countries into a single integrated model befitting the continent. In these light, new technologies, provides great opportunities for Africa but these technologies are only a tool. Innovation will not come from there but from developing human capacity as well developing the continent's leadership. Such a leadership must focus on education. Africa remains underdeveloped due to its poor human capital transformation. How else can we explain why Africa is not producing entrepreneurs, inventors, scientist's engineers and so forth to kick-start the economic transformation of the region? Yet within the Diaspora there are Africans and people of African descent excelling in various fields. They are excelling because of the education system and environment which permits creative and critical thinking and to explore the environment which stimulates and demands progressive actions not backstabbing, and repeating the old story, John is a boy taught to children; and Who is John the teacher will ask; he is a boy, the students will answer at the top of their voices. That has to change with the students, asking why he or a boy is. The education system is repetitive and thus has failed and would continue to fail the majority of African people. The continent needs a new education system designed to be progressive, inquisitive and enables them to graduate with usable skills, become job-creators (entrepreneurs, inventors Etc.) and not job-seekers in public offices. The continent for now is whitewashed with an education system that does not stimulate creative, inquisitive thinking and neither stimulates nor demand action, which unfortunately makes us churning out graduates with beautiful paper certificates and nothing tangent to contribute to the society, In Cameroon, the education system is tilted towards what is called the ***"number pay slip syndrome"*** getting employed by government. An education system that breeds corruption, eschews corruption (Forje 2004).

An approach of this nature makes it necessary to exceed the contradictions and the assumptions of modern capitalism and socialism and to situate Africa within an emerging context of finding its own path to development. By adopting a middle-of the road way, is already a controversial issue in the eyes of many. In short, the paper attempts to construct a 'middle-of-the-way' road between the theories of Rostow's Stages of Growth (1960) and of the Economic Backwardness of (Gerschenkron, 1962) constituting the late-comer advantage of states. How relevant is it to replace any stretch of explanation of the evolutions in the history of the development of the two systems? It boils down to locate and explain the induced socioeconomic transformation in present day context. It is not a question of moving away from capitalist to the socialist mode of development, but what best practices can be deduced from the two systems much relevant to the need and aspiration of the African continent in its transformation process. Could the developmental approach fashioned in" Ujamaa" (Nyerere, Hyden 1968) and the South Africa" Ubuntu" be the way for a new developmental construct of African states. How do these or a combination of these approach tie within the 'globalisation' banwagon of the 21st century and beyond? The capitalist mode of development is based on the nationalisation of the collective activities of the people for the good of a select few. And the socialist ideological orientation is nationalisation of the collective activities of the people for the collective good of the people. The vices of capitalism are what are being forced down the throats of African countries. Africa has so far accepted the vices of capitalism, or capitalism without a human face which places the continent on the wrong side of capitalist development. And the underdevelopment continuum in general. There has to be a change - constructive, positive and rewarding to all.

"Capital" means wealth and 'wealth' is considered as the means of production. With the two concepts playing a pivotal role, the critical works of scholars like Marx capitalism as mode of production, in which, the fundamental social report is the wage-owner, when part of the population can remain only to selling its working strength in goods which is the heart of capitalism The works of Max Weber, Adam Smith, Schumpeter, Samir Amin, Walter Rodney among others become pertinent in analysing the developmental path of African countries. The underdevelopment of Africa is correlated to be inferior trading position with the developed countries. Because of their poor human capital development, these countries are exploited and made to remain raw material producing and export nations. It was for these reasons that the colonial master did very little in translating science and technology related books into local languages; or disciplines like biology, chemistry, biology, physics engineering etc. were given little prominence in the school curriculum in Africa. A conscious collective mobilisation was adopted to keep Africa as supplier and consuming entity. The plurality of the vices of capitalism and socialism gives evidence of differences and the need to fashion out a new way (even though it may have its weakness) for Africa to start rebuilding and exploiting the virtues of the 'late-comer advantage.' Colonialism has not ended. The new ruling elites are growing steady and fuelling the 'neo-liberalism' doctrine, the historic mission which" Franz Fanon aptly expressed in The Wretched of the Earth, has nothing to do with transformation of the nation; it consists, prosaically, of being the transmission line between the nation and a capitalism rampant through camouflaged" (Pilger, 2012).

Africa's development is enveloped in the hot air of in corporate speak, with Wall Street determining bother the macroeconomic and microeconomic development path delivered into the hands of international capital. This new economic apartheid is now being strengthened as African countries complies with the demands of 'western 'interests' is opposed to their own. In addition, the arrival of China as a new colonial power and contender for the resources of the continent, though without the economic and military threats of Europe and America, has provided new impetuses for further western military expansion to accelerate the commerce, Christianity and civilisation mission much more aggressive than ever before. Nwokeabia (2009) argues that with private and unrewarded knowledge bearers innovating in isolation and dyeing in the same fashion, the continent has experienced "continuous but non-additive innovation system" as against "continuous and additive innovation system." This differentiates innovation in Africa and in the developed countries. Malungu (2009) offers a creative innovative and holistic approach to understanding organisational leadership using the principles embodied in the African philosophy of personhood known as 'ubuntu' - or the essence of being human. It is a principle that includes sharing and collective ownership of opportunities, responsibilities and challenges, the importance of people and relationship and decision-making, loyalty, reconciliation, experimental learning and knowledge management. Pushing the discourse further, Varlet (2008) in the Human Peron, tak3s the stand point of the clash of civilisation, illustrating the potential of a dialogue based on the dignity of the human person, i.e. a person is a person through other persons, which is the central idea of the (South) African 'Ubuntu' philosophy, contrasting the views or Senghor, Nkrumah and Nyerere; points out how 'ubuntu' not only shares similar concerns about interpersonal relations but also attempts to come to terms with present-day requirements and hindsight. It highlights 'ubuntu's potential to p4omote corporat3 life and reconcile it with African concerns for consultation and participation. It widens the debate on western perception on development in transitional polities on corporate culture, social pluralism and sustainable development.

While Chlbanda (2010) Entrepreneurship in Africa explores how mindset and attitude affect our enterprises. It offers a 3-dimensional approach to entrepreneurship, management financial and spiritual, that entrepreneurship is a journey full of surprises - joy, trials and tribulations. It penetrates into questions of how to survive in business; what money is; how does sin affect business; does positive thinking really help in this situation. Transformation in Africa is often juxtapose with myths and other othe4r factors that often hold back creativity and innovation. Hence the call for change in mindset, attitude and behaviour is very pertinent in the sustainable transformation of the continent. The capitalist economy is regulated by the market and profit is often heard as economy of companies. The socialist economy is return power to the people and for the collective good. We have to understand these concepts to better sketch the various process and connotations even their transformation from time past to link with the world of the 21st century. How can the suggested middle of the road approach fit in the technological advances of this century governed by a knowledge-based economy is what this paper attempt to ravel with.

Fundamental Issues and Challenges

Africa cannot afford to remain recluse of the emerging national and global realities and social economic challenges of the time. There is an urgent need for strategic long-term transformative reforms in its knowledge structures (from mono-disciplinary certificate education to trans-disciplinary systems studies, entrepreneurship and innovation capacity development) institutions and governance structures (from neo-colonial knowledge dependence to governance structures that are fully embedded in Africa's socio-political, economic and cultural realities). It is time added value be given to indigenous knowledge and cultural values in the development process to increase knowledge circulation and networks (i.e., enhance intra-Africa knowledge flows and networks), and development pathways to enhance transition towards poverty reduction and wealth-creation for inclusive growth and development of the continent.

A new paradigm shift is imperative in the institutional and social structures needed to deliver on sustainable structural transformation towards inclusive growth and shared prosperity in Africa. This includes new forms of public policies shaped by new models of innovation that enhances resources efficiency, resources productivity, greening economics, greening industries and decoupling economic growth from social and environmental impacts, among others. Achieving such goals require comprehensive interface participation among the various stakeholders, promoting privatisation and commercialisation of enterprises, innovation incubation, entrepreneurship and private-public partnership (PPP) in both national, intra-African and new global economy.

It requires building indigenous knowledge and linking it with modern science and technology that Africa can own its development path. The true path for Africa is through fair and trade with Europe and not aid from Europe. 'Fragmenting Africa and remaining through deadly trade arrangements in a manner that undermines internal African integration literally enslaves the African economy' (Soludo 2012:14) which perpetuates the state of abject poverty and corruption. Through education, research, science and technology, innovation, fair trade and good governance endurable change and sustainable development would come the way of African countries. Visionary leadership is imperative to pilot the way towards a new Africa.

This is the only way we can have the Africa we want. An Africa that makes use of its resources to promote the wellbeing of its people and humanity. An Africa that has sovereignty over its resources, development path and future as well as wield respect and is respected within the community of nations. It is only by investing in human capital (education), good governance, science and technology, innovation, entrepreneurship and developing our indigenous knowledge in line with technological advancement to give added value to our human and natural resources. This requires opening up space for participation and integration so that the peoples' voices are heard and inclusion of all the stakeholders will inform the new development agenda, owned, executed and prioritised by the people.

Soul searching and hard questioning must be asked to seek the correct solutions and make the right choices that best transform a backward economy into quality services delivery economy in order to attain and ensure sustainable quality livelihood for the citizens? This begs the following question;

- How Africa can surmount its underdevelopment, exploitation and marginalisation saga.
- How to make Africa felt in the world apart from its abundant natural resource's wealth? And sow the seeds that the future of the world is Africa.
- How do we ensure that all people especially the most vulnerable and marginalised have the food, water, energy, healthcare, shelter and education that is needed to turn around their current predicaments to betting living standards?
- How can employment be meaningfully approached in Africa? How can job-creation be stimulated and sustained?
- How do we empower the largest population group (woken who constitute more fifty-two percent of the population in many countries, with abort seventy percent involved in the private or informal economy sector) to be an integral part of the transformation process?
- What plans has the continent for its bursting and energetic youthful population (the largest youth group in the world) in preparing them as the future custodians of the continent?

- What policies and practices best promote equitable empowerment of the weak and marginalised to ensure adequate standards of living?
- What has Africa learned from existing Millennium Development Goals (MDGs) and what should be added/updated/modified, or is a different approach needed? (Thigo 2012).
- What does the private sector in Africa need to unlock its innovated potentials to get the economy of the group?
- What form of public/private/civil society interface to strengthen participation, change development, progress and sustainability for the continent?
- How can the continent's natural resources presently a curse is converted into a blessing for the good of the region?
- What are the twists and turns of the continent's transformation process?

The right answers, choices and proactive action strategy must be the goal in reviving a continent stuck on the run-way for take-off to a quality services delivery society. This can only be achieved when the people are empowered with the tool and weapon of information and knowledge, the use of science and technology, positively exploiting their potentials and creating a new mindset of the people of Africa nourished by the devotion and sense of purpose of all stakeholders including the Diaspora quietly working together for the common good of the continent. The secret for Africa's sustainable transformation is to have no fear, but put to rest the colonial saga; while drawing valuable lessons from its dark past to forge ahead with the construction of a united continent - Pan-Africanism and African Renaissance (Forje 2011). One can only but agrees with Balfour (2012:8): 'its s quite frustrating that we do not seem to learn from history, and as a result, aspiring African leaders continue to be use by the big powers. If we are to change tomorrow, we are going to have to look back in order to look forward. We will have to look back with some courage, warm our hands on the revolutionary fires of those who came before us, and understand what we have lost and to build a new humanity for ourselves

Exploiting the Late-comer Advantage

The quadruple challenges of imploding economics, deepening and widening poverty, social injustices within countries and between North and South necessitates a careful rethinking of knowledge platforms and development pathways at global, continental and national scales. Given that a pragmatic assessment of global development trends and resource potentials suggest Africa is on the move (UNDP 2012), and the natural and technical resource and productivity potentials for green growth is substantial. Africa is the future. Vast opportunities exist for home grown development on the continent, but the STI capacities and human capital potentials of African countries remain dismal (Urjama et al.2010). Though Africa's scientific capacities and Gross Domestic Products (GDP) growth have improved during the past decade, technological and innovation capacities remain low and the requisite institutional and governance infrastructures are only just emerging (UNESCO 2010, UNDP 2012). The rest of world has noticed. These trends; foreign direct investment in Africa has more than doubled over the last decade. Africa has emerged as one of the favoured global investment destinations, especially by investors seeding portfolio diversification or to tap into the continent's high economic growth that is expected in coming decades. The Diaspora has equally intensified its interest in the continent looping at remittances sent back which are more than foreign aid to the continent. 'There is no doubt that Africa's economic take-off is well under way, and there are compelling reasons to believe it will continue' (Newson 2012:24).

The successful application of pockets of research, STI within the information and communication and other factors, is contributing to the sustained economic growth in the continent over the last decade; generally, the continent lags behind in skills and competencies required to fully reap the benefits offered by STI and the virtues of globalisation. This is attributed to many factors, but key among these are the lack of skills and capacities in the area of STI to guide and foster an African development agenda, inadequate implementation of STI policies and programmes, and limited political commitment. Africa is suffering from the vices of globalisation because of its weak science and technology base which makes it impossible for the continent to benefit from the late-comer advantage (Gerschenkron 1962). On the Other hand, the pockets of successes of STI in Africa indicate the virtues of being a late-comer. Africa has to tape to the phenomenon of Gerschenkron thesis of a "late-comer advantage."

African countries do not have to thread on Rostow's (1960) Stages of Development Thus research, science, technology and human capital development has changed the dynamics of change, development and progress process as well as improving the living standards of citizens. Of course, this implies building her human capacity and infrastructure as well as making proper use of its resources. Visionary leadership with a citizen-focused agenda is an imperative input in the crusade of converting a backward economy into a service delivery economic society. A responsive international community towards the emerging aspiration of people in Africa is also part of the deal. Fair trade and respect for the sovereignty of these countries, aid without conditions and good governance remain integral components for pushing forward an equitable and shared-prosperity society. It is only through participations, partnership between the public/private sector and civil society that inequality and abject poverty can be successfully fought and eradicated.

The key to unlock underdevelopment and Africa's potential is investment in social entrepreneurship and education. Across the continent, advancement in science and technology is having profound impact across all sectors of the economy and society: from nomads using mobile phones to check livestock prices, farmers using this gadget to check the price of coffee in different markets, to members of the Diaspora being able to stay in close contact with their business partners and to transfer money to wherever it is needed. Unfortunately, industrial growth is limited by the poor state of infrastructure in the region. That is why targeted investments in all facets of development - in close partnership with African business community - should be a top priority for national government, Regional Economic Communities (RECs) the African Union (AU) and the international community.

Just as the world's economic centre of gravity is shirting North to South and West to East, and traditional donors deal with a financial crisis that is impacting their aid assistance to Africa (and the Diaspora fill the gap), the (BRICS) nations (Brazil, Russia, India, China and South Africa, are developing a new focus on South-South relationship is developing and exerting their ever-increasing influence in a number of key areas, not just within the global economy. More South nations like Nigeria, Egypt, Morocco, Ghana and Mexico can join the club to give more clout to African countries in their struggle to overcome their transformation predicament.

Deepening Africa's regional integration will be crucial in building its trade capacity and forging greater unity among states. As late-comers, these countries can draw valuable lessons from others that have gone through the debacles of underdevelopment and should be able to adopt the best practices, thereby making natural resources a total blessing to the continent. A particular area is the agricultural sector of ensuring food security in the continent and the rest of the world. Unfortunately, for now, Africa is still a net importer of food, with Egypt being the world's biggest importer of wheat, and Nigeria the world's biggest importer of tomato paste, even as 300,000 metric tons of tomatoes perish across the country every year. Interestingly, agriculture dominants the economies of most African countries, including large oil producers such as Nigeria. But yields remain the lowest in the world. The African Human Development Report commissioned by the UNDP (2012) notes: "countries must put into place policies which provide farmers with the inputs, infrastructures, and incentives that will enable them to lift productivity." Prioritising agriculture is the way forward for food security on the continent. The issue of agricultural transformation and food security in Africa is strongly linked to capacity development, infrastructure, labour and growth. This will also accelerate innovation, entrepreneurship and the creation of industries

The 2012 African Capacity Indicators Report (ACBF) points out that 'the Economics of most African countries are agricultural (and) agricultural labour comprises 59% of the total labour force in Africa (this in fact is the figure quoted in 2011 by the UN Food and Agricultural Organisation) and 13% of value added to GDP in 2009 (World Bank Report, 2011). Thus, agricultural growth holds the key to overall growth and development in Africa.' It is imperative for continent to prioritise agricultural transformation and Food processing as the key to kick-start the growth of entrepreneurship and job creation. For this and other reasons why improving the productivity and economic returns of agriculture will have profound impact on poverty reduction and hunger elimination in at least three important ways: (i) increase in the productivity and incomes of the majority of Africa's poor who work primarily in agriculture - woken for example: (ii) reduction in food Prices which affect real incomes and poverty in urban areas: (iii) generates important spill over to the rest of the economy. Empowering women through education, credits, assess to land titles and good farm to market connectivity will go a long way in accelerating agricultural productivity. Agriculture as a key sector for sustainable transformation of the continent cannot be left in private sector caretaker management and peasants.

The state must play the active role by focusing on implementing a comprehensive agriculture policy strategy with infrastructure development as the key pillar. The views of the Mo Ibrahim, founder and chair of the Mo Ibrahim Foundation should be serious taken: 'Africa is a rich continent. Our poverty is self-inflicted. How cans agriculture which provides 59% of the total labour force in Africa and yet we do not have the political will to improve the sector is really a problem. Agriculture is not backward it can be an engine for growth. All developed economics have powerful agricultural sectors. In fact, food production is more strategic than oil; and food is going to be very important and strategic factor in development in the future. So, African governments had better have their acts together. Therefore, public/private sector/civil society and international community participation and partnership interface constitute the backbone that can uplift the continent out of its backwards or underdevelopment debacle at a time when the continent is fast emerging as the fastest urbanising region in the world and currently with some of the world's fastest growing economies.

Again, the gender gap or disparity is a worrisome factor in the development process of the continent. A new attitude and strategy towards agriculture and female gender participation in the development process is imperative. It is pertinently vital for research institutions in the region to uncover critical factors in the political economy of change, development and progress including the long-term commitment of decision-makers to national development goals, accountability, food security, and good governance. The views of Frannie Leautier (2012) (CEO, ACBF) summaries the place of agriculture as the key capacity development issues and challenges facing African countries; *'the issue of agricultural reform and food security in Africa is strongly linked to capacity development, labour and Growth.' She adds that 'The ACI Report constitutes a definitive knowledge product targeting policymaker, public sector officials, the private sector and civil society, guiding the development of their priorities by providing practical recommendations.'*

In short, together, the public/private/ civil society and the international community provides a comprehensive interface in making Africa's voice heard and presence felt positively across the world. The problems of the continent must be tackled simultaneously. Poverty, corruption famine, poor leadership and governance fuels misery which, in turn, breeds despair, rejection, hopelessness and destructive frustration. With regards to conflicts and wars, there is no chance of lasting peace and good governance without development. Without change, development, and social justice there can be development, progress and sustainability (DPS) ensuring endurable quality livelihood for all. Neglecting the agricultural sector is neglecting and depopulating the rural areas, as the young are not interested in farming with agriculture being undertaken largely by the old or very young. The fast-growing young population prefers living in urban areas only to add to the problems of social exclusion, crimes, poor housing, and other factors contributing to poor living standards. The root causes of poor living standards are many and varies (poverty of knowledge, material/financial, moral, ethics and governance, poor use of resources) to list but a few.

What is rally at stake today? A new well-articulated approach to development, innovation, entrepreneurship, public/private/civil society partnership and political culture. For sure, we know a lot of the historical past and the legacies of colonial rule. We know of the commonality of the African people but failed to utilise this in advancing policy strategies that constructively addresses the vices of foreign rule and exploitation. Both at the national, sub-regional and continental levels, as well as within the countries and communities, our main headache is in the field of politics and leadership (good governance). The political arena should have helped the continent in forging common political values, economic science, technological capabilities, norms and forums that could formalise and cement the myriads of submerged as well as still visible traditional /cultural heritage bonds that manifest along all our national borders and inside Rather, Africa has engaged in the same paths like the colonial masters of the bygone era and even invent new ones (presidents for life) to cause more bloodletting for the sole purpose of remaining in power. Take the Nordic countries for example, how people have prospered in peace and cooperation. They succeeded to leave behind them and forged new bonds. Cross-border co-operation in peace and development needs political will and new sense of leadership direction as well as understanding, creating a new cooperative political and people-focused development mindset.

For now, we operate on the principles of survival of the fittest. Africa should move away from the guiding principle of survival of the fittest to survival of all. That is what a citizen-centred development strategy is all about. Africa should incorporate the Concert of *'ubuntu,'* a South Africa philosophical term that imbues attitudes of reconciliation and forgiveness in the process to heal the wounds of 50 years of destructive development, exploitation and marginalisation at the national and global levels. African states have over the past half-a-century alienated itself from one another. Yet the fulfilment of one becomes a condition for the fulfilment of the other, hence the first article of the Universal Declaration of Human rights urges us in the direction of: *'All human beings are free and equal in dignity and rights. They are endowed with reason and conscience and should act towards one another in a spirit of brothers/sisterhood.'* Most African constitutions are endowed with these words or concepts, but never make efforts in the genuine process of implementation. Can all the stakeholders local and international operate within a new citizen-focused paradigm for Africa to regain its place within the community of nations?

African Capacity Building Index

With a low human capacity development, the continent cannot derive many benefits either from its natural resources or from the science and technology advancement and the globalisation bandwagon of the 21st century. Reliable information from the African Capacity Building Foundation (ACBF) in its African Capacity Indicators Report (ACIR), flagship document launched in London on 3rd April 2012, shows that in developmental states such as China, *'the world has seen rapid growth, which has resulted from the State playing a controlling role in development while permitting private ownership and entrepreneurship at the same time. An active state is not necessarily a repressive one. The world is beginning to realise that so-called 'free market' government's (mostly in the West) also exercise a tremendous amount of control through protectionist measures - and these are primarily to do with agricultural trade.'* the livewire of African countries. The West injects imbalances in trade which African countries mostly need to spur their socio-economic and technological transformation.

In the long saga of transforming Africa into a developmental service delivery state, 'capacity building' is the key. The New Partnership for Africa's Development (NEPAD), sees its development trajectory moving in the direction of a winning strategy for building the continent's capacity in at least the following areas:

- *The efficacy of the African Peer Review Mechanism (APRM) where good governance is being instilled as the best practice in the governance system of African states.*
- *In the agricultural structure where NEPAD has designed the Comprehensive Africa Agriculture Development Plan (CAADP) which all African countries have now joined:*
- *Progress in developing Africa's transport infrastructure, where in cooperation with the African Development Bank / (ADB) implementation of the Short-Term Action Plan and regional projects throughout Africa has already received more than USA 3bn dollars in investment:*
- *Initiative and action plan designed to ensure sustainable development and poverty eradication (Mayaki 2012)*

The African Capacity Index (ACI) ranks countries according to the way they have implemented their capacity building strategies. Ghana which was ranked 5th in 2011 based on 2009-10 performance now occupies the number 1 high ranking position with 60.2 points. Madagascar is ranked 42nd. No country apart from Ghana with 'high' has the 'very high grade' which is a score from 80 and above. Most countries fall within the category of medium (13), 22 countries as low, and six countries with the ranking of 'very low' which include Angola, Djibouti, Guinea, Madagascar, Mauritania and Mauritius. The following North African countries convulsed by the Arab Spring revolution in 2011 were not included. Tunisia, Libya, Egypt, Algeria, and others such as Sudan, Somalia, Comoros and Seychelles were not surveyed and included. See Table 1 with some of the selected countries. The ACI Index measures the policy environment, the processes for implementation, the development results at country level, and the capacity development outcome. It is a very rigorous ranking system that includes figures from the World Bank and the African Development Bank / (ADB)

Table 1 Country Capacity Levels in 2012

Country	ACI 2012 Value	Rank
Ghana	60.2	1
Kenya	58.1	2
Burkina Faso	53.4	3
Ethiopia	52.8	4
Rwanda	51.9	5
Nigeria	50.5	6
Mali	50.3	7
Zambia	49.7	8
Zimbabwe	48.6	9
Uganda	45.2	10
Benin	43, 4	11
Senegal	42.7	12
Gabon	40.4	13
Cape Verde	40.2	14
Burundi	39.5	15
Tanzania	37.6	16
Cameroon	37.3	17
Morocco	36.2	18
Liberia	35.6	18
South Africa	26.0	28
Lesotho	24.6	31
Botswana	23.1	33
Togo	20.7	35
Chad	20.2	36
Angola	17.2	38
Mauritius	14.8	40
Mauritania	14.6	41
Madagascar	10.2	42

Source. Compiled from New Africa (2012) see article by Baffour Ankomah (2012) 'The way Forward - Prioritising Agriculture, No.517, 46th 2012, p61

The Diaspora as a Veritable Partner.

The poor state of Africa's capacity building and agricultural setting calls for a new strategy of 'rethink, reorganise, reinvent and reorganise state construct, policy formulation and implementation action. It equally calls on the role of the Diaspora as the sixth region of the continent to be more constructively engaged in the *rethink, reorganise, reinvent and reorganise* construct. The Diaspora, no doubts has much to contribute in the (4Rs) development strategy in uplifting the pathetic situation of the continent within the rapidly changing global environment. On the one hand is loss of human strength – drain; on the other, have a gain in the case of what the physical loss of human resources injects into society – gain; which in short is 'brain drain' and 'bran gain.'

In an age of scientific and technological advancement and with Africa constrained within the confines of shrinking agriculture and underdevelopment, it is only but wise that all resources be mobilised for comprehensive implementation policies on the 4Rs. While there has been some degree of positive political surprises on the continent (Ghana's election and smooth leadership transition and capacity ranking, see Table 1, Senegal's election and leadership transition (2012) and leadership transition in Ethiopia after the death of President Meles Zenawi, 2012) and other developments in recent years, the continent is backsliding in quality livelihood and capacity building in such critical areas as education, poverty alleviation, corruption eradication, innovation, press freedom, the rule of law, and the rights of civil society - is a sobering reminder that the institutions anchoring democratic governance cannot achieved by protests at one. Given all these setbacks notwithstanding, if there is an overwhelming message for the years ahead, it is one of hope and not of reversal. That message of hope is what all lovers, friends and sympathisers of the continent must capitalise on to ensure that Africa is constructively engaged and benefits from the new knowledge-based global economy. A new strategic compass for redirecting the predicament of the region towards a service delivery society is most needed.

The Diaspora seems to present that hope. Just as the Diaspora championed the struggle for self-determination, the optimism for the Diaspora repeating that trend is more pronounced today than ever before. The new mood of cooperation between Africa and the Diaspora is because in 2003 the AU decided to recognise the Diaspora as its sixth region. The creation of Africa's six regions by the AU is a critical move in recognising the role of the Diaspora in the constructive transformation of the continent. The last Global African Diaspora Summit (GADS) in South Africa, May 2012, brought the Diaspora and the continent much closer in shaping a new strategy for Africa. From remittances to human capacity skills the Diaspora stand a good chance of stimulating Small and Medium Enterprises (SME), promoting innovation and resurrecting disappearing indigenous knowledge as the peoples' contribution developing a developmental emerging polity. To what extent is the continent making proper use of this emerging connection?

Remittance inflows remain a major and stable source of external Finance for Africa

For many African countries, funds sent by migrants represent a lifeline that helps to smooth household consumption, increase foreign exchange reserves and allow for investments, including in small businesses and education. In 2016, the remittances-to-GDP ratio was 10% or more in seven countries, including Gambia, Lesotho, Liberia and Senegal – countries that tend to have large diasporas –, while remittances per capita were higher than USD 100 in nine African countries: See Table. Fifteen Largest Recipient Countries in Africa (ranked by % GDP 2016)

Table: Fifteen Largest Recipient Countries in Africa Ranked by % GDP 2016

Country	% GDP	USA Per Capital	Current USD	
Liberia	30.4		150.0	0.66
Comoros	21.4		161.4	0.13
Gambia	21.0		19.3	0.19
Lesotho	17.7		165.3	0.32
Senegal	13.2		127.4	1.96
Cape Verde	12.1		384.7	0.20
Togo	10.1		60.3	0.45
Morocco	6.8		209.9	7.10
Mali	6.6		55.6	0.94
Egypt	5.7		204.9	18.66
Guinea-Bissau	5.6		36.3	0.07
Sao Tome & Principe	5.5		93.5	0.02
Ghana	5.0		78.1	2.15
Nigeria	4.8		108.9	20.00
Tunisia	4.8		180.0	2.02

Source: Adapted from IMF (2016a) and World Bank (2016b)

Remittances remain an important source of external finance for Africa. They accounted for about 37% of total external financial flows in 2016. Migrant remittances to Africa have increased steadily since the mid-1990s, rising from USD 11 billion in 2000 to USD 64.8 billion in 2015. In 2016, total remittance inflows to Africa were USD 64.6 billion, about the same level as the year before. In addition to being less volatile than development aid and FDI, migrant remittance flows have the advantage of increasing inversely with the economic situation of recipients. Migrants are likely to send more money when difficult situations arise in their country of origin. This counter-cyclical nature of remittances can help to sustain consumption and domestic investment during headwinds. **Egypt and Nigeria continue to receive the bulk of remittance flows to Africa** the relative stability of remittance inflows to Africa hides important country and regional differences. At the regional level, West Africa and North Africa remain the biggest recipients of remittances (Figure 2.5). In 2016, these two regions accounted for 90% of remittances in the continent with Nigeria and Egypt accounting for 71% and 63% of remittances in West Africa and North Africa, respectively. The largest recipients of remittances in 2016 were Nigeria (USD 20 billion), Egypt (USD 18.7 billion), Morocco (USD 7.1 billion), Ghana (USD 2.2 billion), Algeria (USD 2.1 billion), Tunisia (2 billion) and Senegal (1.9 billion). Kenya and Uganda were the only countries in East Africa to surpass the USD 1 billion threshold, accounting for USD 1.6 and 1.1 billion, respectively. In Southern Africa, the largest recipient was South Africa, receiving USD 0.8 billion.

Each country should move from words to actions by creating critical enabling environments for the input roles of the Diaspora. Taking one or two examples, the role of the BRACED Commission (Bayelsa, Rivers, Akwa Boom, Cross River, Edu and Delta State, of Nigeria which has taken a bold initiative in shaping a new Nigeria to devise by devising a master economic plan that boost the six states of the Niger Delta region and the country itself. Planning the right strategy for investment, security and sustainable development, is vital for these states and Nigeria's take-off. It cannot be denied that people want to invest in Africa, as it has immense growth possibilities compared to other parts of the world. We just have to do our homework in order to take advantage of the opportunities.' (BRACED Commission, (2012) Leadership plays an important party. What these six states have demonstrated, is citizen-focused development approach.

Joe Keshi (2012) notes: 'if we promote the region as an investment haven, considering the resources we have in Oil and gas as well as agriculture, I believe that investors will come. The governors of the six states realise the importance of economic integration and are determined to drive the processes required to transform the region.' The Delta has created the Warri Industrial Business Park. In Calabar, Cross River State, the Tinapa Free Trade Zone exists, as part of the strategies for transforming the states into an ideal business destination, and as an integrated park comprising industrial and residential developments. The Tinapa Free Trade Zone is a Public Private Partnership (PPP) that establishes exciting and fruitful opportunities for trade, leisure and entertainment hub for Africa. This is national economic integration at work and with a difference. It should be emulated by other countries in strengthening and fostering Regional Economic Communities (RECs) and the eventual creation of an African Common Market. (Forje 1969).

The other example comes from the role being played by the Mo Ibrahim Foundation and other such institutions promoting the socioeconomic transformation as part of taping into the skills and knowledge capacities of the Diaspora. The case of Phil Emeagwalia (the Father of Internet or Africa's Bill Gate) for example is a thing for the continent to look into. According to Emeagwali (2003) 'ten million Africans now constitute an invisible nation that resides outsides Africa. Although invisible, invisible it is a nation as populous as Angola, Malawi, Zambia or Zimbabwe. If it were to be a nation with direct borders, it would have an income roughly equivalent to Africa's gross domestic product (24 October 2003). Take for example, "Mark Dean, an African-American inventor and computer expert who played the key role in the development of the PC and David Adjaye, the award-winning, world-renowned architect." (Djanie, 2011:45-46); Kwame Anthony Appiah, the 'post-modern Socrates' (Agyeman-Dush, 2012) or Lord Boateng, the First African - British Minister, (Gyasi 21011) or Barrack Obama (first African-American USA President). This is just a tip of the vast potential and resources of the Diaspora to be exploited to the maximum. It must therefore be because there is something seriously wrong with education system and the political environment of the continent. Mwamvenda and Lukhele-Olovenju (eds.) (2013) look at the Triumph and Prosperity of Education in Africa exposes the strides that the continent has made at all levels of the education system; expressing the concern that much has yet to be done to meet the rising needs and challenges of the continent. What medium of language is to be used given Africa's historical past with the imposition of the coloniser's language – English, French, Portuguese, and Spanish? These foreign languages have become predominant over existing indigenous languages to the point that it becomes the official language medium of institutions, a power message is registered and conveyed regarding the states of which language a country adopts. Local la use (Mwamvenda et al. 2013:50).

Presently, there are 1,400 languages spoken in 54 African countries. Which language to use becomes problem – politically and administratively; which may be a source for political instability. Whatever the case, the AU has to look into the issue, set up at least the notion of a regional language (e.g.) Swahili which has become a dominant language in Eastern, parts of Southern Africa, Central African Sub-region. We have to look for a common language that covers West Africa Sub-region. Africa, north of the Saharan region as Arabic which can be developed to cover the West African Economic region. The African Cultural Renaissance and the African Academy of Language has a heavy and noble task before it to come up with some common languages (say at least four that can be used within the continent; to organize for the regions, West Africa, East and Southern Africa; Central African sub-region and Northern Africa. For now, it looks like Swahili is fast making good breaking grounds in Easter, Southern and the Central African Sub-region. The Arabic language remains one that cannot be challenged in Northern African region.

Real education for colonial people would have inevitably meant unrest and revolt against the colonial order and as such colonial education was designed to inculcate obedience, servility and inferiority complex in the Africa. The new inheritors of power after the departure of the colonial master pursue the same old colonial policies to remain in power and as stooges of their masters. Why our educational system has not been reconstituted to give science and technology disciplines greater preference? Why are we shying away from these subjects, from introducing our mother tongue in the education curricula? Why do we continue to stress on ethnicity and tribalism as a factor in the political jig-saw when an election is lost, and not seeing ethnicity and tribalism asset contributing to the holistic development of society?

Africa has more academics with foreign degrees and more graduates with study abroad experience and has imported knowledge and Concerts from abroad than any other continent, making it possibly the most internationalised high education system in the world. Hence, innovation and change in internationalisation should come from Africa. (De Wit (2012). Unfortunately, Africa keeps copying wrongly western concepts, strategies and policies developed by their western counterparts without developing their own innovative ideas about how to internationalise their education systems. For the coming years, Africa's greatest resources will be its relatively large but young population. It should be cause for optimism, yet the current stampede for talent could contribute to ever more global polarisation, and comprise the negative impacts of brain drain for African universities. (Jowi, 2012). By creating an enabling environment for the Diaspora, the continent will be turning the brain drain into brain gain phenomenon hence increasing the human capacity building and innovative strength and entrepreneurial skills of the continent.

In May and June 2010, the Global University Network for Innovation (GUNI), the International Association of Universities (IAU) and the Association of African Universities (AAU) jointly carried out a survey of higher education institutions in Sub-Sahara Africa to determine what contribution they were making towards sustainable development. The initiativ3e was in response to a declaration by leaders of Africa Education Institutions (AHEI) at the 12th General Conference of the AAU in Nigeria in May 2009 calling on all stakeholders to take necessary steps to enable African Universities play a meaningful role in promoting sustainable development. Seventy-three institutions (response rate (18%) room 23 countries. Among the respondents, 69% were publicly funded institutions and 70% were Anglophone. From their responses it showed that:

- 41% had mainstream development degree course, most of these courses were run in public institutions and well over half offered compulsory development courses;
- 40% interdisciplinary sustainable courses most of these run-in public institutions and over half were offered as compulsory course:
- 26% institutions reported running specific sustainable development degree course of these institutions: 27% had courses in social sciences. 23% in natural sciences: 9% in engineering and: 7% in physical sciences.

Some of the barriers encountered hindering the introduction of sustainable development course were (i) lack of funding or finances-23%: (ii) lack of qualified staff 25%: and (iii) lack of awareness and information on sustainable development (17%. In addition, only 31% of the responding institutions have a faculty of education, and of these 30% was producing learning materials for schools of education for sustainable development. In terms of research, 60% of the respondent's institutions research and development represented 20% to 40% of all research undertaken in the institutions. Only 70% of the institutions were sustainable development research greater than 40% of all research.

In respect to partnership and community engagement, 60% partnered with local or national bodies, 55% with regional and international ones, 55% had developed non-formal or informal sustainable development activities targeting a variety of audiences such as government, the general public, industry, and teachers, students and others. Two-thirds (63%) of the respondents were also engaged in activities related to peace, security, and conflict resolution. Student - Staff exchange programmes 49% and internship 44%. And direct collaboration with the communities concerned 28% about 60% of the institutions were equally engaged in various activities to promote cultural diversity and inter-cultural dialogue and understanding (Mohamedbhal, 2012).

After decades of neglect and under-funding, African universities need serious restructuring, revitalisation and refunding to integrate their curriculum with the realities of the continent. There is an urgent need to teach and graduate students who go out to be job-creators (entrepre3nuership) and not as job seekers in the public sector. African institutions must ensure a comprehensive teaching of the realities of underdevelopment development related issues, science technology and cultural development. This fails in line with post Rio+20 ideas of reinvigorating political will and international community to implementing the goals and ideals of sustainable development and the urge for developing countries to proactively fulfil previous commitments and pledges to help Africa's effort to achieve sustainable development. It is not a question of policy formulation that the continent lacks (the Lagos Plan of Action 1980, AUC 2007, AUC 2011 for example), but the political will for constructive engagement and action is lacking. Adopting an Afro-centric strategic position - provides the alternative way forward.

Shaping the Future - Being Afro-Centric

Shaping the future of the continent requires building on African community, good governance, new leadership style and a serious change in mindset, attitude, behaviour and mentality towards their wellbeing. This should contribute to a more inclusive path to sustainability with unity, hard work, sense of direction, development and progress as the anvil on which to achieve new goals and objectives.

The Renaissance African Community (RAC) would make an extensive and continuous request to African governments to be proactive and citizen-focused in their policy articulation and implementation related activities. The Renaissance African Community (RAC) must emphasis as a priority right the best education tool about the change the people need and accept that impact on their wellbeing; government must stress and establish in all ministries a directory of Essential Services, Peace, Unity and Progress which should seek priority sustainable and social integration though out the continent;

- *seek new ways of thinking and behaviour and to eliminate all forms of discrimination, disunity, exploitation, poverty, corruption, social inequality;*
- *nurture a deep respect for life and the wellbeing of one and another;*
- *create unity and harmony, sense of common vision and purpose in fighting the light of the underdevelopment of the continent as one networking group;*
- *work towards sustainable peace, wellbeing and progress of the nation under the confines of good governance, rule of law, justice and equality - power to the people with equal opportunities for all to attain a perfect livelihood.;*
- *promoting social and solidarity economy (SSE) as alternative economic path*
- *building a climate trust, hope and confidence, equitable partnership and social relationship between Africa and Europe not a traumatic hegemonic centralised authoritarian relationship of domination, stigmatisation and exploitation of Africa by the North.*

Social and solidarity economic and alternative finance can provide a different development model as an alternative approach to socioeconomic transformation of Africa. This should be an approach centred on the values of genuine partnership, participation, cooperation and complementing mutual support, human rights and democratic principles. A new social contract for the 21st century is necessary and should evolve on the following pathways as response to the underdevelopment, global crises and challenges challenged of sustainability namely;

- Stabilising markets liberalism;
- Developing the African agricultural sector and market space;
- Embedded liberalism;
- Globalisation with a human face.

To better understand the developmental and emancipation impacts and implications of (SSE,) it is crucial to underscore how this connects to the state, the market, and to civil society networks and movements. In times of multiple crises and insecurity, a societal reaction of coping and transforming occurs to accelerate SSE initiatives. According to

Utting (2012), 'in crises times, three things happen; people assume more direct control of production they mobilise and attempt to change institutions and mainstream organisation, and elites adapt or at least in some form. This dynamic paradigm is now playing out in the field of social and solidarity economy.' In Africa, one in seven persons belongs to a cooperative. The cooperative model has been central in development and has adapted to include new forms of organising, such as women's self-help initiative organisations. Social and solidarity enterprises could represent the 'most advanced pole' in a strategy of up-grading informal economic enterprises. Informal economies (the backbone for the livelihood of the vast majority of the people and the country's economic enterprises) has significant levels of economic growth, but no improvements in employment conditions and many workers in the informal sector are subjected to great risk. Proper policy strategies can turn the deficiency into profitable avenue for the economic growth of the country. The informal sector is embedded with wide diversity of activities offering opportunities of 'making, innovating and producing. It is a Pandora box. Open it, explore, exploit and utilise the vast opportunities that it holds in terms of job-creation, innovation, small-scale enterprises and see how it can transform the wellbeing of citizens.

The Commonwealth Economic Forum (CEF 2012) and other such. Encounters provide a veritable platform for knowledge creation and awareness of public/private/civil society interface for shaping capitalism or socialism for national and global prosperity and economic growth. The universities provide the most enabling environments for pushing forward serious scientific discourses and bipartisan approaches seeking common grounds in galvanising the society towards a new direction in building a new country and continent. Unfortunately, the universities are so politicised that objective non-partisan dialogue can hardly take place. African universities and research centres have lost their sense of direction and roles as centres of scientific and critical excellence for society development. Instead, they have become breeding grounds for political party sing-praises, hand-clapping, motions of support to the governing party, corruption and articulate self-interests. These institutions should undergo serious mindset change paradigm shift and play the right role required of them. - To develop critical scientific minds for the advancement of society and humanity. The diamond jubilee of the Commonwealth Forum July 2012, Mansion House London, had essential sessions like:

- Improving the relationship between business and society;

- Small Medium Enterprise (SME) and entrepreneurship development.
- Learning from doing business in Emerging Markets.
- Developing successful Domestic capital markets.
- Utilising natural and human resources.
- The role of Financial Services in creating growth in the real economy, and
- Promoting the role of women in business

This is a forum which should attract Heads of States, Ministers, top policy-makers, public and private sector Chief Executive Officers (CEOs) and civil society organisations for building a better- and forward-looking platform for citizens-focused strategy in the participation, partnership, development dichotomy for change, progress and sustainable wellbeing of the citizens. Europe should not be the place for these kinds of awareness creation. Sessions for the sustainable transformation of the continent. National governments, the university environment, regional organisations should spear head conferences of these kinds with NEPAD, ECOWAS, CEMAC, SADC etc. playing vital roles of educating the people of their roles, responsibilities and obligations in the development process. A holistic strategic approach is required. Getting all the stake holders on board is essential, as well as ensuring social justice in the dividends of the fallout -shared-prosperity. The concerted effort and determination of all the people should lay the foundation necessary in building a strong progressive continent. So far, the individuals and the states have been too busy individualistic clamouring for self-basic needs. That should change towards the direction of nursing the basic needs of all citizens and our nations, rooted in common purpose, common planning and common endeavour. There is need for innovative communication to spread the ideals of 'make, create, innovate and endorse the entrepreneurial spirit for the progress of the region.

Social Economy Enterprises and Organisation (SEEOs) put people and their surrounding community, rather than financial profit, at the centre of their activities. They aim at creating both economic and social benefits. In a long-term prospect, the social economy can provide complementary paths to bring together in a coherent manner the concerns of economic sustainability, decent works, social justice, ecological balance, political stability, conflict resolution and gender equality. Social and solidarity enterprises could represent the most advanced pole in a strategy of up-grading informal economy enterprises' (Lapayre 2012).

Conclusion

Reviving the fortunes and Tapping into the Potentials of the Continent

Africa is confronted with vast challenges and opportunities. Whether it likes it not the challenges of the changing global economic space are numerous and growing by the day and propelled by the rapid advancement in research, innovation, science and technology. This constitutes Africa's greatest deficit given its poor human capital development. Faced with economic progress within the ambit of western economic meltdown and other financial crisis; it is poised to articulate new forward citizen-focused strategies to improve on its growth rate in the past couple of years. So far, the region remains mired in poverty, inequality, poor human development, poor healthcare, bad governance, and erratic and inefficient energy supply, weak linkages to the domestic and international economies with a skewed distribution of growth dividends. Equity in shared-prosperity does not exist. The continent is blessed with a rich agricultural sector but ineffectively and inefficiently used to ensure food security. Not more than 40% of its agricultural output is processed. Although agro-processing makes for 70% of manufacturing value added and nearly half of all exports in most less developed countries (LDC). To reap the benefits of its vast potential, it must go through a profound transformation of rural hinterland from subsistent household economy to modern industry, and a shift of resources and functions from farm to firm, with some entrepreneurship playing an equally important role.

A holistic approach that effectively mobilises the continent's productive potentials and addresses preconditions for agribusinesses growth by identifying the weakest links of the value chain (human capital development, science, technology, innovation, infrastructure) from farm to market and binding constraints for policy and investment must be adequately addressed. A number of strategies seem pertinent in the process of constructing a sustainable developmental society, namely:

- building the human capital capacity and other skills necessary as inputs to accelerate and consolidate the process of change;
- exploiting indigenous knowledge, local, regional and international demand and know-how:
- strengthening technological efforts and innovation capabilities:
- promoting effective and innovative financing

- stimulating public-private sector-civil society participation and partnership:
- improving infrastructure and access to efficient, infective and sustainable energy:
- promoting good governance.

An enabling business climate and good governance systems a prerequisite for nurturing participation through a mix of created competitiveness and intensified comparative advantage; the promotion of private sector development through development through investment supported by public goods; increasing the efficiency and productivity of local enterprises as well as encouraging entrepreneurship by ramming legal, financial and structural constraints as well as empowering the female gender participation in the process. It cannot be denied that strong visionary people-oriented leadership and public governance are more than ever necessary, including positive responding civil society towards such leadership that promotes openness, macroeconomic stability, mobilising domestic resources, high savings and investment rates, and market allocation of resources. Such policies will address education, market failures, promote fair trade and giving financial assistance to farmers especially women; support public/private sector partnership, dialogue and cooperation, as well as coordination among the stakeholders/actors in value-chains, regional integration, exchanges of best practices and South-South cooperation. The continent needs to link smallholder farmers to medium and large-scale agribusinesses. It needs to disconnect to reconnect in the overall interests of the people.

Africa's present and future needs fixing and quick too. This is the century for her to make concrete difference, create, innovate, and produce and sustainable progress (CIPSP). The 21st century offers the window of opportunity for the continent to unlock its human and natural resources potentials for its people and humanity. The caveat here is that the importance of the issue of the predicament and transformation of these states are well known by the Heads of States. The instruments for development exist and the continent can draw lessons from best practices - the late-comer advantaged (Gerschenkron 1962). In short, the important role for research, science, technology and innovation in fostering socio-economic development has been recognised by African Heads of States in their various declarations including the Lagos Plan of Action, the African Union/New Partnership for Africa's Development (AU/NEPAD).

A Consolidated Plan of Action and Policies of the Regional Economic Commission (RECs) and Member States are needed. Unfortunately, like most of policies, implementation has been constrained by a number of factors including the lack of political will, financial crises, political instability, imposed western financial trade etc. This is the age and time to be more imaginative, proactive, and action-oriented. Action-oriented does not exclude the pathways of being 'Afro-centric' with a strong difference. Being 'Afro-centric' entails taking into concrete actions issues, of indigenous knowledge, make, create, innovate, knowledge, influence improvement and progress.

It is time we face truism and not deny realty by grabbing the bull by the horns. Africa is underdeveloped, unable to feed its population, not able to process its raw materials, still lacking behind in terms of human capital development, the gap between the rich and poor widening more than ever, the gap between north and South not showing any signs of closing. A centre of the road has to be adopted. Convergence of opinions is necessary to find common grounds for the good of humanity, Are the leaders North and South ready to sink articulate self-interests and work for the common good? Will leaders of the South, Africa in particular stop bleeding their citizens to death?

Divergence and Convergence

The diversities of African states should be blessing not a curse. Politicians have made diversity a curse. The continent's economic and diversity should be a blessing as well. Countries should make efforts to diversify the economy, not to be dependent on one source of foreign exchange earnings. It means developing an entrepreneurial spirit, educating citizens, creating jobs, incorporating other stakeholders in the development process. The recent financial collapse indicates a taste of things to come. There has to be interplay between agency and structure. Equally important, the existence of a double inter-play - or between individuals and their physical and social environment producing institutions, then institutions themselves governor at least influence individual behaviour.

Change does not occur in a vacuum, but proceeds from socio-economic behaviours taking place in cultural contexts and mediated by institutions (Polanyi 1945, Granovetter 1985, Zukin and DIMaggio 1990). Africa has forgotten its cultural heritage. Yet culture can be defined as the product of 'specific interaction of human king and environment through time and it evolves not according to some rigid universal schemes, but according to a logic peculiar to each culture

(Mayhew 1989:321). First culture is the answer to the needs of human beings - a way of life through which communities survive and adopt (Hodgson 2001:292) Culture also play a major role in explaining growth and change in specific situations, as it has occurred for institutions such as family and religion (Basile 2005) Any country moves along a path defined by its own culture and history. Africa lost is cultural heritage and history totally distorted as a result of colonial rule. The continent must draw valuable lessons from that. It has to define its own development strategy and how to effectuate it.

Path development derives from choice and decisions of the past concealed in the institutions of today, while institutions are model themselves in cultures. These Africa's development (individual nations and the continent) should move along a path that they defined according to their past and taking cognizance of the global connectivity in which, all initial differences are assimilated and social relations converge towards a common pattern or goal which ought to be for the common good. The world is evolving fast. Thanks to strong investments in human capital development, especially the North and a few countries in the South in research, innovation, science and technology. As already noted, Africa has been wanting in this area. But quick to embrace the ideas of Wall Street which Pranab Bardhan (2007) aptly points out in these words: "A little decade ago, the American model of capitalism was triumphant. For many developing and transition economies in search of a model, there was only one prescription: liberalise, privatise and copy the Anglo-American institutions of legal, financial and corporate governance. Today there is less certainty. A standardised policy prescription that ignores social institutional diversities or the complexities of a particular society is a recipe for failure. The advocates of capitalism should try to protect it from the enthusiasts for a variety of capitalism."

Lessons Learned and Recommendations

The paper shows that the development debacle of Africa lies in the court of African countries to play the crucial role of introducing, re-enforcing and constructively implementing strategic people-focused development policy programmes. There is an indication for the rising importance of Africa in particular and in general South-South Coalition Cooperation (SSCC) in development cooperation: and the changing dynamics of the nature of transformation architecture itself to shift the discourse and processes from North- South to a stronger African focus (Afro-centric) and focus on South - South Cooperation (SSC). Of course, North-South dialogue and cooperation must be fostered as we are inhabitants of a common global village. It is question of de connecting to reconnect or what Samir Amin terms 'de-linking to re-linking.' A concerted policy of 'constructive disengagement' from the North as well as a comprehensive policy of 'constructive re-engagement' after some time could present the breakthrough - the Chinese example, may provide the way out.

The study travel discourse highlights the issue of visionary leadership and policy-makers need to do more; and that civil society should positively respond to policy strategies that make significant impact and changes in their wellbeing. There should be an African as well as global responsibility towards constructive engagement, change and progress for the common good. It has been demonstrated that the number one issue is developing the human capacity of the people to give added value to its abundant natural resources, empower all, financing, promoting social justice, enforcing the rule of law and closing all the gaps and weak links that perpetuates the underdevelopment of the continent. Yet these changes cannot be realised successfully without positive responses from the international community working in concert with Africa and the South. To focus on social humanity mainstreaming is essential. Importantly, the people must take the vital first move. The obligations and responsibilities are theirs. Whether the forces of colonialism have contributed to their plight is not the outstanding issue now. The issue in question is how to provide quality services to the people. Who does what, when where, why, and how is fundamental in the quality livelihood of the vast majority of citizens?

We live in a global community; humanity should be the goal for North and South. The global village is for present and future generations without the current generations compromising the rights and wellbeing of generations yet to come. It is within the possibility of science and technology to make even the Sahara bloom into a vast field with verdant vegetation for agricultural and industrial development. Time and space have been reduced to unimportant abstractions - thanks to science and technology and for the continent to exploit the "late-comer advantage." There are still many challenges, and Africans cannot afford to be complacent. With good leadership there are compelling reasons to believe that the continent would rise up to the challenges it faces. But it must start now to seriously ponder over what has to be done.

Africa should move away from developmental capitalism "without a human face" or centralised socialism that gives too much power to an individual to structural peoples' socialism that addresses the urgent need of the people, through and with the people and for the people in partnership with a cooperating and responsive private sector as well as a positive responding international community in addressing the urgent needs of the people. Therefore, a comprehensive structured people-oriented development strategy should be articulated and implemented. Concerted "political will" is needed and urgently too. People have to be galvanised, empowered and should take the challenges of development seriously now. All the development issues challenge as well as windows of opportunities must be appropriately communicated to the citizens. State-private sector-civil society and the international community must find common grounds how to move out of the underdevelopment construct and move forward to a sustainable quality service society for all. The challenge now is to ensure that Africa's renaissance does indeed continue. Efforts should be exerted to ascertain the economic growth rate stay high and, indeed, accelerate even further. Growth should be fair, inclusive and sustainable. That is why the continent should continue building on her young, growing - and increasingly healthy, well-educated and urbanised - population; as well as on its rich endowment of its natural resources. Or these reasons, articulate policies measures must be formulated and implemented towards political, economic, social and market reforms, which should make the future look attractive for a continent hoping to realise its development aspirations as well as for investors who wish to be part of that growth. Some of the strategic policy measures envisioned includes the following;

- Put in place comprehensive proactive policy strategies at home and targeting the Diaspora to improve competitiveness, public health, education and to provide other public goods,
- Visionary leadership for open governance and strong citizen-focused programmes.
- Concerted and comprehensive policy strategies on public-private sector-civil society development strategy; based on science, technology, innovation, entrepreneurship and development of indigenous knowledge;
- Female gender empowerment in all facet or aspects of life including the involvement of youths;
- Reforms and re-enforcing government policy on fighting corruption, poverty, injustice and exclusion; and job creation for the youths

- Fostering, national cohesion, unity and regional integration - the unity of the continent and sustainable wellbeing of citizens as the target.
- Improving the governance structure through free, fair, clean, competitive and transparent elections

References

Africa Capacity Building Foundation (ACBF) (2012) Africa Capacity Indicators Report (2012)

African Union Commission (2011) African Charter on the Values and Principles of Public Service and Administration, Addis Ababa, Ethiopia.

African Union Commission (2007) African Charter for Democracy, Elections and Governance, Addis Ababa, Ethiopia

Agyeman-Duah Ivor (2012) "Kwame Anthony Appiah - the 'Post-modern Socrates' Gets his honour," New African, April 2012, London, pp64-67

Baffour Ankomah (2012) 'NEPAD 10 Years and Counting', New African, No.517, 46th Year, May 2012, London, pp64-66

Baffour Ankomah (2012) 'The way Forward - Prioritising Agriculture', New African No. 517, .46th Year, May 2012, London, pp58-61

Baffour Ankomah (2012) 'Baffour's Briefs - Why Are We So Blessed?' New African, No. 519, 46th Year, July 2012, London, pp8-9.

Bardhan, Pranab (2007) "21st Century Capitalisms in Europe and Asia: Towards Convergence, Collision or Mitigation of Development Paradigms", (University of California, Berkeley and Chief Editor of the Journal of Development Economics, quoted from Yale Global Online and International Herald Tribune, 9 January 2007

Berbe Maria, Banji Oyeyinka et al (eds.) (2003) Africa Dot Edu. Its Opportunities and Higher Education in Africa. The McGraw Hill Publishing Company Limited, New Delhi, India

Biko Steve (1978). I Write What I Like. The Bowerdean Press and Harper & Row, Publisher, Inc.

BRACED Commission (2012) 'Braced for Impact' Special Report in New Africa, No. 517, 46th Year, May 2012, London, pp71-78

Chibanda Stewart /2010) Entrepre3nuership in Africa. The Spir4itual Dimension. Adonis & Abbey Publishing Limited, London &Nigeria

Djanie Akua (2011) "Education in Africa is Failing its People, - Reflections of an ordinary Woman" New African, 45th Year, No. 512, December 2011, pp46-47

Emeagwali Phil (2003) 'How Do We Reverse the Brain Drain? Keynote Speech delivered on 24 October 2003 at the Pan African Conference on Brain Drain, Elseh, Illinois, USA. See Renaissance World 1st May 2010, pp31-32 and 74

Forje W. John (2011) Century of Change: Symposium on African Unity, Nova Science Publishers Inc, New York, USA

Forje W. John (1989) Science and Technology in Africa. Vol. 10. Longmans Series on Science and Technology, Longmans Science Publishers, London.

Forje W. John (2012) 'Innovation that Matters: Towards Pro-Poor Innovation - Putting Public Policy and Values into Science and Technology for the Benefit of All in Emerging Polities. (Unpublished Paper, CARAD, Buea - Cameroon).

Forje W. John (2012)'The Interface Between the University, Research Institutes and the Private Sector as Appropriate Technological Links for Africa's Developmental Take-off. Changing Attitudes, Changing Behaviours and Pushing Forward Development' (Unpublished Paper, CARAD, BUEA – Cameroon

Forje W. John (2004) Cameroon Without Corruption. The Search for a New Vision. Niba Publishers, Bamenda, Cameroon. (New Enlarged edition forthcoming, Lambert Publishers, Germany)

Forje W. John (1998). "Developing a Science Culture in Africa" in N. Pillay and C.H. Prinsloo (eds.) (1998). Science and Technology and Africa, Proceedings of a seminar organized by the Centre for Science Development of the Human Sciences Research Council, HSRC Publishers, Pretoria, South Africa, pp33-41

Gerschenkron, A (1962) Economic Backwardness in Historical Perspective. The Belknap Press of Harvard University Press, Cambridge, USA

Granovetter (1985)

Gyasi Stephen (2011) "One Day, Britain Too Will Get Its Black Prime Minister," New Africa, 45th Year No.503, February 2011, London, pp36-43

International Labour Organisation (ILO) (2011) 'Social and Solidarity Economy: Our Common Road Towards Decent Living, Geneva

Hodgson (2001:292)

Jowi James (2012) 'Counting the Gains and Losses: Africa and the Global Talent Race', The European Association for International Education for its 202 Conference in Dublin

Lagos Plan of Action (LPA) (1980) Lagos Plan of Action

Lapayre, (2012) 'Statement at the Conference on Solidarity Economy and alternative Finance: A different Development Model. NGLS, 25 October 2012 (www.vick.org)

Malunga Chiku (2009) Understanding Organisational Leadership through Ubuntu. Adonis & Abbey Publishing Ltd, London & Nigeria

Malunga Chiku (2008) Making Strategic Plans Work. Insights from Indigenous African Wisdom. Adonis & Abbey Publishing Limited, London & Nigeria

Mayaki Assane Ibrahim (2012) 'Capacity is Key'. Mayaki is the CEO, Nepad Planning and Coordinating Agency. (See interview by Stephen Williams, (2012) New African, No. 517, 46th Year, May 2012, London, pp62-63).

Mayhew (1989:321)

Mohamedbhal Goolam (2012) 'Promoting Sustainable Development - How Are Universities Farin', World University News, Issue No. 00244, 25 October 2012.

Mwamvenda Tunfufye and Phindili Lukhele-Oloranju (eds.) (2013). The Triumph and Prosperity of Education in Africa. Africa Institute of South Africa, Pretoria, South Africa.

Newson Chris (2012) 'Africa's Future Has Never Looked Brighter', New African, No.519, 46th year, July 2012, London, pp24-25

New Partnership for Africa's Development (NEPAD) Consolidated Plan of Action and Policies of the Regional Economic Communities (RECs)

Nwokeabia, U. Hilary (2009) Why Industrial Revolution By-Passes Africa. Adonis & Abbey Publicising Ltd, London and Nigeria

Pilger John (2012)'Apartheid didn't Die in South Africa. It Inspired a Global Order Upheld by Force,' New Staesman, 21+25 September 2012, p57

Polanyi (1945)

Soludo C. Chukwuma (2012) 'From Berlin to Brussels: Will Europe Underdeveloped Africa Alain?' New African No.516, 46th Year, April 2012, London, pp10-17

Rostow, W.W. (1960) The Stages of Economic Growth. London

Thigo Philip (2012) http://www.infonet.or.ke

UNCTAD (2012 Economic Development in Africa 2012. Report. (See website below)
(http://unctad.org/en/PublicationsLibrary/aldcafrica201 embargo en.pdf)
United Nations Development Programme (UNDP) (2012) African Human Development Report 2012: Towards A Food Secure Future. /http://mirror.undp.org/angola/LinkRtf/Afhdr 2012 pdf)
United Nations Environmental Programme (UNEP) (2012) The Fifth Edition of the Global Environmental Outlook (GEO-5) (http://www.unep.org/geo/geo5.asp)
UNESCO (2012) Science Report 2010: Sub-Saharan Africa Chapter, Paris-France, UNESCO Publishing: 279-322
Urama, K, O. Ogbu, W. Bijker, A. Alfonsi, N. Gomes, & Nicholas Ozor (2010) The Africa Manifesto for Science, technology and Innovation. Nairobi - Kenya: African Technology Policy Studies Network (ATPS) (http://www.atpsnet.org/Files/the African manifesto for st&i.pdf)
Utting (2012) Statement made at the Conference on 'Solidarity Economy and Alternative Finance: A Different Development Model. NGLS, 25 October, 23012 (www.vick.org)
Vervliet Chris (2008) The HUMAN PERSON. African Ubuntu and the Dialogue of Civilisations. Adonis & Abbey Publishing Limited London & Nigeria
Wit de Haris (2012) 'Africa Must Lead in Innovation in Internationalisation', University World News, Issue 0239, 16 September, 2012 - World Blog.
World Bank (2012) Inclusive Green Growth: A Pathway to Sustainable Development. (http://sitersources.worldbank.org/EXTSDNET/Resources/Inclusive Green Growth, May 2012 pdf
Zubin and DiMaggio

Chapter 9

Emerging Perspectives on Democracy, Governance and Development in Africa: Reforms, Challenges and Prospects for a Beleaguered Continent

Abstract

More than five decades has elapsed since former dependencies gain independence from their colonial masters. Given Africa's turbulent political history, the spread of democracy is an extraordinary development that has brought tremendous benefits to citizens, including to some extent the guarantee of fundamental political freedoms, civil liberties and human rights. The paper probes into the growing consensus that modernising the state and consolidating broader and functional institutional framework is at the foundation of a market centred economy, essential to accelerate the pace of social progress and quality livelihood of the citizens. It argues that the task of building the legitimate representative and effective democratic system is not something that can be put off, or even worse subverted, along the road of development. The conceptual premises depart from the premises of system analysis and change using the triple helix model - democracy, governance and development – as a way forward for the continent to consolidate its hard-won independence. As for the design, methodology and approach the paper relies heavily on desk materials, and interviews to delineate and situate the interface of the triple-helix model for the sustainable transformation of the continent. Democracy, governance and development should be people-focused, or else the quality livelihood of the people will not be improved. It concludes that a well-functioning democracy remains indispensable and that strengthening institutions, ensuring participation, deepening the governance process and implementing efficient and sustainable public policies will ultimately lead to sustainable quality livelihood of the population

Keywords: governance, civil society, democracy, policy, shared-prosperity, rule of law

Introduction

"State fragility in sub-Saharan Africa is mainly a product of weak state institutions established under extractive colonialism. Many Sub-Saharan African states, including Nigeria and Ivory Coast, previously thought to be strong, have fallen into 'situations of fragility'. African leaders need to make concerted efforts and adopt effective measures to build state resilience. Although Africans themselves should bear this responsibility, there is no denying the complementary role of the international community and any assistance it may offer to overcome the combination of political fragmentation and weak state

institutions in postcolonial sub-Saharan Africa. State resilience, the opposite of state fragility, implies the ability of states to cope with change while maintaining the bargain of the social contract. Resilience is the ability of a system to adjust to a perpetuation and maintain its core functions unaltered. Efforts at building resilience tend to focus on the endogenous process of state-building. Efforts by national actors to establish reform and strengthen state institutions, where these have been eroded or are missing. State-building has often been a top-down approach focussing on state actors and national elites. And neglecting local concerns" (Maurice O. Dassah, 2012:111)

Gauging the Rationale of the Triple Helix System

The relationship between democracy, governance and development has often elicited discourses among scholars and policy-makers throughout history taking greater controversy and impetus following the granting of independence to former colonies. The failure of state-building looms large in Africa. The continent faces its greatest challenges in post-independence ethno-plural societies divided and mobilised along ethnic, religious and cultural lines. Simply attributing these problems to the societies, cultures and socio-political and economic structures in Africa would be highly delusive. Rather we should question the nature of governance system, leadership, the role of civil society in reconstruction processes, which this paper addresses. Democracy is one of the few systems in which learning is embedded as a fundamental tenet, and democratic institutions have built in processes for continuous reflection and perfection. In addition, the trajectory of democracy, governance and development requires systems for monitoring transitions and developing further analytical tools to assess linkages between the three to allow policy makers to develop and sharpen their tools or policies to ensure the smooth functioning of the state and for the state deliver the needs of the citizens.

During the past fifty years or more, major changes have occurred on the continent and in Rwanda in particular. From the Cold War through Africa's Lost decade of the 1980s, the imposed World Bank/IMF structural adjustment programme, to the gradual recovery process of the continent in the late 1990s and early 2000s only to be confronted by the economic crisis and food shocks of 2008, like the rest of the world, Africa is not isolated from the impact of the global financial crisis, which inadvertently jolted these positive developments made in the recovery process. Rwanda has had its share of ups and downs. Reconciliation and working together as one people, one nation with one destiny provides the structural-functional construct of a united and strong country, embedded with the vital human and institutional capacities to sail through the stormy globalisation ocean of the period. In 2011 the Arab Spring shocked the world for good or worse; but significantly it brought to the fore, the issue of the triple-helix of democracy, governance and development. A new revolution, the architecture of Africa's post-independence development is a clear sign of rising frustration of a new generation of marginalised and socially excluded population, mostly young people exposed to and exploiting the wonders of information and communication technologies (ICTs) in the fight for their basic human rights. In short, ICTs has created a new kind of social movement for the promotion and consolidation of the democratic process. Whether it is an Arab Spring, the genocide in Rwanda, or the apartheid system, the failed state construct in Somalia and on, the underlying factor is the gross absence of a democratic governance that fail to give the people a voice and place in the governance process of the society. Democracy demands that every one of use must be part and parcel in their consciousness of who is leading us and in the way we develop the country.

The continent is riddle with growing abject poverty, institutionalised and legalised viruses of escalating corruption pandemic. These are the results of vulnerability to both inappropriate internal policy articulation and aggregation; externally influenced factors including resources stocks suffered by emerging economies, even though Africa came out slightly better than most other regions at the peak of the economic meltdown. Africa is in turmoil with many people living in abject poverty, tossed around in a national boom for a select few and bust for the silent majority. Gains from the export of natural resources or economic growth are unevenly shared. The rich have become richer at the expense of the suffering lower income population and the poor.

Unfettered economic growth characterised by accumulation and wealth concentration has further increased social inequalities even though the resources it has generated could do the opposite. And finance more equitable access to essential public services. Persistent poverty, unemployment, social exclusion, and higher levels of inequality and insecurity are threatening the governance system, social cohesion and political stability. Africa is experiencing rapid changes requiring a good governance system to see through and sustain these numerous changes.

What is significant with the Arab revolution and the numerous conflicts, coups and counter coups, military and dictatorial regimes which Africa has and will continue to experience will plague the continent unless and until a structure of good governance becomes an entrenched component of the governance system in the transformation process of society, and seriously addressing any dysfunctional dichotomy in the triple-helix - democracy, governance and development (DGD) as currently witnessed throughout the continent. On the other hand, the connectivity between the triple-helix - *democracy, governance and development* - is a stimulus providing the right path for the sustainable transformation of Africa. Sustainable transformation implies a holy marriage or significant consensus or interface in the DGD triple-helix in improving the quality livelihood of the population. The central question is not whether there is a development advantage from democratisation but how to maximize developmental performance in new democratisers.

Rwanda like all other African countries stands at the cross-road of making or marring state construct for present and future generations. No other person can construct that future except the people and leaders of the continent working in synergy for the common good. A weak constructed foundation and divided house cannot hold. To withstand the challenges and construct a solid house is to ensure that the foundation and pillars of the building are well planted and with the right mixture of sand, cement and water. State construct in Rwanda must build on this virtue – the triple helix – a proper mixture of democracy, governance and development. It is within these premises that the conceptual hypothesis is contextualised as the framework for state construct not only for Rwanda but the entire continent. The historical and present construct of Rwanda makes it imperative to choose the transition of reconciliation, inclusion and shared prosperity for all. Its survival is through a people-oriented or focused governance system respecting the basic tenets of virtues of democracy and all that it entails.

Many of the 54 countries in this diverse continent face considerable political, social, and economic and cultural challenges. Some still contend with severe poverty, disease, and civil war. In this context what future can Africa and Rwanda in particular expect in the globalised world? How can the continent become technologically and economically viable and competitive? Can the continent produce its share of countries like the Asian tigers and BRIC – the African Lions? Therefore, the story that must be told is of a reframed continent, an aspiring economic trading bloc, the home of progressive democratic governance system and of future leading global economies. But the path of African politics, governance and democracy and economic growth in the decades ahead depends on the political will, mindset of the people and vision of leadership. It is a question of tapping into the potentials of the people and the natural resources of the continent for the good of the people.

Conceptual Departure Premises

The conceptual frame and departure premises are anchored on this hypothesis as depicted in Fig. 1. It should also be pointed out that only Africans can construct their continent. Any form of external assistance only adds or subtracts on the input efforts of the people. Therefore, fading democracy and economic growth of the continent can only be rectified by the people, and for the people; and under the strategic direction of whether or not the people want to develop. The often-heard word is "marginalisation." Claude Ake (1994) takes a view that: "it may well be that threaten Africa is not so much marginalisation as her negative prominence her construction as the ultimate loser." The phrase Africa is inevitably marginal, whereas, for Africans it is primary. In reality, the phrase covers up the economic forces at work which has brought Africa to its knees – the historic colonial assignment of the continent to primary production of materials for processing in Europe and North America. Combined with these economic forces has been the division of Africa between the great powers into separate colonial states, with each producing one, two or three primary products for export, with their boundaries artificially drawn across ethnic homelands and accepting the coloniser language as medium of expression. The native language was relegated to the back ground – cultural domination. With independence we inherited the colonial state rather transforming it in accordance with the democratic aspirations of the nationalist movement. Whether this could have led to greater chaos than what exist today in a topic of greater and serious debate that cannot be accommodated here.

Former Executive Secretary General of the Economic Commission for Africa (ECA), Prof Adebayo Adedeji (1993:8) write of the "personalisation and monopolisation of power" in African states leading to "marginalisation process which has aggravated severely by the SAPs. The cumulative effect is a state set apart from its society, in which 80 percent of the population are at the margin." Claude Ake further notes "marginalisation will not, of course, guarantee development. But it will give it a chance; for as people develops itself or not at all…will it go a long way towards overcoming the problem posed by the difficulty of crystallising a development agenda which expresses the aspirations of the people and can therefore elicit support." Basel Davidson and Colin Ley in defining "marginalisation" points out that the value of understanding the past, the pre-colonial African experience for Africans to find their own way into the future. While Bayart (1992) sees "Africans on having overcome the centuries always been subordinate players in relation to the outside world; but players nevertheless engaged in a process of 'extraversion'. To which they sought to draw on resources or alliances available in the external environment in furtherance of their community internal competitions and conflicts…"

Fig 1: Departure Premises

Any form of dysfunctionality in the triple-helix contributes and breeds instability leading to failed state;

Conversely, consensus or proper interface in the triple helix or DGD construct leads to sustainable development and quality livelihood of the people

Therefore, a democratic, open and accountable governance system, respecting and practicing the basic virtues or tenets of democracy provides the panacea for providing, protecting, promoting and sustaining peace, stability and quality wellbeing of the state and citizens. Coming from its traumatic past, the best option for Africa in general and Rwanda in particular, is to gun for an all-inclusive governance system.

Democracy-Governance-Development Linkages

The democracy-governance-development nexus is what Africa must reach out for. To begin with, not everyone wants Africa to succeed. In a broader sense, African nations have many strategic adversaries. The natural resources potential is the objective of big-power hegemonic ambitions of the developed economies and established democracies welcoming African states only to gain access to the vast natural resource's potential. It is quite obvious that the old democracies and economies do not look forward to the day when Africa ends its dependence on economic development. The day Africa gains its genuine sovereignty will imply a new global construct. The key to this brief prognosis lies chiefly among African states to demonstrate a determine effort towards a new state construct on the foundations and virtues of good governance and shared-prosperity.

It is clear that the political system of choice, which engineered the 'African one-party state,' proved all encompassing, including all citizens as party members from birth. Civil society, the singularly important countervailing power that constitutes the back-bone of democracy, was co-opted into the monolithic party structure. The state/party, which prohibited political opposition, owned all media. The party structure became a huge bureaucracy that constituted a parallel state within a state. Without opposition, the single political party became the most important route to fame and fortune. Without multiparty elections, the single party could not be defeated. Hence, careers within the single party provided security as well as power [Cohen, 2010; Forje 2009]. While the monolithic party structure could be argued on the basis that African countries at independence inherited a bureaucracy with less qualified persons, it was necessary to consolidate the independence of the country by pulling all forces together for the common good. Human beings being what we are, articulate self-interests took upper hand and the collective good was destroyed. Things started falling apart from people's departure from the collective interests to articulate self-interests. The monolithic party structure, having no fear of being voted out by the populace, enjoying total control and monopoly of government bureaucracies, officials of the monolithic party condemned themselves into the sanctuary of corruption and malfeasance. Paraphrasing Lord Acton's unchecked power is always abused. It was and has remained a futile exercise to get these people out of the sanctuary to the mortuary of corruption. The tendency to bend or severely diminish the rule of law rendered those societies uninviting to private investors, both home-grown and foreign [Le Vine, 2004; Etunga-Manguelle, 2000].

Therefore, democracy-governance- development nexus must be the starting premises and basis for state construct, as the platform on which to avoid rising destructive frustration in society. It should be noted that the generation of leaders who championed the anti-colonial movement faulted on some important decisions about their political and economic policies that eventually caused serious damage to their nations. The rejection of the western-styled democracy inherited from their colonial masters and condemning multiparty democracy incompatible with African cultural norms was wrongly used to stifle the growth of critical opinions needed in shaping the developmental path. The literature exploring the democracy-governance–development nexus is both abundant and inconclusive. Though these concepts continue to undergo a semantic evolution, development is understood as the synonym of economic growth. Development today is broadly understood within a wider context as a process leading to continuous improvement of the quality of life of the vast majority of the people. Equally the concept of democracy has broadly undergone important changes from liberal democracy – concerned essentially with individual freedoms, electoral mechanisms and processes and of course, the non-interference of the state in the economy – towards participatory democracy and, also towards social democracy, (not in the sense of the programme implemented by a specific political party), but as a system of governance that is expected to deliver on social and economic rights and development of the broadest sense to the largest possible segment of society [IDEA 2008; Forje 2009].

This failure to delivery is the cause of dissatisfaction, instability, chaos, conflicts and wars that continue plaguing the continent. *The nexus between democracy-governance-development is call for a new paradigm which should marry state-civil society-private sector interlude for providing and sustaining the quality wellbeing of the people and constructing a new continent* A number of factors must be exploited in this connection, namely (a) the private sector taking the lead and stimulating economic growth. The African private sector must be encouraged to attract foreign investors. The African entrepreneur in conjunction with the Diaspora if allowed to invest with security will become the driving economic force and engine of growth for an emerging Africa. Unfortunately, African countries have not created an enabling environment for the Diaspora to reconnect home and inject their intellectual prowess and entrepreneurial skills to kick start the economic, technological revival of the lost potential and contribution of the continent to global development [see Emekalam 2010]; and (b) developing infrastructure and its multiplier effect represent a key link to the revival of agriculture (farm to market roads) and to the rise of private sector. Rural areas need infrastructure to provide irrigation, roads, reliable power, water, efficient communication systems and other basic social amenities to halt the rapid drift from the rural areas into the big cities. As the saying goes, where a road passes, development follows.

For now, Africa has not failed in developing its intellectual capital nor has it exploited existing intellectual capital of the huge Diaspora population for its development. The trajectory in the triple helix - democracy-governance-development - is crumbling due to poor leadership, poor policy priority and greed. This attitude must change through a new mindset focused towards ending dependency, exploitation and marginalisation. No doubt, foreign aid with is visible or invisible conditionality has developed a dependency that tends to dull other needed efforts promoting rapid growth. Whatever the case, there is growing consensus about a universal acceptance of the following three points concerning the interface between *democracy, governance and development;* See Fig 2. On the Interface between Democracy-Governance-Development.

Fig.2: Interface between Democracy-Governance-Development

1	2	3
Development, governance Democracy is desirable values to be pursued in themselves.	Development is more than economic growth Governance linkage between democracy and development	Democracy is more than the institutions and mechanism of democracy, i.e. democracy are also expected to deliver in terms of a quality of livelihood
//	//	//
	// **Inclusive National Ownership And Quality Wellbeing of Citizens Through Political Processes**	

Forje [2012]

Larry Diamond [2010:26] contends that democratic and economic development are linked by policy imperatives, or governance and the barrage of academic literature leads one to question (a) the long standing proposition that the prospects for democracy are closely linked to the level of economic development, and therefore, democratic prospects are poor in poor countries; related to this is: (b)the poor careless about political and civil rights, or they are in no position to care until their basic economic needs are met. The type of regime structure impacts on the economic and democratic development. There is need to look at the institutional features of the regime and leadership form or style, which leads us to: (c) what, is the impact on democracy of the economic performance of the system. The assumption is that democracy must deliver the economic goods if it is to survive. The rising euphoria or expectations at the dawn of independence was that the granting of self-rule was going to rapidly transform the society from the scourges of poverty to the realms of wealth. This did not happen. And destructive frustration quickly replaced rising expectation. The issue of political process and of distributive equity should not be neglected. In this regard, the poor care about and need democracy as much as the wealthy. Of course, poor countries are gradually being democratic today than ever before, and that the survival in low-income countries and lower-middle income countries depends heavily not exclusively or even immediately on economic performance.

And that the key challenges are (i) to improve the quality and accountability of democracy; (ii)devise specific and effective policies to reduce poverty, corruption and social injustice; and (iii)use the capacity and capabilities of the Diaspora as significant future source of development capital – human and financial – the transformation of Africa. The rule of law must reign supreme as well. Unfortunately, corruption, patronage / clienteles, injustice and poverty are widespread undemocratic practises in Africa. The return to democratic transition in the 1990s has affected little to replace or at least curb these bad practices and other vices that impede the nation from moving forward in a consolidated pattern. The dysfunction of the state contributes to the exploitation and owes of the continent. Participatory democracy and shared-prosperity are highly recommended for transitional polities in their bid for state construct. Most African countries have failed to create a business climate that allows healthy competition and sustainable exploitation of the country's natural and human resources to accelerate development and thus deepen the democratic process. Poor business environment inhibits both foreign and domestic investors and slows down economic development. The economic reasons why the delivery aspect of democracy is in short supply in most African countries are naturally intimately linked to the political system and the institutions on which it rests.

The institutionalisation of the monolithic party governance system constrained the rise of strong and independent institutions as checks and balances on government. Government had a field day and governed with all impunity in the governance process which eventually became less relevant in piloting the affairs of the country. State failure was imminent as witnessed in many African countries. The survival and consolidation of democracy and the advancement of economic development and social justice constitute serious challenges to these countries thereby impeding them to claim full ownership to national development policies. The imposed World Bank/IMF structural adjustment programme could partly be seen within this context. The interface between *democracy-governance-development* faces the following dimensions of challenges, namely;

- the role of the political society – political parties, parliaments, civil society and other actors;

- the failure to bring the female gender on the development continuum construct;
- poor leadership and inappropriate education curriculum not pattern to the developmental priority of the country/continent.
- the role of the international community contributing to the opening of broader spaces for the political in transitional polities in shaping of national development priorities, poverty reduction and corruption reduction strategies [Forje 2004];
- the impact of globalisation on democracy, governance and development – as an opportunity for building more open democratic societies whose citizens are enlightened and aware of the global challenges as well as internal constraints and are ideologically oriented and well-schooled to face these challenges.

Apart from deficits in delivery there are other categories of democratic shortcomings plaguing the African continent, namely, the structural-functional political system of African countries which have not proved resilient and resistant to change. These are inimical as poor economic and social delivery to the thriving of democracy and constitute what could be termed as non-competitive political system - the one-party construct for example - that hinders efficient and effective decision-making process but encourages serious divide and conflict among the various actors, or failures to incorporate effective ways of overcoming differences and promoting reconciliation and consensus.

Reconciliation, consensus and dialogue heal wounds. Examples can be drawn from South Africa and Rwanda which puts these countries on the right rail for state construct. Therefore, in terms of political design, it is imperative that the political system must move away from a divided to a unified government structure that returns power to the people and creates equal opportunities for all. It means that constitutional design must seriously address the following shortcomings among others:

- shortcomings of constitutions enshrined with the contours of functioning only in context of large majorities and excluding minorities or working only for the president's party, Cameron for example as compared to the South African constitution:
- difficulties in constituting the majority needed to reach agreement within parliament – for example, the case of Cameroon, where a de facto one-party construct exist in parliament;

- the absence of a mechanism to promote cooperation and break deadlocks
- existence of centralised authoritarian ethnic hegemonic governance system;
- gross absence for the respect of the rule of law; and the entrenchment of exclusive governance system that intensify the great divide people regions, peoples, the rich and poor, urban and rural areas and others.

Social Change Paving New Attitudes and Values

The rising expectation that never was constrained the sustainable transformation of the African society. People become poorer than ever before, and their natural resources exploited as never has been known in history with very little dividend accruing to the people. It is assumed that economic development transforms a society in several ways making it difficult to sustain he concentration of power in one person, one party, or a self-centred unaccountable elite corp. The globalisation of wealth alters the social and economic structure of a society, as it widely dispenses power and resources.

Human capital development is a vital key in the process of consolidating and impacting positively on the democracy-governance-development dichotomy. The more educated the people are, the greater the pressure on government for open, transparent and accountable government and for meeting its social contract with the citizens in terms of quality services delivery. Thus, economic development raises and enlarges the middle class and it equally raises the levels of education and information among the youths in particular and the general public in general. Increase in the middle-class levels leads to fall in the social distance or divide and political polarisation, between classes. In addition, it shifts attitudes profoundly and values in a democratic direction. It can also raise a great deal of apathy towards the system. Widespread use of ICTs gives new perception, political and social orientation especially to the younger generation who now constitute the majority population and are vested with the use and intricacies of ICTs for various reasons. As the youth acquire more information through the wonders of ICTs and often restricted at home through the state hoarding information, new attitudes, perceptions are acquired as the structural basis for social movements restructuring the governance process and society. A new social movement is in construction but this new movement should be used to bring about constructive social changes not stir destructive frustration that only hampers the progress of the continent. On the dawn of independence, Africa had great synergy for social justices, freedom. Most unfortunately, and disheartening, where have these values gone?

Understanding the horror, they had inherited from colonial rule, getting people educated was a high priority, addressing the tragedy and phenomenon wasted through poor governance. Rising expectations have been overtaken by unemployment, absence of economic opportunities, social injustice and poor governance. All activities have been overtaken by Wall Street, the exploitation of money usage for personal values. African governments are playing the Wall Street game giving a blind eye to the emergence and consolidation of the basic values and tenets of democracy and democratic governance.

Conclusion

Towards Maturation, Transformation and Development

The continent of Africa is caught between the devil and deep blue sea. It stands the chance of developing or decaying. These are the hard choices the leaders and people must make now and be owners or not of their development. If there is anything to go by, the ongoing global financial crisis is an eye-opener for the serious soul-searching towards the reconstruction and transformation of the continent. Attempts have been made through this paper to pinpoint the challenges, changes, opportunities and prospects for reform; instituting good governance; servant visionary leadership; the need for intensive Regional Corporation, national reconciliation and continental unity as the structural basis for facing adversaries. Democratic governance, inclusive government, shared-prosperity are some of the essential ingredients that best prepare a country in addressing the numerous challenges faced in state transformation and providing quality livelihood for its citizens. The global financial crisis is a litmus test on how to fashion out a new development strategic approach. African states may still be small and perhaps weak but they are no longer new and in part in a function of learning – for fifty years should have given the structural learning background to own their own development path. These resources – human and natural – are there but the political will is lacking in converting and properly utilising resources to the benefit of the people. Rather these input resources for development have become a curse not a blessing.

Fifty or more years should have given the continent a new experience – moving from the idealistic and aggressive stances of the early years of independence to have yielded more pragmatic and reasoned positions. Fifty years seem to have contributed to greater marginalisation and exploitation and even created an attitude or sense of resignation rather than expectation. Rising destructive frustration is a reflection of the failure of the state to respond positively to the needs of the people, be their defender rather than the oppressor's most African states have become. The state has failed to deliver quality services to the people. The public service needs renewal. The essence of public service renewal is the creation of a new mindset in the public service, a new outlook that shifts its focus from means to ends. This change of mindset is not limited to any particular level of the public service, or any part of it. The public service and society need to undergo a constructive and structural x-ray and thematic change. The reality is that African states individually and collectively continue to blame and berate the developed world, especially Western Europe – (old colonial lords) for both imperialistic and disinterested policies towards the continent without fashioning alternative strategic approach to contain the invading forces of the old democracies and economies. Only Africans can develop their continent. But this equally implies developing new mindsets, attitude and behaviour towards their developmental construct. The purpose of state or public service renewal, the, is not to make government more like the private sector but to make it more true to itself, better equipped to serve the people and to provide the public goods they expect and need from it.

There is a lack of constructive and explicit link between public service reform and a fiscal agenda creates both a problem and strength. Weakness in correcting the fiscal agenda leads the situation of endemic corruption prevalent and perpetuating the state of abject poverty throughout and inhibiting the development of the continent. Lack of stringent fiscal control undermines efforts at public sector reform and renewal, with its original emphasis on restoring morale in public service. On the other hand, public servants are told that they are the government's most important asset. Yet on the other hand their wages were frozen, resources were cut, for example, the World Bank/IMF imposed Structural Adjustment Programme and the poor policies strategies of the government. This disjunction spawn's cynicism, to say the least, about public service reform and about the sincerity of those who lead it. Only good governance and a government committed to bringing these two objectives into alignment can restore trust, confidence, credibility and legitimacy in the state. The bottom line is democratic governance system to restore order and advanced the sustainable transformation of the continent. There is greater urge in making the Diaspora contribute for Africa's development.

Given the prevalent and seemingly irreversible trend towards globalisation - and let alone, national and regional inequalities – the state has assumed even more important and influential roles than other actors without delivering the necessary goods sustaining quality livelihood for the vast majority of citizens. Two salient factors are pregnant, namely: the pregnant division of African states into majority at the periphery and minority at the semi-periphery; and second, the emergent distinction between the centre and periphery. These divisions have to be addressed as bringing other actors into the development construct remains imperative. The growing division between the rich and poor (centre and periphery) is more fundamental in injecting frustration, weakening state capacity in addressing fundamental problems. Confronting the global financial crisis and developing new strategies for the continent's sustaining transformation requires bringing on board new actors or strengthening state-civil society-private sector partnerships. State-Civil Society-Private sector is currently absent in the developmental nexus of African states. A progressive and inclusive state-civil society-private sector partnership is Africa's best joker for sustainable development. The continent should intensify, develop and build on it as the gateway for an emerging Africa of today and tomorrow. In that vein, bringing the female gender and the youths on board, without which, efforts to development will be in vain.

To enhance the continent's transformation, we cannot ignore the youths and women as the essential ingredients of the continent's development. The youths constitute 65% of the African population; and in most African countries the female gender makes up more than 52% of the population. Africa cannot, and should not play with this population group. It is up to the people of Africa if they want to develop and build a better continent to tap seriously in this population group. We are all challenged to create a continent that enables everyone to have their voices heard and respected. Africa is a continent of wide variety of backgrounds and resources which should make it proud to stand together and champion for our shared cause and values; with this in mind and put into concrete action the future will be truly bright and prosperous for generations to come. We need our youths and women to fight for a better tomorrow. The traditional concept of democratic accountability, transparency and service delivery emphasis the supervision and control of public authorities by citizens through elections, and by the other branches of government should be reinforced.

Even though, elections, however, have long been recognised to be insufficient, though still important, in terms of accountability, it must be encouraged to ensure full and inclusive representation of the voices and will of the people to better create trust, legitimacy, credibility and confidence in the governance system. To a great extent, it should be noted that the circumstance in which African democracies have operated since independence have also influenced the approach to policymaking. A new lease of life should be injected in the governance and policy-making mechanisms of African countries. The chains of colonial rule can be said to be gone, but in reality, in some cases, our minds are still enslaved and we have accepted the myth of the superiority of Europe. Our policies strong ingrained with a Eurocentric agenda. We have to operate from an informed African perspective (Afro-centricism), thinking globally but acting locally or continentally. We continue to believe in the myth that Africa is a poor continent in dire need of support. But why was and there is a scramble for Africa. The new scramble is taking place in the wake of globalisation and advanced technological superiority and dominance. The challenge for Africa is to embrace visionary leaders who will ensure that the people of the continent benefit from their vast resources.

Economic crisis and growing problems of destructive frustration, public safety and insecurity, poverty, corruption have provided incentives and justification for external bodies to exploit and shape the policy direction of the continent. Admittedly, it is high time to avoid the *"blame theory"* and concentrate on the *'realities'* on the ground if the continent is to make significant progress. There has been constitutional breakthrough in the continent since the collapse of the centralised authoritarian regime structure in the Soviet Union. The return to multiparty political pluralism, the holding of free, fair, clean, competitive and transparent elections though still crowded with flaws and rigging mechanisms points towards serious changes for the better. These are positive developments that the continent must build on and consolidate in its endeavours towards building a capable developmental state. It is most desirable for African countries to create a situation of bipolarity, with a strong and unified opposition that can play its role of providing checks and balances. In short, Africa needs strong governments, institutions and strong opposition parties. We are currently short of independent "Think Tanks" like Chatham House (UK), Foreign Policy Council (USA) etc. than can independently, scientifically and academically offer policy outline to the people without political influence from the governing class. The African centre for development and Strategic Studies (ACDESS) Ijebu Ode, Nigeria was envisioned to play such a role. The Founding Board Chair, President Julius Nyerere of Tanzania, notes: "There is no poverty of ideas about what Africa's problems are, nor how to deal with them – either within or outside the continent. But it was felt that there was a lack of opportunity to express debate and test these ideals in an environment in an African context, and under African leadership which is dedicated to thinking about and for Africa's future. It is to fill that gap that ACDESS was set up. Its task is that of providing a firm foundation of ideas tested against African realties, on the time basis of which African can develop and pursue its own strategies". Weak governance holds back infrastructure development in Africa.

Democratic governance should lead towards building an innovative nation. In an increasingly global knowledge-based economy, innovation assumes a greater importance than ever before. The global competitiveness of the continent depends to a large extent to the ability of the different sections of the economy to meet challenges and changing needs and conditions as quickly, effectively and efficiently as possible. For now, the political and economic trajectory is lacking. Not many African countries can pride themselves as foreign investor's destination. Few African countries are well ranked on the Global Competitiveness Index scale. The same goes for the Global Democracy Index scale. The continent needs innovative government that should usher long-term success and quality wellbeing for its citizens. Africa cannot move forward without freeing its minds from the agony of western slavery, colonialism, apartheid, neo-colonialism, as well as from archaic traditional values or taboos inhibiting the valuable contribution of the female gender towards the progress of the continent. Echoing the views of Marcus Garvey and Bob Marley; "none but ourselves can free us from mental slavery." We have to sing songs of struggles, songs of despair, songs of survival and now songs of hope and confidence for a better tomorrow. It is the responsibility of this generation to lift up the flag of Africa through responsible governance structures and people-oriented economic related activities.

Africa should be concentrating in this direction; as well as mobilising domestic resources; building the human capital and forging new relationships on the basis of 'win-win' strategic approach with other nations as countries become more and more submerge into the inevitable knowledge-based global economy. The states should gun for a functional democratic and inclusive governance system ensuring power to the people [Forje 2009], with equal opportunities for all.

Recommendations

- build the human capital of African states and make proper use of the knowledge and capacity of the Diaspora in the transformation process;
- intensify state-civil society-private-sector partnership as veritable factors in the development construct of the continent;
- accelerating the process of mobilising domestic resources and promote the diversification of the African economy;
- bring the female gender into the plus-side of the development continuum; as it is important to restructure some archaic traditional values that impede constructive development;
- intensify regional economic integration the movement or prelude towards a United Africa construct.
- ensure the practice of democratic and inclusive governance system and the rule of law;
- construct strong institutions to safeguard the separation of powers between the three branches of government;
- consolidate the idea of basic human rights – freedom and liberty of speech for the individual and within the media industry;
- the need of a free media industry, objective and responsive reporting cannot be ruled to ensure and safeguard the democratic process;
- consolidate and deepen on the good progress made so far;
- democratic accountability, transparency and leadership remains a serious deficit in the African governance construct which must be rectified to ensure the integrity, respect and confidence in the African state formation and of its role in sustainable transformation of the continent

References

Adedeji Adebayo (1993) "Marginalisation and Marginality" in Adebayo Adedeji (ed.) Africa Within the World. Beyond Dispossession and Dependence. Zed Books, United Kingdom

Ake Claude (1994) "The Marginalisation of Africa. Notes on a Productive Confusion," A Paper Prepared for the Council on Foreign relations Africa Studies seminar, 18February 1994, New York, USA

Bayart Jean-Francois (1992) The State in Africa; The Politics of the Belly. Longman Publishers

Cohen J. Herman [2010] "Africa: A Light at the End of the Tunnel?" Africa and Francophonie, Vol.1. No.3. Fall, 2010, pp6-15

Dassah O. Maurice (2012). "Locating the Image of Postcolonial Sub-Saharan African State Fragility in the Mirror of Colonialism (pp97-117)" in Mammo Muchie, Sanya Osha and Matlotleng P. Matlou, (eds.) (2012). The African World. From Fragmentation to Unity and Resistance, African Institute of South Africa, Pretoria,

Diamond Larry [2008) Democratic Development and Economic Development – Linkages and Policy Imperatives" in IDEA [2008] Democracy and Development in A Globalised World, Stockholm – Sweden, pp26-35

Emekalam Kelechi [2010] "Meet Phil Emeagwali, 'Africa's Bill Gates' and 'Father of the Internet', Renaissance World, 1st April – 31st May 2010, pp42 Etunga-Manguelle, Daniel [2000] "Does Africa Need a Cultural Adjustment Programme?" in Lawrence F. Harrison & Samuel P. Huntington (eds.) Culture Matters: How Values Shape Human Programs, Basic Books, New York, USA, pp65-77

European Development Report (2009). Overcoming Fragility in Africa.

Forje W. John (ed.) Cameroon Without Corruption. The Search for A New Vision. Niba Publishers, Bamenda – Cameroon [New Enlarged Version Forthcoming, Lambert Academic Publishers - Germany)

Forje W. John [Forthcoming] Cameroon Without Poverty, Lambert Academic Publishers

Forje W. John [2009] State Building and Democracy in Africa. A Comparative and Developmental Approach. NOVA Science Publishers Inc, New York, USA.

Forje W. John [2009]. Here the People Rule: Political Transition and Challenges for Democratic Consolidation in Africa, NOVA Science Publishers Inc. New York, USA

IDEA [2008] Democracy and Development in a Globalised World International IDEA Democracy Round Table in Partnership with CSDS, New Delhi, 17-18 June 2008.

Le Vine T. Victor [2004] Politics in Francophone Africa. Lynne Rienner Publishers, Boulder, CO. USA

Organisation for Economic Cooperation and Development (OECD). Concepts and dilemmas of State-building in Fragile Situations.

Chapter 10

Re-imagining Human Capacity Development as Input Nexus to Performance Management and Quality Services Delivery in Africa

Abstract

Performance management and service delivery is a thorny issue in the developmental construct of the African continent. This paper argues that human capital development is sine quad non for performance management and service delivery, the absence of well-trained human personnel undercuts performance management and services delivery. Therefore, African countries have to look more critically and objectively in the education curriculum which must respond and reflect the developmental realties of the continent. It goes further to stress on the issue of ethics, morality and creating the enabling environment to accelerate the process of performance management and quality services delivery to better improve and sustainable the quality livelihood of citizens. Sustaining the quality livelihood of the people through performance management requires constructive, collaborative and dialogical interface between the state-civil-society-private sectors. Performance management requires capacity building. And capacity building is seen as a crucial factor to promoting and sustaining service delivery. It also requires strengthening the moral, ethical and spiritual capacities of individuals and communities. Efforts to eradicate poor services delivery must be guided by a vision of human prosperity in the fullest sense of the term-a dynamic coherence between the material and spiritual dimensions of human life. The paper ends by advancing strategic policy approaches to enhance and harness performance management for quality service delivery. It is within this context that the hypothesis of structural changes in the education curriculum is advanced. And with the conclusion that performance management is governing modern society which requires a dialogical approach towards a participatory governance through an interface between state-civil society and the private sector

Keywords: human capital development, utilisation of human resources, new education curriculum, ethics, services delivery, policy, state institution, leadership

Introduction

The Challenges and Truth We Fail to Accept

African public and private sectors cannot pride themselves of quality services delivery. Much has been written on the state of African public service administration. We have yet to hear and read the last word on this crucial topic for the sustainable transformation of Africa from a developing to a developed polity. As long as human capital remains underdeveloped, so also will be performance management and service delivery with a stagnant or deteriorating citizenry quality livelihood. In line with global trends both the government and private sectors are moving from the endless discourse to some form of effective implementation on how to make the sector accountable and responsive to the basic needs of citizens, to give the satisfaction and ensure trust and confidence in the output functions of the public and private sectors. Human capital development [education] has a positive effect on every aspect of human health, wealth, and wellbeing. Educational attainment impacts on economic growth. The transition of societies into modern democracies is rooted in widening educational participation among the citizens especially the young. But strong further investment in education [human capital development] in the developing world is needed. The link between education and performance management is clear. Unfortunately, the wider significance of education is perhaps less well understood. Better educated people are better empowered to perform better and deliver effective and efficient service as well to properly use the services delivered which improves the livelihood of the people.

The paper takes a critical but objective and analytical x-ray at the series of reform measures that the public service sector has been subjected to since the granting of independence to former colonies and of recent the World Bank/International Monetary(IMF)imposed structural adjustment programme (SAP).It penetrates into an emerging new African Public Service as fashioned by the African Charter on the "Values And Principles of the Public Service And Administration [AUC 2011] which is committed to:(i) promoting a public service and administration that uses the optimum conditions of equity and efficiency;(ii) modify, improve and entrench a new values of governance in public service; and (iii) ensure effective and efficient quality services delivery among others, indicates a determined effort by African States to ensure quality services delivery to the population. The Charter if properly applied will change lives, ensure productivity and growth as well as make Africa competitive in the global knowledge-based capitalist economy. In short, the people receive quality services that build trust, and confidence in the state. Any form of deviation on the part of government breeds conflict, decline, chaos, insecurity and instability, factors threatening the existence of the state. The paper insinuates that the success of the African Charter on the Values and Principles of the Public Service and Administration in conjunction with other relevant documents geared towards an improved public service delivery requires trained human capital development, hard choices and shared determinants to achieve a 'step change' in performance management for improving public services delivery in Africa. It goes on to argue that a 'step change' in growth and transformation economic conditions to be successful has to undergo a new form of human and institutional capacity building. This requires new curriculum and educated corps and committed citizenry incorporating and inculcating new mindset of honesty, transparency, duty consciousness, accountability and building trust and confidence in the public service as the appropriate channel for improving the quality wellbeing of citizens. Quality wellbeing depends on performance management and improved service delivery. And quality services delivery depends on human capital development. African public service must understand and act on the virtues of the triple helix that could be seen as a kind of panacea for transforming the livelihood of the people from misery to riches and satisfaction.

Producing quality human capacity ensures staffing the public service with the requisite manpower schooled within the ethics and values most needed for a functioning and performing public service every ready to deliver. The introduction and success of a performance management agreement rests solely on the quality and integrity of those called upon to deliver required services. The paper argues that the main thrust of performance management systems rests on creating and sustaining enlightened public servants imbued with the relevant skills and mindset necessary for the achievement of desired functions that leads to quality services output. Performance management rests on sharing and understanding what is to be provided, how and when achieved and properly utilised by the receivers. When the people are not enlightened, they cannot properly use the services delivered. By all means, education cuts across users and suppliers. Our academic and research institutions as well as health facilities and the material conditions of intellectual workers must be improved. Otherwise, we shall remain mere buyers and consumers of knowledge developed elsewhere and not producers of original contextualised knowledge.

Performance management for improving public service delivery rests on quality human capital development as well as institutional building. As the jargon goes, 'garbage in, garbage out.' Poor human capital development leads to poor quality services delivery and vice-versa. The focus is building a solid human capital base to ensure quality services delivery through performance management and backing this with motivation and creating an enabling environment for a constructive dialogical, harmonious relationship between state-civil society-private sector interfaces or the "triple helix" for the country to own its developmental path as well as ensure quality wellbeing for its citizens. Therefore, the aim for all government and people – is to work towards a common goal that constantly improves upon the quality livelihood of the population. The challenge is formidable, because making services work for poor people involves changing not only service delivery arrangements but also public sector institutions. It also involves changing the way much foreign aid is transferred and projects contracted. As governments, citizens, and donors create incentives for these changes, they should be selective in the problems they choose to address. All development related activities must be people-focused.

The African continent is trapped in the unrelenting mire of grinding poverty and corruption because of its poor human capital development, poor policy priority and development not people-oriented. It is no wonder that the quality of public services, accordingly, is often a dominant determinant of citizens' perception of government. When government institutions fail to perform, great apathy develops among citizens toward the state. The public service sector as the output functions or arm of government has the impact of colouring citizen's perception and opinions; poor human capital development in the civil services helps to blur the image of public administration. It bears, therefore, to reflect and invest on quality human development as critical input for the proper realisation of performance management for improving public service delivery in Africa and making the continent competitive in the world. We should take cognisance of the importance of history, bearing in mind that the continent has gone through upheavals and changes, but importantly, to ensure that we progress by correcting past mistakes in order to construct a better and sustained tomorrow for generations yet to come. Therefore, a new education curriculum is needed instilling the spirit of 'hard work, duty consciousness, honesty, trust, integrity, respect and love for one another or 'positive humanity'. The current inherited education curriculum has been polluted producing just the opposites of what has been mentioned. It is an education system that fans hatred instils articulate self-interests, accelerates the widening gap between the rich and poor. Proper quality human capital will lead to enhanced;

- performance monitoring and evaluation for improved service delivery;
- local service delivery and development – bringing development and administration closer to the people;
- proper insights in charge of management frameworks;
- enhance accountability, transparency and integrity in performance management;
- creating an enabling environment for civil servants [good salaries, incentives, working conditions, etc.
- building trust and confidence in the government;
- building and sustaining a culture of 'positive' humanity

Good performance management for improving public service delivery in Africa should imply putting in place instruments that lead to:

- articulating basic administrative systems to facilitate the provision of basic services;
- building governance systems that are open, accountable and honest and working to ensure the distribution of limited /scarce resources to those most in need;
- constructing partnership to mobilise additional support (financial, logistics, and technological) to better move things forward;
- prioritising actions plans and services delivery according to the needs of society;
- ensure responsible leadership at the political level and a people galvanised to apply themselves to create nurture and equitably-share wealth to better create conditions that retain the top brains and skilled Africans at home for the sustainable transformation of the continent;

Departing Hypothesis

The departing hypothesis is that improved human capital development backed by motivation, incentives and visionary leadership contributes to better performance management and service delivery and eventual improved and sustained quality livelihood for all citizens.

The absence of these input factors derails performance management, service delivery and quality wellbeing of the people plunging the people into endemic poverty and underdevelopment.

Conceptual Framework and Background Context

The continent is besieged by interferences from all corners. Political party interferences constitute a major drawback to performance management and quality services delivery. Poor human capital development constitutes a serious input factor inhibiting performance management and service delivery. Global economic influences have impacted seriously as important background variables in considering administrative reform. The point of departure is that the quest for qualitative services is far dire in Africa where the majority of the populations are still trapped in the unrelenting mire of grinding poverty and illiteracy. It is no wonder that the quality of public services, accordingly, is often a dominant determinant of citizen perceptions of government. When the people are not enlightened and constantly informed, provided services will not be used properly to improve and sustained their quality wellbeing.

In old democracies, public service delivery also colours citizens' opinions of and support for their elected leaders. In young democracies as is the case with Africa, the effectiveness of public services has even deeper implications, shaping citizens' affinity with their government and popular commitment to democracy. It bears, therefore, to reflect on emerging models and approaches that stake claim unlocking bottlenecks to efficient and effective services to populations [AAPAM 2012:4; Forje 2009:22] The mediating effect of job satisfaction and organisational skills and commitments on self-reported performance is contributing factors to performance management and service delivery [Meyer, 1997; Vandenabeele, 2009; Ritz 2009; Bouckaert & Halligan 2008; Moyniham, 2008; Dooren & Walle 2008]. Olaopa Tunji [2009] sets out guidelines, strategies, ideas and conditions, in short, an institutional blueprint for redirecting the focus of public service in Africa and for making bureaucracy and the African state globally competitive and development-oriented, especially with regards to service delivery. Critical here is that domestication and establishing successful reforms requires knowledge, human resources, capacity-building and good governance as well as foot soldiers determined to bring about changes for the common good.

The capacity to transform knowledge into effective decisions and actions that solve development problems for both the short and long-term is critical to the development of society. McLennan and Munslow [2009] extends the debate on human capital further by noting that sustainable development requires building a knowledge-based economy and the ability to innovate continually in a rapidly evolving process of globalisation. Therefore, competing in a world of constant innovation and fierce market competitions requires the production of highly skilled workers. This is not only true for the private sector but equally critical for public sector organisation. Simply stated, the book highlights the need for the country to produce its own skilled workforce to meet the demand of economic development as well as ensure sustainable quality livelihood for all the citizens. Considering the scale of poor service delivery that exacerbate social inequalities in society, performance management, in managing change requires good knowledge [education] to significantly contribute to quality-based reform. A reform of the educational curriculum to meet the challenges and exigencies of the transformation process remains imperative. The Conference of African Ministers for Public/Civil Service (CAMPS); The Commission of Political Affairs of the African Union [AUC]: The New Partnership for Africa's Development [NEPAD), Regional Economic Communities (RECs) and national governments have insisted on the importance of establishing the centrality of governance and public administration in development. Performance management is seen in light of the services delivered to the people.

A number of measuring yard stick can be used to access or measure performance management, beginning with (i) measuring the performance of the delivers: (ii) whether the delivers are performing their functions effectively and efficiently; and (iii) improving the political-administrative nexus between politicians and the civil service. Clear performance objectives should be defined in order to direct the management of public organisation. Traditional public administration such as security, fairness and equality have to a large extent been replaced with values such as 'economy, efficiency and effectiveness' to better enhance productivity and eventually sustainable quality livelihood. Unfortunately, self-articulate interests override these virtues. With the results that Africa is stuck with a mediocrity civil service structure unable to play the proper output role expected of it in delivering services to the citizens and not being innovative and competitive in the global economy.

The literary world is whitewash with thousands of publications on the subject. As noted by Hondeghen & Perry [2009:5] published materials on performance, performance measurement and performance management, scrolling through Google Scholar runs into more than 1,860.000; limiting it only to the public sector, we find over 300.000 entries. Seldon [2000], Brewer [2008], Kim [2005] and others look at internal and external factors of effectiveness, fairness and efficiency, motivation and other factors contributing to performance. Motivation in Public Management [Perry & Hondeghem 2008] joins a long-standing debate about what drives the behaviour of government employees and others who are engaged in the public business. Performance management is linked to motivation. Public servants are not angels, but neither is they self-aggrandising opportunists. The motivation theory should be grounded not only in rational choice models but altruistic and pro-social perceptions as well. Performance management and services delivery is simply governing modern societies [Heinelt, 2011]. Eymeri-Douzans and John Pierre [2011] notes that after a quarter of century of implementation of New Public Management (NPM) reform strategies, this book assesses the major outcomes of these reforms on states and public sectors, of both at the organisational level and a more practical level.

To attain quality performance management and service delivery, the organisation must ask three interrelated questions in order to develop its strategy towards achieving its objectives*; where are we, where do we want to be; and how will we get there?* While these questions do not change over time, the realities and environments that the public service sector faces. Given today's realities, how should the public service sector answer these questions [Galavan, Murray and Markides, 2008]? It is clear that some countries have made progress in restructuring the public service sector towards performance management and others have not. Those that have not should learn from best practices. Africa is challenged to move towards shared-values and experiences which underscore the past or ancient Africanness we once practised. Unfortunately, we have lost that value and virtues through articulate self-interests. The linkage between performance management democracy and education must be intensified to produce quality services delivery. Issues such as an enabling working environment, recognition, motivation, rewards are some of the encouraging sign posts towards performance and delivery. These are some of the absent indicators that skilled African professionals are lured by the glitter of the developed economies. Sharma and Mhlalauli [1993] note that *"the principal thrust of human resources development is to create a strong human resources base with the right knowledge, skills, attitudes and values, which enhance productivity and competitiveness"*. This challenges government and those involved in human capital development to articulate and aggregate new education curriculum responding to the needs of the society. Botswana's experience in public administration education and training is interesting

[Sharma and Lekorwe, 2007]. The education sector can only respond when there is proper utilisation of trained human capacity, and when it is designed to produce the requisite manpower. Rwanda has drastically cut down the time it takes to register an enterprise as compared to some countries that the exercise takes months on end.

With the state of emigration as depicted in Fig 1, poor performance management becomes a reality on the continent. A new attitude towards human capital development becomes imperative if the continent has to attained quality management for its citizens. Poor performance management as often been stated is not merely the lack of material resources, but also the absence of those ethical, moral and social resources that create an environment in which individuals, through social institutions and communities, can develop to their fullest capacity. Such efforts at capacity building should stress on helping people cultivate ethical and moral values and capacities to become protagonists of their development and wellbeing. More often than not, managers fail to effectively manage their human resources due to the following factors:

- failure of management to provide good quality of life and failure to carry employees along with them;
- management's inability to provide fair working conditions;
- poor remuneration in relation to profits made by organisation, unjustifiable wage differential between high- and low-income earners in different sectors, which often contribute to low morale, lack of commitment, low productivity, and poor services delivery
- worker's inability to meeting their obligations and responsibilities to ensure the progress of the organisation and even to develop their own skills, to become pro-innovative;

Poor utilisation of human capital resources leads to serious drainage of potential human potential that can contribute to performance management and serviced delivery. Fig 1. Emigration from Sub-Saharan Africa depicts a tip of the iceberg.

The situation is even worse, calling for serious policy actions in the proper utilisation of human capital in the development process. Proper training and utilisation breed proper public sector effectiveness. A critical challenge for performance management and higher education in Africa is reversing the brain drain even though the 'brain drain' can be 'brain gain' for the continent in the long-run. In many cases attracting these skilled human capitals have failed, the trend is now moving towards using intellectual's migrants in host countries to strengthen teaching and research back home through graduate advising, joint research schemes, and creating networking skills and opportunities. For example, the South Africa Network of Skills Abroad aims to link highly-skilled South Africans living abroad and working in academic, cultural and commercial sectors. The African Computer Wizard Dr Philip Emeagwali [2010] opines that "ten million Africans now constitute an invisible nation that resides outside Africa. Although invisible, it is a nation as populous as Angola, Malawi, Zambia or Zimbabwe. If it were to be a nation with distinct borders, it would have an income roughly equivalent to Africa's gross domestic product. According to the United Nations, an African professional working in the United States contributes about USA$150,000 per year to the US economy. The brain drain phenomenon explains, in part, why affluent Africans fly abroad for their medical treatment. Secondly because a significant percentage of African doctors and nurses practice abroad in hospitals, we can reasonably conclude that African medical schools or institutions of higher learning are de facto serving the European population, not Africans. African universities are exporting a large percentage of their graduating manpower to Europe".

Fig 1 Emigration from Sub-Saharan Africa

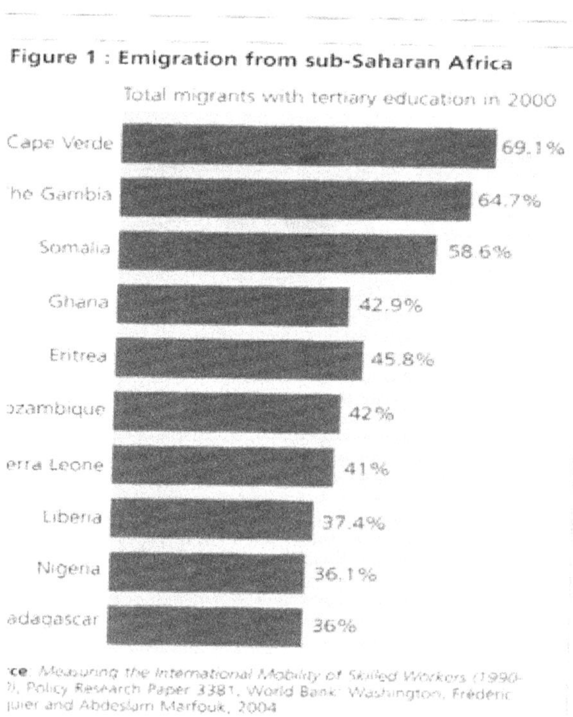

In a given year, the World Bank estimated that 70.000 skilled Africans immigrate to the developed economies, Europe and the United States. These are skilled manpower needed to deliver quality services to the people back home. Poor performance management and services delivery leads to a query, why would the optimism or rising expectations of the 1960s give way to the despair and destructive frustration of 2012? Most African countries achieved independence in the 1960s, but by 2012, these countries have not yet achieved technological and economic independence. Poor performance management and poor services delivery are the continent's greatest deficit. These deficiencies have to be adequately addressed if the continent is to become a meaningful play in the knowledge-based competitive economy of the 21s century and beyond. Globalisation is here to stay. Globalisation process is increasing the foreign debts of developing countries, accelerating the flight of financial and intellectual capital to western economies. To make the best out of it is by deepening our human capital and governance system, creating room for participation and benefit-sharing. Africa at the down of independence was a beacon for great synergy for social justice. It had to understand and undo the horror it has d inherited from many years of slavery and colonial rule. Therefore, getting people educated was a high priority. Unfortunately, the "greed phenomenon or articulate self-interests" derailed the rising expectations of the people with serious danger in the horizon. Today, the rising expectation has been overtaking by the forces of Wall Street, leaving Main Street in abject poverty and despair.

It has been illustrated that knowledge is the engine that drives economic growth, and Africa cannot eliminate poverty, underdevelopment and exploitation without first increasing and nurturing its intellectual capital. Reversing the 'brain drain' will enhance and increase Africa's intellectual capital while also increasing its wealth in many different ways. It cannot be gainsaid that education holds the key to sustainable transformation of the continent and for African owning its development path.

Strengthening Public Sector Effectiveness

Performance management and improving services delivery calls for a new mindset, the need to think innovatively on the African developmental agenda and the nature of the state and public administration required to drive it. The driving slogan or agenda should focus on the notion 'good enough governance' and 'good enough public administration.' Whether a strategy is construed to meet the expediencies of New Public Management (NPM) or Performance Management Systems (PMS), the underlying input factor is human capital development as the positive effects on service delivery. Human capital development remains the important element of the process of establishing effective and efficient public service. To broaden the issue further, Geyer and Rihani [2011] looks at the complexity in public policy and administration, noting that public policies aimed at simplification and rationalisation of social structures, and on the high social costs of their inevitable failure; what public policy can do and cannot do in performance management and service delivery.

In spite of the existence of numerous training institutions, public servants are not adequately trained and qualified nor properly prepared for public services. In many instances there is a tendency to forget that 'good enough governance requires that there be proper training and pre-assessment of individuals for public services. The recent recruitment of 25000 Cameroonians into the public service solves the political agenda of the ruling party and solves short-term unemployment but does not inject efficiency and effectiveness into the public service delivery system. On the contrarily, poor services delivery is being noted within services delivery due to the inadequacies of personnel injected into the public service. There is a failure of adopting the principle of 'the right person for the right job' attitude. Since the public service is responsible for the output functions of government for delivery, emphasis also needs to be placed on their roles as custodians of the values of 'public service' and their accountability to the broader society.

The government avoids the inherent input factor of accountability, transparency and integrity by hanging on and the exigencies of meeting its political agenda to galvanise more votes in order to remain in power at the expense of a sinking society. What is required to better gain more votes is aggressive, coherent and comprehensive people-oriented policy action must be taken before the window of opportunity closes. On the other hand, we must equally question whether skilled Africans have the moral obligation to remain and work in Africa? African governments must encourage and reward skilled citizens to stay, work, and raise their families in Africa. People need to put bread and butter on the table daily for the survival of the family. On the other hand, should skilled African emigrants be compelled to return to Africa? We cannot control immigration. Or should we blame the Diaspora for Africa's problems? We have seen the beneficial side of the "brain drain-brain gain" phenomenon. The final answers rest with African governments – creating the necessary enabling environment for citizens to be part and parcel of state construct and shared-prosperity.

Performance management must have two cardinal factors – performing the job to offer services and customer relationship which ensures that the customer is satisfied with the services so offered. Performance management must be married with customer satisfaction to obtain quality service delivery. This is gyrostatically lacking in the public service sector in most African countries. Services and satisfaction must be improved immensely for improved quality wellbeing of citizens. If the two concepts were properly coordinated, the idea of a Millennium Development Goals [MDGs] would not have seen daylight or would have come to reinforce what exists. The absence of performance management and customer's satisfaction shows that Africa cannot meet the MDGs by 2015. Official reports and anecdotal evidence suggest that at the current pace (poor performance management, poor service delivery and poor customer satisfaction) even by 2050 the goals may still remain unmet by these states.

Africa's progress is at best very slow and patchy – the results of bad governance, inadequate performance management and poor service delivery and poor governance. Poor education (human capital development) accounts for the rate of poor service delivery. *But Africa can meet the MDGs if only it seriously improves on its education system which in turn should impact of performance management and greatly enhances service delivery which improves the quality livelihood of citizens.* There has been remarkable progress in education in terms of enrolment in schools, colleges and universities all over the continent. However, the education curriculum is unfortunately not designed to respond the specific needs of the continent. Africa has to intensify efforts to improve on and jerked up leadership and governance considerably as well as ensures a fairly activist society.

In plain language, our education system, university in particular are not organically linked to our societies. Party politics seem to dominate the orientation of university education. Students do not read creative works that can turn their anger into a positive force for creativity and social transformation. There is a crude way in which the university has become integrated into the vulgarity that is dominating our societies. Higher institutions for public management like the Advance School for Public Management and Magistracy [ENAM) in Cameroon is losing its focus due to over centralised political indoctrination that blurs issues of performance management and services delivery. Here I agree in-toto with Raheem [Biney & Olukoshi 2010], "When universities merely reflect the vulgar side of society instead of providing original reflection on the society, they cease to be a universe of ideas and are doomed to become irrelevant" Education is the foot solider in the war for performance management and quality service delivery.

As a consequence, several countries around the world are attempting to revitalise their public administration and make it more proactive, more efficient, more accountable, and especially more service oriented. To accomplish this transformation, governments are introducing innovation in their organisational structure, practices, capacities, and working on how to mobilise, deploy, and utilise the human, material, information, technological, and financial resources for service delivery to remote, disadvantaged, and challenged people. The public service must reinvent itself with skilled human capital. An efficient and performing public service is a critical factor in enhancing the economic growth and prosperity of a country. Without that critical mass, without a solid human capital development, performance management cannot deliver the need services to the population. Education leaves lasting legacy and imprint in the transformation of a society.

In contrast to the recruitment of 25000 into the public service, Cameroon, winner of the "**AQUARIUM Project of the Sigipes"** that won the 2004 Category 2 Awards of UN Good Governance and Innovations in Public Governance, attributed to the structural reforms undertaken in the Ministry of Public Civil Service and Administrative Reform [MINFORPA). The rigorous in-house training of personnel contributed to the success of the project, aimed at modernising the civil service in order to increase flexibility, accountability and transparency in respect of:

- boosting efficiency and achieving results that match the expectations of public service users;
- implementing good governance in public service;
- raising the responsibility and responsiveness of civil servants; and
- rationalising public sector organisation and the management of their employees [UN 2009:226-228; Forje 2009]. See also: email. aquarium@spm.govt.cm

Or take the case of Kenya, Winner of the 2007 Performance Contracts Committee Secretariat, Category 1. **"Improving Transparency, Accountability, and Responsiveness in the Public Service,"** through an extensive system of performance-based contracting to ensure a style of public sector management emphasising results over process compliance fostering greater responsiveness and accountability of the civil service. Like the Cameroon Civil Service, performance in the Kenyan civil sector was deteriorating. To restore order, efficiency and effectiveness in the sector, Government strategy included a concerted and comprehensive structural adjustment, privatisation, commercialisation, contracting out new budgeting and planning systems. Through the Economic Recovery Strategy (ERS) government decided that performance contract process is adopted as a management tool of public resources. Today Kenya has implemented one of the most extensive systems of Performance Contracts (PCs). This success rests also on the calibre of its human capital, vision and commitment of the staff towards change [UN 2009:131-133]. Sharing knowledge and best practices in the public service

A third example, comes from Morocco, the **'eFez Project'** of ensuring access of all citizens to civil records services through the creation of an online portal. It was hell to say the least, in obtaining the necessary documents to acquire a passport or the papers needed for voter registration; such documents were only obtainable through government offices in the capital, Rabat or big cities like Casablanca. Apparently, Morocco has a highly developed telephone and Internet system, and government is using ICTs to improve programme coordination, tax administration, and auditing among other services. In response to the challenges, researchers from the ICT-for-Development Laboratory [ICT4D Lab] at the Al Akhawayn University in Ifrane, Morocco and officials at the municipality of Fez designed, implemented, and deployed a replicable local e-government system transforming Fez's archaic municipal service delivery into a modern online system. Again, the issue of human capital development through the researchers at the University improved on the performance management which changed and improved public service delivery in the Fez region [UN 2009:154-156].

These and numerous other success stories confirm the issues highlighted under the advanced hypothesis and conceptual framework; namely access performance management, determining how performing civil servants are, and improving the political administrative interface between politicians and management; i.e., improving the output functions between the state and citizens. We cannot escape from the fact that several factors underscore the intense interest in performance management and qualitative services delivery throughout the continent ridden with poverty, inequality and social injustice. The introduction of performance management as a reform tool and output mechanism was a response to increasing calls for governments to become more open, improve accountability, transparency and demonstrate values for money. What is most outstanding in the increasing citizen demand for the government to meet up the standards of service delivery to the levels seen in the private sector? Related to this popular mantra is the legitimate expectation that tangible outputs must justify the resources outlay. This heightened performance scrutiny translates into intense accountability demands on government to deliver discernible quality services to the people [AAPAM 2012:5]. The people are becoming more and more aware of their rights, the values and role of democratic governance can play in meeting basic needs.

But governance by itself is not sufficient when the people are not proactive within the system. And that "governance without effective implementation renders nugatory the intent of policy as much as unaccounted for investment into government projects is a scar on the democratic edifice" [AAPAM 2012:6]. This could be seen in terms of what Ramesh et al [2011] see as Reasserting the Public in the Public Service Performance Management and Service Delivery. This is depicted in what may be termed an Integrated Model for Education Performance and Service delivery.

Education Performance and Service delivery

Education Curriculum ==============➔ <===============	**Performance Management** ================➔ <================	**Quality Service Delivery**
Education governance is about setting a curriculum for quality training that enhances performmance and management output	Performance Management is about promoting output functions of state in advancing and enhancing service delivery	Quality service delivery that leads quality livelyhood

Source: [Forje] 2012

In light of the above, member states are encouraged to exert more efforts to improve public sector performance and to capitalise and share existing knowledge on how to achieve best performance in the public sector. Strengthening public service effectiveness given African context and challenges requires a flexible and phased capacity development strategy, premised on the notion of good enough governance which builds off existing strategies and interventions [Hyden 2001, McLennan 2005;]. No doubt, poor performance management and service delivery could be seen as a violation of human rights; that the most excluded and stigmatized members of society challenge us to think of the world in a different way. Therefore, justice, equity and collective action must be exercised to ensure that all citizens have inputs into decisions that affect the entire community. It can no longer be emphasised that education and empowerment, particularly of women and youth – would help to develop skills and confidence needed for performance management and service delivery. It is within this frame that one can contextualise AAPAM's Annual roundtable conference to improve on the public service performance, management and service delivery

An agenda for strengthening public service effectiveness would necessitate:

- institutionalisation;
- realigned power relations reflected in regulatory frameworks and respect for all stakeholders;
- participation, access and inclusion; engagement; shared control
- greater influence from different stakeholder over the decision-making about the distribution of resources: shared prosperity;
- readiness and ability of stakeholders to make their own decisions about the use of shared resources;
- real participation in decision-making and planning through social mobilisation and civic engagement;

It therefore implies that successful performance management and services delivery requires a cohort of interrelated input factors as depicted here:

Performance Management
And Service Delivery ==========➔
cohort of interrelated input factors

Human Capital Development
Behaviour/Mindset
Internal-efficiency
Internal-effectiveness
Internal fairness
Prevailing governance system
Motivation, rewards and incentives
Role of the media industry {informing, educating, acting as watch dog}
Leadership
Conducive environment
Consumer usage/input {proper usage of services provided}
Information – free or hoarding
The use of media industry to educate society on their rights within the system
External input factors (positive or negative)
External-efficiency, fairness, effectiveness

Source: Forje [2012]

Education and training of human beings are critical to performance management and service delivery and advancement of society for the common good. Access to knowledge is the right of every human being, as is the duty of government to ensure its social contract with the people, and for the people to properly protect and utilise the services so rendered by the state. Efforts towards human capital development must be intensified. Only when people are educated and working in consonant with one another can good performance management and service delivery be attained. With proper human capital development raised can the true potential of the human spirit begin to be tapped for the benefit of all. Seen in this regard, the transformation of individuals and societies be realised, and should include the following;

- moral and ethical education;
- rethinking students, rethinking teachers, rethinking society;
- systematic learning and participation;
- individual and social transformation'
- continental and global solidarity

Enabling an increasing number of people get educated, the more they play an active role in performance management, in the production of knowledge that contributes to more efficient, effective management and service delivery the present education curriculum is not transformative enough for it to change the lives of the people. What needs to happen instead, is to ensure that education is tailored to the developmental needs of the society; that education ensure that opportunities for the job market exists especially for the increasing population of youths. The United States creates a "brain drain" by issuing 135,000 H1-B visas to "outstanding researchers" and persons with 'extraordinary skills. Africa institutions are training people for the American/European job market. At the same time importing external labour as experts at high costs. Take for example, foreign football coaches who are highly paid but African countries will not employ their own citizens who have graduated from the same schools as foreign coaches.

As the principles of equity, justice, efficiency, effectiveness, transparency, accountability become the metrics of service delivery, the human nature in its totality, rather than just its material dimension, it is considered, will true performance management and service delivery begin. It is only then that a new dawn of Africa's public service can begin to emerge in the 21st century era of knowledge based global economy. Human capital development provides a beacon of hope for the future of Africa's public service sector. This valuable input factor is not the panacea for service delivery and performance management but must be constructively linked with other linkage factors to obtain maximum results.

Conclusion

Poor education curriculum leads to poor human capital development. Proper human capital development backed with institutional capacity building is the gateway to performance management and quality services delivery the paper argues. It is appropriate for Africa to take a moment of pause ponder under the kind of education curriculum for the transformation of continent as well as delve into SWOT analysis on Performance Management for Improving Public Service Delivery in Africa. Current debates conclude that the African Public Service is in a state of crisis, or in recession, because it operates failed democratic governance system, (and vice-versa) with inadequate skills, poor working environment and other impeding inputs factors and therefore unable to perform well. Quality service delivery becomes a major problem.

From the discussions so far presented supports the hypothesis that as people become more educated, they also become more politically aware and more inclined to participate in the political and administrative process which enhances performance management and service delivery. In addition, unprecedented increases in education levels, particularly among females – as is taking place in many African countries does suggest, quicken a country's move towards a more democratic political system. Female education appears to matter more as they have been marginalised when it comes to the effects of education on governance, services delivery and the transition to free democracies. Obviously, women have a different touch to livelihood and therefore play a key role when it comes to exerting the checks and balances on the in power that is necessary for a free democracy and performance management and service delivery. Human capital development contributes significantly to performance management which should be viewed as a deliberate attempt to close the yawning gap between governance and policy intendment as improvement measures manifested and amplified at the coalface of service delivery leading better livelihood for the population.

The problem today is not the lack of popular support for an ideal public service sector, but the way in which human-beings are trained and how some vital institutions of state are functioning; elections are being stolen; political parties and the administrative system are often perceived as top-heavy, corrupt, male-dominated and ineffective; parliaments are powerless, and complacent, and fail to exercise their oversight role; civil society is passive and embedded with destructive frustration. The major challengers for the public service sector and democracy are to deliver on its promises and to generate inclusion, more equitable development and better-quality livelihood for the population at large. Performance Management and Service Delivery require participatory governance - constructive collaboration and dialogue between the state-civil society-and private sector - working as team for the common good. Developing human capital is not enough. What is important is putting knowledge at the services of the masses at all times – performance management and service delivery. Not human capital development or knowledge that makes peace with poor governance, corruption and poor service delivery. Human capital development, i.e., acquisition of knowledge must go deeper and become the effectiveness of public services shaping citizen's affinity with their government and popular commitment to unlocking bottlenecks to efficient and effective services delivery to the population. Human capital development must lead to performance delivery or else all is lost in attaining the goals of effective and efficient service delivery. The people are increasingly demanding that their governments demonstrate results – that is making deeper impact and real differences to their material conditions and concomitantly that there is demonstrable value for their inputs into the functioning of government.

The positive results of these achievements show the degree, depth and consequences of performance management on the African continent. Has Africa made progress in performance management? Has performance management impacted on the life of the people? Performance management for whom, and by whom and what purpose? The paper has not provided all the answers to these soul search questions. However, it has no doubt shown that performance management is one measure toward addressing governance logjams that impede implementation and stymie efforts at improved service delivery. It has shown that human capital development is an important input mechanism and implementation vehicle and affirms the governance system as it exposes those that fail for relegation or realignment to ensure government components justifying their existence and resources allocated for their sustenance.

Human capital development should be seen as an essential input that harnesses and enhances performance management as a critical cog in the policy implementation machinery not only for improved service delivery but more appropriately for a definitive impact in citizens' quality well-being. Africa's development challenges demand that the education enterprise sector should stand up as the leading place to prepare the continent for the expected leap forward. For now, education sector remains ill-prepared. Given the role of human capital development (education) there is a strong case to pay special attention to the education sector in nation-building. A holistic approach should be adopted by all stakeholders to ensure good performance management and quality service delivery to improve the quality livelihood of all citizens.

Democratisation which is on the move in Africa has also prompted an ongoing process of change in the relationship between citizens and the state. While citizens previously took a more passive stance toward the state, they now increasingly expect public officials and the government to be accountable to them, and they demand a voice in the decision-making process. There is more free and diverse media that can inform citizens about the problems facing society and the actions of public officials and the government as a whole. Just as democracy has raised expectations for better living standards, improved public services and more responsive efficient and honest government, it has also enhanced the productivity and capacity of the public to examine whether those expectations are being addressed in practice. Human capital development and democracy enhances performance management and confidence in institutions contributing to quality wellbeing.

The public service sector in Africa has been important pillars managing national affairs. The sector has combined traditional role of governance and provision of social services within the implementation of policies and programmes for socioeconomic transformation. Many challenges lie ahead of Africa, implying greater pressure on the public service to improve on its performance management and services delivery. These challenges range from poverty alleviation; promoting economic development, improving on infrastructure, protecting the environment, developing human resources, fostering an enabling environment for popular participation in development and governance, promoting economic cooperation to creating sustaining institutions for political stability. This list of challenges is not exhaustive. Nonetheless, the responsibility for harnessing and enhancing national efforts to managing these challenges rest mostly with the public service. A critical test is how the public services assist the government in fulfilling these obligations and how the public services assist the government in ensuring the articulation of the priority policies need for comprehensive and sustainable changes in society.

Recommendations

- Reconstruct the education curriculum to meet the developmental exigencies of the country/continent;
- Substantial financial assistance and other logistics should be extended to the educational sector;
- Prioritise human capital development as the nexus to improving performance management and quality services delivery
- Proper utilisation of Information and communication Technologies (ICTs) gadgets in enhancing and improving performance management and quality services delivery;
- Improved conditions of service will immensely motivate workers towards better performance
- Sensitisation of society on the proper utilisation of facilities provided by the state in enhancing quality livelihood;
- Intensify democratic and good governance reform processes and initiatives;
- Ownership of development needs to be 'democratised' - i.e., those who 'do democracy' – political parties and legislators, as well as civil society and the media – need to assume a key role in the debating and shaping of development strategies and agendas;
- Holistic or integrated approaches such as the sustainable economic, community, political and livelihood development policies must be put in place;
- Implement all policies documents agreed upon, for example:
    - *The African Charter on the Values and Principles of Public Service and Administration*
    - *Recommendations on the African Management Development Institutes Network [AMDIN];*
    - *Recommendations of the Ministers for National Education/Higher Education and Scientific Research*
    - *Recommendations of the Conference of Ministers for Public/Civil Service (CAMPS); Regional Economic Communities; New Partnership for Africa's Development (NEPAD) and others.*
    - *Recommendations from the United Nations, Commonwealth of Nations and other international organisations.*

References

AAPAM [2012] "Aide Memoire" for the 34th AAPAM Annual Roundtable Conference, Zanzibar, Tanzania, November 12-16, 2012 0n the Theme, Performance Management for Improving Public Services delivery in Africa

African Union Commission (AUC). [2011] African Charter on the Values and Principles of the Public Service and Administration, Addis Ababa, Ethiopia.

Biney Ama & Adebayo Olukoshi (eds.) [2010] Speaking Truth to Power. Selected Pan-Africa Postcards Abdul Tajudeen Raheem. Pambazuka Press, Britain.

See also [http://uww.pambazuka.org/en/issue/259]

Bouckaert Geert & Halligan John [2008] Managing Performance, International Comparisons, Routledge, London

Brewer, Gene A. [2008] Employee and Organisational Performance", in James L. Perry and Annie Hondeghem (eds.) Motivation in Public Management. The Call of Public Service, Oxford University Press, Oxford, pp136-56

Dooren Wouter van & Steven van de Walle (eds.) Performance Information in the Public Sector. How it is Used. Palgrave, Macmillan, London

Emeagwali Philip [2010] "How Do we reverse The Brain Drain?", Renaissance World – Restoring Black and African Dignity, 1st April b- 31st May, 2010, pp31-32-and 74.

Eymeri-Douzans Jean-Michel and Jon Pierre [2011] Administrative Reforms and Democratic Governance. Routledge Taylor & Francis Group, UK.

Forje W. John [2009]. The Challenges of Administrative Political and Developmental Renewal in Africa: Essays on Rethinking Government and Reorganisation. Nova Science Publishers Inc, New York. USA

Forje W. John [2009]. The Challenges of Administrative Political and Developmental Renewal in Africa. Emerging Issues. Nova Science Publishers Inc. New York, USA

Galavan Robert, Murray John, Markides Costas (eds.) [2008] Strategy, Innovation, and Change: Challenges for Management. Oxford University Press, Oxford, United Kingdom

Geyer Robert and Rihani Samir [2011] Complexity and Public Policy: A New Approach to 21st Century Politics, Policy and Society. Oxford University Press, Oxford, United Kingdom

Heinelt Hubert [2011] Governing Modern Societies: Towards Participatory Governance. Oxford University Press, Oxford, United Kingdom.

Hondeghem Annie and Perry l. James [2009] "EGPA Symposium on Public Service Motivation and Performance: Introduction", International Review of Administrative Sciences, Vol.75, No. 1. March 2009, pp5-9

Hyden Goran [2001] Operationalising Governance to Sustainable Development, Perspectives on Global Development and Technology, 17, 3. p13+

Kim Sangmock [2005] "Individual Level Factors and Operational Performance in Government Organisation", Journal of Public Administration Research and Theory 15 (2): 245-61

McLennan, A. [2005] Changing the Mainstream: Political Mechanisms to Enhance Inclusion. Input Provided to DSPD/DESA Expert Group Meeting: Towards an Inclusive Society. Shaping the Policy Process, United Nations, New York, July 13-15.

McLennan Anne & Munslow Barry (eds.) [2009] The Politics of Service Delivery. Wits University Press, Johannesburg, South Africa.

Meyer, J.P. &Allen NU [1997] Commitment in the Workplace, Sage Publication, Thousand Oaks, CA, London, New York,

Moynihan P. Donald [2008] The Dynamics of Performance Management. Constructing Information and Reform. Georgetown University Press, Washington, DC.

Olaopa Tunji [2009] Innovation and Best Practices in Public Sector Reforms: Ideas, Strategies and Conditions. University Press Plc, Nigeria

Perry L. James & Annie Hondeghem [2008] Motivation in Public Management: The Call of Public Service. Oxford University Press, Oxford, United Kingdom

Ramesh M, Eduardo Araral & Xun Wu (eds.) [2011] Reasserting the Public in Public Services: New Public Management Reforms. Oxford University Press, Oxford, United Kingdom.

Ritz Adrian [2009]. "Public Service Motivation and Organisational Performance in Swiss Federal Government," International Review of Administrative Sciences," Vol. 75, No. 1. March 2009, pp53-78

Seldon C. Sally & Brewer Gene A. [2000] "Why Elephants Gallop: Assessing and Predicting Organisation Performance in Federal Agencies". Journal of Public Administration Research and Theory. 10(4). 685-711

Sharma, K. C. and Mhaluali [1993] "Botswana Confronting the Realities of Capacity Building", in L. Picard (ed.) Capacity Building for Policy Change and Sustainability: Lessons from African Experience, Lynne Reiner Publishers, Boulder and London,

Sharma C. Keshav and Lekorwe H. Mogopodt [2007] "Institution-Building for Human Resource Development – Lessons of the Centre for Specialisation in Public Administrations and Management (CESPAM) in Botswana", African Journal of Public Administration and Management, Vol. XVIII, No.2 – July 2007, Nairobi, Kenya, pp51-58

Thomsen Alex [2010[An Introduction to African Political parties. RoutledgeTaylor & Francis Group, London.

United Nations [2009] Good Practices and Innovations in Public Governance. United Nations Public Service Awards Winners and Finalists, 2003-2009. United Nations Publications, New York, USA

Vandenabeele Wouter [2009] "The Mediating Effect of Job Satisfaction and Organisational Commitment on Self-Reported Performance: More Robust Evidence of the PSM-Performance Relationship", International Review of Administrative Sciences, Vol.75, No.1. March 2009, pp12-34

World Bank [2000] Higher Education in Developing Countries: Peril and Promise, The Task Force on Higher Education and Society. World Bank, Washington DC
(www.tfhe.net/report/downloads/download.report.htm)

Chapter 11

The Triumphant Agony and Tragedy of Globalisation and Africa's Socioeconomic Transformation: Challenges, Changes and Prospects for the Future

Abstract

Perpetrated by individuals and nations

Globalisation is now the catch sing-song for Africa's socio-economic transformation. The paper adopts an Afrocentric approach to the topic in question. The argumental scenarios are that by participating in the global economy, it is believed Africa's poverty level will be reduced. The second perspective is that poverty and inequality are rational to globalisation. The third is that only by adopting a progressive focused Afrocentric approach would Africa transcend itself from a backward into a quality services delivery society. Poverty and repression remain dynamic: low-income countries are caught in a trap of dependency, and will never progress without fundamental structural and institutional changes. It argues that globalisation provides a phase for economic transformation. This cannot happen when a society is totally a raw-material resources exporter and lacking the technological know-how and competitive edge giving added value to its natural resources. In a world of sharply divided, intractable political and economic interests and conflicts, brutalities and violence, especially against those regarded as poor and underdeveloped will continue to live uneasily on the threshold between life and death. Theoretically and practically the threshold is a fecund place for building possibilities in one's capacity and capabilities for converting backwardness into wealth. Presently globalisation for Africa is nothing short of being the highest stage of scientific imperialism and the tsunami for consolidating exploitation and dependency of territories that suffered from the yoke of imperialism, slavery and colonialism. Within its present context and structural-functional realities, globalisation remains the hidden tsunami agenda for reinforcing and deepening the underdevelopment and humiliation of Africa. The question is how does Africa fit into the rapidly changing globalising technological structures? The crucial struggle is not between the West and globalisation. It is within Africa developing a new mind set, political will and strong determination to carve and build the Africa she wants within the rapidly changing socio-technological world construct. How can the continent take advantage of the 'late-comer advantage' (Geschenkron, 1962) in the new world of our time in shaping its development and quality services delivery nexus? Looking backwards and forwards tells us that globalisation is a long and complex historical process, weaving continents together. It is cultural, political and technological, as well as economic (Smith, 2006; Kaplinsky 2005). Given that capitalism has finally triumphed, what kind of economic and political order must African countries articulate and constructively deploy in their struggle for sustainable development? It is argued that a progressive, forward looking and focused Afrocentric strategic agenda provides the dynamics for constructive change and changing the game of Africa's humiliation in spite of its vast natural resource's potentials. Poverty and underdevelopment in the midst of plenty can only be addressed through concerted and comprehensive attack on the root causes of the dynamics of humiliation. Globalisation positively executed provides deeper creativity and evokes a middle ground for all countries transcend common grounds for the good of all humanity. O'Donohue (2009) concludes that 'the divided mind separates each from the other and can never participate in the challenge and journey of their conversation, conflict and creativity'. A thoroughly Afrocentric human-centred development dedicated to the fullest promotion of human welfare and wellbeing when it is conceived and implemented to bring the greatest good to the greatest possible number of citizens.

Keywords: Afrocentric, poverty, policy, inequality, globalisation, leadership, (under)development, science and technology, resources, quality services delivery and governance

Introduction

Facing the Realities of the Changing Circumstances

It is generally taken that globalisation offers many benefits but is also the source of major risks facing all societies' particularly transitional polities in Africa. The process of change cannot be held back. The ingenuity of human-beings is on the progressive track, and must be utilised for the good of all. Here lies the positivism of globalisation. The negativisms of globalisation abound as well. Of course, the situation of these transitional polities is made precarious due to their low state of scientific and technological capabilities and capacity as well as low knowledge capacities. Absence of scientific and technological capabilities, democratic governance, and visionary leadership impedes the sustainable transformation of a society as it inhibits the path to quality livelihood to the citizens in spite of its vast abundance of natural resources. These countries remain poor, underdeveloped and exploited in the midst of plenty. The progressive ingenuity of human intellect goes a long way in redressing the peculiarities and disadvantage of African states, provided they know what they want and are ready to work for it.

African countries are faced with the issues of what Dicken (2003) calls the *'Global shift'* characterised by a number of interrelated factors; (i) systematic reduction in the barriers to cross-border flow of labour and capital, (ii) purposeful pursuit of objectives; and (ii) the complex web of scientific and technological advances (Kaplinsky 2005, Smith 2006). The scientific discourses of these authors and others constitute a clarion call for restructuring the foundations of the development trajectories of African countries. A development trajectory that strongly appeals for a progressive Afrocentric approach to its developmental construct. Indeed, the present underdevelopment of African states exposes the inherent fault-lines and structural deficiencies of the existing economic model which brings the fall the icing of Hamlet's deeper perception that all is not well within the African continent. Therefore, a shift of focus is needed from efforts to reinforce an inherently flawed and failing system to conceptualising a better one. That necessitates a re-examination of the social and political foundations of modern economic systems to fathom the underlying forces that have shaped their development and are now driving evolution to something else (Jacobs, 2018:71). Globalisation drives development and poverty in different intensities and directions.

The conceptual and theoretical framework builds on a number of drivers underpinning the global society of the 21st century and beyond. To begin with, Smith (2006) notes that the globalisation agenda is well known, as it focuses on market opportunities, business interests and access to key material, the gradual forging of links between groups and societies and the way economic and technological, military, political and cultural forces and mechanisms 'become global, i.e., anchored in institutions at the global lever, over historical time. Kaplinsky (2005:8) looks at globalisation as a complex and multidimensional process which can be viewed through a variety of lenses. As such, the 'boundary definition,' is one which focuses on the reduction of obstacles to mobility. Therefore, the following hypothesis can be advanced;

(i) Globalisation as characterised by the systematic reduction in the barriers to the cross-border flow of factors (labour, capital), products, technology, knowledge, information, belief systems, ideas and values;

(ii) Globalisation as the purposeful pursuit of objectives – personal, economic, social or political – which leads individuals, institutions and nations to widen their activities across national boundaries;

(iii) Globalisation arises as a natural outcome of the growth complexity and reach of scientific and technological advances;

(iv) As technology and communications allows a widening of personal and social horizons, globalisation is a natural outcome of the curiosity of the human species (Kaplinsky, op cit.)

(v) Africa is in dare need of an Afrocentric balanced globalisation construct to trigger its transformation but must do so by building its capacity in all spheres of transformation requiring new mind set, attitude and behaviour.

Bekkers et al (2017:20-22) posits that the process of globalisation specialisation has radicalised the already existing process of structural differentiation, which can be witnessed since the start of the industrial revolution triggering a number of interrelated factors, for example; (a) specialisation leading to an increasing degree of interdependence of a network; (b) the consequences of this specialisation has been institutionalised; (c) the complexity arising from interdependencies places knowledge and information being locked up in a rather autonomous highly specialised organisations; (d) exchange relationships exist as result of interdependency. Technological progress leads to the advance of global processes in the production of knowledge. Africa is in great need of technological progress, knowledge production as well as increase in productivity of quality goods that attracts foreign demands and investments as well as meeting the people's demands needs and aspirations.

It means and compels the continent progressing in the direction of establishing its identity by understanding its past in order to discover its compound complexity of the present, and to better construct its present in preparation for its future progress. As such, interdependency becomes the watch word for a win-win accord in the globalised world in which we find ourselves - the struggle or competition for survival and advantage in society requires African countries working together in a community by developing and expanding existing socio-cultural heritage values and conceptual believes like Ubuntu, Harambee and Batho Pelo amongst others as the foundation in accelerating the socio-economic transformation of the continent. We have to understand globalisation's hidden agenda under the canopy of humiliation, oppression, subjection, exclusion and supremacy but also as providing a way to further the progress of the continent. The views of Jacobs (op cit. p73) points out that all social accomplishment is the result of the process of generating, releasing, directing and channelling human energies by organising and coordinating the interactions and relationships between individuals, activists and institutions. Without working in synergy progress cannot be made by African countries. Every individual achievement is founded on the cumulative achievement of all humanity over millennia. We all, developing and developed world, are each other's keeper and should therefore work together to better express, invent produce or use without drawing on that universal reservoir of social wealth to promote, develop and sustain our wellbeing on Planet Earth.

Equally, there can be no social advancement, discovery, innovation or creativity without aspiration, inspiration and invention of creative individuals. As a latecomer, Africa has to constructively deplore the now witnessing exponential growth of the various forms of social power – democracy, human rights, rule of law, open markets, entrepreneurship, scientific discovery, technological innovation, globalisation, higher education, and access to information have been major drivers of growth. Africa cannot afford to stay aloof as these changes bring significant progress in enhancing human security, welfare and wellbeing on planet earth. It is from this construct that the paper strongly advocates a progressive Afrocentric developmental synergic approach (human-centred) as the unique role in the sustainable transformation of the continent.

The Journey So Far

What has been Africa's journey so far in the globalisation saga? Given the continent's deficiencies in scientific and technological development, the fall-outs of globalisation is not impacting on the quality of livelihood of citizens compared to the developed polities. Africa has to meticulously, constructively and comprehensively beef up its scientific and technological base to benefit from the fallouts of the globalisation construct. The scientific and technological backwardness of Africa is a combination of many intertwined factors which should be addressed simultaneously to ensure the continent benefits appropriately from advances generated by the forces of globalisation.

Kaplinsky asserts that globalisation arises as a natural outcome of growing complexity and reach of scientific and technological advances. The producers of technology widen their global reach in order to sustain their profitability which they do by intensifying the production of weapons of human destruction and other consumer goods in order to defray the costs of their technological complexity and to strengthen their grip on technological deficient nations. Scientific and technological progress leads to advances of global processes in the production of knowledge. With improved human capital development in many third world countries, Africa in particular, we discover some degree of trickling down effects of globalisation on these countries. The greatest impact has been in the domain of Information and Communication Technologies (ICTs) which, is impacting in different ways on the quality livelihood of citizens.

This alone indicates to African countries to start mapping a new development order in addressing and understanding these important contributions which are critical issues of our time; and how they will convergence between the developed and developing countries. Reinert (2017) notes that globalisation offers many benefits but it is also the source of major risks facing all societies. Altenburg and Lutkenhorst (2017) points out that those countries that need industrial policy the most typically have the worst governance. While Jwa (2017) makes the bold attempt at proposing a new general economic development premised on that economic institutions and policies must embody 'economic discrimination' if there is to be any chance of real economic development. By economic discrimination, is entail 'treating differences differently' by selecting and supporting economic entities and behaviour that contribute positively to the economy. African should undertake a vigorous process of discriminating in treating differences differently, between a destructive Eurocentric and a progressive Afrocentric approach to transforming the continent from a third into a first world.

What Must African Countries Do?

African countries are caught between a rock and a hard place. They have either to accept globalisation as it is under the dictates of western conceptualisation, (Eurocentric development Approach) or enact a new development policy approach (progressive Afrocentric approach) geared towards facing the challenges of globalisation which should focused in the direction of a purposeful pursuit of objectives, be they personal, economic, social or political – which leads individuals, institutions, and nations to widen their activities across national boundaries. Africa is challenged to widen its activities across, local, national, regional and continental boundaries and academic disciplines as well. Karlsson et all (2018) assert that as a consequence of globalisation, news, ideas and knowledge are moving rapidly across national borders and generating international spill overs. Emerging new ideas should spur structural changes impacting on the livelihood of the people. In this respect, Muchie (2017) points out how globalisation has changed our lives and will continue doing so positively or negatively.

Changing our lives positively and sustainably is what we all crave for. That is why we need a progressive Afrocentric developmental and strategic approach under the canopy of a New African Economic Social and Political Order (NAESPO). Only through such a strategic people-oriented focused development geared towards the common good of all can progress be made. Unfortunately, the apparent hidden agenda of globalisation so invested with vested interest voluntarily supporting and pushing ahead widening economic inequality legalising social injustice. Historical precedent is no justification for rational basis for the future persistence of social injustice. It is high time African leaders and people examine themselves critically to better put-in-place comprehensive economic institutions and mechanisms for economic, social and political activities to fully engineer the right changes that move the continent the right way forward.

Unfortunately, the appetite for power, wealth accumulation and greed prohibit any form of creating an NAESPO for the continent. Africa remains the only continent in the world long-serving presidents. For these reasons, the continent can neither find its way out of the Eurocentric development agenda nor capable of embracing a progressive Afrocentric development approach that should give the globalisation nexus the kind of impetus to uplift the quality livelihood of the vast majority of people. To benefit from globalisation, Africa needs a New Economic, Political and Order (NEPSO) that enshrines the respect and practice of the basic tents of democracy. This falls in line with the views earlier expresses under (ii) i.e., globalisation as objectives that leads, individuals, institutions and nations to widen activities within and across national borders; and (v) triggers transformation in building capacity in all spheres of mind set, attitude and behaviour (MAB). Mbaku (2018) characterises this as a way of ensuring a peaceful coexistence of people for inclusive growth and development. Bache and Reardon (2016) go further to conceptualise this as well-being for all citizens.

Therefore, a progressive Afrocentric developmental approach under the umbrella of democratic and administrative governance provides the potentials of globalisation as a win-win developmental approach to the reconstruction of the continent's underdevelopment status. By using the lenses of the democratic governance – accountability, transparency, rule of law, and justice etc., would provide the avenue towards the promise and realisation that 'no one is left behind.' Given that our current world construct is unjust, and a more just world is possible provided we have the political will for constructive and meaningful change exist, Africa can transform itself into a respectable polity. Globalisation should engender a process of global social justice (Craig 2018).

Empowering in an Era of disempowering

Colonial rule piloted the way for Eurocentricism. This seriously contributed to the disempowering of the African people. Globalisation without a progressive Afrocentric input will only sustain the disempowering of African countries. What is required is globalisation that empowers the people in the era of growing disempowering of the African continent. Empowering all segments of society is crucial in fighting inequality, poverty and underdevelopment. There is urgent need for a capability-oriented human-focused policy approach. It should be noted that the current Eurocentric approach creates a situation whereby employment and training opportunities have been reduced or not tailored to the real needs and aspirations of the people. At the same time, the level of poverty, inequality, injustice and social exclusion is on the increase. Independence was expected to pilot the way for an Afro-centric agenda. The Afro-centric agenda implied the continent take control over its development process; put an end to being a material producing and exporting continent; diversify its economic; building the necessary infrastructure and institutions to pilot the developmental changes of the continent.

This is why the imperativeness to critically and judiciously look into the institutional policy frameworks and programmes that should accelerate the quantitative and qualitative human capital development of the continent creates vast opportunities for job creation, employment among others to better curtail the out flux of existing human flight out of the continent. Empowering the young people (Otto et.al eds. (2017) are essential in beating the negative sides of globalisation and in preparing them to face the challenges of globalisation and make it work for the good of the continent. The tidal waves of the tsunami of globalisation cannot be reversed; we only need to see how to make the best of its fall outs. Here we need to beef up the human capacity, scientific, technological and entrepreneurial base of the continent. Presently, the impact of globalisation on different regions and types of low-income economies varies. To be candid, there are significant differences in regional and continental experiences with globalisation. For example, Asia has gained and is gaining, while Latin America and the Caribbean and (especially) Africa and central Asia have lost. This challenges Africa as a wake-up call to seriously rethink its current development strategy. In East Asia, the locational imperatives of modern production systems mean that countries which together participate in regional value chains have been able to reap complementary and systemic gains. In Africa, only countries like South Africa, Egypt, and Nigeria are on the path of sipping some benefits. Generally, Africa as the bastion of the supply of raw resources, should have gained, but due to its low technological, infrastructural and skilled human capacity is not benefiting from the volume of globalisation. Baba A. Buntu (2012:289-290) states: "Africa is one of the richest geographical areas in the world, abundant with minerals, flora and natural resources. Resources that, even by narrow definitions, should constitute a foundation for a superpower. So, why is Africa not a superpower? And moreover, why is Africa seen by many as nowhere close to becoming one?" We should bear in mind that globalisation arises as a natural outcome of the growing complexity and reach of scientific and technological advances. Thus, scientific technological progress leads to the advance of global processes in the production of knowledge. The production of knowledge and of its use in African remains extremely low.

It is time for the continent to sit up and face the realities of its development predicament; to try to understand why the rapid progress of globalisation is not doing more to reduce the stubbornly level of world poverty. What we see is a growing increase in the polarisation of riches and poverty between and within the developed and developing countries as well as within the developing polities in Africa. Africa need to uncover the perils as well as the promise and benefits of globalisation in an unvarnished look at wines, losers and the new rules of the game in the national and global economy of our time. The continent continues hovering in poverty as the developed polities shine in growth and riches. It is now imperative for African countries to understand development and globalisation from an altogether new perspective, one which takes into consideration short-term, middle-term and long-term socio-eco-political development, the dynamics of liberation, and the consequences of humiliation. Against this background, it is time for

African countries to start looking afresh the dynamics of globalisation, the positive and negative sides, the fear, joy, anger, resentment that it impacts on society and the people. Apparently, we have through this section looked at the magnitude of the challenges of oppression, exploitation and benefits that manifest itself in the African continent. Attempts have been made to locate some of the historical root cause of predicaments, some of the social challenges bedevilling the region; as well as pointed out some of the things needed to addressing the plight of the continent. In short, we have looked at the continent within the premises of both the blame-and reality tack games, pointing out some of the best way forward in overcoming the challenges as well as laying down a solid foundation for a better tomorrow. The ball is in our courtyard. Are we ready to take the first shot at the right target? Or continue on the 'blame' pathway and o how long? Are we ready to address the major internal major cankers that beset he continent – the sacralisation of political power, corruption and poo governance. The abuse of power in Africa has become an entrenched aspect of the body politics of the continent. That abuse of power has much to do with our strong attachment to titles as symbols of power. For example, in Cameroon, during the reign of Ahmadou Ahidjo behaved in the manner of the title 'Le Pere de la Nation' like the current president Paul Biya and also the title of 'Osagefor' accorded to Kwame Nkrumah of Ghana. The institutionalisation of the 'dominant - one-party system' as a form of democracy has even made things worse with the proliferation of 'presidents for life' which has gained strong-hold in Africa. Titles are good and give dignify status, but we should make proper and not destructive use of these titles. Titles should be rallying sign-post for mobilising society to progressively move forward in the right direction and tempo (Bayart, 1989, Bjornson 2001, Fanon 1963, French 2004).

Multiparty politics under the dominance of an entrenched dominant single party system is nothing but window dressing of the continent and passport of turning a blind eye to wanton abuse of office and a contributing factor to the plague of corruption that has beseeched the continent. The cancer underpinning the continent's underdevelopment is 'corruption,' lack of accountability and transparency. Honesty, Accountability and Transparency (HAT) are taboo concepts in the body politics of the continent. According Forje (2018) like many other publications (Ngwane, 2005) hammer on the issues of corruption. "The prevalence problem of the corrupt practices poses serious developmental problems on the continent. It is the canker worm that is eating deep into the fabric of the African society. According to the findings of international watchdogs such as the Berlin-based Transparency International (TI), postcolonial Africa is one of the worst victims of political corruption on the globe. This trend has to be reversed in order to give Africa the chance to develop. In spite of the abundance of natural resources in Africa – gold, crude oil, diamonds. Bauxite, aluminium, copper, uranium, manganese, phosphates, iron ore, tin, limestone, coffee, cocoa, maize, cotton, wheat, rice, livestock, rubber, sorghum, timber, tea, fish, to name but a few – Africa remains the poorest continent on earth" (Vakunta, 2006:33). The sad side of all this is the state of poor governance which contributes to a state of inferiority complexes, dependency, exploitation and domination of the region. It pins Africa to the abyss of underdevelopment for entirety. It is a painful good-bye to becoming a member of the select club of quality livelihood for all citizens. Are we surprise as many of our citizens flee the continent for greener pastures abroad? The answer is blowing in the wind, but Adedeji Adebayo (1999:41) was clear when he opined that "what African countries have lacked during most of their history as independent states are leaders who are unifiers, chiefs in the true sense, who bind wounds, hold everything and everyone together, mobilise and innovate their people, pursue policy of inclusion rather that exclusion and are seen by and all to be of the highest integrity and beyond suspicion."

References

Adebayo Adedeji (ed.) (1999) Comprehending and Mastering African Conflicts. The Search for Sustainable Peace and good Governance, Zed Books, London.

Altenburg Tilman and Wilfred Lutkenhorst (2017) Industrial Policy in Developing Countries: failing Market, Weak States. Edward Elgar Publishing Limited, Cheltenham Gloss, United Kingdom.

Bache Ian and Reardon Louise (2018). The Politics of Well-Being. Understanding the Rise and Significance of a New Agenda. Edward Elgar Publishing Ltd. UK

Bayart, Jean-Francois (1999), The Criminalisation of the State in Africa, Indiana University Press, Indianapolis, USA

Bekkers Victor, Menno Fenger and Peter Scholten (2017). Public Policy in Action; Perspectives on The Policy Process, Edward Elgar Publishing Limited, United Kingdom.

Bjornson, Richard (2001) The African Quest for Freedom and Identity. Cameroonian Writing and the National Experience, Indiana University Press, Indianapolis, USA

Buntu A. Baba (2012). "Unscrambling Africa's Future: The Role of African Youth in Pan-Africa Empowerment|," in Mammo Muchie, Sanya Osha and Matlotleng P. Matlou (eds.) (2012) The African World and Renaissance, African Institute of South Africa, Pretoria, South Africa, pp289-310

Craig Gary (2018). Handbook on Global Social Justice. Edward Elgar Publishing Ltd. UK

Dicken P (2003) Global Shift: Reshaping the Global Economic Map in the 21st Century, 4th edition, Sage Publications, London

Fanon Frantz (1963) The Wretched of the Earth, Grove Press, New York

Forje W. John (2018) Cameroon Without Corruption. The Search for A New Vision and Shared-Values. Challenges for Policy Choices, Articulations and Implementations. Lambert Academic Publishing, Germany.

French Howard (2004) A, Continent for the Taking. The Tragedy and Hope of Africa. Knopf, New York, USA

Gerschenkron Alexander (1962) Economic Backwardness in Historical Perspectives. The Belknap

Press, Harvard University Press, Cambridge. MA. United States of America

Jacobs Garry (2018) 'Foundations of Economic Theory: Money, Markets and Social Power', ASPJ – Africa and Francophonie, Ist Quarter 2018, Vol. 9, No.1 USA, pp71-94 (see also Jacobs Garry, 'Money, Markets and Social Power,' Cadmus 6, No.2 (May 2016):20-42. Available at: http://cadmusjournal.org

Jwa Sung-Hee (2017). A General Theory of Economic development: Towards a Capitalist Manifesto. Edward Elgar Publishing Limited, Cheltenham Gloss, United Kingdom

Kaplinsky Raphael, (2005). Globalisation, Poverty and Inequality Between a Rock and a Hard Place. Polity Press, Cambridge, UK

Karlsson Charlie, Andreas P. Cornett and Tina Wallin (2018). Globalisation, International Spill overs and Sectorial Changes. Implications for Regions and Industries, Edward Elgar Publishing Limited, Cheltenham Gloss, United Kingdom

Mbaku Mukum John (2018) protecting Minority Rights in African Countries: A Constitutional Political Economic Approach, Edward Elgar Publishing Ltd. UK

Michie Jonathan (2016) Globalisation and Democracy. Edward Elgar Publishing Limited. Cheltenham Glos, United Kingdom

Michie Jonathan (2017). Advanced Introduction to Globalisation. Edward Elgar Publishing Limited, Cheltenham Gloss, United Kingdom.

Muchie Mamo, Sanya Osaha and Matlotleng P. Matlou (eds) (2012) The African World. From Fragmentation to Unity and Renaissance. Africa Institute of South Africa, Pretoria, South Africa.

Ngwane, Jeff (2005) |" Corruption is a Plague Affecting Everyone", November 21, <www postnewsline.com/2005/11 corruption/html.

O'Donohue (2009)

Otto Hans-Uwe, Egdell Valerie, Bonvin Jean-Michel and Atzmfiler Roland (eds.) (2017). Empowering Young People in Disempowering Times. Fighting Inequality Through capability-oriented Policy. Edward Elgar Publishing Ltd. UK

Reinert A. Kenneth (2017) Handbook of Globalisation and Development. Edward Elgar Publishing Limited Cheltenham Gloss, United Kingdom

Smith Dennis (2006) Globalisation: The Hidden Agenda, Polity Press, Cambridge, United Kingdom

Vakunta Peter (2006) "The Trouble with Africa" COSESRIA Bulletin, Nos.3 and 4 Dakar - Senegal. Pp32-34

Chapter 12

Unleashing Peoples Power: The Promise of a New Democratic Revolution and Evolution for Africa

Abstract

Historical events do not come with labels upon them, telling us precisely how important they are. Only the passage of time can do that, and it may take years. The sad but heroic act of the hawker in Tunis and the subsequent spell-over effect in early February 2011 unleashed the power of the people, creating a new political and governance dawn in the annals of Africa's democratisation and governance process. Anew Africa in the making can no longer be stopped. The end of dictatorial, life serving presidency in Africa is over. The paper critically and objectively looks at the challenges and promise of a new democratisation process in Africa since the collapse of the global bipolar system: the intensification of the globalisation process which mobilises and enhances peoples' power to regain lost and rightful authority as the true custodians of power in society and the only force capable of dismantling entrenched centralised authoritarian regime structures under the canopy of President for Life Syndrome [PFLS] It argues that building strong institutions and political processes such as elections, strong and vibrant civil society, and not strong individuals remains critical in ensuring a sustainable democratisation and governance process for the continent. Strong institutions and not strong individuals provide the take-off for a continent that has stuck on the political/ development runway for five decades. The African democratisation and governance architecture through the unleashing of "Peoples Power" should be seen as providing an opportunity to engage and develop appropriate capacity and responses to the continent's governance and development challenges. But the emergence of peoples' power should convert to constructing or perpetuating a state of anarchy. It should be for the liberation of the people from the bondage of centralised authoritarian regime structure characteristic of many African countries. The paper concludes that the principal governance challenge facing Africa is visionary servant leadership deficit and how to embrace a self-nourishing relationship between authority, accountability, participation, inclusion and responsibility. Sustaining the unleashed power of the people acts as checks and balances to the emerging geo-political-governance for a beleaguered continent stuck on the runway for too long. Unleashing people's power is the start of a new political era. Change is coming to Africa. The people must embrace change and be conduit to the new transformation process.

Key words: strong institutions, political process, inclusion, civil society, electoral process, change

Introduction

Understanding the Political Dynamics of Change

> *"We believe in the rights of all people to govern themselves. We affirm the right of all colonial peoples to control their own destiny. All colonies must be free from foreign imperialist control, whether political or economic. The peoples of the colonies must have the right to elect their own government, a government without restrictions from a foreign power...The object of the imperialist powers is to exploit. By granting the right to the colonial peoples to govern themselves they are defeating that objective. Therefore, the struggle for political power by colonial and subject peoples is the first step towards, and the necessary prerequisite to complete social, economic and political emancipation"* **(Kwame Nkrumah)**

The Arab Spring of 2011 unleashed an avalanche of chain events. A new continent was in the making. Significantly, the event brought to the forefront the consequences of the politics of neglect, exclusion, and articulate-self-interest. Above all, it accelerated the need for and process of institutional reforms in the governance structure of African countries. A new revolution and new continent were in the making through the dynamic forces and power of the people [Forje 2009]. The take home message is clear – a new dynamic political evolution, "Flight 2011 Peoples Power" is on the runway ready for take-off to a new state construct on the continent. When Presidents are brought into a Court of Law in a cage, or on stretchers, no condition can be deemed to be permanent. Importantly, no one is above the law. The state is the people. And the people as custodian of the state possess the final say in state construction. The "Arab Spring" or the fall of any regime should be seen within this context. Things fall apart; Achebe [1958] was categorical on the way things were crumbling in the political construct of the continent. With independence came what Dumont classified as "False Start" in Africa. The independence of the continent started on a wrong note; how to recover and build prosperous continent constitute a daunting task before the people. It is the Mount Kilimanjaro to be conquered collectively, not individually.

Western mounted conspiracy to eliminate leaders critical to western colonialism, exploitation, marginalisation, remains to glaring today. In 2016, Southern Cameroons launched its movement back to climb Mount Fako – reacting to the results of the politics and policies of more than fifty years of the gruesome practice of forced assimilation, annexation, exclusion, marginalisation, injustice, bad faith, discrimination, inequality and name the rest. Bad governance taking centre stage in the structure-functioning of the system. A once beautiful, peace-loving country turned into a nightmare of genocide and destruction. In 2021, Susan Williams sums up Africa's independence in an eloquently and analytically breathe catching book – "White Malice : The CIA and Neocolonisation of Africa" which reveals new shocking details of western covert programmes and actions in Africa; how western intelligence services crawled over the continent, poisoning the hopes of the 1958 All African Peoples Conference in Accra-Ghana with secret agents and informants; surreptitious UN lobbying; cultural infiltration and bribery; assassinations and coups. As the Europeans pretentiously moved out of the continent, the Americans and others swept in with bitter consequences that reverberate throughout the continent today. On the other hand, we equally to be critical of our behaviour, attitude towards ourselves and stop placing our short-comings on others. What have we done or are doing to show that the Euro-centric agenda is wrong and bad for the continent? For fifty years, our actions point in the direction of accepting and condoning to the Euro-centric agenda? They help and continue dividing us; pushing us to practicing on ethnic centred authoritarian governance system. We have failed to find a common ground between the ruling elites and the ordinary citizen; we have only created a colony or nation state of 'forgotten Africans' – the poor, vulnerable and destitute.

The new challenge is to create a common and unified ground for all the people – students, trade unionist, intellectuals, layers, teachers, professional organisations and the large army of have-nots to re-strategise towards a united front for the total liberation of the continent with the goals of some of ideas that was envisioned in the Lagos Plan of Action (LPA) aptly outline by Bade Onimode (1993:54) as:

- Achievement of regional food self-sufficiency through domestic food production – not just food security that can be achieved through volatile food and food imports;
- Elimination or alleviation of poverty;
- Satisfaction of critical needs, safe drinking water, clothing, housing, health care, education and transportation;
- Achievement of effective integration through national and collective self-reliance.

All these essential achievements which constitute the valuable ingredients for sustainable quality livelihood have to be attained under the canopy of democratic governance, justice, rule of law, equality and respect for people, learning of how too living and eating together as one nation, one continent in unity in diversity all focused on the process of nation-building. Africa needs development with a human face. Development with a human face means putting people and country first, and not putting money and power first as it is currently practiced in many African countries. This is the only countervailing strategy that can be adopted as a weapon against Eurocentricism in Africa. Africa has to break out of the downward spiral of the centre-periphery agenda. We can make proper use of Diaspora – 'the bush fellows' or the 'been-tos' by creating the necessary conducive environment for the 'brain-drain' turn 'brain gain' to look back home and impart he knowledge or wealth gained. An enabling environment should create as pulling factors for the Diaspora return home. Creating an enabling environment, "demystification and democratisation of elite-oriented science and technology and also of formal higher education… and the slow but steady increase in local expertise and innovations replacing 'formal' technical assistance programmes… thus reducing the gap between the formally trained scientist and technologist on the one hand and the indigenous (informal) technocrats on the other (Brown, 1995:227). Africa need to create an *"Open Society"* which according to Montesquieu (Thomson, 1969:85) 'open society founded on the belief, deep seated in the 18th century servants, that private interests did ultimately harmonise, that, through benevolent dispensation of Nature, men could be rogues or frauds individually but decent or honest in a mass."

The African state following views advanced by Montesquieu "the state owes to every citizen, an assumed subsistence, proper nourishment, suitable clothing, and a mode of life not incompatible with healthcare. Wealth in a state implies large scale industry. Whenever this happened the state must provide them with immediate help… whether it be to prevent the people from suffering or whether it be to prevent them from revolting" (Thomson op cit. p91). This boils down to what President Franklin D. Roosevelt coined as *"freedom from want"* and *"freedom from fear."* In short, the state is a community of communities, and one of its chief functions is to serve as an adjustment centre for the claims of individuals and societies upon one another. National, continental and world politics are now to a great extent, the result of clash between conditions of inequality and the ideals of equality. As African countries started shaking the yoke of colonialism, political independence and equality of status have been won by people of Africa and Asia formally subject to European rule, dramatic inequality of standard of living have become more important. It is important, we all live like brothers and sisters remains of the most persistent of all political and social ideas in our present civilisation. Africa should present itself differently in the current world context. That can only be done through a progressive Afro-centric agenda totally embraced by the 54 or more countries on the continent.

When will constructive and encompassing change begin to take hold on the continent? The question is when will the African "summer or winter" begin? Regime change being is touted as not just about government, but also will systematic regime change take hold on the continent. For now, good governance is touted as not just about government, but also about political parties, parliament, the judiciary, the media, and civil society. It is about how citizens, leaders and public institutions galvanised and relate to each other in order to make democratic change successful and sustainable [Ngwa in Tanjong 2012 xiii] When will the "Arab Spring" or "calm before the storm" start its South of the Sahara descent? Or has south of the Sahara witnessed its share of the Arab Spring and what results did it produced? The rise of peoples' power in search of a new holistic and inclusive governance system constitutes a new political development in Africa fifty years after independence. The continent descended into a 'bottomless pit' with centralised dictatorial regimes having a free playing ground. The 'Arab Spring' resurrected a new political jig-saw. Governance system and politics will never be the same again on the continent. Understanding the secret of democratic governance in Africa; unlocking the continent's future requires a proper understanding of the past, to better understand the present and gunning for a governance system of inclusion, shared-government, shared-obligations, responsibilities, and shared-prosperity in the construction of a sustainable future [Forje 2011:128].

A new renewal in the public sphere construed on the inalienable dictum and synergy of 'inclusion'; and 'popular participation through polycentric planning replacing the structurally-defective centralised governance arrangements since independence no longer could be stopped. The challenge now is to avert a resurgence of the strong-man phenomenon. Above all, for Africans to understand and appreciate the long-term consequences and implications of NATO's assault on Africa North of the Sahara. Unleashing of peoples' power must have a vision and a focus geared towards (a) creating a capable and sustainable state: (b) sustainability in the living standards of the population: (c) protecting its independence and owning its development roadmap: (d) ensuring the rule of law, justice, equity in the distribution of the wealth of the nation: and (e) national unity, cohesion, constructive engagement of the various stakeholders, among others. The "Arab Spring 2011", leading to NATO's destruction of Libya constitutes a challenge of global democracy. Above all, African solidarity and unity is put into serious questioning. While unleashing peoples' power for redressing the ills inflicted to society by centralised authoritarian regime structures is welcome: but unleashing peoples' only to permit foreign re-colonialisation is absorbed and defeats the good intention that goes along with the ideal orientation of "power to the people and equal opportunities" for all in a new social construct. Unleashing peoples' power represents the final authoritative allocation of values for the common good, or else the purpose is defeated. Contrast the rapid mobilisation of forces by the UN and NATO towards Libya compared with the slow response by these bodies towards the plight of the suffering masses in Somalia or during the genocide in Rwanda. Few countries are coming to the aid of Kenya currently bearing the burden of refuges from Somalia. The international community has become a community of paradoxes. Articulate self-interest takes priority over collective interests. The West is not interested about the future of Libya but what it stands to gain from the conflict of destabilisation. No one supports a centralised authoritarian regime structure that defines the basic fundamental human rights and liberties of people. The double standards of the West are what are questionable. The hypocrisy of African unity is questionable at this stage. Is the agenda of African unity by 2017 still tenable [Forje 2011?].

Akinola, [2011:1] is explicit on this point. His assessment is that centralised authoritarian governance system engendered orchestrated politics of exclusion, neglect and increasing deprivation in the continent. The public sphere dominated by the few elites with 'particularistic' concerns at the exclusion of the people, the trend of corruption among public officials clearly points in the failure of centralised governance arrangements underlines the inherent facts behind the "Arab Spring" and may be South of Sahara's "Hot Autumn" or whatever may occur. African leaders for decades adopted a governance system of disconnect, contradictions, and dissonance between the political subcultures of the postcolonial [state] on the one hand and that of 'the people' on the other. A governance system of 'president for life (PFL) was established under the canopy of a monolithic party structure which rested on ethnic hegemonic forces. "Majority of citizens were pushed to live outside the post-colonial state, but also under the currents of the continuous struggle of groups within the state to redefine political spaces and identities in order to have a place and a voice in the public sphere, as well as a share in the allocation of public resources" [Pul 2011:163-4]. In short, inclusion and shared-prosperity were denied the vast majority of citizens. There is no trickle-down effect from top (or haves) to the bottom (have not's).

Apparently, democracy and state construction seem to have evolved on a wrong note in Africa. In addition, the question of visionary leadership remains a thorny sore in the transformation process of the continent. For now, Africa is littered with "served" and not "servant" leadership. In the face of existing mosaic of predatorialism there is need for responsible leadership and the implanting of a democratic and good governance culture in Africa, including the development of and appropriate utilisation of human capacity and natural resources. Why the urge of maintaining the status-quo of holding on to power for too long in Africa? Political sociology has an important contribution to make to the understanding of the inter-relations between political power and other institutions as the feature of the functioning of the political system. This is a very worrying aspect of the output functions of the governance structure in Africa. The political gurus and other analysts must begin the search for the right cure to the endemic cancer of 'sit-tight presidents' that has gripped the structure-functional dynamics of politics and governance on the continent.

Stay-Put Presidents in the World 2012

Country	Leader	Years in Office
Angola*	Eduardo des Santos	32
Burkina Faso*	Blasé Compaore	24
Cambodia	Hun Sen	26
Cameroon*	Paul Biya	37
Chad*	Idriss Derby	21
Ethiopia*	Meles Zenawi+	20
Equatorial Guinea*	Obiang Nguema	32
Gambia*	Yahya Jammeh	18
Kazakhstan	Nurusltan Nazarbayey	21
Iran	Ali Khamemi	30
Sudan*	Mar al-Bashir	22
Uganda*	Yoweri Museveni	26
Yemen	Ali Abdullah	33
Zimbabwe*	Robert Mugabe	32

Source; Forje (2013) Complied from different sources including international database, US Census Bureau 2011; ***Indicate African Countries; + Meles Zenawi died in August 2012**. The current dynamics shows a change at the helm of the state structure with a number of these heads of states being thrown out by coups or by natural acts (death) for example Ethiopia (Meles Zenawi; Zimbabwe, Robert Mugabe; Chad, Idriss Derby; military coups in countries like Burkina Faso, Sudan, Gambia drove out the long-standing presidents; while Cameroon, Equatorial Guinea and Uganda still hang on to President for Life nexus. In Cameroon, Paul Biya will in November 2022 cloak 40 years in power.

Africa is locked in the vicious cycle of poor governance which accelerates the state of underdevelopment. Since the 1990s, issues of 'Good Governance and Democratisation' have taken centre stage in the transformation process of the continent. Currently, the continent is submerged in witnessing the new onslaught of "people's power" to counter the action of 'hegemonic centralised authoritarian regime system.' Served leadership in Africa failed in responding appropriately to the needs and aspiration of the citizens. Popular participation [Adedeji 1997] was denied the people. The ruling regimes shied away for a people-centred developmental approach [Adedeji 2000]. They went for a foreign dominated and control developmental approach that paid-off for the ruling elites and regime structure and foreign articulate self-interest. That is why Africa is stuck on the runway compared to the Asian Tigers.

The ongoing events in North Africa are indication of the uncompleted activities of the 1990s return to democratic governance and the imperative need for constructing a capable developmental state. The pending question is whether the 'Arab Spring' will generate new optimism, momentum and hope for change in Africa's fragile states within the contextual framework of "Good Governance" [Mkandawire 1995; Shivji 2006:338-220]. The trajectory of post-colonial African democracy currently stuck within the realm of dictatorship and in light of the growing quest towards new forms of democratic governance has been subject to fundamental discourses calling for significant reconstruction and a new mindset. The analytical frameworks, three in number, are construed on exclusion, marginalisation and leadership. Poor leadership contributes to articulate self-interests paving the way for structured exclusion, exploitation, marginalisation and underdevelopment. The rule of law is shelved aside to ensure maximum exploitation of the people by a handful elite class. The revolt by the people is clear; beginning with the western colonial powers were compelled to withdraw, not so much because their power position became their power position became untenable, but because the Asian and later African peoples withdrew their assent to their legitimacy. It should be noted that all regimes, then, function within a political environment. The political leadership is gradually shifting from 'ascriptive' to 'achievement' standards: men are ceasing to be accepted as leaders mainly because of hereditary status; and are beginning to make their impact through their own talents.

Conceptual Premises

The conceptual framework and premises of departure builds on 'problem-solving and problem-seeking' in view of Pye's six crisis of development approach. As a result of inherent weakness in centralised-authoritarian structurally-defective governance system, people are provided with the vast opportunities to recapture their stolen inalienable rights or custodianship and as the focal-point of effecting constructive change as well as accelerating the process of development. As a result of the inability to resolve these crises of development, the continent is stuck on the runway unable to take-off to an industrial and eventually, a service delivery society.

		Legitimacy	legal construct of leaders
		Distribution	equity in wealth-sharing
		Penetration	reaching all aspects of society
State Construct	=======➔	Identity ======➔	who we are and belong
Crisis		Participation	constructive engagement
		Integration	sense of belonging
			// //

Sequences of development => **varying as events evolve**

Holding citizens under a state of siege for a long-time, is bound to back-fire especially with the penetrating impact of the power of information and communication technologies [ICT's'] in the era of a global village gaining more grounds and educating the people on their basic needs and fundamental rights. A form of disconnect exists between leadership and society which affects the orientation and realisation of a capable developmental state guaranteeing sustainable quality livelihood for its citizens. Sit-tight or Presidents for Life makes the government to lose its legitimacy. Fraudulent or dirty elections contributes to citizens' losing confidence and trust in the regime structure. Citizens' harbour and rightly so, the belief that their votes do not count: they are not participants in the transformation process.

Their sense of belonging and identity is seriously question and challenged. Apathy is ensued and frustration arise creating and injecting elements of destabilisation in the smooth functioning of the state machinery. When services delivery does not exist or pitched on ethnic lines, distribution and identity crisis begin showing its ugly face. The call for national unity goes unanswered. This equally reflects on the call for an African federation which goes on answered. No wonder many of Africa's secessionist movements are finding their way online to bring their plight to a wider audience. These secessionist groups arise due to government's inability in addressing the crisis of development in a most satisfactory way encompassing the best possible distribution, and inclusion indicators. There are too many foreign interests with varied hidden agendas but with the common goal of destabilising the sustainable socioeconomic-political transformation of the continent. Two factors stand out clearly in this disconnect or destabilisation process.

- First, the ruling elite are disconnected from the realities of the society within the global context. The ruling class operates on the agenda of self-articulate interests which often is the interests of foreign bodies – part of the forces of neo-colonialism:
- Second these foreign bodies operate under a hidden agenda made to represent the interests of the ruling class. This problem of alienation tends to affect the mental picture, decisions-making ways of life and behaviour of these actors in their day-to-day operations. Politically, the public sphere is dominated by the few elites with 'particularistic' concerns at the exclusion of the silent majority of the people.

These alienating divisions between stakeholders in development (the elite and the people) are legacies of colonialism which were adopted by successive post-colonial African governments. As expected, most economic and political decisions in the continent do not reflect the aspirations of the people simply because government operations are excessively centralised and not people-focused. Without the citizens playing active roles in decision-making, governance process would continue to exclude and marginalised them" [Akinola 2011:3]. It is equally important to guard against the 'blame theory' fifty years after independence. Rather the blame theory runs the risk of being a boomerang to the continent. Africa was ahead or at par with some Asian Tiger countries fifty years ago. Where is Africa compared to the Asian Tiger region today? How objective is western media presenting the true image of Africa's struggle for sovereignty and independence? Has Africa felt encouraged from the Western media coverage? Developing a positive mindset is one of the most powerful life strategies there is to achieving anything. Therefore, if the aim of unleashing people's power is to bring about constructive and inclusive restructuralisation or meaningful change, which is the mindset of the people, positive affirmation and coverage by Western media, would help develop a powerful and positive attitude to the quality of the living standards of the now oppressed majority. With such power and mindset, we can turn failure around into success.

It is no secret that Africa has long been deprived of affirmation from the Western media: it would not be much to ask if we request that the continent be given proper and correct coverage for a change; expose those leaders bleeding their countries to death and are in the good books of the West for the inherent silent destruction of the continent. Africans are now tired of the protection and support given by the West to African dictatorial regimes that have no interest in their citizens but theirs and foreign articulate self-interests in mind. The 'blame theory' cannot be rejected in this case. Western developmental approach towards the African people is biased, but positive towards African leaders who are stooges of the West. Any African leader vocal and positive towards the development of the people is toppled within a twinkle of a second. On the other hand, Africans themselves must learn to distinguish between the leaders working for the collective good, not for the good of the West. The constant negative reports on the continent break the spirit and undermine people's ability to make positive change or attract goodness into their life. On the other hand, these negative reports should be a determinant factor for the people to unleash their power and take full control, own their development and show the world the real side of the African continent. The state construct model advanced by [Edigheji 2010; Mkandawire 1995; Akinola 2011] in various ways streamline the missing links between African governments and African realities in the process of state construction. The missing dimension in the development process of the continent being the people. Applying the International Analysis and Development (IAD) framework, the paper situates and discusses the recent structural changes in Africa North of the Sahara and eventual fundamental changes likely to occur in other parts of the continent. Mainstreaming models of state building assumes establishing state legitimacy and avoiding state collapse through international intervention combined with military presence, huge amounts of aid, and democratic elections. The event in North Africa calls for a serious rethinking of the foundations of state construct in Africa.

Developments in North Africa are part of the uncompleted political structural changes of the 1990s and state inability to deliver quality services to citizens. The peoples' revolt for change constitutes a paradigm shift, from maladjusted states to democratic service delivery states. The paper is grounded on three structural changes; namely: (a) new growth theory or capability expansion; (b) institutional approaches;

and(c) capability theory. The credibility of many African leaders can be faulted on these interrelated approaches to transformation. Sharing the views of Akinola [2011], regardless of the system of government practised, the type of relationship that a state has with the people and their community institutions, to a large extent, determines the outcome of democratic process. In short, a country gets the type of government it deserves. But a country can equally work itself out of the predicaments created. Unleashing people's power is an attempt to redress the existing impasse between the state, government, leadership, civil society and the private sector. The inability of many African states to consolidate democratic governance or even simply create some form of stable political order invites a range of questions: Such as the reasons for the chronic crisis of legitimacy and participation afflicting Africa states. The failure to develop a sense of collective identity, vision and goal as the way forward for the people to reclaim their dignity and livelihood in building a sustainable and viable c The failure of formal political institutions; widespread exclusion of substantive groups harbouring critical opinions about the existing governance system and the need to put in place of functional system addressing the press8ing needs of the people. Such questions require in analysis that goes beyond formal institutional evolution and perhaps delves into the more sustentative socio-cultural dimensions of African governance conundrum" [Bujra and Lando, 2011: xii].

African states in their present constellations are uncheckable with unfettered power and thus become predatory as well as destructive to the sustainable transformation of the country. Foreign aid, economic and technological dependence is institutionalised through the *"donor-sustainability dichotomy"* with increased poverty in spite of the vast natural resource's potential of the continent. Wrong priorities, the misuse of funds and dependence on foreign assistance leads to disconnect between state and civil society. The "donor – sustainability dichotomy" (DSD) must be adequately addressed. Dependence on 'donors' for development restrains any form of sustainability, rather this increases dependency and vulnerability of the state as it exposes it to external exploitation and manipulation. Chaos, discontent, loss of trust and confidence in the government prevails, leading to a structurally-defective pattern of governance. The continent must get rid of the "donor dependency" attitude to cultivating a "sustainability – development" attitude. The present "donor-sustainability" dichotomy is destroying the continent. Dependency on donor is not healthy for the socio-economic transformation of the continent. Africa should move away from the 'donor' mentality to greater reliance on mobilising and proper utilisation of domestic resources. Dependency on indigenous effort is a sustainable development approach which must be encouraged. North "Africa's Spring" unleashing of peoples' power and its eventual spill-over on the continent should be localised and contextualised within the following factor areas characterising the continent's governance style.;

Wrong priorities, wrong development strategies, wrong approaches;
Political party patronage, clienteles, and winner-takes-all attitude, ethnic affiliation, personality cult-worship;
Poor Prevalence of centralised, authoritarian, ethnic regime structures, Governance
========➔ Failure of civil society acting as custodians of the state, people's power, and rights:
Failure of governments in meeting the basic needs of the people;
Interferences from external bodies condoned by governing elites for articulate self-interests;
// // // //
Discontent, exclusion, alienation, fear, mistrust, and social injustice manifesting in various sectors of society and seriously impacting on the health of the state thereby jeopardising its legitimacy, sovereignty, independence, functionality and existence
// // // //
Failed States; Collapsed States; Under-developed Economies; Exploitation, Inequality, Injustice, Endemic Poverty and Misery

The people of Africa deserve better than what their leaders have crafted for them. Unleashing their powers should be a constructive and sustainable developmental approach and not for destructive purposes. The *"black man's burden"* should be converted into the *"black man's pride, governance and development."* It means rethinking Kwame Nkrumah [1965] in its true perspective like rethinking Karl Marx to better understand Adam Smith's 'Wealth of the Nation', and the degree of rising frustration of the people. Karl Marx writes: Modern bourgeois society, with its relation of production, of exchange and of property, a society that has conjured up such gigantic means of production and of exchange, is like the sorcerer who has no longer able to control the powers of neither world that he has called up by his spells" While the ruling elites may rejoice in their current victory, they have cast a black spell they cannot recall – "The Arab Spring" may be just the beginning. Recent events during the past couple of months in Mali, Burkina Faso, and Equatorial Genuine are indications of what awaits the continent. The forces behind unleashing the power of the people should equally draw valuable lessons from Myrdal's [1957:99] assertion: *"Underdeveloped countries should not accept the inherited Western economic theory uncritically but remould it to fit their own problems and interests"* If Africa has a dearth of good leadership is it God's design? The truth remains, if we want to clean things up, we need to be clean ourselves. The absence of many local services, government must reflect its development priorities and provide meaningful strategic answers to the plight of the people. To be candid is it *government of, by and for the people* or ***government against the people.*** Africa has to work against the governance style of **"government against the people" and promote the ideals government, "of, by and for the people"**

Is There an Emerging African Lion?

These and other related inadequacies ties with serious development challenges facing the continent as well as the inadequacies of these response over the years – the leadership problem and positive citizenry responses to good leadership. What were the responses to the brilliant ideological ideals of "Nyerere's Ujamma? How did Africans react to Nkrumah's stand on a Union Government for Africa? This is the continent's greatest deficit. Is there something within the African environment that is so unique as to make the development challenge especially intimidating? Is the environment too 'hard' or 'harsh' to permit the occurrence of anything positive for the sustainable development and transformation of the continent? Is the "Arab Spring" the type of activities promoting a mindset that is antagonistic or favourably disposed to change – the type of change that uplifted the Asian Tigers from poverty to affluence, and from authoritarian rule to increasingly open government. It equally challenges the reader to ponder over the relationship between the prevailing chid-rearing practices, on the one hand, and the emergence of visionary leadership (as against follower-sycophant) personality type or personality cult worship, on the other [Balogun 2011.see also Bjura and Buthelezi 2002].

Constructive structural changes in mindset, behaviour, attitude and style of work are imperative for the emergence of an African Elephant, Lion or Leopard. For now, the very opposite of these virtues are at work It was hoped the collapse of the East-West conflict will drive a new sense of direction into the minds and behaviour of the people of the continent to constructively engage themselves towards a new beginning in a long walk to genuine independence and sovereignty. Two decades after it is still the old sing-song. Things not only continue "falling apart," but it remains a 'long walk to freedom.' The harsh reality is the very opposite of rising standards of living and new freedoms for the African poor. There are severe, potentially catastrophic economic inequities between the North and South. The G-7 powers have very largely ignored these, but they have not conveniently gone away, rather they have become steadily worse. With such widening gap why should the oppressed not revolt – The Arab Spring for example. Following Erskine Childers, the statistics show,

- for example, in 1960 the richest one-fifth of the world's population enjoyed 30 times the income of the poorest fifth;
- by 1989 the richest fifth was receiving 50 times the income of the poorest:
- the ratio of 20:80 or worse, dominates our world today:
- as the 1990s opened, the 20 per cent Northern minority of humankind had 82.7 percent of world gross national product: 81.2 per cent of world trade. Had 94:6 per cent of all commercial lending: 80.6 per cent of all domestic savings: 80.5 per cent of all domestic investment: and 94 per cent of all research and development:
- the 60 per cent majority of humanity in the South get the 20 per cent (or less) scraps from the tables of the affluent:
- in the South, some 1.2 billion people now live-in absolute poverty, on the very margins of survival itself:
- more are driven into this condition every day, 40 per cent more in the last 20 years: they include over 560 million rural women whose numbers in such misery are running faster than men, with 75 million women the sole heads of rural households containing over 500 million children and older people.
- over 15 million of the rural poor die each year from starvation and disease aggravated by malnutrition;
- not less than 24000 children still die wholly unnecessarily every day:
- an African woman has a 1 in 14 chance of dying in childbirth, and in large parts of Asia a scarcely better chance:
- here in the North a woman has only 2:1 in 4000 chances:
- in many Northern countries only 2:1 in 7000 chances of dying while giving birth:
- new pandemic health threats like AIDS made 20000 children orphans in 1992 in Uganda alone, while mosquitoes breeding their own immunity against pesticides have made malaria present again in over 100 countries infecting over 260 million people, especially in Africa [Childers Erskine 2011:19: UNDP Human Development Report 1992:] show the state of gross inequality between the two worlds.

On almost every indicator of social and ecological life – from health protection, literacy development, pipe born water supply, and future vocations for the youths to maintenance of biodiversity and the planet's security of air, water, soil and climate – the restructuring of societies for corporate globalisation has been increasingly life-destructive. Africa is most vulnerable in this setting. The road is indeed long and winding, requiring perseverance, patience and many other virtues to cope with the setbacks and disappointments without capitulating or resignation. Importantly, is bridging the deepening North-South divide. Both North and South must be undergoing comprehensive structural reforms (CSR) to achieve equality among nations and peoples, small and big. Such a move will have sealed the jigsaw puzzle causing conflicts, wars and instability within the global system. There is need to holistically tackle the system's weaknesses – poor governance, inequality and uneven development enhancing the divide between nations and peoples of the world.

Given such a structural setting, how can an African elephant, lion, leopard emerge? There is no disease without a cure. The plants, roots, are there and provide the hidden answer to the problems. We need just a determined will to search for the cure. We lack that determined will and mind for research and solution seeking. Our solution search is dependence on "handouts" which further subjects us to greater dependency and exploitation. The cult of dependency and exploitation is built on the endless repetition of "free-market mantras (liberalisation, privatisation and encouraged foreign trade and transnational corporation) combined with attacks on the cult's enemies – protectionism, government interference, capital controls, in short centralised authoritarian regime structures. Increase citizen participation by revamping, strengthening and deepening the governance system provides the way for constructive engagement leading to sustainable development. The salience of the preceding sections raises the issue of a conflicting situation between unleashing people's power and centralised authoritarian regime structure in Africa. As earlier noted, failing to address the crisis of development subjects the people to the state of rising destructive frustration against the rise of collocation of personalities and circumstances whose behaviour cannot be logically explained or predicted with any degree of certainty. Apparently, the behaviour of such leadership is overcrowded with the vices of inherent powers of articulate self-interests. On the other hand, these actions depict two things; (i) frustration with their leaders for failing to deliver the quality services needed; and (ii) their poor judgement in selecting their leaders. Based on these postulations, one can deduce the following hypothesis.

- Poor judgement on the part of citizens produces leadership selection that can be disastrous to society in the long-end;
- The relation between leadership and development arises from the realisation that the latter is most unlikely to happen unless the leadership selection, succession and development questions facing many African countries are fully resolved.
- External influences are a contributing factor to the continent's crisis of development.

The marriage between these three areas is simply, a country gets the type of government it deserves. External factors (the blame theory) at these stage some fifty years or more after independence does not hold in my opinion. It is a contributing factor depending on the angle of approach and space in time. Available evidence indicates that Africa's record in effecting smooth transfer of power has been largely dismal. Between 1960 and 2004, over half (51.5 percent) of the continent's heads of state lost their jobs in military coups, wars or invasions; with only 7.8 percent leaving office after electoral defeat, and another 12.2 percent opting for voluntary retirement. Military coups and one-party dictatorships have become an anachronism, but they continue to cast an ominous shadow on the leadership selection process in a number of African countries [Balogun, 2011:11]. In some countries, multi-party politics has been a curse not a blessing to the people. Cameroon presents a good example. The monolithic party was disastrous to the country just as multi-party politics today. The spell of a dominant leader sends the other parties into the slumber land of acceptance of whatever is handed down from the centre-to-the periphery. Existing leadership takes advantage of the peculiarity of party politics in the country to prolong the stay in office. Africans need to device new vision of political leadership, party-role and power-sharing paradigm that would ensure good governance. For now, Cameroonians continue turning a blind-eye to wanton abuse of office and corrupt parties that plagues the society.

Staying too long in office without proper service delivering and people's participation is a good recipe for chaos and violent system change. The top-bottom approach cannot satisfy the aspiration of the people: rather it alienates as it destroys a sense of national unity, cohesion and belonging. The two hypotheses merge into a blame theory based on the articulate self-interests of former colonial lords. Adopting this theory is an escapist approach to the problem. Because the citizens are unable to fashion a comprehensive and concerted inward looking approach for their well-being, room is created for external bodies to advance their articulate self-interests. Incidentally, local governing elites join the bandwagon of foreign articulate interests in bleeding their own society to death. In short, the ruling elites are stealing from the future, thereby impoverishing future generations. The governing elites have adopted what could be called 'appropriated carrying capacity" (ACC) which basically means the rich are living off the resources of the poor.

Analytically, the people demonstrate poor judgement in the selection of their leaders. The leaders when selected or elected respond inadequately to the demands of society. When basic needs are not provided people respond in a violent destructive frustrated manner. Incorporating the second hypothesis, Africa lacks visionary transformational leadership to inspire motivation, facing existing challenges from a holistic perspective and in the ultimate interest of the people. The relation between leadership and development arises from the realisation that the latter is most unlikely to happen unless the leadership selection, succession and development questions facing many African countries are fully resolved.

Leadership hinges on personalities, and, by implication, on accidents of history. It will take a long time for the continent to have visionary leadership style like that rendered by Nelson Mandela, Kwame Nkrumah, and Julius Nyerere (3Ns) as persons capable of transforming environments and influencing the course of history or at the very least, guaranteeing political order in rapidly changing societies and circumstances. These three African personalities exhibited what may be termed visionary political-will hypothesis which holds that the viability of the environment and of existing institutional arrangements depends on the protective cover provided by the incumbents.

Visionary servant leadership is a necessary but insufficient condition for the transformation of social systems. It must incorporate constructive engagement with the people as an inherent part and the beneficiary of change. Citizens must be ideologically and psychologically educated on their roles and missions for constructive change. The failure to harness and integrate leadership talents from different sources accounts for the lack of progress on various fronts in Africa. Corruption is one big challenge that remains impregnable due to the prevailing assumption that all it takes is 'leadership' or 'political commitment' [Forje 2003]. Leadership is not sufficient. The leader as a "general" needs strong support from the 'foot soldiers. The marriage between a "visionary servant leadership" and "proactive positive responsive citizenry" constitutes the anvil for the emergence of a capable developmental state. Africa has to learn from the experiences of the East Asian Tigers – Singapore, Hong Kong, South Korea, Taiwan, Malaysia, Indonesia and Thailand within a generation transformed their economies significantly contributing to improving the quality of livelihood of the citizens. Some of these countries were a par or below the economic status of some African countries in the 1960s. In the eyes of the developed countries, East Asian states were dirt-poor and contemptible.

By the 1990s the debt-poor countries had exhibited phenomenal growth rates that bypassed those of the developed economies. With this, they gained their respectability and sustained their sovereignty. These countries are the envy the world over. Africa remains an eye sore in spite of its vast natural resource's potentials. But natural resources require added value through human capital development, which Africa has failed to develop. Adam Smith [1776] is explicit on the correlation between natural resources and human capital development. The Asian Tigers transformed themselves from a "third" into a "first" world status within a couple of decades. The government and people of Libya failed to learn from the Japanese and South Korean development approach. With the vast revenues flowing from oil, human capital development was not given a priority. Dependency on external workers only helped in fuelling animosity against the government. The crisis of penetration was not properly handled and resolved. The two salient input factors driving these countries were "visionary leadership" and "responsible responsive citizenry" accelerating their sprint into economic supremacy, namely: -

Building the ethos of discipline, hard work, and alertness into leadership and management selection and development programmes

Pursuing a state-led, and export-oriented growth strategy, rather than wait until "market forces determined when and how fast import substitutes would be produced;

Remaining focused on internally charted courses and being constantly alert to, nay, prickly towards, external interference or distractions;

Useful tips from the Asian Tigers to ==➔ African Countries

Developing a zero-tolerance for mediocrity, ineptitude, slackness, and slovenly behaviour;

Bartering democratic participation for the benefits of economic growth, and imposing discipline in place of organisational laxity;

Giving high priority importance to thrift and savings at the initial stage, to allow for 'conspicuous consumption' later

(Sources: collude from Balogun 2011)

Of course, external input factors equally played an important role. But these external factors were aided by internal forces looking for a sell-out on thirty pieces of silver, internal discontent and other related developments. A vibrant country-centred civil society would have stood its ground against external invasion, placed articulate national or collective interests first is what is expected for a progressive Afro-centric governance style should offer the people. The time is now for the continent to show the red card to the destructive Euro-centric / Ego-centric post-colonial Africa. Post-colonial leaders and administrators have intensified Euro-centric agenda with ego-centricism.

Conclusion: Strategies and Visions for the Future: Hope or Despair?

Confronted with social and economic inequalities, the people have rediscovered their power, a possible solace to change existing state construct. In short, theirs is a move of existential realism than an ideological socialism. This move should be backed by clear doctrinaire orientation broadly conceptualised with a new economic, legal and political order where the country's resources are equitably distributed and aggregated for the all over development of the country/continent. Political as well as economic vision is sustained by a corresponding education system currently lacking in Africa. The cloud of despair hangs over the continent. Despair can easily lead to rising destructive frustration.

The take home message for Africa is simple: Hard work and sustainability (self-reliance) and not "donor inclined to sustainability". Short and simple, with the determination of the leaders and backed with the commitment of the citizens (leadership and popular participation or constructive engagement with civil society and the private sector) an anaemic economy can grow into a manufacturing powerhouse producing first class products for the world market like the Asian Tigers. Where is Africa today? Still running around with a begging cap in hand. The "donor driven development" attitude cannot lead to sustainability and improved quality living standards for the population. There is an urgent need for strong institutions to help democracy to emerge and be consolidated on the continent.

A new mindset, behaviour and attitude are called for. The first step is to ask ourselves whether we want transformation, how, when and by whom? Facing the reality is to understand and appreciate the fact that only Africans can develop Africa. External assistance is only assistance not the real thing. The Asian Tigers did not sit with folded arms waiting for 'aid' to flow in from Europe. They took the bull by the horn. China did the same. Why can't Africa? No other country can do that for another country. Articulate national self-interests play a key role. The new found power of the people should be directed in that direction. We should change 'the ideal or reality of false start' into a genuine reconstruction for the birth and growth of a new continent.

Is the *"Arab Spring"* the forerunner to the emergence of an 'indigenous sustainability development strategy' or what? A third African revolution becomes imperative. The first revolution triggered the independence of the continent. The second saw the failed attempt towards genuine return to democratisation as witnessed in Cameroon in the early 1990s, Rwanda 1994; Kenya 2007, Zimbabwe 2008, and Ivory Coast 2010 for example. "Democratisation instead of allowing African citizens to re-appropriate the apparatus of the State had if anything reinforced the most destructive tendencies of African polities. In particular, democratic reforms imposed from the West had precipitated a string of failed states. Despite the rapid spread of competitive 'multi-party' politics and various other state institutions designed to moderate power; the formal political structures of the state system are more than ever alienated from African citizens. Moreover, the constraints on African government's formal powers of patronage imposed by economic liberalisation have not starved clientelist networks embedded in the state system" [Bujra op cit.]. For now, the crisis of underdevelopment in Africa and globalisation in the world is a unique opportunity for addressing some core issues of democracy and human development. Like centralised authoritarian regime structure practised by many African countries, it has invigorated a worldwide peoples' movement whose loud demands for change are attracting more and more attention and support from grassroots movements. The "Arab Spring" for example may or may not lead to a true "African reconstituted democratic governance system." A governance system structured to break the camel's back of endemic poverty, wanton corruption, inertia, exploitation, marginalisation and underdevelopment. Rwanda, under the leadership of Paul Kigama after the gruesome genocide of the 1990s is turning the tables for the common good of the people. Can Rwanda become the continent's success story? How many of such success stories do we expect to emerge from the continent?

Africa is in urgent need of radical innovation, "Economics as Anatomy" (Swann, 2019); it needs "Innovation, Economic Development and Progressive Policy" (Fagerberg, 2018), it requires to thread on the path of a new governing science and technology (Shin-yi Peng, 2018) that should focus on questions of creativity, innovation, entrepreneurialship, production, how to be active participant in the growing new dynamic of the international economic order of time which is a knowledge based economy. As a knowledge-based economy requires that Africa should beefed up its educational system, producing both in quality and quantity requisite human capital and capacities to propel the economic transformation from a backward to a quality services delivery economy. Africa needs sustainable growth through strategic innovation (Kodama, 2018), it needs entrepreneurship, innovation and education (Ulla Hytti et al. (2018); it needs 'accelerators' in venture creation and growth; developing innovative capabilities and engaging in globalisation as active not passive participants to better harvest the best of the process. There are vast opportunities outside in the global context for exploitation requiring African countries to use their wits and resources to improve on the quality of livelihood of the vast majority of its population.

The collective power of the people to shape the present and construct a better future is greater now than ever before, and the need to exercise it is more compelling. However, mobilising that power to make life in the 21st century and beyond more democratic, more secure and more sustainable is the foremost challenge of this generation. Fifty years ago, as the wind of change blew across Africa; the continent was on the road to recover from the cataclysmic events of the 'Slave trade" and "colonial rule" African leaders were inspired by the vision that a united, independent free Africa back with its vast natural resource's potentials will be empowered politically and economically to construct a new society with vast opportunities and promise for a better future to be handed down to the next generation. These "founding fathers" agreed in principles and set up an institution (Organisation of African Unity – OAU) to give effect to their vision. Over the past five decades, that good vision crumbled into centralised authoritarian regime structures denying basic needs to the vast majority of people. Today, the people have no choice but to regain their stolen freedom. Karl Marx notes: *"the redeeming feature of war is that it puts a nation to the test. As exposure to the atmosphere reduces all mummies to instant dissolution, so war passes extreme judgement on social system that have outlived their vitality."* Unleashing peoples' power puts the continent to test. Will the new power brokers make or mar the emerging political construct in a direction for the common good or will they go the same way as the disposed old guards? The continent is entrenched in a "conflict situation" which must be resolved amicably to the good of all. Some vital issues to be seriously addressed include:

- the uneven distribution of benefits:
- developing its human capital as added value to its natural resources:
- the current ambiguous role of the state:
- the North-South divide as well as internal rich-poor, male-female dichotomy:
- the place of Africa within the global construct:
- Africa articulating, aggregating and owning its developmental path;
- taking cognisance that the continent's interests are given top-most priorities:

The plutocratic management of the African state suppresses the emergence of the African Lion, Leopard, Crocodile or Elephant; constraining any form of the emergence of an engine of growth or the take-off to a capable developmental state structure. Africa's development is held back by the 'dependency theory;' the donor-development approach and the privatisation of the state approach adopted by the governing elites including even the means of coercion [Ake 1998]. Choices for good governance and sustainability must be articulated by the people, each stakeholder taking its share of responsibility. Are the people well equipped to make the necessary choices and stand by it? Has the state created the requisite environment for the people to operate and regained their stolen liberties and rights? Currently, "Africa is dismissed as a continent void of power. And, too often, this assertion is made without interrogating its truth, or investigating how it could be that Africa, once associated with great civilisations, has been so firmly engraved in the human psyche as a peripheral continent. Peripheral, but obviously not insignificant, if the relentless efforts of rich nations to 'get a piece' of Africa is anything to go by. For, 'getting a piece' of Africa has been, and continues to be, the dominating factor in many African countries' interactions with the rest of the world" (Buntu, 2012:289). John Henrik Clarke (1992) notes that: "the most dangerous of all dependencies is to depend on your powerful oppressor to free you and share power with you, because powerful people never train powerless people to take their power away from them." Thomas Sankara (1988; 89) ascertains; "we chose to risk new paths to achieve greater happiness. We chose to apply new techniques and to look for forms of organisation better suited to our civilisation."

Without which unleashing ***"Peoples' Power"*** will fail to achieve the envisioned goals. What a shame if the new uprising for a new state construct falls on the way side. Remember, policies represent the final authoritative allocation of values. Peoples' Power is a reality in today's national and global politics. At the national level, it sends a clear signal to "sit-tight presidents for life" to drastically readjust to the virtues of the basic tents of democracy. The new generation of leaders must gun for open and accountable government that ensures transparency, inclusion, and quality services delivery, rule of law, justice and constructive engagement of the various stake-holders. The six crises of development must be holistically addressed. Democracy maps the pressing needs of good governance in a perilous age. Africa is entering this new age of "Here the People Rule" [Forje 2009] for the ultimate good of the country.

In the light of Africa's protean environment, one can but emphasise 'self-reliance' and a well-thought open development approach as the means of meeting the peoples demands while still meeting the challenge of the major contradiction, it is part of planet earth with vast natural resources but underdeveloped and the people poor in the midst of plenty. On the other hand: Europe belongs to Europeans. Europe exploited Africa for its development. Similarly, Africa belongs to the African people and cannot change the excellent situation in which the African people win successive victories in the struggle for sovereignty, liberation, liberty and development. Unlike Europe, Africa is not exploiting any part of the world for its development take-off. We must understand the aspirations of the African people and the realities of Africans held captive for centuries by external forces. Any form of analysis must be firmly grounded in recognition of the depth of African nationalism, unity, integration and sensitivity to the historical forces of imperialism and racism. Africa is a large and complex continent that has its own dynamics, a feature most noticeable among the grassroots for liberty and freedom.

Unleashing people's power has to be seen as a process aimed at the fulfilment of an ideal, the creation of a democratic and egalitarian society. Unleashing peoples' power is an ongoing process like democracy as a means to end of authoritarian or bad governance. To this extent, it is a process that seeks to attain an ideal. Because of the massive power of the state that is predicated on inequalities and a strong will to protect privilege, actors engaged in unleashing people's power is trapped in a very difficult situation. Popular aspirations demand of them great sacrifices whereas the state denies them opportunity to realise the ideal. We need to contextualise fundamental policies in respect of:

i. equality of opportunity and access to all training and reward system:
ii. equitable distribution of resources:
iii. Ownership of our development path

Democracy is beginning to emerge on the African continent. It is imperative for the people to mobilise the fighting spirit like in the old-days of the independence struggle and ensure the consolidation of the virtues of democratic governance throughout the continent. The Arab Spring beacons for constructive reckoning and comprehensive reform to re-rail the continent on the right track of governance. The need to unlock the leadership deficit in Africa is now but with an ideological agenda for constructing a capable developmental state. But the situation in Cameroon, Sudan, Mali, Central African Republic and other parts of Africa are doing destructive damage to the progress of the democratisation and good governance on the continent.

Recommendations

The paper strongly argues that *'unleashing people's power'* properly articulated and implanted rightly should promote a new era in the construct of African states to better promote: -

- the concept of oneness, belonging, unity and national cohesion:
- the need not only to dwell on problems, but to strive in a more constructive, comprehensive, inclusive and consensual ways of finding solutions to problems in order to accelerate African unity and integration;
- bearing in mind that in solving the problems of the continent, we must excavate the roots and not dwell superficially at the surface;
- the building of democratic organs where the people shall participate not only in the administration, but also in the planning of their education human capital:
- the development of an alternative curriculum moulded to suit the socio-economic and political environment in which education takes place:
- the ethos and practice of the rule of law, social justice and equity in prosperity-sharing:

- democratic management of the factors in the life of human society and ensuring sustainability in the living standard of the people:
- people of the same planet, and should co-habit as such:
- democratically governed world community and proper management of international cooperation for the wellbeing of all;
- that is imperative for the continent to achieve envisaged goals to adopt and implement a progressive and inclusive Afro-centric agenda, one that places the 'People in the Centre" of development; comprehensive policies moving Africa from fragmentation to Unity and Renaissance
- Africa needs to define itself far beyond the twenty-first century, to open up by combing indigenous and scientific knowledge, creating a multi-way dialogue and enhancing cooperation and participation among the various actors; drawing and making use of the Diaspora population for the successful transformation of the continent.

References

Achebe Chinua [1958] Things Fall Apart. London.

Ake Claude [1998] "The Feasibility of Democracy in Africa", African Books Collection & CODESRIA, UK and Senegal

Alexei Adebayo [1997] "Popular Participation, Democracy and Development: Is there a Dialectical Linkage?" in Adebayo Adedeji and Otter Oniga [1997] Nigeria Renewal and the Roots. Seed Books, London and New York in association with African Centre for Development and Strategic Studies (ACDESS), Ijebu-Ode, Nigeria, pp3-39,

Adedeji Adebayo [2008]" The Way Forward: Operationalising the Six Fundamental Principles of People-Centred Systems of Local Government", in Adedeji Adebayo and Samidele Ayo (eds.) [2000] People-Centred Democracy in Nigeria? The Search for Alternative Systems of Governance at the Grassroots. Heinemann Educational Books, Nigeria Plc, Ibadan, pp135-251

Akinola, S. R. [2011] "Restructuring the Public Sphere for Democratic Governance and Development in Africa: The Polycentric Planning Approach", in Abdalla Bujra (ed.) [2011] Political Culture

Governance & The State in Africa. DMPF Nairobi – Kenya, pp1-61.

Balogun, M. J. [2011] A Framework for Leadership and Management Development in the African Public Service. CAMPS Secretariat/UNDP, Nairobi, Kenya

Balogun, M.J. [2009] The Route to Power in Nigeria: A Dynamic Engagement Options for Current and Aspiring Leaders. Palgrave, New York.

Brown Barratt Michael (19995) Africa's Choices. After Thirty Years of the World Bank. Penguin Books, London. UK

Bujra Abdalla & Samuel Lando [2011] "Introduction", in Bujra Abdalla (ed.)2011 Political Culture Governance & The State in Africa. DMPF, Nairobi-Kenya

Bujra Abdalla & Buthelezi Sipho (eds.) [2002] Leadership, Civil Society and Decentralisation in Africa. DMPF, Nairobi – Kenya

Buntu Baba (2012) "Unscrambling Africa's Future: The Role of African Youth in Pan-African Empowerment" in Mammo Muchie, Sanya Osha & Matlotleng P. Matlou (eds.) (2012) The African World: From Fragmentation to Unity and Renaissance, African Institute of South Africa, pp289-310

Childers B. Erskine [2011] "In a Time Beyond Warnings – Strengthening the United Nations System" in Marjolijn Snippe, Vijay Melita and Henning Melber (eds.) [2011] Erskine Barton Childers – For a Democratic United Nations and the Rule of Law. Development Dialogue No.56, June 2011, Dag Hammarskjöld Foundation, Uppsala – Sweden

Clarke, J.H. (1992) "Blue Skies for Africans: Life and Death Choices for Africa Liberation quoted in P.L. Grant (2005), Navig8or Press, Nottingham,

Edigheji Omano (ed.) [2010] Constructing a Democratic Developmental State in South Africa: Potentials and Challenges, Human Science Research Council Press, Cape Town, South Africa

Fagerberg Jan (2018). Innovation, Economic Development and Policy. Edward Elgar Publishing Limited, Cheltenham, Glos. U.K.

Forje W. John [Forthcoming: 2013] Architecture of Democracy, Governance and Development; Challenges, Prospects and Opportunities: A Strategy for Africa – Finding the Way Foreword.

Forje W. John [2011]. Century of Change. Symposium on African Unity. Nova Science Publishers Inc, New York

Forje W. John [2011] "Rethinking Political Culture, Governance and the state in Africa. Situating Cameroon Within the Context of

Getting Systems Right – Governance and Capacity Building" in Abdalla Bujra (ed.) 2011. Political Culture Governance & The State in Africa, DMPF, Nairobi-Kenya, pp127-161

Forje W. John [2003] Cameroon Without Corruption. The Search for a New Vision, Niba Publishing House, Bamenda, Cameroon (New and enlarged edition forthcoming)

Kodama Mitsuru (2018) Sustainable Growth Through Strategic Innovation. Driving Congruence in Capabilities. Edward Elgar Publishing Limited, Cheltenham, Glos. U.K.

Marx Karl [] The Communist Manifesto

Mkandawire, T. [1995] "Beyond Crisis's Towards Democratic Development States" 8th CODESRIA General Assembly, Dakar-Senegal, 26 June – 2July 199

Myrdal Gunnar [1957] Economic Theory and Underdeveloped Nations._Duckworth_Publishers_London

Ngwa George [2012] "Foreword" in Tanjong Enoh [2012] Media Balance in Sub-Saharan Africa's Fragile Democracy. Analysis of Journalism Practice in Cameroon. Design House, Limbe – Cameroon

Nkrumah Kwame [1965] Neo-Colonialism: The Last Stage of Imperialism. Heinemann, London

Pul A. S. Hippolyt [2011] "Cropping and Aning to the Promised Land: Cultural Disconnects and The Challenges to Nationhood, Governance and Development in Africa", in Abdalla Bujra (ed.) [2011] Political Culture Governance & The State in Africa. DMPF, Nairobi-Kenya, pp163-202

Onimode Bade (1992) A Future for Africa: Beyond the Politics of Adjustment. Earthscan, London

Sankara, Thomas (1988) Thomas Sankara Speaks: The Burkina Faso Revolution 1983-87. Pathfinder, New York/London/Sydney/Toronto:

Shin-yi Peng, Han-Wei Liu & Ching-Fu Lin (2018) Governing Science and Technology under the International Economic Order: Regulatory Divergence and Convergence in the Age of Megaregionals. Edward Elgar Publishing Limited, Cheltenham, Glos. U.K.

Shivji, G. Is [2006] "Pan-Africanism or Imperialism? Unity and Struggle Towards a New Democratic Africa," African Sociological Review 10(1) pp208-220

Smith Adam [1776] The Wealth of a Nation, London

Susan Williams (2021). White Malice: The CIA and the Neocolonisation of Africa. Hurst Publishers, London, United Kingdom

Swann G. M. Peter (2019) Economic as Anatomy: Radical Innovation in Empirical Economics, Edward Elgar Publishing Limited, Cheltenham, Glos. U.K.

Thomson David (ed.) Political Ideas. A Pelican Book, London,

Ulla Hytti, Robert Blackburn & Eddy Laveren (2018) Entrepreneurship, Innovation and Education. Frontiers in European Entrepreneurship Research. Edward Elgar Publishing Limited, Cheltenham, Glos. U.K.

Chapter 13

Leadership Ethos: The Need for Paradigm Shift for Africa's Unity and Development

Africa remains underdeveloped, exploited and marginalized due to the absence of a servant visionary leadership style in a region rich in cultural diversity and heterogeneity and the ethos of tolerance and intellectual creativity that should generate progressive ideas or social justice, democracy, and reconciliation that eventually should reverberate throughout the continent with each nation state. The current leadership construct has failed to exploit the hidden assets of culture diversity and heterogeneity as assets for development, rather existing leadership construct, role and style has made diversity a liability in transforming the society.

Looking at the state of development found within the continent, one can argue that lessons are "indispensable for inculcating in their citizens right from birth the values of good citizenry and leadership necessary to create a capable developmental state and civilization. Leadership is a fundamental part of the human condition and, as such, can only be understood by learning from others around the globe, adapting and practicing best examples. Unfortunately, the continent is confronted with leadership failures that impact seriously on the socio-economic transformation of the region. It is not uncommon to hear many Africans angrily complaining of corrupt and destructive leadership in the continent. At the same time, Africans seem to be slow or reluctant to seek leadership models in their own past, especially during the period just before and the early phases of colonial rule. The situation has become worse after the return to political pluralism in the early 1990s (Preez 2012:7).

Leadership style and ethics in Africa is the theorems facing serious challenges of the inability to meet the basic needs of the people. Why is ethical and servant leadership in African countries such a major problem and difficult to address? Why have African countries to have what could be described as "bad" leaders? More often than not, people trace bad or poor leadership on the continent on corruption, greed, poverty, ethnicity or colonial rule. Temple (2012) points out: "whenever we attempt to interrogate these perspectives, we find ourselves sailing through a labyrinth. In the end, we are led into a vicious circle where we know not whether these factors are causes, or are in themselves, effects of unethical leadership in Africa." Temple goes further to show how cults, clans and religions cause many of the leadership problems in Africa because of their worldviews and ideas about reality.

Leadership and political commitment are critical factors that would shape Africa's future and determine the success of Agenda 2063 and the SDGs. The leadership challenge for accelerated economic growth, transformation and sustainable development that Africa faces today is more complex, albeit no less demanding, than at the time of the struggle for independence from colonialism. There is a need for transformed and visionary leadership in all fields and at all levels: politics, business, industry, science, religion, education, and culture. The style of leadership that prevails, and the ways in which management and governance structures change and interact with national resources, will play an enormous role in shaping Africa's development trajectory. The dwindling and unpredictability of development assistance compels Africa to look inwards for domestic resources for the care of her people. The sustainable and efficient management of national resources is now an imperative for the achievement of at least 12 out of the 17 United Nations Sustainable Development Goals (SDGs). Restoring and maintaining the health of the natural resource base is not only needed to adequately feed current and projected populations, but to provide a better quality of life in the years to come.

There are a variety of leadership theories that emerged in the 19th Century which include: Transformational Leadership, burns (1978) and Bass (1985), the Attributional theory of Charismatic Leadership (Conger et al, 1987), Visionary Leadership propagated by Kouzes and Posner (2007) and Bennis and Nanus (1985). Then there is the Value Based Theory of Leadership (Ulrich et al, 199) which is essentially an extension of the earlier work on the Theory of Charismatic Leadership. Of these, the focus on the current discourse is on the transformational leadership and how this can impact the effective and efficient management of national resources. This is significant because according to Burns, transformational Leadership brings significant changes in the perceptions, values, expectations and aspirations 4 of followers. Much of this is achieved due to the leader's personality and traits – which leads to articulating the organization's vision and setting challenging goals.

In supporting claims for good leadership, Oliver (2012) talks of "leadership" appeals to the justice of symmetrical power relations; arguing that people do not follow or represent each other, "but rather they are all to take full responsibility to sustaining the bode they share and bear together; thus, each according to his/her own interests and capacities, is to be empowered to participate as a bearer of sustainable justice. "With no hesitation, the ethical challenges facing leaders in Africa, and for that matter the rest of the world, are best met by educating citizens who are capable and willing to share the responsibility for creating just and prosperous societies with each other and with their leaders. Africa is said to be littered with "toxic" leadership. Lipman-Blumen (2005) confirms that toxic leadership violates the basic human rights of their citizens, engage in corrupt, criminal and unethical activities, lack integrity and mislead their followers; such a type of leadership is described as "emotionally illiterate, unfit and shallow" (Ngambi 2002). Therefore, the continent needs to develop leaders who are able to embrace the rich and verse heritage of the continent, which can learn from the past, accommodate the present, but determine and engaged in crafting a better future of the continent.

While diversity is pregnant on the continent, the issues embedded in the meaning of diversity are the mind-set and climate of the organization, and the different perspectives people bring to the continent. Whatever are the liabilities of "diversity" it can be turned around as assets? Here we can define 'diversity' as "the mosaic of the people who bring a variety of backgrounds, styles, perspectives, values and beliefs as assets to the groups organization or country with which they interact" (Ngambi in Smith et al. 2007:240). The assets of diversity are such that visionary leadership motivates everyone to rally behind the vision. It is integrity and respects, culture and focuses attention on the developmental needs of the people and community/nation it serves.

As such, the continent needs a new breed of leadership rightly labelled as 'responsible, Accountable, Relevance, Ethical, visionary (RAREV) (Ngambi 2010 who talks of RARE). Africa needs effective leaders that are trustworthy and dependable exhibiting a sense of integrity, morality and sense of direction. These virtues will keep away dishonesty as well as empower the person execute assigned duties and responsibilities to the best of his/her abilities and in the total interest of society. In this regard, visionary servant leadership can be depicted as illustrated in Fig.1: Visionary Servant Leadership.

Fig.1 Visionary Servant Leadership

	Responsible		
	Accountable		**Capable**
Leadership ========➔	Relevance =====➔	Vibrant Civil =====➔	
(Visionary – Servant)	Ethical	Society	**Developmental**
	Visionary		**State**
	Servant		//
	//		//
	Improved Quality Livelihood for Citizens		

Source: Forje 2013

A vibrant civil society with an encompassing progressive attitude, behaviour and change (ABC) perspective will accelerate the attainment of a capable developmental state as the take-off to an industrial and service delivery society. Therefore, Africa needs a holistic approach to solving problems and ensuring the unity, integration and development of the continent and within the countries of an interdependently which as an equivalent in how human beings/Africans approach their problems. Integrating different aspects, breaking down walls and recognizing the mid-expanding and dynamic effects of crossing borders in all aspects are relevant both on policy and personal level. Leadership matters especially in a delicate subject matter like the unity and integration of Africa. Kwame Nkrumah was a visionary leader, far ahead of this time and era; and his colleagues in leadership position as Heads of States or Government failed in keeping an open-mind on the struggle, differences and controversies over African unity. Unfortunately, the 'Walls of Distrust' clouded the minds that shared different opinions on the "Africa Must Unite Project." President Julius Nyerere's speech at the 40th Anniversary of the Independence of Ghana is true reflection and confession of this. For fifty years or more, Africa has been living in an age of mistrust. That wall of mistrust must be broken before real progress can be made on the Africa Must Unite Agenda. That same vision of mistrust was extended to Gadhafi's radical approach to establishing a Union Government for Africa (UGA). Tearing down the 'wall of mistrust' is what should characterise the minds of Africa as the continent celebrates the fifty anniversaries of the formation of the Organisation of African Unity and the publication of the book "Africa Must Unity' by Kwame Nkrumah (1963).

It is not out of place to state that the Golden Jubilee of the founding of the OAU is celebrated at this era and point in time: "when there is said to be peace which is no peace, in time of technological advancement which does not benefit the masses but threatens its own masters with destruction. The celebration of the OAU is at a time when the idea evoked in our minds by the term "diversity globalization, destruction and exploitation' that has switched to a turbulent political fragmentation reality from the rising expectations and hopeful dreams of the coming of independence. The widening of our political horizons to embrace in a new sense the whole of Africa should have meant a to the ideal of "Tolls and Sweat of Labour, Freedom is at last, but it has paradoxically contributed to slavery of the worse dimension, corruption by the powers that be; and abject poverty for the masses; instigated conflicts; fanned ethnic diversities and contributed to new difficulties preventing the establishment of bridge-building human contacts and communication across the divide.

It is only hoped that matters will gradually change, and the AU will initiate viable reforms that will accelerate and sustain the process of 2017 for a Union Government for the continent before and after. It is a question of and the implementation of shared-obligations, responsibility and division of labour. No one country can solve the problem. Region Economic Communities cannot do it either. It has to be holistic involvement – state, civil society, private sector, you name it. Nobody can do everything: but everybody can do something for the common good. It is important to avoid the cult of violence, which most politicians in the states in Africa condemn in principle but do not renounce in practice, can be deployed under various controls. A most dangerous form of pressure is the uncontrolled appeal to the mob. Without appropriate policy measures the situation can get out of hand and the whole structure of public order and recognised authority crumpled like a cardboard, and a menace without a face or name held sway. The situation in Southern Cameroons is pointing in that direction.

To translate the formula or ideological orientation advanced by Nkrumah, "Africa must Unite" into peace, development and sustainable livelihood, is a great challenge, not for a single nation, region, but for the entire continent and its people. It requires total mass mobilisation around the problems and bringing the different stakeholders or actors to consolidate their wisdom, skills, and energies towards a common course. To achieve the "Africa Must Unite" agenda, the AU henceforth must strive to reconcile existing differences and articulate policies that should substantially move the continent further along the right path. It requires translating into common understanding a foundation of cooperation and action plans geared towards the integration of the continent.

One important factor, we cannot achieve the envisaged goal of Africa Must Unite when the policy of exclusion is high on the action strategy and agenda of leaders; when inequality and ethnic and social diversity is perpetuated; when poverty and corruption reigns supreme in society. The "Africa Must Unite" ideological orientation and agenda must remember that the *'haves'* and *'have-nots'* are linked like men and women are more alike than separate. But importantly they must be respected and whatever roles played must be recognised. Unfortunately, the policy has been to exclude the vulnerable. The 'haves' must not exclude the 'have-nots' and treat them like non-human-beings. Such attitude and marginalisation do more harm than good to the course of African Unity and development.

The statement by the Norwegian Noble Peace Committee in the award of the 2011 Peace Prize to Ellen Johnson Sirleaf, Leymah Gbowee and Tawakkol Karman says it all: *"We cannot achieve democracy and lasting peace in the world unless women obtain the same opportunities as men to influence developments at all levels of society."* This statement is symbolic as it is an important acknowledgement of the link between female gender empowerment, peace, security and unity of the continent. In short, the Africa Must Unite Agendas cannot be realized if women and vulnerable groups are not empowered and made part of the evolving process. The active participation of all actors is a prerequisite for change, progress, development, unity and sustainable quality of livelihood for all.

With Ellen John Sirleaf and Joyce Banda as Heads of States, a new dimension of leadership has surged into the political landscape and dispensation for the continent to craft a new vision and direction of governance. The reality is that Africa political leadership exhibit the reality of women marginalization from decision-making and power hierarchies and existence of male chauvinism throughout the continent. Seen within this backdrop, it is wrong to postulate that the issue of 'state collapse, state failure, fragile state and extreme state weaknesses' has roots in the ongoing politics of marginalization and exclusion of some key players.

As Africa celebrates the *'golden jubilee'* of the creation of the OAU and the launching of *"Africa Must Unite"* Project within the auspices of the African Union and its determination geared towards a Union Government in 2017, a new visionary leadership is required to further the ideals inscribed in the quest for the unity and integration of the continent. Presently, the continent is in turmoil, needing a new Messiah or a Noah's Arch to rescue the continent. Too many people especially the marginalized are fussed around continental or state boom and bust. Africa has been turned into a global casino, gambling with the livelihood, security and future of the continent. Africa must bear the blunt of its inapt and inconsistent policies and actions. All too often, neither national nor continental policies have been at reducing inequalities, poverty and corruption and bad governance. Rather the dedication of stimulating economic growth has provided incentives for corruption, undermining the provision of essential services to the need.

Fifty years of independence has further widened the gap between the rich and poor as well as exacerbated inequities and inequalities, not the least, regarding access to resources and inequity in the distribution of the wealth of the nation. Unfettered economic growth, characterized by accumulation and wealth concentration in the hands of a select few further increase's social inequalities in society. Persistent poverty, unemployment, social exclusion, and higher levels of inequality and insecurity are threatening care systems, social cohesion and political stability. There is need therefore to redirect policies towards present and future social justices in society. African governments have so far failed to bring their policies into line with the basic needs and aspirations of the people effectively and spur the desire for continental unity. Rather policies have been narrowly conceived to meet the needs of a select few thereby widening the gap between the 'haves' and 'have-nots'. A Union Government must not commit the same mistakes being carried out by state governments. Continental interest and wellbeing of the people should stand tall on the priority list of activities. No state should be seen as dominating or given special privileged status. Skilled conscious leadership and constructive cooperation from member states is needed to guide the process through. That Nkrumah's statue stands significantly in front of the newly constructed AU Head Quarters in Addis Ababa, is a befitting appreciation and tribute by African leaders in recognition for the role he played in steering and driving home the idea of African Unity.

The tradition of basing political solutions and constructive cooperation across the political, natural and other borders (of the time) should parallel in today's efforts, and responses to the challenges of constructing African Union Government; unrestrained integration and senseless violence of poverty, corruption and environmental destruction. The creation of the OAU and later the AU should be an expression of the aims and ideals for unity proves to be even more farsighted than the founding fathers may have realized. True, total unity has not been achieved yet. However, it will be some day. For now, there is a constant need for flexibility and comprehensive reform but keeping with the original ideals. There is need for seeking a 'delicate balance' between the asserting the need for Euro-centric protection and aid assistance for a resource endowed continent that has become vulnerable and he need for constructive engagement through Afro-centric governments geared towards the goals of an interdependent global community. Francis Deng (2010:19-20) is clear on this point by noting: *"that this is not the approach favoured by those who believe that on these matters we should cry out loud, stand on the mountain-top and preach what is right and condemn what is wrong. However, when we do that, we might satisfy our conscience, but how much can we help the people who need to be helped in a practical way."*

Paraphrasing Dag Hammarskjold's speech to the University of California's Convocation on 13 May 1954, "The United Nations – (in my interpretation, OAU/AU) was created not created in order to bring Africa to Heaven, but in order to save the continent from Hell." Indeed, this sums up as well as anything we have heard the essential role of the AU and why *Africa Must Unite* with all efforts directed towards integration and sustainable quality services delivery for the people. The OAU/AU was created to save Africa from the demons of external exploitation and marginalisation. In this light, African leaders must ensure accountability; obligations and responsibility to their constituencies in the task assigned them of leading the people from the drainages of hell to the gates of heaven. The level of trust is essential and the leaders should respond accordingly to their constituencies. Africa Must Unite with all efforts directed towards the welfare of the people, integration and sustainable quality services delivery to the people.

Quality services delivery entails meeting the challenges of today's and tomorrow's Africa. Meeting these challenges implies putting people first at the centre of every development related activities. In short, what Kofi Annan (Former UN Secretary General) sees as "no calling is more noble, and no responsibility greater, than that of enabling men, women and children, in cities and villages (across Africa) and the world to make their lives better. Only when this begins will we know that (unity) globalization is indeed becoming inclusive, allowing everyone to share in opportunities." Kofi Annan's statement should also be seen in tandem with that of Jan Eliasson, (President of the United Nations 60th General Assembly in 2005);" lasting *solutions require that the pursuit of peace, development and human rights must take place in parallel. There is no peace without development; there is no development without peace; and there is no sustainable peace and development without respect for human rights. If one of these three pillars are weak in a nation or region, the whole structure is weak. Therefore, walls and barriers between these areas must be taken down."*

Given the trend of development, it is only imperative for African leaders and governments to adapt binding commitments to policy coherence for sustainability as well as strategies for implementation, monitoring and evaluation. Seen in this light, the continent needs a Charter on the Right to Sustainable Development to improve on the quality wellbeing of the people. It is this absence of security in quality wellbeing that drives many people to risk their lives across the deserts and oceans in search for greener pastures in Europe. More weight should be focused to a 'people-oriented development approach' and to build strong and robust social protection systems within the limits of the available resources of the continent; and as a tool for addressing peoples' vulnerability and promoting their resilience to crises, especially fighting the state of abject poverty and corruption and ethnic divide in society.

Stamping out factors that accelerate the great divide in society should occupy top place in government actions. This implies that African states must strive to move towards inclusive and accountable democratic governance. In respect of the underlined issues, namely;

- Strengthening democratic governance and by overcoming fragmentation;
- Strengthening institutions to promote coherence fir sustainable development;
- Promoting national and continental unity, cohesion and integration more and better cooperation as well as recognizing existing cultural diversities of people as asset not a liability to development;
- Enforcing the rule of law and justice

  // //

  Freedom, Equality, Justice, Diversity, and Respect for the Views and Cultures of Others

So far, African governments have to a large extent failed to translate agreed policies into enforceable obligations, actions and implementation policies. If governments had adopted a 'people-oriented or focused' policy approach, the unity of the continent would progress in a holistic and constructive pattern, leading to serious reduction in poverty and hunger, corruption and exploitation could have radically and dramatically reduced. To ensure the functioning of society and create safeguards against tyranny, values have to be translated into laws, rights and legally binding obligations to all parties. The urgent concern is to strike a harmonious and sustainable balance or relationship between the various stakeholders for the benefit of present and future generations. This is the challenge that awaits the leaders and African governments and they must face and find long-lasting solutions. The paradigm of ethical development should come into play as the basis for ameliorating conditions in Africa.

The 1990 OAU declaration on the political and socio-economic situation in Africa and the fundamental changes ongoing in the world, is significant here as the Heads of State and Government of OAU member states stated: "We reaffirm our commitment to revive the ideals of Pan-Africanism and commit ourselves, individually and collectively, on behalf of our governments and peoples to maintain and strengthen our unity and solidarity and to pool our resources and wisdom in order to face the challenges of the decade of the 1990s and beyond, change the bleak socio-economic prospects of our continent and guarantee a better life for all peoples and future generations yet unborn. These objectives are well within our capabilities. We, therefore, pledge to apply ourselves fully to the achievement of these objectives (OAU 1990: para.12).

Without unity and visionary leadership, Africa remains vulnerably weak. Nkrumah had strongly argued for a concerted effort by African leaders to implement the policy of "African solutions to African problems" which met many stumbling impediments. The major one being, the sheer number of constraints present in the continent that defy and challenge the pursuit of this ideal. Capacity, ignorance and resources limitations are often cited as being major in this regard. While these are no doubt crucial, the most important constraints to pursuit this ideal are in the realm of politics. Here we should cite the nature of the global political order and importantly the sheer inadequacies of the African political leadership. The point is that Africa states cannot pursue its peace and security agenda independently. A united front is needed for continent. And even with this peace and security issues cannot under existing circumstances and the global structure be undertaken independently by a Union Government. In such a context, any attempt on the part of Africa to pursue its own solutions will face resistance that will frustrate and ultimately abort it. The post-Cold War global political context, or more accurately the multi-polar global order of the 21st century is such that Africa remains weak to remove 'the danger that the ability of the peoples of Africa to determine their destiny would be severely compromised and undermined' (Mbeki 2012; Dersso 2012:42).

Because of the Euro-centric approach that leads to dependence served outside powers to exert enormous influence on the actions of African countries. By this Euro-centric attitude, the cost for Africa is loss of political control and authority over its action plans. Unfortunately, the history of Pan-Africanism since independence shows that it is only when there are leaders (like Nkrumah, Nyerere, Mbeki, etc.) that champion it and make it a priority in continental politics that the ideals of African Unity / Pan-Africanism such as "African solutions to African problems' galvanise the support of the countries of the continent. There are times, such as the Libyan case, when the continent happens to be without leaders committed to pushing the agenda of Africa Must Unite and the ideals of Pan-Africanism. The difficulties are many, varied and enormous requiring vigilant leadership, consensus and cooperation among member states to address the situation. He people must learn to contend with both internal and external forces that militate against the genuine independence of Africa. An issue which prompted former AU Commission Chairperson (Jean Ping) to rightly draw the attention of African countries to the reality that: "lasting peace on the continent can only be achieved if efforts to that end are based on the full involvement of Africa and a recognition of its leadership role because, as stressed by the Summit in August 2009, without such a role, there will be no ownership and sustainability; because we understand the problems far better; because we know which solutions will work, and because, fundamentally, these problems are ours, and our peoples will live with their consequences (AU Commission (2011:4).

For the past years one has only witnessed the following;

Fifty Years of the Failure of African States to implement a Policy of Good And the realization of the Africa Must ====➔

- Lack of control of the territory within its inscribed international borders;
- Low levels of state/leadership legitimacy;
- Low levels of social cohesion and quality livelihood
- frail and ineffective public institutions;
- limited extractive and growth promotion capacities
- growing influence and dictate of the developed polities as a result of the increasing weakness of African states;
- Escalating state of abject poverty and entrenched corruption

Leading to

//

//

Failed, Collapsed and Fragile States

Africa Must Unite and good leadership is not just the panacea for development. The true panacea for development is the people; their resolve to and how they change and relate to governance, leadership and development. It should be understood that the Africa Must Unite Project is to address the potential effects of externalities in subduing the continent into further misery and exploitation. The credibility of "Africa Must Unite" or "Vision 2017" rests on the most complex mix of efforts the process of change, progress and development. Strong and focused independent institutions are needed. Only the decisions and right choices made in the appropriate window of opportunity will accelerate the Africa Must Unite and Renaissance Project. The behaviour of African people is the push and pulls for the realization of or failure Africa Must Unite and Renaissance Agenda of course; we cannot bypass the anarchic nature of international life and the growing influence of the West as an inescapable condition that thwarts the essence of the unity of the continent as well as it thwarts the respect for self-determination and sovereignty of the continent.

Progress in Africa Unity and overall socioeconomic transformation has been seriously hampered by poor leadership and widespread corruption and fraud backed by egocentricity, greed and mindlessness resulting in violence, instability, destruction, hunger, want, disease and ignorance. The basic tenets of the paradigm of ethical and sustainable development (see Salawu 2012:19-20) include;

- ensuring the cultivation and regeneration of mind;
- enhancing the African traditional value system;
- encouraging good citizenship and patriotism;
- promoting the virtues of honesty, discipline, morality, responsibility, integrity and hard work;
- promoting merit and competence over mediocrity;
- promoting learning and intellectualism; and making proper use of indigenous knowledge;
- promoting creativity, innovation and entrepreneurship

Presently, the state of African leadership has emerged as destroyers of institution. They have **succeeded in building a mass followership of power-worshippers, genuine patriots and faithful** supports of self-articulate interests and the destruction of institutions. Happy as they are to the gospel of destroyers of institutions, and praise singers, all they know is what Nigerians call *"Any Government in Power"* (AGIP) or charlatans serving the country in the interest of imperialism, colonialism and neo-colonialism. Imperialism is at work as social groups and communities across the continent have been destroyed or reduced to penny by improper Structural Adjustment Policies (SAP) imposed by the Breton Woods Financial Conglomerates (World Bank, International Monetary Fund and the European Union).

Imperialism has taken up a New Jersey and technology – globalization – the highest stage of scientific imperialism – as the most acceptable vocabulary for greed, exploitation, domination and oppression. The answer to this destructive moving train is to 'jumping off.' Jumping off entails an Afro-centric African Unity/ Renaissance and visionary servant leadership to pilot the affairs of the continent. The triumphalism 'unity and renaissance' will force every black citizen or descendant behind its hegemony, re-establish lost faith, hope and promote 'Afro-centrism and Afro-optimism' for a brighter destiny, the Africanness of the continent. What is required between now and 2017 is the mobilization with vigour of all available forces for the last lap of the struggle for self-determination and construction of an African Union Government.

The continent cannot continuously be ridiculing itself by accepting the Euro-centric invitation to remain zombies and exporter of human capital and raw materials or be the dumping ground for western industrial toxic wastes. Or should the continent expect a Messiah, for their self-determination and liberation. The time is over to continuously ridiculing ourselves by hanging on colonialism as our problem. The alternate is the realization of the ideals of a Union Government by 2017 (Forje 2011). Any society that embarks on exporting its human capital and natural resources like Africa is doom to perpetual exploitation and underdevelopment. Visionary leadership is needed to convert exported human capital (brain drain) into veritable sources for development (brain gain). The move by the AU to create the sixth region of the continent is welcome move in the right direction. This is a challenge for African governments to properly utilize the Diaspora to lift up the plane currently stuck on the runway. The Diaspora is embedded with the financial power, knowledge and experience needed for engine of development and growth lacking on the continent. However, there is a note of caution here. Africa cannot totally rely on the financial prowess of the Diaspora. It is not sustainable due to financial crisis that can be generated by the forces of capitalism once they see their roles in Africa being capitulated by the Diaspora. At best we can rely on their human capital and skills to kick start entrepreneurial related activities for job creation and income generating activities on the continent. This will give added values to the continent's natural resources potentials.

Apparently, the realization of a Union Government could be seen in Fukuyama's "end of history' postulation of colonial rule and the beginning of a more realistic development dialogue strengthening the African Renaissance Agenda. A new agenda for a new society is in the making, creating a society that the youths are proud to belong too and not wanting to leave. Not a colonized society where Africans are permanently trapped in the viruses of poverty, misery and exploitation. The target date of 2017 should not be an end process of adventurism. There is an urgent need for a new focus, a departure from the debates of the 1960s about how far and fast African Unity should proceed. Rephrased, our painful historical past should teach us that *"slow progress leads us to the slaughter house of neo-colonialism and impoverishment in the midst of abundant human and material resources We have no choice but to move faster because the rest of the world will not wait for us?"* (Tajudeen in Biney & Olukoshi, 2010:232).

Achieving the ideals set out in 2017 will not be on a 'platter of gold.' Like the self-determination struggle, there is still a long-road to travel with many hurdles to overcome. African Unity, Pan-Africanism and Renaissance Africa Project must now leave the drawing board, conferences and executive mansions of leaders to real execution, by building from below-upwards, mobilizing the masses as part and parcel of their lives. A union of the people must come first before the Union of States. This should be followed by a club of the willing to forge ahead the unity of the continent. States ready for Union should go ahead and the *'doubting Thomas's"* will follow later though this not the right way to move ahead. There has to be consensus to show the seriousness and unity of the continent. Ghadaffi's ideals and vigour towards the realization of a Union Government could have been misunderstood by many like Nkrumah's aggressive approach could not be navigated through the minds of African leaders. Now that Ghadaffi is out of the way, over taken by the machination of Western fire-power, doubting states may have a new mind set. In addition, the Libyan ideal needs to be marketed in a different style to attract more converts into the fold.

Who is going to do the marketing with Ghadaffi out of the way? A vacuum is likely to exist like what followed after the overthrow of Nkrumah. Nonetheless, Africa is not Nkrumah or Ghadaffi that comes to an end. There are hidden fighters to be discovered to continue the fight. The continent expects the emergence of new leaders to take over the relay baton. A new thought-provoking strategic approach of mobilizing both the leaders and civil society (the population) instead of wasting enormous resources as sweeteners to reluctant Heads of States is required. Good proposals will sell with good crafted strategic approach. Broader alliance building among the people and owned by them will release better results from a creative union that serves the interest of the African people. The principle of the sovereignty of states - the corner stone of the Westphalian international code has to be redefined by African states if they are to craft a Union Government. Sovereignty has two aspects:

First, sovereignty defines the legal identity of states within the international system as equal entities and possessing the same legal capacities. Second, sovereignty signifies independent political authority over the people and territory within the jurisdiction of a state. This is associated with 'the capacity to make authoritative decisions with regard to the people and resources within the territory of a state (ICISS 2001:12). Sovereignty and its corollary, the principle of non-intervention, are the most important principles on which the OAU was founded. Of the seven basic principles outlined under Article 3 of the OAU Charter, four were about the sovereignty and territorial integrity of African states (OAU 1963). In elucidating the impact of this, the stance on sovereignty was perhaps the main weakness of the OAU when it came to conflict management, and one that threatened to render the organization irrelevant in the new international environment (Olonisakin 2000:42; Aneme 2008; Yusuf 2005)

Neither the 'golden jubilee of the OAU nor the envisaged date of 2017b for a Union Government will solve the problems of the continent without the inherent resolve by the people to see the through the proper functioning of the Union. However, 2017 an attained goal of the AU will be a means an end provided the vision, objective and purpose are not derailed by destroyers of institutions. We can continue to argue about the process, historical, structural, attitudinal, personal and institutional causes plaguing African countries; the reality remains that the majority of citizens remain stuck in need amidst plenty. Fifty or more years of independence seem to have changed little of their livelihood for the better. It comes as no surprise that that rising destructive frustration is in the increase threatening the stability and progress of the continent.

Africa needs a Union Government that is one hundred percent concerned and committed to improving the quality of the livelihood of citizens; not a Union government more interested in elite power-struggles. "Any society that threatens the livelihood of its citizen's risks permanently threatening its own survival and security" (Tajudeen 2009). Presently, the global balance of political and economic power is changing rapidly, and Africa must not be left out of the changing construct. But inadequacies of the African political leadership points in a direction that does not make the continent proud. The Libyan episode presents a good case. Speaking to the UN Security Council, South Africa's President Jacob Zuma (2012) stated: *"The AU's plan was completely ignored in favour of bombing Libya by NATO forces."* Only constructive commitment towards a unified continent can salvage the situation. Ratifying the Protocol on Amendments to its Constitutive Act dated 3 February 2010 indicates that out of 53 countries then, 47 had signed and there were 25 ratifications and deposits falling short of the two thirds (35-36) required for the Protocol to come into force.

Fifty years after the creation of the OAU, the unity project as suffering of a malaise of weakening of internal or national borders does not seem to have progressed far or deep enough. Sad enough, Africa is more fragmented with irredentism rearing its ugly head so often, with the last successful example being the creation of South Sudan in 2011 and Mali which was at the brink of fracturing as the Tuaregs and other groups fighting the central government made significant progress in 2012. (Atallah 2013; Matlou et al 2012:351-2). The fifty-four or more African states should put the interest of Africa first. This should be the challenge requiring urgent attention and addressed from a position of strength, consensus and unity and from the background perspective that never again must the continent be subjected to the humiliation of the worse crime ever committed against humanity. Having examined the forces that subjected Africa to colonial, the weaknesses of the continent, it is time to make a comprehensive structural turn-around by adopting a progressive Afro-centric agenda that should carry the country to highest standards of quality livelihood; and banish existing abject poverty, exploitation by external forces. Resolving the plight of the continent requires constructive policy measures and strategies towards building a solid foundation in areas of;

Intelligence	realization	hard work
capability	innovation	new mind-set
courage	learning	human capital development
knowledge	optimism	responsibility
justice	good governance	obligations
leadership	vibrant civil society	rule of law

Africa's unity is meaningless unless all Africans are sure of a sustainable quality livelihood and to strengthen the practice of the spirit of 'ubuntu.' A new mind set is required (Afro-centric with a purpose and focus) – dismantling the colonial mentality – (Euro-centric), forging a new image and role of the continent is imperative. The opportunity for the widest possible expansion of the ideological orientation of African Unity is reinforcing the education and knowledge base of the unity of the continent. In the words of Nelson Mandela; 'education is the most powerful weapon which you can use to change the world.'

Apparently, Africa's weakness is Europe's strength. Africa's new strength in conjunction with the strength of the developing countries will effectuate a dramatic change of political power base in the world. In all, the deficiencies that beset African states underscore the need for special assumptions about their international capabilities, the feasibility of all regional and certainly all continental organizations – perhaps most important – the chances that African states will develop on an essentially independent basis if only they unit, ensure good governance and promote the wellbeing of their citizens.

Not many words need to be expanded to demonstrate that the power of the gun made Africa safe for colonial rule and sealed the continent's fate for centuries. Reversing that fate constitutes the highest challenges faced by this and coming generations. A Union Government should enhance the bargaining position of the continent in that direction. In addition, unity should be enhanced and crafted from a stronger bargaining position – the gift of nature to the continent – as certain natural resources found on the continent are vital and giving it comparative advantage to some or all of the world powers. Even if the latter does not require the resources, it may be in their best interests at least, to deny them to adversaries.

The point is that the legal-constitutional structure under which the former colonies were granted independence was obsolete long before the ink dried on the relevant documents. Politically these documents may have been irrelevant even before. This book attempts to demonstrate why political thought on African unity and development went astray. The challenges now are to pick up the pieces, and reincarnate a new strategic approach to address the spectacular but developmental consequential factional squabbles, personality conflicts, fear, uncertainly or the effervescent phenomena of the passing and present political parade. Fear, uncertainty, personality conflicts guide the mind-set of African leaders derailing them from establishing a vibrant proactive organization in 1963. Africa continues to trail in the mode of thinking.

Sad enough, the strong do what their will, while the weak suffer what they must. Majority may be right with no solutions, but minority may have the right long-term answers to issues at hand. Africa made itself and thus suffers from its weakness and disunity. No doubt, a new mind-set is required. The Unity of Africa must never be impaired. Can much be gained in the way of gauging the future by theorizing about contemporary regime shifts, the paper – thin ritual of international diplomacy, the complexity of domestic politics and its aimless military coups, or the throes of legal, political party or administrative systems that are already doom in birth? That is the question for the current African leadership policy-makers and civil society should address if in reality they want to become a sovereign continent active participant within the global community of nations. Neither the visions of the future nor the lessons of the past, but the tyranny of today's commitments imposes constraints on our thinking. Our thinking therefore needs redemption from impoverished colonial thinking and brainwashing to cultivating a new line of thinking based on the orientation of Afro-centricism - Africa Must Unite and African Renaissance must be the way forward. It would be to Africa's credit to develop its own home-grown innovations to reduce dependency on the developed countries and be self-reliant, independent and sovereign.

It is pious not to expect a colonial government to have contemplated the long-term consequences of its decision on the future. Colonisation was to make the colonies their permanent abhor for cheap and free raw materials and the dumping ground for their industrial waste. For that reason, the people were not to be civilised in a way that they could restrain the progress advancement of the West. Europe was and is not ready for 'highly trained savages' from Africa. In a way, one can argue that by enthusiastically adopting western's educational system, language, religion destroyed our cultural value heritage. Rephrased differently and in a way, the introduction and acceptance of Christianity and Western style of education stunted the progress of and, in most cases, replaced indigenous systems of education, writing and language.

Indeed, the years between now and 2017 should be defined by a programme of orders and deliveries that scales the format of a United Continent ready to be an active player in world politics and economic transformation. Consequently, any modification remains subjected to the social contract between the people and their leaders, not an imposition from above. Consensus, reconciliation, and the policy of give and take to harmonious our diversities as a veritable force of development, not an instrument should take centre stage in all deliberations and activities and focused on the endurable wellbeing of the people. The rule by today's tyranny of the minority must no longer prevail in the governance system of 2017. The relevance of strategic platforms and importance of good governance and the rule of law must prevail.

The publication demonstrates that improvisation, series of ad hoc measures, all of an emergency kind and defensive or reactive in nature remains the style of government and politics of African states for some time to come. Therefore, change and constructive engagement with the various stakeholders is imperative to move the continent forward and in the right direction. Those immediately involved and concern – leaders, policy-makers, elites – should start rethinking how to engage with civil society in a way beneficial to the continent. Civil society should change – become proactive and Afro-centric with a suitcase of optimism in constructing or crafting a new society and being a world player of significance. There has to be an end to the cover-the-shoulder gratuitous advice yet destructive in a way from outside.

If this publication and the concerns of the contributors are to have a sustentative bearing on the outcome of Africa's present travails our sight and actions must be raised high above to allow the people to come to grips with the analytically more rewarding long-range aspects of sustainable transformation of the continent and ensure the wellbeing of the people. To that end, realism must replace 'idealism' wishful thinking, or at least idealism ideology and euphuistic visions must be heavily discounted and more diligently examined for their economic and political contents.

Beyond that, political thought and actions on and above Africa must be cut adrift from its traditional Western moorings and replaced with something more purposeful in serving Africa's interest. Afro-centricism without a purpose could just be as meaningless and destructive to the cause of the continent. Most importantly to lather it to the already calcifying tenets of the defunct Soviet Union communist style or the invading Chinese thought or to the mummified remnants of outdated Marxist doctrine would be no improvement at all. A new way of speaking to power, to crafting a new ideological orientation on the future of the continent is needed in facing the future of unity, social progress and democratic governance.

It is the fervent hope of this book, though limited in scope to enhance its reliability but encompassing and broad enough to be representative, will spur as well as serve Africans and Africa's sincere friends the world over to a joint quest for a better understanding of the continent's role and contribution to continental and global socioeconomic transformation for the common good. So far, there has been a tremendous waste of opportunities and goodwill to craft a Union Government for Africa. The difficult and controversial subject which divides the moderates, conservatives and radicals, in short, the

Afro-centric and Euro-centric Africans will certainly not be solved by prejudices, or by wishful thinking. African Unity – a necessity – must be approached with an open mind and constructive discourses for and against to overcome dangerous tensions and to produce significant and useful results for nations and regions, but first and foremost, for human-beings (Africans in particular) and as the greatest victims and parts of the world.

African unity cannot take place in a one-way street; it must be the grand work of all stakeholders – governments, civil society, private sector and the international community. If the New Africa is honest, determined for change and wants to promote national, continental and international understanding, it should not avoid any serious exchange of views, Cross-fertilisation of ideas is important to avoid loop holes and other trappings that could derail the process of unity. Waste and corruption, oppression and violence, greed and affluence are unfortunately to be found in many parts of the continent and world at large. This should not stop or hinder the long-term goal – unity and African renaissance. This is the time for meaningful dialogue and paradigm shift in the direction of constructing a Union Government for Africa.

We have jot underestimated the difficulties and challenges in constructing or establishing a Union Government for Africa. We strongly believe these obstacles can be overcome through dialogue, cooperation, understanding, reconciliation, consensus, constructive engagement, political will, popular participation and constructive actions which should be successfully broadened and implanted into the mind-set of the African people. The ideological orientation of Afro-centric approach is not the panacea without a comprehensive well thought focus and purpose, hard work, determination to succeed and make the best out situation or issues that will render the evolving situation as it is better to deal with the devil you know than the unknown angel. Purposely crafted Afro-centric strategy could turn out to be the *'unknown angle'* thus giving the Euro-centric approach the *'devil'* you know the advantage.

Undoubtedly, it should be made known that the major share of the burden for effectively attacking poverty, corruption, poor services delivery and bad governance among other ills lies with African people and their governments. This awareness is gaining grounds that egalitarian reforms and increased participation by all sections of the society can substantially improve conditions for more rapid, stable growth and quality livelihood of the people. We also believe that with unity Africa would ensure greater influence in world affairs. A good testimony here is the recent overthrow, bombing of Libya and the killing of Ghadaffi despite Africa's stand on the issue which the West and NATO military might failed to listen to. After all, the future of the world lies in Africa. But the continent should move from dependency into independence and interdependency and global cooperation not domination and oppression.

Together with my colleagues, they believe is that African nations and the people of African descent will not only have to but are able to live together in peace and harmony for the good of the continent and humanity. We think that the task is to free Africans from dependence and oppression, from hunger and diseases and distress, insecurity and uncertainty. We also believe that new links and channels of communication must be developed which will substantially increase the chance of achieving freedom, justice, unity and solidarity for all – the *'Ubuntu Spirit."* This constitutes the greatest task and challenges for both the present generation and for the next.

The shaping of Africa's common future in unity is much too important to be left to governments and experts alone. Therefore, our appeal goes to the youths, to women and civil society organizations, to political, intellectual and religious leaders, to scientists and educators, to members of the rural and business communities, as well as friends of Africa to craft a new mind-set for changing the face and role the of continent. May they try to appreciate and understand the plight of the continent and to conduct their affairs in the light of these new challenges and wonderful opportunities offered for a meaningful restructuring process? The world is changing, and fast too, propelled by the forces of scientific and technological development. Africa has to change in light of these developments. This is the time engendered such a new outlook for the continent and its people.

To state that a catastrophic consequence awaits Africa if there is no paradigm shift could be an over statement, but there is some twist in it as long as the continent embarks on the path of Euro-centrism and not Afro-centrism. No one prays for a 'catastrophic consequence,' but it cannot be brushed aside. The challenge for the world is to move towards a new world order of cooperation, interdependency, equality and respect for each other's diversities. Yet the struggles continue; the search for more substantial African sovereignty and independence and the Africa Must United Agenda gathers momentum, often under pressure, the quest and desire of the people and stimulated by the attitude of the international community towards the treatment of people of Africa and of African descent. That Africa Must Unite promises to yield anything of lasting value for present and future generations. It must not be delayed or toiled with.

On the occasion of OAU's 50 anniversary, each African state should create a reliable ally with the AU with strong institutions and a modernization democracy and good governance system. This should be the present to be offered by the 54 or more sovereign Africa states as a commitment for a stronger and united continent fifty years on. Fifty years gone, Africa now needs the *"great leap forward"* - Agenda of change, progress, development and sustainability (CPDS). The prevailing situation now is that Africa has not achieved either one, but standing on the threshold. Therefore, African leadership and state must focus on building a legitimate government that addresses the peoples' concerns. In all, the states in tandem with AU and its institutions should look at the importance of African unity from this light. "It is fundamental to build the political legitimacy and effectiveness of a government or union not affected by an insurgency. Political reform and development are the hard-core of any counter insurgency and provides a framework for all other counter insurgency programmes and initiatives. An effective political strategy is designed to undermine support for insurgents, win over their sympathisers to the government side, and co-opt local community leaders to ally themselves with the government" (Querze 2012:53).

The state of military coups in Africa during the cold war era contributed partly to the slowness in the realization of a United Continent. Up to the post-cold war period, the capacity and legitimacy of most African states was of a doubtful character. Though this has not change much, the post-cold war era saw the introduction of political party pluralism, even though most states like Cameroon continue to function under a dominant one-party structure and its institutions likewise making it to be weak, captive and vulnerable under the control of a power executive. The existence of strong articulate selfish leadership, weak state institutions and a passive civil society organisation construct, the ideal of a United Africa is hijacked by 'sit-tight presidents' for selfish interests and under the pretext of state sovereignty. "The Pan-Africanist Project was conceived in broad perspectives and premised on the concept of African citizenship not on Kenyan, Ghanaian, Tanzania or Algerian citizenship. It did not discriminate because one's pigment; it embraced because of one's commitment. Pan-Africanism was literally and figuratively, a continental project. It was a grand political vision, not a puny economistic design. Unity will not make us automatically rich, but it can make it difficult for Africa and the African peoples to disregarded and humiliated. The Pan-Africanist project was laboratory, anti-imperialist and democratic (Shivji 2008: xvii).

Therefore, sovereignty should be Africanist, less nationalistic. To build a Union Government for Africa and the Pan-Africanist Projects in the 21st century or age of globalization, the continent needs to understand its ideological drive and political practices of the period. This book is meant to contribute to that understanding. And with the hope that a Union Government for Africa will operate from the basis of reconciling and coordinating the differing positions and interests of member states into consensus that African Unity speaks for the common good of all the people. It is for these reasons that it is most important for African states to gun for the 'ballot box' rather than the 'bayonet' (see Hugh Tinker, 1964).

From this background the power of the union government or African Unity should oscillate from the premises of shared-values, shared-vision and a shared-purpose to deal and respond to challenges that confront each member state. What this means is that African states should draw valuable lessons from the inaptness concerning Libya and the fall of Gaddiffi. On this issue, one can but strongly share the views of Muchie et al (2012:4); *"the capability to develop, maintain and sustain inter-African strategic Alliance in order to manifest a robust and United African Agency, the expression of United African Power that other an only ignore at their own peril."* The Union Government must be embedded with the much need political capacity to counter any form of external obstacles and power geared towards destabilizing or affecting the destiny of the continent from outside or from within.

The Union Government must be embedded with the much-needed political capacity to counter any form of external obstacles and power geared towards destabilising or affecting the destiny of the continent from outside or from within. A major factor minimizing Africa's dignity from time immemorial is the absence of a common stand or unified strategic presence and action. The sovereignty of the region is constantly violated and abused because the penetration of foreign bodies is not met will a unified strategic policy approach and a determined unified strategic response. More often than not, Africa has allowed foreign intrusion gone unchallenged. The new foreign social strategic offensive is now in the area of 'same sex-marriage' which is an African taboo (even though homosexuality exists and practiced), will easily be condoned by poor leadership. The West is even trying to link 'aid assistance' with homosexuality and lesbianism. Countries not supporting this aspect of social contract will not be given foreign assistance. It is a divisive factor that will play into the psychic of African unity. Hence the disunity of Africa contributes to the marginalization and exploitation of the continent. Fifty or more years after independence, disunity has prevailed, the more reason why African leadership should rethink, reconstruct and reconstitute a new strategic road based on an Afro-centric perspective to counter any form of intrusion and destabilization activities.

Continued failure to articulate and manifest a united from and response to policies working against the interests of the continent wellbeing of the people is costing Africa heavily. Africa is underdeveloped and exploited because poor leadership and a passive condescending civil society has yielded to the dictates of foreign forces. Stuck with this manifest disunity, it is imperative to hasten the sustainable contraction of a robust unity and renaissance strategic agenda for the continent. Without such a united front, Africa will for long remain vulnerable fragmented by weak, failed and collapse state construct leading to recolonisation. How many African states overcome the colonial albatross? Why must the desire for a United Africa, fifty years after independence remain a dream?

Echoing Nkrumah's view in 1963, *"Ghana's liberty is meaningless unless all Africans are free."* Therefore, African Unity should be anchored with a value and dignity for all Africans. Here lays the first step in constructing progressive Afro-centric manifestos in a build a continent of people living and eating together. This means fighting the seeds of disunity and liberating themselves mentally and physically from the yoke of servitude, colonialism, dependency and the fragmentation of Africa as illustrated by (Koka 1985:3) in the following words; "The seeds of disunity that Europe had planted in Africa through balkanization and acculturalisation of the whole continent, followed by artificial territorial boundaries they imposed to divide brother from brother, will finally be destroyed by a process of the decolonization of the African mind. Then Africa will once more experience its *"Golden Age"* of development and restore its leadership in the forum of nations as the creator and preserver of those values that once benefited humankind"

Linking a country's independence with the total independence of the continent illustrated Nkrumah's visionary leadership and love for the continent and determination to sacrifice whatever there was for the total freedom of Africa. Few leaders on the continent, if not the world have demonstrated such visionary servant leadership style for the freedom of people far beyond the frontiers of his/her country. The common interest of the people took precedence, while most people will place articulate self-interest first. Kwame Nkrumah did not as far as the unity, independence and socio-economic transformation of the continent was concerned. Of course, as human being, he had weaknesses. He was a hardened yet a visionary, committed, conscious, constructive and positively inclined fanatic for the unity of the continent. Can we blame him for that? I wonder.

We can however attribute the fact that "Africa's destiny lies in Africa's hands;" the message Nkrumah struggled so hard to drive through the minds of African leaders. May be his energetic strive to force this down the throats of other leaders who did not understand and appreciate the usefulness of the continent's unity scared many leaders who hung on the 'state sovereignty' issue. By hanging on the *'state sovereignty'* these leaders waved goodbye to African Unity. But that is not what the people want. Of course, 'Not.' They want 'free movement of persons and goods, respect with dignity and quality livelihood. Fifty years after everybody has suddenly started to realize there is a new generation of really switched-on, clever people. It is only a matter of time before they come through and start taking positions of leadership in government and in business and society. It is time now for African governments to build effective systems in their capacity to govern, thereby helping to reduce poverty and corruption through improved governance and human capital development.

African leadership should be such that it is capable of innovating and navigating the continent out of underdevelopment, exploitation and poverty. It should do so by being Afro-centric, by injecting moral, ethical and African values, concepts, beliefs, moral and ethical standards into all sectors of society and human activities – including the workplace, economic, political and cultural activities, educational and health activities, among others. In spite of existing odds, we can assume that there is a new generation of leadership, a new sense of hope and optimism and a new feeling within the continent which is not only encouraging but exciting towards African Unity and integration. Yet, it is crystal clear that only education, discipline and good leaders can save Africa. The Africa of tomorrow needs answers that last; and wipe the slate clean of the idea and situation where 'the rich get richer and more Westernised and the poor, who constitute 90 percent of the population get poorer and more desperate. With this in mind, Africa is awakening;

only the pace of movement looks slow and not clearly sketched. It will one day reach the Promised Land.

A strategic thrust to rapidly focus on Afro-centrism is on human capital development and with strong emphasis on science and technology. A structural but deliberate policy towards improved science and technology capability is necessary for the transformation of the African continent into a supper paradise given its already existing resources potentials. The emphasis is on strategic leadership backed by a vibrant, pro-active, pro-centric civil society with a committed community engagement for change, progress, development and sustainable quality livelihood for all. The new vision of change means hard work, competition, motivation and reward done with openness and clear development intensions for the common good. The ideal of an African Union Government cannot be realized if many ideological patterns of powers continue to exist; trust flies out of the window, confidence in leadership is lost; state governments lack legitimacy and the entire continent is weakening nationally and internationally.

An African Union Government will strive and succeed with well-articulated models of effective good governance leadership and civil society shows how economy, polity and culture and culture work hand in gloves in the emerging state construct and particularly diffuse the idea that Africa is inferior to everything else. The colonial entrenched idea that the culture of the West is superior to everything else should be diffused. The emphasis for the new African construct should be focused in developing and operating a political system with good leadership and governance aimed at a people-centred development as the only hope for its economic sustainability.

The world construct of today demands a hegemonic organization capable of diffusing, enforcing and protecting it harmonious interest but working with other regions to ensure the sustainability of the human-race. Africa has to be part of the international community through international cooperation efforts, movements of people, trade and other humanitarian related activities. The new African leadership and Union Government must focus on self-reliance and local economic initiatives, or else westernization, imperialism and capitalism will recolonize the continent. Through colonial rule western leadership essentially created a paradigm for post-colonial Africa to specialize in poverty by inhibiting the development of technology in areas of increasing returns. What should Africa do now? It is time to craft a new governance system and efficient institutional capacity which is currently lacking administrative capacities, but more so one of lacking legal authority for the regulatory frame work including the civil service which should be apolitical to push forward a more balanced form of development. An effective and corporative alliance between the state, civil society and the private sector should put in place a solid, inclusive, comprehensive plan that progressively advance African countries to a better status than what currently prevails. State, civil society and private sector intercourse must be maximized to the fullest

Africa by now should understand and develop a strategic focus on maximizing land ownership across the economy (DE Soto, 2000:20) and intensify investments in science and technology education and other factors that ensure rapid development (Bernstein 1992:16). Lessons should be drawn from China, India and Brazil. The African debt burden shows that the "debt vultures" – the rich countries – are financed by the poor countries (Hertz 2004, Moyo 2009). The 'debt vultures' are destroying the continent. Brazil, India and China are gradually escaping from the mess African finds itself entrench in. Note that between Brazil, India and China accounts for half the world's poorest people and even bigger share of those who have escaped poverty. In 1981, 84 percent of China's population lived below the poverty line of USA$1.25 per day in (2005 price); in 2005 the share was just 16 percent. This amounted to a 6.6 percent proportionate annual rate of poverty reduction – the difference between the growth rates of the number of poor and the total population (Ngara 2011:185). The Brazilian situation is not different. The 'Bolsa Familia' cash transfer programme is providing income support to poor families, subject to their fulfilling certain human development requirements such as school attendance (ILO 2009:5) had by 2008 reached around 11.3 million families, 46 million people, around 75 percent of the estimated number of poor families corresponding to a quarter of Brazil's population at an annual cost of US$4.5 billion about 0.4 percent of GDP. Turning to China, which reduced poverty significantly, mainly by fusing on agriculture first and then on manufacturing (Miller 2002:3; The Economist 2009:15). A key strategy for India has been growing entrepreneurship; incubator established to provide skills training, financing, employment and marketing for entrepreneurs with the results that 45 percent of industrial employment, 35 percent of exports and 40 percent of industrial output came from small and micro enterprises (Ngara 2011:67, Prahalad 2005:185).

These dramatic changes own much to leadership and a willing citizenry determined to overcome inadequacies. And this requires as noted by Mbeki (2000:90); *"The act of leadership that we were all called upon to exercise in the management of change and not conservation of the past. It therefore becomes necessary that, as individuals and as partiers, we contextualise whatever position we take with regard to any specific act or action and measure its correctness by the degree to which it contributes to the social transform"* of the African continent. African leadership should articulate and aggregate an Afro-centric and a human-centred model of development. This paradigm shifts; Euro-centric to Afro-centric or from a narrow quantitative concern for growth to an inclusive social development policy regime in Africa is essential to get the continent currently stuck on the runway off to a proper domesticated, integrated and unitary development.

On the other hand, the world is witnessing a new mode4 – Africa reeling under political patriotism – the famous "I am an African" statement by Thabo Mbeki, (Former President of South Africa) could be seen as a new sign of patriotism (2010:7-14) stimulating the African Renaissance Agenda, implying that:

> *"Africa Fifty Years on Need to Mary "Africa Must Unite with I am an African; to push forward the Afro-centric Agenda by getting the Euro-centric influence out of each and every Africa government policy strategy. We need to unite and be proud of who we are"*

Into a new holistic agenda that prioritise and energizes the awakening of a new African continent; or what Wa Thiong'o (2009:71) categorizes as *"a monumental historical shift"* in the life of the people, the nation, the region and continent. But when people implicitly support autocratic governments for the clear reason of protecting articulate-self-interests to the detriment of the people, then we get foreign exploitation through the process of disunity. To achieve legitimate aspirations of dignity and freedom, stability and peace, unity is needed even within the context of our diversities. Our diversities should be our strength not weakness. The quality of leaders in Africa is what is holding the continent back. Africa does not need a lot of people to prosper, just a few visionary leaders.

The publication has considered several of the major changes which must take place for the realisation of "Africa Must Unite and the Renaissance Project" and their influence on development related issues. What limits our response to this challenge on which the destiny of Africa depends? Nor primarily the technical solutions which are largely already familiar, but the non-existence of a clear and generalized awareness of the realities and dangers and the urgency and essence of political will to face up to them and take corrective actions. Only in q spirit of solidarity, consensus, unity, compromise, give and take based on respect for the individual, each nation and the common good will it be possible to achieve craft the common and endurable the solutions that are needed for the take-off to a service delivery society. We need to shape our ploughshares and elevate the Afro-centric strategy as the collar pillar of African power and as part of a strategy of exercising 'smart power' internationally. This is the time to launch a new kind of war on African unity and development, and why now? The war for self-determination has been fought and it continues unabated because underdevelopment conveys the gravity of the challenge and the totality of power and resources employed in the pursuit of victory, freedom and human respect, dignity and quality living standards. The unity metaphor intentionally illuminates one additional aspect of these contest – they can be lost if articulate self-interest prevails. The principal axes of underdevelopment and exploitation in this struggle for African Unity are the fronts of economic and social development, democratisation, development and empowerment of civil society.

Seen with these perspectives, African governments and the people will be failing by not showing their ability to perform their obligations and responsibilities to their constituents; such weakness enables others to undermine the legitimacy of African governments even without the commission of violent or disruptive acts. Rather, failing to unite, like corruption, simple incompetence or a lack of administrative capacity proves that, like a cancer, an 'enemy' needs not be malicious to be malignant. Against such a foe, Africa must bring to bear new and unconventional tools with which to fight a conventional battle – one in which effective local partnerships, proactive diplomacy, and, most importantly, capacity building in all sectors stand in for ever-greater challenges to be encountered. Democratic governance and quality living standards are thus far, promises unfulfilled. And this weakens government stance, legitimacy, authority and image before the people and the wider international community. Therefore, Africa must start putting in place counter insurgency (Afro-centric Approach) and bearing in mind that development and quality livelihood is for the long. State building is a long-term vocation that can cause many problems if not properly tailored to the needs of the people. Therefore, sharpening our ploughshares rather than hanging on the 'blame theory' or turning back into swords of confrontation will do more harm than good.

That said, Africa should play through a united front a vital role in shaping a more equitable and stable continent and then the world – a role that the force of arms cannot play. Within this context, Africa can draw valuable lessons and draw upon a pool of experience from other countries – The Asian Countries – which were behind African countries in the 1960s and today occupy a different but strategic economic position in global politics. This is particularly true when lessons concerning standing up to the realities and working with all stakeholders (e.g., state, civil society, private sector and the international community) and when knowledge is at a premium. This is the time to work in a consensual process toward a useful cross-fertilisation of lessons, ideas and experiences between all African countries no matter their different opinions on the unity of the continent but that, ironically, increasingly face overlapping problems within each of their external relations with the Grand West.

It is undeniable that these solutions call for complete readjustment on various planes as aspects of individuals and of each nation; of course, inevitable sacrifices will have to be made. It is the joint responsibility of all to act without further delay. The action is simple but demanding: "Africa Must Unite: I am an African" all working in unionism for the common good to avoid a dangerous future and to construct a strong and prosperous continent. This is the pledge must all make, to see that we leave behind a better continent to future generations that what we met.

References

African Union Commission. (AU) (2011). Letter from the Chairperson of the Commission, Issue No. 1, November 2011.

Aneme, Girmachew Alemu (2008). A Study of the African Union's Right of Intervention Against Genocide, Crime Against Humanity and War Crimes. Faculty of Law, University of Oslo, Oslo – Norway.

Atallah Rudolph (2013). "The Tuareg Revolt and the Mali Coup," ASPJ: Africa and Francophone, First Quarter, Vol. 4, No. 1, 2013, pp66-79

Bennis W. & Nanus B. Harper (1985) The Most Successful Leaders Do 15 Things Automatically Every Day. Josef Baw, Francisco, CA, USA

Bernstein, P. L. (1992) Capital Ideas. The Improbable Origins of Modern Wall Street. The Free Press, New York

Burns, J. M. (1978). Leadership. Harper & Row, Publishers, New York, USA

Conger, J. M & Kanango, R. N. (1998) Charismatic Leadership in Organisation, Sage Thousand Ok, CA, USA

Dahl Birgitta (2012). "From the Inside: We Must Not Fail," %0 years of Dag Hammarskjöld Foundation, Development Dialogue, No.60, August 2012, Uppsala Sweden, pp15-25

Deng Francis (2010). Idealism and Realism. Negotiating Sovereignty in Divided Nations" the Dag Hammarskjold Lectures. Development Dialogue No.55 March 2010 Dag Hammarskjold Foundation, Uppsala-Sweden,

De Soto (200) The Mystery of Capital: Why Capitalism Triumph in the West and Fails Everywhere Else, Basic Books, New York.

Dersso A. Solomon (2012). "The Quest for Pax Africana; The Case of the African Union's Peace and Security Regime" African Journal of Conflict Resolution: Special Issue on the African Union, Vol.12, Number 2, 2012. ACCORD, South Africa, pp11-47

Eliasson Jan (2011). "Peace, development and Human Rights: The Indispensable Connection" The Dag Hammarskjold Lecture 2011. Dag Hammarskjold Foundation Uppsala-Sweden

Forje W. John (ed.) (2011) Century of Change, Symposium for African Unity, Nova Science Publishers Inc., New York

Hertz, N. (2004) The Debt Threat: How Debt is Destroying the Developing World. Harper Business, New York.

International Commission on Intervention and State Sovereignty (ICISS) (2001). The Responsibility to Protect. Report of the ICISS.

Koka, K. M. (1985) "The Concept of Black Star and Pan-African Unity". Unpublished paper delivered on the 40th Anniversary of the Pan African Conference, Manchester, England

Kouzes, J. M. & Posner, B. (2007) The Leadership Challenge. 4th edition, B. Harper, Joessef Bass, Francisco, USA

International Labour Organisation (ILO) (2009) Bolsa Familiar in Brazil: Context, Concept and Impacts. Social Security Department, ILO Office, Geneva

Lipman-Blumen, J. (2005) Toxic Leadership. A Conceptual Framework.

Matlou P. Matlotleng, Sanya Osha & Mammo Muchie (2012) Renascent and United Africans: Never Again to Any Form of Scramble for Africa", in Mammo Muchie et al (eds.) (2012) The Africa World from Fragmentation to Unity and Renaissance, Africa Institute of South Africa, Pretoria, South Africa

Mbeki M. Thabo (2009) Africa: The Time Has Come. University of South Africa Press (UNISA), Pretoria. South Africa

Mbeki, Thabo (2012). Address by Thabo Mbeki at the Makerere University Institute of Social Research Conference on the Architecture of Post-Cold War Africa – Between Internal reform and External Intervention, Makerere University, Kampala, January 19, 2012.

Mbeki Thabo (2010) Reflections ON African Challenges and Prospects. Kyosti Bookbinders, South Africa

Moyo, D. (2009) Dead Aid: Why Aid is not Working and How There is Another Way for Africa. Strauss and Giroux, Farrar, New York

Muller, H.L. (2002) China's Upcoming Leadership Changes and the PLA. Centre for Contemporary Conflict, California, USA.

Muchie Mammo, Sanya Osha & Matlotleng P. Matlou (eds.) (2012). The African World: From Fragmentation to Unity and Renaissance. Africa Institute of South Africa, Pretoria, South Africa.

Ngambi, H.C. (2002). "The Role of Emotional Intelligence in Transforming South African Organisations. Proceedings of the International Economic and management Sciences Conferences, Vanderbijlpark RSA, pp221-231

Ngambi H.C. (2010). Leadership in Marketing. In Management: A South Africa Perspective (eds.) M.C. Can't, C.H. van Heedrden & H.C. Ngambi (2010) Cape Town, South Africa, Juta.

Ngara Shinga (2011) "Bennu: Africa Innovating Itself Out of Underdevelopment", in International Journal of African Renaissance Studies, Vol. 6. No.1, June 2011, Unisa, Pretoria, South Africa, pp60-77

Oliver Abraham (2012). "How Ethical is Leadership?" in Leadership, Vol. 8. No.1, February 2012, Sage Publications, pp67-84

Olonisakin, Funmi (2000). Conflict Management in Africa: The Role of the OAU and Sub-regional organizations. In Gilliers, Jakkie & Annika Hilding-Norberg (eds.) Building Stability in Africa: Challenges for the New Millennium, ISS Monograph No. 46, Institute for Security Studies, Pretoria, South Africa.

Oliver Abraham (2012) "How Ethical is Leadership" in Leadership, Vo.8. No.1, February 2012, sage Publications, pp67-84

Organisation of African Unity (OAU) (1990). OAU Declaration on the Political and Socio-economic Solutions in Africa and the Fundamental Changes taking place in the world. Adopted at thec26th Ordinary Session of the OAU Heads of State and Government on 9-11 July in Addis Ababa, Ethiopia, OAU Doc.AHG/Decl.1 [XXV1)

Organisation of African Unity (OAU) (1963). Article 111, Sections, 1. 2. 3. And 5

Prahalad (2005) The Fortune at the Bottom of the Pyramid. Penguin Books, London

Preez du Max (2012) "The Socrates of Africa and His Students. A Case Study of the Pre-colonial African Leadership," in Leadership, Vol.8. No.1, February 2012, Sage Publications.

Querze R. Alana (2012) "Assessing the Claims of State-Building Sceptics. Occupation and Counter Insurgency in Iraq," Africa and Francophone, ASPJ, 2nd Quarter, Vol.3

Salawu Abiodun (2012). "The Paradigm of Ethical Development for Civilised Leadership in Africa," Leaders Vol.8, No.1. February 2012, sage Publications, pp17-27

Shivji G. Issa (2008) Pan-Africanism or Pragmatism? Mkubi na Nyota Publishers, Dar es Salaam, Tanzania

Smit, P.G. de J. Cronje; T. Brevis, M.T. Vrba and H.C. Ngambi (2007). Management Principles. A Contemporary Edition for Africa. Fourth Edition, Cape Town, South Africa, Juta

Tajudeen, Abdul-Raheem (2005). "Talking Pan-Africanism to the People" 24 November 2005, Compiled by Ama Biney & Adebayo Olukoshi (2010) Speaking Truth to Power. Selected Pan-African Postcards, Pambazuka Press UK

Tajudeen Abdul-Raheem (2009). "Tajudeen's Last Pan-African Post Card" in Biney and Olukoshi (2010) Speaking Truth to Power, Pambazuka Press, UK

Temple Edwin O'Sarn (2012). "Metaphysical Challenges of Ethical Leadership in Africa," in Leadership, Vol. 8. No. 1. February 2012, Sage Publications, pp47-65.

The Economist (2009). The Economist, 26 November 2009, The Economist Group: 18

Tinker Hugh (1964) Ballot Box and Bayonet. People and Government in Emergent Asian Countries. Chatham House Essays, Oxford University Press, London, New York and Toronto

Yusuf, Abdulqawi A. (2005). The Right of Intervention by the African Union: A New Paradigm in Regional Enforcement Action? African Yearbook of International Law. Martins Nijhoff, The Hague, Netherlands.

Wa Thiong'o (2009) Something Torn and New: An African Renaissance, Basic Civitas Books, New York

Zuma, Jacob (2012). "Speech of President Jacob Zuma of South Africa delivered at the UN Security Council on 12 January 2012.

Chapter 14

Wrong Education Reinforces Exploitation, Inequality And Underdevelopment: What Must Africa Do?

Abstract

Africa's sustainable development rests on its human capacity (human capital development) and a strong structural-functional institutional construct to propel, and manage the transformation processes and challenges. Weak human capital development and fragile institutions are recipes for disaster and underdevelopment. The paper argues that without a pool of skilled human capital value cannot be added to existing vast natural resources as the ingredient for transforming the welfare of the people. Jamshed Tata, an Indian industrialist noted way back in 1876 that, 'priority list of preconditions for industrialisation: are knowledge and skills and experience. Then in addition some iron and steel; plus, cheap domestically produced electricity.' This tells us of a skill mismatch and with organisations seeking graduates to employ. The education system is not tailored to the actual needs of the continent. The paper argues that Africa has to create and fulfil real structural transformation needs by redesigning African education with creativity, innovation and entrepreneurship (Muchie 2015; Lema Catherine Forje). Inappropriate education only fans underdevelopment, divisive tendencies, marginalisation, inferiority complex and inequality. Education creates unprecedented opportunities with important implications for Africa's ability to identify and exploit opportunities of transforming its economies and for the employability of its rapidly growing youth population. With education, the continent can leapfrog the industrialisation stage and bridge technological divides as well as adding value to its vast natural resource's potentials. The paper examines the narratives (both positive and negative) Africa's search for owning its development trajectories and being a veritable player in global politics and improving the wellbeing of its citizens. Centuries of colonial rule destroyed indigenous knowledge and cultural values forcing an inferiority complex and dependency syndrome on the people which has helped in retarding the progress of the continent. The paper concludes by advocating for new impetus into the education curricula ensuring that education is home grown without losing the universally accepted scientific norms, inquiries, objectivity and credibility. Why more African scientists, engineers and medical doctors are working in the United States than in the whole of Africa it is questioned? The current curricula are tailored to meet the needs of the developed world and not to address the continent's wants and aspirations Curriculum should be construed with a progressive Afrocentric orientation in mind without sacrificing academic excellence. How do we reconcile Eurocentric and Afrocentric ideologies (i.e., marrying the world of scientific research and indigenous people's cultural heritage ad values) for the good of humankind? The two worlds cannot be isolated or separated but bridges built across. Building bridges across the two worlds entails 'talking back to' and 'talking up to' thereby building up an institution of knowledge for a better world construct. Decolonising the curriculum is a thing that must be done to lead Africa on the right path of development.

Keywords: curriculum development, human capital building, The Africa We Want, indigenous knowledge, dependency

Introduction

Facing the Realities – Time to Act

"Until Africans are willing and able to curb abuse of power, Africa will never have peace and stability, end poverty, or find its rightful place in a globalising world" ***(Nelson Mandela).***

"A Riot is the Language of the Unheard" ***(Martin Luther King, Jr.)***

"The structure of world order is not rigidly constrained by present patterns, at least not overlong time cycles. Nevertheless, positive forms of transformation depend upon active politics. Any transformation of this sort will result from mass social movements and hard political struggles. This prospect presupposes suitable awareness" ***(Richard Falk, et. al.1982)***

Since the colonisation of Africa, external bodies have and continue to have the upper strata in the continent's transformation nexus. To begin with, the colonial powers laid down the modalities for the education, political and economic structures of African states. Cecil Rhodes outlining the case for colonialism in the1890s noted: *"we must find lands from which we can easily obtain raw materials and at the same time exploit the cheap slave labour that is available from the natives of the colonies. The colonies will also provide a dumping ground for the surplus goods produced in our factories."* (Ellwood, 2001:13). A new development concept - the Eurocentric Agenda - was established under the nexus of destroying everything in use empowering the people and making them susceptible as slaves to foreign cultures and values. The cultural heritage, values and indigenous knowledge system of the people were destroyed. This destructive agenda was undertaken under the notion of civilising the uncivilised and designed to render the people poor and dependent on the metropolis.

The education structure was specifically designed like the economic structure to benefit metropolitan countries. "This was irrespective of whether the resource base of a given African country was mineral resources, agriculture, and land to be populated by colonial settlers or a combination of any of these resources. The result was the same; i.e., an African economy that was outward oriented to suit the needs of metropolitan countries" (Bjura, 2004:21). What rationale underlies our interests for the topic? What are the fundamental arguments advanced for a new approach to human capital development? It cannot be denied that with education, "people's quality of life is greatly enhanced, as it contributes to their capacity and ability to achieve; people become better at identifying and solving their problems, creating jobs and increasing income, thus contributing to quality of life. Education is liberating, both for a given individual and the society at large" (Asmal 2004).

Gasu John (2018) notes that, "Higher education institutions in Africa, since the 1990s, have been operating within a context that is discernibly different from the preceding periods. The landscape for higher education, as it exists today, has been reconfigured by a conjuncture of mutually reinforcing factors that include globalisation, neoliberalism, Information and Communication Technology (ICT), privatisation and new public management system. This has led to the liberalisation of higher education landscape, in which private sector actors have become important players and the public ones corporatized. As a result, public and private higher education institutions have come to share commonality in their adoption of managerialism. The arrival of private sector providers and the infusion of capitalist culture into institutional governance have drawn much concern. Prior to the current situation, public higher education governance in Africa was largely absolved from the stress of seeking alternative sources of funding as the state was supposed to take up that responsibility. The academia was also not distracted by moonlighting activities that has become so enervating on faculty. However, the downscaling of state funding for university education at the instance of the World Bank has generated new challenges for higher education leadership to deal with so as to sustain their institutions. The concerns that have been raised centre around the fear that quality service could be guaranteed within a competitive liberalised higher education system. Another source of fear has been that commercialisation of teaching services, which has become the main source of income generation for the universities, would draw back research activities. Whether higher education leadership in Africa has the capacity to transcend these challenges to restore confidence in stakeholders by assuring quality service has remained a nagging question."

Clotete Nico et al (2018) attest to the issue of higher education in these words; "It is now widely accepted that for a country to thrive in the knowledge economy, it must develop high-level skills and competencies (human capital), as well as its scientific research, innovation and technological development capacity. Higher education and universities in particular, are regarded as key to delivering these knowledge capabilities for development, based on their traditional role of producing, applying and disseminating knowledge, as well as educating the next generation of knowledgeable and suitably qualified workers. Research has suggested a strong association between higher education participation rates and levels of development." Africa stands at the cross-roads of building its human capital capacity and higher education or face the wrath of perishing in this fast-growing global knowledge-based economy.

"The leadership roles in universities are dispersed among various actors; as universities are polycentric in nature. These institutions, nevertheless, have an integrative organic structure from which their governance systems emerge. And in higher educational context where roles change frequently, it is safe to posit that leadership in universities is not permanently lodged in the hands of a given set of individuals. The governance culture that was traditionally associated with universities was primarily established on a consensus building mechanism" (Gasu, 2018:4). As a consensus building mechanism, our institutions of higher learning should take the lead and be the platform or epic centre for building the society. It is either we build or perish. African countries need to master a broad complex set of skills while operating in an increasingly and complex world environment.

Education creates unprecedented opportunities with important implications for Africa's ability to identify and exploit opportunities of transforming its economies and for the employability of its rapidly growing youth population. With education, the continent can leapfrog the industrialisation stage and bridge technological divides as well as adding value to its vast natural resource's potentials. The paper examines the narratives (both positive and negative) Africa's search for owning its development trajectories and being a veritable player in global politics and improving the wellbeing of its citizens. Centuries of colonial rule destroyed indigenous knowledge and cultural values forcing an inferiority complex and dependency syndrome on the people which has helped in retarding the progress of the continent. Priority must be given to meeting the basic needs of the people, hence there be strong emphasis health, education, employment and food security are essential for enhancing human capacities to meet the challenge of sustained development.

Wrong education means a development strategy designed to imitate the life-styles of the consumption patterns of affluent industrial societies is clearly inconsistent with the Afrocentric vision of the development African wants. Eurocentric development without a human-face is a replica of capitalism which accentuates inequalities as the high consumption levels would be possible to secure for only a small minority of the population in each African country. Concern for social justice is an integral part of genuine development that unfortunately has bypassed Africa. A fairer distribution of income and productive assets like land remains essential as the means for speeding up development and making it sustainable. A people-oriented development strategy (Afrocentric) will have to pay much greater note to women; a nation cannot genuinely develop so long as half its population remains marginalised and suffers discrimination.

The result of Africa's education curriculum should be seen within the lenses of imperialism perpetuated through the ways in which knowledge about indigenous peoples was collected, classified and assessed and then represented in various ways back to the West, and then through the eyes of the West, back to those who have been colonised and accepted by the colonised. The paper argues that the significance of indigenous curriculum and perspectives of a progressive Afrocentric human capital development should account for how, and why, such perspectives must form the corner stone for the sustainable transformation of Africa – developing Africa through the lenses of Africans for Africans. Our unfortunate illiterate brothers and sisters should not be left behind. Progressive adult education training should be extended, bearing in mind that a literate population is more productive than an illiterate one. Therefore, revamping and expanding primary education to reach all is imperative. The quality of primary education, the first step in the long-chain in human capital development plays a key role in determining the quality of all higher levels of education, as well as improving the productivity of other economic and social programmes, health for example.

Colonial education was used as a mechanism for creating new indigenous elites. It was not the only mechanism for producing elite groups who converted to the Eurocentric ideology to continue the hegemony and domination. The challenge always is to demystify, to decolonise and to constitute a new mind-set for developing the underdeveloped continent. Africa should not develop through imperial or Eurocentric eyes. Africa needs African strategies. School knowledge systems must be informed by a much more comprehensive system of knowledge which links universities, scholarly societies and indigenous cultural heritage and value systems to the evolving views of development on the ultimate interest of Africa. An Afrocentric curriculum should be one trading with other knowledge systems, putting an end to the old system and starting a new road or agenda of another on its own right.

The words of former Executive Secretary of the Economic commission for Africa, Prof. Adebayo Adedeji (1982) should sink deep into the policy orientations of African policy makers; "...African countries cannot continue to pursue economic policies and strategies as if all they want to be is a poor imitation of America, France, England, USSR, or China....the time has come for us to think seriously about evolving a genuinely authentic strategy for development – a strategy for development that is not externally oriented, that is not based on copying other societies hook, line and sinker, and that does not lead to acculturative modernisation." It is extremely wrong for the continent's efforts towards development to be structured primarily on inherited theories of transformation with dismal developmental prospect for the future of Africa. Our current standing within the global economic context calls for an urgent redefinition of the development approaches, priorities and strategies for the continent. Why must Africa, after more than half-a-century of political independence, continue to sustain the wrong aspects of colonial policy, particularly the raw material export, non-industrialisation and dependency syndromes, which was and is encouraged, nourished, sustained and even enshrined in the constitution by the departing colonial powers for their own articulate interests? Overhauling our educational curriculum to meet the development needs of the continent is imperative if Africa is to be part of rapidly changing globalised knowledge-based economy of our time.

Conceptual Construct –The Overarching Purpose Facing the Perils of Education Underdevelopment

Why is Africa poor in the midst of vast natural resources endowment? What role can human capital development play in transforming the poor image of the country? Why has democratic governance failed on the continent? What can be done to reverse the current poor imagine of the continent as well as ensure sustainable welfare to the vast majority of the population? These and many cross cutting-edge questions need soul-searching answers in addressing the plight of the people. Based on the adage the '*knowledge is power,*' so also it can be stated that '*education is development,* and '*development is power.*' Africa has no education, and therefore cannot develop, but exploited by those with requisite know-how; and without development, the welfare of the people is seriously compromised as the continent is undermined by those with the know-how.

The Eurocentric curriculum is identified and idealised as the '*saviours of the African people.*' But Fanon (1990:193) argues that the problem of creating and legitimating a national culture represents a special battlefield and intellectuals are important to this battle in a number of different ways (Smith 2012:73). First, African intellectuals were assimilated into the culture of the occupying power; (the emergence of the 'negritude' orientation); second, the struggle for independence instigated into the minds of some of these assimilated Africans, or created the stage of a period of disturbance and the urgent need for the intellectuals to remember who they actually are, a time for remembering the past. And thirdly, the consequences of assimilation and era of remembering who they are constitute the new stage producing a revolutionary and realignment – progressive Afrocentric orientation which should put an end to the idea of '*they came, they saw, they named, they claimed and they owned.*'

The orientation through a progressive Afrocentric education curriculum should be '*we were, we are, we will progress, develop and own our development trajectories' for our wellbeing.* Building on our key history that encompasses colonial violence, post-colonial domination, and internal and externally generated underdevelopment, we have the capacity to discuss our development and security in a far more holistic and nuanced ways. We must empower our institutions at the national, regional and continental levels to handle the new development challenges. The people must be mobilised to ensure they partner with the state to ensure a holistic front in addressing the development challenges. Partnerships and cooperation with each other and the rest of the world should arise from internal cohesion. Confronted by suck complex issues, it is argued for radical departures from existing development paradigms and policies that retards the progress of the continent – an urgent but radical changes in attitudes, mind-set, political will and approaches to development as well as the restructuring of the pattern of production, distribution and lifestyles – leading to individual and collective self-reliance and self-sustainability.

With an institutionalised Euro-centric oriented developmental agenda, Africans remain 'extras or beggars,' and that they do not play a role they would have chosen themselves. They are not mastering of their destinies. Their real structure and role its, its physiological functions as an organ in the vast body of the global construct is to remain a raw material supplier to the developed economies. With a progressive Afro-centric ideological orientation, Africa will be what it should be; the continent will no longer be ambiguous; be independent taking its own destinies into her hands. The people are challenged to foster the ideals of a Renaissance Africa, Pan-Africanism, the clarion call of people like Kwame Nkrumah, Nelson Mandel, Nnamdi Azikiwe, Tom Mboya, Sankara, Fanon, Mazrui, Achebe, Nassar, Sekou Touré, Soyinka and many others

Fig.1: The Afrocentric Curriculum Agenda

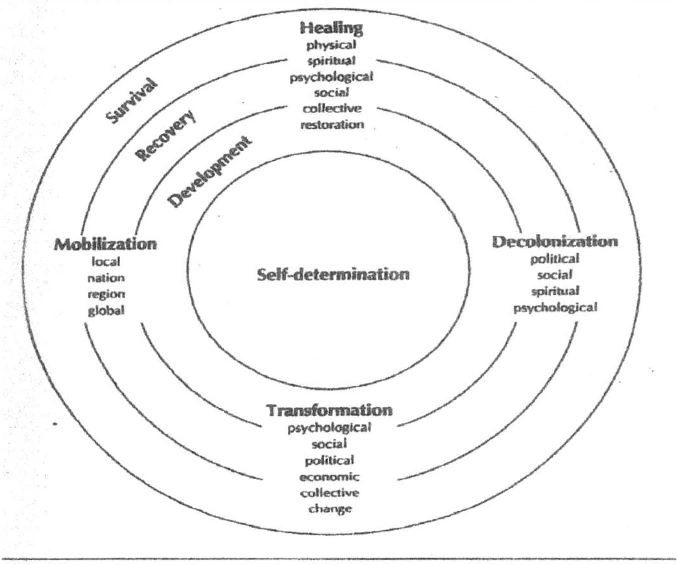

Source: Credit Smith Linda (2012:121) – The Indigenous Research Agenda
[Note: Afrocentric Curriculum Agenda, my conversion)

It is evident that Africa needs to rally around a unified and amplified voice if it is to assert its own interests in national, continental and global development. The Afrocentric education curriculum setup should dig deep into an agenda that puts into its true perspectives four cardinal issues of; [i] '*survival, [ii] recovery, [iii]development and[iv] self-determination*' as illustrated in **Figure 1: An Afrocentric Curriculum**. Expounding on these four cardinal tides, Smith (2012:121) notes that 'survival of peoples as physical beings, of languages, of social and spiritual practices, of social relations; recovery of territories, of indigenous rights, and histories; recovery is a selective process, often responding to immediate crises rather than a planned approach. Self-determination is the right of the people to define the shape of their destiny and own it. Self-determination in a research agenda becomes something more than a political goal. It becomes a goal of social justice expressed through and across a wide range of psychological, social justice which is expressed across a wide range of psychological, social, cultural and economic terrains. These four major areas are backed by for cardinal points, namely, *'healing, mobilisation, decolonisation, and transformation'* represent processes, not goals or ends in themselves. They are processes which connect, inform and clarify the tensions in society as well as give visions and directions at the national, continental and global levels for constructive changes to occur.

Africa's new education curriculum needs [a] Healing: physical, spiritual, psychological, social, collective, restoration etc.; [b] Mobilisation requiring; local, nation, region, continent and global; [c] Decolonisation: political, social, spiritual and psychological; and [d] Transformation: psychological, social, political, economic, collective, change. In short, the new curriculum calls for a new mind-set, comprehensive political will towards a new era for the development of Africa. This provides the way for a winning Africa in the battle against underdevelopment, exclusion, marginalisation, exploitation and undermining of the sovereignty of the African people. Undermining results from Africa's encounter with Euro-colonialism, a reflection of the nexus between indigenous knowledge, culture and development, and indeed a call for the revival and reinstitution of indigenous knowledge, not as a challenge to Western science, but a complementary form of knowledge necessary to steer and promote sustainable development in Africa and beyond' (Mawere, 2014). Hammering on the role of indigenous knowledge, Awuah-Nyamekye (2015) notes that Eurocentric scholars even viewed indigenous knowledge as superstitious, irrational and anti-development. He goes on to discuss an interesting and insightful discourse on the state and role that indigenous knowledge can play in addressing a tapestry of problems of the world and challenges connected with the application of indigenous knowledge n enlightenment science-dominated contexts.

Zeleza (1997) asserts western writings on Africa clearly demonstrates the regimes of representation are suffused with Africa's implacable 'otherness' and pathology.... Africa remains a deeply contested intellectual and ideological terrain, a continent that is perhaps still as misrepresented and misunderstood as it was at the beginning of the century. Muchie (2015:36) asserts that regardless of the different phases African universities have passed through, what is clear is that higher education institutions in Africa have not been home-grown. Universities in Africa still do not include the rich sources of indigenous knowledge. Just as the post-colonial state became largely a legacy of colonialism, the universities also became part of the institutions where the varieties of knowledge that originated in Africa from time immemorial have been bypassed, ignore, and suppressed rather than being used to serve as building blocks for developing Africa's own authentic African higher education systems. But alas, research, knowledge, higher education and learning rooted in African values and philosophies have routinely been discontinued.' A serious rethinking of how to galvanize the education sector of the continent is urgently need as we are in great need of quality and quantity of human capital to accelerate the sustainable transformation of the continent. Gasu (2018) further states that the leadership roles in universities are dispersed among various actors; as universities are polycentric in nature. These institutions, nevertheless, have an integrative organic structure from which their governance systems emerge. And in higher educational context where roles change frequently, it is safe to posit

Michelle Romo et al (2011) looking at the university in African democratic citizens notes that higher education in Africa contributes to democratisation, beyond producing the professionals that are necessary for developing and sustaining a modern political system, remains an unresolved question. ...the potential of a university to act as a training ground for democratic citizenship is best realised by supporting students' exercise of democratic leadership on campus. This in turn, develops and fosters democratic leadership in civil society. In boundaries of the education imagination, Hugo Wayne (2011) puts out that explorations of the limits of education reveal what education is, what it does, and how it works, providing the reader with an overarching vision of individual and collective development as well as systematic principles to recognise what is specifically educational in these processes. While Mouton et al (2015) writes about a resurgence of interest in training programmes for higher education leaders and management [HELM] at African universities.

Lema (2016) posits that "human capital education is central to economic development of a nation". While Mwamwenda and Lukkele-Olorunju (2013:1) notes; "only through education will Africans be in a position to address the demands and challenges of this century." The Deputy Chair of the African Union Commission, (Erastus Mwench, in Lukkele-Olorunji) states that Africa has for some time now, decided to anchor its development of education." Do we anchor the right kind of human capital development to enhance our welfare? Cloete et al (2014) posit that "the dominant global discourse in higher education now focuses on 'world-class' universities – inevitably located in North America, Europe and, increasingly, East Asia. The rest of the world, including Africa, is left to play 'catch-up.' But that discourse should focus rather on the tensions, even contradictions, between 'excellence' and 'engagement' with which all universities must grapple. Here the African experience has much to offer the high-participation and generously resourced systems of the so-called 'developed' world."

True the continent has made great strides in the field of education since independence. Nigeria for example, which had three universities at the time today boost of over 120 such institutions. The same can be traced throughout the continent. For a country or a continent, there is no greater wealth than well-trained human resources. Former South Africa's Minister of Education (Asmal Kadar) argues that education is not only critical, but also a solid foundation for both the reconstruction and development of Africa, adding that providing education is investing in economic development, given that sustainable development calls for adequate and ever-increasing skills and knowledge base, which are inherently products of education. While Langa (2014) looks at the landscape and dynamics of change in the higher education system by describing the attest developments of trends of expansion, financing, governance and policy reforms closely linked to the development of higher education in Portuguese speaking African countries.

Speaking on developing human resources, Margaret Joan Anstee (Director General of UN Office at Vienna and as Under Secretary-General responsible for UN activities relating to social policy and development in Africa) notes: "...The challenge to planners and practitioners is to maintain wherever possible the vitality of this cultural legacy and of traditional support systems during this period of social change... Redressing the social ills of African society and improving the distribution of social services can be achieved in the context of social planning...The ultimate purpose of development, it should not be forgotten, is to improve the well-being of people...all people...."

Africa developing and owning its own development trajectories requires a new *development thinking and a comprehensive and progressive education curriculum*; one construed within the contextual frame of an encompassing Afrocentric science-techno-entrepreneurial developmental approach premised under the umbrella of a *'people-first or people-centred'* development. The education curriculum left behind by the colonial masters with its hidden and even exposed agenda of furthering the underdevelopment and dependency of Africa has to be given a new face lift and test of life making the continent productive and competitive within the global based-knowledge economy of our time. Why must Africa be at the bottom step of the development ladder? That has to change and challenges African academics to spearhead the drive towards a new development episode and epoch for the continent (Adedeji, 1989). What this entails, points in the direction of the continent's education system tailored [a] producing a modern African responding to the material, cultural, social, spiritual and human needs of the people; [b] meeting the challenges of the African people within the global community where science and technology has attained a level of profundity and within a conducive environment that ensures quality services delivery and welfare to all citizens.

The new development thinking of Africa articulated in AU Agenda 2063 – *Building the Africa We Want,* cannot evolve on the colonial imposed form of education curriculum that focused on the liberal arts relegating technical and entrepreneurial education to the background. Africa of today and tomorrow needs a progressive and well-articulated curriculum with a strong orientation on science, technology and entrepreneurial education without which the anvil for industrialisation neither can be structured nor sustainable welfare attained for the population. Taking advantage of Gerschenkron's (1962) *"the late-comer advantage',* and with the vast opportunities offered in the global world, Africa has to streamline and tailor its human capital development in a way that its educational system graduate's students who are *'job-creators'* and not *'job-seekers'* in the public sector.

Forje (2013:149) posits that human capital development faces serious challenges, ranging from the absence of an enabling environment, poor infrastructure, inadequate teaching staff, political interference and financial problems to the centralised nature of the administrative establishment that must be holistically and comprehensively addressed to yield credibility, functionality and quality service delivery. Only a new curriculum teaching methods and management styles adapted to the needs of the society is urgently required. Articulating and implementing a comprehensive progressive Afrocentric education curriculum should evolve within the premises of scientific excellence and academic objectivity and credibility that restores the region back into the heydays of when *"Africa civilised Europe"* (Ankomah, 2015:72-77).

Currently, the education system in practice reduces the African into a 'neo-Europe' minus economic development and sustainable welfare for the vast majority of citizens. Entrepreneurship education and the innovation journey which Africa needs involves educating, motivating and coordinating people to develop and implement ideas by engaging in transactions with others while making the adaptations needed to achieve desired outcomes within changing global context. Skilled manpower in all discipline and spheres of activities are needed to move the continent from its current to a higher status of welfare. The African challenge is failures of 'development' and failures in the management of the continent's human environment. The gap between the rich and poor nations is widening – not shrinking – and there is little prospect, given present trends and institutional arrangements that this process will be reversed. Therefore, African countries need to re-examine the critical role of education in the development process and to formulate realistic policy measures to dealing with them – a new education curriculum is needed; to ensure that the appropriate institutions, equipment's, infrastructures are in place to facilitate the new curriculum in place; and to raise the level of those working in the sector to perform well.

Wrong education reinforces poverty and inequality as it equally intensifies under-development and poor resources utilisation. Africa with vast natural resources benefits very little since added value is not given to these resources. Most state spending in Africa is wasteful, low priority being accorded to those sectors as education and health which provide the necessary inputs for the building up of human capital, improving productive and creating the basis for an industrial society. The solution to Africa's predicament lies in the development and improvement of indigenous managerial skills (a not in) selling off state enterprises into private hands. By denuding the existence of meagre stocks of human capital the continent has, it acts as a long-term constraint on development. Improving its human capital base is prelude to building and entrepreneurial and an industrial base.

The Khartoum Declaration presented a clear perspective of investments in health and education; regrettably, over the past decade human conditions of most Africans have deteriorated calamitously; the unemployment and underemployment situation has worsened markedly." The development of human resources is seen not as the hoped-for product of measures of economic development, but as the very means of development. The disastrous effect of structural adjustment programmes in Africa in the last couple of decades has been that they have been implemented at human cost and sacrifices to the point that they have been 'rending the fabric of African society,' weakening the very capacity of the people to engage in socio-economic recovery and development (Brown, 1995:264-5). Why is Africa underdeveloped in spite of being the centre of academic excellence following the establishment of the first university in the world in 859 BC? We have to dispel the fact or thinking that "the curious idea that a great white race has been responsible for all the great civilisations of the past is nothing more than a crude superstition propagated mainly by European-oriented racist historians. Because for 781 years, between 711 AD and 1492, Africans from ancient Northwest and West Africa, together with their Islamic fellows from Arabia, had put Southern Europe to the sword, conquered it, governed it, and brought civilisation, education, and general enlightenment to Europe as a whole" (Ankomah, 2015:72).

Tabaro (2015:82) writing on tracing African civilisation "...Count Volney remarked that although the black people were slave of the Europeans, they were the source of science, philosophy, technology, astronomy, medicine, mathematics, the arts, etc. that were so beneficial to Europe at the time. The African origin of civilisation in Europe, Asia and America is beyond contention. I hope following Cheik Anta Diop (1923-1986), Chancellor Williams (1893-1992), from his book, Destruction of Black Civilisation) and Martin Bernal (1937-2013, in Black Athena). George James in *'Stolen Legacy,'* it is possible to demonstrate how Africa lost its civilisation and why Europeans denied and continue to do so that Africans enjoyed advanced human culture and civilisation" (Ubuntu). Adding his voice, Pheko Motsoko (2014 – New African July) made an important commentary; "how can the Ubuntu philosophy be restored for the benefit of humanity in general, and not just for Africans alone"?

Africa has to explore its past in building a new society through a genuine Afrocentric curriculum centred education development strategic approach. The African Development Goals (ADGs) requires resources mobilisation and utilisation and building a solid human capital base that covert and gives added value to its vast natural resources base. Former World Bank President, Barber Conable (1988), asserts: "Without education, development will not occur. Only an educated people can command skills necessary for sustainable economic growth and for a better quality of life." To move forward Africa needs education or a critical mass backed by the political will to develop. Getting the critical mass in quantity and quality entails building up a solid educational system (see Fayolle, 2018; Colin Jones, 2019; Ferreira, 2018;

Many reasons can be advanced highlighting the cardinal role of education in the continent's development. It goes without saying that human capital development means helping to meet other basic needs, and helps sustain and accelerates overall development. In addition, the important role of education lies in the fact that it helps to determine the distribution of employment and income for both present and future generations. No doubt, education influences social welfare through its indirect effects of health, fertility and life expectancy. The only way to empower the rapidly increasing youth population is through education so that they meet the challenges of and fit well in demands of the job market. African countries should invest more on human capacity development if they are to be part of the rapidly advancing global knowledge-based economy of the time. Sad to state that African countries are investing in weapons of human destruction than in knowledge and research building as the roadmap to creating employment opportunities through the proper utilisation of and giving added value to its vast abundant natural resources.

Therefore, education creates unprecedented opportunities with important implications for Africa's ability to identify and exploit opportunities of transforming its economies and for the employability of its rapidly growing youth population. With education, the continent can leapfrog the industrialisation stage and bridge technological divides as well as adding value to its vast natural resource's potentials. The paper examines the narratives (both positive and negative) Africa's search for owning its development trajectories and being a veritable player in global politics and improving the wellbeing of its citizens. It strongly emphasises that the creation, mastery, and utilisation of modern science and technology are basic achievements that distinguishes the developed from the developing polities. The widening gap in overall development and wealth between the African nations and the developed countries is to a large extent the science and technology gap. Africa's future development policies will need to address with greater vigour the closing of the knowledge gap with the North.

Knowledge is vital to the future of the continent, for development depends more and more on the benefits derived from the advances of science and technology. Progress here calls for the overhaul of education systems, so that greater attention is given to education in science and technology and to training in engineering and technical skills. It therefore, requires a comprehensive science and technology policies with clear sectorial priorities, integrating science and technology in national plans, as well as provide adequate resources for strengthening scientific and technological capability (Forje 1989; Skorov, G. E. 1978; OAU 1980).

Centuries of colonial rule destroyed indigenous knowledge and cultural values forcing an inferiority complex and dependency syndrome on the people which has helped in retarding the progress of the continent. The new centres of power have not fared better either than the departed colonial masters. It is business as usual. Rather, the belief is that existing status-quo should not undergo change but consolidated through false promises – the West and African ruling elites as the sole provider of the welfare of the people. Colonial curriculum established the positional superiority of western knowledge. An Afrocentric curriculum should focus on the individual and society with capacity to reason, on a society which promotes collective autonomy and collective-interests, and in constructing a state that is built on the rational rule of law and justice regulating the public sphere of life for all citizens.

Africa's new education curriculum should strongly focus on the following critical issues; (i) education must provide to the younger segments of the African society as fast as human and financial resources permit with the ultimate goal of developing a comprehensive system of human capital development for all age groups – free education for all; (ii) placing strong emphasis on a more equitable distribution of education opportunities and on the reduction of existing inequalities based on economic status, geographic location, and sex; (iii) the attainment of greater internal efficiency of the education system and priority reduction to the misuse of resources (students dropping out, corruption, poor infrastructures, etc.); (iv) education focused or directed to greater internal efficiency and tailored to the needs of the society, to the job market and ensuring that the students are properly equipped with the necessary skills that qualify them for the employment or embarking on the road of entrepreneurial related activities; and (v) develop the capacity of maintenance of an institutional capacity to formulate and carry out education policy, as well as to plan, analyse, manage and evaluate education and training programmes and projects at all levels. In line with this, Africa's future is inescapably linked to its ability to create an effective marriage between culture and science and technology – a challenge in which education plays a decisive part. Therefore, suitable education innovation for the continent calls for political and cultural authenticity, not a pale imitation of ex-colonial models, with specific country situations designed, implemented and owned by African countries themselves (World Bank, 1989; Akilu et all (eds. 1983). Invest in research to discover most of the hidden secrets in indigenous knowledge and the pharmacopoeia of the continent. How can traditional medicine contribute to modern science and the entire health system in enhancing the quality livelihood of citizens (Logmo,1985, Lantum, 1985)?

Breaking out of the current downward spiral of the Eurocentric education partly requires drawing up a progressive Afrocentric education curriculum and turning swords into ploughshares by making proper us of the 'conversion of the *'brain-drain into brain gain'* (Glaser, 1978; Adams, 1968; Kannappan, 1968; Seers 1969; UNITAR, 1971; Henderson, 1968; Castells 2016) for the sustainable transformation of Africa. It is interesting, but ironically to note that Africa which lacks the human capital for its development continue to export this valuable scare resources to the developed North. Any country exporting both its raw materials and human resources is doomed to perpetual underdevelopment, exploitation and dependency. Here is where Africa is facing serious underdevelopment/development dichotomy problems. A new education curriculum should provide the requisite game changer for the development of the region.

One can question rightly who is developing who? Is the introduction of the USA *"Green Card"* for example, not a deliberate attempt to drain the continent of its valuable human capital and render the region permanently underdeveloped? Are the inappropriate policies and implementation strategies of African countries that lead to poor utilisation of its human capital, creating jobs and employment opportunities for the bustling youth population not a deliberate strategy of the Eurocentric underdevelopment agenda for the continent? Whilst imperialism is often thought of as a system which drew everything back into the centre, it was also a system which distributed materials and ideas outwards. With its developed human capital Europe developed a 'positional superiority' as a useful tool in which knowledge and culture were as much part of imperialism as raw materials and military strength. Knowledge was also there to be discovered, extracted, appropriated and distributed. There is an escalating spectacle of an unholy alliance between the governing elites and the West to under develop the continent.

The 'brain drain' phenomena cannot be stopped; but it can be usefully converted into a '*brain gain*' factor accelerating the development of Africa. This of course requires African governments creating the necessary enabling environment attracting its exported human capital back home. The existence of failed states (Asonganyi 2015, Ghani & Lockhart, 2008) on the continent does not create the attractive pull factors for the '*brain gained*' return dichotomy. There is an urgent need for policy articulation and implementation strategies of bringing back our Diasporas as the engine of growth for the sustainable transformation of Africa. If the AU Agenda 2063 - '*Building the Africa we want*'- is to be realised, the African Diasporas must be encouraged to return and invest home. Tapping into the vast potentials and prowess of the Diasporas as the '*connectors*' is what could be the vital game changer for Africa's progress. The Diaspora is the termite accelerating the underdevelopment as it equally provides the much needed fertilise for fuelling economic growth and the way forward for closing the development gap, stimulating entrepreneurship, innovation, creativity and industrialisation as stimulants to growth and sustainable livelihood.

Human capital development is crying for change, for without change there can be no development. Can anyone hear and listen to the voices of the poor, the illiterate and disadvantaged? Education is a much-needed wake-up call for the development of the continent. Economic development can accelerate social development by providing opportunities for underprivileged groups or by spreading education more rapidly. Africa is caught up in a series of downward spirals, particularly poverty and lack of education for example. These have to be addressed and done so correctly through new technology and knowledge and properly used for the good of the people. The seriousness of the African crisis and human capital development cannot be overemphasised. Something is rotten in the continent of Africa. Without a thorough decolonisation of the education curriculum there can be movement towards a capable development states in Africa.

What is emphasised is comprehensive proactive actions to righting the wrongs of the current education system. Developing a new political will through which change can be brought is important. This should begin with critical self-reflection directed by knowing ourselves, understanding ourselves, interrogating where our focus should be, and developing cognizance of the need to change, how to change and to move forward. Without understanding what we want, constructive changes cannot be undertaken that benefits the people. Importantly, we should develop solidarity with the struggles to be the game changer in developing a new education curriculum from a realistic perspective considering important debates that are unfolded within them.

In respect of higher education, efforts should be directed towards improving academic standards of the universities. Presently, no African university is within the barometer of the first 100 universities in the world; there is need to increase their efficiency and quantity; change their output mix by controlling enrolments in certain fields of study and increasing them in others; and to reduce the serious burden on public resources through sharing of costs between the beneficiaries and users, on the one hand, and the governments on the other (Kwapong, op cit.187). Priority of science and technology, entrepreneurial education must be strengthened. With the private sector encouraged to invest in research and development geared towards the development and transformation of the continent's resources for the industrialisation and wellbeing of the people. Fighting corruption in the education sector is important in improving quality and efficiency. Here Cameroon has to make extra efforts in streamlining the way degrees and certificates are issued which has and continues to be a great source of confusion and sources of corruption national and international.

Unlocking the Human-Resources Potential: Strategy, Innovation and Change

In 2000, over 160 countries committed to vastly expand education opportunities for children, youth, and adults by 2015. The Millennium Development Goals MDGs has come and gone with not much achieved. In 2013, the African Union advanced the AU 2063 Agenda - ***The Africa We Want,*** and in 2015, the United Nations propagated its Sustainable Development Goals (SDGs 2030) following the non-achievement of the Millennium Development Goals (MDGs). The success or failure of these development agenda pivots on *'leadership;' 'political will'* and the kind of *'citizen's responses'* towards human capital development and of its usage in the transformation process. In Africa, one of its greatest deficits has been that of 'leadership.'

Leadership we are told is always necessary in any endeavour, applying equally to politics, business, economics, society and culture. In today's global context and national development, the perception of effective leadership is fast changing calling for participatory and consensual servant leadership as the inspiration for effective development attainment. The older model of a heroic, authoritarian, served leader-picture the hard charging demanding and worship is outdated. The new conventional wisdom, though, tells us that this model has given way to the *'servant, soft'* leader ideal, where leaders inspire their followers and avoid acting like dictators or semi-gods (Nye 2008; Mouton et al (2015; Jowl James et al; 2015).

Any society must ask three interrelated questions in order to develop its strategy: *where are we, where do we want to be, and how will we get there?* While the questions do not change over time, the realities and environments that countries face do. Given today's realities, how should African countries answer these questions? What form of education curriculum is needed for the continent to get out of its current doldrums of a developing and dependent continent and to improve the quality of livelihood of the people? To get to where Africa wants to be, requires that the education sector (primary, secondary and tertiary) institutions and curriculum in Africa have to be home-grown addressing the critical needs of the continent. From time immemorial, education on the continent has failed to include the rich sources of indigenous knowledge, culture and value systems.

Knowledge and skills are critical ingredients of economic development and societal transformation. If only Africans could be educated to a higher level and their skills developed, the productive potential of the continent - and its strength in the global economy - would be vastly enhanced. Though many countries have acquired impressive educational capabilities in the past many decades, serious deficiencies in human capital development exist in particularly in science and technology related disciplines throughout the continent. Educational policies place wrong emphasis on disciplines that do not accelerate the socio-economic transformation of the region. In many cases, indigenous knowledge is related to the background. The foundation for development is (i) building national consciousness and awareness; (ii) development of human resources; and (iii) the proper utilisation of human and natural resources in effecting appropriate changes in society.

What role has concepts like *(Ubuntu, Harambee, Batho Pele, Ujamaa, etc.,)* played in the epistemology of the educational curriculum and transformation process of the continent? As noted by Muchie (2015:36-37) "universities became institutions where the varieties of knowledge that originated in Africa have been bypassed, ignored and suppressed rather than being used to serve as building blocks for developing

Africa's own authentic African higher education systems. But alas, research, knowledge, higher education and learning rooted in African values and philosophies have routinely been disconnected." Sad enough, the education construct of Africa evolves on the lines set in the past by colonial masters, and has been too academic and unsuited to the scientific, vocational, and others needs of societies in the process of modernisation. This is not a call for inculcating purely materialistic values; education should focus at producing young people who are not alienated from their own culture and community but are equipped to contribute to, and benefit from, the progress of their societies.

Lessons can be drawn from Japan and other countries of the Asian region that are technologizing and not losing their cultural roots. Africa is fast losing its cultural heritage or has even lost this crucial ingredient in the transformation process. It is now the most unculturalised continent in the world; neither knowing whether it is African nor European. A society without its cultural roots is easily derailed by the penetration of external cultural values as Africa has become. This compromises its development orientation. Apparently, this is the pattern of education the current curriculum imparts on the people. We do not need to go further to see why Africa is underdeveloped. African education system is in a gross state of despair lacking substance in its cultural heritage and value system. It is necessary to look into the role of local knowledge and its effects and contribution on the adoption of technologies. New technologies like other innovations face resistance prior to their adoption. What is important is to put the blame game aside and assume responsibility for our future. Individual Africans must take initiatives and commit ourselves to engaging in activities that changes us and the continent, for the better. What is important is the proper usage of the continent's resources to impact on the welfare of the people.

Statistically, 33 million children did not attend school in 2012, 56% of whom were girls. This includes 5.5 million in Nigeria and more than one million in Ethiopia. The realisation of MDG 2 – Achieve universal primary education - shows that in 2012, 10 countries, including Rwanda, Benin, Algeria, Cameroon, Cape Verde, Congo, Mauritius South Africa, Tunisia and Zambia, were able to get more than 90% of their school-age children into classrooms (Africa MDG Report). Rwanda for example, made remarkable progress with 97% school enrolment on the continent in 2012. Girl's enrolment (98%) exceeding boys (95%), while the percentage of children completing their primary school cycle stood at 73% - 'a dramatic increase from 53% in 2008'.

Chad, Cote d'Ivoire and Niger were the only African countries in 2012 with youth literacy rate below 50% (Kuwonu, 2015:23). Due to a combination of many interrelated factors, Africa remains the only continent where more than half of parents are not able to help their children with homework. The illiteracy population rate on the continent needs to be radically brought down.

African universities are open to a sort of *"Scramble for Africa"* as these institutions are starved of funds, research equipment's, infrastructures etc. and become beggars robbed off their research opportunities and results. To a large extent, research results gather dust on the shelves and drawers of researchers, with no avenues for innovation, entrepreneurship, production and transformation of these results to the benefit of society. For now, "we study what we do not need, and need what we do not study. After inheriting an educational system from the colonial-powers who wanted not more than paper-pushers and lots of messengers and cooks, the newly independent African countries just carried on with the inherited educational system as if no independence had come at all, and as if the agendas and aspirations of the colonial governments and the African governments were one and the same" (Ankomah, 2013:25). All these impede the successful transformation of the continent. Investing in human capital development is turning opportunities into reality; making the long and difficult road shorter and easier for the continent suffering abject poverty in the midst of plenty.

Unlocking the continent's human resource potentials gives added value to its huge natural resources exploited by the developed countries. African governments should seize all available opportunity to improve the on its human capital development. The focus is on Africa. If you are down, there is nowhere else to move but up. The process of acceleration has started and there is no turning back. Poor education or human capital development is holding the continent back and our leaders are poised to take action. The people are gradually graduating from their current status of ignorance and getting to know their inherent rights. Just as they are demanding probity and accountability, the people will demand good education for all as a right. African countries must organise themselves and push with a common voice and purpose for the support they need to address the state of poor human capital development. Addressing poor human capital development must be positioned as a regional and national agenda, protected by national constitutions and to be pursued irrespective of which political party is in power. This is critical to ensuring that the momentum is not lost as a result of changes in government. Finally, we owe it to ourselves and future generations to ensure political and economic stability on the continent.

Breaking this vicious circle requires a committed effort to improve education and other essential basic needs - health, water supplies, sanitation etc.; particularly in poverty-stricken areas. Expanding educational opportunities means enrolling many children in primary schools, limiting the number of children dropping out of school; and getting more females on the education bandwagon. Through large-scale literacy programmes several African countries; and parental literacy has in turn helped the increase in literacy rate. There has been significant expansion in secondary and higher education. Today, focus is being directed to technical and vocation training including entrepreneurship. This gradual shift is important as prelude to industrialisation. A shift in the pattern of production and exports from raw materials to manufactures and, within the latter, to products with high and medium R&D intensity, is required to counteract the adverse consequences of the decline in prices of Africa's commodities including '*the black gold*' – oil (The South Commission 1990:109).

The greatest obstacle to development is ignorance. Education curriculum should break that barrier and build consciousness, awareness and erase the growing state of ignorance that bedevils the region. Acceptance of an Afrocentric developmental approach as a strategic objective should be promoted and actively inculcated among policy-maker's political leaders, civil servants, business people, academics and all other groups in society. The support of the people and participation in the development process are an essential part of the foundation in building a quality services delivery society. Therefore, promoting the 'Afrocentric consciousness and awareness' among the people and across the continent, strengthens their belief, mutual trust, confidence building and commitment towards constructing a brave continent within the global-knowledge-based economic context. Developing a new mind-set and consciousness is the fundamental game changer in transforming Africa from a so-called backward into a developed polity. The progress and achievements of the developed countries rest on their degree of awareness and consciousness of society. This is the miracle or medicine for the sustainable transformation of a society. Africa has to cultivate that spirit or else perish in the wallows of exploitation and underdevelopment.

However, African countries need to raise the quality and quantity of primary, secondary and tertiary education and to adapt it to its development needs. It has already been alluded to the issue of insufficient attention given to the importance of science and technology culture through the education system. Most importantly getting the female gender interested in science related disciplines is crucial. University education of a higher standard constitutes an important instrument of modernisation and development. The research and development (R&D) component, innovation, creativity, productivity and entrepreneurship should be emphasised in the education curriculum as these constitute the structural basis for industrialisation. Strengthening the educational systems is essential for narrowing the knowledge gap between Africa and the rest of the world as well as building the needed consciousness and awareness needed in transforming the society. Building the right critical mass is crucial for the transformation of the continent.

Therefore, the reform of curricula, particularly fostering technical and scientific skills, the development of entrepreneurship and management capacities at all levels of education must be adapted to the cultural, economic and developmental requirements of African countries. They must seek a new era of economic growth by investing into the areas mentioned by ensuring that the level of spending on weapons or arsenals of human destruction is greatly diminished. Such constructive changes should be geared towards enhancing the welfare of citizen's rests on political will, consciousness, change in mind-set and commitments of leaders and civil society towards making the vital changes required.

It is time African nations turn away from the destructive Eurocentric developmental agenda and approach so entrenched within the mind-set of African countries and focus instead on their common future through an Afrocentric agenda. African countries must not become prisoners of their own making – policy articulation and implementation strategies. They must face the common challenge of providing for sustainable development and act in concert to remove all factors constraining the progress of the region. By beating ignorance through building the necessary human capitals they can successfully achieve AU Agenda 2063. Therefore, with quality human sciences development, problems of underdevelopment can be addressed through the following channels;

- Getting at the sources;
- Dealing with the effects;
- Assessing national and continental risk;
- Making informed choices;

- Providing the necessary financial means, infrastructure, equipment's, institutional and legal frame works; and
- Investing in the continent's future.

Together these priorities provide the gateway to building the Africa We Want. Concerted holistic actions are needed to achieve envisaged goals. Wrong education generates poverty, tensions and conflicts nationally and across the continent. The people are still awaiting concrete solutions for their problems; which can best come through a people-focused development approach; erasing their state of ignorance, enhancing their status of consciousness and awareness remains imperative. The severity of the crises of development hanging over the continent can be attributed to a variety of factors including articulated self-interests of those on the corridors of power who strongly belief in military power solutions to socio-eco-politico problems. Yet they fail to understand as noted by President Eisenhower (1953) "that every gun that is made, every warship launched, every rocket fired represents, in the final analysis, a theft from those who hunger and are not fed, who are cold and not clothed." We find both national and global military expenditure well in excess of expenditure on human capital development; agricultural technologies, among others. Without substantial increased investments on education, research and development they can be no economic growth and sustainable welfare. Africa is in great need of a new education curriculum focusing on the following areas; -

- *Human capital development in the basic sciences, engineering. Medicine and public health;*
- *Technical and vocational training, including the development of entrepreneurship and management skills, and industrial apprenticeships;*
- *Taking advantage of the 'late-comer advantage' in promoting distance-education programmes within and across borders*

There is a failure on the part of African governments in tapping from the existing human capital potentials found within and beyond the frontiers of the continent. How do we bring the wealth of talents outside to accelerate the transformation process in the African region? The brain drain needs to be converted in a brain gain phenomenon. But to benefit from the Diasporas requires the establishment of an enabling environment for all to operate without harassment. Striving for good governance is a prerequisite for the sustainable transformation of the continent. The knowledge of the Diasporas wealth lost, just as the failure to give added value to existing natural resources. Once a system of good governance is put in place, the Diasporas will respond positively in the reconstruction of the continent. For now, much as they try to be active and serious participants in the transformation, poor administrative system and corruption stands as rock towards their active and positive engagement.

Quality versus Quantity

The challenge to emerging generation of African leaders is to put in place a functional and democratic governance system that assures among others, openness and transparency; efficiency and effectiveness, separation of powers, and the rule of law etc. (Forje 2004) to effectively and efficiently utilise its human and natural resources for the common good of the people. Development is a process of profound structural transformation. It cannot simply be imported. By now, there is ample evidence that successful development is vitally linked to education and the resilience of the economy, polity, and civil society, all functioning in a spirit of harmony to promote shared goals and objectives. Thus, the success of Africa's struggle against underdevelopment, exploitation, marginalisation and poverty depends on the ability of the continent to reform and regenerate its economies, polities, and societies in l tone with its basic development goals. The AU Agenda 2063 provides such a guide line backed by the global UN Agenda 2030 (SDGs) and the national development objectives of each of the 54 member countries of the African Union. Africa should develop one voice, goal and work towards common objectives from a strong and united clear position, using the AU 2063 agenda as the road map.

Infrastructure deficit is a major drawback on the continent. There is general acceptance that economic infrastructure is critical for economic growth and poverty reduction, given its pivotal role in improving competitiveness, facilitating both domestic and international trade and integration of the continent of Africa to the global economy. However, in Africa there is large infrastructure deficit in terms of access and quality, to be filled in the sector of education, energy, transport, information and communication technology (ICT) (Anyanwu and Erhijakpor 2009; Ncube 2013-72-80). Africa is in urgent need of both quality and quantity. We also need to develop self-understanding and to decolonise the mind (Ngugi wa Thiong'o, 1986) to get free of the effects of Eurocentric assault on the 'African mind'. We need collective and public political action aimed at addressing structural changes on the development of this emerging continent.

It is most critical as imperative that each African country takes a critical self-examination to ensure its institutional health is sufficiently sound to be able to respond to the vigorous demands presented by contemporary world construct. One of these challenges which underscore this paper is that of overcoming the knowledge gap. And in the words of Prime Minister Hailemariam Desalegn (Ethiopia): "today in our globalised world, no country can achieve development in isolation" *(Speech at the 2016, Africa Forum in Sharm-el-Sheikh, Egypt)* Structural transformation in the education sector is needed to develop the requisite human capital the continent needs in addressing what The President of the African Development Bank, Akinwumi Adesina (2016) sees as High 5s – five major priorities for the continent; (i) light up and power Africa: (ii) Feed Africa; (iii) Industrialise Africa: (iv) Integrate Africa; and (v) improve the quality of life for Africans *(Speech at Africa Forum, February 2016 Forum, Sharm el-Sheikh, Egypt).*

Increase in the number of institutions of learning education is important to give access to education to the widest number of the continent's fast-growing population. Equally important in this direction is the '*issue of quality of education*' to drive up the continent's expertise, productive and competitively in the global market. Undeniably, the education architecture of the continent is extricable linked to the political/governance culture of the 54 countries making up the continent. Given the need of the continent, there is the desire to pursue both quantity and quality without sacrificing the essence of quality and scientific objectivity. Scholars find it difficult to agree on the exact meaning of quality in education. If the continent is to compete, the issue of quality cannot be relegated to the back ground. The multiplicity of institutions of learning shows also a high degree of falling quality of education in virtually all levels. The challenge for human capital development in Africa is to improve on quality and quantity as well as proper utilisation.

The recent students' protests that have erupted across South Africa's university campuses demanding an end to colonialist education curriculum and mentalities should ring a bell into the minds and souls of policymakers across the continent for an urgent change in the education curriculum of the continent. African countries north of the Limpopo and South of the Sahara need to sharpen their tools and act in concert in creating functional units of educational technology knowledge for their development break through as well as engagement with which all universities must grapple. African universities should in concert begin discoursing an addressing the tensions, even contradictions, between Eurocentric and Afrocentric curriculum, between 'excellence' and 'engagement' to better place the continent on the right path of human capital development in the development of Africa and of the world at large. We have to reshape the debate on development on the global information economy for years to come.

A random sample indicates the following increase, for example, Botswana during 2000-04 academic year had a record of 11,121 university students, and in 2008/9 the number increased to 15,000; South Africa should the following increase 2000 with 670000 increased to 834000 in 2009; Kenya with 53 state and private universities in 2010 with an enrolment that increased from 118,230 (2007) to 142,356 in 208/2010; Rwanda tertiary education increased from 1 to 30 (2010) with a student enrolment of 60,000; Uganda with one higher institution in 1922 , now has over 100 tertiary institutions; Zimbabwe with the creation of the University of Zimbabwe (1980) to having nine public and three church-based universities with 12 institutes of technology colleges and over 400 private vocational institutions. Since 1980, Tanzania can pride itself with 40 public universities; Nigeria had three universities at independence in 1960, and by 2010 boosts of 110 universities, 183 polytechnics, and 86 colleges of education; in 1961 Ethiopia with a single university now has 22 public universities and this number is expected to increase to 33. Cameroon that had a lone State university in 1963 today boosts of 8 state universities and a growing number of higher institutes of Learning with over 25 private universities and technical Institutes (Forje 2013). Obanya (2014) in Educationeering defines as directing the triple academic functions of research, teaching, and responsive social engagement towards the education challenges of society. Research and development are imperative for the entrepreneurial take-off of Africa. Susan Robertson et al (201) make an appeal between the ever-open possibilities of the global space, and the nation-state with still seemingly irreducible hold on territory and imagination, lies the region. In higher education there are many kinds of region and we need to understand the importance of global higher education as providing an invaluable geo-spatial lens that complements analyses based on political economy and culture.

A number of reasons can be attributed to existing falling standards. These include drastic increase in enrolment and inadequacy of teachers, less classrooms, inadequate equipment's/ infrastructures, poor teaching environment poor pay-packets, among others; the rapid increase in educational establishments contributes to the use of under-qualified or unprofessional academics. In addition, the issue of curriculum is crucial to quality in education. Many of the private institutions are *'profit-making focus*ed.' Proprietors of these institutions are more focused on money-making rather than producing quality teaching standards. Government should put a strict control over these institutions and also formulate country centred excellence curricula that meets national needs and universal standards. Even though in some countries these private universities are monitored by state universities, the state universities are not properly equipped either. Finally, the quality of education has much to do with the competence or incompetence of the administrators and managers of education institutions. How some of these private institutions receive their accreditations is questionable. There is also the issue of poor financial investments in the sector. Financial sustainability is crucial in ensuring quality and quantity. In all, most countries have not been aggressive or pro-Afrocentric in character in giving a broad spectrum of the needs of the continent in the education sector and in meeting national needs and the job market.

The good news in the continent's education is the rapid increase of the female gender obtaining education and doing extremely well in nearly all disciplines. The science, maths, physics, engineering and other disciplines; vocation and technical education once the exclusive domain of the male gender, has been invaded successfully and rightly by women. Rwanda is making great strides here, and was a good performer towards achieving the MDGs and education for all by 2015. This falls in line with the government's focus on education which among others is on *educating citizens who are liberated from all kinds of discrimination, including gender-based discrimination, exclusion and favouritism; transform the Rwandan population into human capital for development through the acquisition of skills development; develop the Rwandan citizen an autonomy of thought, patriotic spirit, sense of civic pride, love of work well done and awareness.* This could be contrasted with the position of Nigeria as the country is confronted with issues such as (i) low levels of political will and commitment of some state governments on basic education issues; (ii) low and poor motivations/attitude of the trainees ...with no intention of working as teachers in the future; (iii) a high rate of unqualified teachers in the system; (iv) dearth of institutional materials and teaching aids; (Yazani and Magwanda 2014:117). So, a progressively construed and implemented Afrocentric curriculum is a rallying call and cry for a more just and sustainable future for the continent.

Apparently, any definition of development is incomplete if it fails to comprehend the role and contribution of women in development and the consequences of development for the lives of women and society.

Women should be encouraged and engaged in opportunities for creative work and economic development. Empowering women is very crucial in the process of change. Development in Africa depends on women; policy articulation and implementation on development objectives have added values and benefits when women's interest and role are taken into account. Progress on gender equality has been unacceptably slow and uneven. Widespread and persistent gender inequalities are holding back progress for all. To achieve full gender parity in Africa, African countries need to address structural barriers that discriminate against women and girls in accessing education, employment and finance, as well as restrictions on the right of women to use or own land. Early marriages, female genital mutilation (FGM) and violence against women are some of the cultural impediments that hold back progress and the gender front in Africa today (Musau, 2015:24).

The African Capacity Building Foundation (ACBF: celebrating its 25th anniversary this year) as one of Africa's most effective Pan-African organisation should intensify its training capacity to positively impact on building human capital and critical skills most needed to support government policy articulation and policy implementation as well as strengthen the voice of civil society and the relationship between civil society and the government and private sector for the sustainable transformation of the continent. Developing the capacity of the continent and its major institution is imperative for promoting and consolidating the development of the continent. Going forward means a relentless effort of upholding the virtues of productivity, efficiency and effectiveness, harnessing knowledge and developing skills, ensuring cost-effectiveness and focusing on the welfare of all citizens.

The Scourge of Unemployment: An Avenue for Migration.

The *'brain drain –gain phenomenon'* is triggered by the considerable scourge of unemployment. Only with considerable increase in human capital development that can substantially lead to increases in vestment; and with more effective employment creating putting incomes in the hands of the poor, can African countries hope to increase the desperately slow pace of improvement of the livelihood of the population. Therefore, there is in urgent need of restructuring not only the educational sector but the job creation sector and the entire government structure. Restructuring is a continuous process in all economies through which more productive activities replace less productive ones; or through which archaic ideas are replaced with new and progressive ones. In short, restructuring is always needed as nations change their competitiveness, but equally required for domestic economic efficiency.

Bariagaber Assefaw (2014) analysis the nature and type of South-South migration, focusing on issues, such as brain gain and/or brain drain, remittance flows, technical know-how transfer, violations of the right of Africa migrants and gender dimensions of migration. He further shows the dynamics of migration from Eastern and Southern Africa to the Arab Gulf States as well as to developed countries, focusing on the skills of migrants, brain gain and/or drain, remittance flows, technical know-how transfer, violations of the rights of African migrants and gender dimension of migrants; and assesses the successes, impediments and challenges of African international migrants from Easter and Southern Africa and to formulate policy recommendations to maximize the gains and minimise the cost associated with international migration in Africa.

Restructuring and Renewal should be a positive progressive process. The North depends on the South and vice versa. Therefore, common grounds of mutual interest and benefit to both parties must be established to create a just, stable, peaceful and secured world. Without such a common understanding in the interest of the people, the poorest in Africa will for an unforeseeable future remain outside the realm of quality living standards. United Nations Sustainable Development Goals (UN SDG 2030) goal [Four] calls for inclusive and equitable education and learning opportunities for all' and goal [Nine] 'calls for building resilient infrastructure, promote inclusive and sustainable industrialisation and foster innovation'.

Converting the *'brain drain'* into a *'brain gain'* will help keep at bay most of the skilled human potentials on the continent. There are a number of countries on the continent having more medical personnel - doctors, pharmacists, nurses and other health workers abroad than at home, the case of Botswana. Gambia, Liberia speaks for themselves (Dugger 2003; McKaiser 2016; Maassen, 2011). Williams (2016) points out that there are more African engineers and scientists in the US than on the continent, and studies are suggesting that Africa will need 2.5 million engineers to sustain its current level of economic growth, for infrastructure development, for technological innovation etc. In a number of countries, the cost of 'brain drain' is high, for example, in Uganda the replacement of departing Ugandans costs USA$4 billion on an annual basis expatriate have to be contracted to carry out the work left behind. On the other hand, remittances from the Diaspora far outweigh what is given as foreign aid assistance to African countries. But we should bear mind that it takes years to train a medical doctor or a civil engineer. Why should Africa lose this human capital through a twinkle of second as a result of the poor policy? In a society that is already bifurcated by inequality, the ever-growing youth unemployment statistics represent a poisoned chalice and this contributes seriously for the youths fleeing the continent to greener pastures in other parts of the world. Not even the emerging petro-developmental state in Africa (Ovadia 2016) is able to halt the flight saga. Many African countries are confronted with the ever-growing unemployment curse, and government failures to address this would eventually lead inexorably to disaster (Mills and Herbst, 2016). For now, there are no signs of curbing the unemployment rate and averting the brain drain saga.

The reality is that Africa will need their citizens – whether educated at home or abroad – who will serve their society. Africa is not well served by emigrants who remit no benefits from abroad. On the other hand, professionals working overseas could become more valuable resources for the home country as they might provide higher remittances or loans for development related activities back home. What is important is creating the enabling environment as the attracting pull factor for the Diasporas to develop interest of actively involved in the process of development in the home country. Africa cannot afford to lose or waste is human capital. Every African country needs skilled human power intimate with its own needs. Educational and manpower planning should coordinate more closely with the job market providers to ensure the employment prospects in the country.

Conclusion: Decolonising and Triumphally Moving Forward

It is argued that poor education is under developing the continent. Notwithstanding the remarkable achievements of higher education, it can be concluded that Africa as a continent is confronted with serious challenges of attaining the education goals it has set itself and the international community, (Mwamwenda 2013, 42; UN MDGs 2015; Thomas 2010). The issue of poor curriculum has been stressed as well as the neglect of indigenous knowledge systems and concepts in enhancing the transformation agenda of the continent.

Smith (2012) is categorical in showing the relationship between knowledge research and imperialism and the ways in which it has come to structure our own ways of knowing, though the development of academic disciplines and through the education of colonial elites and of indigenous or 'native' intellectuals. Western knowledge and science are 'beneficiaries' of the colonisation of indigenous peoples. The knowledge gained through our colonisation has been used, in turn, to colonise us in what Ngugi wa Thiong'o calls the colonisation 'of the mind.' A new curriculum conceived and executed under the umbrella of progressive Afrocentric ideology should put that to rest once and for ever.

Even with its meagre human capital, Africa has become the continent exporting its scarce human capital. The brain drain is draining the region of its skilled human power, just as it can be a blessing to the transformation of the region and improving the welfare of its citizens. In terms of remittances, the Diaspora is a fundamental funder to improving the living conditions of many fellows back home. Africa cannot develop on remittances. The diasporas or 'returners are often portrayed as agents of development who bring with them economic capital, knowledge and skills as well as social connections and experience gained in the 'developed North' (Akesson & Baaz, 2015). The continent needs vital human capital to ensure sustainable development. A progressive Afrocentric education curriculum constitutes the greatest arsenal in changing everything and transforming the continent's failed economic and political systems. On this should the continent build the future it wants.

The views expounded by Kwapong (1995:193) should be seriously taken by all states; 'to meet the challenge of capacity building that will enable the African nations to move confidently into the 21st century and beyond and to better share in the benefits of the information and biological revolutions, African nations must give pride of place to a total overhaul of their education systems. Education must, therefore, be brought back to centre stage and given the highest priority in the current programmes of economic and social reform and reconstruction. Nothing short of a high quality, cost-effective, efficient and equitable education available to the populations of the African nations will ensure this transition from the present state of distress and malaise into a prosperous and confident 21st century. For all of this, leadership, democratic participatory institutions and processes and, above all, good governance will ensure a bright and prosperous future for an educated Africa."

By way of conclusion, the paper has only scratched the surface of the problem and the need for radical structural changes in our education system and curriculum development... It addresses a number of important issues. First it explains why a new education curriculum is necessary. Second, it outlines some of the key ways in which the politics for education curriculum is needed. Third, it points in the direction and strongly emphasises the need for African countries to exert themselves to be independent to a certain extent. Even though we live in an interdependent world context, Africa should equally move in the direction of self-reliant development. By discussing the politics of change the importance for the continent's sustainable transformation is highlighted and streamlined. Africa is not an island or cannot develop in isolation. Interaction with other communities and solidarity within and across national frontiers is imperative. The paper cannot claim to have covered the entire structural categories undermining the current curriculum. We need a critical and progressive education curriculum for the renewal of an emerging Africa. An Africa that bids not farewell to Eurocentricism but fare forward voyagers to Afrocentricism in the 21st century. The COVID-19 Pandemic that brought the entire world to its knees should be a serious lesson for African countries to invest in higher education, science and technology, the private sector as well as develop indigenous knowledge and cultural heritage values. How can we tape into traditional knowledge/medicine and its pharmacopoeia and other aspects of our cultural heritage and activities and marry this with modern science and technology in improving on the health status of the population? Africa has for too long undervalued its indigenous knowledge system especially in the health sector food sector and other areas. The COVID-19 pandemic challenges Africa Governments, researcher, scientists and the universities to develop a new vision of the continent's pharmacopoeia, penetrate into the activities of traditional medicine in order that this priceless cultural heritage should be better developed and placed at the disposal for the benefit of humankind. We need to beef-up training in human capital and skills development, improve institutional infrastructures. Here at least five major challenges are central to giving national development programmes some impetus. Namely:

- The need for viable national and regional institutions to create, adapt and apply technologies to the developmental problems of the continent;
- The need for significant technological breakthroughs with s few key commodities;
- The use of indigenous knowledge systems (IKS) to advance the transformation process by marrying these aspects of knowledge with modern scientific advancements;

- The need for appropriately trained human skills at all levels: to plan, manage and to do research; and influence national policy and resource allocation decisions;
- The need for the total mobilisation of all citizens to be active players in the development process;
- The need for mechanism for sharing research outputs across the continent;
- The need for equity in benefit-sharing of the wealth of the nation;
- The need for coordination and consistency among donor programmes and institutions in line with African needs and interests;
- The policy strategy for self-reliance and less dependency on external aids in directing the developmental goals of the continent.

References

Adams Walter (ed.) (1968). The Brain Drain. The Macmillan Publishing Company, United Kingdom

Adedeji Adebayo (1989). "The African University and the Engineering of Structural Change and Transformation," National University of Lesotho 1989 Convocation Lecture, 27 September 1989, Roma

Adedeji Adebayo (1982). "Development and Economic Growth in Africa to the Year 2000: Alternative Projections and Policies", in Timothy M. Shaw (ed.) (1982) Alternative Future for Africa, Westview Press, Boulder, Colorado, USA

Africa Millennium Development Gap Report (2015), United Nations, New York

Akesson Lisa & Maria Eriksson Baaz (eds.) (2015). Africa's Return Migrants. The New Developers? Zed Books, London, UK.

Akilu Lemma, M. S. Swaminathan, E. W.von Weizsacker (eds.) (1983). New Frontiers in Technology Development: Integration of Emerging and Traditional Technologies. United Nations, Tycooly International Publishing, Dublin, p.ixv.

Ankomah Baffour (2015)" When Africa Civilised Europe", New African, No.554, October 2015, IC Publication, London, pp72-77

Ankomah Baffour (2013)." What Africa Can Learn from Singapore (Part 1), New African No. 526, March 2013, IC Publication, London, pp24-28

Anstee Joan Margaret (1990). Social Development in Africa: Perspective, Reality and Promise," in James Pickett & Hans Singer, (1990). Towards Economic Recovery in Sub-Saharan Africa: Essays in Honour of Robert Gardiner, Routledge Publishers, UK.

Anyanwu, J. C. & Erhijakpor, A. E. O. (2009) "The Impact of Road Infrastructure on Poverty Reduction in Africa', in Thomas W. Beasley (ed.) Poverty in Africa, Nova Science Publishers, Inc. Pp1-40

Asonganyi Tazoacha (2015) Cameroon: Difficult Choices in A Failed Democracy, - A Memoir, NGT Publishing, Madison, USA.

Awuah-Nyameke Samuel & Munyaradzi Mawere (eds.) (2015). Between Rhetoric and Reality: The State and Use of Indigenous Knowledge in Post-Colonial Africa. Langaa RPCIG, Bamenda, Cameron Republic.

Bariagaber Assefaw (ed.) (2014). International Migration and Development in Eastern and Southern Africa. OSSREA Publishers, Addis Ababa, Ethiopia.

Bjura Abdalla (2004). Pan-African Political and Economic Visions of Development. From the OAU to the AU: From the Lagos Plan of Action (LPA) to the New Partnership for African Development (NEPAD)), Development Policy Management Forum (DPMF) Occasional Paper, No.13, Addis Ababa, Ethiopia.

Brown Barratt Michael (1995) Africa Choices – After Thirty Years of the World Bank, Penguin Books, Wright Lane, London, United Kingdom

Castells Manuel (2016). Higher Education and Development. African Minds Publishers, Cape Town, Republic of South Africa

Cloete Nico, Peter Massen and Tracy Bailey (eds.) (2014) Knowledge Production and Contradictory Functions in African Higher Education. African Minds Publishers, South Africa,

Conable Barber (1988) Education in Sub-Saharan Africa: Policies for Adjustment, Revitalisation and Expansion, World Bank, Washington D.C. p.5

Dugger, C. W. (2003) Botswana's Brain Drain Cripples War on AIDS. New York Times.
(Available at: http:
www.nytimes.com/2003/11/13/world/Botswana)

Ellwood Wayne (2001). The No-Nonsense Guide to Globalisation. Verso Publishers and New International Publications Ltd, London

Falk Richard, Samuel S. Kim, & Saul H. Mendlovitz (eds.) (1982) Toward a Jut World Order, Vol. 1. Westview Press, Boulder, Colorado, USA

Fanon Frantz (1990). The Wretched of the Earth. Penguin Books, London

Fayolle Alain (2018). A Research Agenda for Entrepreneurship Education. Edward Elgar Publishing Limited, Cheltenham, Glos. UK

Ferreira J. Joio, Vanessa Ratten, Alain Fayolle and Mario Raposo (eds.) (2018) Entrepreneurial Universities: Collaboration, Education and Policies. Edward Elgar Publishing Limited, Cheltenham, Glos. UK

Forje W. John (2013) "The Triumph and Prosperity of Education in Cameroon" in Mwamwend & Lukhele-Olorunju (eds.) (2013). The Triumph and Prosperity of Education in Africa, Africa Institute of South Africa, Pretoria, South Africa, pp98-157

Forje W. John (2004) The Wind of Change: A Journey Through Africa's Political Landscape and A Search for an Alternative. The Archie Mafeje Lectures, 19 October 2004, Africa Institute of South Africa, Pretoria, South Africa.

Forje W. John (1989). Science and Technology in Africa. Vol.10. Longman Guide to World Series on Science and Technology. Longman Publishing Group, Essex, United Kingdom

Gasu John (2018) Strengthening Higher Education Leadership in Africa. A Study of Ghana's Situation. CODESRIA, Dakar, Senegal.

Gerschenkron Alexander (1962) Economic Backwardness in Historical Perspectives, Cambridge, MA. The Belknap Press, Harvard University Press, USA

Ghani Ashraf & Clare Lockhart (2008) Fixing Failed States. Oxford University Press, United States of America and Oxford, UK

Glaser A. William & G. Christopher Habers (1978). The Brain Drain – Emigration and Return. Pergamon Press, London, United Kingdom (Findings of a UNITAR multinational comparative survey of professional personnel of developing countries who study abroad).

Henderson Gregory (1970). Emigration of Highly-Skilled Manpower from the Developing Countries, UNITAR, Research Report No.3, 1970.

Jones Colin (2019). How to Teach Entrepreneurship. Edward Elgar Publishers Limited, Cheltenham, Glos. UK

Jowi James, Manya Klemencic & Thierry Lueschr-Mamashela (2015). Student Politics in Africa: Representation and Activism. African

Higher Education Dynamics Series Vol.2, African Minds Publishers, Cape Town. South Africa

Kannappan Subbiah (1968). "The Brain Drain and Developing countries," International Labour Review, Vol. 98. No. 1, July 1968, pp.1-26

Kuwonu Franck (2015). "MDG2: Achieve Universal Primary Education. More Students in Schools but Still Not All," Africa Renewal, Vol. 29, No. 3, December 2015, New York, pp. 23

Kwapong A. Alexander (1995). "Meeting the Challenge of Education in Africa," in Bade Onimode & Richard Synge (eds.) (1995) Issues in African Development: Essays in Honour of Adebayo Adedeji at 65. Heinemann Education Books (Nigeria) PLC, Ibadan, Nigeria, pp181-193

Langa Victorino Patricio (2014). Higher Education in Portuguese Speaking Africa Countries. African Minds African Minds Publishers, South Africa

Lantum N. Dan (1985) "Cameroonian Cultural Identity Expressed Through Science and Technology", in (Cameroon Government, Ministry of Information and Culture) Papers presented at the Colloquium of the Second National Cultural Week, 13-20 May,1985. The Cultural Identity of Cameroon, Yaoundé, Cameroon, pp401-408.

Lema Catherine Forje (2018) "Entrepreneurship Education Human Capital Development and Quality Livelihood" in Forje W. John (ed.) Shaping Africa's Future: Transforming African and Global Relations for A Just and Stable World. Centre for Action-Oriented Research on Africa's Development (CARAD), Lambert Academic Publishing, pp214-229

Logmo Bienvenu (1985) "The Contribution of Traditional Medicine and its Pharmacopoeia", in Cameroon Government, Ministry of Information and Culture) Papers presented at the Colloquium of the Second National Cultural Week, 13-20 May, 1985, Yaoundé, Cameroon, pp409-424.

Maassen Peter, Ian Bunting, Pundy Pillay, Bailey Tracy & Cloete Nico (2011). Universities and Economic Development in Africa. African Minds Publishers, Cape Town, South Africa.

Mawere Munyaradzi (2014). Culture, Indigenous Knowledge and Development in Africa. Reviving Interconnections for Sustainable Development. Langaa RPCIG, Bamenda, Cameroon Republic

McKaiser Eusebius (2016). Run Racist Run. Journeys into The Heart of Racism, Bookstorm (SA)

Mills Greg & Herbst Jeffrey (2016). How South Africa Works: And Must Do Better. McMillan Publishers, South Africa

Mouton Johann & Lauren Wildschut (2015). Leadership and Management. Case Studies in Training in Higher Education in Africa. African Minds Publishers, cape Town, South Africa

Muchie Mammo (2015). "Time for Universities Made in the Image of Africa," New African, No.554, October 2015, London, pp36-7

Musau Zipporah (2015). "MDG 3: Promote Gender Equality and Empower Women: Closing Africa's 'Elusive' Gender Gap', Africa Renewal, Vol.29, No.3, December 2015, United Nations, New York, United States of America, pp24

Mwamwenda Tuntufye & Phindile Lukhele-Olorunju (eds.) (2013). The Triumph and Prosperity of Education in Africa, Africa Institute of South Africa (AISA), Pretoria, South Africa

Mwamwenda S. Tuntufye (2013). "Some Important Aspects of Triumph and Prosperity of Education in Africa" in Mwamwenda et al. (2013), pp42-59

Myezwa Hellen, Lilian Mariga & Roy McConkey (2014). Inclusive Education in Low-Income Countries. A Resource Book for Teachers educators, parent's trainers and Community Development. Disability Innovations Africa, South Africa.

Ncube Mthuli (2013). "Infrastructure Deficit, Financing Needs and the Post-2015 MDG Framework in Africa", Institute of Development Studies (IDS), Vol. 44, No.5-6, September 2013, John Wiley & Sons, UK, pp72-80

Ngugi Wa Thiong'o (1986) Decolonising the Mind: The Politics of Language in African Literature, James Curry Publishers, London

Nico Clotete, Ian Bunting &Francois van Schalkwyk (2018). Research Universities in Africa. African Minds Publishers, Cape Town, South Africa

Nye Joseph (2008). The Powers to Lead: Soft, Hard, and Smart. Oxford University Press, United States of America

Obanya Pai (2014). Educationeering. HEBN Publishers, Nigeria

Organisation of African Unity (OAU) (1980). The Lagos Plan of Action for the Socio-economic Development of Africa 1980-2000. Addis Ababa, Ethiopian

Ovadia Salah Jesse (2016). The Petro-Developmental State in Africa: Making Oil Work in Angola, Nigeria and The Gulf of Guinea. Hurst Publishers, United Kingdom

President Eisenhower (April 1953): Quote taken from his final valedictory speech to the American Society of Newspaper Editors,

Washington DC. Eisenhower is remembered for his catch reference to the 'military-industrial complex' concept)

Robertson L. Susan, Kris Olds, Roger Dale & Que Anh Dang (eds.) (2016). Global Regionalism and Higher Education. Projects, Processes, Politics. Edward Elgar Publishing, Cheltenham, Glos, UK

Room Michelle, Thierry M. Luescher-Mamashella, Robert Mattes, Angolwisye Mwollo-ntallima & Njuguna Ng'ethe (2011). The University in Africa and Democratic Citizenship: Hothouse or Training Ground? African Minds Publishers, Cape Town, South Africa

Seers Dudley (1969). "The Brain Drain from the Developing Countries," (Brighton: Institute of Development Studies, University of Sussex, 1969, Britain, UK

Skorov G. E. (1978). Science, Technology and Economic Growth in Developing Countries. Pergamon Press, United Kingdom

Smith Tuhiwai Linda (1212). Decolonising Methodologies: Research and Indigenous Peoples. (2nd edition), Zed Books, London and Otago University Press, Dunedin

Tabaro Patrick Justice (2015). "Civilisation: Tracing African Civilisation," New African, No.554, October 2015, AN IPC Publication, London, pp82

The South Commission (1990). The Challenge to The South – The Report of the South Commission, under the chairmanship of President Julius Nyerere Oxford University Press, United States of America

Thomas C. (2010) Higher Education in Africa. Time to Pull Out the Steps. See (http://allafrica.com/stories/201004300680.html)

United Nations (2010). United Nations University Revitalising Higher Education in Sub- Saharan Africa. (See http.//www.edu/Africa/files/UNU-RevitalisingHigherEducation-pdf)

United Nations Institute for Training and Research (UNITAR) (1971). The Brain Drain from Five Developing Countries: Cameroon, Colombia, Lebanon, The Philippines, Trinidad and Tobago, UNITAR Research Report No.5, 1971

Williams Stephen (2015) "Next Einstein Forum", New African, No. 561, May 2016, IC Publication, London pp12-13

World Bank (1989). A Joint Statement on Africa's Long-term Development, May 1989, Washington D.C. USA, para.8

Wayne Hugo (2015). Boundaries of The Educational Imagination. African Minds Publishers, Cape Town, South Africa.

Yazani F. April & Janelle Mangwanda (2014)" A Snapshot View of Consolidated Democracy in South Africa and Nigeria", in Africa Insight, Vol. 44(2) September 2014, Pretoria, South Africa, p108-124

Zeleza T. Paul (1997) Manufacturing African Studies and Crises. CODESRIA Book Series, Antony Rowe Ltd, Codesria, Dakar, Senegal

Chapter 15

Articulating A New Public Sector Reform: Towards Enhancing Good Governance and Quality Services Delivery in Africa. Challenges and Prospects

Abstract

The African Public Service Charter streamlines a new way forward in improving public administration in Africa. This paper based on the views in this and other related documents goes further to add its opinion on how to improve this vital institution as a veritable body in meeting the social contract between the State and the People. The focus is on agenda setting to policy decision-making, implementation and evaluation as an important denominator through the political / administrative interface. The link between dysfunctional political/administrative relations constitutes a malfunctioning administration and stagnation in economic and social development has become increasingly acknowledge. The exploration of factors that impeded and those that catalyse the interface between politician and bureaucratic leaders for effective and efficient policy articulation, implementation and evaluation therefore present a fertile prospect for a robust discourse in this dicey yet useful area of public administration. Conceptually and theoretically, the paper is premised within the framework and confines of 'self-reliance,' 'participation,' 'partnership,' 'collaboration,' 'and 'shared-prosperity' in putting into proper perspectives the search for African Solutions to African Problems (ASAP)and for the continent owing its development trajectories. It is argued and proposed that Africa's New Public Service Policy (ANPS) trajectory should incorporate constructive elements of an interface between the politicians and bureaucrats, distinct from the centralised authoritarian structure-functional systems practised in China or Russia for example. The bureaucracy as the provider of impartial and professional expertise to elected politicians should ideally serve as a 'bridge' between politics and society. The paper maintains that such a constructive act of partnership and participation within the confines of the rule of law and separation of powers provides the best condition (a sine-qua-non) for the development of democratic systems of governance and service delivery in improving the quality of livelihood of citizens. Africa is on the move and should craft its development trajectories that improves policy articulation, implementation and evaluation in fostering public services delivery as a veritable output functions of government in improving and sustaining the quality wellbeing of citizens. Hence, a political/administrative interface clearly articulated provides the way forward in seeking African Solutions to African Problems (ASAP). An analytical and comparative approach is adopted. In conclusion, Africa can only move forward by claiming ownership of its development and by adapting best practices that brings greater dividends to citizens.

Keywords: Political, administrative, policy, service delivery, innovation, shared-prosperity; reform

Introduction

"Democracy offers the possibility to organise a collective decision-making process in such that is considered by the members of the political community as being legitimate, without causing substantial disorder.

(Victor Bekkers et al. 2017:5)

"Africa remains a polarise and demobilised society plagued with the legacies of centralised authoritarian structures promoting greed, scarcity, grievance and governance system driven by a socio-existential imperative" ***(John W. Forje, 21st April, 2022)***

The Search for A New Way

The field of public administration is a vast area with many tons of articles, books, and monographs produced every year. During the past couple of decades, the civil service has taken centre stage in the governance dichotomy. As the output function of government, it is constantly under the microscope for critical analysis and evaluation. In the United States, the central preoccupations of this field are directed towards "managerial," whereas in Europe it is largely judicial. It is hardly surprising; therefore, we know so little about the role of bureaucracy in a political system. It can make or mar government activities.

Two views concerning the role of the bureaucracy in different political systems have gained especially wide currency. The first, mostly applicable to the Anglo-Saxon countries, holds that the bureaucracy is totally subordinate to the political institutions. Rephrased differently, the bureaucracy is not recognised as having any degree of autonomy, All the literature on the British civil service has accepted this point of view (Kingsley 1944) recently begun to receive attention. This is in large part because the Federal bureaucracy has usually been regarded as unquestionably subordinate and obedient to the directives of the political.

In the United States, the bureaucracy's role in society and in the political process has only begun to receive attention. This is in large part because the Federal bureaucracy has usually been regarded as unquestionably subordinate and obedient to the directives of political elites (Sisson 1959). The development of the administrative system in the US displays a paradoxical mixture of continued political selection and control at higher levels and commitment to merit and de-politicisation at lower levels. On the one hand, almost all the top positions in government – at present over 4000 positions – are held by political appointees; on the other hand, the remaining public employees are selected by a rigorously enforced merit system. The two versions of public employment have existed side by side for years in the United States but there has been pressure on that co-existence since the 1980s resulting from the debate as to what extent the political appointments should be expanded or contracted (Peters and Pierre, 2004). The Canadian situation is one displaying a high degree of politicisation of the county's civil service. For a very long time, (since 1935, the country operated virtually as a one-party state. Domination of the Liberal Party forged a special relationship between politicians and career officials. The account of the situation in Canada is somewhat depressing as the civil service is riddled with low morale, loss of confidence in its leaders and themselves, and dissatisfaction with managerial practices (Peters and Pierre, 2004).

The bureaucracy in France is generally regarded as an all-powerful institution (Sharp 1931). The French higher civil service is seen as an integral part of the politico-administrative system as is practiced in former French colonial territories. In Britain, the civil service is seen as an impartial body ready to render services to which ever political party that assumes governance stewardship. The tradition for its political neutrality is well respected. Therefore, adherence to the merit principle for selection, promotion and decision-making and objectivity in tendering of advice to political masters well respected (Peters and Pierre, 2004). The former Soviet Union and its Satellites states see no difference between the political party and the public service – for these states, the two are one and indivisible.

In Greece for example, the civil service has always been heavily politicised, probably to a greater extent than any other Western European country. Over politicisation of the Greek civil service is often manifested in the many in which personnel are hired and promoted. While officially all relevant procedures are standardised and meritocratic, unofficially it is widely admitted that politicisation is quite extensive. While the seniority and professional capacities play an important role, their political opinions are personal contacts as matter as much, if not more. The Greek situation shows how polarised political system and political culture have been conducive to the penetration of the civil service by successive incoming governments (top-down politicisation) and the involvement of civil servants in politics (bottom-up politicisation) Thus in the Greek case, politicisation 'from above' is promoted through the duplication of administrative structures, efforts to change the behaviour of civil servants, waves of new appointments in the civil service and politicisation of promotions to the top positions in the hierarchy . What makes politicisation in Greece different from elsewhere is its pervasiveness, persistence, and strength of clientelistic practices, combined with an egalitarian spirit, which make the country somewhat different from other core western democracies (Sharma 2007:82).

Therefore, the distinction between politics and administration, or between politicians and administrators, was effaced under the Fifth Republic of General de Gaulle's appointment of civil servants (Couve de Murville, Chenot, Pisani, Charic, Giscard d'Estaing etc.) to key ministerial posts. A pattern copied in Cameroon, from Mbida through Ahidjo to Biya (see Ridley and Blondel 1965; Vedel (ed.) 1962). In a way such appointments create contradictory atmospheres. First, it brings in technocrats with a better understanding of the field. Second, it creates a kind of elitism and exclusion of the masses from being participants in the governance process which is not healthy for services delivery. Third, the technocrats hold allegiance to whoever appoints them. This creates a centralised top-down administrative approach.

In a country with a centralised authoritarian dominant monolithic political party construct, (Cameroon) for example, does aggravates ethnic, regional and class difference; and politicisation of the public service by the ruling elites. Constructive decentralisation, we must admit is inhibited with success and failures to which each state gives continent it deems appropriate to its national contingencies; and as the process of power and responsibility sharing between the state and its constituencies; and decentralisation as a learning instrument for the promotion and strengthening of democracy at various levels, i.e. promoting a 'bottom-up' or an all-inclusive decision-making processes and involvement of the vast majority of the population.

It is argued that the post-independent African state because of the colonial legacy developed a centralised hegemonic power state. The state, civil society and private sector were not critical partners in the political, economic and service delivery trajectory. Throughout Africa 'the public sector initially grew relatively fast because the post-colonial state was under enormous pressure to Africanise or indigenises and expand the civil service. For the masses 'uhuru' meant more social services and jobs. It was in the interest of the new political class to satisfy this hunger for social and economic development and to contain the swelling ranks of the unemployed. And it also served their accumulative interests to expand the state apparatuses' (Zeleza 1997:333). The state dominated everything and yet was not fully equipped in undertaking the necessary changes (Forje 2006; 2009; 2011) thereby creating negatives impacting on service delivery in three aspects; namely;

- *failure of the existing state institutional structure to provide dynamism for an inclusive society;*
- *the need to care and nurture democracy engaging communities and citizens, accountability, equity and inclusiveness; and*
- *the need for institutions that command respect, legitimacy, accountability and could instil confidence and trust within society on state institutions*

Within this context, one could argue that due to the centralised nature of the state construct and of its *'top-down'* policy approach, the strategy of decentralisation created opportunities to improve efficiency in governance and service delivery, required the politics and policies of decentralisation as such approach creates opportunities by;

- *enhancing effectiveness through de-bureaucratisation and serious reduction in the number of interacting mechanisms of forces involved in service delivery;*
- *empowering stakeholder to be active partners in the process of quality service delivery, to ensure a social contract between the state, civil society and private sector*

The nature and training of these top public civil servants equally matters as to how they relate to society. Public administration within the Anglo-Saxon world falls as a university discipline, in contrast to the French-speaking world carried out in specialised schools – Ecole Nationale d'Administration (ENA); for example, in Cameroon the main and dominant elite body is Ecole Nationale d'Administration et Magistracy (ENAM) National Advanced School of Administration and Magistracy, which creates an administrative elite corps (Suleiman (1974) that significantly widens the social basis of the higher civil service and the rest of the people.

In Africa for example, a situation existed with the coming of independence where development economics shared the policy optimism of emerging generation of African political leaders. It also shared with them the respect of using the state to redress economic and social imbalances caused by colonial policy. The situation where the indigenous private sector was very weak, it makes perfect political sense to embrace the notion that the state ought to serve as the catalyst of the development process. While the political agenda was shaped by nationalist leaders of Africa, economic policies were fashioned by external advisors. The extensive role of the state in development posed a special challenge to the public service especially in Africa where capacities were low. The cadre of trained and experience public servants was very small in these countries and it was necessary to make the best use of scarce human resources.

A call was made for a new style of administration that met the development needs of the new style of administration that met the development needs of the new states better than conventional public administration. This 'development administration' refers to the administration of development programmes, the method used by large-scale organisations, notably governments, to implement policies and plans designed to meet developmental objectives, (Hyden, 1995:73: Fred, 1970:6-7). Development administration which is control-oriented and stresses regularity. The new development style of administration is viewed as placing emphasis on flexibility and innovativeness (Gant 1979; Schaffer 1969).

Here higher civil servants in general, assume roles that are at once administrative and political. The concept, 'politique' in French covers both 'politics' and 'policy' and to the extent that higher civil servants formulate policies, with all the social and political implications that this entails. Their functions are interlinked with administrative and political activities (Chapman 1959). The Cameroon system encourages and involves higher civil servants to be engaged in party politics; thereby making the public service to be highly politicised and influenced by political party and ethnic affiliations and ideologies. One cannot avoid posing questions about 'the right kind of society;' the purpose of the state, the basis and justification of government business and of its responsibility to the people. British top civil servants do not abandon their official duties and join the political party campaign bandwagon like in Cameroon. It is assumed once appointed to high public bureaucratic post to become a member of the ruling party.

Importantly, Africa countries must fashion their own public service construct that comprehensively addresses their needs without compromising the ideals of equality and service delivery to every citizen. Here a 'bottom-up' approach provides the ways and means of inclusion, participation and equity in benefit-sharing. The public bureaucracy remains the key instrument in the national development process of the continent. Underlining the characteristics hindering the public service to deliver effectively and efficiently and the relationship between the service and other actors and the impact on the State's ability to formulate and deliver on its development agenda.

Failure to deliver increases the number of poor; and growing poverty and inequality can also be attributed to the dysfunctional and poorly developed bureaucracies throughout the continent. Breaking existing barriers requires states to be supported by a highly competent, professional and meritocratic public administration similar to those of the East Asian countries. The African public service needs constructive reforms aimed at transforming the bureaucracy and positioning it to be the lead actor in the development agenda. The public service should be constructed and operated on the principles of accountability, openness, transparency and good governance.

Fig: 1. A New Public Bureaucracy Reform for Africa

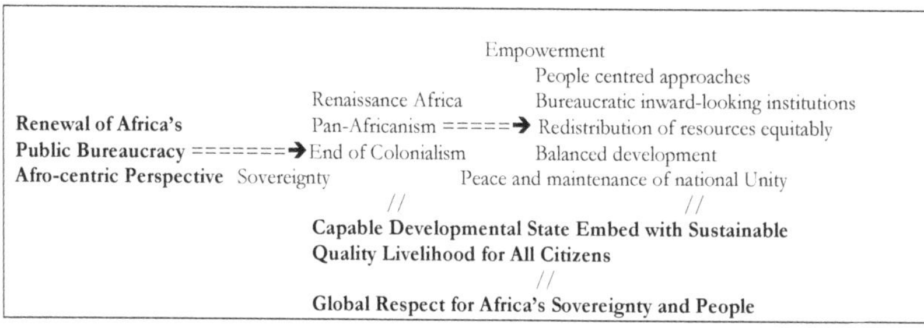

Source: Forje (2015)

A properly structure-functional public service is a veritable system / development changer. This is what the continent most need for its articulating a new public service reform that should be construed from the perspectives of a progressive Afro-centric orientation. In short, Africa is not cursed but blessed with poor leadership. Africa needs a new public bureaucracy and leadership as depicted in Fig 1: A New Public Bureaucracy Reform for Africa.

There are numerous challenges the continent faces in the process of reforming and building a healthy apolitical, professional bureaucracy at the services of the people. Achieving such a reform requires visionary leadership and a proactive citizenry. What are the challenges; what capacities do the people need to develop? What should the people do to develop the needed capacity of its bureaucratic set-up? An Afro-centric approach is required to address the numerous challenges. The leadership and bureaucracy that Africa need is one which must work with people to develop a path that development should take requiring a genuine vision and action plan focused on African solutions for African problems.

- human capital development.
- democratic and good governance
- empowerment of the people
- proper utilisation of resources
- exploiting the late-comer advantage (Gerschenkron 1962)
- putting in place corrective measures addressing past mistakes
- mobilising the masses to engage in development of indigenous policies;
- drastic movements from the 'blame' to the 'reality' factors inhibiting the development of the continent;
- putting in a place a free, objective, mass media out to inform, and educate the people on the problems of societal socio-economic-politico transformation
- promoting innovation, entrepreneurship, science and technology for an improved service delivery
- building necessary institutions and infrastructures
- building links with the diasporas and ensuring African unity

Indeed, the determination of ends, the choice of means, the balance of social forces, are the stuff of politics. In these terms it is clear that some civil servants are engaged in politics. This partly explains why a number of members of parliament and senate are retired civil servants. Very often, the relations between the political and administrative leadership tend to be conflictual and tense. As a result, the policy-making and policy-implementation processes became problematic and ineffective, making the state of affairs not healthy which requires that both sides of the leadership divide find ways and means of minimising conflicts and tensions to ensure smooth administrative procedures.

The continent needs strong state institutions as well as creating systems to enhance service delivery. Strategic objectives and action plans are required for building strong state institutions and creating systems to enhance service delivery requiring actions as indicated in Fig 2: Building Strong State Institutions. It also needs a proactive intellectual community to advance the discourse on good governance and improved quality livelihood. The role of the public intellectual is to raise the level of public discourse so that it might better grapple with the complex issues of the day. To a large extent, African intellectuals seem to shy away from such obligations and responsibilities due to the nature of political construct in the country. What is clear as noted by Skwati (2014): "The commitment by the public sector to embrace innovation as a new way of thinking around possible solutions to service delivery challenges is inarguably on the rise" and by no means improved service delivery improvement can change a country's fortunes to the better. Even though these institutions of higher-learning are largely funded by the government (tax-payers money) party politics and ideology should stay-off university campuses in African countries. The structure-functioning of the universities must have a great latitude of freedom, pay attention to academic matters and promote academic excellence. Therefore, as noted by Akilagpa Sawyerr (2004), "The principal contribution of a university to society tuns on the quality of knowledge it generates and imparts the habit of critical thoughts and problem solving it institutionalises and inculcates in its graduates..." Gasu (2018):4) points out that the global drive to redefine the essence of higher education...regarding whether leadership of African universities have the capacity of manage the consequences..." The other problem is what latitude do the officials have in exercising their duties without serious interferences from the political machinery of the country. Can political leaders say clear-off with their party politics from the university campuses? The academic independence of universities must be highly respected especially within the African context.

Fig. 2: Building Strong State Institutions

Strategic Objectives	Action
	Establish centres of good practice to support improvement of public administration institutions
Creating Systems to enhance service	Strong state institutions central to constructing and delivery strengthen capacity and management of a capable developmental state Reengineer services processes
Building State capacity Requires Sound systems	Develop sound financial management services Human resources information systems Information Technology Management systems e-Government Supply chain management systems
	Public service census establishes legitimate public servants
Public Service Reconstruction	Redefine missions of ministries to pave the way for effective output
Restructure and Reorganise the state reorganisation and reconstruction of the state	

Forje (2013) Emerging Perspectives on Capacity Building, Lambert Academic Publishing, Germany, pp41-42

A critical interface between State and the rest of society is necessary to hammer out differences and create the much needed enabling environment for a functional public bureaucracy capable of addressing the socio-economic crisis, incarceration, the wealth gap or any of the urgent political and administrative issues plaguing the sustainable transformation of the continent from a backward to a service delivery polity. There are also important arguments about the intellectual and his/her relationship to the polity.

The South African initiative is an attempt of blending the divergent views expressed here to better create a unique response and process crafting a public service that is accountable, transparent, responsible and delivering services much needed by society. This unique approach is possible and yield more dividends because more Africans are now living under democratic rule compared to the situation in the late 1970s and 1980s when only a handful of African countries were considered democratic. The politician is thus one who can fight, plead and convince; but, above all, (s) he is guided by an ethic responsibility' which Weber opposed to the 'ethic of ultimate ends." The civil servant who replaces the politician is a specialist, guided by rational standards and hence oblivious to the political implications. The replacement of the politician by the civil servant gives rise, it is argued, to a technocracy, which is seen 'as the rise to power of those who possess technical knowledge or ability, to the detriment of the traditional type of politician. According to Meynaud (1965), it is technical competence that determines influence. Technocracy is the combined result of the competence and infiltration of the technocrat at an appropriate point or sector of the deliberation machine. It is this combination of circumstances which favours and permits the technologists' penetration into the political sector.

Another, arising from the first, is the vital factor responsible for attacks on the administration is the ubiquity of civil servants not only in the State apparatus, where they are naturally to be found, but in the parastatal and in the private sector. The large part of attacks on the administration could be regarded as emanating from these factors where a clique of few, and all the charges of nepotism, personal gain or articulate self-interests, collusion etc., brings into sharp focus the class divisions and distinctions in service delivery in African societies; in addition, pointing to the undemocratic recruitment of for example, Cameroon ethnic ruling elites and to the undemocratic of the (African) or Cameroon society. Still another important reason for the persistent questioning of the administrator's traditional authority has to do with the decline of representative institutions, particularly the political parties and parliament.

The importance of parliament and of the political parties is in sharp contrast to the dominant features of the single-party State, and especially where the State is in some measures associated with the ruling party. In the case of Cameroon, the authoritarian nature of the administration is mirrored in the authoritarian disposition of the ruling government. In attacking the government and the administration, one is actually attacking the State. The State's influence on the Cameroon society has not changed much over the past couple of decades, i.e., since the return to multi-party pluralism. The marriage between the politician and the administrator is seen by the centralised governance structure of creating a kind of stability of political and administrative personnel which reflects the authoritarian disposition of the regime.

The initiative by the African Association for Public Administration and Management (AAPAM) introducing at its annual Roundtable Conference a Ministerial Panel Platform to engage Ministers and Cabinet Secretaries in continental issue affecting the continent's administration and development by delving into navigating the conundrum that is the political/administrative interface by infusing a Ministerial perspective to conference deliberations is welcome and this could be extended to the participation of political parties It is necessary for African countries to adhere to the African Charter on the Values and Principles of Public Service and administration especially in the areas of leadership and management development; performance management and measurement; and human resources development, planning and policy architecture.

In the case of Cameroon, it is probably the stability or longevity of the presidency and the authoritarian disposition of the holder of that office for more than three decades that reflects a greater administrative and political stability than actually exists. To a large extent, it has harnessed, enhanced and influenced the institutionalisation of 'centralised ethnic hegemonic authoritarian governance structure and seriously contributed to the flourishing of malpractices and corruption. Focus on a strong executive lead to reduction in parliament's powers with reduced powers and role of the administration (Neustadt 1964:53). No one will deny that the technicians, whatever their differences, share with other groups, justified in the African society a commitment to the existing political and social system. To the degree that such differences do affect the shape of public, however, it is difficult to call them merely differences of tactics.

These divergent views, 'subordinate' and autonomous' of the role of the bureaucracy in a political system have adverse an unfortunate consequence. - - they have hindered the study of the bureaucracy as an integral, and dynamic part of the political system in other words, the bureaucracy has seldom been seen as an institution that operates within the higher politico-administrative framework. If the bureaucracy is seen as an institution that interacts with other institutions in a society, it becomes easier to understand why a governmental bureaucracy cannot be characterised as either totally subservient or totally autonomous.

Far-reaching administrative reforms are urgently needed in many African countries today is a matter that hardly anyone questions. The Conference of African Ministers of the Public Service and Administration has injected new blood to improve the structure and output functions and service delivery of the sector. Two key factors here relate to (i) institutional capacity and (ii) overall strategic orientation. At the level of strategy there is always the tension between application of shared-values and particularities and specificities of each member state. Hence there are always constraints and established parameters on what can be done in governance and democracy.

Cardinal in the objectives of the Conference of African Minister of the Public Service and Administration is the need to move forward as a collective, compliance to adopted shared-values is not a choice but a necessity. More often than not, states aspirations and indeed to manage strategic tension that exists between the collective and individual interests largely depends on the available capacity – i.e., the capacity and resources made available have never matched expectations. Added to this, is the *'implementation'* question or challenges on a-day-to-day basis. Generally, one can state that institutional transformation is on track, the foundations are being laid for more effective, efficient and responsive delivery to improve on the quality wellbeing of citizens. Therefore, institutions should be at the services of its people. These institutions should be manned by competent, professional, citizens to deliver effective and efficient services. These institutions at all levels of government must be people-oriented, developmental, democratic, responsible, accountable and merit-based

This ultimately imply a new public service trajectory conceived within the framework of improving the living standards of the people, without *'denying, delaying and perverting'* services delivery to anyone. This credo fits into the framework or motto of the Association of African Public Administration and Management (AAPAM) and should be the catechism of every African citizen to advance the role of the civil service in providing the needed services for the peoples' well-being. The challenging question for the African public service is how to reconcile the highly centralised authoritarian system with a people-oriented and focused decentralised structure that ensures quality services delivery to all. The people are challenged, that with highly centralised or highly decentralised system split into multitudinous groups, each of which pursues its own interests to reconcile differences to ensure that social justice prevails. The living inequality (of various sectors of the administration), which is fundamentality in an administrative system as differentiated as that of the African continent and which alone maintains it as a system, forbids that the standard of measure be reduced to simple calculation.

In the case of Cameroon and other African countries, best described as *'a stalemate society,'* this is generally thought sufficient to point to its centralised authoritarian administrative structure, hence the call for decentralisation and democratic governance. The justification and need for decentralisation and good governance is premised on a priori grounds that centralisation and authoritarian governance system has failed to deliver the services much needed by the people to have a sustainable quality of livelihood.

Ultimately there is a fundamental, perhaps irreconcilable, contradiction between the search for objective, rational policies, contradiction between the search for objective, rational policies, and the widespread practice of basing public policies on the compromises that are affected between the various administrations. For if public policy is the lowest common denominator of conflicts among opposing groups (politicians and administrators) for example, within the administration, is this not the surest negation of objectivity and rationality? It could even be said that administrators fear rationality because of its possible adverse effects on the autonomy of their institutions. (Suleiman 1974:383; Bertucci 2001; Forje2012).

It is true that old habits or methods and ideas die slowing in African countries. But if progress entails 'mobility, competition and negotiation' - i.e., modernisation and democratisation, - then it is not difficult to conclude that Africa is catching up. The undemocratic recruitment of the administrative elite may be equally deplorable. There are a number of paradoxes of the African political community and administrative system that have to be understood to better draw meaningful conclusions. Administrative inefficiency and poor governance constitute other perpetual themes of the proponents of the 'stalemate society' thesis, a theme very closely related to the pleas for decentralisation, democratisation and good governance as the gateway (Africa's New Public Service) trajectory for quality services delivery.

We can see that interest groups play a very important role in the policy-making process and greater consolidation among these groups is occurring, with the encouragement of the administration (the South Africa experience or new initiative of partnership between the political and administrative bodies) should receive greater attention. The behaviour of the administrative corps in a society must be seen in the context of the larger social and political framework of which it is part. Administration is not an activity that is separate from politics. It becomes all the more difficult to argue, that the reasons for Africa's resistance to change are to be found in the colonial heritage and character and to equally argue at the same time that the centralised authoritarian administration constitutes the chief obstacle to change in the society.

Of course, the administration is part of the society; it shares the values of the society; it reflects and sometimes exaggerates some of society's defects. In the same vein, the rising level of centralised authoritarian power of the Executive is paralleled by the rapid descent of the powers of Parliament, backed by a corrupt Judiciary contradictions between wanting a weak Executive (in the sense of power-sharing with the other branches of government – judiciary and legislative) which strengthens the role of the bureaucracy as an independent and impartial institution ready to serve which ever shade of political party that assumes government office. This is the only way of having merit-based public institutions providing the most conducive enabling environment for its citizens to exploit, flourish and attain their full potentials. The continent failed in attaining MDGs 2015. We should not fail on the post-2015 Development Agenda in lifting huge sections of the population out of the scourges of poverty and misery. A well-structured and functional public service can radically transform, using the varied opportunities as springboards to ensure its transformation from a backward to quality service delivery society. Currently, there is inadequate engagement of citizens in governance and development making the social welfare gap between the bottom-up and top-down divide to widen. The rich are getting richer as the poor get poorer for each passing day.

People's Governance as Prelude to Quality Services

One of the most crucial challenges ahead of the continent relates to the issue of democratic governance from the community level through the divisional, national, and regional up to the continental and global level. At the nation-state level, the challenge is to deepen systems of democratic governance within and between countries, to reduce the power and influence of bureaucracies, to improve public and service delivery systems, among others. But these tasks of internal democratisation must go hand in hand with the democratisation of the institutions of global governance, particularly the international and regional financial institutions.

Accountability is the necessary counterpart to voice. When accountable authorities answer to engaged communities, social justice is served, service delivery improved and human welfare enhanced, and citizens will develop trust and confidence in the State and its institutions. Participation and voice grow stronger when political, economic and social power is widely dispersed. Locally determined solutions are usually more sustainable than top-down decisions. Public administration must be widely dispersed to ensure that people to people build alliances that actively intervene in the existing institutions of power and decision-making the local, divisional, provincial, and national levels.

Such empowered intervention should have as its goal the reorientation and making transparent and democratic the functioning of processes and institutions of power and decision-making. The South African approach of building linkages between the politician and administrator provides a way of building trust between the two blocks and forging constructive new alternatives between the various stakeholders. The growing number of credible elections compared to the 1980s ***[The African Charter on democratic Elections and Governance, The African Public Service Charter and the African Peer Review Mechanism (of NEPAD)]*** are pointers in the direction of tangible testimony of the gradual movements towards a consolidated partnership between politicians and administrators for the common welfare of society.

Only by understanding the differences that separate the two and seeking common solutions and common grounds can the quality of services delivery be improved to enhance and sustain the living standards of citizens. The centrality here is the quality wellbeing of citizens. This centrality should be rooted in our daily lives and in steering our ways through the chaotic currents stirred up in the dominant centralised authoritarian ethnic hegemonic system of governance widely spread across the continent.

Peoples' government incorporates decentralisation, public-private partnership participation; and creating vast opportunities for improving and enhancing service delivery. It also empowers the different stakeholders to be active partners in the governance process; as it introduces as well as challenges the different actors to cultivate a sense of leadership, moral, ethical and good sense of citizenship. A closed governance system is a recipe for underdevelopment; an open governance form signals development and progress – progress eventually entails sustainable quality livelihood. The African people have a right to better living standards.

Africa is rising. Change must occur. Africa is not an Island. Africa cannot remain static. Change is the message of this paper. A progressive Afro-centric vision is in great and urgent need. It appeals to the African Public Service Sector to gear up towards the vital implementation of a 'Service-Oriented Architecture Strategy (SOAS) to confront the challenges of the 21st century and beyond. The public bureaucracy is the engine of government and pivotal to all sectors of society. The centrality of the public service in bringing about good governance and development can no longer be emphasised. Strongly emphasised that the public administration should say clear of party-politics. When pay politics become an inherent part of the public bureaucracy, corruption is entrenched and poor-quality services delivery the order of the day. An impartial public service that serves which ever political that runs government is most required. Governments come and go, but the public service remains serving which ever party that assumes the reign of power. Thus, a new millennium dawns on Africa, challenging the people and leaders in particular to be constantly reminded of certain traits making up for good leadership and collective progress of society. We are at the break of a new dawn requiring strategic policy approaches without which the leadership of the continent's nation will become increasingly more authoritarian and the citizens ever more polarised and demobilised. Fig 3. Attributes of Leadership in Crafting a new Society takes up some of the issues involved.

Fig. 3: Attributes of Leadership in Crafting a New Society

- Self-confidence =→ the ability to overcome fear and failure and inspire confidence in their followers;
- Persistence ====→ remaining inwardly optimistic and not being shattered by frequent turndowns;
- Resilience =====→ the inner strength that enables leaders to bounce back after suffering frequent defeats;
- Independence ===→ getting satisfaction from being responsible to oneself
- Daring =======→ Not gambling, but calmly evaluating risks and not being afraid of risk-taking

Source: Forje (2015) Compiled from D'Souza, 2008

One should at this juncture emphasise that leadership is cause, everything else is effect. Thus, urging for competence, effectiveness, and efficiency, visionary and pro-active leaders in their respective domains or constituencies. The significance of democratic and good governance principles is vital in piloting the continent out of its current mess. No doubt, the popular and effective participation of citizens in public policy processes, transparency, and accountability of government in all its undertakings, particularly in the management of the extractive sector are critical for sustainable socio-economic development. One of the most serious factors plaguing the sustainable transformation of the continent is that of corruption. The status of the continent as a weak capable developmental and democratic region has roots in decades past with corruption playing a critical role. Aside from corruption characterising the colonial and post-colonial governments in Africa, the menace, unfortunately continues unabated. For example, in a 2009 Report of the African Union (AU) and the African Development Bank (AfDB), corruption cost Africa USA$159 billion a year. And this was estimated to be more than the entire international development aid to Africa that year. Objectively and critically, the continent does not really need aid from the international development partners if only corruption is tackled to its roots on the continent. Even though corruption is a world-wide phenomenon, for example, it is estimated that the act costs the European Union (EU) economy EUR120 billion per year, which is just a little less than the annual budget of the Union.

Apparently, this finding is mind-boggling and underscores the urgent need for Africa countries to seriously address the issue. It is not fictitious claiming that the continent's public service through the Conference of African Ministers for Public Service and Administrative together with other organisations like the African Association for Public administration and management (AAPAM) enormously bought into the idea of thinking and working innovatively. However, there is a serious concern and constraint to effective implementation of national and continental visions by African countries being the inadequate engagement of citizens in governance and development through decentralisation of powers, resources, functions and responsibilities to autonomous local government (Scot & Wallis 2013). Inadequate engagement of citizens in governance and development constitutes a major constraint to effective implementation of national visions by African countries. The country and continent we want also means involving all citizens participating. Development should not be the preserved of a select few. The fall-outs of development should be equitably shared. No one should be excluded or left behind. Building the human capacity knowledge and skills is essential. Therefore, African countries need new approaches to education. The continent has to think of the new role of education or the 21st century and far beyond. It has to think of those 21st century skills that are so crucial for advancing the transition from an underdeveloped to a quality services delivery society. African population needs to acquire new knowledge. Leaning involves developing and practising civic, social and emotional skills – learning to know, learning to do and learning to live together are the bases of justice, security, peace and development. As a continent with a fast-growing large youth population, the youths need the means to cope and integrate within the modern world. They need to acquire the latest knowledge and skills that are necessary to prepare them to be active participants within the new global knowledge society.

Fashioning an Afro-centric Approach

Africa's positive way forward is fashioning and building bridges across existing divide. It means fostering collaboration for sustainable governance for Africa to move forward. Answers to the social, economic and political development problems facing Africa are not self-evident. However, what is clear, is first, the incontestable reality that Africa itself must have a major role in the decisions that affect its future; solutions cannot be imposed unilaterally from outside. Second, important as it may be to respond to immediate problems [for example, famine and drought, poverty eradication, employment] or find ways to deal with balance of payments deficits and debt obligations in the short run, many responses do not represent permanent or long-term solutions. Even if the immediate and short-term problems are being dealt with, a long-term strategy must be developed and acted upon. If not, the short-terms problems are likely to repeat themselves (Kwapong & Lesser 1990: ix; in Forje 2013:61).

The Afro-centric should be able to address fundamental problems plaguing the region within the context of Africa Power and Politics Programme (APPP) of what works, and pursuing the idea of good governance and development for the collective good of the citizens. The African Charter on the Values and Principles of the Public Service and Administration backed the African Peer Review mechanism (of NEPAD) among other such documents like the African Charter on Democracy, Elections and Governance provide new guides for the renewal and implementation of a functional public service sector geared towards meeting the aspirations and needs of the people. Since independence one notices the symptoms of gradual system's collapse. Across the African continent we notice the 'decay and decline of the public bureaucracy, the total politicisation of the public service all contributing to poor services delivery, with things getting worse during the decades of the World Bank imposed Structural Adjustment Programme (SAP) of the 1980s.

A progressive Afro-centric approach will require A New Public Service Policy [ANPS] focused on constructively addressing the underdevelopment/development problematique of the continent. Some of critical issues involved are expressed on Fig 4: Towards A Renewal Bureaucracy for Africa. The fragilities of the continent's current Public Service sector have to be addressed from within every nation state and collectively at the African Union to work in unionism. Building strong institutions is very necessary. The African economy is rife with imbalances that cannot be fixed under the inherited bureaucracy an efficient and effective public bureaucracy is imperative if the continent want to be part of an emerging economy. Education, migration, employment and redistribution are key elements of a long-term solution to quality services delivery in Africa. In addition, African businesses must produce more jobs to fulfil the continent's promises and of claiming the future. African universities should play a key role in the process – teaching, research, knowledge and technology transfer as major contributing in put actors to economic growth and while cautioning decision-makes no to rely overmuch to popular statistical indicators of that performance (Geuna and Rossi, 2015).

Fig. 4: Towards A Renewal Bureaucracy Policy for Africa

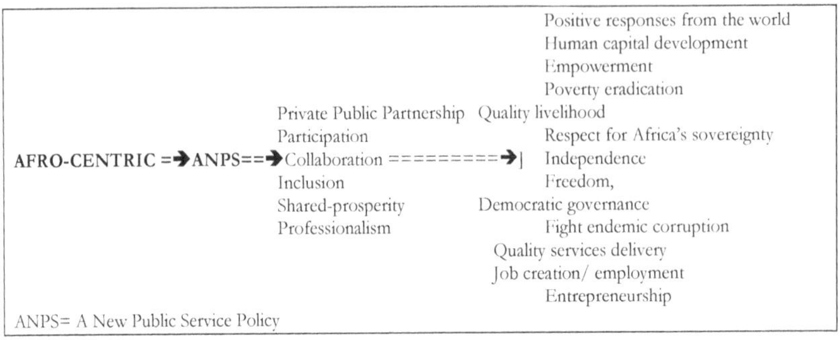

Source: [Forje] 2015

During this period at least two key public administration values which suffered unconscionable assault included issues of transparency and accountability.' Many African countries are currently paying dearly for the collapse of transparency and accountability in the civil service and public life in general (Olaopa 2008). It is not surprising that many African countries are consistently rated very low by Transparency International as corrupt polities. This decay and decline lead to the bureaucracy becoming an institutionalised 'maze of inaction' rather than an institutional pathway for development.

While the wave of Africanisation of the bureaucracy (Cameroonisation, Nigerinisation, Gabonisation, Ethipoianasation etc.) ushered the civil service into a dawn of glory, the decay and decline of bureaucracy became most noticeable in authoritarian civilian governments or in military administered states. Africa's lost decade the 1980s to mid-1990s saw the gradual systems collapse necessitating a renewal when the continent gradually stated returning to the values of democratic governance in the 1990s. With the economic recover of most African countries in the 1990s the state of decay and decline emphasised desire to reengineering managerial revolution in the public service with a strong focus on re-professionalization, which emerged as a 'management challenge and a panacea' to the state of decay and decline within the sector. Afro-centric renewal strategic approach requires further strengthening the development of discipline with the goal to improve the capacity and institutional and infrastructure throughout the continent. To begin with, what was the existing infrastructure for human capital development? What was and is the strength of the existing manpower in the sector? Given that there were few institutions of higher learning.

The continent depended for its modern public administration on institution inherited from the (i) era of colonial tutelage; (ii) the beginning of colonial administration; and (iii) the introduction of central administration to the era of institutional transfer and home rule. With independence the few existing institutions played pioneer role as training institutions, in the case of Nigeria, the Institute of Public Administrations at the University of Ife and the University of Zaria, which today are full faculties; and the Administrative Staff College of Nigeria (ASCON); in Ghana, the University of Legion (Olaopa 2008), Institutions like the Ghana Institute of Management and Public Administration (GIMPA), Kenya Institute of Administration (KIA); Uganda Management Institute (UMI) among other institutions now scattered around the continent. Other bodies responsible for training include The African association for Public Administration and Management (AAPAM); the Commonwealth Association for Public Administration and Management (CAPAM) among others in promoting professional and scholarly development of the discipline.

The Africa of tomorrow needs answers that are effective and lasting. That is why building the continent's human capital and functional bureaucratic public service and other logistics now remains imperative. A new mind-set demystifying Africa as a failed or rouge continent can only be corrected through visionary servant leadership, a proactive civil society and a functional service delivery bureaucratic setup. A new Africa has to be constructed capable of utilising its natural endowment for the collective good of the people. The Conference of African Minsters for Public/Civil Service (CAMPS) through its African Charter on the Values and Principles of Public Service and Administration must redouble efforts in ensuring that African countries adhere strictly to the Charter.

The Renewal of the continent's bureaucracy should facilitate the emergence of a new type of Public Service, more capable of solving contemporary African problems as well as comply with a certain number of principles, for example the equality of clients of the Public Service and Administration, the prohibition of discrimination; impartiality, equity and respect for the law in Public Services delivery; the continuity of the Public service in all circumstance; adaptation to the needs of the users; professionalism and ethics in Public Service and Administration; the promotion and the protection of the users and Public Service Agents' rights; accountability, integrity and transparency in Public Service and Administration equality between men and women in the Public Service and Administration; reinforcement of international co-operation for the improvement of Public Service and the sharing of good practices and experiences among Member States and the effective and efficient use of resources.

The continental body Africa Union (AU) stepped in to fashion a continental approach directed towards the eradication of abuses or distortions in the existing system with a focus on restructuring, reorganising and renovating the system. It is not just an issue of investing more resources, but building institutional capacity and human capability in the public bureaucracy to better manage diversities in the public service, mobilise, and manage available resources to ensure increased investments in services delivery and improved outcomes. Fig. 5 An Afrocentric Renewal Approach to Confronting the Challenges of Poor Service delivery and underdevelopment.

Fig 5: Afro centric Approach Confronting the Challenges of Poor Public Service

inefficiency in the delivery of social welfare;

- insensitivity in general welfare
- indifference to the norms guiding the conduct of public officials
- rampant corruption

//

Gave rise to

- weakening of public institutions
- distrust of government and institutions by citizens
- collapse of infrastructures;
- development of a sense of despair among the people
- poor external image of the continent

Renewal Reform Focusing on

- addressing the crisis in public management being a
- restructuring, reorganising and renovating the system
- key aspect of the deterioration in the quality of governance
- civil service reform
- anti-corruption reform
- pension reform
- improved working conditions for civil servants
- public expenditure management reform
- intensification human capital development
- encourage public-private sector participation and partnership
- establishment of professional and ethical values in the conduct of government business

// //

Requiring

- **State legitimacy**
- **Clear vision and strategic development direction;**
- **Visionary servant leadership and proactive civil society & productive private sector**
- **Implementation capacity and a focus on development outcomes**
- **Positive response from the international community**

Source [Forje 2015]

The African Charter on the Values and the Principles of the Public Service and Administration provides the guidelines to attaining a bureaucracy that cares and protects the welfare of citizens through the delivery of innovating and quality services, the modernisation and reinforcement of the Public Administration's capacities, the participation of the users in the administrative processes, the promotion of moral values in the Public Service, the improvement of working conditions of the Public Service Agents and the protection of their rights, the harmonisation of public policies and procedures of African Union Member States relating to Public Service, the equality between men and women in the Public Service and Administration, the reinforcement of international co-operation for the improvement of Public Service and the sharing of good practices and experiences amongst Member States. Thus, the African Charter on the Values and the Principles of the Public Service and Administration is geared towards an effective public service delivery towards a capable developmental state (CDS) in Africa. As such, member state of the African Union is urgently called upon to align their public service practices with the provision of the Charter and take the anti-corruption fight extremely serious and in line with the AU Convention on Preventing and Combating Corruption.

African countries are entrenched with problems because representation through the choice of the people and voices of the people are constantly thwarted. Society today is 'knowledge-driven' requiring skilled human resources potential, sense of direction, quality and style of leadership, accountability, transparency, productivity, far competition, and equity in the distribution of national wealth. (Forje 2007). The need for creating a civil service (like in Britain known traditionally) for its political neutrality; impartiality; adherence to merit principles for selection, promotion and decision-making; objectivity in tendering of advice to political masters, should at least be a point of reference. The cause and consequences of the politicisation of the public service in developed countries (Peters and Pierre, 2004) provides an appropriate launching-pad for understanding the developments elsewhere in the world. Africa in particular.

We cannot ignore, therefore, that politicisation can negate the merit principle in the organisation and functioning of the public services. T can undermine the morale and legitimacy of public bureaucracy and public confidence in it. Apparently, de-politicising the public service promotes merit, stability, continuity, professionalism and rationality; it persists despite political and social upheavals and violent swings in the political pendulum; and the public receives uniform and impartial treatment... However, some potentially positive features of politicisation of the public service could be recognised. Greater political commitment, for instance, may energise the public service in a way that may not be possible with a more neutral public service (Sharma, 2007:85)

To ensure good governance and reduce poverty and corruption, ensure proper service delivery, it is crucial to promote a harmonious state—civil society-private sector partnership and participation, as well as it is imperative to reduce existing opportunities for discretionary intervention by state authorities that use these mechanisms for their own benefits. Keeping the public service as much as possible clear from political ethnic and religious interferences and influences is a plus to effective and efficient services delivery

Conclusions

Shaping Our Future and Celebrating Diversity.

As we share the diversity of our struggles and celebrate the plurality of our resistance, our hopes and our aspirations, we are strengthened through comprehensive policies and the will to succeed. African countries share the diversity of their struggles; it is time to celebrate the plurality of its diversity as asset in the transformation process. This can only be done through good policies (input and output) functions of the state and the people. The end result is for the people and state to have trust in one another. Such developments show that administrative efficiency will increase with increased human capital development and with increases in specialisation (Simon 1976; Bertucci 2001). Our diversity is equally our strength and must be positively exploited to our best advantage.

The argument has been on developing a progressive Afro-centric approach. To attain this, the people must commit themselves to build people to people alliances (The Ubuntu, Batho Pele, and Harambe Spirit) to actively intervene in the existing institutions of power and decision-making, at the local, national and continental levels. Such empowered intervention will have as its goal the reorientation and building of a one and indivisible society, nation and continent. This is the foundations of African solutions to African problems. It creates the pathway for Africa articulating and owning its development for the benefit and good of the people. Seen within this perspective, Africa will celebrate its perseverance and struggle against large destructive development projects that dispossess and displace the people, making them refugees in their own continent

Successes towards such an envisioned goal require commitments and resolve to overcome all hurdles. Therefore, the political and administrative construct of the continent should be one that will not, and need not, wait only for our elected representatives and political leaders to address and resolve the multifarious economic, political, cultural, social and ecological crises that he continent faces. The emerging relationship between the *politician and administrator* should not be limited to a dialogue between the ruling party and administrators but extended to all political parties to better have an inside perspective of the structure and functioning of state apparatus. Where quality leadership exists, political leadership looms highest in the minds of many for a number of very important reasons, namely that of shaping the national vision and overseeing priority strategic policies for change and development for the collective good of society.

After all, the opposition parties constitute a *"government in waiting"* and should equally be schooled to properly understand and take-over the reigns of governance when the opportunity offers itself. This is what makes the *'bureaucracy'* an *impartial and independent institution* ready to serve whichever political party that takes over the reign of governance. The relationship should be an ongoing process of *renewal, reconciliation, reconstructing and the constant* search for best practices that improves the political and administrative apparatus to attain greater heights of efficiency and effectiveness in quality services delivery. The continent's institutions of higher learning play an important role in this aspect of 'training' the political parties and society.

The challenge is of such magnitude that Africans must begin first to acknowledge inherent weaknesses and failures as actors of social change. It entails accepting the reality of the evolving situation and to accept the reality of consistent honest, humble and self-reflecting, and never be stooges to national and international institutions and structures of power out to destroy the continent. It is, therefore, necessary to develop appropriate mechanisms for de-emphasising the negative aspects of centralisation and hierarchy. The challenge that Africa has to restructure itself into a capable development state as prelude to transcending into a service delivery polity is now The need to reinforce the effectiveness of government and encourage the development of the rule of law, justice, legal reforms and other measures to move the continent forward cannot be overemphasised.

Africa must now start envisioning the possible; by recognising that it is only through continuous efforts in building alliances and movements through active linking and resisting that can sustain and further the development of the continent. Apparently, it is from such a dynamic vision that the continent must assess, confront and transform the dominant political, economic, social and cultural systems that impoverishes the people of Africa. African leaders have expressed the desire for continental unity and have equally affirmed on many occasions that the continent has a common destiny.

Now is the time to ensure the realisation of those aspirations that Africa no longer can be on the valley of the death but on the avenue of the living. African states are challenged to recreate and re-design their states and make them development focused. Excellent and pragmatic development agenda has never been in want on the continent, the challenge has always been the political will for implementation and ensuring proper management of resources, creating more wealth and eliminating social inequalities and ethnic diversities. The journey for a New Africa starts here and now. On this basis, we advance the following recommendations.

Recommendations

Articulating a new good governance trajectory for service delivery in Africa does require among others the following policy recommendations;

- Human capital development (education) and creating awareness of the roles of stake holders in quality service delivery;
- Empowering stakeholders to be active partners in the process of service delivery as well as ensure a social contract between the state, civil society and the private sector;
- Lack of visionary leadership and a proactive citizenry – cultivating a new mind-set – attitude, behaviour and concern;
- Developing new curricular for human capital development from a progressive Afrocentric perspective and within the context of global scientific knowledge;
- Over-centralisation and authoritarian governance decision-making system is also demodulating; decentralisation and participatory promotes motivations as it encourages effectiveness and efficiency

- Cultivating a new mind-set for honesty, trustworthiness and seeking positive proactive forward-looking solutions to the plethora of African problems;
- Weakness of both leadership and citizens in the following; vision, transparency, ethics, goal orientation, team building leads to poor delivery of services;
- The future of public service rest upon innovation, creativity change and doing things differently through taking calculated risks in the overall interests of the people
- Create a professional, non-apolitical bureaucracy ready to serve which ever political party that assumes office;
- Challenges facing public service can be solved through home grown solutions;
- Encourage efforts in mainstreaming gender empowerment and other concerns;
- Failure to mobilise the people to engage in development of indigenous policies, instead leaders impose policies which have been copied from the developed world which are not adaptable to local people;
- Eradicating poverty, unemployment, endemic diseases, promoting and sustaining the welfare of citizens – people first before profit.

References

African Association for Public Administration and Management (AAPAM) (2007). Proceedings of the 29th Roundtable Conference of the African Association for public Administration and Management Proceedings on the Them Political and Managerial Leadership for Change and Development in Africa, 3-7 September 2007, Mbabane – Swaziland

African Association for Public Administration and Management (AAPAM) (2008), Proceeding of the 30th Roundtable Conference (AAPAM) on the Theme, Enhancing the Performance of the Public Service in a Developmental State, 6-10 October 2008, Accra-Ghana.

African Public Service: New Challenges, Professionalism and Ethics in cooperation with the Africa Training and Research Centre in Administration for Development [CAFRAD]. ST/ESA/PAD/SER.E/20. New York (in English and French]

African Union (2008) African Charter on democracy, Elections and Governance. Addis Ababa, Ethiopia

Bertucci Guido (2001) Managing Diversity in the Civil Service: UDESA-IIAS Joint Publication, IOS Press, Oxford, Washington, Tokyo

Chapman Brain (1959) The Profession of Government, Unwin University Books, London

D'Souza A. Anthony (2008) Leaders for Today: Hope for Tomorrow. Pauline Publications Africa, Nairobi - Kenya

Forje W. John (2006) "Rethinking Decentralisation and Devolution of Power Within the African Context: Challenges and Opportunities", Paper presented at the 28th Roundtable Conference of the Africa Association for Public Administration and Management (AAPAM), Arusha, Tanzania 4-8 December 2006, on the Theme: Towards and Effective Delivery of Public Services in Africa.

Forje W. John (2007) "Enhancing Sustainable Governance and Development in Africa – A Reassessment of Current Challenges and Future Prospects", African Journal of Public Administration and Management, Vol. XV111, No. 1, January 2007, pp43-54

Forje W. John (2009) The Challenges of Administrative Political and Developmental Renewal in Africa – Essays on Rethinking Government and Reorganisation, Nova Science Publishers, Inc., New York, USA

Forje W. John (2011) State Building and Democracy in Africa. A Comparative and Developmental Approach. Nova Science Publishers, Inc. New York

Forje W. John (2012). Emerging Perspectives on Capacity-Building and Quality Public Services Delivery in Africa; Challenges, Prospects and Opportunities for the Future Lambert Academic Publishing, Germany

Forje W. John (2015) Cameroon Without Corruption. The Search for A New Vision. Lambert Academic Publishing, Germany

Gant, G. (1979) Development Administration: Concepts, Goals, Methods. The University of Wisconsin Press, Madison, WI

Gasu John (2018) Strengthening Higher Education Leadership in Africa. A Study of Ghana's Situation, CODERSIA Book Publication, Dakar – Senegal.

Gerschenkron Alexander (1962) Economic Backwardness in Historical Perspectives the Belknap Press, Harvard University Press, Cambridge, MA

Geuna Aido And Rossi Federica (2015) The University and the Economy. Pathways to Growth and Economic Development. Edward Elgar Publishing, Cheltenham, Gloss, UK

Hyden Goran (1995) "The Changing Nature of the State and Public Management in Africa" in Bade Onimode & Richard Synge (eds.) (1995). Issues in African Development. Essays in Honour of Adebayo Adedeji at 65. Heinemann Educational Books (Nigeria) Plc. pp69-85

Kingsley J. Donald (1944) Representative Bureaucracy. The Antioch Press, Yellow Springs, Ohio

Mills Wright (1857). The Power Elite. Oxford University Press, p237

Meynaud Jean (1965) Technocracy, Faber and Faber, London,

Neustadt, Richard (1964). Presidential Power: The Politics of Leadership. Signet Books, New York.

Olaopa Tunji (2008) Theory and Practice of Public Administration and Civil Service Reforms in Nigeria. Spectrum Books Limited, Ibadan - Nigeria

Peters Guy & Pierre Jon (2004) Politicisation of the Public Service in Comparative Perspective: The Quest for Control, Routledge Taylor and Francis Group, London and New York

Riggs, Fred (1970) Frontiers of Development Administration. Duke University Press, Durham, NC.

Ridley, F. and Blondel, J. (1965) Public Administration in France, Barnes and Noble Publishers, New York New

Sawyerr Akilagpa (2004) "Challenges Facing African Universities. Selected Issues" African Studies Review, 47 (1), 1-59

Schaffer, B. Bernhard (1969). "The Deadlock in Development Administration," in: Politics and Change in Developing Countries, in Ley Colin (ed.) (1969), Cambridge University Press, Cambridge.

Scott K. George & Malcolm Wallis (eds.) [2014] Citizen Engagement, Decentralisation and Service Delivery in Africa, AAPAM Book Series, Nairobi - Kenya

Sharma C. Keshav (2007) "Trends in the Politicisation of the Public Service', African Journal of Public Administration and Management, Vol. XV111, No.1, January 2007, pp78-86

Sharp R. Walter (1931). The French Civil Service: Bureaucracy in Transition, Macmillan, New York

Simon A. Herbert (1976) Administrative Behaviour – A Study of Decision-Making Processes in Administrative Organisation. The Free Press, London

Sisson C. H. (1959). The Spirit of British Administration, Faber and Faber, London

Suleiman N. Ezra (1974) Politics, Power, Ad Bureaucracy in France. The Administrative Elite. Princeton University Press, USA

Victor Bekkers, Menno Fenger and Peter Scholten (2017 Public Policy in Action. Perspectives on the Policy Process, Edward Elgar Publishing Limited, UK

Vedel Georges (ed.) (1962) La Depolarisation, Mythe ou Réalité, Armand Colins, Paris.

Weber Max, (1958) "Politics as a Vocation," in H. H. Gerth and C. Wright Mills (eds.) From Max Weber: Essays in Sociology, Oxford University Press, New York

Zeleza Tiyanbe Paul (1997). Manufacturing African Studies and Crises. Codesira Book Series, Dakar – Senegal

Chapter 16

Conclusion

Looking Back and Facing Forward Challenges:

"Africa's first great crisis, for she will have to decide whether to go forward or backward. She must understand that it is no longer possible to advance by regions, that, like a great body that refuses any mutilation, she must advance in totality, that there will not be one Africa that fights against colonialism and another that attempts to make arrangements with colonialism. Africa, that is to say the Africans, must understand that there is never and greatness in procrastination and that there is never any dishonour in saying what one is and what and what one wants and that in reality the cleverness of the colonized can in the last analysis only be his courage, the lucid consciousness of his objectives and of his alliances, the tenacity that he brings to his liberation. Lumumba believed in his mission. He had an exaggerated confidence in the people. The people, for him, not only could not deceive themselves but could not be deceived. And, in fact, everything seemed to prove him right" (Fanon, 1970:202-3). *"A people now forgotten, discovered while others were yet barbarians, the elements of the arts and science. A race of men, now rejected from society for their babble skin and frizzled hair, founded on the study of the laws of nature those civil and religious systems which still govern the universe." (Count C. Volney – French Historical Researcher. "Africa needs fundamental change and transformation, not just adjustment. The change and transformation required are not just narrow, economic and mechanical ones. They are the broader and fundamental changes that will bring about, over time, the new Africa of our vision where there is development and economic justice, not just growth. A new revolution is in progress – democratic revolution that will give full rein to popular participation. Will we, the Africans, stand by and allow this wind of change to pass us by? We stood by during the period of the renaissance. We were even less than onlookers in the era of the industrial and technological revolutions… are we going to allow the continent to be further marginalized, to be out of the new mainstream? **(Adebayo Adedeji**), in The Closing statement at International Conference on Popular Participation)*

Mapping a New Domestic and Foreign Order for Africa

We started the book by placing the cards on the table; telling the story how it is, for inevitably a complex story, for many of the issues are inter-related and impact on one another and cannot sensibly be addressed in isolation. The story is surveyed through the thicket of an

African eye, to offer some solutions, especially concerning governance, justice, peace, security and development. We need to build a new mind-set, and change behaviour. The call is extended to the developed countries to reciprocate and cultivate a new attitude and approach towards the developing states in Africa. Africa made a bold step by transforming from the Organisation of African Unity to the African Union with the hope of creating something new out of the continent. It is not the place of this publication to judge whether that something new actually emerged out of the policy of 'non-interference' to 'non-indifference.' Is the continent faced with Construction and Development or Collapse and Decay dichotomy? There is an ongoing economic growth that is attracting investors from the emerging economies. These investors pose serious threats to the established partners of the continent - the former colonial powers. At the same time there is a rising clash of development approach between gang of the old and the collection or a coalition of the new. While their approaches may differ, both sides have one common interest - convergence on exploiting of the resources of the continent. In this game of interest, exploitation, and profit, power and knowledge play an important role. Who Rules Africa Now? Frantz Fanon (1969:121-123) writes: "The national economy of the period of independence is not set on a new footing. It is still concerned with the ground-nut harvest, with the cocoa crop and olive yield. In the same way there is no change in the marketing of basic products, and not a single industry is set up in the country. We go on exporting raw materials; we go on being Europe's small farmers who specialise in unfinished products."

Looking back, we see why the old parent states withdrawal from their possessions in Africa created and established law and order among what they called barbarians, for the protection of the concessions and interests. In the case of France, her defeat in Vietnam created a different situation for their African expedition. All sorts of means were deployed to cling to her colonies. The Franco-Algerian war, because of its size and intensity, enables us to see in close-up, by the very reason of her successive failures, the attempts made by France to maintain domination by imposing the assimilation and annexation construct. The situation in Cameroon, the Central African Sub-region and what is happening in French West Africa paints an unforgettable picture of French administration in Africa. The struggle for the liberation of Africa remains imperative. The general idea is that the Maghreb region and the Central African sub-region must remain under French imperialistic governance. Extending the debate further, and bringing in the Cameroon political debacle, the French army and its cohort in Cameroon have distinguished themselves only by pillaging or massacring civilians as a means of subduing the people to accepting French dominance (Forje, 2020, 2021).

The state of rising destructive frustration is the result of the pitfalls of national and individual consciousness. Here, Fanon (1969:119) is categorical when he states: "national consciousness, instead of being the all-embracing crystallization of the innermost hopes of the whole people, instead of being the immediate and most obvious result of the mobilization of the people, will be in any case only an empty shell, a crude and fragile travesty of what it might have been." There are just too many faults with our independence; making the nation to be classified and passed over for race and tribe instead of the country or state. These are some of the cracks in the edifice of our so-called independence which has created the process of retrogression that is harmful to prejudicial to national effort and nation unity. Today, more than sixty years after independence, we are more disunited, with the weaknesses and serious dangers that entail to the advancement of a country and the continent. We have over the years, and especially following the lowering of the colonial flag and hoisting of the new national flag destroy national and individual consciousness; giving rise to the mutilation of national pride and sovereignty; but by this act only given credit to the departed colonial regime, hence we worship and adore the Euro-centric ideology in total disregard to the vision and doctrine of the Afro-centric ideological orientation, making us suffer from a cultural and spiritual penury and destroying our thinking capacity in cultivating a new mindset for our sustainable transformation. As a result, our national economy has never been set on a new footing, nor our political governance undergone a structural-functional change that brings the outputs government closer to the people.

Africa is still with the raw material exporting continent we are. Immediately after independence, those who live in more prosperous areas suddenly realized the good luck and showed hatred or resistance, profound reaction in refusing to share their wealth with others. This explains why the coastal people will hate those from the hinterlands; those from resources rich areas do not want to see those from resource poor regions, all contributing to envy and covetousness as well as homicidal impulses. Old rivalries which existed before colonialism, old inter-racial hatred come to the surface and are being perpetuated by the departed colonial masters or the emerging new governing elites who replaced the departed who colonial lords. In Cameroon for example, following the Anglophone crisis, the people from South-West do not want to see those from the North-West, but prefer to inter-relate with people from the Littoral region even though this will place them under greater suppression that never existed during the colonial era. And so, African Unity, that vague formula, yet one to which the men and women of Africa are passionately attached, and whose operative value served to bring immense pressure to bear on colonialism, and supposed with an Afro-centric approach to unity, African unity fails to take off the march, and crumbles into ethnic, authoritarian rule, regionalism inside the hollow shell of nationality itself.

The result as noted by Fanon is that: "Colonialism which had been shaken to its very foundation, by the birth of African Unity, recovers its balance and tries now to break that will to unity by using all the movement's weakness. Colonialism and neo-colonialism set the African peoples moving by revealing to them the existence of their cultural rivalries and spiritual weakness as destroying the transformation of the region. Neo-colonialism pulls the every strong shamelessly; and is only too content to set at loggerheads those Africans who only yesterday was leagued against the settlers. A new state form takes shape in certain minds and quarters, and the "advocates of colonialism/neo-colonialism laugh to themselves derisively when they her magnificent declaration on African Unity" (Fanon, 1968:129). It is not surprising for every passing day; the economic channels of African states sink back inevitably into neo-colonialist lines. The national economy formerly protected, is today, literally controlled. The former colonial masters, France in particular, has total hegemony over its former colonies, increases its grip and demands, accumulates, concessions and guarantees and takes fewer and fewer pains to mask the hold over the national government. The ongoing senseless war and genocide in Southern Cameroons has roots in French manipulations of its former colonial territory – Republique du Cameroun. Southern Cameroons is paying the heavy price of wanting to uphold the two Federated government structure agreed in 1961; they want to set the record clean and clear to ensure the reign of rule of law persist and to guarantee that democracy return and takes shape in the country. What strategies are they using to arrive at them envisage goals? France and its cohorts do not want any change in the current status-quo

Governments must be answerable to all their people, including the poorest and most vulnerable. The political leaders should be held accountable; citizens must be fed with all the necessary and right information about government income and expenditure. Openness in government makes it more likely that resources will be deployed and used more efficiently. By contrast, lake of transparency and accountability breeds corruption. Corruption is systemic throughout the continent. This is another of Africa's vicious circles; corruption has a corrosive effect on efforts to improve governance; and yet, improved governance remains essential in reducing the scope and degree for corruption to begin with. The African Peer Review Mechanisms (APRM) and the country Anti-corruption institution are good instruments for waging the war against corruption. The Blair Report (2005:44) states that "the rot of corruption has spread throughout society at all levels. But to send a strong signal it is worth tackling the most egregious examples." It is not only corruption in which we have distinguished ourselves, but become the best users of western arms in destroying ourselves. Africans have become experts in the acts of 'genocide,' the killings in Cameroon as if one is killing animals is just the tip of the iceberg in keeping in rotation of western arms factories. Too many Africans have died and will continue to die prematurely as Susan Williams (2021:502) points out, "for there not to be questions raised about the now well-known employment of insidious ways of silencing those who threaten the established order." Again, in page 511 she goes further to state following the publication of The Spymasters (2020); "if you know what the CIA is doing, you know what the president wants; and if you know what the president wants you know what the CIA is doing".

For all the frightening and horrible stories about the continent, interest is growing about the region with the imposition mainstream liberal thinking and a coalition of the willing to push ahead a mixed of shady nets and free-market capitalism. A new balkanization of the continent ill emerged when the interest of the old power economies merged with the interests of the emerging economies led by China. The struggle of infighting for the continent's resources and markets between the economic powers - western Economic Powers and the Emerging Economies will or may destroy the economic growth and break-through for the economic take-off if African countries do not master the intricacies of power politics (Kennedy, Kissinger, and Niebuhr). Indeed, Africa has yet to master the intricacies of western politics on Africa. The sad side of the story is that western mercenaries in partnership with our people are operating in the destruction of the continent. We have to blame ourselves for the ongoing predicaments that have befallen on us. Our hands are dripping in blood to please western interests. For how long, I wonder?! Yet the struggle continues, for national and world politics are now, to a great extent, the result of a clash between conditions of inequality ad the ideals of equality. David Thomson (1969:200-201) opines in this lengthy quote that; "As political independence and equality of status have been won by peoples of Asia and Africa formerly subjects to European rule, dramatic inequalities of standard of living have become more important.

Retarded in their economic progress by the 'population explosion' happening whilst their natural resources were still underdeveloped, the peoples of the 'Third World' remain dependent upon financial and technical aid from the more technologically advanced countries. The fact that that are 'coloured' peoples makes for racial inequalities on a global scale. It may come to seem, in the future, that current conflicts of political ideas are concerned less with issues of dictatorship versus democracy, the claims of the community as against the rights of the individual, and in the complex of issues usually associated with the ideal of Liberty: and that they are even more directly concerned with the ideal of Equality…." For now, Africa is in turmoil and great pains requiring serious surgical treatment. The 'fire' next time and on the mountain calls for practical solutions that challenges with relentless power the pervasive elements of fear. We have to know and address the hell of the continents, underdevelopment, the problem of inequality, suppression, why and the urgent need of articulating and implementing a proactive progressive Afro-centric agenda, the priority for change. We have to keep singing "change we can and change we must" for survival and well-being.

The coalition of new is gaining grounds, building on the failure of colonial master for having neglected the continent during their reign. The gang of the old is exploiting the colonial legacy - neo-colonialism - to maintain a hegemonic advantage. The key to the situation lies in the role of the ruling elites. On whose side, are they? Of course, it is said that the devil you know is better to deal with than the angel you know not. But who is going to supply the needs of the people best? Again, it is a question of interests - where the ruling elites stand? And working in whose interests? The economic and political ups and downs of the continent are what make it such an interesting entity. One the hand, it is an example of a region that has and continues to succumb to several of the issues traditionally associated with 'weakness, disunity poor organisation underdevelopment, exploitation, by-per inflation, failed market, corruption, violent military dictatorship and centralised authoritarian civil administration. One the other hand, it is a continent with vast natural resources attractive to the industrial countries, backed by the fact that it is an untapped market potential with a very rich and prosperous economy. Africa is the bride everyone wants but may be difficult to marry once the terms are set-out. Whatever the politics and choices made, to what extents will these choices and implementation processes be to the benefit of the broadest segment of society?

What is Government more than the management of the affairs of a Nation? It is not, and from its nature cannot be, the property of any particular man or family, but of the whole community, at whose expense it is supported; and though by force and contrivance it has been usurped into an inheritance, the usurpation cannot alter the right of things. Our leaders have usurped for themselves the nation as personal property – the leader is the state and the state are the leader – which underscores the problems nations in Africa are suffering from. Governments are founded on the principles of the people. Therefore, every citizen is a member of the sovereignty, and as such, can acknowledge no personal subjection: and his/her can only be to the laws of the nation. The nation should be construed on the foundation of good governance, justice and respect for the rule of law. Elected government, as representative of the people, is the only form of rule of government by direct democracy which grossly absent on the continent

Everyone knows that with good governance, peace, stability and an educated labour force, Africa will emerge as a world economic power. For now, the continent is being manipulated into forced recession, come to think of the World Bank /IMF imposed structural adjustment (SAP) which target those areas essential to development - education, healthcare sectors unemployment through the retrenchment of able workers, serious devaluation of the currency, (for example 50% bin CFA zones) and other areas just to safe the devaluation of the French Francs. Francophone African countries were made to bail out France whenever France is in financial difficulties. The gross effect has been political turmoil with the West giving their unflinching support to dictatorial regimes across the continent. The alternation between civilian and military governments seems to be the pattern of governance on the continent with the full blessing and support from the old democracies. It is not surprising that political instability has increased on the continent. Political violence culminated with the Rwanda genocide, the war in Somalia, Sudan, Cameroon, Mali, Central African Republic, Chad and of not-too-distant a past the Arab Spring. To a large extent, Africa's political climate looms with uncertainties while is economy is the state of a boom with future prospects of growth. How to move the state of political disaster to one of one of political recovery, maturity to sustainability, and to move from 'served leaders' to 'servant' leadership is the question? Politics and the economy are interrelated. The existing mismatch on African politics and economy needs serious redressing. Without a proper mix and understanding it will be difficult for the continent to forge ahead politically and economically

Africa has 60% of the world's unused arable land. Which implies that in the end the world will be running towards the continent as it has all that Europe, the Asian Tigers and the Chinese Dragons need? If the first scramble was for historians to make their imprint and ensure territorial expansion building strategy (and with Africans being ignorant or uneducated), the second scramble (undertaken within the context of an enlightened population) opens up windows of opportunities for Africa to reconstruct and re-establish itself as a meaningful player in global politics. Here lays the best hope, requiring forward looking strategic designs. The more needed Africa is, the less needy - and more powerful - it can be. African governments and peoples have the capacity and capability to do marvellous things if they want to. Tough days are ahead; tough decisions and choices beacon for an evolution to occur that will reborn the forgotten and awaken sleeping continent. Out of the old will grow a new, strong and prosperous continent if only the right decisions and choices are made and implemented. There is an ongoing alienation of civil society by government. There is strong mistrust of the government and legislation continues to be serious problem. Most parliaments are clapping institutions represent not the interest of their electors but that of government. The system of checks and balances are non-existent. Voter's apathy reigns high as the introduction of multiparty system has only produced a monopolistic party structure in most countries, Cameroon for example. The multiplicity of political parties has not contributed to free and fair elections and good governance. Election rigging is common even with the advent of modern electronic process of registration, voting and counting.

Africa remains the last authentic place on 'planet earth,' but when everyone wants a piece of paradise, can paradise remain intact? At the same time, the world is changing, very fast and rapidly in all directions. Africa as part of that changing world must join the bandwagon on its own foresight, capacity and capability. The continent needs seeds of change - servant visionary leadership and a responsive proactive civil society with a forward moving productive, innovative and competitive

sector as seeds of change to invigorate the fertile lands with good and healthy seeds for a bounty harvest. The continent is inhabited with the trajectories of inequalities within and between each of 54 states or more, and between Africa and the rest of the world. The Mugs expands these inequalities in greater dimension, showing how vulnerable the region is and why an Afro-centric proactive policy strategy must be articulated and aggregated with all genuine sincerity now. First, there is going to be an emerging consensus concerning 'interests' between the emerging economies and the old colonial guards. The state of poverty and underdevelopment absence of justice and good governance gives ample room for exploitation and consensus interest building between the coalitions of the willing. Divided as the continent is on presenting a common and united consensus and given that dependency on the West has been the guiding factor of each country, African states will fall prey to the 'interest' articulation of the coalition of the willing. Of particular importance is the degree to which the poorer and middle-class of the various social groupings are integrated or disintegrated given the centrality of this dimension to the longer term social and political agenda of the interest of the coalition of the willing. The continent blacks a powerful media channel house - BBC, CNN, CBC etc. to create awareness, educate the population of the intensions of the 'interest' of the coalition of the willing. There is no strong media house or channel to sell the continent and count-act the false image or the hidden agenda of the new colonial powers.

Second, there is a gross absence of any meaningful independent "Think Tank" to dissect, aggregated and formulate counter attack policies by advancing critical, scientific and objective scholarship for African governments on which to base their strategic approach in dealing with the invading forces from all velocity, intensions and angles. The politicization of African academics, think tanks adds to the polarization of policy debate and decision-making over fundamental on the development path to be adopted; the state of inequality, exclusion and the marginalization, infect, hinders Africa's ability to revise, rethink and reconstruct as well as recalibrate their development agenda away from any move towards an Afro-centric comfort zone. Third, African countries are not focusing on a people-oriented development agenda. In other words, there is no focus on the 'inequality and ethno-centric divisional dichotomy of the continent. The focus is on dependency theory to meet the articulate self-interests of the ruling elites and the old guards soon to be joined by the forces of the emerging economies. In addition to this common insight of a neglected people-oriented development policy, there is a wide range of social process occurring across the rising middle class and the poor through the 'connectivity' forces of 'internet' which again can be manipulated by the developed economies to suit their best interests. All these developments have important consequences on mobility, stratification and cohesion. Indeed, a lack of attention to the poor and emerging middle class can inadvertently reinforce a tendency to attribute various inequality induce social disorder to poverty, ethno-centric divide, thereby reinforcing the invading forces exploitative phobia impulse to segregate and further divide an already divided continent even though the opposite is arguably required in order to move towards lasting socially inclusive or people-oriented development.

From this perspective, it is imperative to integrate a holistic socially policy based on an Afro-centric perspective into the discourse on inequality and division in the post-2015 Mugs, 2017, 2030, 2035 or whatever development agenda adopted by the various countries, and, in particular, the key role of an Afro-centric modes of social and development policy by all African countries, the regional and the continental bodies (ECOWAS, CEMAC, ECCAS, SADC, NEPAD, AU etc.) as the most powerful tool in dealing with the plight add predicaments to the continent; and simultaneously in seeking the continent's alliances with other global forces on a broader development agenda. The contention here is a force shifting towards more African principles bit also keeping a universalistic open-door approach in mind. Africa cannot be an Island, especially in the 21s century world of growing interconnectivity. China succeeded because interconnectivity was basically unknown. Time and space have changed everything. The continent is coming on the scene at a different historical time period. The equations are not the same and never will be.

Science and technology are important components of the wall dividing poverty and prosperity. Today, there are unusual opportunities for Africa countries, especially those bypassed by the great benefits of science and technology, to improve the quality of life of the rural and urban poor through the integration of traditional or indigenous knowledge and emerging technologies. The marriage of indigenous knowledge know-how technology and the advances in modern science and technology should create a national, continental and global effort of introducing placing S&T at the centre of development. Africa and the rest of the world stand to benefit from this 'new moral and social contract' in bringing the benefits of development to all citizens. Seen within this context, Africa's future is inescapably linked to its ability to create an effective relationship between indigenous knowledge system and modern science and technology – a challenge in which education will play a decisive role. This calls for a rethinking and re modification of the current educational curriculum in African countries - i.e., putting in place suitable educational innovation system or developmental authenticity not continuing with the pale imitation of colonial models.

The key requirements for the success of all economic and social policy reforms is that the educational curriculum should not only be relevant to the specific country situations, but that, they must be articulated, designed, implemented and owned by African countries themselves. In short, success requires, the imperative input of the necessary human resources – the scientists, the technologists, the scholar and others who can effectively operate within the necessary institutional framework such as institutions of higher learning, scientific research and development institution. Africa's institutions of learning have to be more proactive, creative, research innovative just as government has to invest more or research, infrastructure, as well as creating an enabling environment for the smooth functioning of the educational system. African governments must show greater willingness more than ever before in considering alternative approaches to development. African governments should fully engage with the private sector to facilitate lasting societal and economic transformation. The relationship between the government, universities, research institutes and the private sector should be intensified. Building a research, development, scientific, and technology power (RSTP) should be the priority focus of African governments. A progressive Afro-centric agenda is a philosophy that promotes the idea that Africa can truly become transformed as a sovereign, independent and sustainable developed entity. It calls for long-term investing in Africa by Africa's own private sector as a means to solving the continent's most pressing challenges. It's also an ideology that believes in a model of growth that is all-inclusive. Lessons should be learned from countries in the Asian region.

China did isolate itself from the world to build its current infrastructure and economic power base. Its homogeneity made it possible. Africa has not got that advantage. Today, a new school of thought is fast awakening in Chinese thinking - that science and technology are not enough? To stay competitive and abreast with the developed countries, the next generation of Chinese students is heading into the future armed with liberal arts degree. Their horizon is much wider. What we see in the African youth (those who have not been poisoned with western values and cultures) is impatience for a new Africa, not some throwback to authoritarian past. The Internet or social media is creating thinking of the new young and progressive youths for the future of Africa. How do we invest in this new line of thinking and the youths that espouse such proactive vision for the continent regaining its position in the world? A renaissance continent is the answer. Currently, the continent is confronted with a clash of paradigms but must select the paradigm that puts the continent on the right path. African countries must focus on the need for a development strategy that is people-oriented, more disciplined bottom-up approach which is inclusive. The obvious dominance of western system of education, research, academic publishing, patents, mobility flow, translational operation and partnership places Africa at a disadvantage, as there these areas are not properly developed on the continent. This leads to a state of dependency on external forces. Added to the fact that the African continent with its 55 or more countries lacks a common economic, political and cultural platform as face as face different challenges and complexities make it impossible to talk of a single African higher education and political system as well as a single or common approach to internationalization.

For the coming years Africa's biggest resources will be its relatively large but young population. This should be cause for concern as well as optimism; yet the current stampede for talent could contribute to even more global polarisation and compound the negative impacts of brain drain for African universities and its efforts to develop. There are also opportunities - encourage 'brain gain '- tapping into the potential capacity and capability of the diasporas., and creating back home an enabling environment to attract the growing academic mobility within Africa and a 'healthy balance' for Africa in the global race for talents as well as building a string and sustainable continent. There is no silver bullet when it comes to employment. Otherwise, all except the unwilling will signed up. But it is a good idea to invest in education and research in order to create a knowledge-based and sustainable economy, and economy that not only creates jobs but contributes to the quality of society as a whole. The first step is obviously not to cut public funding on health and education (as World Bank imposed SAP did in Africa in the 1990s). Such destructive disastrous or short-term economic interests and the crises continue to block the road forward to the continent's recovery and development. Good health, education and research should be used to create enterprises, jobs and sustainable economy of tomorrow. Bear in mind that you cannot force someone to learn, but you can place them in a conducive and enabling environment as possible and hope for the best. Likewise, you cannot force innovation and creativity. All the state can do is to create the right the right condition. And no state can definitely force a new economic paradigm, especially if you do not even know what it is supposed to look like. You cannot climb to do either. China and India may present an exception. Nothing stops Africa from fashioning its own pathway to sustainable transformation. All it needs is the 'will and collectiveness' to do so. We are by this publication like others, challenged to starting a new history for the continent and we should not continue paying tribute to Euro-centric ideals by creating states, institutions and societies which draw wrong inspirations from the West.

The old structures of universities are irrecusably gone; universities can no longer be beacons for the elites but need to fully take on their roles as the foundation as centres of excellence of a knowledge-based economy. This will lead to a new level of social inclusion never seen before. Therefore, constructive partnership with the private sector should lead to good investment for tomorrow: but will also help industries, technologies and education of yesterday's economic paradigm to develop. It is time for critical reflection, but also for new ideas to turn existing destruction into creative process. The future should not be constructed not on 'fear,' but on 'hope' and proper restructuring and sustainability, creating employment and growth is imperative for a sustainable future. In the end, employment is the main mechanism of economic growth in an individual's as well as a nation's life. For Africa's developmental approach requires a political, economic, and cultural engagement with all the different strata at home and abroad before facing the invading forces from a position of strength, unity and cohesion. The risk of not explicitly anchoring future development agenda with an inclusive politicised policy debate and socio-cultural and eco-political engagement of the people is that these agenda can be subverted towards the policy interest agendas of the invading parties that will eventually and possibly undermine the development efforts of a fragmented continent and citizens in many contexts.

Building consensus is what is required now. It is only through inclusion, constructive engagement of people that the volatile political and economic mi can benefit the people. Exclusion experienced by those higher up in a social hierarchy can lead to a variety of knock-on effects lower down in the social hierarchy, for example, in terms of outright obstructions to upward mobility or ideational influences regarding the perceived value of education among lower social start, ethno-centrism, inequality, injustice etc. is a can be a higher revolution, and the continent hiss had enough of its share in this dolman. Hence, the challenge with the transformation discourse of the continent centres on how to create genuinely redistributive structures and strong institutions at the local, national, regional and continental levels. These are the political challenges that cannot be resolved through military style might solutions, but require right choices to be made politically and with the consent of the people on what they wish to inhabit and how they wish to relate and treat each there within and between countries (see Fischer 2012).

Does the Arab-Spring make Africa more dangerous or it gives wider publicity to the potential riches of the continent for further invasion, military, political and economic? For now, Africa is the sacrificial lamb for the West, the Asian Tigers and the Chinese Dragons. Indeed, we see that in their aggressive or subtitle policies to exploit the rich potential resources of the continent, they have to be treated or settled properly as both sides of the same coin with more in common than not. If something is going to come out of the new rush to Africa, the people must sharpen their tools, strategies and decision-making mechanisms; make the right choices to get what they want in a skilful but harried manner. It is a game of the survival of the fittest. For now, the continent is faced with a managed democracy that plays into the hands of the invaders. Democratic progress appears to be reverted. Good governance is crucified. Development on the continent is stagnated. Poverty and corruption increase. It opens the Pandora box for exploitation by external forces. We become dependent on foreign aid. And so, continues the vicious circle. Stability is the single most important factor in boosting an emerging economy which Africa is about to become in no distant future.

Fear, uncertainty and insecurity famously are the antithesis of trust, confidence and hope. But it is trust that we need. We need trust, hope and confidence in our governments, leadership and strong institutions. If we are able to make change in political discourse from fearful "efficiency" desires to a partnership of trust between the state, civil society and private sector, policy-makers will undoubtedly find that the framework established will be to the common human benefit of all, universities will take on a greater social and economic role. The continent's education system must be heading towards that direction. To what extent are African leaders committed to democracy, development and the quality well-being of the people? Therefore, the leaders must gun for sound inclusive and sustainable development in an age of a knowledge-based economy. For now, Africa is sustaining the avenue of financial resources transfer to the metropolis; (a) thereby improving the social services and employment levels as well as the general standards of their peoples': (b) the independent economies equally enmeshed in non-productive dependent structures as micro-colonies, undergoing serious declines in their economic performance, employment and poor living standards.

Economic growth, poverty reduction, job creation and putting people to work open up the avenues for a better future for the continent. Can policymakers make poverty, corruption, bad governance, underdevelopment history? These are the prevailing challenges. Can the leaders deal with the currents of democracy, development and destruction? Whatever the case, any country/ leadership that uses authoritarian principles, guns and violence to suppress freedom of expression and quality livelihood for others does not deserve respect and credibility. But what Africa does Africans what? For now, it remains a continent divided against it. This division is destructive to the continent. Africa's greatest problem is preparing its future; and the way we treat the coming generation. There is need to profoundly reform the education system to ensure proper training of youths according to the needs of society; and to give added value to the rich natural resources potential of the continent for the good of the people. Disparities and regional inequalities must be corrected. To achieve the goals for the future, a break with policies of the past decades and a repeal of destructive laws so far in practice to stop the deepening of inequalities between institutions, regions, localities and ethnic constellations.

The country/continent needs policy measures, opening changes for hope for all in society. The solution for the continent is to gear up towards genuine independence; towards the creation of a united and strong continent with a civilisation that is based on a pro-Afro-centric vision and quality living standards for its population. Therefore, Africa must work for the construction of an economy and guided by the principle of delivering an acceptable quality livelihood to all its citizens. The vision of a united continent must be upheld. So far, Africa presents a picture of a relatively emerging continent but based on an economic sub-structure of "dependent development" since it has adopted the Eurocentric designed development ideological orientation that constantly bleeds the region to death. And inherent in those sub-structures of dependent development are a number of specific mortal dangers for the people which this paper attempts to address and highlight. The continent is caught in a trap of "dependent independence" otherwise known as "neo-colonialism." No doubt the continent still has some distances to cover to attain genuine independence, self-respect, sovereignty, dignity, strength, self-sufficiency, mental and psychological emancipation. For now, it is stuck on the run-way unable to take-off to destination, 'quality livelihood and independence.'

Listen to the French President Jacques Charics who in his 1996 official address to mark the 50th anniversary of the departmentalisation of the French Antilles, referred to the French colonies, as "bridgeheads" of francophone culture that provides France with a presence in the four corners of the world and that 'must be ardent to defend and promote the cultural patrimony of France, calling the overseas departments 'messengers' of French messengers in their respective regional organisations such as the Association of Caribbean states (or the French-speaking African countries). All of these dangers are intensified by the fact that the internationalist capitalist economy is in throes of profound recession and Africa provides the backup or rescue team like it did when the French Franc was in serious trouble in the late 1980s, and the currencies of former French colonies in Africa had to be devalued to rescue it. African challenges, African Solutions is whistle for the goal the leaders must work for and in a constructively and strategic manner. Trade should replace aid. The continent stands in the midst of serious African challenges, hard choices and the right decisions to be; at the same time, African problems are global challenges requiring global solutions. The two must converge as a major input factor is good trade replacing trade. The promise of innovative trade with good prices is by and large unfulfilled. Trade gap or unbalanced trade between North and South remains large especially with respect to supporting development, including achieving quality livelihood for the people. The international community must recognise that it is to the common interest to provide stable and contractual resources for these purposes.

Politically, tapping revenue from global resources and raising taxes internationally to address global problems are much more difficult than taxing for purely domestic purposes. But like all political decisions taken for the next generation and not just for the next elections; this should be assessed carefully against alternative scenarios, including the very dangerous one of continuing polarisation, exclusion, confrontation and insecurity in the world. The time has come for world leaders to confront the challenges. For now, the ball is squarely placed in the centre position of African governments. It is time they take their leadership roles seriously and responsibly. It is not out of place to question whether, there is a cure of Africa's problems. The civilisation of the continent was destroyed through the slave trade and colonial rule and today through neo-colonialism. It is time for the people to reconnect with its continent, nature and to reconstruct a condition of its true part within the evolving world context; be a dialogue between the great past and the evolving future. Here we need to build on the following; truth, justice, respect, freedom, honesty, loves for one another and hard work. There is the need to change, which embodies the desire to want to change others and progressively move forward with the changes of the day.

To transform the continent, which should pay attention by serious questioning and accepting its past mistakes backed by a determined constructive will for comprehensive and constructive change? A change that must generate essentially from inside and not from outside or is imposed and directed by external forces. In this regard, there is no room for a Eurocentric approach or solution to the plight of the people. There has to be some form of mental decolonisation to better harness ourselves and to gun for interior transforming their human revolutions for quality well-being. Delinking from the world to relinking to the world. Africans must care for themselves and from their sufferings; to propose the logic of the power of their cultural heritage; the use of their natural resources by the care of the heart and love for each other which is that of the social logic. As pointed out many times, the hope of the continent lies with the youths as the means of reflections and exchanges; by the acknowledgement put at their disposal which will support, stimulate and energise with wisdom and the intelligence to grow.

African governments must be committed to locally, nationally, continentally and internationally to the promotion of sustainable development. Progress in this regard is constrained by the lack of popular participation and shared prosperity. We leave in an interconnected but create discriminative barriers and racists policies destroying the humankind. There is a need to unmask racist World Bank and the developed countries hold to exploitative capitalism without a human face that strong aggregates' the poverty and corruption worldwide creating endless economic stagnation and stipulations circling the globe. The scale and speed of the emerging destructive challenges manifest not only in the state of growing poverty of the continent, constitute irrefutable evidence that the root cause of the problem of the continent lies in the socioeconomic and political system, and particularly in the capitalist scale of capitalist accumulation and in the politics of 'greed' self-articulate interests. Africa is more vulnerable to external exploitation than fifty years ago. Modern science and technology gadgets accelerate its vulnerability. There are no measures put in place to countervail the vulnerability of the continent. Leadership style and attitude of the people accelerates the exploitation and vulnerability of the continent within the international community

Faced with these intractable problems, the response of the dominant interest has always been the capitalist or top-down solution by decoding the people as genuine participants and beneficiaries in the process of development. We fail to realise the importance of all working together in an effective and efficient way of balancing development with quality wellbeing for all. If we look at the abolition of slavery, or the end of colonial rule, it is clear that both formally speaking, were brought to an end. But any serious examination of the last 50 years since independence has been achieved in Africa; it is clear that colonisation by other means has been successfully maintained and reinforced with the connivance of Africa governments. The crimes against humanity committed during slavery and during colonial rule were never brought to a tribunal of any kind. The crimes were committed with impunity. And impunity of the most powerful, not just in Africa, but the world over, has become a way of life almost taken for granted. The mindset that has grown from the impunity that has accompanied so many humanities, has kept humanity on the course of self-annihilation.

As a result, other mantras have grown aimed at forgetting history, forgetting humanity and anything connected to keep them - the commons of history, humanity - alive and well. The tragedy unfolding in front of our eyes is not just about the excesses of one financial environment disaster. It is about the continued and deliberate fraction that, for centuries and generation has always gotten away literally with murder. The enemies of Africa realise with a certain fear and trembling that an afro-centric agenda deeply planted in the minds and hearts of the people will greatly offset the balance of power and the colonialist empire will come tumbling down like a big-bang especially in French Africa will become a transformed and renovated community. The great success of the enemies of Africa is to have compromised the Africans themselves. We see this in the ongoing crisis in Cameroon, where French conspiracy succeeds in dividing the two Anglophone regions of

Southern Cameroons. They have succeeded in using Southern Cameroons elites in the destruction of the region. The French have a precise plan of destabilisation and these governing elites are directly interested in the murder of Southern Cameroons.

What struck me the most about the papers pierced here is the unwillingness of leaders who shouted at the top of their voices against colonial rule and are today doing things far more badly than the departed colonial masters did? Much as we try to dissect the Black Code, it is just a reminder that the mindset at work today assumed the plight of the people, was born during historical processes that current rulers do not like to refer to, at the risk having to own up to a history of devastation of humanity whose responsibility was not nature but irresponsible cruelty, call it genocide against the people. Today, these leaders prefer to fudge the historical record, however, where it becomes alarming is when highly respected intellectuals from many different parts of the world seem to have accepted the framings and formatting of history according to those who have become too powerful and too rich to be questioned. The most distressing face of all is the apparent complete and total absence of African voices articling how the current mindset was set in motion. These voices should not just come from Africa, they should be coming from any corner of the planet that has endured what the African continent and indigenous people the world over have endured for centuries, to this day (Depelchin 2011)

The challenge, of course, is what next for Africa? Getting rid of the dark clouds hanging over the continent, the question mark-shaped continent begins here and now with a new determined soul-searching mindset of correcting past mistakes; revitalising its civil society organisations in the direction of creativeness, ensuring that leaders become visionary and servant oriented towards serving the masses not themselves and above all how African governments can best governed? It remains an uphill task that does not exclude anyone. We are all enmeshed in a boat far into the sea with the compass map of either sailing to the shore or sinking. It has to be the great escape to development. For now, the continent is confronted with a series of options on inadequate ambition on mitigation. The solution here is developing a new shared-vision. Under shared-vision, plunges Africa to continuous exploitation and will never overcome the entrenched hurdles – therefore, the clarion call is - Africa Must Unite - which Nkrumah sounded some fifty-five years ago. Current loopholes must be sealed from a constructed, comprehensive and consensus manner and in the ultimate interest of the people. Anything short of that vision is null and void. Shall Africa focus on the real problems and get back to serious and committed work?

It is Africa and development challenges and changes - spin, facts and real constructive politic. Africa has to be serious about developmental challenges and changes - how to roll back exploitation, marginalisation and underdevelopment, poverty, corruption, initial, injustice and embrace the virtues of justice, rule of law, ethical, democratic governance, ethical and moral values, equality, inclusive sustainable development for the common well-being of the people and not a select few. We cannot claim to have offered a solution that is elegant, and we are not generally pleased with the fact that we are not able to reach the wishes and desires of all the people. But what we are happy with is that the publication should stimulate critical discourses on issues raised and those that have not been touched upon. Most importantly, it should be a discourse involving all cross-sections of society and sharing our thoughts with others no matter what our different views are to create the baseline for consensus and to better move forward in common agreement for the well-being of all. I must admit, though, it is a slippery slope, that with the involvement of all, things can change for the better; a new political will is imperative to sail through the difficulties and challenges faced. Africa has no choice but to radically and constructively change in the direction of sustainable transformation for the common well-being of all. The Tony Blair Commission (2005) reminds of one important issue: "The end of apartheid reminds Africa, and the world, that no injustice can last forever. More darkly, the evens in New York and Washington on September 11th 2001 have caused many in the rich world to reflect on the relationship between global poverty and homeland security. What happens to the poorest citizen in the poorest country can directly affect the richest citizen in the richest country? 'If a free society cannot help the many, who are poor,' as the US President John F. Kennedy once said. 'It cannot save the few who are rich.' Take all that together and this document becomes a declaration of our common interest." Adding his voice, George W. Bush said: "Persistent poverty and oppression can lead to hopelessness and despair. And when governments fail to meet the most basic needs of their people, these failed states can become havens for terror… in many states around the world, poverty prevents governments from controlling their borders, policing their territory, and enforcing their laws. Development provides the resources to build hope, prosperity and security."

In this specifically superficially rationalised continent and world at large, in which all the bits and bytes and flashing lights have blinded us, to the power of the sacred in the midst of the social, it is more important than ever before to know this. The publication can be seen as whistleblower like others before it; is a sacred act to state the least, clothed in the sense of rationality and geared towards the well-being and common good of all citizens. We should be blessed with the feeling of creating new knowledge under the canopy of a committed seriousness this newly acquired knowledge brings to the advancement of the continent. Let us try to listen to one another, with the seriousness this new knowledge in this publication deserves. The publication challenges us all to the African society from a new perspective and in the basic values of each one being the 'keeper of the other,' not just its power centres, but the communality of the commonness and oneness of everybody in society, then it is easier to see that challenging forces as geared towards a common solution of which we must all subscribed to. For each state, or individual, there is a kind of chaos to overcome by a new order and mindset; the physical world may be overcome by the human. Feast replaces famine, abundance poverty, light darkness, and, of course, good triumphs over evil. Each disjunctive occasion then, represents overcoming and transcendence, that is, from a lower to a higher condition, from a worse to a better status. Here the state must blend with civil society and the private sector to locate, identify, particularise, and prioritise the continent's development efforts. Africa must overcome what Patrick Chabal (2016) describes as the Politics of Suffering and Smiling. The people must embrace the politics of being, working hard and enjoying the fruits of their labour and resources. "The Commission for Africa finds the conditions of the lives of the majority of Africans to be intolerable and an affront to the dignity of all mankind. We insist upon an alteration of these conditions through a change of policy in favour of the weak" (Blair, 2005). Prof. Olukoshi Adebayo (2006:45-50) lambast the Commission for Africa Report in the following cross-cutting edge observations;

- Why was it deemed imperative to create the Commission in the first place at a time when African governments had adopted NEPAD and were seeking to unite themselves behind it?
- Was it a deliberate decision so conspicuously to exclude the Africa Union which, politically, is by far the most credible organ of the collective will of the African people and which, on all the issues covered by the Commission, has had a clear point of view developed?

- Is it really possible to change the fortunes of Africa from externally-driven initiatives such as those represented by the Commission?
- Of what use is the plea for an increase in aid flows to Africa if no commensurate effort is made fundamentally to reform the aid system itself?
- Would not a lot be gained by increasing not just African access to Western markets but equally importantly, also improving the terms of trade for African agricultural exports?
- In all matters pertaining to the development of Africa within an environment of peace, security, and stability, has not the time come to stop chasing shadows (such as those associated with the omnibus notion of 'conflict resources', corruption, and resources' flows) and re-focus attention on fundamental issues that speak to the structural roots of the problems addressed by the Commission, issues such as the whole scale re-invention of the state beyond the watch-dog role that is too frequently attributed to it, the thorny issue of citizenship and the urgent need for a workable macro-economic and macro-social policy environment that will promote domestic accumulation?
- The recognition by the Commission of the central place of higher education in the development prospects of all countries represented a welcome re-statement of a position that was obvious to all except the World Bank which strove in the 1980s and part of the 1990s both to undermine African higher education and shift attention to primary and vocational education, dragging many donors along.

We can in this connection question whether the Blair Commission was another strategic plan to catapult NEPAD like was done in derailing the Lagos Plan of Action with SAP and other measures articulated by the World Bank? Can we find solace in the views of Prof. Adebayo Adedeji (1999-41) "what African countries lacked during most of their history as independent states are leaders who are unifiers, chiefs in the true sense, who bind wounds, hold everything and everyone together, mobilise and motivate their people, pursue a policy of inclusion rather than exclusion and are seen by one and all to be of the highest integrity and beyond suspicion". According to Mustapha Raufu Abdul (2006:3-9), "At play here, of course, are the interactions between power and knowledge; between the desire to shape Africa's future along particular paths and the deployment of explanations of her past and present. Of equal importance is the fact the 'African crisis' which heralded these shifts has continued if not intensified despite decades of intense socioeconomic engineering. The continuing problems of African societies can partly be traced to the intellectual crises concerning our understanding of the nexus between these three dominant conceptual pillars in contemporary Africa.

Unlocking Africa's Contaminated Political and Economic Heart!

Unlocking Africa's fewer volatile sources of growth to spur human development will require greater investment in human capital – such as in health, education and skills –, stronger capacities to diversify financing and more effective efforts to promote structural transformation. Despite a decade of progress, 54% of the populations in 46 African countries are still living in poverty. It is essential to double efforts to empower Africans with the necessary skills to promote development from the bottom up, driven by domestic innovation and investment. This is why the *African Economic Outlook* focuses this year on the role of entrepreneurs in Africa's industrialisation. We need to help African countries address the challenges of low human development and social exclusion, and this is what we are doing. Industrialisation is one of the High 5 priority areas of the African Development Bank. It is also in line with the African Union's proclamation of industrialisation as the main strategy to promote inclusive economic transformation, and it is the ninth Sustainable Development Goal. In addition, in July 2016, the United Nations General Assembly proclaimed 2016-25 as the Third Industrial Development Decade for Africa; and under China's leadership, the G20 also agreed in September 2016 to support Africa's industrialisation as part of its Action Plan on the 2030 Agenda for Sustainable Development. To bolster this momentum, this year's *African Economic Outlook* proposes several concrete steps for action. Africa's industrialisation will differ from the experience of other world regions. First, the 54 African countries are diverse and will thus follow various pathways to industrialisation. Second, industrialisation will not rely solely on the manufacturing sector, which remains modest at 11% of the continent's GDP. Twenty-first century industrial policies can target additional sectors with high-growth potential, such as agroprocessing and services with higher value added. Third, policies must promote "green

Industrialisation," as technological and market changes have made it possible to achieve industrialisation with lower environmental costs. Greater efforts should also be made in ha direction.

So far, Africa remains a continent in crisis; and the 'Dark Clouds' will continue hanging over it for an unforeseeable future until the people wake up from slumber land, prepared to consciously, comprehensively and concerted take-up the battle against its chequered predicaments. Only a new mindset, consensus and cordially inter-relationship will facilitate its transformation nexus. Such a linkage or inter-relationship between the interior with the coastal, the rich and poor will a new Africa be discovered and sustained; it will give the new kind fertility and riches in improving the welfare of the people. It will put an end or take Africa from the ghetto of poverty, marginalisation and exploitation. That is why we need a successfully implemented grand Afro-centric design agenda under the canopy of a consolidated policy concepts to change the face and image of the continent for the better. The need for an African Internal and External New Order (AIENO) can no longer be emphasused; it is urgent and imperative (Forje, 2019:277). According to the Maurice Blondel, "The Future cannot be forecasted, it is prepared" and only Africa can prepare its future which was hijacked by imperialism and colonialism, and held in perpetual check by the forces of neo-colonialism and globalisation – the new form of scientific imperialism. The time is ripe for Africa to start looking into its crystal ball, put an end to the going top-bottom development approach; develop and consolidate a new progressive mindset, and by consolidating a bottom-up development approach under the inherent canopy of Afro-centric agenda. Time to bid fare-voyage to the entrenched Euro-centric agenda. The greatest pride a country/continent has is its sovereignty, independence, freedom, security and social cohesion under the umbrella of democratic governance. Sad enough, Africans are suffering from the lack of this golden and great treasure, but they worship and love everything foreign; conversely, the hate anything local, home grown or manufactured, which helps in destroying their potential, creativity, capacity and ability to progress as it equally entrenches and deepens their dependency, exploitation and marginalisation. We waste our time hanging on the blame theory instead of concentrating on the 'reality theory' in order to critically understand, evaluate the situation in order to move forward.

In short, our problem is that of dispossessing ourselves and the glorification of external values which have plunge and continue derailing us into a state perpetual poverty, exploitation and dependency.

Can we develop a new mentality and mindset for a transformation that leaves no one behind but propels Africa into the kind of future we prepare for!? We need to unleash people's power for constructive development. Following Mawere (2018), Forje (2020; xxxi), one of the fundamental challenges in rethinking and remaking development in Africa from an Afro-centric perspective is that too much 'more talk' and 'blame game' have played and continue to play out in our psychic at the expense of 'real and genuine actions'. The 'blame game and more talk continue playing at Africa's poverty, marginalisation, exploitation, exclusion and marginalization underdevelopment jam which remain printed in bold on the face of the continent, yet Africa's dire situation warrants nothing less than real and concrete emphatic action. This should be the priority and focus of the continent. In the final analysis, we have to prepare ourselves in facing all sides; 'top-bottom, bottom-up' approach; 'developed and developing world 'nexus; 'rich and poor'; 'strong and weak'; 'open and closed structure-functional governance system'; 'Eurocentric and Afrocentric' all which put us at the centre of crisis of 'discontinuity and continuity' which we ae living through at the moment. We are suffering from our greed, failure to reach-out and share equitably for the benefit of the common good. We should restore the concept of 'Batho pele, ubuntu, interdependency' its real meaning of cooperation, participation, partnership in conditions of real equality. It requires a North-South and an inter-African dialogue to avoid us sinking into helpless despair.

The apocalypse is not for tomorrow, provided we know how to manage nature's patrimony rationally and we put a stop to its destruction. Rephrased differently, provide our intentions are with the visible hand of planning in good faith, trust and confidence rather than relying on the invisible hands of destruction and greed so dear to us and which execute with all zeal. Let us turn to the Afro-centric developmental approach and help establish an African nexus communication network establishing a cordial relation between the various social actors involved in the battle against underdevelopment, poverty, injustice, inequality and marginalisation. We must learn more of what is happening at the grassroots level. The pessimism presenting the African situation in a uniform negative light is not acceptable. We have to construct by building a profoundly positive aspect and image of the continent through an Afro-centric orientation, action plan and create a positive silent revolution to force a serious reverse of the Euro-centric attitude that is consuming Africa. Strictly speaking, we have to advocate and invent our own development model in tandem with the prevailing situation and funded on the mastery of the time past, and time present with great attention paid to nature and building a strong capacity for human development as well as taking advantage of scientific and technological advancement places at our door steps.

Our first contribution in this journey of a long walk to freedom would why we are poor in the midst of plenty and to try situation out original solutions founded on the criteria of justice, truth and social interest in our respective countries and in the overall interest of the continent. Vladimir Popov, and Piotr Dutkiewicz (2017) challenges us to Mapping a New World Order that provide appropriate conceptual and policy responses for a rapidly changing world situation. Africa needs a new general theory of economic and political development, whereas Jwa Sung-Hee (2017) points out; 'treating difference differently by selecting and supporting economic entities and behaviour that contribute positively to the economy" and the well-being of the people. We end with a strong appeal to the people, to mobilise forces for a common goal; the battle to end poverty, underdevelopment, injustice, inequality, discrimination; to fight and sustain our sovereignty and dignity as human-beings, promoting quality livelihood for all. We cannot and will never claim to have addressed the problems of the continent.

As we move along, other challenging issues will surface requiring solutions. What are essential are laying the solid foundation and having the right tools, positive critical mindset, capacity and capability in tackling these challenges as they surface. It is important to note seriously that the principles of development, like globalisation, are no guide to the viability of their development because too many questions of value ad politics are involved. African countries should not accept developmental theories uncritically, for much of these theories are designed to benefit their interests. Here we see the need and value for an Afro-centric agenda as being instructive and beneficial to the people and country. Co-operating and working together offers potentially powerful means to provide the sort of joint creativity, action-plans and capacity-pooling needed to advance and apply knowledge to the problems we encounter. We are obliged in our endeavour to achieve the following goals which is not exhaustive:

- substantial growth in income and productivity and employment;
- capability of managing political, social, economic and environmental issues;
- attending to the needs of the millions of poor and destitute in society;

- eliminating and curbing poverty, inertia and deprivation;
- building the human capacity and intellect of the people;
- creation of employment opportunities and making proper use of available resources and traditional skills;
- direct exchange of information and transfer of infrastructural technologies, development of indigenous knowledge
- bringing the female gender to the plus side of the development continuum;
- building infrastructures and strong institutions; not strong individuals;
- promoting partnership, cooperation, participation and sharing spirit among and within the people;
- international support and co-operation for ongoing efforts being made by African countries
- avoid building a destructive climate of hatred, destructive competition, but create an optimal level of interaction;
- broadening the concept of development and ensuring participation and equity in benefit-sharing
- instil hope, trust, confidence in the people;
- provide lasting and secure livelihood that minimise resources depletion, environmental degradation, cultural disruption and social instability;
- instil the idea of cultural and ethnic diversity as asset and not liability to the transformation of society;
- ensuring the accountability, transparency, responsibility of government to the society;
- avoid building social stresses in the society; etc.

Are we prepared to have a new mindset based on the common good - the *'ubuntu, harambee, batho pele and the nhimbe spirits'* to move the continent forward? Moving forward requires commitments, obligations and responsibilities from all sides. Indeed, obligation works only when myth and theory reinforce each other and together offer explanations of what is in order to demonstrate what ought to be. This is not to suggest some easy functional connections or automatic relationships between a political economy of needs and a set of mythological 'interests.' African states must consolidate their efforts during this disjunctive era of development, i.e., how civil society, and how the polis (the state) was founded, how it was transformed, and how it is redeemed (from the faults and lapses of its members). Africa can change, and must change, for the better. To recapitulate, the continents transformation as the term is being used today is a function of innovation, but innovation can lead to substantial transformation of the region. Creativity and critical thinking are most needed. Africa needs a holistic and inclusive transformation process initiated and implemented by the people for the good of the people and humanity. This book in its simplest way sets out the arguments and recommendations for a strong, prosperous and united Africa.

It exposes the political economic and psychological degradation of imperialism, colonialism, neo-colonialism and points the way forward for a better Africa of tomorrow. Our people are waiting for something new other than the continuation of the Euro-centric agenda which would be almost an obscene caricature. We are not gunning through this publication to turn Africa into Europe. The goal is to advance Africa a step farther, and to bring it up to a different level than that which the developed polities have shown it; we must invent, be creative, innovative, and entrepreneurial and be proactive; and to live up to our people's expectations, we are obliged to work and seek the response from within us. We are all challenged to turn over a new leaf, be ourselves, and work out new concepts and strategies and setting afoot a new Africa of our choice, not one imposed from Europe. Yes, we can do that; we have to begin now. Come brothers and sisters, there is much work to be done; to do for us and to play and replay the game for real change; for our wellbeing and that of future generations. Interpolating the iconic views of Fanon (1970:183) "Africa shall be free. Yes, but it must get to work; it must not lose sight of its own unity. It is in this one of the most important among a number of points at the First Congress of African Peoples in Africa in 1958 was adopted, that of creating a militia which will have the duty to support the African peoples fighting for their independence." Questions of 'slavery, colonialism, neocolonialism, poverty etc.' are quite understandably capable of evoking a heated, emphatic, and vigorous show of strength against what is identified as the colonialist policy or action.

The African Union (AU) is not different from the UN, as sharp cleavages develop between the strong advocates of the Euro-centric agenda and those calling for a strong afro-centric approach to seeking African solutions to African problems. The common silver lining among African countries is that of 'self-determination', a common sense of national consciousness stirs them towards a common good, but divided on how self-determination should take shape. The old dividing line between the 'Casablanca, Monrovia, and the Brazzaville groups still exist impeding a common consensual ground for African countries to act in unionism in seeking solutions to their predicaments. Without such common unity and purpose of direction, Africa cannot make significant progress towards national unity and development. Though African countries to a certain extent agree and demonstrate their commitment to the anticolonial cause very vigorous opposition to any effort on the part of Europeans blocking further independence movement, they are unable to agree about political union among themselves. The next decade remains a special crucial period for African countries in determining whether the continent is to be spared more violence, evoke more economic growth and work consciously, purposefully and energetically toward unity.

Africa is now faced with a self-evolving situation and governance system, which it has to do everything possible stop. "There are dangers and advantages in this situation. It is obvious that the gain in material power affords opportunity for social betterment. But material power in itself is ethically neutral. It can equally well work in the wrong direction. The problem is not how to produce great men, but how to produce great societies. The great society will put up the men for the occasions…There is another picture of the possibilities of decadence. At the present moment a discussion is raging as the future of civilisation in the novel circumstance of rapid scientific and technological advance. The evils of ...have been diagnosed in various ways, the loss of… the malignant use of material power, the degradation attending a differential rate favouring the lower types of humanity, the suppression of aesthetic creativeness. Without doubt, these are all evils, dangerous and threatening" opines Whitehead Alfred (1985:255). If only Africa can rise to the occasion, there lies in front a golden age of beneficent creativeness. We are challenged to take action towards positive change for the golden age of the continent that lies ahead.

There is a new Africa to come. "Africans must remember that there is no an objective optimism that is more or less mechanically inevitable, but that optimism must be the sentiment that accompanies the revolutionary commitment and the combat. Under these conditions, yes we can be optimistic" (Fanon; 1970.183). We have to support ourselves resolutely. For no one knows the name of next Nkrumah, Lumumba, Azikiwe, Sankara, Moumie, Biko, Nyerere, Mandela, Nasser, Sekou Toure, Achebe, Fanon, Soyinka, Mazrui, and hundreds of thousands of others. There can be no better way of ending this book than with the views expressed by Fanon; "There is in Africa a certain tendency represented by certain men. It is this tendency, dangerous but good for imperialism, which is t issue. Let us be sure never to forget it;

the fate of all of us is at stake in Africa." We can also question whether the agitation for independence only sowed the seeds of destruction as African leaders spearheading the struggle for self-rule, Kwame Nkrumah, Lumumba, Steve Biko, Sekou Toure, Thomas Sankara, Felix Moumie, Amilcar Cabral etc., were objects for assassination and the colonialists, neo-colonialist and cohorts succeeded

In the final analysis, we have to prepare ourselves in acing all sides: "top-bottom, "bottom-top" approach; "developing and developed world nexus"; "rich and poor"; "strong and weak"; "open and closed" transformation; "Euro-centric and Afro-centric" approaches all of which put us at the crisis of discontinuity and continuity which we are living through at the moment. We ae suffering from our greed and failure to reach out and share equitably for the common good. We should restore as well as practice the concepts of inter-dependency, Batho Pele, ubuntu etc. and of the real meaning of cooperation, participation, partnership in conditions of genuine equality and justice. It requires a North-South dialogue to avoid us sinking into a helpless despair of no return. The apocalypse is no for tomorrow, provided we know how to manage nature's patrimony rationally and we put a stop to its destruction. In other words; provided our intentions are with the visible hands of good planning in good faith, justice, trust and confidence rather than relying on the invisible hands of destruction, greed, inequality and injustice currently so implanted and dear to us. Let us turn to the Afro-centric developmental approach and help establish an African nexus communication network; establishing a cordial and functional relation between the various social actors involved in the battle against underdevelopment, injustice, inequality, marginalisation, discrimination and exclusion. It is time for us all to learn more of what is actually happening at the grass-roots level, to live their experiences, sha ether pains as well as happy moments.

The pessimism of presenting the African situation in a uniform negative light is not acceptable. We have to rebuild ha image by constructing a profoundly positive aspect of the continent through a progressive Afro-centric orientation as well as creating a positive silent revolution that forces us to seriously reverse the Euro-centric attitude that has consumed Africa. Our fears of the Africa we want deepened because for over fifty years, our independence has been a bumpy ride. Our leaders seemed unconcerned. We have by this attitude of our leaders taken every pitch of the journey to freedom as the beginning of the end. Finally, we have landed on the runway unable to take-off to the next destination the destination of quality livelihood and services delivery to the people. We are today struck as much by darkness, endemic corruption, miseries and poverty as by the heat of the dangerous acts of the colonial powers. Africa has never seen a dark period of its history as black as this. James Weldon Johnson in a poem called "The Creation," tells it all;

"...far as the eye of God could see
Darkness covered everything,
Blacker than a hundred midnights
Down in a cypress swamp."

The hopes of poverty-stricken people in Africa have been dashed by the African Klux-Klu-Klan or governing elites ready to slaughter their fellow citizens as they are doing in Southern Cameroons to preserve what is best known as a failed government. And so, the journey to the 'promised land' is strategically and tactically but constantly derailed and destroyed. The majority of the people is ignorant or fails to see the delaying tactics being employed the ruling elites who are agents of imperial powers cloth in wolf attire to deceive the people. This is Africa's song but a dilemma. With such events ongoing, we all have to be angry and mad. It was Martin Luther King who pointed out that anger was a necessary ingredient for change. There is no way we cannot subscribe completely to that. The African people are very angry with what is afflicting them. We have to understand our anger and make true value of it. With our true cause, we can redirect it and to make it productive and rewarding to the people. We have to believe and be aware that we live a world over-run by cruelty and destruction, Africa disintegrates and her spirits numb, the people lose moral and ethical purpose and creative vision. Just imagine that the data of most African countries (passports, identity cards, etc., etc.,) are with the foreign companies that the government contracts for the production of such documents. How independent are African countries when our raw statistical data are in the keepings of the powers behind SIC?

The True and Genuine Africa Lies Ahead

This is what the architect of the continent's independence intended the independence of the continent to be. The truth and reality are that the best of Africa lie ahead and that in the final analysis along the way, Africa shall triumph and we shall be comforted by one another in the true African spirit of Batho Pele, Ubuntu, and Harambee etc. This is Africa's song, desire and wish! We should all look up for a positive and progressive dawn for Africa. It will come, may be, not in our live time. There is going to be a new dawn for Africa of tomorrow. It is a transformation that no earthly power can stop. The sixties had taken a toll on the freedom fights for the independence of the continent leaving the African struggle for sovereignty naked and weakened but not out for the fight had to be continued. There was need for a balancing act to keep the struggle alive and floating for future counter-attack. A new song of defiance was puffing up on the continent – the Arab Spring for example; geared towards the independence and freedom of the continent. In Southern Cameroons, after sixty years of the unification of the two United Nations Trust-territories under the British and French Administration, the unholy marriage can no longer hold with all indications of the two parts going their separate ways. The centre can no longer hold; with smaller part – Southern Cameroons - seeking for its own identification, justice, equity, respect, sovereignty and identification that an end to a marriage that the world body forced the people into such a marriage could no longer. Here, the traditional medical doctors are needed to restore the marriage to the desires and abilities of living together and eating together. With all the calamities besieging the continent, we can ask ourselves, whether there is any hope for Africa; will the dark clouds clear? What kind of tsunami would be needed to do a clean job? As we have heard, and seen the dark clouds, so much we hope for the dark clouds to fade away for us to see the blue sky over the continent once again.

Africa is what she is and will always be what she was made to be. It has to be true to itself in spite of foreign mechanisation of what the continent is and has to offer to the world and humanity. Africa got independence, ended the horrors of the apartheid governance system in South Africa in the nineties. But Africa has not been closing behind in meeting the needs of the newly independent African nations, tipping between hope and despair. The mid-fifties saw the independence of Ghana, and the sixties saw the plethora of African states becoming independent but unable to move and make a significant shift in the balance of power in African and global politics. While the decades of the fifties and sixties saw the rapid transformation of from a colonized to a decolonized (so to speak), the countries have failed to speak with one consorted voice. That weakness saw the demise of the Congo and the destruction of Africa. In spite of the efforts of progressive leaders like Kwame Nkrumah, Lumumba, Sekou Toure and others, Congo fell apart, showing the substantial distances separating them leading to what can be called the Balkanisation of the continent. Indeed, this could be

seen as another neocolonial device to perpetuate the substance of colonial rule through the manipulation of small, unviable states. Making the United Nations to be inevitably dominated by a passionate anticolonialism, by a demand for social and economic development, and by a neutralism whose manifestations may often seem capricious. The Congo crisis exhibited the true colours of the United Nations. In short, the emergence of the African peoples to independence tested the strengths and weaknesses of the new international order as thy have never been tested before. The outcome of the test remains crucial, and issues raised incalculably important – not only for the hope of peace and security on the African continent, but also for the future of world order. Africa is a litmus test for the world, and as the dynamics of international politics. The Southern Cameroons predicament evolved during the pandemic of the Congo conflict. Like the unresolved Congo Crisis, the Southern Cameroons struggle for self-determination is taking the same direction. It points in the direction that Africa has not learned from historical evolution and unable to seek Africa solutions to African problem.

Therefore, any discussion of Africa's place in the world order would be unthinkable without including the Africans' own concept of it. Fearing this, the African voice was destroyed with the Congo crisis that left Africa naked. Today, where amid the many voices of Africa, is there one that has captured the span of the African political mind as to be able to reflect it in full? One thing remains candid – the emergence of Africa from colonial rule and bondage has had and continues to have both a stimulating and disruptive effect upon the new world order. No doubt, great new spheres of activity have been opened to it, but there is yet no clear indication or evidence that the U.N. itself and the specialized institutions or agencies with it are capable of responding successfully to the overwhelming challenges being put before them. The Congo crisis exposed its weakness or hidden agenda in addressing the problems of the continent. Padelford and Emerson writing in 1962 noted that: "Nowhere have the potentialities and pitfalls of the new order of things been more starkly disclosed than in the Congo, which, while it certainly cannot be taken as typical of all of Africa, represents some features of Africa in an exaggerated form – indeed, as a shocking caricature of African hopes and fears."

The ongoing crisis in Cameroon caused by the UN in 1961, speaks volumes of the failed attitude of the UN system as it concerns political developments on the continent. We still await the coming of the shift of balance of power that will usher the true and genuine independence of the Africa continent. The shift of balance of power must be initiated and executed by the people or else there is no shift of balance of power. Is Africa domed to perpetual slavery, colonization and destruction? Only time will tell! And remember that democracy is neither East nor west; neither north nor South; it is an evolution of human experience in struggle. Democracy is about freedom, but not unconditional freedom. It recognizes the necessity to safe guard the peace and security of the nation and the state; to safeguard public order, the rights of the citizens and public morals; but such restrictions being allowed only within limits, to the flowering of individual initiative and freedom is not thereby restricted. The architect of present day for the struggle for freedom and sovereignty did not sacrificed their lives and did not seek to replace colonialism with political and economic irresponsibility, moral decay, inequality, and injustice as spiritual blackout. Will Africa be free or destroyed with time?

There is the blue sky beaconing the people to move forward. Are the people ready to see, exploit and enjoy 'the blue sky' or let again they sky disappear into a much thicker darker cloud? Banseka Cage (2006:35) holds the view that: "In Africa inefficiency and exploitation are less dramatic phenomena that state violence, but they are the most recurrent. The extractive role of the state and the degree to which it extorts revenues from the common man in order to provide benefits to a privileged group of government employees or loyalists and clients is very much more evident than its efforts to achieve a better life for all. Unlike in the industrial capitalist states where one of the functions of the government is to divert resources from producers to consumers, and from those with more to those with less. Africa governments more often than not make the transfer in the opposite direction. Resources are transferred from those with little political influence on those with more political influence. In this way Africa leadership makes itself distinctive from others through the self-perpetuating nature of groups of beneficiaries." For now, it is *"Cry thy Beloved Continent,"* when will the continent be free? In the lamenting words of Ndeh Ntumazah (2001), the freedom fighters like Nkrumah, Amiclar Cabral, Sekoue, Toure, Nasser, Fanon, Mouime, and many others: *"Nkrumah did not have time to plant the tree of freedom, which would have borne new flowers', adding, these freedom fighters "were good men in a world where few had the strength to resist the corroding influence of power, wealth and vanity at the expense of the weak and helpless."*

It is within Africa's competence to banish hunger, misery, poverty, ignorance, disease, insecurity and autocracy. Africa's inhabitants everywhere long for the day when these scourges will be banished forever from their midst. Do their leaders have the will, vision, courage and commitment to lead them across today's wasteland to the green pastures that lie on the other side? With the picture painted, we are bound to ask whether Africa be transformed into a land of integrity, rather than moral deprivation; of hope, rather than despair; of tranquillity, rather than turmoil; of abundance and social justice, rather than abject poverty and injustice; a continent where an individual's talents can fully develop and be fully utilized (Were, 1981:22-24). We cannot banish abject poverty, exploitation, marginalization and underdevelopment by trading on the path of a Euro-centric agenda, and developing the endless going around 'begging attitude' instead of articulating and implementing a progressive Afro-centric and self-reliant agenda. We continue championing the sad sides of the Euro-centric agenda on Africa with this lengthy quote from Jacques Chirac's address to President Thabo Mbeki in Senegal on the 02/10/2005 telling us how we learn nothing from past historical incidents as reported by (Nfamewih Aseh, 2006:248-250).

"I have the power to decide where and when I want war to break out and with the helping hand of the West African psychology, the war will happen. If I am bored, I call them for a Francofolie meeting. (I am sure you are familiar with the word. Francofolie is a monitoring tool to ensure that the prescribed West African psychology is working and if anybody needs resetting, we reset them) they will all be there. I have the power to manipulate them, they gave that power to me because I remember when I was a cab driver in New York many of these Africans were presidents, barristers, ministers you name it. I used to lick their boots but you can see that they have not grown up at all; they have not matured at all. My dear Mbeki, I can see that you have a good intention for your African brother, BUT they will not listen to you because you are not a WHITE MAN. What you could possibly do is to hand your mission over to a white tramp, dress him up and it would do the business. They will listen to him because he is a white man; otherwise, you are wasting your time. You are not a white man, your mission is a failure, and your own African brothers in blood will never listen to you because you are not a white man. It is sad but it is also the sad truth. That's why I said that before you get involved you must know and understand the West African psychology. To better understand my thesis on African Psychology, let's together go through some historic facts. As you well know, Africa has been through the worst atrocities the world has ever known and especially this part of Africa, which has suffered and is still suffering. Africans have been chased, poached, caught and tied like animals and piled up like sardines and shipped across the world for sale. That period was the period of slavery of which Senegal is bearing the fresh scars. What lessons have Africans learned from it? NONE. Then we invented the invasion called (colonization) during which Africans suffered worse. Africans were forced to work for us; they went through the same atrocities and humiliations. What lesson have Africans learned from it? NONE. During the two European wars (World War 1&11), the poor Africans under some derogatory names of Senegalese fusiliers (of which Senegal is still bearing the scars) were used as sniffer dogs in the snow to free our trapped and dispirited parents from the Nazis. Many Africans lost their lives under the French flag. When we celebrate the liberation of Europe who mentions them? NOBODY. These Africans dared to ask us to compensate them, we French told them to get lost. What lessons have Africans learned from it? NONE. They wanted their independence; we gave them their independence with small prints tagged at the bottom and on the conditions that they stay our slaves. What lesson have Africans learned from it? NONE. All Africans have witnessed and still remembers how Giscard Desting and his government treated Jean Bedel Bokassa from the Republic of Central Africa was proclaimed emperor, he was humiliated, after all the riches from the country were transferred to France, he was then deposed by the same French government. What lesson have Africans learned from it? NONE. Then came the genocide of Rwanda when millions and millions of Africans fought against each other for no apparent reasons. Millions and millions of Africans lost their lives. All these African leaders including the UN SG know very well the role France played in this genocide. But what lessons have African learned from it. NONE. Then there have been the following cases; Congo Brazzaville (the president was democratically elected and deposed by France), the Republic of Central Africa (the president was democratically elected and deposed by France), Democratic Republic of Congo, Chad. I could give you example until year 20yx. But what lessons have Africans learned from these unfortunate events? NONE…. You kill one European we will kill millions of yours. What do Africans believe in? NOTHING. The West African is an F***** slave to the white man, my dear Mbeki, you are wasting your time. Your own brothers in flesh and blood will not listen to you for you are not a white man and you have not come to destroy. AFRICANS ARE NOT TAKING ANY HINT AT ALL." What is, and has been the reaction of African leaders to this statement? Their hands are tight. They know what they have been doing and would continue doing. Foreign leaders continue creating some kind of barriers between the citizens of a country and their leaders to ensure that the white supremacy status-quo is upheld for entirety. I strong believe that it is only a well-articulated progressive Afro-centric manifesto backed with a well structure mind-set that the current table can be overturn to the benefit of the people. We are all in our different corners challenged to do just that. With Euro-centric agenda, we internalize colonialism (i.e., a structure of social relations based on domination and exploitation among culturally heterogenous, distinct groups, Casanova (1965) or as pointed out by Berghe (1978) of "internal colonialism that involves the rule of one ethnic group over other ethnic groups combined with territorial separation of the subordinate groups…" and, hence, fail in our development nexus.

Ange Bergson Lendja Ngnemzue (2008:62) adds further dimensions to the views of French perception of the Africa, following a speech President Sarkozy delivered in Dakar on 26 July 2007. "…this time, the faith in a Franco-French government ideology, both complex and unscrupulous in regard to French colonial policy, is accompanied by an attempt to theoretically justify African underdevelopment." The author goes further to point out that "the historical, cultural and ideological resources that the French president contributed towards the construction of his perception of the causes of underdevelopment in Black Africa were fraught with 'substantialism' and a revisiting of the fantasies that marked the dawn of the colonial era. And this leads fatally to the Sarkozian theory of the 'African,' whose timeless soul is damned: *'the African tragedy,' the French president asserts, 'is that the African is not sufficiently integrated in history.*

In this mindset whereby everything always starts afresh, there is neither room for the human adventure nor for the idea of progress. In such a universe where nature reigns supreme, the African remain immobile amid an unchanging order in which everything seems to be predetermined. Here human beings never take a leap into the future. It never dawns on them that they can get out of the humdrum repetitiveness and forge their destiny." These and other perception of the Africa, and other views about the continent beacons the question – Will Africa ever be free, independent and sovereign as well as treated as human-beings? This should teach Africa to looking back and to prepare for the future!

GHANA

DAILY GRAPHIC

INDEPENDENCE DAY

NO. 2,007 ACCRA, WEDNESDAY, MARCH 6, 1957 PRICE: TWOPENCE

The birth of Ghana

'OUR BELOVED COUNTRY IS FREE FOR EVER'

NKRUMAH'S MIDNIGHT MESSAGE

GHANA was born at midnight. The Union Jack was lowered at the National Assembly building in Accra and the red, gold and green flag of Ghana fluttered into the night air. The Gold Coast was no more. Prime Minister Kwame Nkrumah was carried shoulder high out of the Assembly and passed through the tens of thousands of cheering Ghanaians to a stand in the Old Polo Ground. And there he started to highlife to music from the Police Band. Then the vast audience was hushed. And Dr. Nkrumah made his dramatic midnight message announcing freedom. He said: "At long last the battle has ended. And thus Ghana, our beloved country is free for ever."

Source: Credit Susan Williams (2021) White Malice. The CIA and the Neocolonisation of Africa. Hurst Publishers, UK

These and other incidents show how weak and vulnerable the continent is and will continue to be. The reader is left to make and draw his/her conclusions and content analysis of this speech which is not only insulting, derogating but speak the truth of existing realities on ground zero. Was President Jacques Chirac's address an attempt to drive a wedge of division between South Africa and the rest of Africa? Is the EU/AU summit meeting in Brussels, 19-20 February 2022 a new strategic build-up to destroy the new African Free Trade Area or what? Remember what happened to the Lagos Plan of Action (LPA). Why must Africans remain fools and slaves forever under servitude for the Euro-centric agenda or will they implement a progressive Afro-centric agenda and regain their freedom by completely casting off the "White Man's Burden?" For the French President, "It is not an insult when I say that your mediation has failed. Here is the psychology of the West

Africa; *THE WHITE MAN IS THE ABSOLUTE MASTER AND THE BLACK MAN IS THE SLAVE AND THE SERVANT.* Do you really think that any African leader, who behaves like me, can set foot on European soil or European country? God created Africa and put these West Africans here to serve us. These Africans do not grow up, do not mature and will never grow up nor mature whatever their level of education and age...From my position, I can ask them to fight, and they will fight without asking a question as you have already noticed."

Sixty or more years after independence, even though with the continuous penetrating inputs of the Euro-centric agenda, the Africa we want can neither afford nor need to sink into the luxury of despair and hopelessness. Hopelessness, despair and pessimism should be out in the minds of the people, even though we have to admit that the rising expectations and the high hopes inspired with the hoisting of the 'Black Star' of Ghana in 1957 has not been fully achieved, despair should be cast out of the minds of Africans. We have to blossomed with the vision and the wonderful words and works of Nkrumah, Nyerere, Nasser, Nelson Mandela, Sekou Touré, Samoa Machel, Thomas Sankara, Lumumba, Ghaddafi, Thabo Mbeki, Obasanjo Olusegun, Wade, Steve Biko, Azikiwe, Awolowo and hundreds many others in the struggle o he independence, sovereignty and respect o he human dignity of the black people. On their good work depends on the continent faring forward into the 21st century and far beyond.

This is a challenge that can only be attained in Africa by Africans and for Africans and for the rest of humanity. That is why we need a progressive Afro-centric ideological orientation, action plan to be deeply rooted in the significant soil geographic context and community hearts strategic agenda and action plans of, by and for the people are not something to be bought off the shelf from Euro-centric experts. Outside institutions and other bodies cannot be committed to developing Africa without putting their articulate interests first. Only Africans can develop Africa in the first place. External assistance though welcome have limits. It is imperative for Africa to have its strategic plans through the umbrella of a progressive Afro-centric agenda that requires us to be patriotic, determined and well organized in all he endeavours undertaken, for example, in the domain of: -

- justice and the rule of law;
- peace, security, poverty alienation and corruption eradication;
- good governance, democratisation, and economic growth;
- public services and public servants;

- innovation, productivity and wealth creation
- African agendas and an African coordinated agenda

Good governance means putting an end to existing endemic corrupt practices. Our bad governance means we are hurting ourselves. Good governance means we are developing and improving ourselves in all facets of life. Good governance means accountability, transparency, responsibility, order and capacity. Accountability, responsibility and transparency entails holding those who take or implement decisions to account; and of course, with the end result of showing the red card to corrupt practices. Corruption is clearly an absence of ethical and moral values, accountability, transparency and the rule of law and order. Corruption increases the poverty and underdevelopment status-quo of the African society and continent. Accountability requires not merely transparency but freedom to query, to criticise and to propose changes that moves society forward.

Currently, several African countries are among the fastest growing economies in the world. Africa's regional debt-to-GDP ratio is extremely low. Africa is also blessed with abundant natural resources, and a young vibrant population. Africa is one of the regions that continue to grow at rates of 5 to 7% in the face of the global financial crisis. To borrow a cliché; "Africa capitalism's next frontier;" Africa is the future of the world. Africans should not cast doubts or throw that future away. Africa's entrepreneurs hold the key to unlocking sustainable economic growth for the region. The private sector holds the key in paving the way for long-term development. One can with the progressive Afro-centric agenda hope as well as have faith – that the Afro-Pessimist and Chaos Theory Schools of Thought will have to accept that 'out of Africa there is always something new.' That something new is the 'Progressive Afro-centric agenda' that should usher a 'new dawn' for the continent and humanity. The Progressive Afro-centric Agenda should be guided by 'placing the people first.' War against absolute poverty and endemic corruption; providing sustainable quality livelihood to all citizens.

In spite of the numerous and increasing disastrous se backs aced since 1957, and especially with the passing to glory of Nkrumah, Biko, Sankara, Touré, Ghaddafi, Mandela, Nyerere, Lumumba and others; no doubt, some progress can equally be recorded. However, Africa is going through interesting time, new things will happen that will witness a most impudent daydreams and some of the old dispensations (Euro-centric agenda) agonisingly slow in dying. Yet, in all, the signs of hope and a sense of a better and brighter future are more evident and beaconing than a decade or more ago. The course of history will not remain stagnant; things will change; a new and progressive dawn will be Africa's. Any draw-back recorded means had front towards a fare forward voyagers – Africa into the 21st /22nd century.

Strictly speaking, we have to advocate and invent our own development model in tandem with the prevailing world situation and founded on the mastery of time past, and time present with great attention paid to nature, and building a strong capacity anvil for human capital development, as well as taking advantage of scientific and technological advancement that places all avenues for development at our door steps. Our first contribution in this journey of a long walk to freedom, positive transformation and sovereignty would then be to agree to call ourselves to order, to question why we are poor in the midst of plenty; why we are underdeveloped in the midst of vast natural resources; and to try our original solutions founded on the criteria of justice, truth and social interest in our respective countries and in the overall interest of the continent. "Change we need" as Barack Obama (2020) points out. Such a change must begin in us here and now with greater determination of a 'no return' to the past and the existing status-quo, but looking forward. And in the words of ***Kwame Nkrumah:***

"Forward Ever, Backward Never." \

References

Aseh Nfamewih (2006) Political Philosophies and Nation-Building in Cameroon. Grounds for the Second National Liberation Struggle, Unique Printers, Bamenda-Cameroon

Banseka Cage (2006) "Painful Good-Bye to Home: Governance failures as a Precipitant to emigration from Africa", CODERSIA Bulleting, no. 3&4, 2006, pp34-36, Dakar - Senegal

Blair Tony (2005) Commission for Africa – Our Common Interest, Penguin Books, UK.

Berghe, Pierre Van den (1978) Education, Class and Ethnicity in Southern Peru: Revolutionary Colonialism", In Altbach G. and Kelly, Gail P. (eds.) Education and Colonialism: Comparative Perspectives, Longman Publishes Limited. New York, USA

Casanova Pablo Gonzalez (1965) "Internal Colonialism and National Development" Studies in Comparative International Development, 1 (4)

Chabal Patrick (2016). The Politics of Suffering and Smiling. Zed Books. London.

Chan Lincoln and Xu Dong (2012) "Trends in China's Reform: The Rashomon Effect," The Lancet 379, March 3, pp 782-3

Depelchin Jacques (2011) "It is All in the connected, Why Pretend Otherwise?"http://www.Lemnde fr/idees/article/2011/03/23/japon_alerte_verte-et-rouge1497021_3232-htm/

Fanon Frantz (1969). The Wretched of the Earth, Penguin Books, United Kingdom

Fanon Frantz (1970). Toward the Africa Revolution. Pelican Books, United Kingdom

Fisher M. Andrew (2012) Addressing Inequality and the Universalism Principle in the Post-2015 Development Agenda

Forje W, John (2020). There was Another Cameroon, Vol.1. Lambert Academic Publishers, Germany.

Forje W. John (2020) Unravelling the Mysteries of Africa's Underdevelopment: Changing Africa, One Idea at a Time. Langaa Publishers, Mankon – Bamenda, Cameroon

Forje W. John (2021) There Was Another Country – Southern Cameroons, Langaa Publishers, Mankon, Bamenda-Cameroon

Forje W. John (2019) In the Heat of Africa's Underdevelopment: Africa at the Crossroads – Time to Deliver. Langaa Publishers, Mankon – Bamenda, Cameroon

Forje W. John (2918) Cameroon Without Corruption. The Search for a New Vision and Shared Values. Challenges for Policy Choices, Articulations and Implementations. Lambert Academic Publishing, Germany.

Fukuyams Francis () A Probative Post Cold Era. The End of History and the Last Man

Gosh Jayati (2301) "Dealing with 'The Poor,'" Development and Change 42(3) pp849-858

Kennedy Paul () Why in the End, Money Makes Right. The Rise and Fall of Great Powers

Jwa Sung-Hee (2017). A General Theory of Economic Development. Towards a Capitalist Manifesto. Edward Elgar Publishing United Kingdom.

Kissinger Henry () A Primer on Power and Politics. Diplomacy, USA

Mawere Munyaradzi (2018) Jostling Between 'Mere Talk and Blame Game'? Beyond Africa's Poverty and Underdevelopment Game Talk. Langaa PRICG, Bamenda – Cameroon

McNamara Robert R. (2012) If You can handle The Truth. In Retrospect Cutting Peter, Shari Zukav, Rebecca Buchholz (eds.) (2012). The Global Crisis and Transformative Social Change. Palgrave, Macmillan Publishers, Basingstoke, UK

Mustapha Raufu Abdul (2006). "Rethinking Africanist Political Science," CODESRIA Bulletin, Nos. 3 & 4, 2006, pp3-10, Dakar – Senegal.

Niebuhr Reinhold () Why Governments Need Enemies. Moral Man and Immoral Society.

Nguemzue Lendja Bergson Ange (2008) "French Policy on Immigration and Co-development in Light of the Dakar Speech", CODERSIA Bulletin, Nos 1 and 2 Dakar-Senegal, pp62-67

Ntumazah Ndeh (2001). A Conversational Auto Biography. Edited by Linus T. Asong and Simon Ndeh Chi. Langaa Research and Publishing, Mankon, Bamenda - Cameroon

Obama Barack (2020) A Promised Land. Viking – Penguin Books, USA

Olukoshi Adebayo (2006) "African Perspectives on the Commission for Africa Report", CODERSIA Bulleting, No.3&4, 2006, pp45-50, Dakar - Senegal

Padelford J. Norman & Emerson Rupert (eds.) (1962) Africa and World Order. Fredrick A. Praeger Publishers, New York (USA) and London (UK).

Thomson David (1969) Political Ideas. Pelican – Penguin Books, Harmondsworth, Middlesex, England.

Vladimir Popov and Piotr Dutkiewicz (2017). Mapping a New World Order. The Rest Beyond the West. Edward Elgar Publishing Limited, United Kingdom

Warren Penn Robert () How to Corrupt a Politician. The Entire King's Men

Whitehead North Alfred (1985) Science and The Modern World. Free Association Books, London

Williams Susan (2021) White Malice: The CIA and The Neocolonisation of Africa. Hurst Publishers, United Kingdom

CARAD Publications

- There Was Another Country Southern Cameroons: Popular Resistance, Resurrection or Betrayal of a People; Fighting for Change Vol.2 (2021), Langaa Research & Publishing Common Initiative Group, Mankon-Bamenda, Cameroon. **ISBN: 978 9956 552 382.**
- There Was Another Country Southern Cameroons: The Rape of Freedom, Justice, and Rule of Law, Equality, Accountability and Good Management. Vol. 1. (2020) Lambert Academic Publishing, Germany **(ISBN:978-620-2-67225-2)**
- The Future of Africa. Reform, Development, Progress or Progressive Decline (2020) Langaa Research & Publishing Common Initiative Group, Mankon, Bamenda-Cameroon **(ISBN:13:978-9956-551-89-7**
- Unravelling the Mysteries of African Underdevelopment. Changing Africa, One Idea at a Time (2020) Langaa RPCIG Publishing, Bamenda-Cameroon. **(ISBN:978 995 655 1392**) Shaping Africa's Future: Transforming African and Global Relations for A Just and Stable World: (2019) Lambert Academic Publishing, Germany **(ISBN: 978-413-9-4930-4)**
- Unchaining Africa's Economic Development through Entrepreneurship Education. (2019) L'Harmattan Publishers, France/Cameroun, **(ISBN978-2-343-16632-2)**
- In the Heat of Africa's Underdevelopment: Africa at the Crossroads – Time to Deliver (2019) Langaa RPCIG, Bamenda-Cameroon **(ISBN:978-995-655-095-1)**
- Cameroon without Corruption: The Search for a New Vision and Shared-Values. Challenges for Policy Choices, Articulation and Implementations. (Enlarged Edition) **(2018).** Lambert Academic Publishing, Germany **(ISBN:978-613-9-86151-4)**
- Withering or Constructing African Unity Fifty Years after Kwame Nkrumah. Implementing an Action Plan for the Realisation of 'Africa Must Unite' **(2017)** Lambert Academic Publishing, Germany **[ISBN:978-3-330-31786-4]**
- Gender Empowerment, Equality and Economic Development as Africa's Solutions to African Problems.

(2016) Lambert Academic Publishing, Germany **[ISBN: 978-3-659-71046-9]**

- Perspectives on Democracy and Governance in Africa. Reorganising the State and Society for A Better Tomorrow **(2015)** Lambert Academic Publishing, Germany. **[ISBN: 978-3-659-56679-0]**
- Emerging Perspectives on Capacity Building and Quality Public Services Delivery in Africa **(2013)** Lambert Academic Publishing, Germany **[ISBN: 978-3-659-38368-7]**
- State Building and Democracy in Africa: A Comparative and Developmental Approach **(2013).** Nova Science Publishers Inc. New York, USA **[ISBN: 978-1-61209-025-2]**
- Century of Change – Symposium on African Unity, (ed.) **(2011)** Nova Science Publishers Inc., New York – United States of America [**ISBN: 978-1-61122-034—6]**
- Cameroon without Poverty - Civil Society Empowerment: Growth and Poverty Eradication? Mapping New Strategies for the Future **(2010**). Lambert Academic Publishing, Germany **[ISBN: 978-3-8433-6951-0]**
- Here the People Rule: Political Transition and Challenges for Democratic Consolidation in Africa **(2009)** Nova Science Publishers Inc., New York, USA [**ISBN:978-1-60692-706-9]**
- The Challenges of Administrative Political and Developmental Renewal in Africa: Emerging Issues, **(2009)** Nova Science Publishers Inc. New York, USA**[ISBN:978-1-60741-265-6]**
- The Challenges of Administrative and Developmental Renewal in Africa: Essays on Rethinking Government and Reorganisation **(2009).** Nova Science Publishers Inc., New York USA **[ISBN: 978-1-60741-266-3]**
- Consolidating Democratic Governance and Quality Management in Africa**, (2003)** CARAD Readings in Policy, Governance and Management, Yaoundé – Cameroon
- Science and Technology in Africa **(1989)** Vol. 10. Longman World Series on Science and Technology, Longman, Essex, United Kingdom [**ISBN: 0-582-00086-6]**
- Science, Technology and Development Policy in Cameroon, Lund-Sweden, **1986**) [**ISSN:0349-1684] [ISBN:91-7810-970-1]**

- Third World Development and the Myth of International Cooperation, Lund-Sweden, **(1984)**
- Science and Technology for Development in Africa South of the Sahara: A Bibliography **(1982)** Research Policy Institute, University of Lund-Sweden **[ISSN: 0349-1684]**
- The One and Indivisible Republic of Cameroon. Political and Economic Integration in a Fragmented Polity **(1981).** Department of Political Science, Lund Political Studies Series No.35, University of Lund Printing Press, Lund - Sweden **[ISBN:91-7222-450-9]**
- Cameroon's Five-Year Development Plans **(1977).** Publishers, Bokforlaget Doxa, Lund-Sweden
- The Rape of Africa in Vienna. African Participation in the 1979 United Nations Conference on Science and Technology for Development (ARGAD Publication, Lund-Sweden, **1979**)
- The Challenge of African Economic and Technological Development and the Influence of International Forums. **(1978)** ARGAD Publications, Lund, Sweden

Bali Airport Road – T-Junction, Njenka-Hausa,
Post Box 85, Bali Nyonga,
Bali Sub Division, Mezam North West Region,
Republic of Cameroon

CPSIA information can be obtained
at www.ICGtesting.com
Printed in the USA
LVHW040936221222
735718LV00006B/409

9 789956 552351